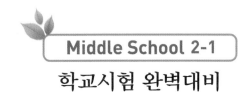
KB086637

1학기 전과정

적중100plus

영어 기출문제집

중2

시사 | 박준언

Best Collection

구성과 특징

교과서의 주요 학습 내용을 중심으로 학습 영역별 특성에 맞춰 단계별로 다양한 학습 기회를 제공하여
단원별 학습능력 평가는 물론 중간 및 기말고사 시험 등에 완벽하게 대비할 수 있도록 내용을 구성

Words & Expressions

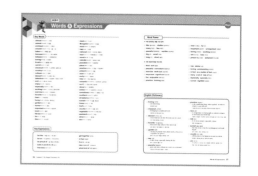

Step1 Key Words 단원별 핵심 단어 설명 및 풀이
Key Expression 단원별 핵심 숙어 및 관용어 설명
Word Power 반대 또는 비슷한 뜻 단어 배우기
English Dictionary 영어로 배우는 영어 단어

Step2 실력평가 단원별 수시평가 대비 주관식, 객관식 문제풀이

Step3 서술형 대비 학업성취도 및 수행능력평가 대비 서술형 문제풀이

Conversation

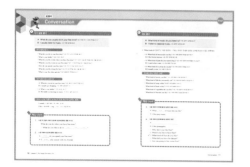

Step1 핵심 의사소통 소통에 필요한 주요 표현 방법 요약
핵심 Check 기본적인 표현 방법 및 활용능력 확인

Step2 대화문 익히기 교과서 대화문 심층 분석 및 확인

Step3 교과서 확인학습 빈칸 채우기를 통한 문장 완성 능력 확인

Step4 기본평가 시험대비 기초 학습 능력 평가

Step5 실력평가 단원별 수시평가 대비 주관식, 객관식 문제풀이

Step6 서술형 대비 학업성취도 및 수행능력평가 대비 서술형 문제풀이

Grammar

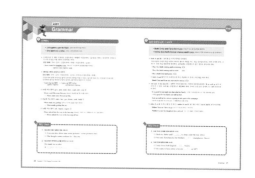

Step1 주요 문법 단원별 주요 문법 사항과 예문을 알기 쉽게 설명
핵심 Check 기본 문법사항에 대한 이해 여부 확인

Step2 기본평가 시험대비 기초 학습 능력 평가

Step3 실력평가 단원별 수시평가 대비 주관식, 객관식 문제풀이

Step4 서술형 대비 학업성취도 및 수행능력평가 대비 서술형 문제풀이

Reading

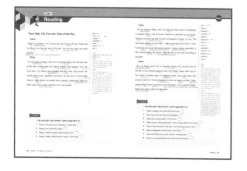

Step1 구문 분석 단원별로 제시된 문장에 대한 구문별 분석과 내용 설명
확인문제 문장에 대한 기본적인 이해와 인지능력 확인

Step2 확인학습A 빈칸 채우기를 통한 문장 완성 능력 확인

Step3 확인학습B 제시된 우리말을 영어로 완성하여 작문 능력 키우기

Step4 실력평가 단원별 수시평가 대비 주관식, 객관식 문제풀이

Step5 서술형 대비 학업성취도 및 수행능력평가 대비 서술형 문제풀이
교과서 구석구석 교과서에 나오는 기타 문장까지 완벽 학습

Composition

|영역별 핵심문제|

단어 및 어휘, 대화문, 문법, 독해 등 각 영역별 기출문제의 출제 유형을 분석하여 실전에 대비하고 연습할 수 있도록 문제를 배열

|단원별 예상문제|

기출문제를 분석한 후 새로운 시험 출제 경향을 더하여 새롭게 출제될 수 있는 문제를 포함하여 시험에 완벽하게 대비할 수 있도록 준비

|서술형 실전 및 창의사고력 문제|

학교 시험에서 점차 늘어나는 서술형 시험에 집중 대비하고 고득점을 취득하는데 만전을 기하기 위한 학습 코너

|단원별 모의고사|

영역별, 단계별 학습을 모두 마친 후 실전 연습을 위한 모의고사

교과서 파헤치기

- **단어Test1~3** 영어 단어 우리말 쓰기, 우리말을 영어 단어로 쓰기, 영영풀이에 해당하는 단어와 우리말 쓰기
- **대화문Test1~2** 대화문 빈칸 완성 및 전체 대화문 쓰기
- **본문Test1~5** 빈칸 완성, 우리말 쓰기, 문장 배열연습, 영어 작문하기 복습 등 단계별 반복 학습을 통해 교과서 지문에 대한 완벽한 습득
- **구석구석지문Test1~2** 지문 빈칸 완성 및 전문 영어로 쓰기

Manage Yourself!

🎤 의사소통 기능

- 슬픔, 불만족, 실망의 원인에 대해 묻기
  What's the matter?
- 제안·권유하기
  I think you should use a planner.

🎤 언어 형식

- to부정사의 형용사적 용법
  You will have more work **to do**.
- 접속사 that
  I think **that** using my time to prepare for my future is important.

Words & Expressions

Key Words

- **achieve**[ətʃíːv] 통 달성하다, 성취하다
- **again**[əgén] 부 다시
- **always**[ɔ́ːlweiz] 부 항상
- **appointment**[əpɔ́intmənt] 명 약속
- **attention**[əténʃən] 명 주의, 집중
- **before**[bifɔ́ːr] 접 ~하기 전에
- **check**[tʃek] 통 확인하다
- **chef**[ʃef] 명 요리사
- **due**[djuː] 형 ~하기로 되어 있는[예정된]
- **easily**[íːzili] 부 쉽게
- **finish**[fíniʃ] 통 끝내다
- **focus**[fóukəs] 통 집중하다
- **forget**[fərgét] 통 잊다
- **free time** 자유 시간
- **future**[fjúːtʃər] 명 미래
- **help**[help] 통 도움이 되다 명 도움
- **helpful**[hélpfəl] 형 도움이 되는
- **history**[hístəri] 명 역사
- **important**[impɔ́ːrtənt] 형 중요한
- **instead**[instéd] 부 대신에
- **join**[dʒɔin] 통 가입하다
- **lesson**[lésn] 명 수업, 강습
- **master**[mǽstər] 통 ~을 완전히 익히다, ~에 숙달하다
- **monthly**[mʌ́nθli] 형 매월의 부 매월
- **nervous**[nɔ́ːrvəs] 형 긴장되는, 불안한
- **planner**[plǽnər] 명 일정 계획표, 플래너
- **posting**[póustiŋ] 명 포스팅, (인터넷이나 SNS에 올리는) 글
- **practice**[prǽktis] 통 연습하다
- **prepare**[pripɛ́ər] 통 준비하다
- **present**[préznt] 명 선물
- **probably**[prábəbli] 부 아마 (= perhaps)
- **quiz**[kwiz] 명 퀴즈, 시험, 테스트
- **recipe**[résəpi] 명 조리[요리]법
- **regularly**[régjulərli] 부 규칙적으로
- **remember**[rimémbər] 통 기억하다
- **save**[seiv] 통 절약하다, 구하다
- **schedule**[skédʒuːl] 명 일정
- **spend**[spend] 통 (돈을) 쓰다, (시간을) 소비하다
- **step**[step] 명 걸음
- **textbook**[tékstbuk] 명 교과서
- **tired**[taiərd] 형 피곤한
- **toward**[tɔːrd] 전 (목적 · 준비) ~을 위해, ~을 향하여
- **try**[trai] 통 해 보다, 노력하다
- **warm**[wɔːrm] 형 따뜻한
- **weekly**[wíːkli] 형 매주의 부 매주
- **while**[hwail] 접 ~하는 동안
- **wisely**[wáizli] 부 현명하게
- **worried**[wɔ́ːrid] 형 걱정하는

Key Expressions

- **a lot of** 많은
- **a type of** 일종의
- **all day long** 온종일
- **at a time** 한 번에
- **be good at** ~을 잘하다, ~에 능숙하다
- **be worried about** ~에 대해 걱정하다
- **because of** ~ 때문에
- **get along with** ~와 잘 지내다
- **have a cold** 감기에 걸리다
- **in front of** ~ 앞에
- **make a plan** 계획을 세우다
- **prepare for** ~을 준비하다
- **put aside** ~을 한쪽에 두다
- **put off** 미루다, 연기하다
- **search for** ~을 찾다
- **see a doctor** 병원에 가다
- **set a goal** 목표를 세우다
- **set the alarm** 알람을 맞춰 놓다
- **stop -ing** ~하는 것을 멈추다
- **take[have] a lesson** 수업[강습]을 받다
- **these days** 요즘
- **used to** ~하곤 했다

Word Power

※ 명사에 -ful, -y 등을 붙여 형용사가 되는 단어

- □ **beauty** (아름다움) → **beautiful** (아름다운)
- □ **care** (주의) → **careful** (주의 깊은)
- □ **cloud** (구름) → **cloudy** (흐린)
- □ **harm** (해) → **harmful** (해로운)
- □ **help** (도움) → **helpful** (도움이 되는)

- □ **luck** (행운) → **lucky** (운이 좋은)
- □ **mess** (엉망인 상태) → **messy** (지저분한)
- □ **star** (별) → **starry** (별이 총총한)
- □ **thirst** (갈증) → **thirsty** (갈증이 나는)
- □ **wonder** (경이) → **wonderful** (경이로운)

※ 형용사에 -ly를 붙여 부사가 되는 단어

- □ **easy** (쉬운) → **easily** (쉽게)
- □ **careful** (주의 깊은) → **carefully** (주의 깊게)
- □ **kind** (친절한) → **kindly** (친절하게)
- □ **loud** (소리가 큰) → **loudly** (큰 소리로)

- □ **special** (특별한) → **specially** (특별히)
- □ **sudden** (갑작스러운) → **suddenly** (갑자기)
- □ **regular** (규칙적인) → **regularly** (규칙적으로)
- □ **wise** (현명한) → **wisely** (현명하게)

English Dictionary

- □ **achieve** 달성하다, 성취하다
  → to get or reach something by working hard
  열심히 일해 뭔가를 얻거나 이루다

- □ **appointment** 약속
  → an arrangement to meet with someone at a particular time
  특정한 때에 어떤 사람을 만나기로 하는 약속

- □ **attention** 주의
  → the act of listening to, looking at, or thinking about something or someone carefully
  어떤 것 또는 누군가에 대해 주의 깊게 듣고, 보고, 생각하는 행위

- □ **due** ~하기로 되어 있는[예정된]
  → expected to happen or arrive at a particular time
  특정 시간에 발생하거나 도착할 것으로 예상되는

- □ **focus** 집중하다
  → to direct your attention or effort at something specific
  관심이나 노력을 특정한 대상에 기울이다

- □ **future** 미래
  → the period of time that will come after the present time
  현재 시간 이후에 올 시간[시기]

- □ **join** 가입하다
  → to become a member of a group or organization
  집단이나 단체의 구성원이 되다

- □ **lesson** 수업, 강습
  → an activity that you do in order to learn something
  어떤 것을 배우기 위해 하는 활동

- □ **master** ~을 완전히 익히다
  → to learn something completely
  어떤 것을 완전히 익히다

- □ **prepare** 준비하다
  → to make yourself ready for something that you will be doing
  앞으로 하려는 일을 위해 자신을 준비시키다

- □ **present** 선물
  → something that you give to someone especially as a way of showing affection or thanks
  특히 애정이나 감사의 표시로 누군가에게 주는 것

- □ **recipe** 조리[요리]법
  → a set of instructions for making food
  음식을 만들기 위한 일련의 지시 사항

- □ **save** 절약하다
  → to keep something from being lost or wasted
  어떤 것이 손실되거나 낭비되지 않게 하다

- □ **schedule** 일정
  → a plan of things that will be done and the times when they will be done
  할 일에 대한 계획 및 그 일을 할 때

 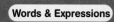

01 다음 중 〈보기〉와 같이 변화하는 단어가 <u>아닌</u> 것은?

┌─── 보기 ───┐
help → helpful
└──────────┘

① harm ② color
③ danger ④ wonder
⑤ beauty

02 다음 빈칸에 공통으로 알맞은 것은?

• There is a church in front _____ the school.
• She closed the door because _____ the rain.

① at ② of
③ on ④ by
⑤ from

03 다음 영영풀이에 해당하는 단어로 알맞은 것은?

to get or reach something by working hard

① check ② focus
③ master ④ achieve
⑤ prepare

서답형

04 다음 짝지어진 두 단어의 관계가 같도록 빈칸에 알맞은 말을 쓰시오.

easy : difficult = remember : _____

05 다음 빈칸에 들어갈 동사가 바르게 짝지어진 것은?

• I _____ the alarm clock for 7 o'clock.
• I will _____ a plan to visit you next year!

① keep – give ② set – take
③ get – make ④ keep – have
⑤ set – make

서답형

06 다음 영영풀이에 해당하는 단어를 쓰시오.

a set of instructions for making food

➡ _____

서답형

07 다음 우리말에 맞게 빈칸에 알맞은 말을 쓰시오.

Ann은 하루 종일 집에 있었어.
➡ Ann stayed home _____ _____ _____.

08 다음 빈칸에 알맞은 말이 바르게 짝지어진 것은?

• I must prepare _____ the exam.
• Carrie never puts _____ doing her homework.

① at – on ② for – off
③ from – up ④ about – out
⑤ with – down

01 다음 짝지어진 두 단어의 관계가 같도록 빈칸에 알맞은 말을 쓰시오.

(1) before : after = _____ : cool
(2) delicious : tasty = gift : _____
(3) cloud : cloudy = help : _____

02 다음 우리말에 맞게 빈칸에 알맞은 말을 쓰시오.

(1) 나는 영어에 능숙하고 싶다.
➡ I want to _____ _____ _____ English.
(2) 나는 반 아이들과 잘 지낼 거야.
➡ I'll _____ _____ _____ my classmates.
(3) 마지막 목표는 스마트폰 게임을 멈추는 것이다.
➡ The last goal is to _____ _____ smartphone games.

03 다음 빈칸에 들어갈 알맞은 말을 〈보기〉에서 골라 쓰시오.

┌─── 보기 ───┐
achieve future manage appointment
└──────────┘

(1) Let's change our _____ to 7 o'clock.
(2) What do you want to be in the _____?
(3) You need to _____ your time well.
(4) I set small goals and _____ them every day.

04 다음 괄호 안의 단어를 문맥에 맞게 고쳐 쓰시오.

(1) I want to spend money _____. (wise)
(2) Listen _____ to what I say. (careful)
(3) We all need to exercise _____. (regular)

05 다음 빈칸에 알맞은 말을 〈보기〉에서 골라 쓰시오.

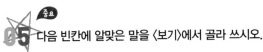

┌─── 보기 ───┐
put aside   put off
at a time   because of
└──────────┘

(1) I was late _____ a traffic jam.
(2) Don't _____ today's work until tomorrow.
(3) I will achieve my big goal, one step _____.
(4) I _____ my smartphone when I do my homework.

06 다음 영영풀이에 해당하는 단어를 주어진 철자로 시작하여 쓰시오.

(1) l_____ : an activity that you do in order to learn something
(2) s_____ : to keep something from being lost or wasted
(3) f_____ : to direct your attention or effort at something specific
(4) d_____ : expected to happen or arrive at a particular time

Conversation

1 슬픔, 불만족, 실망의 원인에 대해 묻기

> **A** Emily, you look sad. What's the matter? Emily, 너 슬퍼 보여. 무슨 일 있니?
> **B** I lost my cat. 고양이를 잃어버렸어.

■ What's the matter?는 '무슨 일 있니?'라는 뜻으로 상대방의 슬픔, 불만족, 실망의 원인에 대해 물을 때 사용하는 표현이다. 상대방의 응답에 이어 That's too bad. 나 I'm sorry to hear that. 등과 같은 동정이나 유감을 나타내는 표현이 주로 이어진다.

> • A: What's the matter? 무슨 일이야?
> B: I broke my smartphone. 내 스마트폰이 고장 났어.
> A: That's too bad. 그것 참 안됐구나.

슬픔, 불만족, 실망의 원인에 대해 묻는 표현

- • What's wrong (with you)? 무슨 일 있니?
- • What's the matter (with you)?
- • What happened (to you)?
- • What's the problem (with you)?
- • What's going on?
- • Is (there) something wrong with you? 무슨 문제라도 있니?
- • Why are you sad[disappointed]? 왜 슬픈[실망한] 거야?

슬픔, 불만족, 실망의 원인에 대해 답하기

- • I have a cold. 감기에 걸렸어.
- • My team lost the game. 우리 팀이 경기에서 졌어.
- • She's in the hospital. 그녀는 지금 병원에 입원해 있어.
- • My puppy is sick. 내 강아지가 아파.
- • I failed the test. 나는 시험에 떨어졌어.

핵심 Check

1. 다음 우리말과 일치하도록 빈칸에 알맞은 말을 쓰시오.

   (1) **A:** What's the _____? (무슨 일 있니?)

   B: I _____ my cellphone. (나는 휴대전화를 잃어버렸어.)

   A: That's _____ _____. (그거 참 안됐구나.)

   (2) **A:** What's wrong _____ Mr. Han? (한 선생님에게 무슨 문제가 있니?)

   B: He _____ his _____. (그분은 손가락을 다치셨어.)

   A: _____ _____ to hear that. (그거 참 안됐구나.)

2 제안 · 권유하기

> **A** I want to be good at speaking English. 나는 영어를 잘하고 싶어.
>
> **B** I think you should join an English conversation club.
> 내 생각에 너는 영어 회화 동아리에 가입해야 할 것 같아.

■ '내 생각에 넌 ~해야 할 것 같아.'라고 상대방에게 무언가를 제안하거나 권유할 때에는 I think you should ~. 표현을 사용하여 말할 수 있다.

- A: I want to be good at cooking. 나는 요리를 잘하고 싶어.
  B: I think you should search for recipes. 내 생각에 넌 조리법을 찾아봐야 할 것 같아.

제안 · 권유하기 표현

- I think (that) you should[ought to]+동사원형 ~. 나는 네가 ~해야 한다고 생각해.
- You should[must / have to] + 동사원형 ~. 너는 ~해야 해.
- You'd better + 동사원형 ~. 너는 ~하는 게 좋겠어.
- I advise you to + 동사원형 ~. 나는 네가 ~하길 조언해.
- If I were you, I'd + 동사원형 ~. 내가 너라면 ~할 텐데.
- Why don't you + 동사원형 ~? ~하는 게 어때?
- How[What] about + -ing ~? ~하는 게 어때?

핵심 Check

2. 다음 우리말과 일치하도록 빈칸에 알맞은 말을 쓰시오.

(1) **A:** I have a _____. (이가 아파.)

   B: I _____ you _____ _____ to a dentist. (내 생각에 넌 치과에 가야 할 것 같아.)

(2) **A:** _____ eat hamburgers. (햄버거를 먹자.)

   B: You'd _____ eat some vegetables. (너는 채소를 좀 먹는 것이 좋겠어.)

(3) **A:** _____ _____ we drink soft drinks? (우리 탄산음료를 마시는 게 어때?)

   B: You _____ _____ milk. (너는 우유를 마셔야 해.)

(4) **A:** Shall we _____ computer games? (컴퓨터 게임을 할까?)

   B: I think you _____ _____ do your homework first.
   (넌 먼저 숙제부터 해야 한다고 난 생각해.)

A. Listen & Speak 1 - A - 1

G: ❶You look worried, Sam. ❷What's the matter?

B: ❸I don't hear my alarm in the morning these days.

G: ❹Why don't you set the alarm on your clock and on your smartphone?

B: ❺That's a good idea.

G: 걱정이 있어 보여, Sam. 무슨 일 있니?
B: 요즘 아침에 알람을 못 들어.
G: 네 시계와 스마트폰에 알람을 맞춰 놓는 게 어때?
B: 좋은 생각이야.

❶ look+형용사: ~하게 보이다
❷ What's the matter?: 무슨 일 있니?(슬픔, 불만족, 실망의 원인에 대해 묻기) = What's the problem?=What's wrong?=Is something wrong?
❸ these days: 요즈음
❹ Why don't you + 동사원형 ~?: ~하는 게 어때? (권유나 제안하기) / set the alarm: 알람을 맞춰 놓다
❺ That's a good idea. = I think so, too.=I'm with you on that.=That sounds good.=You can say that again. (동의하기)

Check(√) True or False

(1) Sam looks happy these days.   T ☐ F ☐

(2) Sam will set the alarm on his clock and on his smartphone.   T ☐ F ☐

Conversation B

Hana: ❶What's the matter, Jiho?

Jiho: I didn't bring my uniform. ❷I forgot I have soccer practice today.

Hana: Again?

Jiho: ❸My second year in middle school is busier than my first year, and ❹I often forget things.

Hana: ❺I think you should use a planner. Here's mine.

Jiho: ❻Oh, can I see it?

Hana: Sure. I write my class schedule and appointment in my planner.

Jiho: That's great. ❼Maybe I should buy one.

하나: 무슨 일 있니, 지호야?
지호: 나는 내 유니폼을 가져오지 않았어. 오늘 축구 연습이 있다는 걸 잊고 있었어.
하나: 또?
지호: 중학교 2학년은 1학년보다 더 바쁘고, 나는 종종 어떤 것들을 잊어버려.
하나: 내 생각에는 너는 일정 계획표를 사용해야 할 것 같아. 여기 내 것이 있어.
지호: 오, 내가 봐도 될까?
하나: 물론. 나는 일정 계획표에 나의 수업 일정과 약속을 적어.
지호: 정말 좋구나. 나도 하나 사야 할까 봐.

❶ What's the matter?: 무슨 일 있니?(슬픔, 불만족, 실망의 원인에 대해 묻기)
❷ I forgot와 I 사이에 목적절을 이끄는 접속사 that 생략
❸ busier than: 비교급 + than(~보다 더 …한)
❹ 빈도부사 often은 일반동사 앞이나 be동사와 조동사 뒤에 위치한다.
❺ I think you should ~.: 내 생각에 너는 ~해야 할 것 같아. (제안이나 권유하기) = You'd better + 동사원형 ~. = Why don't you + 동사원형 ~? = How[What] about + -ing ~?
❻ Can I ~?: 내가 ~해도 될까?(허락 요청하기) / it=a planner
❼ Maybe I should + 동사원형 ~.: (아마) ~해야겠지, ~할까 봐. / one = a planner

Check(√) True or False

(3) Jiho always forgets things.   T ☐ F ☐

(4) Hana advises Jiho to use a planner.   T ☐ F ☐

Listen & Speak 1 - A - 2

G: ❶Phew, what should I do?

B: ❷What's the matter, Julie?

G: I spend money too fast.

B: ❸Well, I always make a plan before I buy things.

G: ❹Maybe I should do the same.

❶ What should I do?: 내가 어떻게 해야 하니? / phew: 휴, 후유
❷ What's the matter? = What's wrong? = What's the problem? = What happened?
❸ 빈도부사 always는 일반동사 앞이나 be동사와 조동사 뒤에 위치한다.
❹ Maybe I should + 동사원형 ~.: (아마) ~해야겠지, ~할까 봐.

Listen & Speak 2 - A - 1

G: ❶Jason, are you okay? You don't look good today.

B: ❷I have a cold.

G: ❸That's too bad. ❹ I think you should see a doctor.

B: You're right. Thank you.

❶ Are you okay?: 너 괜찮니?
❷ have a cold: 감기에 걸리다(=catch[get/take] a cold)
❸ That's too bad.: 그것 참 안됐구나. (유감을 나타내는 표현) = I'm sorry to hear that.
❹ I think you should + 동사원형 ~.: 내 생각에 너는 ~해야 할 것 같아.

Listen & Speak 2 - A - 2

G: You look worried. ❶What's going on?

B: ❷I'm worried about tomorrow's history quiz. What should I do?

G: I think you should read your textbook again.

B: ❸That's a good idea.

❶ What's going on?: 무슨 일 있니?(슬픔, 불만족, 실망의 원인에 대해 묻기)
= What's the problem?=What's wrong?=Is something wrong?
❷ I'm worried about ~: 나는 ~이 걱정돼.
❸ That's a good idea.: 좋은 생각이야.

Listen & Speak 2 - A - 3

B: I'm so tired.

G: Why?

B: ❶I don't sleep well these days.

G: ❷I think you should drink a glass of warm milk before you sleep. ❸It will help.

B: Okay, I will try.

❶ these days: 요즈음
❷ a glass of: 한 잔의
❸ It = to drink a glass of warm milk before you sleep

Conversation A

B: ❶This is a type of book. I write my daily, weekly, and monthly plans here. ❷I also write important dates like my friends' birthdays and homework due dates here. Every night, I check this for the next day. Do you want to remember things easily? ❸Then I think you should use this.

❶ a type of: 일종의(=a kind of, a sort of)
❷ like: ~와 같은 / due: ~하기로 되어 있는[예정된]
❸ I think you should + 동사원형 ~.: 내 생각에 너는 ~해야 할 것 같아.

Wrap Up - ❶

W: ❶What's the matter, Sam? Are you sick?

B: ❷Ms. Green, I think I have a cold.

W: Did you go to the school nurse?

B: Yes. ❸She said I need to go to the hospital. ❹ Can I leave school now?

W: Okay, Sam. I'll call your mom and tell her about it.

❶ What's the matter? = What's wrong? = What's the problem? = What happened?
❷ have a cold: 감기에 걸리다(=catch[get/take] a cold)
❸ need to: ~할 필요가 있다
❹ Can I + 동사원형 ~?: 제가 ~해도 될까요? (허락 요청하기)

Wrap Up - ❷

B: I'm so nervous.

G: Why? ❶Is it because of the dance contest?

B: Yes. I practiced for many days, but I'm still nervous. ❷What should I do?

G: ❸I think you should practice in front of your family. ❹It will be very helpful.

B: That's a good idea. Thank you.

❶ because of: ~ 때문에
❷ What should I do?: 내가 어떻게 해야 하지? (충고 구하기)
❸ in front of: ~ 앞에서
❹ It=to practice in front of your family

• 다음 우리말과 일치하도록 빈칸에 알맞은 말을 쓰시오.

Listen & Speak 1 - A

1. G: You look _____, Sam. What's the _____?

   B: I don't _____ my alarm in the morning _____ _____.

   G: _____ _____ you _____ the alarm on your clock and on your smartphone?

   B: That's a good _____.

2. G: Phew, what _____ I do?

   B: _____ the matter, Julie?

   G: I _____ money too _____.

   B: Well, I always _____ a plan _____ I buy things.

   G: Maybe I _____ do the _____.

Listen & Speak 2 - A

1. G: Jason, are you _____? You _____ _____ good today.

   B: I have a _____.

   G: That's too bad. I _____ you _____ _____ a doctor.

   B: You're _____. Thank you.

2. G: You look _____. What's _____ _____?

   B: I'm _____ _____ tomorrow's history quiz. _____ should I _____?

   G: I think you _____ _____ your textbook again.

   B: That's a good _____.

3. B: I'm so _____.

   G: Why?

   B: I don't sleep well _____ _____.

   G: _____ _____ you should drink _____ _____ _____ warm milk _____ you sleep. It will _____.

   B: Okay, I _____ _____.

Conversation A

B: This is a _____ of book. I write my _____, weekly, and _____ plans here. I also write important dates _____ my friends' birthdays and homework _____ _____ here. Every night, I _____ this for the next day. Do you want _____ _____ things _____? Then I think you _____ _____ this.

Conversation B

Hana: What's the _____, Jiho?

Jiho: I _____ _____ my uniform. I _____ I have soccer practice today.

Hana: Again?

Jiho: My _____ year in middle school is _____ _____ my _____ year, and I often forget things.

Hana: I think _____ _____ _____ a planner. Here's _____.

Jiho: Oh, _____ I see it?

Hana: Sure. I write my class _____ and _____ in my planner.

Jiho: That's great. _____ I _____ buy one.

Wrap Up - ❶

W: _____ the matter, Sam? _____ you _____?

B: Ms. Green, I think I _____ _____ _____.

W: Did you go to the _____ _____?

B: Yes. She said I _____ _____ go to the hospital. _____ I _____ school now?

W: Okay, Sam. I'll _____ your mom and _____ _____ about it.

Wrap Up - ❷

B: I'm so _____.

G: Why? Is it _____ _____ the dance contest?

B: Yes. I practiced _____ many days, but I'm _____ nervous. What _____ I _____?

G: I _____ you _____ practice _____ _____ _____ your family. It will be very _____.

B: That's _____ _____ _____. Thank you.

B: 이것은 일종의 책이야. 나는 여기에 매일, 매주, 그리고 월간 계획을 써. 나는 또한 여기에 내 친구들의 생일이나 숙제 예정일과 같은 중요한 날짜를 적어. 매일 밤, 나는 다음 날을 위해 이것을 확인해. 무언가를 쉽게 기억하고 싶니? 그러면 내 생각에 너는 이것을 사용해야 할 것 같아.

하나: 무슨 일 있니, 지호야?

지호: 나는 내 유니폼을 가져오지 않았어. 오늘 축구 연습이 있다는 걸 잊고 있었어.

하나: 또?

지호: 중학교 2학년은 1학년보다 더 바쁘고, 나는 종종 어떤 것들을 잊어버려.

하나: 내 생각에는 너는 일정 계획표를 사용해야 할 것 같아. 여기 내 것이 있어.

지호: 오, 내가 봐도 될까?

하나: 물론. 나는 일정 계획표에 나의 수업 일정과 약속을 적어.

지호: 정말 좋구나. 나도 하나 사야 할까 봐.

W: 무슨 일이야, Sam? 어디 아파?

B: Green 선생님, 제가 감기에 걸린 것 같아요.

W: 보건 선생님한테 갔었니?

B: 네. 보건 선생님이 병원에 갈 필요가 있다고 하셨어요. 지금 하교를 해도 될까요?

W: 그럼, Sam. 내가 어머니한테 전화해서 그것에 대해 말할게.

B: 나 너무 긴장돼.

G: 왜? 댄스 경연 대회 때문이니?

B: 응. 며칠 동안 연습을 했지만 여전히 긴장돼. 어떻게 해야 하지?

G: 내 생각에 너는 가족 앞에서 연습을 해야 할 것 같아. 그것은 아주 도움이 될 거야.

B: 좋은 생각이야. 고마워.

01 다음 대화의 밑줄 친 말과 바꾸어 쓸 수 있는 것은?

> **A:** You look worried today. <u>What's the matter?</u>
> **B:** My puppy is sick.

① What's wrong?　　② What about you?
③ How are you doing?　　④ What do you do?
⑤ What are you doing?

02 다음 대화의 빈칸에 알맞은 것은?

> **A:** I have a bad cold.
> **B:** _____

① You'd better eat less.
② You'd better study harder.
③ You'd better go to bed late.
④ You'd better go to see a doctor.
⑤ You'd better get up late.

03 다음 중 의도하는 바가 나머지 넷과 <u>다른</u> 것은?

① What's wrong with Jinsu?
② What do you think of Jinsu?
③ What's the matter with Jinsu?
④ What's the problem with Jinsu?
⑤ Is something wrong with Jinsu?

04 다음 대화의 ⓐ~ⓓ를 자연스러운 대화가 되도록 바르게 배열하시오.

see a doctor 병원에 가다

> ⓐ Oh, you are right.
> ⓑ No. I have a bad cold.
> ⓒ You should see a doctor.
> ⓓ You look sick. Are you okay?

➡ _____

[01~05] 다음 대화를 읽고, 물음에 답하시오.

Hana: ⓐWhat's the matter, Jiho?

Jiho: I didn't bring my uniform. I forgot I have soccer practice today.

Hana: Again?

Jiho: My second year in middle school is ⓑbusy than my first year, and I often forget things.

Hana: ⓒI think you should use a planner. Here's mine.

Jiho: Oh, can I see ⓓit?

Hana: Sure. I write my class schedule and appointment in my planner.

Jiho: That's great. Maybe I should buy one.

01 위 대화의 밑줄 친 ⓐ와 같은 의미가 되도록 빈칸에 알맞은 말을 쓰시오.

What's the _____, Jiho?

➡ _____

02 위 대화의 밑줄 친 ⓑ를 알맞은 형태로 고쳐 쓰시오.

➡ _____

위 대화의 밑줄 친 ⓒ와 바꿔 쓸 수 있는 것은?

① Do you think I should use a planner?

② Do you want to use a planner?

③ Why don't you use a planner?

④ Why do you use a planner?

⑤ If I were you, I wouldn't use a planner.

04 위 대화의 밑줄 친 ⓓ가 가리키는 것을 쓰시오.

➡ _____

05 위 대화를 읽고, 답할 수 없는 질문은?

① What didn't Jiho bring today?

② Does Jiho often forget things?

③ Where does Jiho practice soccer?

④ What does Hana think Jiho should use?

⑤ Does Hana write her class schedule in her planner?

[06~09] 다음 대화를 읽고, 물음에 답하시오.

G: You looked worried. What's going ⓐ ?

B: I'm worried about tomorrow's history quiz. ⓑ

G: ⓒI think you should read your textbook again.

B: That's a good idea..

06 위 대화의 빈칸 ⓐ에 알맞은 것을 쓰시오.

➡ _____

위 대화의 빈칸 ⓑ에 알맞은 것은?

① What is it?

② What's the matter?

③ What's wrong?

④ What should I do?

⑤ What happened?

서답형

08 위 대화의 밑줄 친 ⓒ를 다음과 같이 바꿔 쓸 때 빈칸에 알맞은 말을 쓰시오.

> You'd _____ _____ your textbook again.

서답형

09 위 대화를 읽고, 다음 질문에 완전한 문장으로 답하시오.

> Q: What does the girl think the boy should read?
>
> A: _____

[10~12] 다음 대화를 읽고, 물음에 답하시오.

> B: I'm so nervous. (①)
> G: Why? Is it because ____ⓐ____ the dance contest? (②)
> B: Yes. I practiced for many days, but I'm still nervous. (③)
> G: I think you should practice in front ____ⓑ____ your family. ⓒIt will be very helpful. (④)
> B: That's a good idea. Thank you. (⑤)

10 위 대화의 ①~⑤ 중 주어진 문장이 들어갈 알맞은 곳은?

> What should I do?

①   ②   ③   ④   ⑤

서답형

11 위 대화의 빈칸 ⓐ와 ⓑ에 공통으로 알맞은 말을 쓰시오.

➡ _____

서답형

12 위 대화의 밑줄 친 ⓒ가 가리키는 말을 우리말로 구체적으로 쓰시오.

➡ _____

[13~15] 다음 대화를 읽고, 물음에 답하시오.

> G: You look worried, Sam. ____ⓐ____
> B: I don't hear my alarm in the morning these days.
> G: ____ⓑ____ set the alarm on your clock and on your smartphone?
> B: ⓒThat's a good idea.

13 위 대화의 빈칸 ⓐ에 들어갈 말로 적절하지 <u>않은</u> 것은?

① What's wrong?
② What's the problem?
③ What happened to you?
④ What's the matter with you?
⑤ What do you hope to do?

중요

14 위 대화의 빈칸 ⓑ에 알맞은 것은?

① How about   ② How come
③ What about   ④ What makes you
⑤ Why don't you

15 위 대화의 밑줄 친 ⓒ와 바꿔 쓸 수 <u>없는</u> 것은?

① I think so, too.
② I'm afraid I can't.
③ I'm with you on that.
④ That sounds good.
⑤ You're right.

[01~03] 다음 대화를 읽고, 물음에 답하시오.

G: You look worried. <u>What's going on?</u>
B: I'm worried about tomorrow's history quiz. What should I do?
G: ⓑI think you should read your textbook again.
B: That's a good idea.

01 위 대화의 밑줄 친 ⓐ와 바꿔 쓸 수 있는 표현을 두 가지 이상 쓰시오.

➡ _____

_____

02 위 대화의 밑줄 친 ⓑ를 다음과 같이 바꿔 쓸 때 빈칸에 알맞은 말을 쓰시오.

_____ _____ you read your textbook again?

03 What is the boy worried about? Answer in Korean.

➡ _____

[04~05] 다음 대화를 읽고, 물음에 답하시오.

G: Jason, are you okay? You don't look good today.
B: I have a cold.
G: <u>That's too bad.</u> I think you should see a doctor.
B: You're right. Thank you.

04 위 대화의 밑줄 친 ⓐ와 바꿔 쓸 수 있는 표현을 쓰시오.

➡ _____

_____

05 What does the girl think Jason should do? Answer in English.

➡ _____

[06~09] 다음 대화를 읽고, 물음에 답하시오.

W: What's the (A)[wrong / matter], Sam? Are you sick?
B: Ms. Green, ⓐ(cold / a / have / I / I / think).
W: Did you go to the school nurse?
B: Yes. She said I need to go to the hospital. (B)[Can / Should] I leave school now?
W: Okay, Sam. I'll call your mom and tell her about ⓑit.

06 위 대화의 괄호 ⓐ를 의미가 통하도록 단어를 바르게 배열하시오.

➡ _____

07 위 대화의 괄호 (A)와 (B)에서 알맞은 것을 골라 쓰시오.

(A) _____ (B) _____

08 What did the school nurse say to Sam? Answer in English.

➡ _____

09 위 대화의 밑줄 친 ⓑ가 가리키는 것을 우리말로 쓰시오.

➡ _____

Grammar

1 to부정사의 형용사적 용법

- **You will have more work to do.** 너는 할 일이 더 많아질 것이다.
- **He has many books to read.** 그는 읽을 책을 많이 가지고 있다.
- **Would you like something to drink?** 마실 것 좀 드릴까요?

■ to부정사가 명사나 대명사를 뒤에서 꾸며주는 형용사의 역할을 할 때는 '~할', '~해야 할'로 해석한다.
- Seho needs some water **to drink**. 세호는 마실 물이 필요하다.
- He had no friends **to help** him. 그는 자기를 도와줄 친구가 하나도 없었다.
- You feel that you have nothing **to wear**. 너는 입을 것이 아무것도 없다고 느낀다.

■ **명사+to부정사+전치사:** 수식받는 명사가 전치사의 목적어인 경우는 to부정사 뒤에 반드시 전치사를 쓴다.
- I need some paper **to write on**. 나는 쓸 종이가 좀 필요하다.
- She's looking for a chair **to sit on**. 그녀는 앉을 의자를 찾고 있다.
- They will need a house **to live in**. 그들은 살 집이 필요할 것이다.
- He needs a friend **to talk to**. 그는 말할 친구가 필요하다.
- She has a pen **to write with**. 그녀는 쓸 펜을 가지고 있다.

cf. **-thing+형용사+to부정사:** -thing으로 끝나는 부정대명사는 형용사가 뒤에서 수식하며, 이를 다시 to부정사가 뒤에서 수식한다.
- I want something **hot to drink**. 나는 뜨거운 마실 것을 원한다.

핵심 Check

1. 다음 괄호 안에서 알맞은 것을 고르시오.
   (1) It's time (go / to go) to school.
   (2) Jack has a lot of friends (helping / to help).
   (3) Give me a pen (to write / to write with).
   (4) Would you like something (to drink cold / cold to drink)?

2. 다음 괄호 안에서 알맞은 것을 고르시오.
   (1) There are so many places _____ _____ in my town. (visit)
   (2) I have something important _____ _____ you. (tell)
   (3) Is there nobody _____ _____ to my story? (listen)

2 접속사 that

- I think **that** using my time to prepare for my future is important.
  나는 미래를 준비하기 위해 시간을 사용하는 것이 중요하다고 생각한다.

- He knows **that** I want to be a writer. 그는 내가 작가가 되고 싶어 한다는 것을 알고 있다.

- Imagine **that** you can fly like a bird. 새처럼 날 수 있다고 상상해 보라.

■ 접속사는 절과 절을 연결하는 역할을 하므로 접속사 that은 「주어+동사+that+주어+동사 ~」의 형태로 쓰인다.

- I hope **that** she likes the flowers. 그녀가 그 꽃들을 좋아하면 좋겠어.

- I think **that** he is a genius. 나는 그가 천재라고 생각해.

■ 접속사 that이 이끄는 절은 문장 안에서 주어, 목적어, 보어의 역할을 하므로 이때 that을 명사절 접속사라 한다. 목적어 역할을 하는 명사절을 이끄는 that은 생략 가능하다.

- **That** he plays soccer well is true. [주어 역할] 그가 축구를 잘한다는 것은 사실이다.

- He knows (**that**) I got up early this morning. [목적어 역할]
  그는 내가 오늘 아침에 일찍 일어났다는 것을 알고 있다.

- My problem is **that** I'm poor at English. [보어 역할] 내 문제는 내가 영어를 못한다는 것이다.

cf. that은 '저것'을 뜻하는 지시대명사나 지시형용사로 사용될 수도 있으므로, 문장 안에서 명사 역할을 하는 접속사 용법과 구분하도록 한다.

- I need **that** pen. [지시형용사] 나는 저 펜이 필요해.

- I want **that** blue shirt. 나는 저 파란색 셔츠를 원해.

■ 접속사 that 이하의 내용이 부정일 때, that 앞에 있는 주절의 동사를 부정으로 만든다.

- He doesn't think **that** she is rich. 그는 그녀가 부자라고 생각하지 않는다.

- We don't hope **that** you will like it. 우리는 네가 그것을 좋아하기를 바라지 않는다.

핵심 Check

3. 다음 괄호 안에서 알맞은 것을 고르시오.

(1) I think (what / that) he is honest.

(2) I know (that / which) she was a teacher.

4. 다음 문장에서 that이 들어갈 수 있는 곳에 V표 하시오.

(1) I heard she would go to the Philippines.

(2) Our teacher thought we were good at math.

(3) Miss Susan says the Han River is beautiful.

01 다음 문장의 빈칸에 알맞지 <u>않은</u> 것은?

> I _____ that Jane is good at playing the piano.

① think   ② know   ③ mind
④ heard   ⑤ believe

> be good at ~을 잘하다

02 다음 괄호 안에 주어진 단어를 바르게 배열하시오.

(1) There are _____ _____ _____ _____.
(do / things / to / many)
(2) He is the only person _____ _____ _____.
(help / to / us)

03 다음 우리말과 같도록 괄호 안의 단어를 바르게 배열하여 문장을 완성하시오.

(1) 나는 Jenny가 집에 있다고 생각한다.
(at / is / home / Jenny / that)
➡ I think _____.
(2) 그녀는 그가 돌아올 거라고 믿었다.
(he / back / believed / come / that / would)
➡ She _____.
(3) 나는 Alice가 Mason을 좋아할 거라고 생각하지 않았다.
(Mason / didn't / Alice / think / like / that / would)
➡ I _____.

04 다음 우리말과 일치하도록 빈칸에 알맞은 말을 쓰시오.

(1) 우리는 계획을 바꿀 시간이 없다.
➡ We have no time _____ _____ the schedule.
(2) 그는 우리나라를 방문한 최초의 미국인이었다.
➡ He was the first American _____ _____ our country.
(3) 그는 풀어야 할 수학 문제가 많다.
➡ He has a lot of math problems _____ _____.

01 다음 문장의 빈칸에 알맞은 것은?

> We want to introduce _____ water.

① saving a way   ② to save a way

③ a way save   ④ a way saving

⑤ a way to save

02 다음 문장의 빈칸에 알맞지 <u>않은</u> 것은?

> I _____ that he is sick today.

① know   ② believe

③ heard   ④ think

⑤ made

서답형

03 다음 빈칸에 공통으로 알맞은 말을 쓰시오.

> • He knows _____ the room is clean.
> • My mom said _____ the story was true.

04 다음 문장의 빈칸에 알맞은 것은?

> I bought some books _____.

① to read at night

② to drink after running

③ to eat in the morning

④ to wear after swimming

⑤ to keep in the refrigerator

05 다음 중 밑줄 친 부분의 쓰임이 나머지와 <u>다른</u> 하나는?

① It's time <u>to say</u> goodbye.

② I have a lot of work <u>to do</u>.

③ She needs a chair <u>to sit</u> on.

④ Please give me something <u>to eat</u>.

⑤ When does the snow start <u>to melt</u>?

서답형

06 다음 문장의 빈칸에 알맞은 말을 쓰시오.

> 나는 그가 현명한 아빠가 될 것이라고 믿는다.
> ➡ I _____ _____ he will be a wise father.

07 다음 밑줄 친 that 중 쓰임이 <u>다른</u> 하나는?

① I think <u>that</u> the movie was terrible.

② I know <u>that</u> Sally doesn't have a job.

③ I think <u>that</u> bag is yours.

④ I hope <u>that</u> he will be my boyfriend.

⑤ I know <u>that</u> she will go abroad to study.

서답형

08 다음 두 문장을 한 문장으로 바꿀 때, 빈칸에 알맞은 말을 쓰시오.

> I will bring some snacks. + I will eat them during the hike.
> ➡ I will bring some snacks _____ _____ during the hike.

09 다음 문장의 빈칸에 알맞은 것은?

> She has good news _____ you.

① tell
② to tell
③ tells
④ telling
⑤ to telling

10 다음 밑줄 친 that 중 생략할 수 없는 것은?

① I think that you are so beautiful.
② I hope that I will get good grades.
③ I didn't know that Jenny was sick.
④ I believe that he will be a great engineer.
⑤ I know that man is Jack's father.

서답형

11 다음 우리말에 맞도록 빈칸에 알맞은 말을 쓰시오.

> Ann은 그 없이는 살 수 없을 것이라는 사실을 몰랐다.
> ➡ Ann _____ _____ _____ she wouldn't be able to live without him.

12 다음 중 밑줄 친 부분의 쓰임이 다른 하나는?

① I have the project to finish.
② I need some food to eat.
③ We went out to have lunch.
④ She has no money to buy a new dress.
⑤ I have a lot of homework to do today.

서답형

13 다음 우리말과 같도록 주어진 어휘를 바르게 배열하시오.

> 나는 진우가 훌륭한 리더가 될 것이라고 생각한다.
> (Jinwoo / great / be / will / that / think / I / a / leader).

➡ _____

14 다음 중 어법상 어색한 것은?

① He has no friends to talk to.
② I have no time to play.
③ She's looking for something reading.
④ I need something to write on.
⑤ I have lots of homework to do.

서답형

15 다음 우리말과 뜻이 같도록 주어진 단어를 알맞게 배열하시오.

> 너에게는 읽을 흥미로운 것이 있니?
> (interesting / something / you / do / have / read / to)

➡ _____

16 다음 중 밑줄 친 that의 쓰임이 다른 하나는?

① I think that honesty is the most important thing.
② I think that Jinny has a dog.
③ Do you know that woman over there?
④ Susan thinks that he is very smart.
⑤ Runa believes that her hometown is New York.

17 다음 문장의 괄호 안의 말을 바르게 배열한 것은?

> She needs (paper, to, on, write).

① on paper to write
② paper on to write
③ to write paper on
④ paper to write on
⑤ on write to paper

21 다음 빈칸에 들어갈 말로 알맞지 <u>않은</u> 것은?

> I think _____.

① it is easy
② he is honest
③ is she fine
④ that he likes you
⑤ that she is taller than you

[18~19] 다음 괄호 안에 주어진 단어를 이용하여 우리말에 맞도록 문장을 완성하시오.

서답형

18 차가운 마실 것 좀 주세요. (something)

➡ Give me _____.

서답형

22 다음 주어진 단어를 이용하여 우리말을 영어로 바꿔 쓰시오.

> 나는 James가 여행을 갔다고 생각한다.
> (think, go on a trip)

➡ _____

서답형

19 그녀는 앉을 의자가 필요하다. (sit)

➡ She needs _____.

중요

23 다음 중 밑줄 친 부분의 쓰임이 바르지 <u>않은</u> 것은?

① There are no benches <u>to sit</u> on.
② I have no money <u>to give</u> you.
③ Judy has a lot of friends <u>to talk</u>.
④ She doesn't have a house <u>to live</u> in.
⑤ Do you have a pen <u>to write</u> with?

20 다음 중 밑줄 친 that과 쓰임이 같은 것은?

> He thinks <u>that</u> science is a useful subject.

① Look at <u>that</u> old temple.
② Where did you find <u>that</u> pencil?
③ He walked this way and <u>that</u> way.
④ I am not <u>that</u> interested in music.
⑤ I believe <u>that</u> everything will be fine.

서답형

24 다음 우리말과 뜻이 같도록 주어진 단어를 이용하여 영작하시오.

> 그 소녀에게는 그 개에게 먹일 음식이 좀 있다.
> (have, some, feed)

➡ _____

[01~02] 다음 빈칸에 공통으로 알맞은 말을 쓰시오.

01
- Mike had no time _____ do his homework.
- We are going to buy a house _____ live in.

02 〔중요〕
- I believe _____ the story is true.
- I'm reading the book _____ I bought yesterday.
- Does your mother know _____ boy in the room?

03 다음 두 문장을 to부정사를 이용하여 한 문장으로 고쳐 쓰시오.

(1) I bought some cookies. I will eat them in the afternoon.

➡ _____

(2) They need four chairs. They'll sit on the chair.

➡ _____

04 다음 주어진 두 문장을 that을 사용하여 한 문장으로 만드시오.

(1) My brother says something. He didn't eat the bananas.

➡ _____

(2) They think something. They are proud of themselves.

➡ _____

05 〔중요〕 다음 〈보기〉에서 알맞은 단어를 골라 문장을 완성하시오.

┌─ 보기 ─────────────────┐
sit eat drink talk buy wear
└──────────────────────┘

(1) I'm hungry. I need some food _____ _____.

(2) I'm very thirsty. I need something _____ _____.

(3) There's no chair here. I need a chair to _____ _____.

(4) Tony feels lonely. He needs friends to _____ _____.

06 다음 우리말과 같도록 괄호 안의 단어를 바르게 배열하시오.

(1) 나는 네가 모든 것을 할 수 있다고 생각한다.
(everything / do / you / can / that)
➡ I think _____.

(2) 너는 그녀가 예쁘다고 생각하니?
(is / think / she / pretty / that / you)
➡ Do _____?

07 〔중요〕 다음 문장에서 어법상 어색한 부분을 찾아 바르게 고쳐 쓰시오.

(1) He needs a pen to write.

_____ ➡ _____

(2) There are many places visiting in Paris.

_____ ➡ _____

08 다음 괄호 안에 주어진 단어와 that을 이용하여 바르게 배열하시오.

(1) (is / wife / know / I / a / wise / she)

➡ _____ that _____ .

(2) (Chinese / I / is / think / he)

➡ _____ that _____ .

(3) (we / we / world / the / can / change / believe)

➡ _____ that _____ .

09 다음 우리말과 같도록 주어진 단어를 바르게 배열하시오.

> 그녀는 입을 뭔가가 필요하다.
> (put / something / on / she / needs / to)

➡ _____

10 다음 괄호 안에 주어진 단어를 이용하여 우리말을 영어로 옮기시오.

(1) 그녀는 딸이 아프다고 생각한다.
   (think, that, sick)

➡ _____

(2) 나는 Nick이 파티에 올 것이라고 믿지 않는다.
   (believe, that)

➡ _____

11 다음 우리말에 맞게 빈칸에 알맞은 말을 쓰시오.

> 나는 묵을 호텔을 찾고 있다.
> ➡ I'm looking for _____ _____
> _____ _____ _____ .

12 다음 괄호 안에 주어진 단어를 이용하여 우리말을 영어로 옮기시오.

(1) 그녀는 가수가 되려는 강한 욕망을 갖고 있다.
   (strong desire, be, singer)

➡ _____

(2) 우리는 이야기할 것이 있었다.
   (something, talk about)

➡ _____

(3) 나는 쓸 종이를 한 장 원한다.
   (want, write)

➡ _____

(4) 제게 뜨거운 마실 것을 좀 주십시오.
   (please, something, drink)

➡ _____

13 다음 우리말을 괄호 안의 단어를 이용하여 영작하시오.

(1) 나는 나의 영어 선생님이 예쁘다고 생각한다.
   (pretty)

➡ _____

(2) 많은 사람들은 지구가 둥글다고 믿는다.
   (round)

➡ _____

14 다음 주어진 단어를 바르게 배열하여 문장을 완성하시오.

(1) (a / of / to / homework / I / do / have / lot)

➡ _____

(2) (family / your / is / to / introduce / turn / it / your)

➡ _____

Manage Your Time Well

Welcome to the new school year. In the second grade, you will have
more work to do. You need to manage your time well. How do you do
that?

Subin: I set small goals and achieve them every day. I do not say,
"I will master English." With such a big goal, I will probably put off
working on it until tomorrow, next week, or next month. Instead, I say,
"I will learn three new English words every day." I will achieve my big
goal, one step at a time.

work 일	
manage 관리하다	
well 잘	
grade 학년	
goal 목표	
achieve 성취하다, 달성하다	
master ~을 완전히 익히다	
such 그런, 그러한	
probably 아마(=perhaps)	
instead 대신에	
learn 배우다	
step 걸음, 단계	
at a time 한 번에	

 확인문제

- 다음 문장이 본문의 내용과 일치하면 T, 일치하지 <u>않으면</u> F를 쓰시오.

1 First graders will have more work to do. ☐

2 In the second grade, you need to manage your time well. ☐

3 Subin sets big goals and achieves them every day. ☐

4 Subin does not say, "I will master English." ☐

5 Subin says "I will learn a lot of English words every day." ☐

6 Subin will achieve her big goal quickly. ☐

Minsu: When I do <u>something</u>, I give <u>it</u> my full attention. I <u>used to read</u>
시간의 접속사(~할 때)　　　　　= something　　　used to+동사원형: (과거에) ~하곤 했었다

SNS postings <u>while</u> I was <u>doing my homework</u>. It <u>slowed me down</u>
시간의 접속사(~하는 동안)　　do one's homework: 숙제를 하다　　slow down: 속도를 늦추다

because I couldn't focus. Now, I <u>put aside</u> my smartphone <u>when</u> I
접 ~이기 때문에　　　　　　　　~을 한쪽에 놓다　　　　시간의 접속사(~할 때)

do my homework. It saves me <u>a lot of</u> time. <u>These days</u>, I finish my
　　　　　　　　　　　　　　많은(=much)　　　요즘

homework quickly and enjoy my <u>free time</u>.
자유 시간

John: I regularly <u>spend time working</u> toward my dream. I <u>want to</u>
spend time -ing: ~하는 데 시간을 소비하다　　　　want to+동사원형: ~하기를 원하다

become a chef. <u>Every Saturday morning</u>, I go to cooking classes or
토요일 아침마다

<u>search for</u> recipes. I think <u>that</u> <u>using</u> my time <u>to prepare</u> for my future
~을 찾다　　명사절을 이끄는 접속사 동명사 주어　to부정사의 부사적 용법(~ 하기 위하여)

is important.
동명사 주어는 단수 취급

Time is a <u>present</u>. Everyone has the same present <u>to spend</u> every day.
선물(=gift)　　　　　　　　to부정사의 형용사적 용법 (~할)

<u>Manage</u> your time well, <u>and</u> you will <u>be happier</u> in the new school
명령문 ~, and …: ~해라, 그러면 …　　　더 행복해지다

year!

attention 주의, 집중

posting 포스팅, 게시 글

focus 집중하다

save 절약하다

finish 끝내다

regularly 규칙적으로

toward ~을 위하여

chef 요리사

cooking class 요리 강좌

recipe 요리[조리]법

future 미래

important 중요한

present 선물

everyone 모든 사람

every day 매일

확인문제

● 다음 문장이 본문의 내용과 일치하면 T, 일치하지 <u>않으면</u> F를 쓰시오.

1 Minsu used to read SNS postings while he was doing his homework. ☐

2 Minsu uses his smartphone when he does his homework. ☐

3 These days, Minsu finishes his homework quickly. ☐

4 John never spends time working for his dream. ☐

5 John wants to become a chef. ☐

6 John goes to cooking classes every morning. ☐

7 Everyone has different presents to spend every day. ☐

• 우리말을 참고하여 빈칸에 알맞은 말을 쓰시오.

1 _____ _____ the new school year.

2 _____ the _____ grade, you will have more work _____ _____.

3 You_____ _____ manage your time _____.

4 _____ do you _____ that?

5 Subin: I _____ small goals and _____ them every day.

6 I do not say, "I _____ _____ English."

7 _____ such a big goal, I will probably _____ _____ working on it _____ tomorrow, next week, _____ next month.

8 _____, I say, "I _____ _____ three new English words _____ _____.

9 I _____ _____ my big goal, one step _____ _____ _____.

10 Minsu: _____ I do something, I give it my _____ _____.

11 I _____ _____ _____ SNS postings _____ I was doing my homework.

1 새 학년이 된 걸 환영해.

2 2학년에서, 여러분은 할 일이 더 많을 거야.

3 여러분은 시간을 잘 관리할 필요가 있어.

4 여러분은 시간 관리를 어떻게 하는가?

5 수빈: 나는 작은 목표들을 세우고 매일 그것들을 성취해.

6 나는 "나는 영어를 마스터할 거야."라고 말하지 않아.

7 그렇게 큰 목표를 가지면, 나는 아마 그것을 위해 노력하는 걸 내일, 다음 주, 혹은 다음 달까지 미룰 거야.

8 대신에 나는 "나는 매일 세 개의 새로운 영어 단어를 배울 거야." 라고 말해.

9 나는 한 번에 한 단계씩 나의 큰 목표를 달성할 거야.

10 민수: 나는 무언가를 할 때 그것에 모든 주의를 기울여.

11 나는 숙제를 하는 동안 SNS 게시 글을 읽곤 했어.

12 It _____ me down _____ I couldn't focus.

13 Now, I _____ _____ my smartphone _____ I do my homework.

14 It saves me _____ _____ _____ time.

15 _____ _____, I finish my homework quickly and enjoy my _____ _____.

16 John: I regularly _____ time _____ toward my dream.

17 I want _____ _____ a chef.

18 _____ Saturday morning, I go to cooking _____ or _____ _____ recipes.

19 I think _____ using my time _____ _____ for my future is important.

20 Time is a _____.

21 Everyone _____ the same present _____ _____ every day.

22 _____ your time well, _____ you will _____ _____ in the new school year!

12 집중할 수 없었기 때문에 그것은 나의 속도를 늦추었어.

13 지금 나는 숙제를 할 때 스마트폰을 한쪽에 치워 놔.

14 그렇게 하면 시간이 많이 절약돼.

15 요즈음, 나는 숙제를 빨리 끝내고 자유 시간을 즐겨.

16 John: 나는 내 꿈을 위해 노력하며 규칙적으로 시간을 사용해.

17 나는 요리사가 되고 싶어.

18 토요일 아침마다 나는 요리 강습에 가거나 요리법을 찾아봐.

19 나는 나의 미래를 준비하기 위해 시간을 쓰는 것이 중요하다고 생각해.

20 시간은 선물이다.

21 모든 사람은 매일 소비할 똑같은 선물을 가지고 있다.

22 시간을 잘 관리하면 여러분은 새 학년에 더 행복해질 것이다!

Reading **31**

● 우리말을 참고하여 본문을 영작하시오.

1 새 학년이 된 걸 환영해.

➡ _____

2 2학년에서, 여러분은 할 일이 더 많을 거야.

➡ _____

3 여러분은 시간을 잘 관리할 필요가 있어.

➡ _____

4 여러분은 시간 관리를 어떻게 하는가?

➡ _____

5 수빈: 나는 작은 목표를 세우고 매일 그것들을 성취해.

➡ _____

6 나는 "나는 영어를 마스터할 거야."라고 말하지 않아.

➡ _____

7 그렇게 큰 목표를 가지면, 나는 아마 그것을 위해 노력하는 걸 내일, 다음 주, 혹은 다음 달까지 미룰 거야.

➡ _____

8 대신에 나는 "나는 매일 세 개의 새로운 영어 단어를 배울 거야."라고 말해.

➡ _____

9 나는 한 번에 한 단계씩 나의 큰 목표를 달성할 거야.

➡ _____

10 민수: 나는 무언가를 할 때 그것에 모든 주의를 기울여.

➡ _____

11 나는 숙제를 하는 동안 SNS 게시 글을 읽곤 했어.

➡ _____

12 집중할 수 없었기 때문에 그것은 나의 속도를 늦추었어.

➡ _____

13 지금 나는 숙제를 할 때 스마트폰을 한쪽에 치워 놔.

➡ _____

14 그렇게 하면 시간이 많이 절약돼.

➡ _____

15 요즈음, 나는 숙제를 빨리 끝내고 자유 시간을 즐겨.

➡ _____

16 John: 나는 내 꿈을 위해 노력하며 규칙적으로 시간을 사용해.

➡ _____

17 나는 요리사가 되고 싶어.

➡ _____

18 토요일 아침마다 나는 요리 강습에 가거나 요리법을 찾아봐.

➡ _____

19 나는 나의 미래를 준비하기 위해 시간을 쓰는 것이 중요하다고 생각해.

➡ _____

20 시간은 선물이다.

➡ _____

21 모든 사람은 매일 소비할 똑같은 선물을 가지고 있다.

➡ _____

22 시간을 잘 관리하면 여러분은 새 학년에 더 행복해질 것이다!

➡ _____

[01~05] 다음 글을 읽고, 물음에 답하시오.

Subin: I ⓐ small goals and achieve ⓑ them every day. I do not say, "I will master English." With such a big goal, I will probably ⓒput off working on it until tomorrow, next week, or next month. ⓓ , I say, "I will learn three new English words every day." I will achieve my big goal, one step at a time.

01 위 글의 빈칸 ⓐ에 알맞은 것은?

① put　　　② set
③ get　　　④ take
⑤ win

서답형

02 위 글의 밑줄 친 ⓑ가 가리키는 말을 찾아 영어로 쓰시오.

➡ _____

03 위 글의 밑줄 친 ⓒ와 바꿔 쓸 수 있는 것은?

① quit　　　② finish
③ carry　　　④ postpone
⑤ establish

중요

04 문맥상 위 글의 빈칸 ⓓ에 알맞은 것은?

① So　　　② However
③ Instead　　　④ Besides
⑤ Therefore

05 위 글의 내용으로 보아 수빈이에 대한 진술이 올바른 것은?

① 매일 큰 목표들을 성취한다.
② 영어를 빨리 익히고 싶어 한다.
③ 영어 공부하는 것을 자주 미룬다.
④ 매일 많은 영어 단어를 배우고 싶어 한다.
⑤ 차근차근 그녀의 큰 목표를 성취하기를 원한다.

[06~10] 다음 글을 읽고, 물음에 답하시오.

Welcome ⓐ the new school year. In the second grade, you will have more work ⓑto do. You need to manage your time well. How do you do that?
John: I regularly spend time ⓒwork toward my dream. I want to become a chef. Every Saturday morning, I go to cooking classes or search for recipes. I think ⓓ using my time to prepare for my future is important.

서답형

06 위 글의 빈칸 ⓐ에 알맞은 말을 쓰시오.

➡ _____

중요

07 위 글의 밑줄 친 ⓑ와 쓰임이 같은 것은?

① I have no pen to write with.
② My dream is to be a doctor.
③ I did my best to pass the test.
④ They want to go hiking together.
⑤ I went to the bakery to buy some bread.

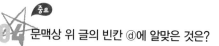

서답형

08 위 글의 밑줄 친 ⓒ를 알맞은 형태로 고쳐 쓰시오.

➡ _____

09 위 글의 빈칸 ⓓ에 알맞은 것은?

① as   ② if

③ that   ④ while

⑤ when

10 위 글의 내용으로 보아 John에 대한 진술이 잘못된 것은?

① 꿈을 위해 시간을 규칙적으로 사용한다.

② 요리사가 되고 싶어 한다.

③ 토요일 아침에 요리 수업을 들을 때가 있다.

④ 매일 요리법을 찾아본다.

⑤ 미래를 준비하기 위해 시간을 사용하는 것이 중요하다고 생각한다.

[11~16] 다음 글을 읽고, 물음에 답하시오.

> **Minsu:** When I do something, ⓐI give it my full attention. (①) I ___ⓑ___ read SNS postings while I was doing my homework. (②) ⓒIt slowed me down ___ⓓ___ I couldn't focus. (③) Now, I put aside my smartphone when I do my homework. (④) These days, I finish my homework quickly and enjoy my free time. (⑤)

11 위 글의 ①~⑤ 중 다음 문장이 들어갈 알맞은 곳은?

> It saves me a lot of time.

①   ②   ③   ④   ⑤

서답형

12 위 글의 밑줄 친 ⓐ를 다음과 같이 바꿔 쓸 때 빈칸에 알맞은 말을 쓰시오.

> I give my full attention _____ it

➡ _____

13 위 글의 빈칸 ⓑ에 문맥상 알맞은 것은?

① could   ② might

③ should   ④ ought to

⑤ used to

서답형

14 위 글의 밑줄 친 ⓒ가 가리키는 것을 우리말로 구체적으로 쓰시오.

➡ _____

15 문맥상 위 글의 빈칸 ⓓ에 알맞은 것은?

① if   ② while

③ when   ④ though

⑤ because

16 위 글의 내용으로 보아 민수에 대해 알 수 없는 것은?

① 어떤 일을 할 때 그것에 모든 주의를 기울인다.

② 숙제하는 동안 SNS 게시 글을 읽곤 했다.

③ 스마트폰을 이용해서 숙제를 하곤 했다.

④ 지금은 숙제할 때 스마트폰을 한쪽에 치워 놓는다.

⑤ 요즈음은 숙제를 빨리 끝낸다.

[17~21] 다음 글을 읽고, 물음에 답하시오.

I regularly spend time working ⓐ_____ my dream. I want ⓑbecome a chef. Every Saturday morning, I go to cooking classes or search ⓓ_____ recipes. ⓔI think that using my time to prepare for my future are important.

※ I = John

중요

17 위 글의 빈칸 ⓐ에 알맞은 것은?

① against   ② within
③ toward   ④ through
⑤ along

서답형

18 위 글의 밑줄 친 ⓑ를 알맞은 형태로 고쳐 쓰시오.

➡ _____

19 위 글의 밑줄 친 ⓒ와 같은 의미로 쓰인 것은?

① I will take a class on play.
② We were in the same class at school.
③ He is the tallest boy in the class.
④ He is ahead of his class in English.
⑤ The class listened and took notes.

20 위 글의 빈칸 ⓓ에 알맞은 것은?

① up   ② for
③ in   ④ into
⑤ with

서답형

21 위 글의 밑줄 친 ⓔ에서 어법상 틀린 부분을 찾아 바르게 고쳐 쓰시오.

_____ ➡ _____

[22~26] 다음 글을 읽고, 물음에 답하시오.

Welcome to the new school year. In the second ⓐgrade, you will have more work to do. You need to _____ⓑ your time well. How do you do that?

Subin: I set small goals and achieve them every day. I do not say, "I will master English." With such a big goal, I will probably put _____ⓒ working on it _____ⓓ tomorrow, next week, or next month. Instead, I say, "I will learn three new English words every day." I will achieve my big goal, one step at a time.

중요

22 위 글의 밑줄 친 ⓐ와 같은 의미로 쓰인 것은?

① I got a terrible grade in math.
② He is one grade above me.
③ His grade is almost at the bottom.
④ She's not in the first grade as a painter.
⑤ 70% of pupils got grade C or above.

23 위 글의 빈칸 ⓑ에 알맞은 것은?

① save   ② spend
③ create   ④ manage
⑤ design

24 위 글의 빈칸 ⓒ에 알맞은 것은?

① on
② out
③ down
④ up
⑤ off

중요
25 위 글의 빈칸 ⓓ에 알맞은 것은?

① to
② within
③ until
④ during
⑤ among

서답형
26 위 글을 다음과 같이 요약할 때 빈칸에 알맞은 말을 쓰시오.

Subin says, "I _____ small goals and _____ them every day. A _____ doesn't help me _____ it."

[27~32] 다음 글을 읽고, 물음에 답하시오.

Minsu: When I do something, I give it my full ___ⓐ___. (①) I ⓑused to read SNS postings ___ⓒ___ I was doing my homework. (②) Now, I put aside my smartphone when I do my homework. (③) It ⓓsaves me a lot of time. (④) These days, I finish my homework quickly and enjoy my free time. (⑤)

27 위 글의 ①~⑤ 중 다음 문장이 들어갈 알맞은 곳은?

It slowed me down because I couldn't focus.

①   ②   ③   ④   ⑤

서답형
28 위 글의 빈칸 ⓐ에 다음 영영풀이에 해당하는 단어를 주어진 철자로 시작하여 쓰시오.

the act of listening to, looking at, or thinking about something or someone carefully

➡ a_____

중요
29 위 글의 밑줄 친 ⓑ와 바꿔 쓸 수 있는 것은?

① might
② could
③ should
④ would
⑤ ought to

30 위 글의 빈칸 ⓒ에 알맞은 것은?

① if
② since
③ because
④ though
⑤ while

중요
31 위 글의 밑줄 친 ⓓ와 같은 의미로 쓰인 것은?

① I wanted to save my dog.
② She has to save this report to a file.
③ He saved many lives from the fire.
④ This is why we need to save energy.
⑤ You should save your work frequently.

서답형
32 위 글을 읽고, 다음 질문에 완전한 문장으로 답하시오.

Q: These days, what does Minsu do after he finishes his homework quickly?

A: _____

[01~06] 다음 글을 읽고, 물음에 답하시오.

Welcome to the new school year. In the second grade, ⓐ너는 할 일이 더 많을 거야. You need to manage your time well. How do you ⓑdo that?

Subin: I set small goals and achieve them every day. I do not say, "I will master English." With such a big goal, I will probably put off ⓒwork on it until tomorrow, next week, or next month. Instead, I say, "I will learn three new English words every day." ⓓI will achieve my big goal, one step at a time.

01 위 글의 밑줄 친 ⓐ의 우리말을 주어진 단어를 이용하여 영어로 옮기시오.

> (will / work / do)

➡ _____

02 위 글의 밑줄 친 ⓑ가 의미하는 것을 우리말로 쓰시오.

➡ _____

03 How often does Subin set small goals and achieve them? Answer in English.

➡ _____

04 위 글의 밑줄 친 ⓒ를 알맞은 형태로 고쳐 쓰시오.

➡ _____

05 How many new English words will Subin learn every day? Answer in English.

➡ _____

06 위 글의 밑줄 친 ⓓ를 우리말로 옮기시오.

➡ _____

[07~10] 다음 글을 읽고, 물음에 답하시오.

Minsu: When I do something, I give ⓐit my full attention. I (A)[used to / ought to] read SNS postings while I was doing my homework. It slowed me down (B)[though / because] I couldn't focus. Now, I put aside my smartphone when I do my homework. ⓑIt saves me a lot of time. These days, I finish my homework quickly and enjoy my free time.

07 위 글의 밑줄 친 ⓐit이 가리키는 것을 찾아 쓰시오.

➡ _____

08 위 글의 괄호 (A)와 (B)에서 알맞은 것을 골라 쓰시오.

(A) _____ (B) _____

09 위 글의 밑줄 친 ⓑIt이 가리키는 것을 우리말로 쓰시오.

➡ _____

10 What did Minsu use to do while he was doing his homework? Answer in English.

➡ _____

_____

13 What does John want to become? Answer in English.

➡ _____

[11~17] 다음 글을 읽고, 물음에 답하시오.

Welcome to the new school year. In the second grade, you will have more work (A) [doing / to do]. You need to manage your time well. How do you do that?

John: I regularly spend time (B)[working / to work] toward my dream. I want to become a chef. Every Saturday morning, I go to cooking classes or search for recipes. ⓐI think (   ) using my time to prepare for my future (   ) important.

Time is a present. Everyone has ⓑ(spend / same / to / the / present) every day. Manage your time well, and you will be happier in the new school year!

14 위 글의 밑줄 친 ⓐ에서 괄호 안에 들어갈 말을 순서대로 쓰시오.

➡ _____

15 What does John do every Saturday morning? Answer in English.

➡ _____

11 위 글의 괄호 (A)와 (B)에서 알맞은 것을 골라 쓰시오.

(A) _____ (B) _____

16 위 글에서 시간의 중요성을 강조하기 위해 시간을 무엇에 비유했는지 우리말로 쓰시오.

➡ _____

12 What do you need to do in the second grade? Answer in English.

➡ _____

17 위 글의 괄호 ⓑ의 단어들을 순서에 맞게 알맞게 배열하시오.

➡ _____

Enjoy Writing B

My Goals for This Year

I have three goals to achieve this year. The first goal is to get along with my
　　　　　　　　　to부정사의 형용사적 용법 (~ 할)　　　　　　　　　　　　　　~와 잘 지내다

new classmates. The second goal is to get an A on the English speaking test.
　　　　　　　　　　　　　　　　　　　　　A를 받다

The last goal is to stop playing smartphone games. I hope that this year is
　　　　　　　　stop -ing: ~하는 것을 멈추다　　　　　　　　명사절을 이끄는 접속사(생략 가능)

better than last year.
비교급+than: ~보다 더 ...한

구문해설　• this year: 올해　• goal: 목표　• second: 두 번째의　• last year: 지난해

올해의 나의 목표

"나는 올해 달성해야 할 목표
가 세 가지 있다. 첫 번째 목표
는 새로운 반 친구들과 잘 지
내는 것이다. 두 번째 목표는
영어 말하기 시험에서 A를 받
는 것이다. 마지막 목표는 스
마트폰 게임을 중단하는 것이
다. 나는 올해가 작년보다 더
낫기를 희망한다.

Project - Step 1

A: I think we should make our group's motto about dreaming and doing.
나는 ~해야 한다고 생각해. (무언가를 제안하거나 권유하는 표현)　　　　　전치사+동명사

B: That's a good idea. I believe that dreaming and doing are different.
상대방의 의견에 동의하는 표현　　명사절을 이끄는 접속사　　동명사 주어

C: Yes. I think that doing is more important than dreaming.
　　　　　　　동명사 주어는 단수 취급　　~보다 더 중요한(비교급)

D: That's right.

구문해설　• motto: 좌우명　• dream: 꿈을 꾸다　• different: 다른

A: 나는 우리가 꿈을 꾸고 행
동하는 것에 대한 우리 모둠의
좌우명을 만들어야 한다고 생
각해.

B: 좋은 생각이야. 나는 꿈과
행동이 다르다고 믿어.

C: 맞아. 나는 꿈을 꾸는 것보
다 행동하는 것이 더 중요하다
고 생각해.

D: 맞아.

Wrap Up - Writing

Jenny is going to go to the grocery store today. She is going to buy three
　　　　is going to ~할 것이다

apples to eat. She is going to buy two bottles of water to drink. She is going to
　　　　to부정사의 형용사적 용법 (~ 할)　　　　　　두 병의　　　to부정사의 형용사적 용법 (~ 할)

buy one fashion magazine to read.
　　　　　　　　to부정사의 형용사적 용법 (~ 할)

구문해설　• grocery: 식료품, 잡화류　• buy: 사다　• magazine: 잡지

Jenny는 오늘 식료품점에 갈
거야. 그녀는 먹을 사과 세 개
를 살 거야. 그녀는 마실 물 두
병을 살 거야. 그녀는 읽을 패
션 잡지를 하나 살 거야.

영역별 핵심문제

Words & Expressions

01 다음 중 단어의 성격이 <u>다른</u> 것은?

① wisely   ② loudly
③ kindly   ④ lovely
⑤ regularly

02 다음 영영풀이에 해당하는 단어는?

> to direct your attention or effort at something specific

① check   ② focus
③ master   ④ join
⑤ prepare

03 다음 짝지어진 두 단어의 관계가 같도록 빈칸에 알맞은 단어를 쓰시오.

> probably : perhaps = gift : _____

04 다음 문장의 빈칸에 알맞은 것은?

> • I want to be good _____ English.
> • Please do one thing _____ a time.

① in   ② on
③ at   ④ by
⑤ for

05 다음 빈칸에 들어갈 말로 적절하지 <u>않은</u> 것은?

> • I will _____ my big goal.
> • I have soccer _____ today.
> • He is in the sixth _____.
> • You need to _____ your time well.

① grade   ② manage
③ finish   ④ practice
⑤ achieve

06 다음 문장의 밑줄 친 부분과 바꿔 쓸 수 있는 것은?

> We cannot <u>put off</u> decisions any longer.

① order   ② postpone
③ achieve   ④ demand
⑤ prepare

Conversation

07 다음 대화의 밑줄 친 부분과 바꿔 쓸 수 <u>없는</u> 것은?

> A: I want to be good at cooking.
> B: <u>I think you should search for recipes.</u>

① What about searching for recipes?
② I advise you to search for recipes.
③ How about searching for recipes?
④ You'd better search for recipes.
⑤ Why didn't you search for recipes?

08 다음 대화의 빈칸에 들어갈 말로 어색한 것은?

> A: What's wrong with Jinsu?
> B: _____
> A: That's too bad.

① He has a terrible headache.
② He lost his new digital camera.
③ He broke his leg in the soccer game.
④ He won first prize on a science contest.
⑤ He got a really bad grade on his English test.

09 다음 대화의 순서를 바르게 배열하시오.

> (A) I have a cold.
> (B) You're right. Thank you.
> (C) That's too bad. I think you should see a doctor.
> (D) Jason, are you okay? You don't look good today.

➡ _____

10 다음 대화의 빈칸에 알맞지 않은 것을 고르면? (2개)

> A: _____
> B: He failed the math test.
> A: I'm sorry to hear that.

① What's wrong with Kevin?
② What subject is Kevin good at?
③ Is something wrong with Kevin?
④ What's the matter with Kevin?
⑤ How do you feel about Kevin?

11 다음 주어진 표현을 이용하여 밑줄 친 우리말을 영작하시오.

> A: You looked worried. What's the matter?
> B: 나는 수학 시험이 걱정돼. (math test)

➡ _____

[12~16] 다음 대화를 읽고, 물음에 답하시오.

> B: I'm so nervous. (①)
> G: Why? (②) Is it because ___ⓐ___ the dance contest?
> B: Yes. I practiced ___ⓑ___ many days, ___ⓒ___ I'm still nervous. (③) What should I do?
> G: I think you should practice ___ⓓ___ front of your family. (④)
> B: That's a good idea. Thank you. (⑤)

12 위 대화의 ①~⑤ 중 다음 문장이 들어갈 위치로 알맞은 것은?

> It will be very helpful.

① ② ③ ④ ⑤

13 위 대화의 빈칸 ⓐ와 ⓑ에 알맞은 말이 바르게 짝지어진 것은?

① of – during ② for – for
③ to – for ④ of – for
⑤ to – during

14 위 대화의 빈칸 ⓒ에 알맞은 것은?

① so ② and ③ but
④ for ⑤ because

15 위 대화의 빈칸 ⓓ에 알맞은 말을 쓰시오.

➡ _____

16 Why is the boy nervous? Answer in English.

➡ _____

Grammar

17 다음 문장의 빈칸에 알맞은 것은?

> I think _____ cars will fly in the sky someday.

① that ② before
③ as ④ after
⑤ when

18 다음 〈보기〉의 우리말을 영어로 바르게 옮긴 것은?

> ┤ 보기 ├
> 그는 살 좋은 집을 갖기를 원한다.

① He wants to have a good house live.
② He wants to have a good house live in.
③ He wants to have live in a good house.
④ He wants to have to live in a good house.
⑤ He wants to have a good house to live in.

19 다음 두 문장의 빈칸에 공통으로 알맞은 말을 쓰시오.

> • I believe _____ I can fly in the air.
> • We don't hope _____ you will like it.

20 다음 밑줄 친 부분의 쓰임이 나머지와 <u>다른</u> 하나는?

① This is the time <u>to study</u>.
② I bought some water <u>to drink</u>.
③ I studied hard <u>to pass</u> the exam.
④ Tom needs some books <u>to read</u>.
⑤ She has no money <u>to buy</u> a new dress.

21 다음 밑줄 친 부분 중 생략할 수 있는 것은?

① You can say <u>that</u> again.
② He said <u>that</u> was a correct answer.
③ She likes <u>that</u> brown bag on the shelf.
④ Do you know <u>that</u> boy in the corner?
⑤ I think <u>that</u> we should respect each other.

22 다음 문장의 밑줄 친 부분의 쓰임이 〈보기〉와 같은 것은?

> ┤ 보기 ├
> She has many bags <u>to carry</u>.

① I went to bed <u>to sleep</u>.
② He has a dog <u>to walk</u>.
③ I want <u>to meet</u> my friends.
④ My hobby is <u>to collect</u> stamps.
⑤ He went to her house <u>to fix</u> the computer.

23 다음 우리말과 일치하도록 주어진 단어를 바르게 배열하시오.

> Jane은 Kevin이 그 파티에 올 것이라고 믿지 않았다. (party / Jane / the / Kevin / come / to / that / would / didn't / believe)

➡ _____

24 다음 문장에서 어법상 어색한 부분을 찾아 바르게 고쳐 쓰시오.

> I need a pen to write.

_____ ➡ _____

25 다음 문장에서 어법상 어색한 부분을 찾아 고쳐 쓰시오.

> I don't know that he will come tomorrow.

_____ ➡ _____

26 다음 문장의 밑줄 친 부분의 쓰임이 나머지와 다른 하나는?

① I have a book to buy.
② There are many places to visit.
③ I went to the store to buy a jacket.
④ Do you have something to eat?
⑤ The man has three dogs to take care of.

27 다음 문장의 빈칸에 들어갈 말이 다른 하나는? (대·소문자 무시)

① Do you know _____ man?
② I think _____ she is pretty.
③ Do you know _____ he is sick?
④ _____ you finish it, let me know.
⑤ _____ he never came back is true.

28 다음 중 밑줄 친 부분의 쓰임이 같은 것끼리 묶인 것은?

> ⓐ I need something to drink.
> ⓑ She wants to become a teacher.
> ⓒ The girl had nothing to wear.
> ⓓ She went out to meet her boyfriend.

① ⓐ, ⓑ   ② ⓑ, ⓓ
③ ⓑ, ⓒ   ④ ⓐ, ⓒ
⑤ ⓒ, ⓓ

Reading

[29~35] 다음 글을 읽고, 물음에 답하시오.

> _____ⓐ_____ I do something, I give it my full attention. I ⓑused to read SNS postings while I was doing my homework. It slowed me down because I couldn't _____ⓒ_____. ⓓNow, I put aside my smartphone when I do my homework. It saves me a lot of time. ⓔThese days, I finish my homework quickly and enjoy my ⓕfree time.   ※ I = Minsu

29 위 글의 빈칸 ⓐ에 알맞은 것은?

① If   ② That
③ When   ④ What
⑤ Because

30 위 글의 밑줄 친 ⓑ를 한 단어로 바꿔 쓰시오.

➡ _____

31 위 글의 빈칸 ⓒ에 다음 영영풀이에 해당하는 단어를 주어진 철자로 시작하여 쓰시오.

> to direct your attention or effort at something specific

➡ f_____

32 위 글의 밑줄 친 ⓓ를 우리말로 옮기시오.

➡ _____

33 위 글의 밑줄 친 ⓔ와 바꿔 쓸 수 있는 것은?

① Instantly　　② At once
③ Right now　　④ Nowadays
⑤ Immediately

34 위 글의 밑줄 친 ⓕ와 의미가 같은 것은?

① Is this seat free?
② He was free as a bird.
③ I am now free from danger.
④ Children under five travel free.
⑤ An excellent lunch is provided free.

35 위 글을 읽고, 답할 수 없는 질문은?

① When Minsu does something, does he give it his full attention?
② What did Minsu use to do while he was doing his homework?
③ How long does Minsu use his smartphone a day?
④ Now, what does Minsu do when he does his homework?
⑤ What does Minsu do after finishing his homework quickly?

[36~40] 다음 글을 읽고, 물음에 답하시오.

I have three goals ⓐto achieve this year. The first goal is to get along _____ⓑ_____ my new classmates. The second goal is to get an A on the English speaking test. The last goal is to stop ⓒplay smartphone games. I hope _____ⓓ_____ this year is better than last year.

36 위 글의 밑줄 친 ⓐ와 쓰임이 같은 것은?

① His dream was to draw pictures.
② It's easy to memorize English words.
③ I have a lot of work to do today.
④ He wants to play tennis after school.
⑤ She studied very hard to pass the exam.

37 위 글의 빈칸 ⓑ에 알맞은 말을 쓰시오.

➡ _____

38 위 글의 밑줄 친 ⓒ를 알맞은 형태로 고쳐 쓰시오.

➡ _____

39 위 글의 빈칸 ⓓ에 알맞은 것은?

① if　　　　② that
③ when　　　④ while
⑤ as

40 위 글을 읽고, 답할 수 없는 질문은?

① Does the writer have three goals to achieve this year?
② What is the first goal the writer wants to achieve?
③ What test does the writer want to get an A on?
④ What goals did the writer achieve last year?
⑤ What is the last goal the writer wants to achieve?

출제율 90%

01 다음 중 짝지어진 두 단어의 관계가 <u>다른</u> 것은?

① future : past
② sad : glad
③ gift : present
④ low : high
⑤ remember : forget

출제율 95%

02 다음 빈칸에 알맞은 말이 바르게 짝지어진 것은?

> • I _____ along with him very well.
> • He _____ aside his smartphone when the teacher came in.

① go – put
② make – got
③ take – made
④ get – turned
⑤ get – put

출제율 100%

03 다음 우리말에 맞게 빈칸에 알맞은 말을 쓰시오.

(1) 나는 많은 사람들 앞에서 말할 수 없다.
➡ I can't speak _____ _____ many people.

(2) 그녀는 매우 슬퍼서 하루 종일 울었습니다.
➡ She was very sad and cried _____ _____ _____.

(3) 수지는 어렸을 때 안경을 썼었다.
➡ Suji _____ _____ wear glasses when she was a child.

(4) 그녀는 그 때문에 매우 화가 났다.
➡ She was very angry _____ _____ him.

출제율 85%

04 다음 중 영영풀이가 <u>잘못된</u> 것은?

① easy: not difficult
② master: to learn something completely
③ recipe: a set of instructions for making food
④ save: to use money to pay for something
⑤ due: expected to happen or arrive at a particular time

출제율 95%

05 다음 대화의 빈칸에 알맞은 것은?

> A: You look worried. What's wrong?
> B: I can't get good grades. _____
> A: How about making a study plan?

① What is it?
② What are you doing?
③ What should I do?
④ What happened?
⑤ What are you looking for?

출제율 90%

06 다음 대화의 빈칸에 알맞은 말이 바르게 짝지어진 것은?

> A: What's wrong?
> B: I have _____.
> A: That's too bad. Why don't you _____?
> B: OK. I will.

① a bad cold — see a doctor
② a pet — get some fresh air
③ a lot of homework — go to sleep
④ some stress — go to see a dentist
⑤ long hair — take some medicine

07 다음 짝지어진 대화 중 어색한 것은?

① A: What should I do?
   B: You should make a new study plan.
② A: You look down. What's wrong?
   B: My computer isn't working.
③ A: Would you give me some advice?
   B: Sure. What is it?
④ A: Why don't you take notes?
   B: Not yet. What should I do?
⑤ A: We should wait for the next showing.
   B: Sorry, it's all my fault.

[08~10] 다음 대화를 읽고, 물음에 답하시오.

> G: You look ⓐworry. ⓑWhat's going on?
> B: I'm ⓒworry about tomorrow's history quiz.
>   What should I do?
> G: _____ⓓ_____ read your textbook again?
> B: That's a good idea.

출제율 95%

08 위 대화의 밑줄 친 ⓐ와 ⓒ의 단어를 올바른 형태로 고쳐 쓰시오.

➡ _____

출제율 85%

09 위 대화의 밑줄 친 ⓑ의 의도로 알맞은 것은?

① 안부 묻기   ② 경험 묻기
③ 주의 끌기   ④ 의견 묻기
⑤ 문제점 파악하기

출제율 100%

10 위 대화의 빈칸 ⓓ에 알맞은 것은?

① Are you   ② How about
③ Do you want   ④ What about
⑤ Why don't you

출제율 95%

11 다음 중 〈보기〉의 밑줄 친 부분과 쓰임이 같은 것은?

> ┤ 보기 ├
> Do you have anything to eat?

① To ride a bike is fun.
② My hobby is to play soccer.
③ I want to go to Jeju-do.
④ She has no money to buy a ticket.
⑤ Tom went to Canada to learn how to snowboard.

출제율 95%

12 다음 빈칸에 공통으로 들어갈 말은?

> • I hope _____ you do well in the spelling bee.
> • I'm sorry to hear _____.

① what   ② this   ③ that
④ it   ⑤ them

출제율 85%

13 다음 문장에서 어법상 어색한 부분을 바르게 고쳐 쓰시오.

> I can't find a peg to hang my coat.

_____ ➡ _____

출제율 90%

14 다음 밑줄 친 부분의 쓰임이 나머지와 다른 것은?

① Look at that parrot.
② I think that boy is Jake's brother.
③ I know that he hurt his arm yesterday.
④ Wash your hands before eating that cake.
⑤ That skirt is more expensive than this one.

출제율 95%

15 다음 문장에서 어법상 어색한 부분을 찾아 바르게 고쳐 쓰시오.

I hope if you will be a famous writer.

_____ ➡ _____

출제율 85%

16 다음 괄호 안에 주어진 단어를 이용하여 우리말에 맞게 문장을 완성하시오.

뜨거운 마실 것 좀 주세요. (something, hot)

➡ Give me _____.

출제율 100%

17 다음 중 밑줄 친 부분을 생략할 수 없는 것은?

① I think that he is American.
② He knows that she is rich.
③ We don't hope that you will like it.
④ I can't believe that you made this.
⑤ It is true that I'm poor at English.

출제율 95%

18 다음 중 어법상 어색한 문장은?

① I need a chair to sit.
② Columbus was the first man to discover the American continent.
③ We have no house to live in.
④ He has a wish to become a pilot.
⑤ She forgot to bring something to write with.

[19~26] 다음 글을 읽고, 물음에 답하시오.

Subin: I set small goals and achieve ⓐthem every day. I do not say, "I will master English." With ⓑ(such / big / a / goal), I will probably put off working on ⓒit until tomorrow, next week, or next month. Instead, I say, "I will learn three new English words every day." I will achieve my big goal, one step ___ⓓ___ a time.

Time is a present. Everyone has the same present ⓔto spend every day. Manage your time well, ___ⓕ___ you will be happier in the new school year!

출제율 90%

19 위 글의 밑줄 친 ⓐthem이 가리키는 것을 우리말로 쓰시오.

➡ _____

출제율 85%

20 위 글의 괄호 ⓑ의 단어들을 순서대로 배열하시오.

➡ _____

출제율 90%

21 위 글에서 다음 영영풀이에 해당하는 말을 찾아 쓰시오.

to decide that something which had been planned for a particular time will be done at a later time instead

➡ _____

출제율 95%

22 위 글의 밑줄 친 ⓒ가 의미하는 것을 우리말로 쓰시오.

➡ _____

출제율 95%

23 위 글의 빈칸 ⓓ에 알맞은 것은?

① at
② with
③ in
④ on
⑤ for

출제율 90%

24 위 글의 밑줄 친 ⓔ와 쓰임이 같은 것은?

① There is no water to drink.
② I must hurry to the bus stop to meet Jack.
③ My hobby is to play computer games.
④ She was very happy to pass the exam.
⑤ We went to the store to buy some snacks.

출제율 100%

25 위 글의 빈칸 ⓕ에 알맞은 말을 쓰시오.

➡ _____

출제율 90%

26 위 글을 읽고, 다음 질문에 완전한 문장으로 답하시오.

Q: Instead of "I will master English," what does Subin say?

A: _____

[27~29] 다음 글을 읽고, 물음에 답하시오.

I regularly spend time working toward my dream. I want to become a chef. Every Saturday morning, I go to cooking classes or search for ⓐ . I think that using my time ⓑto prepare for my future is important.

※ I = John

출제율 95%

27 위 글의 빈칸 ⓐ에 다음 영영풀이에 해당하는 단어를 쓰시오. (복수형으로 쓸 것)

a set of instructions for making food

➡ _____

출제율 100%

28 위 글의 밑줄 친 ⓑ와 쓰임이 다른 것은?

① Ann is coming to Seoul to visit us.
② Give me a pen to write with.
③ I'm going to the park to walk my dogs.
④ Paul drove very quickly to get there on time.
⑤ I went to the post office to send the parcel.

출제율 85%

29 위 글을 읽고, 답할 수 없는 질문은?

① Does John spend time working toward his future every day?
② What does John want to become?
③ Where does John take his cooking classes?
④ Does John search for recipes every day?
⑤ Does John think it is important to use his time to prepare for his future?

01 다음 괄호 ⓐ와 ⓑ 안에 주어진 단어를 이용하여 대화를 완성하시오.

G: You look worried. ⓐ(what, the matter)?
B: I'm worried about tomorrow's history quiz. ⓑ(what, do)?
G: I think you should read your textbook again.
B: That's a good idea.

ⓐ _____
ⓑ _____

02 다음 대화의 순서를 바르게 배열하시오.

(A) OK, I will.
(B) What's wrong?
(C) Well, I have a toothache.
(D) That's too bad. Why don't you go see a dentist?

➡ _____

[03~04] 다음 대화를 읽고, 물음에 답하시오.

A: ⓐWhat's the matter with you?
B: I have a sore throat.
A: That's too bad. ⓑI think you should drink some water.
B: Okay, I will.

03 위 대화의 밑줄 친 부분과 바꿔 쓸 수 있는 표현을 두 가지 이상 쓰시오.

➡ _____
_____

04 위 대화의 밑줄 친 ⓑ와 유사한 표현을 3가지 이상 쓰시오.

➡ _____
_____
_____

05 다음 괄호 안에 주어진 단어를 이용하여 우리말을 영어로 옮기시오.

(1) 그는 그것이 매우 재미있을 것이라고 믿는다.
(believe / that / a lot of fun)
➡ _____

(2) 나는 그가 정직하다고 생각한다.
(think / that / honest)
➡ _____

(3) 나는 그녀가 선생님이었다는 것을 안다.
(know / that / teacher)
➡ _____

06 다음 두 문장을 한 문장으로 쓸 때 빈칸에 알맞은 말을 쓰시오.

I need a friend. + I play with the friend.
➡ I need a friend _____ _____ _____.

07 다음 주어진 단어를 바르게 배열하여 문장을 완성하시오. (필요시 어형을 바꿀 것)

(think / play / enjoy / he / soccer / I / that)

➡ _____

08 다음 〈보기〉에서 알맞은 단어를 골라 올바른 형태로 문장을 완성하시오.

┌─ 보기 ─┐
eat live play take tell
└────────┘

(1) Sumi has good news _____ _____.
(2) He is looking for a house _____ _____
_____.

09 다음 문장에서 어법상 틀린 부분을 찾아 바르게 고쳐 쓰시오.

(1) Here are the questions to answers.

_____ ➡ _____

(2) I'm lonely. I want some friends to talk.

_____ ➡ _____

(3) I'm eating pizza, but I don't have anything drink.

_____ ➡ _____

[10~12] 다음 글을 읽고, 물음에 답하시오.

I have ⓐ(to / goals / achieve / three) this year. The first goal is to get along with Jiho and Sujin. ⓑThe second goal is to stop to play smartphone games. The last goal is to learn taegwondo. I hope that I achieve these goals this year.

10 위 글의 괄호 ⓐ 안의 단어들을 어법에 맞게 바르게 배열하시오.

➡ _____

11 위 글의 밑줄 친 ⓑ에서 어법상 어색한 것을 찾아 바르게 고쳐 쓰시오.

_____ ➡ _____

12 What is the last goal the writer wants to achieve? Answer in English.

➡ _____

[13~17] 다음 글을 읽고, 물음에 답하시오.

I ⓐregular spend time working toward my dream. I want to become a ⓑ_____. Every Saturday morning, I go to cooking classes or search ⓒ_____ recipes. I think that ⓓuse my time to prepare ⓔ_____ my future is important.

※ I = John

13 위 글의 밑줄 친 ⓐ를 알맞은 형태로 고쳐 쓰시오.

➡ _____

14 위 글의 빈칸 ⓑ에 다음 영영풀이에 해당하는 단어를 쓰시오.

a professional cook, especially the most senior cook in a restaurant, hotel, etc.

➡ _____

15 위 글의 빈칸 ⓒ와 ⓔ에 공통으로 알맞은 말을 쓰시오.

➡ _____

16 위 글의 밑줄 친 ⓓ를 알맞은 형태로 고쳐 쓰시오.

➡ _____

17 When does John go to cooking classes? Answer in English.

➡ _____

창의사고력 서술형 문제

01 다음 주어진 상황에 맞게 〈to부정사〉와 괄호 안의 단어를 이용하여 〈보기〉처럼 문장을 완성하시오.

┌─ 보기 ───┐
│ I'm hungry. I need some food to eat. (eat)   │
└──┘

(1) I'm very thirsty. _____ (drink)

(2) There's no chair here. _____ (sit)

(3) Tony feels lonely. _____ (talk)

02 다음 (A), (B), (C)에 주어진 단어를 이용하여 〈보기〉와 같이 문장을 4개 쓰시오.(필요하면 어형을 바꿀 것)

(A)	(B)	(C)
I He She Mike They	say that think that hear that know that hope that	it's delicious Jenny is kind they need help everyone will be happy many children are hungry

┌─ 보기 ───┐
│ I hope that everyone will be happy.   │
└──┘

(1) _____

(2) _____

(3) _____

(4) _____

03 자신의 경우에 맞게 〈to부정사〉를 이용하여 〈보기〉와 같이 지금 필요한 것에 대해 써 보시오. (3문장 이상)

┌─ 보기 ───┐
│ I need something to drink.   │
└──┘

(1) _____

(2) _____

(3) _____

단원별 모의고사

01 다음 영영풀이에 해당하는 단어로 알맞은 것은?

> to make yourself ready for something that you will be doing

① achieve   ② decide

③ prefer   ④ prepare

⑤ practice

02 다음 중 밑줄 친 우리말 뜻이 잘못된 것은?

① You should <u>see a doctor</u>.
   병원에 가다

② He <u>put off</u> his homework.
   끝냈다

③ I want to <u>be good at</u> cooking.
   ~을 잘하다

④ This is <u>a type of</u> book.
   일종의

⑤ I don't sleep well <u>these days</u>.
   요즘

03 다음 빈칸에 공통으로 알맞은 것은?

> • We have to _____ water for the future.
> • We need to _____ pink dolphins in danger.

① recycle   ② share

③ store   ④ save

⑤ protect

04 다음 짝지어진 두 단어의 관계가 같도록 빈칸에 알맞은 말을 쓰시오.

> future : past = forget : _____

05 다음 영영풀이에 해당하는 단어를 쓰시오. (m으로 시작할 것)

> to learn something completely

➡ _____

06 다음 짝지어진 대화가 어색한 것은?

① A: Hey, Jenny. What's the matter?
   B: My bicycle doesn't work.

② A: I want to be friends with her. What should I do?
   B: You should say hello to her first.

③ A: I have too much homework.
   B: Don't worry. I will help you.

④ A: I left my homework at home. What should I do?
   B: You should bring it tomorrow, then.

⑤ A: You look sad today. What's the matter?
   B: I will help you.

07 다음 대화의 밑줄 친 부분과 같은 의미가 되도록 빈칸에 알맞은 말을 쓰시오.

> A: It's very cold outside.
> B: You'd better wear a warm coat.

➡ _____ _____ _____ wear a warm coat?

[08~11] 다음 대화를 읽고, 물음에 답하시오.

Hana: ⓐ<u>What's the matter, Jiho?</u>

Jiho: I didn't bring my uniform. I forgot I have soccer practice today.

Hana: Again?

Jiho: My second year in middle school is busier than my first year, and I often forget things.

Hana: ⓑ<u>I think you should</u> use a planner. Here's mine.

Jiho: Oh, can I see it?

Hana: Sure. I write my class schedule and _____ⓒ_____ in my planner.

Jiho: That's great. Maybe I should buy one.

08 위 대화의 밑줄 친 ⓐ와 같은 의미가 되도록 빈칸에 알맞은 말을 쓰시오.

What's _____, Jiho?

09 위 대화의 밑줄 친 ⓑ와 바꿔 쓸 수 있는 것은?

① You had better
② You must not
③ You can rarely
④ You used to
⑤ You are able to

10 위 대화의 빈칸 ⓒ에 알맞은 단어를 다음 영영풀이를 참조하여 쓰시오. (주어진 철자로 시작할 것)

an arrangement to meet with someone at a particular time

➡ a_____

11 What does Hana think Jiho should use? Answer in English.

➡ _____

12 다음 문장의 빈칸에 알맞은 것은?

I'm looking for a friend to travel _____.

① at
② in
③ with
④ on
⑤ for

13 다음 중 밑줄 친 부분의 쓰임이 나머지와 다른 하나는?

① Do you know <u>that</u> she is from Turkey?
② This is a picture <u>that</u> I took yesterday.
③ We hope <u>that</u> Jenny will get better soon.
④ I believe <u>that</u> he read the book twice.
⑤ I think <u>that</u> Susan is good at playing tennis.

14 다음 괄호 안의 단어 형태가 바르게 짝지어진 것은?

• I have something (tell) you.
• Do you have anything (read)?

① tell – read
② tell – to read
③ to tell – read
④ telling – read
⑤ to tell – to read

15 다음 우리말에 맞게 주어진 단어를 바르게 배열하시오.

나는 나의 영어 선생님이 예쁘시다고 생각한다.
(teacher / is / that / English / think / my / pretty / I)

➡ _____

16 다음 중 어법상 알맞지 <u>않은</u> 것은?

① Let me get you a chair to sit on.

② She has no house to live in.

③ There's nothing to worry about.

④ Give me a pen to write with.

⑤ You seem to have important something to tell me.

17 다음 괄호 안에 주어진 단어를 이용하여 우리말에 맞게 문장을 완성하시오.

수진이는 머무를 호텔을 찾고 있다. (stay)

➡ Sujin is looking for a hotel _____.

18 다음 밑줄 친 부분의 쓰임이 나머지와 <u>다른</u> 하나는?

① I think <u>that</u> he is handsome.

② He believes <u>that</u> he can be a good doctor.

③ She hopes <u>that</u> there will be no more exams.

④ Do you know <u>that</u> handsome guy over there?

⑤ Professor Kim says <u>that</u> we should save energy.

19 다음 중 밑줄 친 부분의 쓰임이 같은 것끼리 묶인 것은?

ⓐ I want something <u>to drink</u>.

ⓑ I want <u>to become</u> a teacher.

ⓒ There are many problems <u>to solve</u>.

ⓓ <u>To clean</u> the house is really fun.

ⓔ I'm standing here for three hours <u>to meet</u> her.

① ⓐ, ⓑ ② ⓑ, ⓓ ③ ⓑ, ⓒ

④ ⓐ, ⓓ ⑤ ⓒ, ⓔ

[20~24] 다음 글을 읽고, 물음에 답하시오.

Minsu: When I do something, I give it my full attention. I ___ⓐ___ read SNS postings while I was doing my homework. ⓑ<u>It slowed down me because I couldn't focus.</u> Now, I put aside my smartphone when I do my homework. ⓒ<u>It</u> saves me ⓓ<u>a lot of</u> time. These days, I finish my homework quickly and enjoy my free time.

20 문맥상 위 글의 빈칸 ⓐ에 알맞은 것은?

① could ② should

③ might ④ used to

⑤ ought to

21 위 글의 밑줄 친 ⓑ에서 어법상 어색한 부분을 찾아 바르게 고쳐 쓰시오.

_____ ➡ _____

22 위 글의 밑줄 친 ⓒ가 의미하는 것은?

① 숙제할 때 SNS 게시 글을 읽는 것

② 숙제할 때 음악을 듣는 것

③ 숙제할 때 스마트폰을 한쪽에 치워 놓는 것

④ 빨리 숙제를 끝내는 것

⑤ 여가 시간을 즐기는 것

23 위 글의 밑줄 친 ⓓ를 한 단어로 바꿔 쓰시오.

➡ _____

24 위 글을 읽고, 다음 질문에 완전한 문장으로 답하시오.

Q: Does Minsu finish his homework late these days?

A: _____

[25~31] 다음 글을 읽고, 물음에 답하시오.

Welcome to the new school year. In the second grade, you will have more work ⓐto do. You need to manage your time well. How do you do that?

John: I regularly spend time ⓑwork toward my dream. I want to become a chef. Every Saturday morning, I go to cooking classes or search for recipes. I think that using my time ⓒ____ for my future is important.

Time is a present. Everyone has the ⓓsame present to spend every day. ⓔManage your time well, and you will be happier in the new school year!

25 위 글의 밑줄 친 ⓐ와 쓰임이 같은 것은?

① He likes to play badminton.
② I didn't have time to think.
③ I want to buy some cheese.
④ To study English is not easy.
⑤ My dream is to be an English teacher.

26 위 글의 밑줄 친 ⓑ를 알맞은 형태로 쓰시오.

➡ _____

27 위 글에서 다음 영영풀이에 해당하는 단어를 찾아 쓰시오.

to use your time, money, etc. sensibly, without wasting it

➡ _____

28 위 글의 빈칸 ⓒ에 알맞은 것은?

① prepare
② preparing
③ to prepare
④ for prepare
⑤ to preparing

29 위 글의 밑줄 친 ⓓ의 반의어를 쓰시오.

➡ _____

30 위 글의 밑줄 친 ⓔ를 다음과 같이 바꿔 쓸 때 빈칸에 알맞은 말을 쓰시오.

➡ _____ you manage your time well, you will be happier in the new school year!

31 위 글을 읽고, 답할 수 없는 질문은?

① What do second graders need to do?
② What does John do to become a chef?
③ Does John take his cooking class every day?
④ Why does John want to become a chef?
⑤ Does everyone have the same present to spend every day?

Lesson 2

All about Safety

 의사소통 기능

- 상기시켜 주기
  Don't forget to get under the desk.
- 금지하기
  You'd better not use the elevator.

언어 형식

- 의문사+to부정사
  I learned **how to do** CPR.
- as + 형용사/부사의 원급 + as
  I was **as** scared **as** the others.

교과서
Words & Expressions

Key Words

- **almost** [ɔ́ːlmoust] 부 거의
- **ambulance** [ǽmbjuləns] 명 구급차
- **angle** [ǽŋgl] 명 각도
- **announcer** [ənáunsər] 명 아나운서
- **around** [əráund] 전 ~ 주위에
- **audience** [ɔ́ːdiəns] 명 청중, 시청자
- **brave** [breiv] 형 용감한(= fearless)
- **breathe** [briːð] 동 숨을 쉬다, 호흡하다
- **carefully** [kɛ́ərfəli] 부 주의 깊게
- **chance** [tʃæns] 명 기회, 가능성
- **chest** [tʃest] 명 가슴
- **CPR** 명 심폐소생술
- **dangerous** [déindʒərəs] 형 위험한(↔ safe)
- **degree** [digríː] 명 (각도의 단위인) 도
- **earthquake** [ɔ́ːrθkweik] 명 지진
- **excited** [iksáitid] 형 신이 난
- **experience** [ikspíəriəns] 명 경험
- **floor** [flɔːr] 명 바닥(↔ ceiling)
- **forget** [fərgét] 동 잊다(↔ remember)
- **gear** [giər] 명 장비, 복장
- **grade** [greid] 명 학년
- **greatly** [gréitli] 부 대단히, 크게
- **hard** [hɑːrd] 부 세게, 힘껏 형 어려운, 딱딱한
- **heart** [hɑːrt] 명 심장
- **important** [impɔ́ːrtənt] 형 중요한(↔ unimportant)
- **impressive** [imprésiv] 형 인상적인

- **join** [dʒɔin] 동 함께하다
- **late** [leit] 부 늦게(↔ early)
- **low** [lou] 부 낮게(↔ high) 형 낮은
- **lower** [lóuər] 동 낮추다, 낮아지다
- **luckily** [lʌ́kili] 부 다행히도
- **open** [óupən] 형 막혀 있지 않은, 개방된
- **perform** [pərfɔ́ːrm] 동 행하다, 실시하다
- **practice** [prǽktis] 동 연습하다
- **protect** [prətékt] 동 보호하다
- **remember** [rimémbər] 동 기억하다
- **safety** [séifti] 명 안전(↔ danger)
- **save** [seiv] 동 구하다
- **scared** [skɛərd] 형 무서워하는, 겁먹은
- **scary** [skɛ́əri] 형 무서운, 겁나는
- **shake** [ʃeip] 동 흔들리다
- **shoulder** [ʃóuldər] 명 어깨
- **shout** [ʃaut] 동 외치다
- **skill** [skil] 명 기술
- **stay** [stei] 동 유지하다
- **suddenly** [sʌ́dnli] 부 갑자기
- **tap** [tæp] 동 (가볍게) 톡톡 두드리다[치다]
- **teenager** [tíːnèidʒər] 명 십대
- **training** [tréiniŋ] 명 교육, 훈련
- **wet** [wet] 형 젖은(↔ dry)
- **within** [wiðín] 전 ~ 이내에, ~ 안에
- **zoo keeper** 동물원 사육사

Key Expressions

- **all the time** 항상
- **as ~ as possible** 가능한 한 ~한[하게]
- **as soon as you can** 가능한 한 빨리
- **at first** 처음에
- **bump into** ~에 부딪히다
- **fall down** 넘어지다
- **get off** ~에서 내리다
- **get out** 나가다
- **get under** 밑에 들어가다, 밑에 숨다
- **hit ~ on the shoulder** ~의 어깨를 치다

- **hold on to** ~을 꼭 잡다, ~을 붙잡다
- **in case of** ~의 경우에
- **in front of** ~ 앞에서
- **out of** ~의 밖으로
- **push down** ~을 꽉[꾹] 누르다
- **put on** ~을 입다
- **run around** 뛰어다니다
- **stand in line** 줄을 서다
- **up and down** 위아래로
- **wait for** ~을 기다리다

Word Power

※ 동사에 -ive를 붙여 형용사로 만드는 단어

□ **act** (행동하다) → **active** (활동적인)

□ **attract** (마음을 끌다) → **attractive** (매력적인)

□ **communicate** (의사소통을 하다) →
　　　　　　communicative (이야기하기 좋아하는)

□ **create** (창조하다) → **creative** (창의적인)

□ **impress** (깊은 인상을 주다) → **impressive** (인상적인)

□ **talk** (수다를 떨다) → **talkative** (수다스러운)

※ 형용사에 -ly를 붙여 부사로 만드는 단어

□ **careful** → **carefully** (주의 깊게)

□ **easy** → **easily** (쉽게)

□ **great** → **greatly** (대단히, 크게)

□ **lucky** → **luckily** (다행히)

□ **slow** → **slowly** (천천히)

□ **sudden** → **suddenly** (갑자기)

English Dictionary

□ **audience** 청중, 시청자
→ the people who watch, read, or listen to something
어떤 것을 보거나 읽거나 듣는 사람들

□ **brave** 용감한
→ feeling or showing no fear
두려움을 느끼거나 나타내지 않는

□ **breathe** 숨을 쉬다, 호흡하다
→ to move air into and out of your lungs
공기를 폐 안으로 들이마셨다가 내쉬다

□ **chest** 가슴
→ the front part of the body between the neck and the stomach
목과 위 사이의 몸의 앞부분

□ **degree** (각도의 단위인) 도
→ a unit for measuring the size of an angle
각의 크기를 측정하는 단위

□ **earthquake** 지진
→ a sudden, violent shaking of the earth's surface
지구 표면의 갑작스럽고 격렬한 진동

□ **experience** 경험
→ the process of doing and seeing things and of having things happen to you
일들을 하고 보고 또한 자신에게 일어나는 일들을 겪는 과정

□ **lower** 낮추다, 낮아지다
→ to reduce something in amount, degree, strength etc, or to become less
양, 정도, 강도 등을 줄이거나 적게 만들다

□ **perform** 행하다, 실시하다
→ to do an action or activity that usually requires training or skill
대개 훈련이나 기술이 필요한 행동이나 활동을 하다

□ **protect** 보호하다
→ to keep someone or something from being harmed, lost, etc.
누군가 또는 어떤 것이 해를 입거나 없어지거나 하지 않게 하다

□ **save** 구하다
→ to keep someone or something safe from death, harm, loss, etc.
누군가 또는 무언가를 죽음, 위해, 상실 등으로부터 안전하게 지키다

□ **shake** 흔들다
→ to move sometimes violently back and forth or up and down with short, quick movements
짧고 빠른 동작으로 때때로 격렬하게 앞뒤로 또는 위아래로 움직이다

□ **skill** 기술
→ the ability to do something that comes from training, experience, or practice
훈련 · 경험 · 연습에서 생기는 어떤 일을 할 수 있는 능력

□ **tap** (가볍게) 톡톡 두드리다[치다]
→ to hit someone or something quickly and lightly
누군가 또는 무언가를 빠르고 가볍게 치다

□ **wet** 젖은
→ not yet dry
아직 마르지 않은

□ **zoo keeper** 동물원 사육사
→ a person who takes care of the animals in a zoo
동물원에서 동물을 돌보는 사람

01 다음 〈보기〉와 같은 형태로 변화하는 단어는?

┌─ 보기 ┐
act : active
└────────┘

① help
② stress
③ scare
④ harm
⑤ impress

05 다음 빈칸에 알맞은 말이 바르게 짝지어진 것은?

• He says he bumped _____ the wall.
• I'll wait _____ you in front of the theater.

① to – on
② up – for
③ in – with
④ into – for
⑤ over – on

서답형
02 다음 두 문장의 뜻이 같도록 빈칸에 알맞은 말을 쓰시오.

You need to call 119 as soon as you can.
= You need to call 119 as soon as _____.

서답형
06 다음 영영풀이에 해당하는 단어를 쓰시오.

a sudden, violent shaking of the earth's surface

➡ _____

중요
03 다음 영영풀이에 해당하는 단어로 알맞은 것은?

to move air into and out of your lungs

① allow
② throw
③ defend
④ breathe
⑤ protect

중요
07 다음 빈칸에 공통으로 알맞은 것은?

• I'll _____ off at the first floor.
• Don't forget to _____ under the desk when the earthquake occurs.

① put
② get
③ take
④ turn
⑤ bring

서답형
04 다음 짝지어진 단어의 관계가 같도록 빈칸에 알맞은 말을 쓰시오.

wrong : right = dry : _____

서답형
08 다음 빈칸에 공통으로 알맞은 말을 쓰시오.

• He's the person who can _____ your life.
• You can _____ money by buying a one-day ticket.

01 다음 짝지어진 두 단어의 관계가 같도록 빈칸에 알맞은 말을 쓰시오.

(1) late : early = important : _____
(2) easy : difficult = forget : _____
(3) strong : weak = floor : _____
(4) trash : waste = _____ : fearless

02 다음 우리말에 맞게 빈칸에 알맞은 말을 쓰시오.

(1) 자동차가 트럭 앞에 있다.
➡ The car is _____ _____ _____ the truck.
(2) 우리는 버스 정류장에서 한 줄로 서야 한다.
➡ We must _____ _____ _____ at a bus stop.
(3) 너무 빨리 뛰지 마. 넘어질 수 있어.
➡ Don't run too fast. You may _____ _____.
(4) 그녀는 항상 행복해 보인다.
➡ She looks happy _____ _____ _____.

03 다음 빈칸에 공통으로 들어갈 말을 〈보기〉에서 골라 쓰시오.

┌─ 보기 ─┐
grade   save   hard
└────────┘

(1) • That test was _____.
• He hit the ball _____.
(2) • He risked his life to _____ her.
• She would rather _____ than spend.
(3) • He is in the second _____.
• I got a good _____ on my math test.

04 다음 빈칸에 들어갈 알맞은 말을 〈보기〉에서 골라 쓰시오.

┌─ 보기 ─┐
scared   breathe   practice
└────────┘

(1) They usually _____ soccer after school.
(2) Humans need oxygen to _____.
(3) The rabbit was _____ when it met the lion.

05 다음 빈칸에 알맞은 말을 〈보기〉에서 골라 쓰시오.

┌─ 보기 ─┐
in case of   put on   run around
└────────┘

(1) You should not _____ indoors.
(2) Don't forget to _____ hiking shoes.
(3) You'd better not use an elevator _____ _____ a fire.

06 다음 영영풀이에 해당하는 단어를 주어진 철자로 시작하여 쓰시오.

(1) d_____ : a unit for measuring the size of an angle
(2) c_____ : the front part of the body between the neck and the stomach
(3) p_____ : to do an action or activity that usually requires training or skill
(4) a_____ : the people who watch, read, or listen to something

Conversation

1 상기시켜 주기

> A I'm going to go hiking. 나는 등산하러 갈 거야.
> B Don't forget to put on hiking shoes. 등산화 신는 걸 잊지 마.
> A Okay, I see. 그래. 알았어.

■ Don't forget to ~.는 '~하는 것을 잊지 마라.'라는 뜻으로 상대방에게 어떤 일을 상기시킬 때 사용하는 표현이다.

- A: I'll buy a cake for my mom's birthday. 엄마 생일을 위해 케이크를 살 거야.
- B: Don't forget to bring some candles. 초 가져 오는 것을 잊지 말아라.

상기시켜 주기 표현

- Don't forget to bring your coat. 코트 가져오는 것을 잊지 마.
- Never forget to bring your coat 코트 가져오는 것을 잊지 마.
- Remember to bring your coat. 코트 가져오는 것을 기억해.
- Make[Be] sure you bring your coat. 코트를 반드시 가져오도록 해.

상기시켜 주는 말에 답하기

- Okay, I see.
- All right. Thank you.
- OK, thanks.
- OK, I won't.
- I will remember (that).
- I'll keep that in mind. 명심하도록 할게.
- Thank you for reminding me. 상기시켜 줘서 고마워요.

핵심 Check

1. 다음 우리말과 일치하도록 빈칸에 알맞은 말을 쓰시오.

(1) A: I'm going bike riding. (나는 자전거를 타러 갈 거야.)

　　B: Have fun and _____ _____ _____ wear a helmet.

　　(재밌게 타고, 헬멧 쓰는 것을 잊지 마.)

(2) A: May I _____ this book? (제가 이 책 빌려가도 될까요?)

　　B: Sure. Just _____ _____ give it back in a week.

　　(그럼요. 일주일 후에 돌려주는 것을 잊지 마세요.)

　　A: Okay. I _____. (네. 그럴게요.)

(3) A: _____ _____ you close the windows. (창문을 반드시 닫도록 해.)

　　B: OK, I _____. (알았어, 잊지 않을게.)

② 금지하기

> **A** Peter, you'd better not play with a ball on the street.
> Peter, 길거리에서 공을 가지고 놀면 안 돼.
>
> **B** Okay, I see. 응, 알았어.

■ You'd better not ~은 '~하지 않는 게 좋겠어., ~하면 안 돼.'라는 뜻으로 어떤 일을 하지 말아야 함을 이야기할 때 사용하는 금지의 표현이다.

- A: Tony, you'd better not run when you cross the street. Tony, 길을 건널 때 뛰지 않는 게 좋겠어.
  B: Okay, I see. 응, 알겠어.

cf. You'd better ~는 '~하는 게 좋겠다.'라는 뜻으로 상대방에게 제안이나 충고를 할 때 사용한다.

- You had better have breakfast every day. 너는 매일 아침식사를 하는 것이 좋겠다.

금지를 나타내는 표현

- You'd better not take pictures at the museum. 박물관에서는 사진을 찍지 않는 것이 좋겠어.
  = You should not take pictures at the museum.
  = You must not take pictures at the museum.
  = Don't[Do not] take pictures at the museum.
  = You can't take pictures at the museum.
  = You're not supposed[allowed/permitted] to take pictures at the museum.

핵심 Check

2. 다음 우리말과 일치하도록 빈칸에 알맞은 말을 쓰시오.

(1) **A:** I _____ I've got a _____. (나 감기에 걸린 것 같아.)

　B: You'd _____ _____ _____ cold water. (너는 차가운 물을 마시지 않는 게 좋겠어.)

(2) **A:** _____ _____ snacks in here. (이 안에서 과자를 드시지 마세요.)

　B: Oh, I'm sorry. (오, 죄송합니다.)

(3) **A:** Excuse me. You _____ _____ your cell phone here.

　(실례합니다. 이곳에서 휴대 전화를 사용하시면 안 됩니다.)

　B: Oh, I'm _____. (오, 죄송합니다.)

A. Listen & Speak 1 - A - 1

B: ❶Mom, can I buy some apple juice?

W: Sure, Chris. ❷Don't forget to check the food label.

B: The food label?

W: Yes. ❸Too much sugar is not good for you.

B: Okay, I will check it.

B: 엄마, 사과 주스 좀 사도 돼요?

W: 물론, Chris. 식품 라벨을 확인하는 것을 잊지 마라.

B: 식품 라벨이요?

W: 그래. 너무 많은 설탕은 너에게 좋지 않아.

B: 네, 확인해 볼게요.

---

❶ Can I ~?: 제가 ~해도 될까요? (허락 요청하기)

❷ Don't forget to+동사원형 ~: ~하는 것을 잊지 마라. (상기시켜 주기)

❸ be good for: ~에 좋다

Check(√) True or False

(1) The boy will buy some apple juice. T ☐ F ☐

(2) The boy forgot to check the food label. T ☐ F ☐

Conversation B

Teacher: ❶I told you a few safety rules for earthquakes today. ❷Now, let's practice. Are you ready?

Amy & Jiho: Yes.

Teacher: Everything is shaking. ❸Don't forget to get under the desk and protect your body first.

Jiho: It's so scary.

Amy: You're doing fine, Jiho. ❹Hold on to the leg of the desk.

Jiho: Oh, the shaking stopped for now. ❺Let's get out!

Teacher: Remember! ❻You'd better not use the elevator. Use the stairs.

Amy: Where should we go now?

Teacher: You need to find an open area with no buildings.

Jiho: Then, let's go to the park.

선생님: 오늘 지진에 대한 몇 가지 안전 수칙들을 말했죠. 자, 실습해 봅시다. 준비됐나요?

Amy와 지호: 네.

선생님: 모든 것이 흔들리고 있어요. 책상 밑에 들어가서 먼저 여러분의 몸을 보호하는 것을 잊지 마세요.

지호: 너무 무서워요.

Amy: 너는 잘하고 있어, 지호야. 책상 다리를 꽉 잡아.

지호: 오, 떨림이 잠시 멈췄어. 나가자!

선생님: 기억하세요! 엘리베이터를 이용하면 안 돼요. 계단을 이용하세요.

Amy: 이제 우린 어디로 가야 하죠?

선생님: 건물이 없는 확 트인 곳을 찾아야 해요.

지호: 그럼, 공원에 가자.

---

❶ a few: 몇 가지 / safety rule: 안전 규칙 / earthquake: 지진

❷ Let's ~: ~하자. / practice: 연습하다

❸ Don't forget to+동사원형 ~: ~하는 것을 잊지 마라.(상기시켜 주기) / get under the desk: 책상 밑에 들어가다

❹ hold on to: ~을 꽉 잡다

❺ get out: 나가다

❻ You'd better not + 동사원형 ~: 너는 ~하지 않는 게 좋겠다.

Check(√) True or False

(3) They learned a few safety rules for earthquakes yesterday. T ☐ F ☐

(4) When the students go out, they should not use the elevator. T ☐ F ☐

Listen & Speak 1 - A - 2

G: Dad, I'm leaving.

M: ❶You need to wear this, Julie. ❷There is a lot of fine dust in the air today.

G: Oh, I didn't know that.

M: ❸It will be bad for your health. ❹So don't forget to wear this mask.

G: ❺All right. Thank you.

❶ need to+동사원형: ~할 필요가 있다 / wear: 쓰다
❷ There is ~: ~이 있다 / fine dust: 미세 먼지
❸ be bad for: ~에 나쁘다
❹ Don't forget to + 동사원형 ~.: ~하는 것을 잊지 마라.

Listen & Speak 2 - A - 1

B: Hi, Amy. ❶What's up?

G: ❷I'm here to buy a shirt. What about you?

B: I have a lunch meeting in this shopping center. ❸Oh, I should go now. I'm late.

G: ❹Okay, but you'd better not run. ❺The sign says the floor is wet.

B: I didn't see it. Thanks.

❶ What's up?: 왠일이야?
❷ to buy: to부정사의 부사적 용법 중 목적(~하기 위하여)
❸ I should + 동사원형 ~: 나는 ~해야겠다.
❹ You'd better not + 동사원형 ~: 너는 ~하지 않는 게 좋겠다.(금지의 표현)
❺ The sign says ~.: 표지판에 ~라고 되어 있어. / wet: 젖은

Listen & Speak 2 - A - 2

G: ❶What does the sign mean?

B: ❷It means that you'd better not look at your smartphone while you are walking.

G: That's interesting, but why?

B: ❸You can bump into people and there are many cars around here. It's so dangerous.

G: Now I see.

❶ What does[do] + 주어 + mean? = ~는 무슨 뜻이야?
❷ It means ~.: 그것은 ~라는 뜻이야. / You'd better not + 동사원형 ~: 너는 ~하지 않는 게 좋겠다.
❸ bump into: ~에 부딪히다 / There are + 복수명사 ~: ~이 있다

Conversation A

B: I was ❶having a good time with my family last night. ❷Suddenly everything started to shake. ❸I couldn't stand still and almost fell down. Dad shouted, "❹Get under the table. ❺ Don't forget to protect your head." Luckily, the shaking soon stopped. ❻It was a scary experience.

❶ have a good time: 좋은 시간을 보내다
❷ suddenly: 갑자기 / shake: 흔들리다
❸ fall down: 넘어지다
❹ get under the table: 책상 밑에 들어가다
❺ Don't forget + 동사원형 ~: ~하는 것을 잊지 마라.(=Remember+동사원형 ~) / protect: 보호하다
❻ scary: 무서운 / experience: 경험

Wrap Up - Listening 1

G: Many people use this almost every day. ❶ People stand in line to enter this. ❷They wait for others to get off before they enter. ❸ They use this to move up and down floors in a building. ❹You'd better not use this in case of a fire.

❶ stand in line: 줄을 서다
❷ wait for: ~을 기다리다 / get off: 내리다
❸ up and down: 위아래로
❹ You'd better not + 동사원형 ~: 너는 ~하지 않는 게 좋겠다. / in case of: ~의 경우에

Wrap Up - Listening 2

B: ❶I'm going to go to Jiri Mountain with my dad tomorrow.

G: It sounds great.

B: ❷I'm excited because we are going to stay there for two days and one night.

G: ❸That'll be great, but don't forget to check the weather.

B: Okay.

❶ be going to: ~할 것이다
❷ excited: 신이 난 / for two days and one night: 1박 2일 동안
❸ Don't forget to+동사원형 ~: ~하는 것을 잊지 마라. / weather: 날씨

다음 우리말과 일치하도록 빈칸에 알맞은 말을 쓰시오.

Listen & Speak 1 - A - 1

B: Mom, _____ I _____ some apple juice?

W: Sure, Chris. Don't _____ _____ check the food label.

B: The _____ _____?

W: Yes. Too much sugar is not good _____ you.

B: Okay, I _____ _____ it.

Listen & Speak 1 - A - 2

G: Dad, I'm _____.

M: You need to _____ this, Julie. There is a lot of _____ _____ in the air today.

G: Oh, I _____ _____ that.

M: It will be _____ _____ your health. So _____ _____ to wear this mask.

G: _____ _____. Thank you.

Listen & Speak 2 - A - 1

B: Hi, Amy. What's _____?

G: I'm here _____ _____ a shirt. What _____ you?

B: I _____ a lunch meeting _____ this shopping center. Oh, I _____ _____ now. I'm _____.

G: Okay, but you'd _____ _____ run. The sign _____ the floor is _____.

B: I _____ see it. Thanks.

Listen & Speak 2 - A - 2

G: What _____ the sign _____?

B: It means that _____ _____ look at your smartphone _____ you are walking.

G: That's interesting, _____ why?

B: You can _____ _____ people and _____ _____ many cars _____ here. It's so _____.

G: Now I _____.

해석

B: 엄마, 사과 주스 좀 사도 돼요?
W: 물론, Chris. 식품 라벨을 확인하는 것을 잊지 마라.
B: 식품 라벨이요?
W: 그래. 너무 많은 설탕은 너에게 좋지 않아.
B: 네, 확인해 볼게요.

G: 아빠, 저 나가요.
M: Julie, 이걸 쓸 필요가 있어. 오늘은 공기 중에 미세먼지가 많아.
G: 오, 전 몰랐어요.
M: 그것은 건강에 나쁠 거야. 그러니 이 마스크 쓰는 걸 잊지 마.
G: 알겠습니다. 감사합니다.

B: 안녕, Amy. 웬일이야?
G: 셔츠를 사러 왔어. 너는?
B: 이 쇼핑센터에서 점심 모임이 있어. 오, 이만 가 봐야겠어. 늦었어.
G: 그래, 하지만 뛰지 않는 게 좋겠어. 표지판에 바닥이 젖었다고 적혀 있어.
B: 난 못 봤어. 고마워.

G: 그 표지판은 무슨 뜻이니?
B: 걷는 동안 스마트폰을 보지 않는 게 낫다는 뜻이야.
G: 재미있네, 그런데 왜지?
B: 사람들과 부딪힐 수 있고 이 근처에는 차도 많아. 너무 위험해.
G: 이제 알겠어.

Conversation A

B: I was _____ a good time _____ my family last night. Suddenly everything started _____ _____. I _____ stand still and almost _____ _____. Dad shouted, "_____ under the table. _____ _____ to protect your head." _____, the shaking soon stopped. It was a _____ _____.

Conversation B

Teacher: I _____ you _____ _____ safety rules for earthquakes today. Now, _____ practice. Are you _____?

Amy & Jiho: Yes.

Teacher: Everything _____ _____. Don't _____ _____ _____ under the desk and _____ your body first.

Jiho: It's so _____.

Amy: You're doing fine, Jiho. _____ _____ _____ the leg of the desk.

Jiho: Oh, the shaking stopped _____ _____. Let's get _____!

Teacher: Remember! You'd _____ _____ _____ the elevator. _____ the stairs.

Amy: Where _____ we _____ now?

Teacher: You _____ _____ find an open area _____ no buildings.

Jiho: Then, _____ go _____ the park.

Wrap Up - Listening 1

G: Many people use this _____ every day. People _____ _____ _____ to enter this. They _____ _____ others to _____ _____ before they enter. They use this to _____ _____ and _____ floors in a building. _____ _____ not use this _____ _____ _____ a fire.

Wrap Up - Listening 2

B: I'm _____ _____ go to Jiri Mountain _____ my dad tomorrow.

G: It _____ great.

B: I'm excited _____ we are going to stay there _____ two days and _____ _____.

G: That'll be great, but _____ _____ _____ _____ the weather.

B: Okay.

해석

B: 나는 어젯밤에 가족과 즐거운 시간을 보내고 있었다. 갑자기 모든 것이 흔들리기 시작했다. 나는 가만히 있을 수가 없어서 하마터면 넘어질 뻔했다. 아빠는 "테이블 밑으로 들어가. 머리를 보호하는 걸 잊지 마."라고 소리쳤다. 다행히도, 흔들림은 곧 멈추었다. 그것은 무서운 경험이었다.

선생님: 오늘 지진에 대한 몇 가지 안전 수칙들을 말했죠. 자, 실습해 봅시다. 준비됐나요?
Amy와 지호: 네.
선생님: 모든 것이 흔들리고 있어요. 책상 밑에 들어가서 먼저 여러분의 몸을 보호하는 것을 잊지 마세요.
지호: 너무 무서워요.
Amy: 너는 잘하고 있어, 지호야. 책상 다리를 꽉 잡아.
지호: 오, 떨림이 잠시 멈췄어. 나가자!
선생님: 기억하세요! 엘리베이터를 이용하면 안 돼요. 계단을 이용하세요.
Amy: 이제 우린 어디로 가야 하죠?
선생님: 건물이 없는 확 트인 곳을 찾아야 해요.
지호: 그럼, 공원에 가자.

G: 많은 사람들이 거의 매일 이것을 사용한다. 사람들이 이것에 들어가기 위해 줄을 선다. 그들은 다른 사람들이 들어오기 전에 내리기를 기다린다. 그들은 건물의 층을 위아래로 움직이기 위해 이것을 사용한다. 화재가 났을 때는 이것을 사용하면 안 된나.

B: 나는 내일 아빠와 지리산에 갈 거야.
G: 멋진데.
B: 우리는 1박 2일 동안 묵을 예정이어서 신나.
G: 그거 좋겠네. 하지만, 날씨를 확인하는 걸 잊지 마.
B: 알았어.

01 다음 대화의 빈칸에 알맞은 것은?

> A: I have a headache. What should I do?
> B: Take some rest and don't _____ to take a medicine.

① mind   ② awake
③ delay   ④ insist
⑤ forget

> take some rest 좀 쉬다

02 다음 대화의 밑줄 친 부분과 바꾸어 쓸 수 있는 것은?

> A: Peter, you'd better not run when you cross the street.
> B: Okay, I will.

① you may run when you cross the street
② you must run when you cross the street
③ you need to run when you cross the street
④ you would run when you cross the street
⑤ you shouldn't run when you cross the street

[03~04] 다음 대화의 빈칸에 알맞은 것을 고르시오.

03

> A: I'm going to swim at the beach.
> B: Don't forget to _____.

① wear safety gear   ② put on hiking shoes
③ wear a helmet   ④ wear a life jacket
⑤ turn on the fan

04

> A: It's going to rain. _____
> B: Okay. If it rains, I'll stay inside.

> stay 머물다

① You will go outside.   ② You shouldn't go outside.
③ You would go outside.   ④ You might not go outside.
⑤ You can go outside.

[01~04] 다음 대화를 읽고, 물음에 답하시오.

G: Dad, I'm leaving.
M: You need to wear this, Julie. There ⓐ a lot of fine dust in the air today.
G: Oh, I didn't know that.
M: It will be bad for your health. ⓑ ⓒdon't forget to wear this mask.
G: All right. Thank you.

서답형

01 위 대화의 빈칸 ⓐ에 알맞은 말을 쓰시오.

➡ _____

02 위 대화의 빈칸 ⓑ에 알맞은 것은?

① Or ② But ③ So
④ And ⑤ Yet

중요
03 위 대화의 밑줄 친 ⓒ의 의도로 알맞은 것은?

① 확신하기 ② 사과하기
③ 불평하기 ④ 상기시켜 주기
⑤ 허락 구하기

04 위 대화의 내용과 일치하지 <u>않는</u> 것은?

① 오늘은 미세 먼지가 많다.
② 소녀는 미세 먼지가 많은 것을 알지 못했다.
③ 미세 먼지는 건강에 나쁘다.
④ 아빠는 소녀에게 마스크를 쓸 것을 당부하고 있다.
⑤ 소녀는 마스크를 쓰지 않을 것이다.

[05~08] 다음 대화를 읽고, 물음에 답하시오.

Teacher: I told you ⓐ safety rules for earthquakes today. Now, let's practice. Are you ready?
Amy & Jiho: Yes.
Teacher: Everything is shaking. Don't forget to get under the desk and protect your body first.
Jiho: It's so scary.
Amy: You're doing fine, Jiho. Hold on ⓑ the leg of the desk.
Jiho: Oh, the shaking stopped for now. Let's get out!
Teacher: Remember! ⓒ use the elevator. Use the stairs.

05 위 대화의 빈칸 ⓐ에 알맞은 것은?

① any ② much
③ little ④ a few
⑤ a little

06 위 대화의 빈칸 ⓑ에 알맞은 것은?

① to ② of
③ for ④ up
⑤ out

중요
07 위 대화의 빈칸 ⓒ에 가장 알맞은 것은?

① You would not
② You'd better not
③ You're supposed to
④ You don't have to
⑤ You're not able to

08 위 대화를 읽고, 다음 질문에 완전한 문장으로 답하시오.

Q: What are Amy and Jiho practicing now?

A: _____

[09~11] 다음 담화문을 읽고, 물음에 답하시오.

I was having a good time with my family last night. (①) I couldn't stand still and almost fell down. (②) Dad shouted, "Get under the table. (③) Don't forget to protect your head." (④) Luckily, the shaking soon stopped. It was a scary experience. (⑤)

09 위 글의 ①~⑤ 중 다음 문장이 들어갈 알맞은 곳은?

Suddenly everything started to shake.

①   ②   ③   ④   ⑤

10 위 글의 밑줄 친 부분을 다음과 같이 바꿔 쓸 때 빈칸에 알맞은 말을 쓰시오.

_____ to protect your head.

11 위 글을 읽고, 답할 수 <u>없는</u> 질문은?

① What is the writer talking about?
② When did the earthquake occur?
③ Were the writer and his/her father in the drawing room?
④ What did the dad shout to the writer?
⑤ Did the shaking stop soon?

[12~15] 다음 대화를 읽고, 물음에 답하시오.

G: What does the sign mean?
B: It means that ⓐyou'd better not look at your smartphone while you are walking.
G: That's interesting,   ⓑ   why?
B: You can bump   ⓒ   people and there are many cars around here. It's so dangerous.
G: Now I see.

12 위 대화의 밑줄 친 ⓐ와 바꿔 쓸 수 있는 것은? (2개)

① you must not
② you don't have to
③ you shouldn't
④ you're permitted to
⑤ you're allowed to

13 위 대화의 빈칸 ⓑ에 알맞은 것은?

① so   ② or   ③ but
④ and   ⑤ for

14 위 대화의 빈칸 ⓒ에 알맞은 것은?

① at   ② with
③ into   ④ for
⑤ from

15 What does the sign mean? Answer in Korean.

➡ _____

[01~02] 다음 우리말에 맞도록 괄호 안에 주어진 단어를 배열하여 문장을 완성하시오.

01

장갑 끼는 것을 잊지 마.
(wear / gloves / don't / to / forget / your).

➡ _____

02 중요

쓰레기를 가져오는 것을 명심해라.
(back / bring / to / your / make / trash / sure).

➡ _____

03 다음 괄호 안에 주어진 단어들을 배열하여 대화를 완성하시오.

A: Tony, (play / better / you'd / not) with a ball near the street.
B: Okay, I see.

➡ _____

04 다음 대화의 순서를 바르게 배열하시오.

A: I'm going to go to Jiri Mountain with my dad tomorrow.
(A) Okay.
(B) It sounds great.
(C) That'll be great, but don't forget to check the weather.
(D) I'm excited because we are going to stay there for two days and one night.

➡ _____

05 다음 대화의 밑줄 친 말과 바꿔 쓸 수 있는 표현을 2개 이상 쓰시오.

A: Jane, you'd better not use your smartphone while you are riding a bike.
B: Okay, I see.

➡ _____
_____

[06~08] 다음 대화를 읽고, 물음에 답하시오.

B: Hi, Amy. What's up?
G: I'm here ⓐbuy a shirt. What about you?
B: I have a lunch meeting in this shopping center. Oh, I should go now. I'm late.
G: Okay, but you'd better not run. The sign says the floor is wet.
B: I didn't see it. Thanks.

06 중요

위 대화의 밑줄 친 ⓐ를 알맞은 형태로 바꿔 쓰시오.

➡ _____

07 Why did the girl come to this shopping center? Answer in English.

➡ _____

08 Why should the boy not run? Answer in English.

➡ _____

Grammar

① 의문사+to부정사

- I learned **how to do** CPR. 나는 심폐소생술을 하는 방법을 배웠다.
- We couldn't decide **what to eat** for dinner. 우리는 저녁으로 무엇을 먹을지 결정할 수 없었다.
- Can you tell me **where to buy** a life jacket? 구명조끼를 어디서 사는지 말해 줄래?

■ 의문사 뒤에 to부정사를 써서 '~해야 하는지, ~하는 것이 좋을지'라는 의무의 뜻을 나타낼 수 있다. 이때 「의문사+to부정사」는 보통 문장 안에서 동사의 목적어 역할을 한다. 또, 의문사 대신 접속사 whether를 쓸 수도 있다.

- I can't decide **what to do**. 나는 무엇을 할지 결정할 수 없다.
- I don't know **where to buy** notebooks. 나는 공책을 어디서 사야 할지 모른다.

■ 의문사와 to부정사 사이에 명사가 오면 의문사와 함께 하나의 의문사(구)를 형성한다.

- I wanted to know **what time to** start. 나는 몇 시에 출발해야 하는지 알고 싶었다.

의문사+to부정사		의문사+명사+to부정사	
what to do where to go when to start which to choose how to swim	무엇을 해야 하는지 어디에 가야 하는지 언제 출발해야 하는지 어느 것을 골라야 할지 어떻게 수영해야 할지	what book to read which way to go what time to get up how many books to read	어떤 책을 읽어야 할지 어느 길로 가야 할지 몇 시에 일어나야 할지 얼마나 많은 책을 읽어야 할지

■ 「의문사+to부정사」는 의무를 나타내므로 should를 써서 「의문사+주어+should+동사 원형」 구문으로 바꿔 쓸 수 있다.

- I don't know **what to make** next. 다음에 무엇을 만들어야 할지 모르겠다.
  → I don't know **what I should make** next.

핵심 Check

1. 다음 괄호 안에서 알맞은 것을 고르시오.

   (1) She doesn't know (which / how) to play chess.

   (2) I asked her (which / where) book to buy.

   (3) Please tell him (why / where) to buy the doll.

   (4) The doctor told me (what / when) to take medicine.

   (5) I want to travel this summer, but I don't know (where / what) to go.

② as + 형용사/부사의 원급 + as

- I was **as** scared **as** the others. 나는 다른 사람들 만큼 무서웠다.
- My shoes are **not as** big **as** yours. 내 신발은 너의 신발만큼 크지 않다.
- Teri studies **as** hard **as** her twin sister. Teri는 그녀의 쌍둥이 여동생만큼 열심히 공부한다.

■ **동등비교**

둘을 비교하여 두 대상의 정도가 같음을 비교하는 표현으로 「as+형용사[부사]의 원급+as」의 형태로 '~만큼 …한[하게]'라는 의미이다.

- I am **as** tall **as** Sam. 나는 Sam만큼 키가 크다.

■ **동등 비교의 부정**

'not as[so]+형용사[부사]의 원급+as'의 형태로 '~만큼 …하지 못한'의 의미이다. 비교급으로 바꿔 쓸 수도 있다.

- Jane is **not as** tall **as** Tony.
  = Tony is **taller than** Jane. Tony는 Jane보다 더 키가 크다.

■ **as+원급+as+사람+can[could]**

'가능한 한 ~하게'의 뜻으로 「as ~ as …」 구문의 관용적인 표현이다. 같은 뜻으로 'as+원급+as possible'의 구문을 쓰기도 한다.

- He swam **as** fast **as he could**. 그는 가능한 한 빨리 수영을 했다.
  = He swam **as** fast **as possible**.

■ **배수 표현**

'…의 몇 배만큼 ~한'이라고 배수 표현을 나타낼 경우 「숫자+times+as+형용사/부사+as」 또는 「배수사+as+형용사/부사+as」의 표현을 사용한다.

- Their house is about **twice as** big **as** ours. 그들의 집은 우리 집보다 두 배 정도 크다.

핵심 Check

2. 다음 괄호 안의 말을 알맞은 순서로 배열하시오.

(1) Sally runs (fast / as / Bora / as).

➡ Sally runs _____.

(2) Is your camera (as, mine, new, as)?

➡ Is your camera _____?

(3) The red pencil is (the, as, not, yellow, as, long, one).

➡ The red pencil is _____.

01 다음 우리말과 일치하도록 빈칸에 알맞은 말을 쓰시오.

> make kimchi 김치를 만들다
> restaurant 식당

(1) Julie는 어디로 가야 할지 모른다.

➡ Julie doesn't know _____ _____ _____.

(2) 그는 김치 만드는 법을 알고 싶어 한다.

➡ He wants to know _____ _____ _____ kimchi.

(3) 우리는 중국 식당에서 무엇을 먹을지 얘기하고 있다.

➡ We're talking about _____ _____ _____ at the Chinese restaurant.

(4) 그 문을 언제 열어야 할지 너의 엄마에게 물어 보아라.

➡ Ask your mother _____ _____ _____ the door.

02 다음 밑줄 친 부분을 바르게 고쳐 쓰시오.

> delicious 맛있는

(1) Your bag is <u>as heavy as me</u>.

➡ _____

(2) I can <u>as run fast as</u> my father.

➡ _____

(3) Tokyo's population is as large as <u>Seoul</u>.

➡ _____

(4) This is <u>as not delicious as</u> it looks.

➡ _____

(5) The second question was <u>more difficult</u> as the first question.

➡ _____

03 다음 두 문장의 의미가 같도록 빈칸에 알맞은 말을 쓰시오.

(1) I want to know where to park my car.

= I want to know _____ _____ _____ _____ my car.

(2) They learned how to use the computer.

= They learned _____ _____ _____ _____ _____ _____.

01 다음 문장의 빈칸에 알맞은 것은?

> Jake is _____ old as my big brother.

① as
② so
③ than
④ very
⑤ much

02 다음 두 문장의 빈칸에 공통으로 알맞은 것은?

> • Can you show me how _____ do it?
> • They knew what _____ buy at the mall.

① on
② to
③ for
④ must
⑤ should

03 다음 주어진 문장에 맞도록 빈칸에 알맞은 것은?

> • Tom is 175 centimeters tall.
> • John is 175 centimeters tall, too.
> ➡ John is _____ Tom.

① shorter than
② as tall as
③ taller than
④ not as tall as
⑤ not taller than

04 다음 문장의 빈칸에 알맞은 것으로 짝지어진 것은?

> • She didn't decide _____ to wear that morning.
> • Can you tell me _____ to cook it?

① what – why
② how – who
③ what – how
④ when – which
⑤ where – what

05 다음 문장의 빈칸에 알맞은 것은?

> I don't know what to say about it.
> = I don't know what I _____ say about it.

① can
② should
③ would
④ may
⑤ could

서답형
06 다음 문장의 빈칸에 알맞은 말을 쓰시오.

	Ted	Minho	Eric
height	175cm	172cm	175cm

➡ Eric is _____ _____ _____ _____.

07 다음 우리말을 영어로 바르게 옮긴 것은?

> 나는 동생에게 중국어 책 읽는 법을 가르쳤다.

① I taught my brother how to read Chinese books.
② I taught my brother where to read Chinese books.
③ I taught my brother why to read Chinese books.
④ I taught my brother what to read Chinese books.
⑤ I taught my brother how he could read Chinese books.

서답형
08 다음 두 문장의 뜻이 같도록 빈칸에 알맞은 말을 쓰시오.

> We could not agree as to where we should go during the holidays.
> = We could not agree as to _____ _____ _____ during the holidays.

서답형

09 다음 두 문장의 뜻이 같도록 빈칸에 알맞은 말을 쓰시오.

I don't have _____ much money _____ you.

➡ I have less money than you.

중요

10 다음 중 어법상 어색한 문장은?

① Can you tell me what to do first?

② She decided what to eat lunch.

③ They showed him how to make it.

④ I didn't know where to find her.

⑤ Jack explains them how to finish it quickly.

11 다음 글에서 가장 빨리 달리는 사람은?

• Eric runs very fast.

• Junho cannot run as fast as Eric.

• Mina and Mike are faster than Eric.

• Mina is slower than Mike.

① Junho ② Mike

③ Mina ④ Eric

⑤ Mina and Mike

12 다음 밑줄 친 부분의 문장 성분이 다른 하나는?

① He told me where to go.

② The important thing is what to read.

③ I don't know which book to buy.

④ I didn't know whether to take this bus or not.

⑤ I have no idea about how to solve this problem.

서답형

13 다음 문장과 뜻이 같도록 빈칸에 알맞은 말을 쓰시오.

He didn't tell them what to read.

➡ He didn't tell them what _____ _____ read.

서답형

14 다음 두 문장의 의미가 같도록 빈칸에 알맞은 말을 쓰시오.

The desk is cheaper than the table.

➡ The table is _____ _____ _____ _____ the desk.

중요

15 다음 밑줄 친 부분이 어색한 것은?

① Can you show me how to cook it?

② I didn't know what to wear.

③ They decided where to go first.

④ Jack explained them how to make next.

⑤ She told me when to start it.

서답형

16 다음 두 문장이 같은 뜻이 되도록 빈칸에 알맞은 말을 쓰시오.

(1) February is colder than March.

➡ March isn't as _____ as Februay.

(2) It wasn't as hot in Pusan as in Taegu.

➡ It was _____ in Taegu _____ in Pusan.

17 다음 중 어법상 잘못된 것은?

① I am as pretty as you.

② You're as tall as me.

③ They are not as scary as lions.

④ English is easier than math.

⑤ Minsu can speak Chinese as good as I do.

18 다음 중 어법상 <u>어색한</u> 문장은?

① Does she know when to start?

② I don't know how use this camera.

③ We don't know which bus to get on.

④ They had no idea where to go.

⑤ I'm wondering what to buy for my mother's birthday.

서답형
19 다음 괄호 안에 주어진 단어를 이용하여 우리말을 영어로 옮기시오.

> 그녀는 너만큼 인기 있지 않다. (as, popular)

➡ _____

20 다음 빈칸에 들어갈 말로 바르게 짝지어진 것은?

> • You may eat as much _____ you like.
> • This picture is _____ beautiful than mine.

① as – much   ② as – more

③ so – few   ④ as – little

⑤ so – much

중요
21 다음 두 문장의 뜻이 같도록 빈칸에 알맞은 것은?

> Seoul is bigger than Incheon.
> = Incheon is _____ Seoul.

① as big as   ② larger than

③ bigger than   ④ not so big as

⑤ not smaller than

서답형
22 다음 우리말과 같도록 괄호 안의 단어들을 이용하여 문장을 쓰시오.

> 카메라 사용법 좀 가르쳐 주실래요?
> (can / show / how)

➡ _____

23 다음 중 어법상 틀린 문장은?

① Can you tell me when to get up?

② They told me where to go.

③ Jack decided what to eat in the morning.

④ Will you tell me who to invite Jack?

⑤ I learned how to make lemonade.

24 다음 빈칸에 들어갈 말이 나머지 넷과 <u>다른</u> 것은?

① What _____ learn in youth is very important.

② I want you to decide where _____ go first.

③ We discussed who _____ take the responsibility.

④ She completely forgot how _____ make a paper crane.

⑤ I will tell you what _____ see in London.

01 다음 빈칸에 알맞은 말을 〈보기〉에서 골라 쓰시오. (중복 사용 금지)

┌─ 보기 ─┐
what   where   which   how
└─────┘

(1) Jim learned _____ to ride a bike.

(2) I wanted to know _____ time to start.

(3) I asked her _____ book to read.

(4) Can I ask you _____ to write my name?

02 다음 표를 보고, 빈칸에 알맞은 말을 고르시오.

	Kevin	Junho	Brian
height(cm)	172	178	172
age(years old)	15	16	16

(1) Brian is (taller than / as tall as) Kevin.

(2) Junho is (taller than / as tall as) Kevin.

(3) Brian is (older than / as old as) Junho.

(4) Kevin is (as old as / not as old as) Junho and Brain.

03 다음 문장에서 어색한 부분을 찾아 바르게 고쳐 쓰시오.

(1) I can't decide what will buy for my mother's birthday.

➡ _____

(2) Bill didn't tell us where to staying.

➡ _____

04 다음 문장을 as ～ as 구문으로 고쳐 쓰시오.

(1) Jimin is shorter than Taemin.

➡ _____

(2) Jane is less heavy than Kirk.

➡ _____

05 주어진 단어를 순서에 맞게 배열하여 문장을 완성하시오.

(1) You don't know about history _____ _____. (I, as, do, much, as)

(2) I got here _____. (as, could, fast, I, as)

(3) This bed is _____. (that, not, as, bed, comfortable, as)

06 다음 문장을 should를 써서 같은 의미의 문장으로 바꿔 쓰시오.

(1) My brother doesn't know where to go.

➡ _____

(2) Alice doesn't know what to cook.

➡ _____

(3) Please tell me when to help you.

➡ _____

(4) The problem is how to escape from here.

➡ _____

07 다음 우리말과 의미가 같도록 문장을 완성하시오.

(1) 어디서 노래 연습을 해야 할지 선생님에게 여쭤 보자.

➡ Let's ask our teacher _____ _____

_____ singing songs.

(2) 나는 언제 서울을 방문해야 할지 결정하지 못했다.

➡ I didn't decide _____ _____

_____ Seoul.

(3) 너는 누구와 그곳에 가야 하는지 아니?

➡ Do you know _____ _____

_____ there with?

(4) 나는 무엇을 사야 할지 몰랐다.

➡ I didn't know _____ _____

_____.

(5) 그녀는 어느 꽃을 살지 정했다.

➡ She decided _____ flower _____

_____.

08 다음 두 문장을 as ~ as를 써서 〈보기〉와 같이 한 문장으로 나타내시오.

┌ 보기 ┐

Jack has six dogs. Kate also has six dogs.

➡ Jack has as many dogs as Kate has.

(1) Ella has nine hats. I also have nine hats.

➡ _____

(2) This new tool is useful. That old one is useful, too.

➡ _____

(3) Tom drank much wine. He also drank much water.

➡ _____

09 다음 문장에서 어법상 <u>어색한</u> 곳을 찾아 바르게 고쳐 쓰시오.

┌─────────────────────────┐
│ Mary didn't know which way she to take. │
└─────────────────────────┘

_____ ➡ _____

10 다음 두 문장을 한 문장으로 만들 때, 괄호 안의 말을 이용해 빈칸에 알맞은 말을 쓰시오.

┌─────────────────────────┐
│ Amy scored 100 on the test. Junsu scored │
│ 90 on it. (well) │
│ ➡ Amy scored _____ than Junsu did. │
│ ➡ Junsu didn't score _____ _____ │
│ _____ Amy did. │
└─────────────────────────┘

11 다음 주어진 단어를 바르게 배열하여 문장을 완성하시오.

(1) (didn't / leave / I / to / when / know).

➡ _____

(2) (do / how / know / the guitar / play / to / you)?

➡ _____

(3) (to / I / her / where / meet / know / don't).

➡ _____

12 다음 빈칸에 알맞은 말을 〈보기〉에서 골라 쓰시오.

┌ 보기 ┐

early   wise   twice   just

(1) This cat is _____ as pretty as that one.

(2) He's not as _____ as he used to be.

(3) This box is _____ as large as that one.

(4) He doesn't get up as _____ as Ann.

Reading

CPR Saves Lives

Announcer: Yesterday, a teenager saved the life of an old man. The
생명
brave student is in the studio with us today. Please introduce yourself.
= fearless   ~와 함께   동사의 목적어가 되는 재귀대명사

Sejin: My name is Kim Sejin. I'm in the second grade at Hanguk
be in the second grade: 2학년이다
Middle School.

Announcer: Could you tell us your experience?
tell+간접목적어+직접목적어: ~에게 ···을 말하다

Sejin: Sure. I was waiting for the bus with my friend, Jinho. A man
wait for: ~을 기다리다   ~와 함께   my friend와 Jinho는 동격 관계
suddenly fell in front of us. Nobody knew what to do. I was as scared
= all of a sudden   ~ 앞에서   what+to부정사: 무엇을 ~해야 할지   as+원급+as: ~만큼 ···한
as the others at first. Then, I ran to him and tapped him on the shoulder.
처음에   = a man   tap ~ on the shoulder: ~의 어깨를 톡톡 치다
He wasn't moving or breathing. I said to Jinho, "Call 119," and started
명령문: 동사원형 ~
CPR.

CPR 심폐소생술

save 구하다

announcer 아나운서

teenager 십대

brave 용감한

introduce 소개하다

grade 학년

experience 경험

suddenly 갑자기

fall 넘어[쓰러]지다

scared 무서워하는, 겁먹은

tap (가볍게) 톡톡 두드리다[치다]

shoulder 어깨

breathe 숨을 쉬다, 호흡하다

 확인문제

- 다음 문장이 본문의 내용과 일치하면 T, 일치하지 않으면 F를 쓰시오.

1   Sejin is in the studio now. ☐

2   Sejin saved the life of an old man today. ☐

3   Sejin is in the second grade at Hanguk Middle School. ☐

4   Sejin wasn't scared when a man fell down. ☐

5   Sejin told Jinho to call 119 before he started CPR. ☐

Announcer: That's impressive. When did you learn such an important

such a/an+형+명=so+형+a/an+명

skill?

Sejin: We had Safety Training Day at school last week. I learned how to

지난주   *how+to부정사: ~하는 방법*

do CPR and had a chance to practice.

to부정사의 형용사적 용법(~할)

Announcer: Can you show the audience how to perform CPR?

how+to부정사: 어떻게 행하는지

Sejin: Yes. Keep your arms straight. Your arms and the other person's

keep+목적어+목적격보어: ~을 …하게 유지하다

chest must be at a 90 degree angle. Push down in the center of the

~해야 한다   *~을 누르다*

chest hard and fast until an ambulance comes.

(부) 세게   *(접) ~할 때까지*

Announcer: Are there any other things to remember?

Are there + 복수명사 ~?: ~이 있니?   *to부정사의 형용사적 용법(~할)*

Sejin: Yes. You need to remember the four minutes of "Golden Time." It

~할 필요가 있다

means that you should start CPR within four minutes after someone's

= the four minutes of "Golden Time"   *~ 이내에[안에]*   *(접) ~한 후에*

heart stops. To begin CPR later than that will greatly lower the chances

= Beginning   *~보다 늦게*

of saving someone's life.

전치사+동명사

Announcer: Timing is as important as doing CPR. Thank you for joining

as+원급+as: ~만큼 …한   *~해서 고맙다*

us.

Sejin: My pleasure.

---

impressive 인상적인

important 중요한

skill 기술

safety 안전

training 훈련

chance 기회, 가능성

practice 연습하다

audience 청중, 시청자

perform 행하다, 실시하다

chest 가슴

degree (각도의 단위인) 도

angle 각도

hard 세게, 힘껏

ambulance 구급차

remember 기억하다

heart 심장

greatly 대단히, 크게

lower 낮추다, 낮아지다

join 함께하다

확인문제

● 다음 문장이 본문의 내용과 일치하면 T, 일치하지 <u>않으면</u> F를 쓰시오.

1 Sejin learned how to do CPR yesterday. ☐

2 Sejin showed the audience how to perform CPR. ☐

3 Your arms and the other person's chest must be at a 45 degree angle. ☐

4 We push down in the center of the chest when we perform CPR. ☐

5 You should start CPR within four minutes after someone's heart stops. ☐

● 우리말을 참고하여 빈칸에 알맞은 말을 쓰시오.

1 Announcer: Yesterday, a teenager _____ the _____ of an old man.

2 The _____ student is in the studio _____ _____ today.

3 Please introduce _____.

4 Sejin: _____ name _____ Kim Sejin.

5 I'm _____ the _____ grade _____ Hanguk Middle School.

6 Announcer: Could you _____ _____ your _____?

7 Sejin: Sure. I was _____ _____ the bus _____ my friend, Jinho.

8 A man suddenly fell _____ _____ _____ us.

9 Nobody knew _____ _____ _____.

10 I was _____ scared _____ the others _____ first.

11 Then, I _____ to him and _____ him _____ the shoulder.

12 He _____ moving or _____.

13 I _____ _____ Jinho, "Call 119," and started _____.

14 Announcer: That's _____.

1 아나운서: 어제, 한 십대가 어떤 노인의 생명을 구했습니다.

2 그 용감한 학생이 오늘 우리와 함께 스튜디오에 있습니다.

3 자기소개를 해 보세요.

4 세진: 제 이름은 김세진입니다.

5 저는 한국중학교 2학년입니다.

6 아나운서: 당신의 경험을 우리에게 말해 줄 수 있나요?

7 세진: 물론이죠. 저는 친구 진호와 버스를 기다리고 있었어요.

8 갑자기 한 남자가 우리 앞에 쓰러졌어요.

9 아무도 무엇을 해야 할지 몰랐어요.

10 저는 처음엔 다른 사람들처럼 겁이 났어요.

11 그러고 나서, 저는 그에게 달려가서 그의 어깨를 두드렸어요.

12 그는 움직이지도 숨을 쉬지도 않았어요.

13 저는 진호에게 " 119에 전화해." 라고 말하고 심폐소생술을 시작했습니다.

14 아나운서: 인상적이네요.

15 When _____ you learn _____ _____ important skill?

16 Sejin: We had _____ _____ Day _____ school last week.

17 I learned _____ _____ _____ CPR and had a chance _____ _____.

18 Announcer: Can you _____ the audience _____ _____ perform CPR?

19 Sejin: Yes. _____ your arms _____.

20 Your arms and the _____ person's chest _____ be _____ a 90 degree _____.

21 _____ _____ in the center of the chest _____ and fast _____ an ambulance comes.

22 Announcer: _____ _____ any other things _____ _____?

23 Sejin: Yes. You _____ _____ remember the four _____ of "Golden Time."

24 It means _____ you _____ start CPR _____ four minutes _____ someone's heart _____.

25 _____ _____ CPR _____ _____ that will greatly lower the chances of _____ someone's life.

26 Announcer: Timing is _____ _____ _____ doing CPR.

27 Thank you _____ _____ us.

28 Sejin: My _____.

---

15 언제 그런 중요한 기술을 배웠나요?

16 세진: 지난주에 학교에서 '안전 교육의 날'이 있었어요.

17 저는 심폐소생술을 하는 방법을 배웠고 연습할 기회도 가졌어요.

18 아나운서: 청중들에게 심폐소생술을 어떻게 하는지 보여줄 수 있나요?

19 세진: 네. 팔을 쭉 펴세요.

20 당신의 팔과 다른 사람의 가슴은 90도 각도여야 합니다.

21 구급차가 올 때까지 가슴 중앙을 세게 그리고 빨리 누르세요.

22 아나운서: 기억해야 할 다른 것이 있나요?

23 세진: 네. "골든타임" 4분을 기억해야 합니다.

24 그것은 여러분이 누군가의 심장이 멈춘 후 4분 안에 심폐소생술을 시작해야 한다는 것을 의미합니다.

25 그보다 늦게 심폐소생술을 시작하는 것은 누군가의 생명을 구할 가능성을 크게 낮출 것입니다.

26 아나운서: 타이밍은 심폐소생술을 하는 것만큼이나 중요하군요.

27 저희와 함께 해 주셔서 감사합니다.

28 세진: 제가 더 고맙습니다.

● 우리말을 참고하여 본문을 영작하시오.

1 아나운서: 어제, 한 십대가 어떤 노인의 생명을 구했습니다.

➡ _____

2 그 용감한 학생이 오늘 우리와 함께 스튜디오에 있습니다.

➡ _____

3 자기소개를 해 보세요.

➡ _____

4 세진: 제 이름은 김세진입니다.

➡ _____

5 저는 한국중학교 2학년입니다.

➡ _____

6 아나운서: 당신의 경험을 우리에게 말해 줄 수 있나요?

➡ _____

7 세진: 물론이죠. 저는 친구 진호와 버스를 기다리고 있었어요.

➡ _____

8 갑자기 한 남자가 우리 앞에 쓰러졌어요.

➡ _____

9 아무도 무엇을 해야 할지 몰랐어요.

➡ _____

10 저는 처음엔 다른 사람들처럼 겁이 났어요.

➡ _____

11 그러고 나서, 저는 그에게 달려가서 그의 어깨를 두드렸어요.

➡ _____

12 그는 움직이지도 숨을 쉬지도 않았어요.

➡ _____

13 저는 진호에게 "119에 전화해."라고 말하고 심폐소생술을 시작했습니다.

➡ _____

14 아나운서: 인상적이네요.

➡ _____

15 언제 그런 중요한 기술을 배웠나요?

➡️ _____

16 세진: 우리는 지난주에 학교에서 '안전 교육의 날'이 있었어요.

➡️ _____

17 저는 심폐소생술을 하는 방법을 배웠고 연습할 기회를 가졌어요.

➡️ _____

18 아나운서: 청중들에게 심폐소생술을 어떻게 하는지 보여줄 수 있나요?

➡️ _____

19 세진: 네. 팔을 쭉 펴세요.

➡️ _____

20 당신의 팔과 다른 사람의 가슴은 90도 각도여야 합니다.

➡️ _____

21 구급차가 올 때까지 가슴 중앙을 세게 그리고 빨리 누르세요.

➡️ _____

22 아나운서: 기억해야 할 다른 것이 있나요?

➡️ _____

23 세진: 네. "골든타임" 4분을 기억해야 합니다.

➡️ _____

24 그것은 여러분이 누군가의 심장이 멈춘 후 4분 안에 심폐소생술을 시작해야 한다는 것을 의미합니다.

➡️ _____

25 그보다 늦게 심폐소생술을 시작하는 것은 누군가의 생명을 구할 가능성을 크게 낮출 것입니다.

➡️ _____

26 아나운서: 타이밍은 심폐소생술을 하는 것만큼이나 중요하군요.

➡️ _____

27 저희와 함께 해 주셔서 감사합니다.

➡️ _____

28 세진: 제가 더 고맙습니다.

➡️ _____

[01~05] 다음 글을 읽고, 물음에 답하시오.

Announcer: Yesterday, a teenager saved the life of an old man. The brave student is in the studio with us today. Please introduce __ⓐ__.

Sejin: My name is Kim Sejin. I'm __ⓑ__ the second grade at Hanguk Middle School.

Announcer: Could you tell us your experience?

Sejin: Sure. I was waiting for the bus with my friend, Jinho. A man ⓒsuddenly fell in front of us. ⓓ아무도 무엇을 해야 할지 몰랐다. I was as scared as the others at first. Then, I ran to him and tapped him on the shoulder. He wasn't moving or breathe. I said to Jinho, "Call 119," and started CPR.

01 위 글의 빈칸 ⓐ에 알맞은 것은?

① him   ② you
③ itself   ④ yourself
⑤ himself

서답형

02 위 글의 빈칸 ⓑ에 알맞은 말을 쓰시오.

➡ _____

중요

03 위 글의 밑줄 친 ⓒ와 뜻이 같은 것은?

① specially   ② exactly
③ actually   ④ certainly
⑤ unexpectedly

서답형

04 위 글의 밑줄 친 ⓓ의 우리말을 주어진 단어를 이용하여 5단어로 영작하시오.

┌─────────────────────────┐
│   (nobody / what)   │
└─────────────────────────┘

➡ _____

05 위 글을 읽고, 답할 수 없는 질문은?

① Whose life did Sejin save?
② Where is Sejin now?
③ Who was Sejin waiting for the bus with?
④ What does the old man do for a living?
⑤ How did Sejin feel when a man fell in front of her?

[06~09] 다음 글을 읽고, 물음에 답하시오.

Announcer: Are there any other things ⓐ remember?

Sejin: Yes. You need to remember the four minutes of "Golden Time." ⓑIt means that you should start CPR within four minutes after someone's heart __ⓒ__. ⓓBegin CPR later than that will greatly __ⓔ__ the chances of saving someone's life.

중요

 위 글의 밑줄 친 ⓐ와 ⓓ의 알맞은 형태로 짝지어진 것은?

① remember – Begin
② to remember – Begin
③ remembering – To begin
④ remembering – Beginning
⑤ to remember – To begin

서답형

07 위 글의 밑줄 친 ⓑ가 가리키는 것을 영어로 쓰시오.

➡ _____

중요

08 위 글의 빈칸 ⓒ에 문맥상 알맞은 것은?

① hurts   ② begins

③ beats   ④ pounds

⑤ stops

09 위 글의 빈칸 ⓔ에 다음 영영풀이에 해당하는 단어를 주어진 철자로 시작하여 쓰시오.

> to reduce something in amount, degree, strength etc, or to become less

➡ l_____

[10~14] 다음 글을 읽고, 물음에 답하시오.

Announcer: When did you learn ⓐ(skill / such / important / an)?

Sejin: We had Safety Training Day at school last week. I learned how ___ⓑ___ do CPR and had a chance ⓒto practice.

Announcer: Can you show the audience how to perform CPR?

Sejin: Yes. Keep your arms straight. Your arms and the other person's chest must be at a 90 degree angle. Push down in the center of the chest hard and fast until an ambulance comes.

서답형

10 위 글의 괄호 ⓐ 안의 단어들을 순서대로 배열하시오.

➡ _____

서답형

11 위 글의 빈칸 ⓑ에 알맞은 말을 쓰시오.

➡ _____

중요

12 위 글의 밑줄 친 ⓒ와 쓰임이 같은 것은?

① I got up early to see her.

② Watch your step not to slip.

③ I have so many friends to help me.

④ You can spend money to help poor people.

⑤ He did his best to solve the problem.

서답형

13 위 글에서 다음 영영풀이에 해당하는 단어를 찾아 쓰시오.

> to do an action or activity that usually requires training or skill

➡ _____

14 위 글을 읽고, 다음 질문에 완전한 문장으로 답하시오.

> Q: When we perform CPR, at how many degree angle must our arms and the other person's chest be?
>
> A: _____
> _____

[15~20] 다음 글을 읽고, 물음에 답하시오.

Sejin: I was waiting for the bus with my friend, Jinho. A man suddenly fell in front of us. Nobody knew what to do. I was as ⓐ   as the others at first. Then, I ran to ⓑhim and tapped him ⓒ   the shoulder. ⓓHe wasn't moving or breathe. I said to Jinho, "Call 119," and started ⓔ   .

15 문맥상 위 글의 빈칸 ⓐ에 알맞은 것은?

① tired   ② scared
③ bored   ④ busy
⑤ excited

서답형

16 위 글의 밑줄 친 ⓑ가 가리키는 말을 찾아 쓰시오.

➡ _____

17 위 글의 빈칸 ⓒ에 알맞은 것은?

① at   ② in
③ on   ④ up
⑤ over

서답형

18 위 글의 밑줄 친 ⓓ에서 어법상 틀린 부분을 찾아 바르게 고쳐 쓰시오.

➡ _____

서답형

19 위 글의 빈칸 ⓔ에 다음 영영풀이에 해당하는 단어를 세 글자로 쓰시오.

a way of trying to save the life of someone who has stopped breathing and whose heart has stopped beating

➡ _____

서답형

20 위 글을 읽고, 다음 질문에 완전한 문장으로 답하시오.

Q: What was Sejin doing when a man fell in front of her?

A: _____

[21~26] 다음 글을 읽고, 물음에 답하시오.

Announcer: ⓐIs there any other things to remember?
Sejin: Yes. You need to remember the four minutes of "Golden Time." It means that you should start CPR ⓑ   four minutes after someone's heart stops. To begin CPR later than ⓒthat will greatly lower the chances ⓓ   saving someone's life.
Announcer: Timing is as ⓔ   as doing CPR. Thank you for ⓕjoin us.
Sejin: My pleasure.

서답형

21 위 글의 밑줄 친 ⓐ에서 어법상 틀린 부분을 찾아 바르게 고쳐 쓰시오.

_____ ➡ _____

22 위 글의 빈칸 ⓑ에 알맞은 것은?

① with   ② for

③ within   ④ during

⑤ between

서답형

23 위 글의 밑줄 친 ⓒthat이 가리키는 것을 우리말로 쓰시오.

➡ _____

중요

24 위 글의 빈칸 ⓓ에 알맞은 것은?

① by   ② of

③ to   ④ on

⑤ for

25 위 글의 빈칸 ⓔ에 문맥상 가장 알맞은 것은?

① easy   ② popular

③ difficult   ④ creative

⑤ important

서답형

26 위 글의 밑줄 친 ⓕ를 알맞은 형태로 고쳐 쓰시오.

➡ _____

[27~30] 다음 글을 읽고, 물음에 답하시오.

> **Announcer:** Can you show the audience ___ⓐ___ ?
>
> **Sejin:** Yes. Keep your arms straight. Your arms and the other person's ___ⓑ___ must be ___ⓒ___ a 90 degree angle. ___ⓓ___ in the center of the chest hard and fast until an ambulance comes.

중요

27 위 글의 빈칸 ⓐ에 알맞은 것은?

① how to call 119

② how to perform CPR

③ how to stand straight

④ how to do safety training

⑤ how to breathe

서답형

28 위 글의 빈칸 ⓑ에 다음 영영풀이에 해당하는 단어를 찾아 쓰시오.

> the front part of the body between the neck and the stomach

➡ _____

서답형

29 위 글의 빈칸 ⓒ에 알맞은 전치사를 쓰시오.

➡ _____

30 위 글의 빈칸 ⓓ에 문맥상 알맞은 것은?

① Put down   ② Push out

③ Push down   ④ Pull up

⑤ Put off

Reading 서술형 시험대비

[01~06] 다음 글을 읽고, 물음에 답하시오.

Sejin: My name is Kim Sejin. I'm in the second grade at Hanguk Middle School.
Announcer: ⓐCould you tell us your experience?
Sejin: Sure. I was waiting for the bus with my friend, Jinho. A man suddenly fell ⓑ~ 앞에서 us. Nobody knew what to do. ⓒ저는 처음엔 다른 사람들처럼 겁이 났어요. Then, I ran to him and tapped him ⓓ the shoulder. He wasn't moving or breathing. I said to Jinho, "Call 119," and started CPR.

01 What grade is Sejin in? Answer in English.

➡ _____

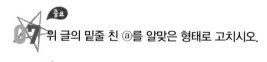

02 위 글의 밑줄 친 ⓐ의 4형식 문장을 3형식 문장으로 바르게 전환하시오.

➡ _____

03 위 글의 밑줄 친 ⓑ의 우리말에 맞게 세 단어로 쓰시오.

➡ _____

04 위 글의 밑줄 친 ⓒ의 우리말에 맞도록 주어진 어구를 순서대로 배열하시오.

> (the others / as / I / first / scared / was / as / at)

➡ _____

05 위 글의 빈칸 ⓓ에 알맞은 전치사를 쓰시오.

➡ _____

06 What did Sejin say to Jinho before starting CPR?

➡ _____

[07~11] 다음 글을 읽고, 물음에 답하시오.

Announcer: Are there any other things ⓐremember?
Sejin: Yes. You need to remember the four minutes of "Golden Time." It means ⓑ you should start CPR within four minutes after someone's heart stops. To begin CPR later than that will greatly lower the ⓒ of saving someone's life.
Announcer: Timing is ⓓ(CPR / as / doing / as / important). Thank you for joining us.
Sejin: My pleasure.

07 위 글의 밑줄 친 ⓐ를 알맞은 형태로 고치시오.

➡ _____

08 위 글의 빈칸 ⓑ에 알맞은 것을 쓰시오.

➡ _____

09 What does the four minutes of "Golden Time" mean? Answer in Korean.

➡ _____

_____

10 (중요) 위 글의 빈칸 ⓒ에 다음 영영풀이에 해당하는 단어를 주어진 철자로 시작하여 쓰시오. (복수형으로 쓸 것)

the possibility that something will happen

➡ c_____

11 위 글의 괄호 ⓓ 안의 단어들을 알맞은 순서로 바르게 배열하시오.

➡ _____

[12~17] 다음 글을 읽고, 물음에 답하시오.

Announcer: When did you learn ⓐsuch an important skill?
Sejin: We had Safety Training Day at school last week. ⓑ나는 심폐소생술을 하는 방법을 배웠다 and had a chance to practice.
Announcer: Can you show the ⓒ how to perform CPR?
Sejin: Yes. Keep your arms straight. Your arms and the other person's chest must be at a 90 degree angle. ⓓPush down in the center of the chest hard and fast until an ambulance will come.

12 위 글의 밑줄 친 ⓐ를 다음과 같이 바꿔 쓸 때 빈칸에 알맞은 것을 쓰시오.

_____ important a skill

13 When and where did Sejin have Safety Training Day? Answer in English.

➡ _____

14 (중요) 위 글의 밑줄 친 ⓑ의 우리말에 맞도록 주어진 단어를 바르게 배열하시오.

(to / CPR / I / do / learned / how)

➡ _____

15 위 글의 빈칸 ⓒ에 다음 영영풀이에 해당하는 단어를 쓰시오.

the group of people who have gathered to watch or listen to something (a play, concert, someone speaking, etc.)

➡ _____

16 (중요) 위 글의 밑줄 친 ⓓ에서 어법상 틀린 부분을 찾아 바르게 고쳐 쓰시오.

_____ ➡ _____

17 위 글을 읽고, 심폐소생술을 하는 과정을 우리말로 쓰시오.

➡ _____

_____

My Writing B

Save Your Life from a Fire

Do you know what to do when there is a fire? You should shout, "Fire!" You
  　　　　　　what+to부정사: 무엇을 ~해야 할지　there is + 단수명사: ~이 있다　　~해야 한다
need to cover your face and body with a wet towel. You have to stay as low
　　　　　　　　　　　　　　　　　~으로　　　　　　　~해야 한다(=must)
as possible and get out. Also, you need to call 119 as soon as you can. Don't
as ~ as possible: 가능한 ~하게　　　　　　　　　　　가능한 한 빨리(=as soon as possible)
forget to use the stairs, not the elevator.
Don't forget to+동사원형 ~: ~하는 것을 잊지 마라

밖으로 나가다

구문해설 · **shout**: 외치다 · **cover**: 덮다 · **wet**: 젖은 · **also**: 또한 · **stair**: 계단

해석

화재로부터 여러분의 생명을 구하라

불이 나면 여러분은 무엇을 해야 하는지 아는가? 여러분은 "불이야!"라고 외쳐야 한다. 여러분은 젖은 수건으로 얼굴과 몸을 가려야 한다. 가능한 한 낮은 자세로 밖으로 나가야 한다. 또한, 가능한 한 빨리 119에 전화해야 한다. 엘리베이터가 아니라 계단을 이용하는 것을 잊지 마라.

Wrap Up

Safety Training Day

Today we had Safety Training Day at school. Teachers taught us what to do
　　　　　　　　　　　　　　　　　　　　　　　　　수여동사(teach)+간접목적어+직접목적어
when an earthquake hits. We learned how to protect our heads and bodies. We
　　　　　　　　　　　　　　　　　how+to부정사: ~하는 방법
also learned where to go when the shaking stops.
　　　　　　　where+to부정사: 어디로 ~할지

구문해설 · **safety**: 안전 · **training**: 교육, 훈련 · **earthquake**: 지진 · **protect**: 보호하다
· **shaking**: 흔들림

안전 교육의 날

오늘은 학교에서 안전 교육의 날이었다. 선생님들은 우리에게 지진이 일어났을 때 무엇을 해야 하는지 가르쳐 주셨다. 우리는 머리와 몸을 보호하는 법을 배웠다. 우리는 또한 흔들림이 멈추었을 때 어디로 가야 하는지 배웠다.

Project - Step 3

We'll tell you what to do for safety in the science room. First, don't forget to
　　　수여동사(tell)+간접목적어+직접목적어　　　　　　　　　　　　　Don't forget to+동사원형 ~: ~하는 것을 잊지 마라
use safety glasses. Second, you'd better not run around.
　　　보안경　　　　　　　You'd better not + 동사원형 ~.: ~하면 안 된다

구문해설 · **science room**: 과학실 · **use**: 사용하다 · **run around**: 뛰어다니다

과학실에서 안전을 위해 무엇을 해야 하는지 알려드리겠습니다. 첫째, 보안경을 쓰는 것을 잊지 마세요. 둘째, 뛰어다니면 안 됩니다.

영역별 핵심문제

01 다음 중 짝지어진 단어의 관계가 나머지 넷과 다른 것은?

① late : early   ② heavy : light
③ cheap : expensive   ④ wet : dry
⑤ brave : fearless

02 다음 빈칸에 공통으로 알맞은 것은? (대·소문자 무시)

- There is a church _____ front of the school.
- _____ case of fire, ring the alarm bell.

① on   ② at
③ from   ④ in
⑤ with

03 다음 우리말과 같도록 빈칸에 알맞은 말을 쓰시오.

넘어져서 발목을 다치지 않도록 조심하라.
➡ Be careful not to _____ _____ and hurt your ankle.

04 다음 우리말과 같도록 빈칸에 알맞은 말을 주어진 철자로 시작하여 쓰시오.

가장 인상적인 것은 사람들이 매우 친절했다는 거야.
➡ The most _____ thing was that the people were very kind.

05 다음 빈칸에 들어갈 말로 적절하지 않은 것은?

- You should _____, "Fire!"
- What does the sign _____?
- Don't forget to _____ the weather.
- You need to _____ your face and body with a wet towel.

① cover   ② check
③ pick   ④ mean
⑤ shout

06 다음 영영풀이에 해당하는 단어로 알맞은 것은?

to do an action or activity that usually requires training or skill

① exercise   ② perform
③ achieve   ④ experience
⑤ protect

07 다음 대화의 빈칸에 들어갈 말로 알맞은 것은?

A: I'm going to go to a taekwondo lesson.
B: Don't _____ to wear a uniform.
A: Okay, thanks.

① remember   ② forget
③ take   ④ bring
⑤ sell

08 다음 대화의 빈칸에 알맞은 것을 <u>모두</u> 고르면? (3개)

> A: I'm going to visit France.
> B: _____ learn some French.

① Don't forget to
② Make sure to
③ He doesn't want you to
④ Remember to
⑤ Are you interested in

09 다음 대화의 밑줄 친 부분과 바꿔 쓸 수 있는 것은?

> A: Is it okay to eat chocolate?
> B: Sure, but <u>don't eat too much.</u>

① you can eat too much
② you don't have to eat too much
③ you won't eat too much
④ you should eat too much
⑤ you'd better not eat too much

10 다음 대화의 빈칸에 알맞은 것은?

> A: Don't forget to take your umbrella.
> B: _____

① No, I'm not.   ② Okay, I see.
③ You're welcome.   ④ Sorry, but I can't.
⑤ I'm sorry to hear that.

[11~14] 다음 대화를 읽고, 물음에 답하시오.

> B: Mom, can I buy some apple juice?
> W: ⓐSure, Chris. ⓑ식품 라벨을 확인하는 것을 잊지 마라.
> B: The food label?
> W: Yes. Too much sugar is not good ⓒ____ you.
> B: Okay, I will check ⓓit.

11 위 대화의 밑줄 친 ⓐ와 바꿔 쓸 수 있는 것은?

① Of course.
② Of course not.
③ That's the problem.
④ Sorry, but I can't.
⑤ I'm afraid I can't.

12 위 대화의 밑줄 친 ⓑ의 우리말에 맞도록 주어진 단어들을 바르게 배열하시오.

> (check / label / forget / the / to / don't / food)

➡ _____

13 위 대화의 빈칸 ⓒ에 알맞은 것은?

① at   ② in
③ of   ④ for
⑤ about

14 위 대화의 밑줄 친 ⓓ가 가리키는 것을 찾아 쓰시오.

➡ _____

15 다음 표의 내용과 일치하도록 빈칸에 알맞은 말을 쓰시오.

	weight(kg)
Insu	65
Kevin	60
Minho	70

➡ Kevin is not _____ heavy _____ Minho.

16 다음 문장의 빈칸에 공통으로 알맞은 말을 쓰시오

- I can't decide what _____ do.
- Can you show me how _____ use this washing machine?

17 다음 중 어법상 어색한 문장은?

① My house is not so large as yours.
② Jenny's mother ran as fast as she could.
③ He is as a great statesman as ever lived.
④ Are you as good at English as her?
⑤ The air is polluted as badly as the rivers.

18 다음 밑줄 친 ①~⑤ 중 어법상 어색한 것은?

①Before winter comes, many different ②kinds of birds ③head south. How do they know ④when to migrate? How do they know ⑤where should go?

① ② ③ ④ ⑤

19 다음 주어진 단어를 이용하여 우리말을 영어로 옮기시오.

그는 Tom만큼 테니스를 잘 친다. (as ~ as)

➡ _____

20 다음 두 문장이 같은 의미가 되도록 빈칸에 알맞은 말을 써 넣으시오.

The teacher told us when to begin the test.
= The teacher told us when we _____ _____ the test.

21 다음 중 어법상 어색한 것은?

① It is not as easy as you think.
② John doesn't work as hard as George do.
③ I don't have so much money as you do.
④ Let me have your answer as soon as possible.
⑤ I don't have as many friends as you do.

22 다음 중 어법상 올바른 문장을 모두 고른 것은?

ⓐ Please show me how to solve this problem.
ⓑ They decided what to do after school.
ⓒ We want to know where to go next time.
ⓓ Do you know who to tell me about it?
ⓔ Let me tell you when to move yesterday.

① ⓐ   ② ⓐ, ⓑ
③ ⓐ, ⓑ, ⓒ   ④ ⓐ, ⓑ, ⓒ, ⓓ
⑤ ⓐ, ⓑ, ⓒ, ⓓ, ⓔ

23 다음 중 밑줄 친 부분의 쓰임이 나머지 넷과 <u>다른</u> 것은?

① They were <u>as</u> busy as bees.

② Tom is not <u>as</u> honest as John.

③ Please come home <u>as</u> quickly as possible.

④ This house is twice <u>as</u> large as that.

⑤ He came up <u>as</u> she was speaking.

24 다음 두 문장의 의미가 같도록 빈칸에 알맞은 말을 쓰시오.

> Sarah is more diligent than Jane.
> = Jane is ＿＿＿＿ ＿＿＿＿ ＿＿＿＿
> ＿＿＿＿ Sarah.

25 다음 문장의 밑줄 친 부분과 의미가 같은 것은?

> I don't know <u>what to write in the letter</u>.

① what I write in the letter

② what I could write in the letter

③ how should I write in the letter

④ what I should write in the letter

⑤ how might I write in the letter

26 다음 두 문장의 의미가 같도록 할 때 빈칸에 알맞은 것은?

> This room is just the same size ＿＿＿＿
> that one.
> = This room is just as large as that one.

① as   ② so

③ from   ④ for

⑤ with

Reading

[27~32] 다음 글을 읽고, 물음에 답하시오.

Announcer: Yesterday, a teenager saved the life of an old man. The brave student is in the studio with us today. Please introduce ⓐyou.

Sejin: My name is Kim Sejin. I'm in the second grade at Hanguk Middle School.

Announcer: ⓑCould you tell us your experience?

Sejin: Sure. I was waiting ＿ⓒ＿ the bus with my friend, Jinho. A man suddenly fell ＿ⓓ＿ front of us. ⓔ아무도 무엇을 해야 할지 몰랐다. I was ＿ⓕ＿ scared as the others at first. Then, I ran to him and tapped him on the shoulder. He wasn't moving or breathing. I said to Jinho, "Call 119," and started CPR.

27 위 글의 밑줄 친 ⓐ를 바르게 고쳐 쓰시오.

➡ ＿＿＿＿＿＿＿＿＿＿＿＿＿＿＿＿＿

28 위 글의 밑줄 친 ⓑ의 4형식 문장을 3형식 문장으로 쓰시오.

➡ ＿＿＿＿＿＿＿＿＿＿＿＿＿＿＿＿＿

29 위 글의 빈칸 ⓒ와 ⓓ에 알맞은 말이 바르게 짝지어진 것은?

① at – in   ② by – on

③ for – in   ④ over – on

⑤ into – at

30 위 글의 밑줄 친 ⓔ의 우리말에 맞게 주어진 단어를 바르게 배열하시오.

(to / nobody / what / knew / do)

➡ _____

31 위 글의 빈칸 ⓕ에 알맞은 것은?

① as   ② so
③ than   ④ very
⑤ much

32 위 글을 읽고, 답할 수 없는 질문은?

① Where is Sejin now?
② What school does Sejin attend?
③ Where was the old man going?
④ How did Sejin feel when a man fell in front of her?
⑤ What did Sejin say to Jinho before starting CPR?

[33~37] 다음 글을 읽고, 물음에 답하시오.

Save Your Life from a Fire
ⓐDo you know what to do when there are a fire? You should shout, "Fire!" You need to cover your face and body ___ⓑ___ a wet towel. ⓒYou have to stay as low as possible and get out. Also, you need to call 119 as soon as you can. ⓓDon't forget to use the stairs, not the elevator.

33 위 글의 밑줄 친 ⓐ에서 어법상 **틀린** 부분을 찾아 바르게 고쳐 쓰시오.

_____ ➡ _____

34 위 글의 빈칸 ⓑ에 알맞은 것은?

① to   ② by
③ for   ④ from
⑤ with

35 위 글의 밑줄 친 ⓒ를 다음과 같이 바꿔 쓸 때 빈칸에 알맞은 말을 쓰시오.

You have to stay _____ _____
_____ _____ _____

36 위 글의 밑줄 친 ⓓ를 다음과 같이 바꿔 쓸 때 빈칸에 알맞은 말을 쓰시오.

_____ to use the stairs

37 위 글을 읽고, 화재 발생 시 대처법으로 옳지 **않은** 것은?

① "불이야!"라고 외쳐야 한다.
② 젖은 수건으로 얼굴과 몸을 가려야 한다.
③ 가능한 한 몸을 낮게 유지하고 밖으로 나간다.
④ 가능한 한 빨리 119를 불러야 한다.
⑤ 엘리베이터를 이용해야 한다.

단원별 예상문제

출제율 95%

01 다음 중 〈보기〉와 같은 형태로 변화하는 단어는?

┌─ 보기 ─┐

impress : impressive

① change   ② act
③ admire   ④ train
⑤ practice

출제율 100%

02 다음 밑줄 친 반의어를 두 단어로 쓰시오.

The man is taking off his hat.

➡ _____

출제율 90%

03 다음 중 영영풀이가 잘못된 것은?

① wet: not yet dry
② scary: causing fear
③ brave: feeling or showing no fear
④ line: a unit for measuring the size of an angle
⑤ tap: to hit someone or something quickly and lightly

출제율 85%

04 다음 우리말과 같도록 빈칸에 알맞은 단어를 주어진 철자로 시작하여 쓰시오.

그는 깨끗한 공기를 마실 수 있는 곳에서 살고 싶어 한다.

➡ He wants to live where he can b_____ clean air.

출제율 90%

05 다음 빈칸에 공통으로 알맞은 것은? (대 · 소문자 무시)

- _____ first, Kate didn't like Korean food, but now she loves it.
- This seatbelt protects the dogs _____ case of an accident.

① at – for   ② in – on
③ in – with   ④ at – in
⑤ of – in

출제율 90%

06 다음 짝지어진 단어의 관계가 같도록 빈칸에 알맞은 말을 쓰시오.

floor : ceiling = _____ : safe

출제율 100%

07 다음 대화에서 밑줄 친 부분의 의도로 알맞은 것은?

A: Can you take a picture of me?
B: Sure.
A: You'd better not use the flash here, David. The baby animals will wake up.
B: I see.

① 질문하기   ② 요청하기
③ 금지하기   ④ 행동 묘사하기
⑤ 미래의 계획 말하기

출제율 90%

08 다음 대화의 밑줄 친 부분과 의미가 같은 것은?

> A: I can't find my seat.
> B: Your seat is right here. <u>Don't forget to turn off your smartphone, please.</u>
> A: OK, I won't.

① You can take off your smartphone.
② Make sure to use your smartphone.
③ Be sure to turn on your smartphone.
④ You should turn on your smartphone.
⑤ Remember to turn off your smartphone.

[09~10] 다음 대화를 읽고, 물음에 답하시오.

> B: Hi, Amy. What's up?
> G: I'm here to buy a shirt. What about you?
> B: I have a lunch meeting in this shopping center. Oh, I should go now. I'm late.
> G: Okay, but ⓐ<u>너는 뛰지 않는 게 좋을 거야.</u> The sign says the floor is wet.
> B: I didn't see ⓑ<u>it</u>. Thanks.

출제율 95%

09 위 대화의 밑줄 친 ⓐ의 우리말을 주어진 단어를 이용하여 영어로 옮기시오. (4단어)

> better

➡ _____

출제율 90%

10 위 대화의 밑줄 친 ⓑ가 가리키는 것을 영어로 쓰시오.

➡ _____

출제율 100%

11 다음 문장의 빈칸에 알맞은 것은?

> Books must be chosen as _____ as friends are.

① care
② caring
③ cared
④ careful
⑤ carefully

출제율 95%

12 다음 문장에서 어법상 <u>어색한</u> 부분을 찾아 바르게 고쳐 쓰시오.

> Let's decide what to buys for Mina's birthday.

_____ ➡ _____

출제율 90%

13 다음 빈칸에 들어갈 말이 나머지와 <u>다른</u> 하나는?

① Can you tell me what _____ buy at the mall?
② They didn't know where _____ go.
③ Let me know how _____ cook bulgogi.
④ He is _____ short to touch the ceiling.
⑤ I can't decide what _____ wear today.

출제율 85%

14 다음 주어진 말을 이용하여 우리말에 맞게 문장을 완성하시오.

> 나는 너만큼 예쁘지 않다. (pretty)

➡ _____

출제율 90%

15 다음 두 문장의 뜻이 같도록 빈칸에 알맞은 말을 쓰시오.

> I want to learn cooking.
> = I want to learn _____ _____
>   _____.

출제율 85%

16 다음 중 어법상 알맞지 <u>않은</u> 것은?

① Kate doesn't speak Korean as well as Mike do.
② The movie is not as interesting as you think.
③ I don't work so hard as you do.
④ Let me have your answer as soon as possible.
⑤ I don't have as much money as my brother does.

출제율 95%

17 다음 중 밑줄 친 부분이 <u>어색한</u> 것은?

① I'm thinking about <u>what to show</u> you.
② Do you know <u>how to make</u> a kite?
③ She wants to know <u>when turn off</u> the oven.
④ Rachel wants to know <u>where to buy</u> a bike.
⑤ Please tell me <u>which to choose</u>.

출제율 85%

18 다음 우리말과 일치하도록 주어진 단어를 바르게 배열하시오.

> 그는 예전만큼 많이 그녀를 미워하지 않는다.
> He doesn't hate her (as / used / he / as / much / to).

➡ _____

[19~23] 다음 글을 읽고, 물음에 답하시오.

> Announcer: When did you learn such an important skill?
> Sejin: We had Safety Training Day at school last week. I learned ⓐ _____ to do CPR and ⓑ연습할 기회가 있었어요.
> Announcer: Can you show the audience ⓒ _____ to perform CPR?
> Sejin: Yes. ⓓ(your / keep / straight / arms). Your arms and the other person's chest must be at a 90 degree angle. Push down in the center of the chest hard and fast ⓔ _____ an ambulance comes.

출제율 95%

19 위 글의 빈칸 ⓐ와 ⓒ에 공통으로 알맞은 것은?

① what   ② how
③ where   ④ why
⑤ when

출제율 90%

20 위 글의 밑줄 친 ⓑ의 우리말에 맞도록 주어진 단어에 한 단어를 추가하여 바르게 배열하시오.

> (practice / a / had / chance)

➡ _____

출제율 90%

21 위 글의 괄호 ⓓ 안의 단어들을 바르게 배열한 것은?

① Straight your arms keep
② Keep straight your arms
③ Your arms straight keep
④ Your arms keep straight
⑤ Keep your arms straight

22 위 글의 빈칸 ⓔ에 알맞은 것은?

① as   ② because

③ since   ④ until

⑤ after

23 위 글을 읽고, 다음 질문에 영어로 답하시오.

> Q: What did Sejin learn on Safety Training Day?
>
> A: _____

[24~28] 다음 글을 읽고, 물음에 답하시오.

Announcer: Are there any other things ⓐto remember?

Sejin: Yes. You need to remember the four minutes of "Golden Time." ⓑIt means that you should start CPR within four minutes _____ⓒ_____ someone's heart stops. ⓓBegin CPR later than that will greatly lower the chances of save someone's life.

Announcer: _____ⓔ_____ is as important as doing CPR. Thank you for joining us.

Sejin: My pleasure.

24 위 글의 밑줄 친 ⓐ와 쓰임이 다른 것은?

① Give me something to drink.

② We need a house to live in.

③ I want a chair to sit on.

④ I sat down to take a break.

⑤ He has no friends to help him.

25 위 글의 밑줄 친 ⓑ가 가리키는 것을 우리말로 쓰시오.

➡ _____

26 위 글의 빈칸 ⓒ에 알맞은 것은?

① though   ② before

③ after   ④ until

⑤ because

27 위 글의 밑줄 친 ⓓ에서 어법상 틀린 부분을 두 군데 찾아 바르게 고쳐 쓰시오.

(1) _____ ➡ _____

(2) _____ ➡ _____

28 위 글의 빈칸 ⓔ에 다음 영영풀이에 해당하는 단어를 쓰시오.

> the time when something happens or is done especially when it is thought of as having a good or bad effect on the result

➡ _____

서술형 실전문제

01 다음 두 문장이 같은 뜻이 되도록 빈칸에 알맞은 말을 쓰시오.

> Make sure to wash your hands.
> = _____ to wash your hands.

➡ _____

02 다음 대화의 밑줄 친 부분과 바꿔 쓸 수 있는 말을 3개 쓰시오.

> A: Is it okay to eat chocolate?
> B: Sure, but you'd better not eat too much.

➡ _____

03 다음 괄호 안의 단어를 바르게 배열하여 대화를 완성하시오.

> A: I'm going to ride a bike.
> B: (gear / wear / don't / safety / to / forget)

➡ _____

04 자연스러운 대화가 되도록 (A)~(E)의 순서를 바르게 배열하시오.

> (A) The food label?
> (B) Okay, I will check it.
> (C) Mom, can I buy some apple juice?
> (D) Yes. Too much sugar is not good for you.
> (E) Sure, Chris. Don't forget to check the food label.

➡ _____

05 다음 〈조건〉에 맞게 괄호 안의 단어를 이용하여 우리말을 영어로 옮기시오.

> ┤ 조건 ├
> 1. 주어진 단어를 모두 이용할 것.
> 2. 필요시 어형 변화를 할 것.
> 3. as ~ as ...를 쓸 것.
> 4. 대·소문자 및 구두점에 유의할 것.

(1) Meg는 너만큼 노래를 잘 부른다. (sing, well)

➡ _____

(2) 이 거리는 저 거리와 아주 똑같은 넓이이다.
(street, just, wide, that one)

➡ _____

(3) 서울 타워는 이 탑보다 약 세 배 높다.
(Seoul Tower, about, time, as)

➡ _____

(4) 나는 나의 언니만큼 요리를 잘하지 못한다.
(can, cook, well, my sister)

➡ _____

06 다음 〈조건〉에 맞게 괄호 안의 단어를 이용하여 우리말을 영어로 옮기시오.

> ┤ 조건 ├
> 1. 주어진 단어를 모두 이용할 것.
> 2. 필요시 어형을 바꾸거나 단어를 추가할 것.
> 3. '의문사+to부정사'를 이용할 것.
> 4. 대·소문자 및 구두점에 유의할 것.

(1) 나는 어느 것을 골라야 할지 결정할 수 없었다.
(make / which / mind / choose / can / my / up)

➡ _____

(2) 그는 언제 공부하고 언제 놀아야 할지 알지 못한다. (when / play / and / he / know / does / study)

➡ _____
➡ _____

Save Your Life from a Fire

Do you know what to do ⓐ불이 나면? You should shout, "Fire!" You need to cover your face and body ___ⓑ___ a wet towel. You have to stay as low as possible and get out. Also, you need to call 119 as soon as you can. Don't forget to use the stairs, not the elevator.

07 위 글의 밑줄 친 ⓐ의 우리말에 맞도록 주어진 단어들을 바르게 배열하시오.

> (a / when / is / fire / there)

➡ _____

08 위 글의 빈칸 ⓑ에 알맞은 말을 쓰시오.

➡ _____

09 위 글에서 다음 영영풀이에 해당하는 단어를 찾아 쓰시오.

> not dry

➡ _____

10 Should we use the elevator instead of the stairs in case of fire? Answer in English.

➡ _____

Announcer: When did you learn such an important skill?
Sejin: We had Safety Training Day at school last week. I learned how ___ⓐ___ do CPR and had a chance ___ⓑ___ practice.
Announcer: Can you show the audience how to perform CPR?
Sejin: Yes. ⓒ당신의 팔을 똑바로 펴세요. Your arms and the other person's chest must be at a 90 degree angle. Push down in the center of the chest hard and fast until an ambulance comes.

11 위 글의 빈칸 ⓐ와 ⓑ에 공통으로 알맞은 것을 쓰시오.

➡ _____

12 위 글의 밑줄 친 ⓒ의 우리말에 맞도록 주어진 단어를 바르게 배열하시오.

> (your / keep / straight / arms)

➡ _____

13 Where on the body do we push down when we perform CPR? Answer in English.

➡ _____

창의사고력 서술형 문제

01 다음 표를 참고하여 허락을 구하는 표현과 당부하는 표현을 넣어 대화를 완성하시오.

May I ~?	Don't forget to ~
• use this computer • borrow this book • ride my bike • use my cell phone here • eat here	• return it • turn it off • talk quietly • ride slowly • pick up any trash

A: Excuse me. May I _____?
B: Yes, you may. But don't forget to _____.
A: All right.

02 다음 〈보기〉와 같이 동등비교 구문(as ~ as / not as ~ as)을 이용하여 자신의 입장에서 문장을 만드시오. (4 문장)

> ─ 보기 ─
>
> I am as tall as Minho.

(1) _____
(2) _____
(3) _____
(4) _____

03 「의문사 + to부정사」 구문을 활용하여 〈보기〉와 같이 자신의 입장에서 문장을 만드시오.

> ─ 보기 ─
>
> I know how to swim.

(1) _____
(2) _____
(3) _____
(4) _____

단원별 모의고사

01 다음 중 짝지어진 단어의 관계가 <u>다른</u> 것은?

① wet : dry
② late : early
③ hard : soft
④ brave : fearless
⑤ dangerous : safe

02 다음 빈칸에 알맞은 말이 바르게 짝지어진 것은?

- She held on _____ his arm for support.
- I bumped _____ a big boy and fell on the ice.

① at – over
② about – to
③ with – in
④ to – into
⑤ of – over

03 다음 영영풀이에 해당하는 단어를 쓰시오.

a person whose job is to take care of animals, especially in a zoo

➡ _____

04 다음 빈칸에 들어갈 말로 적절하지 <u>않은</u> 것은?

- You should _____ a swimming cap.
- You'd better not _____ the animals.
- You should _____ apples and eat them.
- You'd better not play with a ball when you _____ the street.

① pick
② touch
③ cross
④ wear
⑤ shake

[05~06] 다음 우리말에 맞도록 빈칸에 알맞은 말을 쓰시오.

05

나는 버스 정류장에서 너를 기다릴게.
➡ I'll _____ _____ you at the bus stop.

06

가능한 한 빨리 오세요.
➡ Please come _____ soon _____ _____ .

07 다음 대화의 빈칸에 알맞은 것은?

A: Don't forget to take your cellphone.
B: _____

① Don't forget me.
② OK, I won't.
③ I have my cellphone.
④ Thank you for your help.
⑤ I don't remember anything.

08 다음 대화의 밑줄 친 부분과 바꿔 쓸 수 있는 것은?

A: <u>You'd better not to</u> pick flowers here.
B: Oh, I'm sorry. I didn't know that.

① You should
② You don't want to
③ You would like to
④ You're not permitted to
⑤ You might want to

09 다음 대화의 빈칸에 들어갈 말로 알맞은 것은?

> A: What's the weather like there in winter?
> B: It's rainy. _____ take your umbrella.

① Forget to
② Don't forget
③ Don't forget to
④ I would like to
⑤ Don't remember to

[10~11] 다음 대화를 읽고, 물음에 답하시오.

> A: I'm going to make fried eggs.
> B: ⓐDon't forget to turn on the fan.
> A: ⓑOkay, I see.

10 위 대화의 밑줄 친 ⓐ와 바꿔 쓸 수 있는 것은?

① You don't need to turn on the fan.
② Remember to turn on the fan.
③ You can turn on the fan.
④ Make sure to turn on the fan.
⑤ Don't learn to turn on the fan.

11 위 대화의 밑줄 친 ⓑ와 바꿔 쓸 수 있는 <u>모두</u> 고르면?

① No, I won't.
② Sorry, I can't.
③ Thank you for reminding me.
④ You're welcome.
⑤ I'm happy to meet you.

12 다음 대화의 빈칸에 들어갈 말로 알맞은 것은?

> A: You must not _____.
> B: Oh, I'm sorry. I won't do that again.

① walk to school
② recycle plastics
③ reuse gift boxes
④ leave computers on
⑤ take a short shower

13 다음 빈칸에 알맞은 말이 바르게 짝지어진 것은?

> • Can you tell us _____ to play this game?
> • Do you know _____ to get to the ABC shopping mall?

① where – how
② what – where
③ how – what
④ what – how
⑤ when – where

14 다음 중 어법상 <u>틀린</u> 것은?

① Bungee jumping is as exciting as skydiving.
② This apple is as red as a rose.
③ Kevin is twice as old as Brian.
④ Jane is as heavier as Tom.
⑤ My sister can run as fast as my brother.

15 다음 두 문장이 같도록 빈칸에 알맞은 말을 쓰시오. (3 단어)

> He didn't know what he should say.
> = He didn't know _____.

16 다음 중 어법상 어색한 것은?

① You're as brave as I am.

② I'm not as pretty as the actress.

③ She is twice as popular as you.

④ It's not so expensive as your computer.

⑤ Get out of the building so quickly as possible.

17 다음 문장의 잘못된 부분을 고칠 때 빈칸에 알맞은 말을 쓰시오.

> The question is why to go there.
>
> ➡ The question is why we _____
>
> _____ _____.

18 다음 문장에서 어법상 틀린 부분을 찾아 바르게 고쳐 쓰시오.

> I study as harder as you do.

_____ ➡ _____

19 다음 중 어법상 어색한 것은?

① Let's decide where to go.

② I can't decide what to wear.

③ Please tell me which bus to take.

④ Can you tell me what to read a book?

⑤ Can you show me how to use the computer?

20 다음 두 문장을 한 문장으로 만들 때 빈칸에 알맞은 말을 쓰시오.

> He runs fast. I can run fast, too.
>
> ➡ He runs fast, but I can run _____
>
> _____ _____ he does.

[21~24] 다음 글을 읽고, 물음에 답하시오.

Announcer: Yesterday, a teenager saved the life of an old man. The brave student is in the studio with us today. Please introduce yourself.

Sejin: My name is Kim Sejin. I'm ___ⓐ___ the second grade at Hanguk Middle School.

Announcer: Could you tell us your experience?

Sejin: Sure. I was waiting for the bus with my friend, Jinho. A man suddenly fell in front of us. Nobody knew ⓑ무엇을 해야 할지. I was as ___ⓒ___ as the others at first. Then, I ran to him and tapped him ___ⓓ___ the shoulder. He wasn't moving or breathing. I said to Jinho, "Call 119," and started CPR.

21 위 글의 빈칸 ⓐ와 ⓓ에 알맞은 말이 바르게 짝지어진 것은?

① at – over   ② on – to

③ to – by   ④ of – from

⑤ in – on

22 위 글의 밑줄 친 ⓑ의 우리말에 맞도록 세 단어로 쓰시오.

➡ _____

23 위 글의 빈칸 ⓒ에 다음 영영풀이에 해당하는 단어를 주어진 철자로 시작하여 쓰시오.

> frightened of something or afraid that something bad night happen

➡ s_____

24 위 글의 내용과 일치하지 <u>않는</u> 것은?

① 세진이는 어제 노인의 생명을 구했다.

② 세진이는 지금 방송국의 스튜디오에 있다.

③ 세진이는 노인을 구한 경험을 이야기하고 있다.

④ 갑자기 노인이 세진이 앞에서 쓰러졌다.

⑤ 세진이는 노인이 움직이지 않고 있다는 것을 몰랐다.

[25~27] 다음 글을 읽고, 물음에 답하시오.

Announcer: When did you learn (A)[so /such] an important skill?

Sejin: We had Safety Training Day at school last week. I learned how to do CPR and had a chance to practice.

Announcer: Can you show the audience how to perform CPR?

Sejin: Yes. Keep your arms (B)[straight straightly]. Your arms and the other person's chest must be at a 90 degree angle. Push down in the center of the chest hard and fast until an ambulance comes.

Announcer: Are there any other things (C) [remembering / to remember]?

Sejin: Yes. You need to remember the four minutes of "Golden Time." ⓐIt means that you should start CPR within four minutes after someone's heart stops. To begin CPR later than that will greatly lower the chances of saving someone's life.

25 위 글의 괄호 (A)~(C)에서 알맞은 것이 바르게 짝지어진 것은?

① so – straight – remembering

② so – straightly – remembering

③ such – straight – to remember

④ such – straight – remembering

⑤ such – straightly – to remember

26 위 글의 밑줄 친 ⓐ가 가리키는 것을 찾아 영어로 쓰시오.

➡ _____

27 위 글의 내용과 일치하지 <u>않는</u> 것은?

① Sejin learned how to do CPR on Safety Training Day.

② Sejin had a chance to practice CPR on Safety Training Day.

③ Sejin is showing how to perform CPR to the audience.

④ We should push down in the center of the chest when we perform CPR.

⑤ Beginning CPR later than the four minutes increases the chances of saving someone's life.

[28~29] 다음 글을 읽고, 물음에 답하시오.

Today we had Safety Training Day at school. Teachers taught us what to do when an earthquake hits. We learned how to protect our heads and bodies. We also learned ___ⓐ___ to go when the shaking stops.

28 위 글의 빈칸 ⓐ에 알맞은 의문사를 쓰시오.

➡ _____

29 What did the teachers teach us on the Safety Training? Answer in English.

➡ _____

_____

Lesson

3

Living a Healthy Life

 의사소통 기능

- 능력 여부 묻기
  Do you know how to ride a longboard?

- 좋아하는 것 표현하기
  I enjoy riding my longboard because it reduces my stress.

 언어 형식

- 사역동사
  It will **make** your eyes **feel** more comfortable.

- 조건을 나타내는 접속사 if
  If you massage yourself and stretch every day, you will feel healthier.

Words & Expressions

Key Words

- **activity** [æktívəti] 몡 활동
- **advice** [ædváis] 몡 조언, 충고(= tip)
- **already** [ɔːlrédi] 뷔 벌써, 이미
- **back** [bæk] 몡 뒤쪽, 뒷부분
- **backward** [bǽkwərd] 뷔 뒤로(↔ forward)
- **behind** [biháind] 젼 ~ 뒤에
- **bend** [bend] 동 구부리다
- **both** [bouθ] 때 둘 다
- **bowl** [boul] 몡 그릇
- **comfortable** [kʌ́mfərtəbl] 혱 편안한(↔ uncomfortable)
- **count** [kaunt] 동 세다
- **difficult** [dífikʌlt] 혱 어려운(↔ easy)
- **download** [dáunlòud] 동 다운로드하다
- **exercise** [éksərsàiz] 동 운동하다
- **face** [feis] 동 ~을 마주보다[향하다] 몡 얼굴
- **fall** [fɔːl] 동 넘어지다
- **fishing** [fíʃiŋ] 몡 낚시
- **fresh** [freʃ] 혱 신선한
- **habit** [hǽbit] 몡 습관
- **healthy** [hélθi] 혱 건강한, 건강에 좋은
- **hold** [hould] 동 유지하다
- **however** [hauévər] 뷔 그러나
- **life** [laif] 몡 삶
- **light** [lait] 몡 빛
- **like** [laik] 젼 ~와 같은, ~처럼
- **lower** [lóuər] 동 ~을 낮추다, ~을 낮게 하다

- **massage** [məsáːʒ] 몡 마사지 동 마사지를 하다
- **move** [muːv] 동 움직이다
- **nature** [néitʃər] 몡 자연
- **neck** [nek] 몡 목
- **place** [pleis] 동 놓다, 두다
- **position** [pəzíʃən] 몡 자세
- **pour** [pɔːr] 동 붓다
- **pull** [pul] 동 당기다, 끌다
- **push** [puʃ] 동 밀다
- **put** [put] 동 놓다, 두다
- **reduce** [ridjúːs] 동 줄이다(↔ increase)
- **relax** [rilǽks] 동 (근육 등의) 긴장이 풀리다, 긴장을 풀다
- **second** [sékənd] 몡 (시간 단위인) 초
- **shoulder** [ʃóuldər] 몡 어깨
- **show** [ʃou] 동 보여[가르쳐] 주다
- **simple** [símpl] 혱 간단한, 단순한(↔ complicated)
- **softly** [sɔ́ːftli] 뷔 부드럽게
- **step** [step] 몡 걸음
- **stress** [stres] 동 스트레스를 받다[주다]
- **stretch** [stretʃ] 동 스트레칭하다
- **switch** [switʃ] 동 바꾸다(= change)
- **understand** [ʌndərstǽnd] 동 이해하다, 알다
- **usually** [júːʒuəli] 뷔 보통, 대개
- **waist** [weist] 몡 허리
- **warm** [wɔːrm] 혱 따뜻한(↔ cool)
- **way** [wei] 몡 길

Key Expressions

- **a little bit** 조금
- **at the same speed** 같은 속도로
- **be good for** ~에 좋다
- **be worried about** ~에 대해 걱정하다
- **block out** (빛을) 가리다[차단하다]
- **each other** 서로
- **from top to bottom** 위에서 아래까지
- **focus on** ~에 집중하다
- **for a few seconds** 몇 초 동안
- **get over** 회복[극복]하다

- **have a cold** 감기에 걸리다
- **loosen up** 몸을 풀어 주다
- **more than** ~ 이상
- **prepare for** ~을 준비하다
- **straighten up** 똑바로 하다
- **take a walk** 산책하다
- **team up with** ~와 협력하다, ~와 한 팀이 되다
- **three times a week** 일주일에 세 번
- **warm up** 준비 운동을 하다
- **what kind of** 어떤 종류의

Word Power

※ 동사에 접미사 -able를 붙여 형용사가 되는 단어

- □ **comfort** → **comfortable** (편안한)
- □ **change** → **changeable** (바뀔 수 있는)
- □ **use** → **usable** (사용 가능한)

- □ **move** → **movable** (움직이는)
- □ **respect** → **respectable** (존경할 만한)
- □ **desire** → **desirable** (바람직한)

※ 접두사 un-은 형용사 · 부사 · 명사 앞에 붙어 부정이나 반대의 의미를 나타낸다.

- □ **comfortable** (편안한) → **uncomfortable** (불편한)
- □ **easy** (편한) → **uneasy** (불편한)
- □ **fair** (공평한) → **unfair** (불공평한)

- □ **friendly** (친절한) → **unfriendly** (불친절한)
- □ **happy** (행복한) → **unhappy** (행복하지 않은)
- □ **known** (알려진) → **unknown** (알려지지 않은)

English Dictionary

□ **advice** 조언
→ an opinion or suggestion about what someone should do
누군가에게 어떻게 하라고 알려 주는 말이나 제안

□ **bend** 구부리다
→ to move your body so that it is not straight
몸을 움직여 구부리다

□ **comfortable** 편안한
→ making you feel physically relaxed
당신을 신체적으로 편안함을 느끼게 하는

□ **count** 세다
→ to say numbers in order
숫자를 순서대로 말하다

□ **habit** 습관
→ something that a person does often in a regular and repeated way
사람이 규칙적으로 또는 반복적으로 자주 하는 행동

□ **massage** 마사지
→ the action of rubbing and pressing a person's body with the hands to reduce pain in the muscles and joints
근육과 관절의 통증을 줄이기 위해 손으로 사람의 몸을 문지르고 누르는 행동

□ **neck** 목
→ the part of the body between the head and the shoulders
머리와 어깨 사이의 신체 부위

□ **position** 자세
→ the way someone stands, sits, or lies down
어떤 사람이 서거나 앉거나 눕는 방식

□ **pull** 당기다
→ to hold something firmly and use force in order to move it or try to move it toward yourself
뭔가를 단단히 잡고 힘을 사용하여 움직이거나 자신을 향해 움직이려고 하다

□ **reduce** 줄이다
→ to make something smaller in size, amount, number, etc.
어떤 것의 크기, 양, 수 등이 작아지게 하다

□ **relax** (근육 등의) 긴장을 풀다
→ to cause something to become less tense, tight, or stiff
어떤 것이 긴장, 팽팽함 또는 경직성이 줄어들게 하다

□ **simple** 간단한
→ not hard to understand or do
이해하거나 하기가 어렵지 않은

□ **stretch** 스트레칭하다
→ to put your arms, legs, etc., in positions that make the muscles long and tight
근육이 길고 팽팽해지게 하는 자세로 팔, 다리 등을 뻗다

□ **switch** 바꾸다
→ to change or replace something with another thing
어떤 것을 다른 것으로 바꾸다

□ **warm up** 준비 운동을 하다
→ to do gentle physical exercises to prepare your body for a sport or other activity
운동이나 다른 활동을 위해 당신의 몸을 준비하기 위해 가벼운 신체 운동을 하다

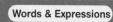

 01 다음 중 〈보기〉와 같이 변화하는 단어가 <u>아닌</u> 것은?

┌─ 보기 ─┐

move – movable

① use ② change
③ respect ④ impress
⑤ comfort

중요

02 다음 빈칸에 알맞은 말이 바르게 짝지어진 것은?

• Fruits are good _____ your health.
• You can focus _____ your studies better.

① at – in ② for – on
③ on – at ④ from – in
⑤ about – on

서답형

03 다음 짝지어진 단어의 관계가 같도록 빈칸에 알맞은 말을 쓰시오.

strong : weak = cool : _____

04 다음 영영풀이에 해당하는 단어로 알맞은 것은?

making you feel physically relaxed

① simple ② comfortable
③ pleasure ④ serious
⑤ popular

서답형

05 다음 우리말에 맞게 빈칸에 알맞은 말을 쓰시오.

너희 둘 다 어린애들 같구나.
➡ _____ _____ you are acting like children.

서답형

06 다음 영영풀이에 해당하는 단어를 쓰시오.

to do gentle physical exercises to prepare your body for a sport or other activity

➡ _____

07 다음 문장의 빈칸에 알맞은 것은?

I hope you will get _____ your cold soon.

① from ② over
③ off ④ up
⑤ through

서답형

08 다음 빈칸에 공통으로 알맞은 말을 쓰시오.

• He runs 100 meters in 13 _____ s.
• He is a _____ year in middle school.

01 다음 짝지어진 두 단어의 관계가 같도록 빈칸에 알맞은 말을 쓰시오.

(1) before : after = backward : _____
(2) wrong : right = reduce : _____
(3) delicious : tasty = tip : _____
(4) appear : disappear = comfortable : _____

02 다음 우리말에 맞도록 빈칸에 알맞은 말을 쓰시오.

(1) 그들은 서로 쳐다보고 웃었다.
➡ They looked at _____ _____ and laughed.
(2) 나는 일주일에 세 번 이상 운동을 한다.
➡ I exercise _____ _____ three times a week.
(3) 그 문제는 조금 어렵다.
➡ The problem is _____ _____ _____ difficult.

03 다음 빈칸에 들어갈 알맞은 말을 〈보기〉에서 골라 쓰시오.

┌─ 보기 ─┐
download   count   reduce   ride
└────────┘

(1) I _____ my longboard when I'm stressed.
(2) The beautiful pictures _____ my stress.
(3) Tom, _____ to ten and open your eyes.
(4) Users can _____ the full image.

04 다음 괄호 안의 단어를 문맥에 맞게 고쳐 쓰시오.

(1) I want to eat something _____. (health)
(2) My bike is very old, but it is still _____. (move)
(3) We should wear _____ shoes for walking for a long time. (comfort)

05 다음 빈칸에 알맞은 말을 〈보기〉에서 골라 쓰시오.

┌─ 보기 ─┐
am worried about / prepare for / get over
└────────┘

(1) Do you know how to _____ a cold?
(2) I will _____ the English speech contest.
(3) I _____ the math quiz on Monday.

06 다음 영영풀이에 해당하는 단어를 주어진 철자로 시작하여 쓰시오.

(1) s_____ : to put your arms, legs, etc., in positions that make the muscles long and tight
(2) h_____ : something that a person does often in a regular and repeated way
(3) s_____ : to change or replace something with another thing
(4) r_____ : to cause something to become less tense, tight, or stiff

Conversation

① 능력 여부 묻기

> **A** Do you know how to play basketball? 너는 농구를 어떻게 하는지 아니?
> **B** Yes, I do. / No, I don't. 응, 알아. / 아니, 몰라.

- Do you know how to+동사원형 ~?은 '너는 ~를 어떻게 하는지 아니?'라는 뜻으로, 어떤 일을 할 수 있는지 물을 때 사용하는 표현이다.
  - A: Do you know how to do rock climbing? 너는 암벽 등반을 어떻게 하는지 아니?
    B: Yes, I do. 응, 알아.

상대방의 능력 여부를 묻는 표현

- Do you know how to + 동사원형 ~? 너는 ~하는 방법을 아니?
- Can you + 동사원형 ~? 너는 ~할 수 있니?
- Are you able to + 동사원형 ~? 너는 ~할 수 있니?
- Are you good at ~? 너는 ~를 잘하니?

능력을 나타내는 표현

- I know how to + 동사원형 ~. 나는 ~하는 방법을 알아.
- I can + 동사원형 ~. 나는 ~할 수 있어.
- I'm able to + 동사원형 ~. 나는 ~할 수 있어.
- I'm good at ~. 나는 ~을 잘해.

능력 여부에 답하기

〈긍정〉 Yes, I do. / Yes, I can. / I'm good at ~. / Yes, I know how to + 동사원형 ~. / Sure. / Of course.

〈부정〉 No, I don't. / No, I can't. / I'm not good at ~. / No, I don't know how to + 동사원형 ~. / No, I'm poor at ~.

핵심 Check

1. 다음 우리말과 일치하도록 빈칸에 알맞은 말을 쓰시오.

  (1) **A:** Do you know _____ _____ fix a computer? (컴퓨터를 어떻게 고치는지 아니?)

  　　B: I'm _____ _____ _____ fixing machines. (난 기계 고치는 일을 잘 못해.)

  (2) **A:** Do you know how to make potato salad? (너는 감자 샐러드를 어떻게 만드는지 아니?)

  　　B: No, I don't know _____ _____ _____ it. (아니, 나는 그것을 만드는 방법을 몰라.)

2 좋아하는 것 표현하기

A Kate, what do you enjoy doing to be healthy?

Kate, 너는 건강해지기 위해 무엇을 하는 걸 즐기니?

B I enjoy riding a bike. 나는 자전거 타는 것을 즐겨.

■ I enjoy ~(very much).는 '나는 ~하는 것을 (매우) 즐겨.'라는 뜻으로, 자신이 좋아하는 것을 말하는 표현이다.

· A: Amy, what do you enjoy doing to be healthy? Amy, 너는 건강해지기 위해 무엇을 하는 걸 즐기니?

B: I enjoy growing vegetables. 나는 채소 기르는 것을 즐겨.

좋아하는 것 말하는 표현

· I enjoy -ing ~. 나는 ~하는 것을 즐겨.

· I love ~. 나는 ~하는 것을 정말 좋아해.

· I like ~. 나는 ~하는 것을 좋아해.

· I feel great when I ~. 나는 ~할 때 기분이 좋아.

관심을 나타내는 표현

· Sounds cool. / That's great. / That's interesting! / How interesting!

· A: I enjoy watching birds. 나는 새를 관찰하는 것을 즐겨.

B: How interesting! 정말 흥미롭구나!

핵심 Check

2. 다음 우리말과 일치하도록 빈칸에 알맞은 말을 쓰시오.

(1) **A:** _____ do you _____ _____ do after school? (넌 방과 후에 무엇 하기를 좋아하니?)

B: I enjoy _____ a bike. (난 자전거 타는 것을 즐겨.)

(2) **A:** David, _____ do you _____ _____ to be healthy?

(David, 너는 건강해지기 위해 무엇을 하는 것을 즐기니?)

B: I enjoy _____. (나는 낚시를 즐겨.)

(3) **A:** What _____ _____ _____ in your free time? (너는 여가 시간에 무엇을 하니?)

B: I _____ _____ cartoons. I post them on the Internet.

(나는 만화 그리는 것을 즐겨. 나는 그것들을 인터넷에 게시하지.)

A: _____ interesting! (정말 흥미롭구나!)

A. Listen & Speak 1 - A - 1

B: ❶I want to eat something healthy. Do you have any advice?

G: I often eat fresh salad. ❷It makes me feel good.

B: Really? ❸Do you know how to make it?

G: Yes, it's quite simple. ❹First, cut many vegetables into small pieces. ❺Next, put them into a bowl. Then, pour some lemon juice on them. Finally, mix everything together.

B: That's it? I should try it.

B: 나는 건강에 좋은 것을 먹고 싶어. 말해 줄 조언이 있니?

G: 나는 신선한 샐러드를 자주 먹어. 그것은 나를 기분 좋게 만들어.

B: 정말? 그것을 어떻게 만드는지 아니?

G: 응. 아주 간단해. 먼저, 많은 채소들을 작은 조각으로 잘라. 다음으로 그것들을 그릇에 담아. 그런 다음, 레몬주스를 조금 부어. 마지막으로 모든 것을 함께 섞어.

B: 그게 다야? 한번 해 봐야겠다.

❶ -thing으로 끝나는 부정대명사는 형용사가 뒤에서 수식한다.
❷ It=fresh salad / make me feel good: 나를 기분 좋게 만들다
❸ Do you know how to+동사원형 ~?: ~하는 방법을 아니?(능력 여부 묻기)
❹ cut A into B: A를 B로 자르다
❺ put A into B: A를 B에 넣다 / them: small pieces

Check(√) True or False

(1) The girl knows how to make fresh salad.　　　　　　　　T☐ F☐

(2) The first step in making fresh salad is to put vegetables into a bowl.　T☐ F☐

Conversation B

Karl: Hana, ❶what's the matter?

Hana: Well, ❷I'm stressed about the test next week.

Karl: I understand. I ride my longboard when I'm stressed. ❸Do you know how to ride a longboard?

Hana: No, I don't.

Karl: Let's go out! I can teach you. Put one foot on the board and push hard with the other.

Hana: Like this? Wow! This is fun. ❹I feel better already.

Karl: See? ❺I enjoy riding my longboard because it reduces my stress.

Hana: That's great!

Karl: 하나야, 무슨 일 있니?

하나: 음, 다음 주에 있을 시험 때문에 스트레스를 받아.

Karl: 난 이해돼. 나는 스트레스를 받을 때 롱보드를 타. 넌 롱보드를 어떻게 타는지 아니?

하나: 아니, 몰라.

Karl: 나가자! 내가 가르쳐 줄 수 있어. 한 발을 보드 위에 올려놓고 다른 한 발로 세게 밀어.

하나: 이렇게? 와! 이거 재밌다. 벌써 기분이 좋아졌어.

Karl: 봤지? 나는 롱보드를 타는 것이 나의 스트레스를 줄여 주기 때문에 즐겨.

하나: 정말 멋진데!

❶ What's the matter?: 슬픔, 불만족, 실망의 원인에 대해 묻기
❷ be stressed about: ~에 대해 스트레스를 받다
❸ Do you know how to + 동사원형 ~? = Can you + 동사원형 ~?
❹ feel better: 기분이 더 좋아지다
❺ I enjoy + (동)명사 ~: 나는 ~하는 것을 즐긴다.(좋아하는 것 말하기) / it=riding my longboard / reduce: 줄이다

Check(√) True or False

(3) Hana doesn't know how to ride a longboard.　　　　　　T☐ F☐

(4) Karl listens to music to reduce his stress.　　　　　　　T☐ F☐

Listen & Speak 1 - A - 2

B: ❶People say that we should walk more than 10,000 steps every day to be healthy. I can't count the number of my steps easily.

G: You can use this smartphone app. ❷Do you know how to use it?

B: No. ❸Can you show me?

G: Sure. First, download the app. Then, walk with your smartphone. Later, you can check the number of steps you took.

B: Thank you. ❹I will start using it today.

❶ more than: ~ 이상 / to be: to부정사의 부사적 용법 중 목적 ❷ Do you know how to + 동사원형 ~?: 너는 ~하는 방법을 아니? (능력 여부 묻기) ❸ Can you + 동사원형 ~?: ~해 줄래? ❹ it = a smartphone app

Listen & Speak 2 - A - 1

G: ❶What do you enjoy doing after school?

B: ❷I enjoy cooking healthy food.

G: ❸Sounds cool. What can you make?

B: I can make salad, Bibimbap, and vegetable juice.

❶ What do you enjoy -ing?: 너는 무엇을 ~하기를 즐기니? (좋아하는 것 묻기) / after school: 방과 후에 ❷ I enjoy -ing ~. 나는 ~하는 것을 즐긴다. (좋아하는 것 말하기) / healthy: 건강에 좋은 ❸ Sounds cool.: 관심을 나타내는 표현이다.

Listen & Speak 2 - A - 2

B: ❶What do you do on weekends?

G: I take pictures.

B: ❷What kind of pictures do you usually take?

G: ❸I enjoy taking pictures of nature, like trees and flowers. ❹The beautiful pictures reduce my stress.

❶ on weekends: 주말에 ❷ What kind of: 어떤 종류의 ❸ I enjoy -ing ~: 나는 ~하는 것을 즐긴다 / take a picture: 사진을 찍다 / like: ~같은 ❹ reduce one's stress: 스트레스를 줄이다

Listen & Speak 2 - A - 3

G: Do you have a puppy?

B: Yes. Her name is Coco. I really like her.

G: ❶What do you do with her?

B: I enjoy ❷taking a walk with her. ❸It makes me healthy.

❶ with: ~와 함께 / her = Coco ❷ take a walk: 산책하다 ❸ It = taking a walk with her / make + 목적어 + 형용사: ~을 …하게 만들다 / healthy: 건강한

Conversation A

B: Tomorrow, I have an English speaking contest. ❶I started preparing for the contest two weeks ago. ❷I enjoy speaking in English, but I am worried about the contest. I cannot sleep well.

❶ start+to부정사[동명사]: ~하기 시작하다 / prepare for: ~을 준비하다 / two weeks ago: 2주 전 ❷ enjoy+동명사: ~하는 것을 즐기다 / be worried about: ~에 대해 걱정하다

Wrap Up - ❶

B: ❶You look sick. ❷What's the matter?

G: ❸Well, I have a cold.

B: ❹Did you see a doctor?

G: Not yet. ❺Do you know how to get over a cold?

B: Well, I usually drink warm water when I have a cold. It makes me feel better.

G: Sounds good. I will try it.

❶ look+형용사: ~하게 보이다 ❷ What's the matter? = What's wrong? = What's the problem? = What happened? ❸ have a cold: 감기에 걸리다 (=catch[get/take] a cold) ❹ see a doctor: 병원에 가 보다 ❺ get over: 회복하다

Wrap Up - ❷

B: My family enjoys many activities. My dad enjoys fishing. ❶Early in the morning, he goes to the lake and comes back with some fish. ❷ My mom enjoys drawing pictures. ❸She likes to draw beautiful mountains and lakes. My brother and I enjoy playing soccer.

❶ early in the morning: 이른 아침 / come back: 돌아오다 ❷ draw a picture: 그림을 그리다 ❸ lake: 호수

● 다음 우리말과 일치하도록 빈칸에 알맞은 말을 쓰시오.

Listen & Speak 1-A-1

B: I want to eat _____ _____. Do you _____ any _____?

G: I _____ _____ fresh salad. It _____ me feel _____.

B: Really? Do you know _____ _____ make it?

G: Yes, it's quite simple. First, _____ many vegetables _____ small pieces. Next, _____ them _____ a bowl. Then, _____ some lemon juice on them. Finally, _____ everything together.

B: That's it? I _____ _____ it.

Listen & Speak 1-A-2

B: People say that we should walk _____ _____ 10,000 steps every day _____ _____ healthy. I can't _____ the number of my _____ easily.

G: You _____ _____ this smartphone app. Do you know _____ _____ _____ it?

B: No. _____ you _____ me?

G: Sure. First, _____ the app. Then, walk _____ your smartphone. Later, you can _____ the number of steps you took.

B: Thank you. I _____ start _____ it today.

Listen & Speak 2 - A - 1

G: _____ do you enjoy _____ after school?

B: I _____ _____ healthy food.

G: _____ cool. What _____ you make?

B: I _____ _____ salad, Bibimbap, and vegetable juice.

Listen & Speak 1-A-1

B: What do you do _____ _____?

G: I _____ pictures.

B: _____ _____ of pictures do you usually _____?

G: I enjoy _____ pictures _____ nature, _____ trees and flowers. The beautiful pictures _____ my stress.

해석

B: 나는 건강에 좋은 것을 먹고 싶어. 말해 줄 조언이 있니?

G: 나는 신선한 샐러드를 자주 먹어. 그것은 나를 기분 좋게 만들어.

B: 정말? 그것을 어떻게 만드는지 아니?

G: 응. 아주 간단해. 먼저, 많은 채소들을 작은 조각으로 잘라. 다음으로 그것들을 그릇에 담아. 그런 다음, 레몬 주스를 조금 부어. 마지막으로 모든 것을 함께 섞어.

B: 그게 다야? 한번 해 봐야겠다.

B: 사람들은 우리가 건강해지기 위해서 매일 10,000 걸음 이상을 걸어야 한다고 말해. 나는 내 걸음 수를 쉽게 셀 수 없어.

G: 너는 이 스마트폰 앱을 사용할 수 있어. 어떻게 사용하는지 아니?

B: 아니. 내게 보여줄 수 있니?

G: 물론. 먼저 앱을 다운로드해. 그런 다음 스마트폰을 가지고 걸어. 나중에 네가 걸은 걸음 수를 확인할 수 있어.

B: 고마워. 오늘부터 그것을 쓰기 시작해야겠어.

G: 너는 방과 후에 뭐 하는 걸 즐기니?

B: 나는 건강에 좋은 음식을 요리하는 것을 즐겨.

G: 멋지구나. 너는 무엇을 만들 수 있니?

B: 나는 샐러드, 비빔밥 그리고 야채 주스를 만들 수 있어.

B: 너는 주말에 무엇을 하니?

G: 나는 사진을 찍어.

B: 너는 보통 어떤 종류의 사진을 찍니?

G: 나는 나무와 꽃 같은 자연의 사진을 찍는 것을 좋아해. 그 아름다운 사진들은 내 스트레스를 줄여주거든.

Listen & Speak 2-A-3

G: Do you have a _____?

B: Yes. _____ name is Coco. I _____ like her.

G: What do you do _____ her?

B: I _____ _____ a walk with her. It _____ me _____.

Conversation A

B: Tomorrow, I _____ an English _____ contest. I started _____ _____ the contest two weeks _____. I enjoy _____ _____ English, but I am worried _____ the contest. I _____ _____ well.

Conversation B

Karl: Hana, what's the _____?

Hana: Well, I'm _____ _____ the test next week.

Karl: I understand. I _____ my longboard _____ I'm stressed. Do you know _____ _____ _____ a longboard?

Hana: No, I don't.

Karl: Let's _____ _____! I _____ teach you. _____ one foot _____ the board and _____ hard _____ the other.

Hana: _____ this? Wow! This is fun. I _____ _____ already.

Karl: See? I enjoy _____ my longboard _____ it reduces my stress.

Hana: That's great!

Wrap Up 1

B: You look _____. _____ the matter?

G: Well, I have a _____.

B: Did you _____ a doctor?

G: Not _____. Do you know how to _____ _____ a cold?

B: Well, I usually drink _____ water _____ I have a cold. It _____ me _____ better.

G: Sounds good. I _____ _____ it.

Wrap Up 2

B: My family _____ many activities. My dad enjoys _____. _____ in the morning, he goes to the lake and _____ _____ with some fish. My mom _____ _____ pictures. She likes _____ _____ beautiful mountains and lakes. My brother and I _____ _____ soccer.

해석

G: 너는 강아지를 기르고 있니?

B: 응. 그녀의 이름은 코코야. 난 코코를 아주 좋아해.

G: 너는 코코와 함께 무엇을 하니?

B: 난 코코와 산책하는 걸 즐겨. 그것은 나를 건강하게 만들어.

B: 내일 영어 말하기 대회가 있어. 나는 2주 전에 대회를 준비하기 시작했어. 나는 영어로 말하는 것을 즐기지만, 난 그 대회가 걱정돼. 나는 잠을 잘 못 자.

Karl: 하나야, 무슨 일 있니?

하나: 음, 다음 주에 있을 시험 때문에 스트레스를 받아.

Karl: 난 이해돼. 나는 스트레스를 받을 때 롱보드를 타. 넌 롱보드를 어떻게 타는지 아니?

하나: 아니, 몰라.

Karl: 나가자! 내가 가르쳐 줄 수 있어. 한 발을 보드 위에 올려놓고 다른 한 발로 세게 밀어.

하나: 이렇게? 와! 이거 재밌다. 벌써 기분이 좋아졌어.

Karl: 봤지? 나는 롱보드를 타는 것이 나의 스트레스를 줄여주기 때문에 즐겨.

하나: 정말 멋진데!

B: 너 아파 보여. 무슨 일 있니?

G: 음, 감기에 걸렸어.

B: 병원에 가봤니?

G: 아직. 넌 감기가 나아지는 방법을 아니?

B: 음, 나는 감기에 걸렸을 때 보통 따뜻한 물을 마셔. 그것은 내 기분을 좋아지게 해.

G: 좋아. 한번 해 볼게.

B: 우리 가족은 많은 활동을 즐겨. 우리 아빠는 낚시를 즐기셔. 이른 아침, 그는 호수에 가셔서 약간의 물고기를 가지고 돌아오셔. 우리 엄마는 그림 그리기를 즐기셔. 그녀는 아름다운 산과 호수를 그리는 것을 좋아하셔. 나의 형과 나는 축구를 즐겨.

01 다음 대화의 빈칸에 알맞은 것은?

> A: Do you know _____ healthy juice?
> B: Yes, I do.

① when to make　　② how to make
③ what to make　　④ where to make
⑤ how to do

healthy 건강한

02 다음 대화의 빈칸에 들어갈 말로 적절하지 <u>않은</u> 것은?

> A: Kate, what do you enjoy doing to be healthy?
> B: I enjoy _____.

① fishing　　　　　② jogging
③ playing catch　　④ riding a bike
⑤ playing computer games

03 다음 문장과 바꿔 쓸 수 있는 것은?

> Do you know how to fix the watering can?

① Are you fixing the watering can?
② Can you fix the watering can?
③ Can I fix the watering can?
④ May I fix the watering can?
⑤ Did you fix the watering can?

04 다음 대화의 ⓐ~ⓓ를 자연스러운 대화가 되도록 바르게 배열하시오.

take a walk 산책하다

> ⓐ What do you do with her?
> ⓑ Yes. Her name is Coco. I really like her.
> ⓒ Do you have a puppy?
> ⓓ I enjoy taking a walk with her. It makes me healthy.

➡ _____

[01~05] 다음 대화를 읽고, 물음에 답하시오.

Karl: Hana, what's the matter?

Hana: Well, I'm stressed ___ⓐ___ the test next week. (①)

Karl: I understand. I ride my longboard when I'm stressed. Do you know how ⓑride a longboard?

Hana: No, I don't. (②)

Karl: Let's go out! I can teach you. (③) Put one foot on the board and push hard ___ⓒ___ the other. (④)

Hana: Like this? Wow! This is fun. (⑤)

Karl: See? I enjoy ⓓride my longboard because ⓔit reduces my stress.

Hana: That's great!

01 위 대화의 ①~⑤ 중 다음 문장이 들어갈 알맞은 곳은?

> I feel better already.

①   ②   ③   ④   ⑤

02 위 대화의 빈칸 ⓐ와 ⓒ에 알맞은 말이 바르게 짝지어진 것은?

① for – to
② of – with
③ on – from
④ from – into
⑤ about – with

서답형

03 위 대화의 밑줄 친 ⓑ와 ⓓ를 알맞은 형태로 각각 고쳐 쓰시오.

ⓑ _____ ⓓ _____

서답형

04 위 대화의 밑줄 친 ⓔ가 가리키는 것을 영어로 쓰시오.

➡ _____

05 위 대화를 읽고, 답할 수 없는 질문은?

① Why is Hana stressed?
② What does Hana do when she's stressed?
③ Did Hana know how to ride a longboard?
④ Does Karl teach Hana how to ride a longboard?
⑤ Why does Karl enjoy riding his longboard?

[06~08] 다음 대화를 읽고, 물음에 답하시오.

B: You look sick. ⓐWhat's the matter?

G: Well, I have a cold.

B: Did you see a doctor?

G: Not yet. ⓑDo you know how to get over a cold?

B: Well, I usually drink warm water when I have a cold. ⓒIt makes me feel better.

G: Sounds good. I will try it.

06 위 대화의 밑줄 친 ⓐ와 바꿔 쓸 수 없는 것은?

① What's wrong?
② What happened?
③ How have you been?
④ What's the problem?
⑤ Is there something wrong?

07 위 대화의 밑줄 친 ⓑ의 의도로 알맞은 것은?

① 제안하기   ② 주제 정하기

③ 능력 여부 묻기   ④ 위로하기

⑤ 반문하기

서답형

08 위 대화의 밑줄 친 ⓒ가 의미하는 것을 우리말로 쓰시오.

➡ _____

[09~11] 다음 대화를 읽고, 물음에 답하시오.

> B: ⓐI want to eat healthy something. Do you have any advice?
>
> G: I often eat fresh salad. ⓑIt makes me feel good.
>
> B: Really? ⓒDo you know how to make it?
>
> G: Yes, it's quite simple. First, cut many vegetables into small pieces. Next, put them into a bowl. Then, pour some lemon juice on them. Finally, mix everything together.
>
> B: That's it? I should try it.

서답형

09 위 대화의 밑줄 친 ⓐ에서 어법상 어색한 부분을 고쳐 문장을 다시 쓰시오.

➡ _____

서답형

10 위 대화의 밑줄 친 ⓑ가 의미하는 것을 영어로 쓰시오.

➡ _____

중요

11 위 대화의 밑줄 친 ⓒ와 의미가 같은 문장은? (2개)

① Can you make it?

② Why don't you make it?

③ Are you good at making it?

④ When did you make it?

⑤ Are you interested in cooking?

[12~14] 다음 글을 읽고, 물음에 답하시오.

> B: Tomorrow, I have an English speaking contest. I started preparing ___ⓐ___ the contest two weeks ago. I enjoy speaking in English, ___ⓑ___ I am worried ___ⓒ___ the contest. I cannot sleep well.

중요

12 위 글의 빈칸 ⓐ와 ⓒ에 알맞은 말이 바르게 짝지어진 것은?

① at – of   ② for – about

③ with – for   ④ of – at

⑤ from – over

13 위 글의 빈칸 ⓑ에 알맞은 것은?

① so   ② but

③ and   ④ for

⑤ or

14 위 글의 글쓴이의 심경으로 알맞은 것은?

① bored   ② excited

③ stressed   ④ pleased

⑤ happy

[01~04] 다음 대화를 읽고, 물음에 답하시오.

B: People say that we should walk more than 10,000 steps every day to be healthy. I can't count the number of my steps easily.

G: You can use this smartphone ____ⓐ____.
ⓑDo you know how to use it?

B: No. Can you show me?

G: Sure. First, download the ____ⓒ____. Then, walk with your smartphone. Later, you can check the number of steps you took.

01 How many steps do people say we should walk every day to be healthy? Answer in English.

➡ _____

02 위 대화의 밑줄 친 ⓑ를 해석하고, 이와 바꿔 쓸 수 있는 표현을 2개 쓰시오.

(1) 해석: _____

(2) 같은 표현: _____

_____

03 위 대화의 빈칸 ⓐ와 ⓒ에 공통으로 들어갈 단어를 다음 영영풀이를 참조하여 쓰시오. (세 글자)

> a computer program designed to do a particular job, especially one that you can use on a smartphone

➡ _____

04 What is the first step in using the smartphone app? Answer in English.

➡ _____

[05~08] 다음 대화를 읽고, 물음에 답하시오.

B: What do you do on weekends?

G: I take pictures.

B: What kind of pictures do you usually take?

G: I enjoy ⓐtake pictures of nature, ⓑlike trees and flowers. The beautiful pictures ____ⓒ____ my stress.

05 위 대화의 밑줄 친 ⓐ를 알맞은 형태로 고쳐 쓰시오.

➡ _____

06 What does the girl enjoy doing? Answer in English.

➡ _____

07 위 대화의 밑줄 친 ⓑ를 두 단어로 바꿔 쓰시오.

➡ _____

08 위 대화의 빈칸 ⓒ에 다음 영영풀이에 해당하는 단어를 주어진 글자로 시작하여 쓰시오

> to make something smaller in size, amount, number, etc.

➡ r_____

Grammar

1 사역동사

- It will **make** your eyes **feel** more comfortable. 그것은 너의 눈을 더 편안하게 할 것이다.
- I will **let** you **ride** my new longboard. 나는 네가 나의 새 롱보드를 타게 해 줄게.
- The massage will **help** you **(to) feel** better. 마사지는 너의 기분이 좋아지도록 도울 것이다.

- 사역동사 make, have, let은 「사역동사+목적어+목적격 보어(동사원형)」의 형태로 '(목적어)에게 ~하게 하다'라는 의미로 목적어의 행동을 설명한다.

  ① let: ~ 하도록 허락하다 / I will **let** you **go**. 네가 가도록 허락해 줄게.

  ② have: ~ 하도록 하다 / I will **have** my brother **clean** my room. 나는 내 남동생이 내 방을 치우도록 할 것이다.

  ③ make: ~ 하게 시키다 / My mom **makes** me **do** the dishes. 엄마는 내가 설거지를 하도록 시킨다.

- help는 목적격 보어로 동사원형이나 to부정사 둘 다 사용할 수 있다.

  - I **helped** Julia **(to) cook** breakfast for the family. 나는 Julia가 가족을 위해 아침식사를 요리하는 것을 도왔다.

- get은 목적격 보어로 to부정사를 사용한다.

  - He **got** our dreams **to come** true. 그는 우리의 꿈이 실현되게 했다.

- have는 목적어와 목적격 보어가 능동 관계이면 동사원형을, 수동 관계이면 과거분사형을 쓴다.

  - I **had** him **repair** my computer. 나는 그에게 내 컴퓨터를 고치게 했다.

  - I **had** my computer **repaired**. 나는 내 컴퓨터를 수리시켰다.

핵심 Check

1. 다음 괄호 안에서 알맞은 것을 고르시오.

   (1) The heat makes the ice (melt / to melt).

   (2) Parents often don't let their children (doing / do) what they want.

   (3) The secretary had the phone (rings / ring) at lunchtime.

   (4) He got her (come / to come) to the meeting.

2 조건을 나타내는 접속사 if

- **If** you massage yourself and stretch every day, you will feel healthier.
  매일 마사지를 하고 스트레칭을 하면, 너는 더 건강하게 느껴질 것이다.

- **If** it is sunny tomorrow, we can go for a bike ride.
  내일 날씨가 맑으면, 우리는 자전거를 타러 갈 수 있다.

- He will get sick **if** he doesn't stop eating fast food.
  패스트푸드 먹는 것을 멈추지 않으면, 그는 병에 걸릴 것이다.

■ 접속사 if는 두 개의 절을 연결하는 접속사이며, '만약 ~하면'이라는 의미로 조건을 나타낸다. if가 이끄는 종속절은 주절의 앞이나 뒤에 올 수 있다.

- **If** we take a taxi, we can get there in ten minutes.
  만약 우리가 택시를 타면, 우리는 그곳에 10분 후에 도착할 수 있다.

- You can win the contest **if** you practice hard. 만약 네가 열심히 연습한다면, 너는 대회에서 우승을 할 수 있다.

■ 조건을 나타내는 접속사 if가 이끄는 절에서는 미래의 일을 나타내는 경우에도 동사는 현재시제를 쓴다.

- **If** it will be sunny tomorrow, we will play soccer. (X)

- **If** it **is** sunny tomorrow, we will play soccer. (○) 만약 내일 날씨가 맑으면, 우리는 축구를 할 것이다.

■ '만약 ~하지 않는다면'이라는 의미의 「if+주어+don't[doesn't]+동사원형 ~」은 「unless+주어+동사의 현재형 ~」으로 바꿔 쓸 수 있다.

- **If** he doesn**'t** study hard, he can't get a high score.
  = **Unless** he studies hard, he can't get a high score.
  만일 그가 열심히 공부하지 않는다면, 그는 높은 점수를 얻을 수 없다.

핵심 Check

2. 다음 괄호 안에서 알맞은 것을 고르시오.

(1) If I see her, I (give / will give) it to her.

(2) (If / Because) you arrive early, you will get a good seat.

(3) If she (takes / will take) the subway, she will be there on time.

(4) Unless you (drink / don't drink) some water, you will feel very thirsty.

01 다음 우리말과 같도록 주어진 단어들을 바르게 배열하시오.

go to a movie 영화 보러 가다

(1) 프랑스에 간다면, 나는 에펠탑을 방문할 거야. (France / I / to / if / go)

➡ _____, I will visit the Eiffel Tower.

(2) 내일 비가 오면 난 영화 보러 갈 거야. (rains, if, tomorrow, it)

➡ _____, I will go to a movie.

02 다음 문장에서 어법상 어색한 부분을 찾아 바르게 고쳐 쓰시오.

(1) The dress makes her to look slim.

_____ ➡ _____

(2) She had her son to write the teacher a letter.

_____ ➡ _____

(3) She won't let me to go there.

_____ ➡ _____

03 다음 두 문장이 같은 뜻이 되도록 빈칸에 알맞은 말을 쓰시오.

leave 떠나다, 출발하다
miss 놓치다

(1) If you don't leave now, you will miss the school bus.

= _____ _____ _____ now, you will miss the school bus.

(2) Unless it rains tomorrow, I will go camping.

= _____ _____ _____ _____ tomorrow, I will go camping.

04 다음 주어진 문장을 〈보기〉와 같이 바꾸어 쓸 때, 빈칸에 알맞은 말을 쓰시오.

┌─ 보기 ├─
I cleaned my hands.
➡ My teacher made me clean my hands.
└──

(1) I went out after dinner.

➡ My mother let _____.

(2) The children played outside.

➡ He had _____.

(3) The bear stood on the ball.

➡ Mr. Brown made _____.

01 다음 문장의 빈칸에 알맞은 것은?

> She had me _____ my work.

① to do　　　　② starting
③ finish　　　　④ done
⑤ be finished

02 다음 빈칸에 공통으로 알맞은 것은?

> • I'm not going to work tomorrow _____
> I don't feel well.
> • I'm not sure _____ he will enter the
> speech contest.

① if　　　　② so
③ that　　　　④ since
⑤ whether

03 다음 문장의 빈칸에 알맞지 <u>않은</u> 것은?

> Eating chocolate can make you _____.

① fat　　　　② happy
③ smile　　　　④ feel better
⑤ feeling good

04 다음 문장의 빈칸에 알맞은 것은?

> If you pass the test, you _____ study
> more.

① has to　　　　② don't
③ had to　　　　④ were to
⑤ won't have to

서답형
05 다음 문장에서 어법상 <u>어색한</u> 부분을 찾아 바르게 고쳐 쓰시오.

> Lisa makes me to do her homework.

_____ ➡ _____

06 다음 문장의 빈칸에 알맞은 것은?

> If you _____ straight two blocks, you
> will find our school.

① will go　　　　② were
③ go　　　　④ must be
⑤ went

서답형
07 다음 주어진 어구를 이용하여 우리말을 영어로 옮기시오.
(필요시 어형 변경할 것)

> 나는 엄마가 설거지하시는 것을 도와 드렸다.
> (do the dishes)

➡ _____

08 다음 우리말과 같도록 할 때, 빈칸에 알맞은 것은?

> 만약 내일 그가 오지 않으면, 나는 매우 슬플 것
> 이다.
> = _____, I will feel very sad.

① If he comes tomorrow
② If he won't come tomorrow
③ If he doesn't come tomorrow
④ Unless he won't come tomorrow
⑤ Unless he doesn't come tomorrow

09 다음 문장의 빈칸에 알맞지 <u>않은</u> 것은?

> My mother _____ me clean the room.

① let   ② had
③ wanted   ④ made
⑤ helped

10 다음 두 문장의 의미가 같도록 빈칸에 알맞은 것은?

> If you don't eat breakfast, you can't focus on your studies.
> = _____ you eat breakfast, you can't focus on your studies.

① When   ② While
③ Because   ④ Unless
⑤ Although

11 다음 중 밑줄 친 부분의 쓰임이 나머지와 <u>다른</u> 하나는?

① I <u>made</u> him wash the dishes.
② Please <u>make</u> me laugh.
③ I <u>made</u> him carry the box.
④ My mom <u>made</u> me some snacks.
⑤ His advice <u>made</u> me do the work.

서답형
12 다음 문장에서 어법상 어색한 부분을 찾아 바르게 고쳐 쓰시오.

> If it will rain tomorrow, I will not go there, either.

_____ ➡ _____

충요
13 다음 문장의 빈칸에 알맞은 것은?

> If it _____, we'll play soccer outside.

① won't rain   ② don't rain
③ doesn't rain   ④ didn't rain
⑤ hadn't rained

서답형
14 다음 우리말과 일치하도록 주어진 표현을 이용하여 영작하시오.

> 그의 미소는 항상 나를 미소 짓게 만든다.
> (make)

➡ _____

15 다음 빈칸에 공통으로 알맞은 것은?

> • I'll _____ him to see a doctor.
> • How can I _____ him to help me?

① let   ② make
③ get   ④ have
⑤ help

충요
16 다음 세 문장의 뜻이 같도록 빈칸에 들어갈 말을 순서대로 짝지은 것은?

> Be careful, or you'll be in danger.
> = _____ you are careful, you'll be in danger.
> = _____ you are careful, you won't be in danger.

① If – If   ② If – Unless
③ Unless – If   ④ As – If
⑤ Unless – As

17 다음 빈칸에 알맞은 말이 바르게 짝지어진 것은?

> Her mother _____ the girl _____ care of her little sister.

① let – to take   ② had – take
③ helped – taking   ④ had – to take
⑤ made – taking

18 다음 두 문장이 같은 뜻이 되도록 빈칸에 알맞은 말을 쓰시오.

> If you don't stop shouting, they will call the police.
> = Unless _____ _____ shouting, they will call the police.

중요

19 다음 밑줄 친 부분 중 어법상 어색한 것은?

① She made me come early.
② My sister let me to go home early.
③ Sumi asked me to call her right now.
④ I will make her go to the party.
⑤ My mother helped me do my homework.

20 다음 우리말과 같도록 주어진 단어를 바르게 배열하여 문장을 완성하시오.

> Judy는 남동생에게 수학 공부를 하도록 시킨다.
> (makes / brother / study / her / math / Judy)

➡ _____

중요

21 다음 중 어법상 어색한 것은?

① If he helps me, I can carry this easily.
② If you don't have breakfast, you will feel hungry soon.
③ If you will leave now, you can get there on time.
④ If she makes a lot of money, she will buy a car.
⑤ If school finishes early today, we'll go to the movies.

22 다음 두 문장의 의미가 같도록 빈칸에 알맞은 말을 쓰시오.

> If you don't like the food, you don't have to pay.
> = _____, you don't have to pay.

23 다음 우리말과 일치하도록 주어진 어구를 바르게 배열하시오.

> 아버지는 내가 무거운 가방 드는 것을 도와 주셨다.
> (me / heavy / my father / bag / carry / helped / the)

➡ _____

24 다음 대화의 밑줄 친 부분과 쓰임이 같은 것은?

> A: Why do you like bright colors?
> B: Because they make me feel happy.

① He made me a toy boat.
② She made us coffee.
③ Wine is made from grapes.
④ She makes her own clothes.
⑤ My mom made me stop playing games.

01 다음 빈칸에 알맞은 말을 〈보기〉에서 골라 쓰시오. (필요시 어형을 바꿀 것)

┌─ 보기 ┤
help   get   carry   show
└──────────────────────┘

(1) He helped me _____ the heavy bag.

(2) I couldn't _____ the car to start this morning.

(3) Please let me _____ you with your homework.

(4) I have lots of pictures _____ _____ you.

02 다음 빈칸에 알맞은 말을 〈보기〉에서 골라 쓰시오. (문장의 앞에 오는 경우 대문자로 쓰시오.)

┌─ 보기 ┤
when   if   unless
└──────────────────────┘

(1) _____ you don't leave now, you will miss the last train.

(2) We had a big party _____ Sarah came home.

(3) _____ you start now, you'll be late for the meeting.

03 다음 문장에서 어법상 어색한 부분을 찾아 바르게 고쳐 쓰시오.

(1) I let Tom to explain why he was late.
_____ ➡ _____

(2) The hot milk will make you fell asleep easily.
_____ ➡ _____

(3) The teacher had his students played outside.
_____ ➡ _____

04 접속사 if를 사용하여 다음 두 문장을 한 문장으로 고쳐 쓰시오. (단, 종속절이 주절의 앞에 오는 문장으로 바꿀 것)

(1) I am late for class. My teacher gets very angry.
➡ _____

(2) The weather is nice. I always walk to school.
➡ _____

(3) It rains on weekends. We watch TV.
➡ _____

[05~06] 다음 주어진 말을 이용하여 우리말을 영작하시오.

05
엄마는 내가 밤에 밖에 나가는 것을 허락하지 않으신다. (let, night)

➡ _____

06
나는 남동생에게 TV를 끄도록 했다.
(make, turn)

➡ _____

07 다음 우리말과 일치하도록 빈칸에 알맞은 말을 넣어 문장을 완성하시오.

(1) 네가 만일 열심히 공부한다면, 너는 그 시험에 합격할 거야.
➡ _____, you'll pass the exam.

(2) 만일 내일 비가 오면 우리는 집에 있을 것이다.
➡ _____ tomorrow, we'll stay home.

08 다음 문장에서 어법상 어색한 부분을 찾아 바르게 고쳐 문장을 다시 쓰시오.

(1) Finally, the police let the thief goes.

➡ _____

(2) Love makes people to do unusual things.

➡ _____

(3) I got my dog wear strange glasses.

➡ _____

(4) My English teacher helps us writing a diary every day.

➡ _____

09 다음 문장에서 어법상 어색한 것을 찾아 바르게 고쳐 쓰시오.

(1) You'll be happy if you'll pass the exam.

_____ ➡ _____

(2) If I won't be free tomorrow, I'll see you on Saturday.

_____ ➡ _____

10 다음 〈보기〉와 같이 문장을 바꿔 쓰시오. (단, make, let을 사용할 것)

┌─ 보기 ┐

My mom: Clean your room.
➡ My mom made me clean my room.

└──────┘

(1) My parents: Play computer games every Friday.

➡ _____

(2) My teacher: Wash your hands.

➡ _____

(3) My mom: Don't go out.

➡ _____

11 다음 문장에서 어법상 어색한 부분을 바르게 고쳐서 문장을 다시 쓰시오.

(1) If it will rain tomorrow, we won't go hiking.

➡ _____

(2) Unless you don't hurry, you will miss the train.

➡ _____

12 다음 우리말과 일치하도록 주어진 어구를 바르게 배열하시오.

(1) Eddie는 남동생에게 그의 장난감을 갖고 놀게 한다. (lets / play / his toys / Eddie / his brother / with)

➡ _____

(2) 그녀는 아이들에게 영어 공부를 시킨다. (English / makes / she / children / study / her)

➡ _____

(3) 아빠는 우리에게 일요일마다 아침을 요리하게 한다. (breakfast / Dad / us / Sundays / cook / on / has)

➡ _____

13 다음 주어진 단어를 바르게 배열하여 문장을 완성하시오.

┌──────────────────────────────┐
(she / will / if / study / the exam / , / she / fail / doesn't / hard)
└──────────────────────────────┘

➡ _____

Reading

Loosen Up!

At school you sit for many hours. Do you get tired? Why don't you
오랜 시간 동안   피곤하다   Why don't you ~?: ~하는 게 어때?(권유)

massage yourself and stretch?
재귀대명사(재귀 용법)

Let's begin with the eyes. Close your eyes and massage them softly
~하자   명령문: 동사원형 ~(~해라)   = your eyes

with your fingers. It will relax your eyes. When you finish, cover your
~으로   = Massaging your eyes softly with your fingers   접 ~하면

eyes with your hands to block out the light. It will make your eyes feel
목적을 나타내는 to부정사의 부사적 용법 / (빛을) 차단하다   사역동사 make+목적어+목적격보어(동사원형)

more comfortable.

Next, massage your neck. Put your fingers on the back of your neck.
명령문: 동사원형 ~(~해라)

Draw small circles with your fingers to massage your neck. Massage
~으로   to부정사의 부사적 용법(목적)

from top to bottom. The massage will help you feel better.
위에서 아래로   help+목적어+목적격보어(동사원형/to부정사)

---

loosen up 몸을 풀어 주다

massage 마사지하다

stretch 스트레칭하다

softly 부드럽게

finger 손가락

relax 편안하게 하다

finish 끝나다

cover 가리다

comfortable 편안한

neck 목

back 뒤쪽, 뒷부분

draw 그리다

circle 원

 확인문제

● 다음 문장이 본문의 내용과 일치하면 T, 일치하지 <u>않으면</u> F를 쓰시오.

1   To massage your eyes softly with your fingers will relax your eyes. ☐

2   We cover our eyes with our arms to block out the light. ☐

3   We draw small circles with our fingers to massage our neck. ☐

4   The neck massage will help you feel better. ☐

Let's work on your waist. Team up with a friend. Stand close to each other and face your partner. Hold each other's wrists. Slowly stretch your head and body backward. Hold that position for three seconds. Then, slowly pull each other to a standing position. You and your partner should move at the same speed. If you don't, both of you will fall!

Place the top of your right foot on the desk behind you. Then, slowly bend your left leg and lower yourself. Hold it for a few seconds and slowly straighten up. This position will loosen up your right leg. Switch your legs and repeat the exercise.

How do you feel now? If you massage yourself and stretch every day, you will feel healthier. Also, you can focus on your studies better.

waist 허리
close 가까이
face ~을 마주보다
slowly 천천히
wrist 손목
position 자세
pull 끌어당기다
fall 넘어지다
behind ~ 뒤에
bend 구부리다
lower 낮추다
hold 유지하다
switch 바꾸다
repeat 반복하다
exercise 운동
healthy 건강한
study 공부

 확인문제

● 다음 문장이 본문의 내용과 일치하면 T, 일치하지 않으면 F를 쓰시오.

1 To work on your waist, you have to team up with a friend. ☐

2 If two people move at the same speed, they will fall. ☐

3 After we place the top of our right foot on the desk behind us, we slowly bend our right leg and lower ourselves. ☐

4 If you massage yourself and stretch every day, you can focus on your studies better. ☐

● 우리말을 참고하여 빈칸에 알맞은 말을 쓰시오.

1 _____ school you sit _____ many hours.

2 Do you _____ _____ ?

3 _____ _____ you massage _____ and stretch?

4 _____ begin _____ the eyes.

5 _____ your eyes and _____ them softly _____ your fingers.

6 It _____ _____ your eyes.

7 _____ you finish, _____ your eyes _____ your hands to _____ _____ the light.

8 It will _____ your eyes _____ more _____ .

9 Next, _____ your neck.

10 _____ your fingers _____ the back of your neck.

11 _____ small circles _____ your fingers _____ massage your neck.

12 Massage _____ top _____ bottom.

13 The massage will _____ you _____ better.

14 _____ work on your _____ .

15 _____ _____ with a friend.

1 학교에서 너는 오랜 시간에 걸쳐 앉아 있다.

2 여러분은 피곤한가?

3 마사지와 스트레칭을 하는 게 어떤가?

4 눈부터 시작하자.

5 눈을 감고 손가락으로 눈을 부드럽게 마사지해라.

6 그것은 여러분의 눈을 편안하게 해줄 것이다.

7 끝나면, 빛을 차단하기 위해 손으로 눈을 가려라.

8 그것은 여러분의 눈을 더 편안하게 해줄 것이다.

9 다음으로, 여러분의 목을 마사지해라.

10 여러분의 목 뒤에 손가락을 대라.

11 여러분의 목을 마사지하기 위해 손가락으로 작은 원을 그려라.

12 위에서 아래로 마사지해라.

13 마사지는 여러분의 기분이 좋아지도록 도울 것이다.

14 허리 운동을 하자.

15 친구와 짝을 이루어라.

16 Stand close to _____ _____ and _____ your partner.

17 _____ each other's wrists.

18 Slowly _____ your head and body _____.

19 _____ that position _____ three seconds.

20 Then, slowly _____ each other _____ a standing position.

21 You and _____ partner should move _____ the same speed.

22 _____ you don't, _____ _____ you will fall!

23 _____ the top of your right foot _____ the desk _____ you.

24 Then, slowly _____ your left leg and _____ yourself.

25 _____ it for _____ _____ seconds and slowly straighten _____.

26 This position will _____ _____ your right leg.

27 _____ your legs and _____ the exercise.

28 _____ do you _____ now?

29 If you _____ yourself and _____ every day, you will _____ _____.

30 Also, you can _____ _____ your studies _____.

16 서로 가까이 서서 여러분의 파트너를 마주 보아라.

17 서로의 손목을 잡아라.

18 천천히 여러분의 머리와 몸을 뒤로 뻗어라.

19 3초 동안 그 자세를 유지해라.

20 그리고 나서, 천천히 서로 선 자세로 끌어 당겨라.

21 너와 너의 파트너는 같은 속도로 움직여야 한다.

22 그렇지 않으면, 너희 둘 다 넘어질 것이다!

23 여러분의 뒤에 있는 책상 위에 오른쪽 발등을 올려놓아라.

24 그리고 나서, 천천히 왼쪽 다리를 구부리고 몸을 낮추어라.

25 몇 초 동안 그 자세를 유지하다가 천천히 몸을 펴라.

26 이 자세는 여러분의 오른쪽 다리를 풀어 줄 것이다.

27 다리를 바꿔서 운동을 반복해라.

28 지금 기분이 어떤가?

29 매일 마사지와 스트레칭을 하면, 여러분은 더 건강해지는 것을 느낄 것이다.

30 또한, 여러분은 공부에 더 집중할 수 있을 것이다.

● 우리말을 참고하여 본문을 영작하시오.

1 학교에서 여러분은 오랜 시간에 걸쳐 앉아 있다.

➡ _____

2 여러분은 피곤한가?

➡ _____

3 마사지와 스트레칭을 하는 게 어떤가?

➡ _____

4 눈부터 시작하자.

➡ _____

5 눈을 감고 손가락으로 눈을 부드럽게 마사지해라.

➡ _____

6 그것은 여러분의 눈을 편안하게 해줄 것이다.

➡ _____

7 끝나면, 빛을 차단하기 위해 손으로 눈을 가려라.

➡ _____

8 그것은 여러분의 눈을 더 편안하게 해줄 것이다.

➡ _____

9 다음으로, 여러분의 목을 마사지해라.

➡ _____

10 여러분의 목 뒤에 손가락을 대라.

➡ _____

11 여러분의 목을 마사지하기 위해 손가락으로 작은 원을 그려라.

➡ _____

12 위에서 아래로 마사지해라.

➡ _____

13 마사지는 여러분의 기분이 좋아지도록 도울 것이다.

➡ _____

14 허리 운동을 하자.

➡ _____

15 친구와 짝을 이루어라.

➡ _____

16 서로 가까이 서서 여러분의 파트너를 마주 보아라.

➡ _____

17 서로의 손목을 잡아라.

➡ _____

18 천천히 여러분의 머리와 몸을 뒤로 뻗어라.

➡ _____

19 3초 동안 그 자세를 유지해라.

➡ _____

20 그러고 나서, 천천히 서로 선 자세로 끌어 당겨라.

➡ _____

21 너와 너의 파트너는 같은 속도로 움직여야 한다.

➡ _____

22 그렇지 않으면, 너희 둘 다 넘어질 것이다!

➡ _____

23 여러분의 뒤에 있는 책상 위에 오른쪽 발등을 올려놓아라.

➡ _____

24 그러고 나서, 천천히 왼쪽 다리를 구부리고 몸을 낮추어라.

➡ _____

25 몇 초 동안 그 자세를 유지하다가 천천히 몸을 펴라.

➡ _____

26 이 자세는 여러분의 오른쪽 다리를 풀어 줄 것이다.

➡ _____

27 다리를 바꿔서 운동을 반복해라.

➡ _____

28 지금 기분이 어떤가?

➡ _____

29 매일 마사지와 스트레칭을 하면, 여러분은 더 건강해지는 것을 느낄 것이다.

➡ _____

30 또한, 여러분은 공부에 더 집중할 수 있을 것이다.

➡ _____

[01~05] 다음 글을 읽고, 물음에 답하시오.

At school you sit ___ⓐ___ many hours. Do you ___ⓑ___ tired? Why don't you massage yourself and stretch?

Let's begin with the eyes. Close your eyes and massage ⓒthem softly with your fingers. It will relax your eyes. When you finish, cover your eyes with your hands to block ___ⓓ___ the light. ⓔIt will make your eyes feel more comfortable.

 01 위 글의 빈칸 ⓐ와 ⓓ에 알맞은 말이 바르게 짝지어진 것은?

① in – up
② by – off
③ for – out
④ over – into
⑤ during – over

02 위 글의 빈칸 ⓑ에 알맞은 것은?

① go
② get
③ put
④ take
⑤ have

서답형

03 위 글의 밑줄 친 ⓒ가 가리키는 것을 찾아 영어로 쓰시오.

➡ _____

서답형

04 위 글에서 다음 영영풀이에 해당하는 단어를 찾아 쓰시오.

to put your arms, legs, etc., in positions that make the muscles long and tight

➡ _____

05 위 글의 밑줄 친 ⓔIt이 의미하는 것은?

① 스트레칭을 하는 것
② 눈을 감는 것
③ 손으로 눈을 비비는 것
④ 손가락으로 눈을 마사지하는 것
⑤ 빛을 차단하기 위해 손으로 눈을 가리는 것

[06~10] 다음 글을 읽고, 물음에 답하시오.

Let's work on your waist. Team up with a friend. Stand close to each other and ⓐface your partner. Hold each other's wrists. Slowly stretch your head and body backward. Hold that position ___ⓑ___ three seconds. Then, slowly pull each other to a standing ___ⓒ___. You and your partner should move at the same speed. ___ⓓ___ you don't, both ___ⓔ___ you will fall!

06 위 글의 밑줄 친 ⓐ와 쓰임이 같은 것은?

① She looks thin in the face.
② She'll face with a difficult decision.
③ I turned the chair to face him.
④ The man is wiping his face.
⑤ The birds build their nests in the rock face.

서답형

07 위 글의 빈칸 ⓑ와 ⓔ에 알맞은 말을 쓰시오.

ⓑ _____   ⓔ _____

서답형

08 위 글의 빈칸 ⓒ에 다음 영영풀이에 해당하는 단어를 쓰시오.

> the way someone stands, sits, or lies down

➡ _____

09 위 글의 빈칸 ⓓ에 알맞은 것은?

① As   ② If
③ That   ④ While
⑤ When

10 위 글의 내용과 일치하지 <u>않는</u> 것은?

① 친구와 함께 협력한다.
② 서로 가까이 서서 파트너를 마주 본다.
③ 서로의 손목을 잡는다.
④ 천천히 머리와 몸을 뒤로 뻗는다.
⑤ 두 사람이 같은 속도로 움직이면 둘 다 넘어진다.

[11~15] 다음 글을 읽고, 물음에 답하시오.

> ①Place the top of your right foot on the desk behind you. Then, ②slowly ⓐbend your left leg and lower ③itself. Hold it ④ for a few seconds and ⓑslow straighten _____ⓒ_____ . This position will loosen _____ⓓ_____ your right leg. Switch your legs and ⑤repeat the exercise.

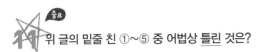

11 위 글의 밑줄 친 ①~⑤ 중 어법상 틀린 것은?

①   ②   ③   ④   ⑤

12 위 글의 밑줄 친 ⓐ의 영영풀이로 알맞은 것은?

① to add something to something else
② to change or replace something with another thing
③ to move your body so that it is not straight
④ to put something or someone in a particular place or position
⑤ to extend your arm, leg, etc., in order to reach something

서답형

13 위 글의 밑줄 친 ⓑ를 알맞은 형태로 고쳐 쓰시오.

➡ _____

14 위 글의 빈칸 ⓒ와 ⓓ에 공통으로 알맞은 것은?

① on   ② out
③ off   ④ up
⑤ over

서답형

15 위 글의 다리를 풀어 주는 방법을 순서대로 배열하시오.

> ⓐ 다리를 구부리고 몸을 낮춘 상태로 몇 초 동안 유지한다.
> ⓑ 뒤에 있는 책상 위에 오른쪽 발의 윗부분을 올려놓는다.
> ⓒ 천천히 왼쪽 다리를 구부리고 몸을 낮춘다.

➡ _____

[16~20] 다음 글을 읽고, 물음에 답하시오.

Let's begin with the eyes. Close your eyes and massage them ⓐsoft with your fingers. ⓑIt will relax your eyes. When you finish, ____ⓒ____ your eyes with your hands ⓓblock out the light. ⓔ그것은 너의 눈을 더 편안하게 해줄 것이다.

서답형

16 위 글의 밑줄 친 ⓐ를 알맞은 형태로 고쳐 쓰시오.

➡ _____

서답형

17 위 글의 밑줄 친 ⓑIt이 가리키는 것을 우리말로 쓰시오.

➡ _____

18 문맥상 위 글의 빈칸 ⓒ에 알맞은 것은?

① open   ② rub
③ cover   ④ close
⑤ massage

19 위 글의 밑줄 친 ⓓ의 형태로 알맞은 것은?

① block   ② blocks
③ blocking   ④ to block
⑤ to blocking

서답형

20 위 글의 밑줄 친 ⓔ의 우리말에 맞게 주어진 어구를 이용하여 문장을 완성하시오.

It will _____.

[21~23] 다음 글을 읽고, 물음에 답하시오.

Next, massage your neck. __ⓐ__ your fingers on the back of your neck. __ⓑ__ small circles with your fingers ⓒto massage your neck. __ⓓ__ from top to bottom. ⓔThe massage will help you feeling better.

21 위 글의 빈칸 ⓐ, ⓑ, ⓓ에 알맞은 말이 바르게 짝지어진 것은?

① Draw – Massage – Put
② Put – Draw – Massage
③ Massage – Put – Draw
④ Draw – Put – Massage
⑤ Put – Massage – Draw

중요

22 위 글의 밑줄 친 ⓒ와 쓰임이 같은 것은?

① The boy wants to drink juice.
② He loves to play outside.
③ She dressed up to meet her boyfriend.
④ To swim in this river is dangerous.
⑤ My plan is to travel around Thailand.

서답형

23 위 글의 밑줄 친 ⓔ에서 어법상 틀린 부분을 찾아 바르게 고쳐 쓰시오.

_____ ➡ _____

[24~27] 다음 글을 읽고, 물음에 답하시오.

Let's work on your ___@___. Team up with a friend. ①Stand close to each other and face your partner. ②Hold each other's wrists. Slowly stretch your head and body ③forward. ④Hold that position for three ⓑ seconds. Then, slowly ⑤pull each other to a standing position. You and your partner ___ⓒ___ move at the same speed. If you don't, both of you ___ⓓ___ fall!

서답형

24 위 글의 빈칸 @에 다음 영영풀이에 해당하는 단어를 쓰시오.

> the area around the middle of the body between the ribs and the hips

➡ _____

25 위 글의 밑줄 친 ①~⑤ 중 문맥상 단어의 쓰임이 <u>어색한</u> 것은?

①   ②   ③   ④   ⑤

26 위 글의 밑줄 친 ⓑ와 뜻이 같은 것은?

① I agreed to speak <u>second</u>.
② The light flashes every 5 <u>seconds</u>.
③ He was the <u>second</u> to arrive.
④ Milan is Italy's <u>second</u> largest city.
⑤ Fill the <u>second</u> bowl with warm water.

중요

27 위 글의 빈칸 ⓒ와 ⓓ에 알맞은 말이 바르게 짝지어진 것은?

① might – will   ② would – can
③ must – may   ④ could – will
⑤ should – will

[28~31] 다음 글을 읽고, 물음에 답하시오.

(①) Place the top of your right foot on the desk behind you. (②) Then, slowly bend your left leg and lower @you. (③) This position will ___ⓑ___ your right leg. (④) Switch your legs and repeat the exercise. (⑤)

중요

28 위 글의 ①~⑤ 중 다음 문장이 들어갈 알맞은 곳은?

> Hold it for a few seconds and slowly straighten up.

①   ②   ③   ④   ⑤

서답형

29 위 글의 밑줄 친 @를 알맞은 형태로 고쳐 쓰시오.

➡ _____

서답형

30 위 글에서 다음 영영풀이에 해당하는 단어를 찾아 쓰시오.

> to make a change from one thing to another

➡ _____

31 위 글의 빈칸 ⓑ에 알맞은 것은?

① get over   ② put on
③ block out   ④ focus on
⑤ loosen up

[01~04] 다음 글을 읽고, 물음에 답하시오.

At school you sit for many hours. Do you get tired? ⓐ(you / why / massage / don't) yourself and stretch?

Let's begin with the eyes. Close your eyes and massage them softly with your fingers. It will relax your eyes. When you finish, cover your eyes with your hands to block out the light. ⓑIt will make your eyes feel more comfortably.

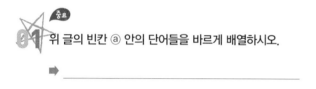 위 글의 빈칸 ⓐ 안의 단어들을 바르게 배열하시오.

➡ _____

02 위 글에서 다음 영영풀이에 해당하는 단어를 찾아 쓰시오.

> to rub or press someone's body in a way that helps muscles to relax or reduces pain in muscles and joints

➡ _____

03 위 글의 밑줄 친 ⓑ에서 어법상 틀린 부분을 찾아 바르게 고쳐 쓰시오.

_____ ➡ _____

04 What can we do to block out the light? Answer in English.

➡ _____

[05~08] 다음 글을 읽고, 물음에 답하시오.

Next, massage your neck. Put your fingers on the back of your neck. Draw small circles with your fingers ⓐmassage your neck. Massage ____ⓑ____ top to bottom. ⓒ마사지는 여러분의 기분이 나아지도록 도울 것이다.

05 위 글의 밑줄 친 ⓐ를 알맞은 형태로 고쳐 쓰시오.

➡ _____

06 위 글의 빈칸 ⓑ에 알맞은 말을 쓰시오.

➡ _____

07 위 글의 밑줄 친 ⓒ의 우리말에 맞도록 주어진 어구를 바르게 배열하시오.

> (you / will / the massage / help / better / feel)

➡ _____

08 목을 마사지하는 방법을 순서대로 배열하시오.

> ⓐ 목을 마사지하기 위해 손가락으로 작은 원을 그린다.
> ⓑ 위에서부터 아래로 마사지한다.
> ⓒ 목 뒷부분에 손가락을 댄다.

➡ _____

[09~12] 다음 글을 읽고, 물음에 답하시오.

Place the top of your right foot on the desk behind you. Then, slowly bend your left leg and _____ⓐ yourself. Hold ⓑit for a few seconds and slowly straighten _____ⓒ. ⓓThis position will loosen up your right leg. Switch your legs and repeat the exercise.

09 위 글의 빈칸 ⓐ에 다음 영영풀이에 해당하는 단어를 주어진 철자로 시작하여 쓰시오.

> to move something down from higher up

➡ l_____

10 위 글의 밑줄 친 ⓑ가 의미하는 것을 우리말로 구체적으로 쓰시오.

➡ _____

11 위 글의 밑줄 친 ⓒ에 '똑바로 하다'라는 의미가 되도록 할 때 빈칸에 알맞은 말을 쓰시오.

➡ _____

12 위 글의 밑줄 친 ⓓ를 우리말로 옮기시오.

➡ _____

[13~16] 다음 글을 읽고, 물음에 답하시오.

Let's work on your waist. Team up with a friend. Stand close to each other and _____ⓐ your partner. Hold each other's wrists. Slowly stretch your head and body backward. Hold ⓑthat position for three seconds. ⓒThen, slowly push each other to a standing position. You and your partner should move at the same speed. If you don't, both of you will fall!

13 위 글의 빈칸 ⓐ에 다음 영영풀이에 해당하는 단어를 주어진 철자로 시작하여 쓰시오.

> to stand or sit with your face and body turned toward something or someone

➡ f_____

14 위 글의 밑줄 친 ⓑ가 의미하는 것을 우리말로 구체적으로 쓰시오.

➡ _____

15 위 글의 밑줄 친 ⓒ에서 문맥상 단어의 쓰임이 어색한 것을 찾아 바르게 고쳐 쓰시오.

_____ ➡ _____

16 If two people don't move at the same speed, what will happen?

➡ _____

Enjoy Writing C

My Plan to Be Healthier

Here is my plan to be healthier.
Here is + 단수 명사 ~: 여기 ~이 있다

1. I will exercise more than three times a week.
~ 이상   일주일에 세 번

2. I will eat breakfast every day.
매일

If I exercise more than three times a week, I will become stronger. Also, if
조건을 나타내는 접속사 if(~한다면)   become+형용사: ~해지다

I eat breakfast every day, I will feel better in the morning. I will change my
기분이 좋아지다

habits, and it will make me live a healthy life.
사역동사 make+목적어+목적격 보어(동사원형): ~을 …하게 하다

구문해설 · healthy: 건강한 · exercise: 운동하다 · change: 바꾸다 · habit: 습관

Project - Step 2

Do you know how to stretch your shoulders? Our stretching exercise is
how+to부정사: 어떻게 ~하는지   ~라고 불리다

called "Number Stretching." First, make a number "1" with your arm to warm
목적을 나타내는 to부정사의 부사적 용법(~하기 위해)

up. Then, make a number "2" with your arms. It will stretch your shoulders.
~으로

Now, make a number "3". If you move your arms in a circle, it will feel nice.
feel+형용사: ~하게 느끼다

Finally, make a number "4". It is a little bit difficult, but it will be good for
조금   ~에 좋다

your shoulders.

구문해설 · stretch: 스트레칭하다 · shoulder: 어깨 · warm up: 준비 운동을 하다 · circle: 원
· finally: 마지막으로 · difficult: 어려운

Wrap Up - Writing

Sumi: I feel stressed these days. What should I do?
요즘

Jiae: When I get stressed, I listen to music. It makes me feel better. If you don't
스트레스를 받다   사역동사 make+목적어+목적격 보어(동사원형): ~을 …하게 하다

know how to download music, I will show you.
다운로드하는 방법

구문해설 · listen to: ~을 듣다 · feel better: 기분이 더 좋아지다 · show: 보여주다, 가르쳐 주다

해석

더 건강해지기 위한 나의 계획
여기 더 건강해지기 위한 나의 계획이 있다.
1. 나는 일주일에 세 번 이상 운동을 할 것이다.
2. 나는 매일 아침을 먹을 것이다. 일주일에 세 번 이상 운동을 하면 더 강해질 것이다. 또한, 매일 아침을 먹으면 아침에 기분이 나아질 것이다. 나는 습관을 바꿀 것이고, 그것은 나를 건강한 삶을 살게 할 것이다.

여러분은 어깨를 어떻게 스트레칭하는지 아는가? 우리의 스트레칭 운동은 "숫자 스트레칭"이라고 부른다. "첫 번째, 준비 운동을 하기 위해 팔로 숫자 "1"를 만들어라. 그런 다음, 팔로 숫자 2를 만들어라. 그것은 여러분의 어깨를 쫙 펴 줄 것이다. 이제 숫자 3을 만들어라. 팔을 동그랗게 움직이면 기분이 좋아질 것이다. 마지막으로, 숫자 4를 만들어라. 그것은 조금 어렵긴 하지만, 여러분의 어깨에 좋을 것이다.

수미: 나는 요즘 스트레스를 받고 있어. 어떻게 해야 하지?
지애: 스트레스를 받을 때, 나는 음악을 들어. 그건 내 기분을 좋아지게 해. 음악을 다운로드하는 방법을 모르면, 내가 가르쳐 줄게.

01 다음 중 짝지어진 단어의 관계가 <u>다른</u> 것은?

① warm : cool
② difficult : easy
③ heavy : light
④ switch : change
⑤ backward : forward

02 다음 영영풀이에 해당하는 단어는?

> to move your body so that it is not straight

① pull
② bend
③ place
④ push
⑤ stretch

03 다음 우리말과 같도록 빈칸에 알맞은 말을 쓰시오.

> 새로운 과학 프로젝트를 위해, 우리는 친구들과 협력할 필요가 있다.
> ➡ For the new science project, we need to _____ _____ with friends.

04 다음 영영풀이에 해당하는 단어를 쓰시오.

> the action of rubbing and pressing a person's body with the hands to reduce pain in the muscles and joints

➡ _____

05 다음 빈칸에 공통으로 알맞은 것은?

> • What is the best _____ to get to City Hall?
> • I don't know the _____ to the stadium.

① tip
② part
③ way
④ top
⑤ choice

06 다음 빈칸에 알맞은 말이 바르게 짝지어진 것은?

> • You have to loosen _____ your arms and legs before swimming.
> • The trees in the park block _____ a lot of sunlight.

① of – in
② over – at
③ to – off
④ from – on
⑤ up – out

07 다음 대화의 빈칸에 알맞지 <u>않은</u> 것은?

> A: What do you enjoy doing after school?
> B: _____

① I like to go hiking.
② I enjoy playing soccer.
③ I enjoy cooking healthy food.
④ I'm interested in science.
⑤ I enjoy listening to music.

08 다음 대화의 빈칸에 알맞은 것은?

> A: How about making paper flowers?
> B: That sounds great. But I don't know _____.

① what to make them
② how to make them
③ how to use them
④ where to get there
⑤ what to use them

09 다음 대화의 빈칸에 알맞은 것은?

> A: _____
> B: I enjoy listening to pop music.

① Can you play music?
② Why don't you listen to music?
③ What kind of music do you like?
④ Do you want to listen to music?
⑤ What's your favorite sport?

10 다음 대화의 빈칸에 들어갈 말로 알맞은 것은?

> A: Are you good at solving math problems?
> B: No, I _____ math.

① am going to
② can get
③ am not good at
④ feel so good
⑤ am looking forward to

11 다음 대화의 순서를 바르게 배열하시오.

> (A) I enjoy cooking healthy food.
> (B) I can make salad, Bibimbap, and vegetable juice.
> (C) What do you enjoy doing after school?
> (D) Sounds cool. What can you make?

➡ _____

[12~15] 다음 대화를 읽고, 물음에 답하시오.

> B: I want to eat something healthy. Do you have any advice?
> G: I often eat fresh salad. It makes me ⓐfeel good.
> B: Really? Do you know how ⓑmake it?
> G: Yes, it's quite simple. __(A)__, cut many vegetables __ⓒ__ small pieces. __(B)__, put them into a bowl. Then, pour some lemon juice on them. __(C)__, mix everything together.
> B: That's it? I should try it.

12 위 대화의 밑줄 친 ⓐ와 ⓑ를 알맞은 형태로 쓰시오.

ⓐ _____ ⓑ _____

13 위 대화의 빈칸 ⓒ에 알맞은 것은?

① by
② on
③ for
④ into
⑤ with

14 위 대화의 빈칸 (A)~(C)에 들어갈 말을 순서대로 나열한 것은?

① Second – Finally – Third
② First – Two – Third
③ First – Then – Finally
④ First – Finally – After then
⑤ Finally – First – End

15 위 대화를 읽고, 다음 물음에 완전한 문장으로 답하시오.

> Q: What is the second step in making fresh salad?
> A: _____
> _____

16 다음 빈칸에 공통으로 알맞은 것은?

> • He _____ me cook dinner.
> • Mom _____ me clean up my room.

① gave   ② wanted

③ made   ④ enjoyed

⑤ asked

17 다음 중 〈보기〉의 밑줄 친 부분과 쓰임이 같은 것은?

> ┤ 보기 ├
> I want to know if it will rain tomorrow.

① If he comes back, I will tell him about it.

② I won't go there if is cold tomorrow.

③ If you turn right, you can see the building.

④ You may go home early if you don't feel well.

⑤ I doubt if the baby can understand your words.

18 다음 밑줄 친 부분의 쓰임이 나머지와 다른 것은?

① Let me tell you about my teacher.

② I made him do his homework last night.

③ The students have many books to read.

④ I helped my dad wash his car.

⑤ My teacher had the students play outside.

19 다음 문장에서 어법상 어색한 부분을 바르게 고쳐서 문장을 다시 쓰시오.

> What do you do if he visits your home tomorrow?

➡ _____

20 다음 중 어법상 어색한 문장은?

① Mom let me go to bed early.

② Mr. Han told me go home early.

③ He made the children wash his car.

④ Jack will help you find the bicycle.

⑤ It lets you know about the price.

21 다음 빈칸에 공통으로 알맞은 것은?

> • You will get one free _____ you buy this.
> • I wonder _____ she is really a middle school student.

① as   ② if

③ that   ④ since

⑤ whether

22 다음 주어진 어구를 바르게 배열하여 문장을 완성하시오.

> 그녀는 아이들에게 축구를 하게 한다.
> (soccer / she / the children / play / has)

➡ _____

23 다음 〈보기〉의 밑줄 친 부분의 의미와 같은 것은?

> ┤ 보기 ├
> He made me do my math homework.

① She made it after all.

② I want to make money to buy the ring.

③ She made pasta for her little son.

④ They make the students do voluntary service at school.

⑤ You have to make an effort to be happy.

24 다음 밑줄 친 부분 중 어법상 어색한 것은?

① Unless he is late, we will start on time.

② Don't open the box until he says it's safe.

③ I'll go swimming if it will be sunny.

④ She will be happy when he sends her some flowers.

⑤ I'll wait here until the concert is over.

25 다음 문장에서 어법상 어색한 부분을 찾아 고쳐 쓰시오.

Nothing will make me changing my mind.

_____ ➡ _____

26 다음 두 문장을 접속사 if를 써서 한 문장으로 바꿔 쓰시오.

Jenny does not get up now. She will miss the train.

➡ _____

_____

27 다음 빈칸에 들어갈 말이 나머지 넷과 다른 것은?

① Mike will stay at home _____ it is cold.

② You can stay at home _____ you're tired.

③ She'll watch TV _____ she finishes her work early.

④ He'll buy a necktie for his dad _____ he goes shopping.

⑤ I think _____ Anderson won't come back.

[28~31] 다음 글을 읽고, 물음에 답하시오.

At school you sit (A)[for / during] many hours. Do you get tired? Why don't you massage (B)[itself / yourself] and stretch?
Let's begin ____ⓐ____ the eyes. ①Close your eyes and ②massage them softly ____ⓑ____ your fingers. It will ③relax your eyes. When you finish, ④open your eyes with your hands (C)[blocking / to block] out the light. It will ⓒ(feel / eyes / make / your) more ⑤comfortable.

28 위 글의 괄호 (A)~(C)에서 알맞은 것이 바르게 짝지어진 것은?

① for – itself – blocking

② for – yourself – to block

③ during – itself – blocking

④ during – yourself – blocking

⑤ during – itself – to block

29 위 글의 빈칸 ⓐ와 ⓑ에 공통으로 알맞은 말을 쓰시오.

➡ _____

30 위 글의 밑줄 친 ①~⑤ 중 흐름상 적절하지 않은 것은?

①   ②   ③   ④   ⑤

31 위 글의 괄호 ⓒ 안의 단어들을 순서대로 바르게 배열하시오.

➡ _____

[32~35] 다음 글을 읽고, 물음에 답하시오.

> Let's ⓐ<u>work</u> on your waist. Team __(A)__ with a friend. (①) Stand close to each other and ⓑ<u>face</u> your partner. (②) Hold each other's __(B)__ . (③) Slowly ⓒ<u>stretch</u> your head and body backward. (④) Then, ⓓ<u>slowly</u> pull each other to a standing position. (⑤) You and your partner should move at the same speed. If you don't, both of you ⓔ<u>fall</u>!

32 위 글의 빈칸 (A)에 알맞은 것은?

① on ② in
③ out ④ up
⑤ down

33 위 글의 빈칸 (B)에 다음 영영풀이에 해당하는 단어를 쓰시오. (복수형으로 쓸 것)

> the part of your body where your hand joins your arm

➡ _____

34 위 글의 ①~⑤ 중 다음 문장이 들어갈 알맞은 곳은?

> Hold that position for three seconds.

① ② ③ ④ ⑤

35 위 글의 밑줄 친 ⓐ~ⓔ 중 어법상 <u>어색한</u> 것은?

① ⓐ ② ⓑ ③ ⓒ ④ ⓓ ⑤ ⓔ

[36~39] 다음 글을 읽고, 물음에 답하시오.

> ⓐ<u>너는 너의 어깨를 스트레칭하는 방법을 아니?</u> Our stretching exercise is called "Number Stretching." __(A)__ , make a number "1" with your arm to warm up. __(B)__ , make a number "2" with your arms. ⓑ<u>It</u> will stretch your shoulders. Now, make a number "3". If you move your arms in a circle, it will feel nice. __(C)__ , make a number "4". It is a little bit difficult, __ⓒ__ it will be good for your shoulders.

36 위 글의 밑줄 친 ⓐ의 우리말과 일치하도록 빈칸에 알맞은 말을 쓰시오.

> Do you know _____ _____ _____ your shoulders?

37 위 글의 빈칸 (A)~(C)에 알맞은 말을 〈보기〉에서 골라 차례대로 쓰시오.

> ┤ 보기 ├
> Finally First Then

(A) _____ (B) _____ (C) _____

38 위 글의 밑줄 친 ⓑ<u>It</u>이 가리키는 것을 우리말로 쓰시오.

➡ _____

39 위 글의 빈칸 ⓒ에 알맞은 것은?

① so ② and
③ for ④ but
⑤ also

단원별 예상문제

01 다음 〈보기〉와 같이 변화하는 단어는?

┌─ 보기 ─────────────┐
│ use → usable │
└────────────────────┘

① create　　　　　② act
③ comfort　　　　④ attract
⑤ impress

02 다음 짝지어진 단어의 관계가 같도록 빈칸에 알맞은 말을 쓰시오.

┌──────────────────────────────┐
│ simple : complicated = top : _____ │
└──────────────────────────────┘

03 다음 빈칸에 알맞은 말이 바르게 짝지어진 것은?

┌──────────────────────────────┐
│ • I want to focus _____ losing │
│   weight. │
│ • Straighten _____ your shoulders │
│   when you walk. │
└──────────────────────────────┘

① in – on　　　　② at – up
③ of – off　　　　④ into – for
⑤ on – up

04 다음 영영풀이에 해당하는 단어는?

┌──────────────────────────────┐
│ to become or to cause something to │
│ become less tense, tight, or stiff │
└──────────────────────────────┘

① bend　　　　　② switch
③ reduce　　　　④ relax
⑤ prepare

05 다음 우리말에 맞게 빈칸에 알맞은 말을 쓰시오.

(1) 몇 초 동안 수프를 저어라.
　➡ Stir the soup for _____ _____
　　 _____.

(2) 나는 항상 저녁 식사 후에 산책을 한다.
　➡ I always _____ _____ _____
　　 after dinner.

(3) 너는 보통 어떤 종류의 사진을 찍니?
　➡ _____ _____ _____ pictures
　　 do you usually take?

06 다음 대화의 밑줄 친 부분의 의도로 알맞은 것은?

┌──────────────────────────────┐
│ **A:** Do you know how to make healthy │
│ 　juice? │
│ **B:** No, I don't. │
└──────────────────────────────┘

① 의견 동의하기　　② 도움 요청하기
③ 능력 여부 묻기　　④ 제안이나 권유하기
⑤ 선호에 대해 묻기

07 다음 대화의 빈칸에 알맞지 <u>않은</u> 것은?

┌──────────────────────────────┐
│ **A:** What do you do in your free time? │
│ **B:** _____ │
│ **A:** How interesting! │
└──────────────────────────────┘

① I ride a bike in the park.
② I hate to study English and math.
③ I take pictures of animals.
④ I enjoy drawing cartoons.
⑤ I play badminton with my sister.

[08~11] 다음 대화를 읽고, 물음에 답하시오.

B: People say that we should walk more than 10,000 steps every day ⓐbe healthy. I can't count the number of my steps easily.

G: You can use this smartphone app. ⓑ(you / how / do / it / use / know / to)?

B: No. Can you show me?

G: Sure. First, download the app. Then, walk with your smartphone. ⓒLate, you can check the number of steps you took.

B: Thank you. I will start using ⓓit today.

출제율 95%

08 위 대화의 밑줄 친 ⓐ를 알맞은 형태로 고쳐 쓰시오.

➡ _____

출제율 90%

09 위 대화의 괄호 ⓑ 안의 단어들을 바르게 배열하시오.

➡ _____

출제율 100%

10 위 대화의 밑줄 친 ⓒ를 알맞은 형태로 고치시오.

➡ _____

출제율 95%

11 위 대화의 밑줄 친 ⓓ가 가리키는 것을 영어로 쓰시오.

➡ _____

출제율 95%

12 다음 빈칸에 들어갈 말로 알맞은 것은?

She won't let me _____ home early.

① to go   ② going
③ went   ④ will go
⑤ go

출제율 100%

13 다음 중 어법상 어색한 것은?

① We can make the robots work better.
② My father made my dog stand up.
③ The house is the biggest in our town.
④ It makes students practicing their English a lot.
⑤ Swimming is the most interesting activity for me.

출제율 95%

14 다음 문장의 빈칸에 알맞은 것은?

If it _____ tomorrow, we won't go fishing.

① rain   ② rains
③ rained   ④ will rain
⑤ would rain

출제율 90%

15 다음 글의 밑줄 친 ①~⑤ 중 어색한 것은?

Sanghui ①loves ②repairing machines. She can ③make any broken machine ④working again. And Mr. Han makes children run away by ⑤shouting at them.

①   ②   ③   ④   ⑤

16 다음 우리말을 영어로 바르게 옮긴 것은?

> 나는 날씨가 좋으면 주말마다 낚시하러 간다.

① I go fishing on weekends because the weather is good.

② The weather is good, so I go fishing on weekends.

③ As the weather is good, I will go fishing on weekends.

④ If the weather will be good, I go fishing on weekends.

⑤ I go fishing on weekends if the weather is good.

17 다음 빈칸에 들어갈 말이 바르게 짝지어진 것은?

> • I was late _____ the bus broke down.
> • I can finish that work _____ I have three days.

① when – how
② when – where
③ if – because
④ because – that
⑤ because – if

18 다음 우리말과 같도록 빈칸에 알맞은 말을 써서 문장을 완성하시오.

> 만약 이번 일요일에 날씨가 맑으면, 우리는 소풍을 갈 것이다.
> = _____ _____ _____ sunny this Sunday, we _____ _____ on a picnic.

19 다음 우리말과 같은 뜻이 되도록 빈칸에 알맞은 말을 쓰시오. (필요하면 어형을 바꾸시오.)

> 선생님은 Martin이 반 아이들 앞에서 그 이야기를 읽도록 하셨다. (have)

➡ The teacher _____ the story in front of the class.

[20~23] 다음 글을 읽고, 물음에 답하시오.

> (①) Place the ____ⓐ____ of your right foot ____ⓑ____ the desk behind you. (②) Then, slowly bend your left leg and lower yourself. (③) Hold it for ____ⓒ____ seconds and slowly straighten up. (④) Switch your legs and repeat the exercise. (⑤)

20 위 글의 빈칸 ⓐ에 다음 영영풀이에 해당하는 단어를 쓰시오.

> an upper surface of something

➡ _____

21 위 글의 빈칸 ⓑ에 알맞은 것은?

① at
② with
③ in
④ on
⑤ for

22 위 글의 빈칸 ⓒ에 알맞은 것은?

① few
② little
③ much
④ a little
⑤ a few

23 위 글의 ①~⑤ 중 다음 문장이 들어갈 알맞은 곳은?

> This position will loosen up your right leg.

① ② ③ ④ ⑤

[24~26] 다음 글을 읽고, 물음에 답하시오.

Do you know how ___ⓐ___ stretch your shoulders? Our stretching exercise is called "Number Stretching." First, make a number "1" with your arm ___ⓑ___ warm up. Then, make a number "2" with your arms. It will stretch your shoulders. Now, make a number "3". If you move your arms in a circle, it will feel nice. Finally, make a number "4". It is a little bit difficult, but it will be good ___ⓒ___ your shoulders.

출제율 95%
24 위 글의 빈칸 ⓐ와 ⓑ에 공통으로 알맞은 말을 쓰시오.

➡ _____

출제율 95%
25 위 글에서 다음 영영풀이에 해당하는 단어를 찾아 쓰시오.

> to do an exercise or set of exercises done to prepare for a sport or other activity

➡ _____

출제율 95%
26 위 글의 빈칸 ⓒ에 알맞은 말을 쓰시오.

➡ _____

[27~30] 다음 글을 읽고, 물음에 답하시오.

___ⓐ___ the top of your right foot on the desk behind you. Then, slowly ___ⓑ___ your left leg and lower yourself. ___ⓒ___ it for a few seconds and slowly straighten ___ⓓ___. This position will ___ⓔ___. Switch your legs and repeat the exercise.

How do you feel now? If you massage yourself and stretch every day, you will feel healthier. ___ⓕ___, you can focus ___ⓖ___ your studies better.

출제율 95%
27 위 글의 빈칸 ⓐ~ⓒ에 알맞은 말을 〈보기〉에서 골라 쓰시오.

┤ 보기 ├
> hold   place   bend

ⓐ _____ ⓑ _____ ⓒ _____

출제율 100%
28 위 글의 빈칸 ⓓ와 ⓖ에 알맞은 말이 바르게 짝지어진 것은?

① up – on
② on – in
③ in – of
④ off – to
⑤ on – about

출제율 90%
29 위 글의 빈칸 ⓔ에 알맞은 것은?

① tighten your right foot
② relax your left leg
③ make your left leg strong
④ straighten up your position
⑤ loosen up your right leg

출제율 85%
30 위 글의 빈칸 ⓕ에 알맞은 것은?

① But
② And
③ Or
④ Also
⑤ So

[01~02] 괄호 안의 단어를 바르게 배열하여 대화를 완성하시오.
(필요하면 어형을 바꿀 것)

01 중요

A: (how / do / massage / know / you / to)
  legs?
B: Yes, I do.

➡ _____

02

A: Kate, what do you enjoy doing to be
  healthy?
B: (catch / enjoy / I / play).

➡ _____

03 다음 대화의 밑줄 친 말을 주어진 표현을 이용하여 영작하시오.

A: Are you good at solving math problems?
B: No, 나는 수학을 잘 못해. (be good at)

➡ _____

04 중요 자연스러운 대화가 되도록 (A)~(D)의 순서를 바르게 배열하시오.

(A) Sounds cool. What can you make?
(B) I can make salad, Bibimbap, and
  vegetable juice.
(C) I enjoy cooking healthy food.
(D) What do you enjoy doing after school?

➡ _____

05 중요 다음 문장에서 어법상 <u>어색한</u> 부분을 고쳐 다시 쓰시오.

(1) I will have my brother cleaned my room.

  ➡ _____

(2) Inhui made her daughter did the dishes.

  ➡ _____

(3) My mother let me to watch the TV drama.

  ➡ _____

06 다음 괄호 안의 어구를 이용하여 우리말을 영어로 옮기시오.

(1) 열이 있으면 너는 의사의 진찰을 받아야 한다.
  (have, you, a, fever, should, see, doctor)

  ➡ _____

(2) 내일 비가 오면 난 영화 보러 갈 거야.
  (rains, tomorrow, it, go, a movie)

  ➡ _____

(3) 파란색에 노란색을 섞으면 초록색이 된다.
  (add, to, blue, green, yellow, you, become)

  ➡ _____

07 다음 주어진 어구를 바르게 배열하시오.

(1) (makes / my / clean / mother / my / me /
  room)

  ➡ _____

(2) (librarian / find / the / a / helped / book /
  me)

  ➡ _____

(3) (safely / her / they / go / let)

  ➡ _____

Let's begin with the eyes. Close your eyes and massage them softly with your fingers. It will relax your eyes. When you finish, cover your eyes with your hands to block out the light. ⓐIt will make your eyes feel more comfortable.

Next, massage your neck. Put your fingers on the back of your neck. Draw small circles with your fingers to massage your neck. Massage from top to bottom. ⓑ마사지는 여러분의 기분이 좋아지도록 도울 것이다.

08 How do we massage our eyes with our fingers? Answer in English.

➡ _____

09 위 글의 밑줄 친 ⓐ를 우리말로 옮기시오.

➡ _____

10 What can we do to massage our neck? Answer in English.

➡ _____

11 위 글의 밑줄 친 ⓑ의 우리말에 맞도록 괄호 안의 어구를 순서대로 배열하시오.

(will / the / feel / help / you / better / massage)

➡ _____

ⓐHere are my plan to be healthier.
1. I will exercise more than three times a week.
2. I will eat breakfast every day.
  If I exercise more than three times a week, I will become stronger. Also, if I eat breakfast every day, I will feel better in the morning. I will change my habits, and ⓑit will ⓒ (healthy / live / a / me / make / life).

12 위 글의 밑줄 친 ⓐ에서 어법상 틀린 부분을 찾아 바르게 고쳐 쓰시오.

_____ ➡ _____

13 How many times a week does the writer plan to exercise? Answer in English.

➡ _____
_____

14 위 글의 밑줄 친 ⓑit이 가리키는 것을 우리말로 쓰시오.

➡ _____

15 위 글의 괄호 ⓒ 안의 단어들을 바르게 배열하시오.

➡ _____

창의사고력 서술형 문제

01 다음 주어진 표현을 보고, 자신이 할 수 있는 일에 ∨표 한 후, 〈보기〉와 같이 대화문을 완성하시오.

- shop on the Internet ( )
- cook instant noodles ( )

┤ 보기 ├

A: Do you know how to make fresh salad?
B: Yes, I know how to make fresh salad. / No, I don't know how to make fresh salad.

(1) A: _____

　　 B: _____

(2) A: _____

　　 B: _____

02 다음과 같은 상황이 벌어진다면 어떨지 상상하여 〈보기〉와 같이 쓰시오.

- get an A on the math test
- go to Paris
- it is sunny tomorrow
- find an abandoned dog on the street

* abandoned dog: 유기견

┤ 보기 ├

If I get an A on the math test, I will be very happy.

(1) _____

(2) _____

(3) _____

03 다음 〈보기〉의 사역동사들을 이용하여 문장을 4개 쓰시오. (필요시 형태를 바꿀 것)

┤ 보기 ├

let　　make　　help　　have

(1) _____

(2) _____

(3) _____

(4) _____

단원별 모의고사

01 다음 영영풀이에 해당하는 단어로 알맞은 것은?

> either of the two parts of the body between the top of each arm and the neck

① hip ② waist
③ back ④ chest
⑤ shoulder

02 다음 중 밑줄 친 우리말 뜻이 잘못된 것은?

① Massage from top to bottom.
　　　　　위에서부터 아래까지
② I think you should see a doctor.
　　　　　　　　　병원에 가다
③ For a few seconds nobody said anything.
　오랫동안
④ You and your partner should move at the same speed. 같은 속도로
⑤ Both of my sisters moved even farther away from home. 둘 다

03 다음 빈칸에 공통으로 알맞은 것은?

> • She has a pretty _____.
> • Stand close to each other and _____ your partner.

① step ② store ③ place
④ face ⑤ switch

04 다음 짝지어진 두 단어의 관계가 같도록 빈칸에 알맞은 말을 쓰시오.

> hungry : full = complicated : _____

05 다음 영영풀이에 해당하는 단어를 주어진 철자로 시작하여 쓰시오.

> an opinion or suggestion about what someone should do

➡ a_____

06 다음 대화의 밑줄 친 부분과 의미가 같은 것은?

> A: Do you know how to download photos from the Internet?
> B: Yes. I do. I'm good at using computers.

① Do you want to download photos?
② Can I download photos from the Internet?
③ May I download photos from the Internet?
④ Would you mind downloading photos from the Internet?
⑤ Can you download photos from the Internet?

07 다음 밑줄 친 말과 바꿔 쓸 수 있는 것을 모두 고르면?

> A: What do you enjoy doing to be healthy?
> B: I enjoy riding a bike.

① I can ride a bike.
② I like to ride a bike.
③ I want to ride a bike.
④ I will ride a bike.
⑤ I feel great when I ride a bike.

[08~11] 다음 대화를 읽고, 물음에 답하시오.

> Karl: Hana, what's the matter?
>
> Hana: Well, I'm stressed about the test next week.
>
> Karl: I understand. I ride my longboard ⓐ ____ I'm stressed. ⓑ<u>Do you know how to ride a longboard?</u>
>
> Hana: No, I don't.
>
> Karl: Let's go out! I can teach you. Put one foot on the board and push hard with ⓒ ____ .
>
> Hana: Like this? Wow! This is fun. I feel better already.
>
> Karl: See? I enjoy riding my longboard ⓓ ____ it reduces my stress.
>
> Hana: That's great!

08 위 대화의 빈칸 ⓐ와 ⓓ에 알맞은 말이 바르게 짝지어진 것은?

① if – as
② when – because
③ as – for
④ if – before
⑤ while – because of

09 위 대화의 밑줄 친 ⓑ와 의미가 <u>다른</u> 것을 <u>모두</u> 고르시오.

① Can you ride a longboard?
② Are you riding a longboard?
③ Are you good at riding a longboard?
④ How can I ride a longboard?
⑤ Are you able to ride a longboard?

10 위 대화의 빈칸 ⓒ에 알맞은 것은?

① two
② others
③ the other
④ the second
⑤ the others

11 Explain how to ride the longboard. Answer in Korean.

➡ _____

12 다음 문장의 빈칸에 알맞은 것은?

> Why don't you cook some soup ____ you're hungry?

① and
② but
③ if
④ where
⑤ because

13 다음 문장에서 어법상 틀린 부분을 찾아 고쳐 쓰시오.

> Brian makes his dad feels comfortable.

_____ ➡ _____

14 다음 문장의 빈칸에 알맞은 것은?

> The police officer let the children ____ the road.

① cross
② crossing
③ to cross
④ to crossing
⑤ crossed

15 다음 밑줄 친 ①~⑤ 중 어법상 틀린 것은?

> My father <u>will buy</u> <u>me</u> a computer <u>if</u> I
> ①   ②   ③
> <u>will get</u> a perfect score <u>in the final exam</u>.
> ④   ⑤

16 다음 괄호 안에 주어진 단어를 이용하여 우리말을 영어로 옮기시오. (필요하면 어형을 바꿀 것)

> 나의 형은 나에게 방을 청소하라고 시켰다.
> (have)

➡ _____

17 다음 두 문장의 뜻이 같도록 빈칸에 알맞은 말을 쓰시오.

> If you don't hurry up, you will miss the bus.
> = _____ you hurry up, you will miss the bus.

18 다음 중 밑줄 친 make의 쓰임이 다른 하나는?

① He made the dog sit down.
② Mom made him some tea.
③ It makes you have more energy.
④ The Reading Club makes you read faster.
⑤ She made us work again.

19 다음 중 어법상 어색한 것은?

① I'll phone you if I'll have time.
② If you don't have a ticket, you can't come in.
③ We can be in Seoul by 10 if we catch the first train.
④ If you don't give me my money, I'm going to the police.
⑤ If it is sunny tomorrow, we'll have the party outside.

[20~21] 다음 글을 읽고, 물음에 답하시오.

> Place the ⓐbottom of your right foot on the desk behind you. Then, slowly ⓑbend your left leg and ⓒlower yourself. ⓓHold it for a few seconds and slowly ⓔstraighten up. This position will _____ your right leg. Switch your legs and repeat the exercise.

20 위 글의 밑줄 친 ⓐ~ⓔ 중 문맥상 어색한 것은?

① ⓐ   ② ⓑ   ③ ⓒ   ④ ⓓ   ⑤ ⓔ

21 위 글의 빈칸에 알맞은 것은?

① block out   ② team up
③ fasten up   ④ loosen up
⑤ get along with

[22~23] 다음 글을 읽고, 물음에 답하시오.

> Next, massage your neck. ⓐ _____ your fingers on the back of your neck. Draw small circles with your fingers to massage your neck. ⓑ위에서 아래로 마사지해라. The massage will help you feel better.

22 문맥상 위 글의 빈칸 ⓐ에 알맞은 것은?

① Put   ② Pull
③ Bend   ④ Move
⑤ Cover

23 위 글의 밑줄 친 ⓑ의 우리말에 맞게 주어진 단어를 바르게 배열하시오.

> (bottom / to / massage / top / from)

➡ _____

[24~27] 다음 글을 읽고, 물음에 답하시오.

Let's work on your waist. Team up with a friend. Stand close to each other and __(A)__ your partner. Hold each other's wrists. Slowly __(B)__ your head and body backward. Hold that position ⓐ three seconds. Then, slowly __(C)__ each other to a standing position. You and your partner should move ⓑ the same speed. ⓒIf you won't, both of you will fall!

24 위 글의 빈칸 (A)~(C)에 알맞은 말이 바르게 짝지어진 것은?

① face – pull – stretch
② pull – stretch – face
③ stretch – face – pull
④ face – stretch – pull
⑤ pull – face – stretch

25 위 글의 빈칸 ⓐ와 ⓑ에 알맞은 말이 바르게 짝지어진 것은?

① at – in
② during – at
③ for – at
④ for – with
⑤ during – with

26 위 글에서 다음 영영풀이에 해당하는 단어를 찾아 쓰시오.

the way someone stands, sits, or lies down

➡ _____

27 위 글의 밑줄 친 ⓒ에서 어법상 틀린 부분을 찾아 바르게 고쳐 쓰시오.

_____ ➡ _____

[28~30] 다음 글을 읽고, 물음에 답하시오.

At school you sit for many hours. (①) Do you get tired? (②) Why don't you massage yourself and stretch?
(③) Let's begin with the eyes. (④) Close your eyes and massage them softly with your fingers. (⑤) When you finish, cover your eyes with your hands to block ⓐ the light. ⓑIt will make your eyes to feel more comfortable.

28 위 글의 ①~⑤ 중 주어진 문장이 들어갈 알맞은 곳은?

It will relax your eyes.

①　　②　　③　　④　　⑤

29 위 글의 빈칸 ⓐ에 알맞은 것은?

① up
② out
③ off
④ into
⑤ over

30 위 글의 밑줄 친 ⓑ에서 어법상 틀린 부분을 찾아 바르게 고쳐 쓰시오.

_____ ➡ _____

To Be a Global Citizen

의사소통 기능

- 의도 묻기
  Are you going to eat all of that?
- 희망 표현하기
  I hope we can save the Earth.

언어 형식

- 주격 관계대명사
  Global citizens are people **who** try to understand different cultures.
- something/anything/nothing/everything + 형용사
  You did **something wonderful**.

Words & Expressions

Key Words

□ **adult**[ədʌ́lt] 명 어른

□ **aim**[eim] 동 ~을 목표로 삼다, 지향하다

□ **alongside**[əlɔ́ŋsáid] 전 ~ 옆에, 나란히

□ **American**[əmérikən] 형 미국의 명 미국인

□ **awesome**[ɔ́:səm] 형 굉장한, 감탄할 만한, 엄청난

□ **bag**[bæg] 명 가방

□ **campaign**[kæmpéin] 명 캠페인, 조직적 활동

□ **celebrate**[séləbrèit] 동 (특별한 날·경사 등을) 축하하다, 기념하다

□ **citizen**[sítəzən] 명 시민

□ **communicate**[kəmjú:nəkèit] 동 의사소통하다

□ **community**[kəmjú:nəti] 명 공동체

□ **education**[èdʒukéiʃən] 명 교육

□ **environment**[inváiərənmənt] 명 자연환경, 환경

□ **far**[fɑːr] 부 멀리 형 먼

□ **fight**[fait] 명 싸움 동 싸우다

□ **flood**[flʌd] 명 홍수

□ **garden**[gɑ́ːrdn] 명 정원

□ **gather**[gǽðər] 동 모으다

□ **global**[glóubəl] 형 전 세계적인, 지구상의

□ **hold**[hould] 동 (회의, 시합 등을) 열다

□ **hunger**[hʌ́ŋgər] 명 기아, 배고픔

□ **hurt**[həːrt] 동 다치게 하다

□ **international**[ìntərnǽʃənəl] 형 국제적인

□ **join**[dʒɔin] 동 참여하다

□ **Kenyan**[kénjən] 형 케냐의

□ **lantern**[lǽntərn] 명 랜턴, 등불, 등

□ **leave**[liːv] 동 남기다

□ **messy**[mési] 형 엉망진창의

□ **nothing**[nʌ́θiŋ] 대 아무것도 ~ 아니다

□ **plate**[pleit] 명 접시

□ **poor**[puər] 형 가난한

□ **produce**[prədjúːs] 동 생산하다

□ **protect**[prətékt] 동 보호하다

□ **raise**[reiz] 동 (자금 등을) 모금하다

□ **recycle**[riːsáikl] 동 (폐기물을) 재활용하다

□ **save**[seiv] 동 살리다, 구하다

□ **sell**[sel] 동 팔다

□ **send**[send] 동 보내다, 전하다

□ **share**[ʃɛər] 동 같이 쓰다, 공유하다

□ **site**[sait] 명 (인터넷의) 사이트

□ **take**[teik] 동 가져가다

□ **trash**[træʃ] 명 쓰레기

□ **upload**[ʌplóud] 동 업로드하다, 올리다

□ **upset**[ʌ́pset] 형 당황한

□ **waste**[weist] 동 낭비하다, 허비하다

Key Expressions

□ **be going to 동사원형** ~할 것이다

□ **be good at** ~을 잘하다

□ **care about** ~에 관심을 가지다

□ **care for** ~을 돌보다, 신경 쓰다

□ **die of** ~으로 죽다

□ **do volunteer work** 자원 봉사를 하다

□ **go well** 잘 되다

□ **in need** 어려움에 처한

□ **send+간접목적어(사람)+직접목적어(사물)**
 …에게 ~을 보내다

□ **share A(사물) with B(사람)**
 A를 B와 나누다[나눠 가지다]

□ **take a shower** 샤워를 하다

□ **thanks to** ~ 덕분에

□ **throw away** ~을 버리다

□ **turn down the heat** (실내) 온도를 낮추다

□ **turn on** (전등·불·텔레비전·라디오 등을) 켜다

□ **watch out (for)** (~에 대해서) 조심하다

Word Power

※ 서로 반대되는 뜻을 가진 단어

□ **far**(멀리; 먼) ↔ **near**(가까운)

□ **sell**(팔다) ↔ **buy**(사다)

□ **poor**(가난한) ↔ **rich**(부유한)

□ **arrive**(도착하다) ↔ **leave**(떠나다)

※ 서로 비슷한 뜻을 가진 단어

□ **gather**(모으다) : **collect**(모으다)

□ **save**(살리다, 구하다) : **rescue**(구출하다, 구조하다)

□ **global**(전 세계적인) : **worldwide**(세계적인)

□ **upset**(당황한) : **worried**(걱정스러운, 당황하는)

English Dictionary

□ **adult** 어른
→ a grown-up person 성인이 된 사람

□ **aim** ~을 목표로 삼다, 지향하다
→ to plan or hope to achieve something
어떤 것을 성취하는 것을 계획하거나 희망하다

□ **alongside** 옆에, 나란히
→ along the side of something, or close to the side of it
어떤 것의 옆을 따라서 혹은 옆에 가까이

□ **celebrate** (특별한 날·경사 등을) 축하하다, 기념하다
→ to do something enjoyable on a special occasion
특별한 경우에 즐거운 어떤 것을 하다

□ **communicate** 의사소통하다
→ to share or exchange information or emotion with someone 다른 사람과 정보나 감정을 나누거나 교환하다

□ **community** 공동체
→ a group of people who live in the same area or who are similar in some way
같은 지역에 사는 사람들이나 어떤 방식으로 비슷한 사람들의 모임

□ **education** 교육
→ the activity of teaching or training students in school, etc. 학교 등에서 학생들을 가르치거나 훈련시키는 활동

□ **environment** 자연환경, 환경
→ the nature where there are land, sea, air, plants, and animals 육지, 바다, 공기, 식물 및 동물이 있는 자연

□ **fight** 싸우다
→ to contend in a battle or physical combat
전투나 육체적 싸움으로 다투다

□ **flood** 홍수
→ an overflow of water 물의 넘쳐흐름

□ **garden** 정원
→ a place where you can grow plants
식물을 기를 수 있는 장소

□ **gather** 모으다
→ to bring people together or collect things together
사람이나 사물을 함께 모이도록 하다

□ **global** 전 세계적인, 지구상의
→ including the whole world 전 세계를 포함하는

□ **hurt** 다치게 하다
→ to injure or cause pain to a part of someone's body
어떤 사람의 신체 일부에 부상을 입히거나 고통을 유발하다

□ **lantern** 랜턴, 등불, 등
→ a lamp in a metal frame with glass sides and with a handle on top so you can carry it
금속 테두리와 유리로 된 옆면 그리고 위에 손잡이가 달려 갖고 다닐 수 있는 램프

□ **messy** 엉망진창의
→ untidy or dirty 깔끔하지 못하거나 더러운

□ **raise** (자금 등을) 모금하다
→ to collect money for a particular purpose
특정한 목적을 위해 돈을 모으다

□ **recycle** (폐기물을) 재활용하다
→ to process used or waste materials so as to make suitable for reuse
사용된 재료나 폐기물을 재사용에 알맞게 되도록 처리하다

□ **sell** 팔다
→ to give goods in exchange for money
돈과 교환하여 물건을 주다

□ **upload** 업로드하다
→ to send documents or programs from your computer to a larger system using the Internet
인터넷을 사용해서 문서나 프로그램을 컴퓨터에서 더 큰 시스템으로 보내다

□ **upset** 당황한
→ emotionally disturbed or agitated
감정적으로 매우 교란되거나 동요된

□ **waste** 낭비하다, 허비하다
→ to fail to use time, money, energy, etc. fully or in the sensible or useful way
시간, 돈, 에너지를 완전히 또는 합리적이거나 유용한 방법으로 사용하지 못하다

서답형

01 다음 짝지어진 두 단어의 관계가 같도록 빈칸에 알맞은 단어를 쓰시오.

> more : less – _____ : near

[02~03] 다음 빈칸에 들어갈 말로 적절한 것은?

02

> The heavy rain resulted in the _____.

① flood   ② earthquake

③ drought   ④ weather

⑤ environment

중요

03

> A very large _____ is called a city.

① population   ② experience

③ site   ④ community

⑤ situation

[04~05] 다음 영영 풀이에 해당하는 단어를 고르시오.

04

> to send documents or programs from your computer to a larger system using the Internet

① take   ② leave

③ update   ④ upload

⑤ post

05

> a person who lives in a country or town legally

① adult   ② citizen

③ lawyer   ④ village

⑤ community

중요

06 밑줄 친 부분의 의미가 잘못된 것은?

① Will you plant roses in your garden this year? (정원)

② Charlie entered a Kenyan middle school. (케냐의)

③ The town will hold a festival this year. (잡다, 쥐다)

④ She saw the light of a lantern in the distance. (등불, 등)

⑤ Many workers come from poor areas. (가난한)

서답형

[07~08] 다음 밑줄 친 부분과 의미가 가장 가까운 것을 주어진 철자로 시작하여 쓰시오.

07

> Teaching and learning is the most important thing to change the world.

➡ E_____

08

> He wants to be the CEO of a worldwide company.

➡ g_____

서답형

09 다음 주어진 우리말에 맞게 빈칸을 채우시오.

(1) 어떤 종류의 가방을 원해?

➡ What _____ of _____ do you want?

(2) 그들은 사과를 판매한다.

➡ They _____ some apples.

01 다음 우리말에 맞게 주어진 단어를 바르게 배열하시오.

(1) 차들이 우리와 나란히 움직이고 있다.

(moving, us, the cars, alongside, are)

➡ _____

(2) 같은 나라의 시민들은 같은 국적을 가지고 있다.

(citizens, the, nationality, the, of, same, country, same, have)

➡ _____
_____

(3) 그 폭우로 홍수가 났다.

(the flood, rain, heavy, in, the, resulted)

➡ _____

(4) 우리는 궁핍한 사람들을 돕기 위해 모금하기로 결정했다.

(to, for, needy, decided, we, people, the, raise, money)

➡ _____
_____

02 다음 빈칸에 알맞은 단어를 〈보기〉에서 골라 쓰시오. (형태 변화 가능)

보기
communicate   leave   gather   celebrate

(1) We _____ with each other in English.

(2) He has _____ information on the Internet.

(3) She _____ my birthday last year.

(4) He _____ food on his plate yesterday.

03 주어진 단어를 활용하여 빈칸에 알맞은 말을 넣으시오.

(1) They will suffer from _____ and air pollution. (hungry)

(2) This is not a _____ but an international issue. (nation)

04 다음 〈보기〉에서 빈칸에 공통으로 들어갈 단어를 골라 쓰시오.

보기
take   be   care   look

• She wanted to _____ for him for two weeks until he got better.

• He should _____ about others' feeling.

05 다음 주어진 우리말에 맞게 빈칸을 채우시오. (철자가 주어진 것도 있음)

(1) 그는 어려운 수학 문제 푸는 것을 잘한다.

➡ He _____ difficult math problems.

(2) 네 도움 덕분에 나는 그것을 할 수 있었다.

➡ _____ your help, I was able to do it.

(3) 너는 실내 온도를 낮출 거니?

➡ Are you _____ to _____ _____ the heat?

(4) 그들은 크리스마스와 새해를 함께 기념해.

➡ They c_____ Christmas and New Year's Day together.

Conversation

1 의도 묻기

Are you going to eat all of that? 너 그걸 다 먹을 거니?

- 의도나 계획을 묻는 표현으로 'Are you planning to 동사원형 ~?', 'Are you going to 동사원형 ~?', 'Are you trying to 동사원형 ~?' 등이 있으며, '너는 ~할 계획이니?' 또는 '너는 ~할 거니?'의 의미로 쓰인다.

- 'I'm planning to 동사원형 ~.'은 '나는 ~할 계획이다.'라는 의미이며 미래의 계획이나 의도에 대해 사용하는 표현으로 to 다음에 동사원형이 온다. 비슷한 표현으로 'I'm going to 동사원형~.', 'I'll 동사원형 ~.' 등이 있다.

의도 묻기

- Are you planning to 동사원형 ~? 너는 ~할 거니?
- Are you trying to 동사원형 ~?
- What are you going to do? 너는 무엇을 할 거니?
- Are you going to 동사원형 ~?
- Do you have a plan to 동사원형 ~?

의도 표현하기

- I'm planning to 동사원형 ~.
- I will 동사원형 ~.
- I'm going to 동사원형 ~.

핵심 Check

1. 다음 우리말과 일치하도록 빈칸에 알맞은 말을 쓰시오. (철자가 주어진 것도 있음)

   (1) A: Are _____ p_____ _____ take a dance class? (너는 무용 수업을 받을 계획이니?)

   B: Yes, I _____. (응. 그래.)

   (2) A: _____ _____ _____ planning _____ _____ this weekend?

   (이번 주말에 무엇을 할 계획이니?)

   B: _____ planning _____ visit my grandparents. (조부모님을 방문할 계획이야.)

2. 대화의 순서를 알맞게 배열하시오.

   (A) I'm planning to go hiking. How about you?

   (B) What are you doing this afternoon?

   (C) I'm going to play table tennis.

   ➡ _____

② 희망 표현하기

I hope we can save the Earth. 나는 우리가 지구를 살리기를 바라.

■ 소망을 표현할 때는 동사 want나 hope를 사용할 수 있다. want와 hope는 둘 다 to부정사를 사용한다. 또한 hope는 that절을 목적어로 사용할 수도 있다.

■ 자신이 희망하는 바를 표현할 때에는 'I hope (that) I can ~.(나는 ~할 수 있기를 바라.)', 'I hope to ~.(나는 ~하고 싶어.)', 'I want to ~.(나는 ~하고 싶어.)', 'I'd like to ~.(나는 ~하고 싶어.) 등으로 말할 수 있다.

• I hope that I can read books to the children. 나는 아이들을 위해 책을 읽어줄 수 있기를 바라.

= I hope to read books to the children.

• I hope I can stay with him. 나는 그와 같이 머무르기를 바라.

= I hope to stay with him.

희망 표현하기

• I hope (that) 주어 can 동사 ~. 나는 ~하기를 바라.　　• I hope to 동사원형 ~. 나는 ~하고 싶어.

• I want to 동사원형 ~.　　• I'd like to 동사원형 ~.

핵심 Check

3. 다음 우리말과 일치하도록 빈칸에 알맞은 말을 쓰시오. (철자가 주어진 것도 있음)

(1) A: _____ _____ p_____ to take a swimming lesson after school?

(방과 후에 수영 강습 받을 거니?)

B: Yes, I hope _____ _____ in the sea. (네, 바다에서 수영하고 싶거든요.)

(2) A: Is this present for Mina? (이 선물이 미나를 위한 것이야?)

B: Yes. _____ _____ _____ will like it.

(그래. 나는 그녀가 그것을 좋아하기를 바라.)

4. 주어진 문장과 바꿔 쓸 수 있는 것을 모두 고르시오.

• I hope that I can go on a picnic with my family.

① I want to go on a picnic with my family.

② I need to go on a picnic with my family.

③ I hope to go on a picnic with my family.

④ I should go on a picnic with my family.

⑤ I can go on a picnic with my family.

Listen & Speak ① A-1

B: Did you watch the news ❶about the flood?

G: Yes, I ❷did. They said ❸a lot of people ❹lost their homes.

B: My club ❺is going to send them some money.

G: How can you do ❻that? Are you going to ❼raise money, Andy?

B: Yes. We're going to make pencil cases and ❽sell them.

B: 홍수에 대한 뉴스를 보았니?

G: 응, 보았어. 많은 사람들이 집을 잃었다고 하더라.

B: 우리 동아리는 그들에게 약간의 돈을 보낼 거야.

G: 그것을 어떻게 할 수 있니? 돈을 모금할 거니, Andy?

B: 응. 우리는 필통을 만들어서 그것들을 팔 거야.

❶ about the flood은 '홍수에 대한'의 의미로 앞의 the news를 수식하고 있다. flood: 홍수

❷ 'Did you ~?'로 질문하고 있으므로, 대답으로 'Yes, I did.' 또는 'No, I didn't.'가 나올 수 있다.

❸ said 뒤에는 접속사 that이 생략되어 있다. a lot of: 많은 (= lots of = many)

❹ lost는 lose(잃다)의 과거형이다. (lose-lost-lost)

❺ 'be going to 동사원형 ~'은 '~할 것이다'의 의미로 의도를 나타낼 때 사용하는 표현이다.

❻ 여기서 that은 앞 문장의 'to send them some money'를 의미한다.

❼ raise: (자금 등을) 모으다, 모금하다

❽ sell은 접속사 and에 의해 make와 병렬 구조를 이루고 있다. them은 pencil cases를 의미한다.

Check(√) True or False

(1) Because of the flood, a few people lost their homes.   T ☐ F ☐

(2) The girl didn't watch the news about the flood.   T ☐ F ☐

Listen & Speak ② A-1

G: ❶What are you doing, Jason?

B: I'm making a poster about ❷global hunger. ❸Many people are dying of hunger.

G: ❹That's too bad. I didn't know that.

B: I hope ❺more people ❻care about global hunger.

G: 무엇을 하고 있니, Jason?

B: 세계의 기아 문제에 대한 포스터를 만드는 중이야. 많은 사람들이 기아로 죽어가고 있어.

G: 정말 안됐다. 난 몰랐어.

B: 더 많은 사람들이 세계의 기아 문제에 관심을 갖기를 바라.

❶ 현재진행형(be동사의 현재형+동사ing)을 사용하여, 지금 진행하고 있는 일이 무엇인지 질문하고 있다.

❷ global: 전 세계적인, 지구상의(= worldwide) hunger: 기아, 배고픔

❸ people은 '사람들'이라는 의미로 much가 아닌 many로 수식한다. dying은 die의 현재분사형이다. hunger: 기아, 배고픔

❹ 'That's too bad.'는 유감을 표현하는 말로 'I'm sorry to hear that.(그 말을 들으니 유감이다.)'으로 바꾸어 쓸 수 있다.

❺ hope와 more 사이에 접속사 that이 생략되어 있다.

❻ care about: ~에 관심을 가지다 global: 전 세계적인, 지구상의

Check(√) True or False

(3) The boy wants many people to care about global hunger.   T ☐ F ☐

(4) The girl didn't know that many people are dying of hunger.   T ☐ F ☐

Listen & Speak ① A-2

B: Do you have any plans for the summer vacation, Suji?

G: Yes. ❶I'm going to the Philippines ❷to ❸do some volunteer work with my family.

B: Oh, ❹I went there and helped some children study last year. ❺Are you going to do that, too?

G: Yes. And I'll also paint walls with the children.

B: That ❻sounds nice.

❶ be going to 동사원형: ∼할 것이다(의도나 계획을 말하는 표현)
❷ to부정사의 부사적 용법 중 목적(∼하기 위해서)의 의미로 사용되었다.
❸ do volunteer work: 자원 봉사를 하다
❹ went와 helped는 접속사 and로 연결되어 있는 동사 병렬구조이고, last year(작년에)라는 과거 시간의 부사구가 있기 때문에 과거형 동사로 사용되었다. there는 to the Philippines를 의미한다.
❺ Are you going to 동사원형 ∼?: 너는 ∼할 계획이니?, 너는 ∼할 거니? (= Are you planning to 동사원형 ∼?)
❻ sound+형용사: ∼하게 들리다

Listen & Speak ② A-2

G: Dad, my class ❶decided to make a vegetable ❷garden.

M: A vegetable garden? ❸What will you grow there, Sena?

G: Carrots. ❹We'll grow them and share them with others.

M: That's a good idea.

G: I hope ❺the carrots grow well.

❶ decide는 동명사가 아닌 to부정사(to 동사원형)를 목적어로 취하는 동사이다.
❷ garden: 정원
❸ What will you grow there?: 거기서 무엇을 기를 거니? (= What are you going to grow there? = What are you planning to grow there?)
❹ grow와 share는 접속사 and로 연결되어 있는 동사 병렬구조이다. them은 carrots를 의미한다. others: 다른 사람들
❺ hope와 the carrots 사이에 접속사 that이 생략되어 있다. hope는 목적어로 to부정사와 that절을 취할 수 있다. grow: 기르다, 재배하다

Listen & Speak ① B-1

A: ❶Are you going to ❷take a short shower?

B: ❸Yes, I am.

❶ Are you going to 동사원형 ∼?: ∼할 거니?(의도나 계획 묻기)
❷ take a shower: 샤워하다
❸ 'Are you ∼?'로 질문하였으므로 'Yes, I am.' 또는 'No, I'm not.'으로 대답할 수 있다.

Listen & Speak ② B-1

A: I hope ❶people don't throw away trash.

B: I hope so, too. ❷Let's ❸hold a Keep the World Clean campaign.

A: ❹That's a good idea.

❶ hope와 people 사이에 접속사 that이 생략되어 있다. throw away: ∼을 버리다 trash: 쓰레기
❷ Let's 동사원형: ∼하자 / 어떤 활동을 함께 하자고 제안할 경우에는 'Why don't we+동사?' 혹은 'Let's+동사'를 사용할 수 있다.
❸ hold: (회의, 시합 등을) 열다
❹ 'That's a good idea.(좋은 생각이야.)'는 상대방이 말한 의견에 대해 동의하는 표현이다.

Wrap Up 1

B: ❶What's your plan for the weekend, Sumin? Are you going to do ❷anything special?

G: Yes. ❸On Saturday, ❹I'm going to visit my grandmother.

B: ❺How about on Sunday?

G: I have no plans for Sunday. Why?

B: I'm going to ❻do volunteer work at the library on Sunday. ❼Would you like to come with me?

❶ What's your plan for the weekend?: 너의 주말 계획은 뭐니?(= What are you going to do this weekend? = What are you planning to do this weekend?)
❷ '-thing', '-body', '-one'으로 끝나는 대명사는 형용사가 뒤에서 수식한다.
❸ 요일 앞에는 전치사 on을 사용한다.
❹ I'm going to 동사원형: 나는 ∼할 거야. (의도 표현)
❺ How about on Sunday?: 일요일은 어때? (= What about on Sunday?)
❻ do volunteer work: 자원 봉사를 하다
❼ Would you like to 동사원형 ∼?: ∼할래?(요청, 제안하는 표현)

● 다음 우리말과 일치하도록 빈칸에 알맞은 말을 쓰시오.

Listen & Speak 1 A

1. **B:** Did you watch the news _____ _____ _____?
   G: Yes, _____ _____. They said a _____ of people _____ their homes.
   B: My club is going _____ _____ them some money.
   G: _____ can you do that? _____ _____ going _____ _____ money, Andy?
   B: Yes. We're _____ _____ make pencil cases and _____ them.

2. **B:** Do you have any _____ for the summer _____, Suji?
   G: Yes. I'm _____ _____ the Philippines to _____ some volunteer work _____ my family.
   B: Oh, I _____ there and _____ some children study last year. _____ _____ _____ _____ _____ that, too?
   G: Yes. And I'll also _____ _____ with the children.
   B: That sounds nice.

Listen & Speak 1 B

1. **A:** Are you going _____ _____ a short shower?
   B: Yes, I _____. / No, _____ _____.

2. **A:** Are you _____ _____ _____ bottles?
   B: Yes, _____ _____. / No, I'm not.

Listen & Speak 2 A

1. **G:** _____ are you doing, Jason?
   B: I'm _____ a poster _____ global _____. Many people are _____ of hunger.
   G: That's _____ _____. I didn't know that.
   B: I _____ more people _____ _____ _____ hunger.

해석

1. **B:** 홍수에 대한 뉴스를 보았니?
   G: 응, 보았어. 많은 사람들이 집을 잃었다고 하더라.
   B: 우리 동아리는 그들에게 약간의 돈을 보낼 거야.
   G: 그것을 어떻게 할 수 있니? 돈을 모금할 거니, Andy?
   B: 응. 우리는 필통을 만들어서 그것들을 팔 거야.

2. **B:** 여름 방학에 어떤 계획이 있니, 수지야?
   G: 응. 나는 나의 가족들과 봉사활동을 하러 필리핀에 갈 거야.
   B: 오, 나는 작년에 그곳에 가서 몇몇 아이들이 공부하는 것을 도와줬어. 너도 그렇게 할 거니?
   G: 응, 그리고 나는 또한 아이들과 벽화를 그릴 거야.
   B: 정말 좋겠다.

1. **A:** 너는 샤워를 짧게 할 거니?
   B: 응, 그럴 거야. / 아니, 그러지 않을 거야.

2. **A:** 너는 병을 재활용할 거니?
   B: 응, 그럴 거야. / 아니, 그러지 않을 거야.

1. **G:** 무엇을 하고 있니, Jason?
   B: 세계의 기아 문제에 대한 포스터를 만드는 중이야. 많은 사람들이 기아로 죽어가고 있어.
   G: 정말 안됐다. 난 몰랐어.
   B: 더 많은 사람들이 세계의 기아 문제에 관심을 갖기를 바라.

2. **G:** Dad, my class decided _____ _____ a vegetable _____.

M: A _____ _____? What _____ you grow there, Sena?

G: Carrots. We'll _____ them and _____ them _____ others.

M: That's a good idea.

G: I _____ the carrots _____ well.

Listen & Speak 2 B

1. **A:** I _____ people _____ _____ _____ trash.

B: I _____ _____, too. _____ _____ a Keep the World Clean _____.

A: That's a good idea.

2. **A:** _____ _____ _____ _____ hurt animals.

B: I hope _____, too. _____ _____ a Love Animals campaign.

A: That's a good idea.

Wrap Up

1. **B:** _____ _____ _____ for the weekend, Sumin? _____ you going _____ _____ _____ _____?

G: Yes. _____ Saturday, I'm _____ _____ visit my grandmother.

B: How _____ _____ Sunday?

G: I _____ no plans for Sunday. Why?

B: I'm _____ _____ _____ _____ _____ at the library on Sunday. Would you _____ _____ _____ with me?

G: Sure.

2. **G:** My club is _____ _____ _____ a green campaign _____ school next Friday.

B: _____ _____ a green campaign?

G: It's a campaign to _____ the environment. Many students _____ _____ _____ the streets. We hope _____ _____ that.

B: I _____ your campaign _____ well.

G: Thanks. I hope so, too.

해석

2. **G:** 아빠, 우리 반은 채소밭을 가꾸기로 했어요.

M: 채소밭? 거기서 무엇을 기를 거니, 세나야?

G: 당근이요. 우리는 그것을 길러서 사람들과 나눌 거예요.

M: 좋은 생각이구나.

G: 당근이 잘 자랐으면 좋겠어요.

1. **A:** 나는 사람들이 쓰레기를 버리지 않기를 바라.

B: 나도 그렇게 생각해. '세상을 깨끗하게 하라'라는 캠페인을 열자.

A: 좋은 생각이야.

2. **A:** 나는 사람들이 동물을 해치지 않기를 바라.

B: 나도 그렇게 생각해. '동물을 사랑하라'라는 캠페인을 열자.

A: 좋은 생각이야.

1. **B:** 너의 주말 계획은 뭐니, 수민아? 특별한 걸 할 거니?

G: 응. 토요일에 할머니를 방문할 거야.

B: 일요일은 어때?

G: 일요일은 아무 계획 없어. 왜?

B: 나는 일요일에 도서관에서 봉사활동을 할 거야. 나와 함께 갈래?

G: 물론이지.

2. **G:** 우리 동아리는 다음 주 금요일에 학교에서 그린 캠페인을 열 거야.

B: 그린 캠페인이 뭐야?

G: 환경을 보호하기 위한 캠페인이야. 많은 학생들이 길에 쓰레기를 버려. 우리는 그걸 멈추길 바라.

B: 네 캠페인이 잘 되길 바라.

G: 고마워. 나도 그러길 바라.

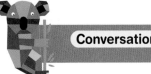

[01~03] 다음 대화의 빈칸에 알맞은 말은?

01

A: Are you going to take a shopping bag?

B: _____

① Yes, I do.　　　　　② No, I don't.
③ Yes, I go.　　　　　④ Yes, I am.
⑤ No, you aren't.

02

A: _____

B: I hope so, too. Let's hold a Love Animals campaign.

① I hope to keep the world clean.
② I'm going to the Philippines to do some volunteer work.
③ I hope people don't hurt animals.
④ I hope that more people care about global hunger.
⑤ I want to turn down the heat.

03

B: What's your plan for the weekend, Sumin? Are you _____ do anything special?

G: Yes. On Saturday, I'm _____ visit my grandmother.

① going to　　② going　　③ planning
④ want　　　　⑤ have to

04 자연스러운 대화가 되도록 순서대로 배열하시오.

(A) Carrots. We'll grow them and share them with others.
(B) Dad, my class decided to make a vegetable garden.
(C) A vegetable garden? What will you grow there, Sena?
(D) That's a good idea.

➡ _____

[01~03] 다음 대화를 읽고 물음에 답하시오.

> G: _____(A)_____, Jason?
> B: I'm making a poster ⓐ global hunger. Many people are dying ⓑ hunger.
> G: _____(B)_____ I didn't know that.
> B: I hope more people care ⓒ global hunger.

01 빈칸 (A)에 알맞은 말을 고르시오.

① What are you planning to do
② What did you do
③ What are you going to do
④ What are you doing
⑤ What will you make

02 빈칸 (B)에 알맞은 말을 모두 고르시오.

① I want to cook food.
② I'm sorry to hear that.
③ Let's hold a Keep the World Clean campaign.
④ I usually like to make a poster.
⑤ That's too bad.

03 빈칸 ⓐ~ⓒ에 알맞은 말로 짝지어진 것은?

	ⓐ	ⓑ	ⓒ
①	about	about	for
②	at	of	for
③	about	about	at
④	about	of	about
⑤	for	for	at

04 다음 중 짝지어진 대화가 <u>어색한</u> 것은?

① A: Are you going to turn down the heat?
　 B: No, I'm not.
② A: I hope to solve this problem.
　 B: I hope so, too.
③ A: Are you going to raise money?
　 B: Yes, we are.
④ A: I hope the air gets cleaner. Let's hold a Plant More Trees campaign.
　 B: That's too bad.
⑤ A: Are you planning to take a swimming lesson after school?
　 B: Yes, I hope to swim in the sea.

[05~06] 다음 대화를 읽고 물음에 답하시오.

> G: Dad, my class decided to make a vegetable garden.
> M: A vegetable garden? What will you grow there, Sena?
> G: ⓐCarrots. We'll grow ⓑthem and share ⓒthem with ⓓothers.
> M: That's a good idea.
> G: I hope ⓔthey grow well.

05 다음 영영풀이에 해당하는 단어를 대화에서 찾아 쓰시오.

> a place where you can grow plants

➡ _____

06 밑줄 친 ⓐ~ⓔ 중 가리키는 것이 <u>다른</u> 것을 고르시오.

① ⓐ　　② ⓑ　　③ ⓒ
④ ⓓ　　⑤ ⓔ

07 밑줄 친 부분과 바꾸어 쓸 수 있는 문장을 <u>모두</u> 고르시오.

> A: <u>Are you going to take a shopping bag?</u>
> B: Yes, I am.

① Do you hope to take a shopping bag?
② Are you planning to take a shopping bag?
③ Do you take a shopping bag?
④ Are you trying to take a shopping bag?
⑤ Do you want to take a shopping bag?

08 빈칸에 알맞은 말을 고르시오.

> A: I hope the air gets cleaner.
> B: I hope so, too. _____

① Let's hold a Plant More Trees campaign.
② Let's hold a Love Animals campaign.
③ Let's hold a Save Water campaign.
④ I'm making a poster about global hunger.
⑤ I hope your campaign goes well.

[09~12] 다음 대화를 읽고 물음에 답하시오.

> Karl: Jiho, isn't that too much? Are you going to eat all of that?
> Jiho: I'm not sure, but Bulgogi is my favorite. (①)
> Karl: Hey! Look at the campaign poster. "Think, Eat, Save!" (②)
> Jiho: What does that mean?
> Karl: It means "Think first before you eat and save the Earth." (③)
> Jiho: I think I took too much Bulgogi. (④)
> Karl: Okay. That's a good idea.

> Jiho: We ate it all. My clean plate makes me feel good. (⑤)
> Karl: Let's not waste ___(A)___ now on. I hope we can save the Earth.

서답형

09 위 대화의 ①~⑤ 중 다음 주어진 말이 들어갈 알맞은 곳은?

> Let's share it.

①   ②   ③   ④   ⑤

서답형

10 다음 영영풀이에 해당하는 단어를 대화에서 찾아 쓰시오.

> to fail to use time, money, energy, etc. fully or in the sensible or useful way

➡ _____

11 빈칸 (A)에 알맞은 것은?

① to   ② from
③ at   ④ of
⑤ with

12 위 대화의 내용과 일치하지 <u>않는</u> 것을 <u>모두</u> 고르시오.

① "Think, Eat, Save!" is on the campaign poster.
② Jiho is sure that he is going to eat all of Bulgogi.
③ Jiho likes Bulgogi.
④ They left some food.
⑤ Karl hopes to save the Earth.

Conversation 서술형 시험대비

[01~03] 다음 대화를 읽고 물음에 답하시오.

B: What's your plan for the weekend, Sumin?
Are you ___(A)___ to do anything special?
G: Yes. On Saturday, I'm ___(B)___ to visit my grandmother.
B: How about on Sunday?
G: I have no ___ⓐ___ for Sunday. Why?
B: I'm ___(C)___ to do volunteer work at the library on Sunday. Would you like to come with me?
G: Sure.

01 (A)~(C)에 공통으로 들어갈 알맞은 말을 두 개 쓰시오. (주어진 철자로 시작할 것)

➡ (1) g_____ (2) p_____

02 빈칸 ⓐ에 알맞은 말을 대화에서 찾아 쓰시오. (복수형으로 쓸 것)

➡ _____

03 According to the dialog, what will Sumin do on the weekend? (Answer in English)

➡ On Saturday, _____,
and on Sunday, _____
_____.

04 대화 속 괄호 안의 단어를 바르게 배열하시오.

A: (own, you, your, cup, going, are, use, to, ?)
B: Yes, I am.

➡ _____

[05~07] 다음 대화를 읽고 물음에 답하시오.

B: Did you watch the news about the flood?
G: Yes, I did. They said a lot of people lost their homes.
B: 우리 동아리는 그들에게 약간의 돈을 보낼 거야.
G: ___(A)___ can you do that? Are you going to raise money, Andy?
B: Yes. We're going to make pencil cases and sell them.

05 다음 영영풀이에 해당하는 단어를 대화에서 찾아 쓰시오.

an overflow of water

➡ _____

06 밑줄 친 우리말을 주어진 단어를 이용하여 영작하시오.

➡ _____
(going, some, them)

07 빈칸 (A)에 알맞은 의문사를 쓰시오.

➡ _____

08 밑줄 친 우리말을 주어진 단어를 이용하여 영작하시오.

A: 나는 사람들이 쓰레기를 버리지 않기를 바라.
(away, don't, hope, trash)
B: I hope so, too. Let's hold a Keep the World Clean campaign.
A: That's a good idea.

➡ _____

Grammar

교과서

① 주격 관계대명사

- Global citizens are people **who** try to understand different cultures.
  세계 시민이란 다른 문화를 이해하려고 노력하는 사람들이다.

- I want to live in a house **that** is not far from the school.
  나는 학교에서 멀지 않은 집에서 살고 싶다.

■ **주격 관계대명사**

앞에 오는 명사를 대신하고 뒤에 오는 절을 선행사에 연결해 주는 대명사와 접속사 역할을 함께하는 것을 관계대명사라고 한다. 관계대명사에는 'who, which, that'이 있다. 관계대명사 뒤에 동사가 나오고 관계대명사가 이끄는 절에서 'who, which, that'이 주어 역할을 할 때 이를 주격 관계대명사라고 한다. 주격 관계대명사가 이끄는 절은 앞에 나온 명사인 선행사를 수식해 준다.

■ **주격 관계대명사의 종류**

선행사	관계대명사
사람	who
사물·동물	which
사람·사물·동물	that

■ **관계대명사로 문장 연결하기**

① 두 문장에서 동일한 대상을 가리키는 단어를 찾는다.

- The man is my friend. He is working in the garden.

② 뒤 문장의 대명사를 관계대명사(who, which, that)로 바꾼다.

- He is working in the garden.
  → who is working in the garden

③ 관계대명사가 이끄는 문장을 선행사 바로 뒤에 붙여 쓴다.

- The man **who** is working in the garden is my friend.

cf. '주격 관계대명사+be동사'는 생략할 수 있다.

e.g. The man (**who is**) working in the garden is my friend.

핵심 Check

1. 괄호 안에서 알맞은 것을 고르시오.

(1) I like the girl (which / who) is wearing a red ribbon.

(2) I like the house which (has / have) big windows.

(3) Ann is the girl (that / which) has blue eyes.

2 something/anything/everything/nothing + 형용사

- You did **something wonderful.** 너는 멋진 일을 했구나.
- Sam didn't do **anything bad.** Sam은 나쁜 일을 하지 않았다.

■ '형용사＋명사'의 어순

명사의 상태나 성격을 나타내는 형용사는 보통 명사 앞에 와서 명사를 꾸며 준다.

- Tom is a **good boy**.
- Ms. Jang is a **nice teacher**.
- This is a very **difficult problem**.

■ 형용사가 뒤에서 꾸며 주는 단어

'something, anything, nothing, everything'처럼 -thing으로 끝나거나 -body, -one으로 끝나는 부정대명사는 형용사가 뒤에서 꾸며 준다.

- I want to eat **something sweet**. 나는 뭔가 단 것이 먹고 싶다.
- Is there **anything interesting**? 뭐 재미있는 것 있니?
- I have **nothing special** to do this weekend. 이번 주말에 해야 할 특별한 일이 없어.
- I did **everything wrong**. 나는 모든 것을 잘못했다.

cf. 'something'은 긍정문에, 'anything'은 부정문과 의문문에 주로 쓰인다.

핵심 Check

2. 괄호 안에서 알맞은 것을 고르시오.

(1) There is (nothing strange / strange nothing) here.

(2) Peter didn't eat (delicious anything / anything delicious) today.

(3) They are holding (anything bright / something bright).

3. 주어진 단어를 바르게 배열하여 문장을 완성하시오.

(1) I need to drink _____. (cool, something)

(2) There is _____ here. (exciting, nothing)

(3) Do you have _____? (sweet, anything)

01 다음 문장에서 어법상 어색한 부분을 바르게 고쳐 쓰시오.

(1) Global citizens are people which try to understand different cultures.

_____ ➡ _____

(2) This is wonderful something.

_____ ➡ _____

(3) I know the girl which is wearing a white dress.

_____ ➡ _____

(4) Kate didn't eat delicious anything yesterday.

_____ ➡ _____

02 다음 빈칸에 들어갈 말로 알맞은 것은?

There is a huge clock _____ called Big Ben.

① who   ② who is   ③ which
④ which is   ⑤ which are

03 두 문장을 한 문장으로 만들 때 빈칸에 알맞은 말을 모두 고르시오.

• I need a woman.
• She can take care of my baby.
➡ I need a woman _____ can take care of my baby.

① whose   ② who   ③ which
④ that   ⑤ what

04 다음 빈칸에 들어갈 말로 알맞은 것은?

Global citizenship education is _____ for the world.

① useful anything   ② useful something
③ something useful   ④ anything useful
⑤ useful nothing

Grammar 시험대비 실력평가

01 다음 중 어법상 어색한 문장은?

① I saw strange something outside.
② I know a girl who wants to be a news reporter.
③ Ben is my neighbor who works in a hospital.
④ Sandra doesn't want to sell anything expensive.
⑤ Look at the dog that is very fat.

서답형

02 다음 우리말에 맞게 주어진 단어를 알맞은 순서로 배열하시오.

(1) 너는 유명한 누군가를 아니?

(do / famous / you / anybody / know)?

➡ _____

(2) 나는 뭔가 다른 것을 해보고 싶다.

(I / want / different / to / something / do).

➡ _____

(3) 너는 무언가 새로운 게 있니?

(have / anything / do / new / you)?

➡ _____

(4) 그는 어제 어떤 아름다운 사람을 만났다.

(he / yesterday / met / beautiful / someone).

➡ _____

서답형

03 다음 대화를 읽고 빈칸에 알맞은 관계대명사를 쓰시오. (that은 제외할 것)

A: The lion _____ is in the cage looks sick.
B: Yes, we should tell this to an animal doctor _____ takes care of animals.

서답형

04 다음 괄호 안에서 알맞은 단어를 고르시오.

(1) Laura was the first woman (who / which) became the president of the country.
(2) Students (who is / who are) good at painting will gather and paint on some walls of schools and parks.
(3) Dave first gave it to the girl (whose / who) was studying history.

05 다음 우리말에 맞게 알맞게 영작한 것은?

옆집에 사는 소녀는 Jenny다.

① Jenny is the girl which live next door.
② The girl which lives next door is Jenny.
③ The girl who live next door is Jenny.
④ Jenny lives next door who is the girl.
⑤ The girl who lives next door is Jenny.

중요

06 다음 문장에서 주격 관계대명사가 쓰인 문장은?

① Ann is the girl whom I was talking to.
② I know a chef who makes great food.
③ I like your jacket whose design is unique.
④ Amy is the girl whose dad is a doctor.
⑤ Jim is the boy who I made friends with.

07 〈보기〉의 밑줄 친 부분과 쓰임이 같은 것은?

> ┤ 보기 ├
> I admire the actress <u>who</u> helps the poor.

① <u>Who</u> won the prize this semester?

② She asked me <u>who</u> you are.

③ Can you tell me <u>who</u> is late for the meeting?

④ He is the man <u>who</u> takes care of some dogs.

⑤ Let me guess <u>who</u> you are thinking of.

08 中요
다음 중 어법상 어색한 것은?

① The company will hire a man that can speak English.

② I met an old lady that showed me the way to the station.

③ This is the girl who gave me the doll.

④ He has two daughters who is doctors.

⑤ I dislike the man that is wearing glasses.

09 서답형
어법상 **틀린** 부분을 찾아 바르게 고치시오.

(1) We have special nothing this weekend.

_____ ➡ _____

(2) Is there something interesting?

_____ ➡ _____

(3) Harry lives in a house who are 100 years old.

_____ ➡ _____

10 中요
다음 빈칸에 들어갈 알맞은 것은?

> There are many people _____ want to take part in the festival.

① who   ② which

③ whose   ④ of which

⑤ whom

11 다음 두 문장을 한 문장으로 바꿀 때 빈칸에 들어갈 말로 바르게 짝지어진 것은?

> • I have two books.
> • The books have many beautiful pictures.
> ➡ I have two books _____ many beautiful pictures.
> • Do you know the man?
> • He is wearing a hat.
> ➡ Do you know the man _____ wearing a hat?

① who have – who is

② who have – which is

③ which have – who is

④ which has – who are

⑤ which has – which is

12 다음 중 어법상 알맞은 것은?

① I like the girl which lives next door.

② Kate sent me a book who was written by Lee Sang.

③ I would like you to meet Ms. Ha whom is a great teacher.

④ Give me the phone whose is on the table.

⑤ They brought my mom the flowers that made her happy.

13 다음 괄호 안에서 알맞은 것을 고르시오.

(1) They enjoy reading books (who / which) are about Abraham Lincoln.
(2) He has two nephews (who / which) live in Rome.
(3) We prepared the surprise party (who / which) was for my daughter.
(4) She is going to meet the woman (who / which) studied abroad with her.

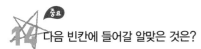

14 다음 빈칸에 들어갈 알맞은 것은?

> I enjoy watching the movie _____ is scary.

① who   ② which
③ whom   ④ whose
⑤ of which

15 다음 우리말에 맞게 주어진 단어를 이용하여 영작하시오.

> 나는 뭔가 단 것이 먹고 싶다.
> (sweet, something)

➡ _____

16 다음 우리말에 맞도록 빈칸에 들어갈 알맞은 말을 쓰시오.

> 우리는 키가 큰 누군가를 찾고 있다.
> ➡ We are looking for _____ _____.

17 다음 밑줄 친 부분과 바꿔 쓸 수 있는 말을 한 단어로 쓰시오.

> There are many people <u>that</u> want to visit Rome.

➡ _____

18 다음 우리말을 바르게 영작한 것은?

> 미진이는 뜨거운 뭔가를 마시기를 원한다.

① Mijin wants to drink something hot.
② Mijin wants to drink hot something.
③ Mijin wants to drink to something hot.
④ Mijin wants to drink for hot something.
⑤ Hot something is wanted to Mijin.

19 다음 두 문장을 한 문장으로 바르게 바꿔 쓴 것은?

> • I like to collect stamps.
> • They were made in 1900s.

① I like to collect stamps who were made in 1900s.
② I like to collect stamps of which were made in 1900s.
③ I like to collect stamps which were made in 1900s.
④ I like to collect stamps which made in 1900s.
⑤ I like to collect stamps who made in 1900s.

20 다음 빈칸에 들어갈 알맞은 것은?

> There is _____ interesting on TV now.

① a talk show   ② a drama
③ the news   ④ a movie
⑤ nothing

21 괄호 안에서 알맞은 것을 고르시오.

(1) He is the boy (who / whose) broke the window.
(2) A nurse is a person (which / that) looks after the sick.

01 다음 문장에서 어법상 틀린 부분을 찾아 바르게 고쳐 쓰시오.

> Did the thief take valuable anything?

➡ _____

02 다음 문장에서 어법상 어색한 부분을 고쳐 문장을 다시 쓰시오.

(1) Both paintings show a couple which are dancing.

➡ _____
_____

(2) In 1883, Renoir completed two paintings whose look very similar.

➡ _____
_____

(3) Jake is wearing a hat who look very old.

➡ _____

03 다음 문장에서 어법상 잘못된 부분을 찾아 바르게 고쳐 쓰시오.

(1) Sally enjoys drinking the tea who smells sweet.

_____ ➡ _____

(2) Kirk wants to live in a house who are not far from the station.

_____ ➡ _____

(3) Picasso is the famous painter whom is loved the most.

_____ ➡ _____

04 〈보기〉의 문장을 참고하여, 그림을 보고 관계대명사를 이용하여 문장을 완성하시오.

┤ 보기 ├
> Sumi is talking to a girl who is wearing glasses.

(1) Jiho is watering the plant _____ _____ yellow flowers.

(2) The girl _____ _____ cleaning the floor is Mina.

(3) Jinsu is reading a book _____ _____ a red cover.

05 두 문장을 관계대명사를 이용하여 한 문장으로 쓰시오. (that은 사용하지 말 것)

(1) Yesterday I met a girl.
  + She is from Mexico.

➡ _____

(2) I want to buy a smartphone.
  + It has a large screen.

➡ _____

(3) John read an article.
  + It was written by his friend.

➡ _____
_____

★06 주어진 단어와 'something, anything, nothing'을 이용하여 대화를 완성하시오.

> A: Do you have any plans this weekend?
> B: I have (1)_____ _____ to do this weekend. (special) Why?
> A: I'm planning to eat (2)_____ _____ with Jenny this weekend. (nice) Can you join us?
> B: Sure.

07 우리말과 일치하도록 주어진 어구를 알맞은 순서로 배열하시오.

(1) 선생님께서 뭔가 다른 것에 대해 말씀하셨다.
(something / talked / about / the / teacher / different)
➡ _____

(2) Sam은 그에게 너무 큰 신발을 신고 있다.
(Sam / big / that / is wearing / shoes / are / too / for him)
➡ _____

(3) 너는 여름 방학 동안 어떤 특별한 것을 할 거니?
(the summer / are / special / you / going / during / to / vacation / do / anything / ?)
➡ _____
_____

08 다음 글에서 어법상 틀린 부분을 찾아 바르게 고쳐 쓰시오.

> My group made a poster which aim to help people understand different cultures. We'll hold an Around the World Cultural Festival. If you want to do special something for other people, join us!

_____ ➡ _____
_____ ➡ _____

09 다음 대화의 밑줄 친 우리말에 맞도록 괄호 안의 단어들을 순서대로 바르게 배열하시오.

> A: I can't solve this science problem. Can you do me a favor?
> B: No, I can't. It's too difficult. <u>우리보다 더 똑똑한 누군가가 필요해.</u> (us / than / need / we / smarter / someone)

➡ _____

10 다음 문장을 어법에 맞게 고쳐 쓰시오.

(1) There is strange something on the roof of the house.
➡ _____
_____

(2) He liked to draw ballet dancers which was moving.
➡ _____
_____

(3) He fell in love with a lady which taught music at the nursing home.
➡ _____
_____

Reading

교과서

Global Citizenship Education

This is the Global Citizenship Education site. Global Citizenship Education helps us grow as global citizens. Global citizens are people who try to understand different cultures. They also care for people in need and work for a better world. Please share your global citizenship education experiences here.

Hello. I am Minhee from Korea. I am a member of the Global Community Club. My club aims to communicate with people from around the world. A week ago we produced a video about the lantern festival in our village. We uploaded it to the Internet and amazingly, we got nearly 5,000 hits. Click here for our video.

└ Alice: Wow, your lantern festival looks fantastic!

└ Sunan: We have a water festival in our village. I'd like to make a video like yours.

Glossary (sidebar):

global 세계적인, 지구의
citizenship 시민 의식, 시민권
education 교육
site 사이트, 장소
citizen 시민
share 나누다, 공유하다
care for 돌보다, 보살피다
in need 어려움에 처한
community 공동체, 사회
aim 목표로 하다, 조준하다
communicate 의사소통하다
produce 생산하다
lantern 등불, 등
upload 올리다, 탑재하다

 확인문제

● 다음 문장이 본문의 내용과 일치하면 T, 일치하지 <u>않으면</u> F를 쓰시오.

1 Global Citizenship Education helps us grow as global citizens. ☐

2 Global citizens try to understand their own cultures first. ☐

3 Global citizens are people who are in need. ☐

4 Global citizens work for a better world. ☐

5 Minhee is a member of the Global Community Club. ☐

6 Minhee's club aims to communicate with their neighbors. ☐

7 Minhee's club produced a video about the lantern festival in their village. ☐

Hi, my name is Jo. I am from Australia. A few weeks ago, my teacher

showed us pictures of students in Kenya. Sadly, they were all using

plastic bags to carry their books. My class decided to raise money to

send them new school bags. We sold cookies and drinks and raised 600

dollars. We hope the Kenyan students are happy with the new bags.

    ↳ **Wang:** Awesome! I'm sure they will like the bags.

    ↳ **Kozo:** You did something wonderful!

I am Afig from Malaysia. My school started a wall painting campaign

to make our village look better. Students who are good at painting

gathered and painted on some walls of schools and parks. Thanks to

this campaign, our village looks much nicer. Now everyone can enjoy

walking alongside the painted walls.

    ↳ **Junho:** What a nice idea!

raise (돈을) 모으다, 기르다, 키우다

Kenyan 케냐의; 케냐인, 케냐어

awesome 감탄할 만한, 엄청난

gather 모이다

campaign 캠페인

alongside ~ 옆에, ~와 나란히

be good at ~을 잘하다, ~에 능숙하다

thanks to ~ 덕분에

확인문제

● 다음 문장이 본문의 내용과 일치하면 T, 일치하지 않으면 F를 쓰시오.

1   Jo is from Austria. ☐

2   Jo's teacher showed students pictures of Kenyan students. ☐

3   The Kenyan students were using school bags to carry books. ☐

4   Jo's class decided to raise money to send the Kenyan students new school bags. ☐

5   Afig's school started a wall painting campaign. ☐

6   Students who are interested in painting gathered and painted. ☐

7   Thanks to this campaign, their school looks much nicer. ☐

8   Now everyone can enjoy walking alongside the painted walls. ☐

● 우리말을 참고하여 빈칸에 알맞은 말을 쓰시오.

1 _____ _____ Education

2 _____ _____ the Global Citizenship Education site.

3 Global Citizenship Education _____ _____ _____ as global citizens.

4 Global citizens are people _____ _____ _____ _____ different cultures.

5 They also _____ _____ people _____ _____ and work for a better world.

6 Please _____ your global citizenship education _____ here.

7 Hello. I am Minhee _____ _____ .

8 I am _____ _____ _____ the Global Community Club.

9 My club aims _____ _____ _____ people from around the world.

10 A week ago we produced a video _____ _____ _____ _____ in our village.

11 We _____ _____ to the Internet and amazingly, we got nearly _____ _____ .

12 Click here _____ _____ _____ .

13 Alice: Wow, your lantern festival _____ _____ !

14 Sunan: We have _____ _____ _____ in our village.

15 I'd like to make a video _____ _____ .

1 세계 시민 교육

2 이곳은 세계 시민 교육 사이트입니다.

3 세계 시민 교육은 우리가 세계 시민으로 자라도록 도와줍니다.

4 세계 시민은 다른 문화를 이해하려고 노력하는 사람들입니다.

5 그들은 또한 어려움에 처한 사람들을 보살피고 더 나은 세상을 위해서 일합니다.

6 당신의 세계 시민 교육 경험을 이곳에 공유해 주세요.

7 안녕. 나는 한국의 민희야.

8 나는 세계 공동체 동아리의 회원이야.

9 우리 동아리는 전 세계의 사람들과 소통하는 것을 목표로 해.

10 일주일 전에 우리는 우리 마을의 등 축제에 관한 비디오를 제작했어.

11 우리는 그것을 인터넷에 올렸는데, 놀랍게도 거의 5,000개의 조회 수를 획득했어.

12 우리 비디오를 보려면 이곳을 클릭해.

13 Alice: 와, 너희 등 축제는 환상적으로 보인다!

14 Sunan: 우리 마을에는 물 축제가 있어.

15 나도 너희 것과 같은 비디오를 만들고 싶어.

16 Hi, _____ _____ is Jo.

17 I _____ _____ Australia.

18 A few weeks ago, my teacher _____ _____ _____ of students in Kenya.

19 Sadly, _____ _____ _____ using plastic bags _____ _____ _____ _____.

20 My class decided _____ _____ _____ to send them new school bags.

21 We sold cookies and drinks and _____ _____ _____.

22 We hope the Kenyan students _____ _____ _____ the new bags.

23 Wang: _____! _____ _____ they will like the bags.

24 Kozo: You did _____ _____!

25 I am Afig _____ Malaysia.

26 My school started _____ _____ _____ campaign to make our village _____ _____.

27 Students who _____ _____ _____ painting _____ and _____ on some walls of schools and parks.

28 _____ _____ this campaign, our village looks _____ _____.

29 Now everyone can enjoy _____ _____ the _____ walls.

30 Junho: _____ _____ _____ _____!

16 안녕, 내 이름은 Jo야.

17 나는 호주 출신이야.

18 몇 주 전에, 선생님이 우리에게 케냐에 있는 학생들의 사진을 보여주셨어.

19 슬프게도, 그들은 모두 책을 들고 다니기 위해서 비닐 봉지를 사용하고 있었어.

20 우리 반은 그들에게 새로운 책 가방을 보내기 위해서 기금을 모금하기로 결정했어.

21 우리는 쿠키와 음료를 팔아서 600달러를 모았어.

22 우리는 케냐의 학생들이 그들의 새 가방을 좋아하기를 바라.

23 Wang: 멋지다! 분명 그들이 가방을 좋아할 거야.

24 Kozo: 훌륭한 일을 했구나!

25 난 말레이시아의 Afig야.

26 우리 학교는 우리 마을을 좀 더 좋아 보이게 하기 위해서 벽화 캠페인을 시작했어.

27 그림을 잘 그리는 학생들이 모여서 학교와 공원 벽에 그림을 그렸어.

28 이 캠페인 덕분에, 우리 마을은 훨씬 멋져 보여.

29 이제 모든 사람들이 그림이 그려진 벽을 따라서 산책하는 것을 즐길 수 있어.

30 Junho: 정말 멋진 생각이다!

우리말을 참고하여 본문을 영작하시오.

1 세계 시민 교육

➡ _____

2 이곳은 세계 시민 교육 사이트입니다.

➡ _____

3 세계 시민 교육은 우리가 세계 시민으로 자라도록 도와줍니다.

➡ _____

4 세계 시민은 다른 문화를 이해하려고 노력하는 사람들입니다.

➡ _____

5 그들은 또한 어려움에 처한 사람들을 보살피고 더 나은 세상을 위해서 일합니다.

➡ _____

6 당신의 세계 시민 교육 경험을 이곳에 공유해 주세요.

➡ _____

7 안녕. 나는 한국의 민희야.

➡ _____

8 나는 세계 공동체 동아리의 회원이야.

➡ _____

9 우리 동아리는 전 세계의 사람들과 소통하는 것을 목표로 해.

➡ _____

10 일주일 전에 우리는 우리 마을의 등 축제에 관한 비디오를 제작했어.

➡ _____

11 우리는 그것을 인터넷에 올렸는데, 놀랍게도 거의 5,000개의 조회 수를 획득했어.

➡ _____

12 우리 비디오를 보려면 이곳을 클릭해.

➡ _____

13 Alice: 와, 너희 등 축제는 환상적으로 보인다!

➡ _____

14 Sunan: 우리 마을에는 물 축제가 있어.

➡ _____

15 나도 너희 것과 같은 비디오를 만들고 싶어.

➡ _____

16 안녕, 내 이름은 Jo야.

➡ _____

17 나는 호주 출신이야.

➡ _____

18 몇 주 전에, 선생님이 우리에게 케냐에 있는 학생들의 사진을 보여주셨어.

➡ _____

19 슬프게도, 그들은 모두 책을 들고 다니기 위해서 비닐 봉지를 사용하고 있었어.

➡ _____

20 우리 반은 그들에게 새로운 책가방을 보내기 위해서 기금을 모금하기로 결정했어.

➡ _____

21 우리는 쿠키와 음료를 팔아서 600달러를 모았어.

➡ _____

22 우리는 케냐의 학생들이 그들의 새 가방을 좋아하기를 바라.

➡ _____

23 Wang: 멋지다! 분명 그들이 가방을 좋아할 거야.

➡ _____

24 Kozo: 훌륭한 일을 했구나!

➡ _____

25 난 말레이시아의 Afig야.

➡ _____

26 우리 학교는 우리 마을을 좀 더 좋아 보이게 하기 위해서 벽화 캠페인을 시작했어.

➡ _____

27 그림을 잘 그리는 학생들이 모여서 학교와 공원 벽에 그림을 그렸어.

➡ _____

28 이 캠페인 덕분에, 우리 마을은 훨씬 멋져 보여.

➡ _____

29 이제 모든 사람들이 그림이 그려진 벽을 따라서 산책하는 것을 즐길 수 있어.

➡ _____

30 Junho: 정말 멋진 생각이다!

➡ _____

[01~03] 다음 글을 읽고 물음에 답하시오.

http://www.global citizen.com
SHARE VIDEO HELP CAMPAIGN

Global Citizenship Education

This is the Global Citizenship Education site. Global Citizenship Education helps us grow ⓐas global citizens. Global citizens are people who try to understand different cultures. ⓑThey also care for people in need and work for a better world. Please share your global citizenship education experiences here.

01 위 글의 종류로 알맞은 것을 고르시오.

① e-mail from the education website
② review of the education experiences
③ article about the education site
④ writing posted on the website
⑤ summary of the citizenship education experience

02 위 글의 밑줄 친 ⓐas와 같은 의미로 쓰인 것을 고르시오.

① As she was tired, she soon fell asleep.
② He runs as fast as you.
③ He is famous as a singer.
④ As you know, he is honest.
⑤ As we go up, the air grows colder.

서답형

03 위 글의 밑줄 친 ⓑThey가 가리키는 것을 본문에서 찾아 쓰시오.

➡ _____

[04~06] 다음 글을 읽고 물음에 답하시오.

Hello. I am Minhee from Korea. I am a member of the Global Community Club. My club aims ⓐto communicate with people from around the world. A week ago we produced a video about the lantern festival in our village. We uploaded it ____ⓑ____ the Internet and amazingly, we got nearly 5,000 hits. Click here ____ⓒ____ our video.

04 아래 보기에서 위 글의 밑줄 친 ⓐto communicate와 to부정사의 용법이 같은 것의 개수를 고르시오.

┤ 보기 ├
① I was glad to meet him at the party.
② He expected to go to Europe.
③ I have some pictures to show you.
④ It is good for the health to eat breakfast.
⑤ Do you want to go there?

① 1개 ② 2개 ③ 3개 ④ 4개 ⑤ 5개

05 위 글의 빈칸 ⓑ와 ⓒ에 들어갈 전치사가 바르게 짝지어진 것은?

① to – for   ② from – in
③ on – from   ④ to – by
⑤ from – for

06 위 글의 제목으로 알맞은 것을 고르시오.

① Join the Global Community Club!
② How to Communicate with Netizens
③ How about Producing a Video?
④ The Most Famous Club in Our School
⑤ Let Me Introduce Our Club Activity

[07~09] 다음 글을 읽고 물음에 답하시오.

  I am Afig from Malaysia. My school started a wall painting campaign to make our village look better. Students who are good at painting gathered and painted on some walls of schools and parks. Thanks to this campaign, our village looks _____ⓐ_____ nicer. Now everyone can enjoy walking alongside the painted walls.
∟ Junho: ⓑWhat a nice idea!

07 위 글의 요지로 알맞은 것을 고르시오.

① Afig의 학교는 다양한 캠페인을 시작했다.
② 그림을 잘 그리는 학생들은 봉사활동을 통해 보람을 얻을 수 있다.
③ 학교와 공원 벽에는 그림을 그려야 한다.
④ Afig의 학교는 벽화 캠페인으로 마을을 더 보기 좋게 만들었다.
⑤ 그림이 그려진 벽을 따라서 산책하는 것은 즐겁다.

08 위 글의 빈칸 ⓐ에 들어갈 수 없는 말을 고르시오.

① very   ② much   ③ even
④ still   ⑤ a lot

서답형
09 위 글의 밑줄 친 ⓑ를 (1) How로 시작하는 감탄문과 (2) 평서문으로 고치시오.

➡ (1) _____
  (2) _____

[10~12] 다음 글을 읽고 물음에 답하시오.

  Hello. I am Minhee from Korea. I am a member of the Global Community Club. My club aims to communicate with people from around the world. A week ago we produced a video about the lantern festival in our village. We uploaded it to the Internet and amazingly, we got nearly 5,000 _____ⓐ_____s. Click here for our video.
∟ Alice: Wow, your lantern festival looks fantastic!
∟ Sunan: We have a water festival in our village. I'd like to make a video ⓑlike yours.

서답형
10 주어진 영영풀이를 참고하여 빈칸 ⓐ에 철자 h로 시작하는 단어를 쓰시오.

┌─────────────────────────────┐
│   a single visit to a website   │
└─────────────────────────────┘

➡ _____s

11 위 글의 밑줄 친 ⓑlike와 다른 의미로 쓰인 것을 고르시오.

① She's wearing a dress like mine.
② Do you like your new house?
③ He drinks like a fish.
④ I cannot cook well like you.
⑤ She looks like an actress.

12 위 글의 내용과 일치하지 않는 것은?

① 민희는 세계 공동체 동아리의 회원이다.
② 세계 공동체 동아리는 전 세계의 사람들과 소통하는 것을 목표로 한다.
③ 세계 공동체 동아리는 민희네 마을의 등 축제에 관한 비디오를 제작했다.
④ Alice는 등 축제가 환상적으로 보인다고 했다.
⑤ Sunan은 자기 마을의 물 축제에 관한 비디오를 만들었다.

[13~15] 다음 Sunan이 살고 있는 태국의 송크란 축제를 소개하는 글을 읽고 물음에 답하시오.

Where: In Thailand
When: from April 13th to 15th
Why: To celebrate the traditional Thai New Year and ⓐhave fun
What you can do at the festival:
- Enjoy the big water fight ___ⓑ___ is very popular
- Watch Songkran parade ___ⓒ___ shows Thai culture and traditions
- Taste traditional Thai food

13 위 글의 밑줄 친 ⓐhave fun과 바꿔 쓸 수 있는 말을 <u>모두</u> 고르시오.

① have a good time
② make fun of it
③ help yourself
④ enjoy yourself
⑤ make a funny face

서답형

14 위 글의 빈칸 ⓑ와 ⓒ에 공통으로 들어갈 말을 쓰시오.

➡ _____

15 다음 중 태국의 송크란 축제에 대한 설명과 일치하지 <u>않는</u> 것은?

① 4월 13일부터 15일까지 열린다.
② 전통적인 태국의 설날을 축하하는 축제이다.
③ 물싸움은 금지되어 있다.
④ 송크란 퍼레이드는 태국의 문화와 전통을 보여 준다.
⑤ 전통적인 태국 음식을 맛볼 수 있다.

[16~19] 다음 글을 읽고 물음에 답하시오.

Hi, my name is Jo. I am from Australia. (①) A few weeks ago, my teacher showed us pictures of students in Kenya. (②) Sadly, they were all using plastic bags ⓐto carry their books. (③) We sold cookies and drinks and raised 600 dollars. (④) We hope the ___ⓑ___ students are happy with the new bags. (⑤)

중요

16 위 글의 흐름으로 보아, 주어진 문장이 들어가기에 가장 적절한 곳은?

My class decided to raise money to send them new school bags.

①   ②   ③   ④   ⑤

17 위 글의 밑줄 친 ⓐto carry와 to부정사의 용법이 <u>다른</u> 것을 <u>모두</u> 고르시오.

① She needs someone to talk with.
② I am sorry to hear the bad news.
③ I use the computer to get information.
④ This book is easy to read.
⑤ To study English is interesting.

서답형

18 본문의 한 단어를 변형하여 위 글의 빈칸 ⓑ에 들어갈 알맞은 말을 쓰시오.

➡ _____

19 위 글을 읽고 대답할 수 <u>없는</u> 질문은?

① Where is Jo from?
② A few weeks ago, what did Jo's teacher show to the students?
③ Did the students in the pictures use school bags to carry their books?
④ Where did Jo's class sell cookies and drinks?
⑤ How much did Jo's class raise?

[20~23] 다음 글을 읽고 물음에 답하시오.

Hi, my name is Jo. I am from Australia. A few weeks ago, my teacher showed us pictures of students in Kenya. Sadly, they were all ①using plastic bags ②to carry their books. My class decided ③raising money to send ⓐthem new school bags. We sold cookies and drinks and ④raised 600 dollars. We hope the Kenyan students are happy with the new bags.

└, **Wang:** Awesome! I'm sure they will like the bags.

└, **Kozo:** You did ⑤something wonderful!

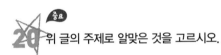

20 위 글의 주제로 알맞은 것을 고르시오.

① the pictures of the Kenyan students
② using plastic bags to carry the books
③ raising money to send new school bags
④ how to sell cookies and drinks
⑤ the difficulty of raising money

서답형

21 위 글의 밑줄 친 ①~⑤ 중 어법상 틀린 것을 찾아 고치시오.

_____ ➡ _____

서답형

22 위 글의 밑줄 친 ⓐthem이 가리키는 것을 본문에서 찾아 쓰시오.

➡ _____

23 위 글을 읽고 알 수 없는 것을 고르시오.

① Jo의 출신 국가
② Jo의 선생님이 보여주신 사진의 숫자
③ 사진의 학생들이 책가방으로 사용한 것
④ Jo의 반이 기금을 모금한 방법
⑤ Jo의 반이 모은 기금의 액수

[24~26] 다음 Sunan이 살고 있는 태국의 송크란 축제를 소개하는 글을 읽고 물음에 답하시오.

To my friend Minhee,

Hi, Minhee. I want to let you ①knowing about Songkran, a big festival in Thailand. It ②is held from April 13th to 15th. People ③hold this festival to celebrate the traditional Thai New Year and have fun. At the festival, you can enjoy the big water fight ④which is very popular. You can also watch Songkran parade ⑤that shows Thai culture and traditions. For food, you can taste traditional Thai food. If you want to experience something special, come and enjoy the Songkran festival.

From Sunan

서답형

24 위 글의 밑줄 친 ①~⑤ 중 어법상 틀린 것을 찾아 고치시오.

_____ ➡ _____

25 다음 빈칸에 들어갈 알맞은 말을 고르시오.

Sunan is _____ Minhee to come to Thailand and enjoy the Songkran festival.

① visiting ② calling
③ ordering ④ forcing
⑤ inviting

26 다음 중 송크란 축제에서 할 수 있는 것을 모두 고르시오.

① 물싸움 ② 장기 자랑
③ 퍼레이드 구경 ④ 민속 씨름
⑤ 태국 전통 음식을 맛보기

[01~03] 다음 글을 읽고 물음에 답하시오.

This is the Global Citizenship Education (A)[cite / site]. Global Citizenship Education helps us (B)[grow / growing] as global citizens. Global citizens are people who try to understand different cultures. They also ⓐcare for people in need and (C)[work / working] for a better world. Please share your global citizenship education experiences here.

01 위 글의 괄호 (A)~(C)에서 문맥이나 어법이나 알맞은 낱말을 골라 쓰시오.

➡ (A) _____ (B) _____ (C) _____

02 위 글을 읽고 Global citizens의 정의를 우리말로 쓰시오.

➡ (1) _____
(2) _____
_____

03 위 글의 밑줄 친 ⓐcare for와 바꿔 쓸 수 있는 말을 쓰시오.

➡ _____

[04~06] 다음 글을 읽고 물음에 답하시오.

Hello. I am Minhee from Korea. I am a member of the Global Community Club. My club aims to communicate with people from around the world. A week ago we produced a video about the lantern festival in our village. We uploaded it to the Internet and amazingly, ⓐ거의 5,000 조회 수를 획득했어. Click here for our video.

⌐ **Alice:** ⓑWow, your lantern festival looks like fantastic!

⌐ **Sunan:** We have a water festival in our village. ⓒI'd like to make a video like yours.

04 위 글의 밑줄 친 ⓐ의 우리말에 맞게 주어진 어휘를 이용하여 5 단어로 영작하시오.

we, got

➡ _____

05 위 글의 밑줄 친 ⓑ에서 어법상 틀린 부분을 찾아 고치시오.

_____ ➡ _____

06 다음 빈칸 (A)와 (B)에 알맞은 단어를 넣어 위 글의 밑줄 친 문장 ⓒ가 말하고 있는 내용을 완성하시오.

Sunan wants to (A)_____ _____
_____ about a water festival in their village like (B)_____ _____ produced a video about the lantern festival in their village.

[07~10] 다음 글을 읽고 물음에 답하시오.

Hi, my name is Jo. ①I am from Australia. A few weeks ago, my teacher ②showed us pictures of students in Kenya. Sadly, they were all using plastic bags ③to carry their books. My class decided to raise money ⓐto send them new school bags. We sold cookies and drinks and ④raised 600 dollars. ⑤We hope the Kenyan students to be happy with the new bags.

07 다음 질문에 대한 알맞은 대답을 주어진 단어로 시작하여 쓰시오. (4 단어)

> Q: What were the Kenyan students in the pictures using to carry their books?
>
> A: They _____ .

➡ _____

08 다음 문장에서 위 글의 내용과 <u>다른</u> 부분을 찾아서 고치시오.

> Jo's class raised 600 dollars to send the Kenyan students new plastic bags by selling cookies and drinks.

_____ ➡ _____

09 위 글의 밑줄 친 ①~⑤ 중 어법상 <u>틀린</u> 것을 찾아 고치시오.

_____ ➡ _____

10 위 글의 밑줄 친 ⓐ를 3형식으로 고치시오.

➡ _____

[11~12] 다음 글을 읽고 물음에 답하시오.

> I am Afig from Malaysia. My school started a wall painting campaign to make our village look better. ⓐ그림을 잘 그리는 학생들이 모여서 학교와 공원 벽에 그림을 그렸어. Thanks to this campaign, our village looks much nicer. Now everyone can enjoy walking alongside the painted walls.

11 다음 질문에 대한 알맞은 대답을 주어진 단어로 시작하여 쓰시오. (5 단어)

> Q: Why did Afig's school start a wall painting campaign?
>
> A: To _____ .

12 위 글의 밑줄 친 ⓐ의 우리말에 맞게 한 단어를 보충하여, 주어진 어휘를 알맞게 배열하시오.

> gathered and painted / students / some walls / on / good / who / painting / schools and parks / are / of

➡ _____
_____

[13~14] 다음 글을 읽고 물음에 답하시오.

> To my friend Minhee,
>
> Hi, Minhee. I want to let you know about Songkran, a big festival in Thailand. It is held from April 13th to 15th. People hold this festival to celebrate the traditional ___ⓐ___ New Year and have fun. At the festival, you can enjoy the big water fight which is very popular. You can also watch Songkran parade that shows ___ⓑ___ culture and traditions. For food, you can taste traditional ___ⓒ___ food. If you want to experience something special, come and enjoy the Songkran festival.
>
> From Sunan

13 다음 빈칸 (A)와 (B)에 알맞은 단어를 넣어 송크란 축제에 대한 소개를 완성하시오.

> Songkran is held to celebrate the traditional (A)_____ _____ of Thailand. At the festival, you can enjoy the big (B)_____ _____ .

14 본문의 한 단어를 변형하여 위 글의 빈칸 ⓐ~ⓒ에 공통으로 들어갈 알맞은 말을 쓰시오.

➡ _____

해석

Conversation B

Karl: Jiho, isn't that too much? <u>Are you going to eat all of that?</u>
= Are you planning to 동사원형 ~?: 너는 ~할 거니?

Jiho: I'm not sure, but Bulgogi is my <u>favorite</u>.
(형) 좋아하는 (명) 좋아하는 것. 여기서는 명사

Karl: Hey! Look at the campaign poster. "Think, Eat, Save!"

Jiho: <u>What does that mean?</u>
의미를 묻는 표현

Karl: It means "Think first before you eat and save the Earth."
'It means ~.'를 사용해서 설명할 수 있다. 몰라서 설명을 하지 못하는 경우에는 'I'm sorry. but I don't know what it means.'

Jiho: I think I took too much Bulgogi. <u>Let's share it.</u>
또는 'I'm not sure what it means.'
Let's 동사원형: ~하자
등으로 답한다.

Karl: Okay. That's a good idea.

Jiho: We ate it all. My clean plate <u>makes me feel good</u>.
make+목적어+동사원형: …가 ~하도록 만들다 feel+형용사: ~하게 느끼다

Karl: Let's not waste food from now on. I hope we can save the Earth.

구문해설 • look at: ~을 보다   • share: 같이 쓰다. 공유하다   • waste: 낭비하다. 허비하다
        • from now on 앞으로는. 이제부터   • save 살리다. 구하다

Karl: 지호야, 너무 많지 않니? 너 그걸 다 먹을 거니?

지호: 잘 모르겠어, 그렇지만 불고기는 내가 가장 좋아하는 음식이야.

Karl: 저기! 캠페인 포스터를 봐. "생각하라, 먹어라, 구하라!"

지호: 저게 무슨 뜻이야?

Karl: 그것은 먹기 전에 먼저 생각하고 지구를 살리자는 뜻이야.

지호: 나 불고기를 너무 많이 담아온 것 같아. 나눠 먹자.

Karl: 그래. 좋은 생각이야.

지호: 우리 다 먹었네. 내 깨끗한 그릇을 보니 기분이 좋아.

Karl: 이제부터 음식을 낭비하지 말자. 나는 우리가 지구를 살리기를 바라.

Project

A: <u>What kind of</u> activity do you like?
어떤 종류의

B: <u>What do you think about</u> sending shoes to poor children?
~하는 게 어때?

C: Good. I hope they are happy with them.

D: Let's make a poster about the activity to find <u>people</u> <u>who want to help</u>.
선행사   주격 관계대명사절(people을 수식)

Sending Shoes of Hope

Why: To help poor children <u>who don't have shoes</u>
주격 관계대명사절로 선행사 poor children을 수식

How: 1. Bring shoes from home.

2. Draw pictures or write caring words on them.

3. Send them to children in need.

When: July 3rd

If you want to do <u>something special</u> for the world, join us!
–thing+형용사

구문해설 • activity 활동   • be happy with ~에 만족하다   • bring 가져오다   • caring 배려하는
        • in need 어려움에 처한

A: 어떤 활동을 하고 싶니?

B: 가난한 아이들에게 신발을 보내는 게 어때?

C: 좋아. 그들이 그것들을 좋아하길 바라.

D: 도움을 주고 싶어 하는 사람들을 찾기 위해서 이 활동에 대한 포스터를 만들자.

희망의 신발 보내기
왜: 신발이 없는 가난한 아이들을 돕기 위해
어떻게:
1. 집에서 신발을 가져오세요.
2. 신발에 그림을 그리거나 배려의 말을 쓰세요.
3. 그것들을 어려움에 처한 아이들에게 보내세요.
언제: 7월 3일
세상을 위해 뭔가 특별한 일을 하고 싶다면, 우리와 함께 해요!

01 〈보기〉에 주어진 두 단어의 관계가 나머지와 <u>다른</u> 것을 고르시오.

┌─ 보기 ├─
ⓐ gather – collect
ⓑ global – worldwide
ⓒ save – rescue
ⓓ upset – worried
ⓔ far – near

① ⓐ   ② ⓑ   ③ ⓒ   ④ ⓓ   ⑤ ⓔ

02 밑줄 친 단어와 의미가 같은 것을 고르시오.

That movie is <u>awesome</u>.

① impressive   ② interesting
③ awful   ④ boring
⑤ popular

03 그림을 보고 대화의 빈칸에 어울리는 단어를 고르시오.

A: Are you going to _____ all your food?
B: Yes, I am.

① hold   ② take   ③ lose
④ leave   ⑤ finish

04 다음 〈보기〉의 단어를 사용하여 자연스러운 문장을 만들 수 <u>없는</u> 것은? (형태 변화 가능)

┌─ 보기 ├─
campaign   bag   garden   trash

① Do you need plastic _____ for food?
② This park will be closing in ten minutes. You must not leave the _____ behind.
③ Do you often have a _____ with your friends?
④ I want you to participate in our new _____.
⑤ Will you plant roses in your _____?

05 다음 대화의 빈칸에 알맞은 단어를 고르시오.

A: I hope people don't waste water.
B: I hope so, too. Let's hold a _____ Water campaign.
A: That's a good idea.

① Hold   ② Save   ③ Hope
④ Eat   ⑤ Waste

[06~08] 다음 대화를 읽고 물음에 답하시오.

B: Do you have any plans for the summer vacation, Suji?
G: Yes. I'm ___(A)___ (go) to the Philippines ___(B)___ (do) some volunteer work with my family.
B: Oh, I went there and ___(C)___ (help) some children study last year. <u>너도 그렇게 할 거니?</u>
G: Yes. And I'll also paint walls with the children.
B: That sounds nice.

06 빈칸 (A)~(C)를 주어진 단어를 이용하여 채우시오.

➡ (A) _____ (B) _____ (C) _____

07 밑줄 친 우리말을 주어진 단어를 이용하여 영작하시오.

➡ _____

(too, that, going, 7단어)

08 위 대화를 읽고 답할 수 없는 질문을 고르시오.

① When did the boy go to the Philippines?
② Where is the girl planning to go for the summer vacation?
③ What did the boy do in the Philippines?
④ Does the boy have any plans for the summer vacation?
⑤ When is the girl going to go to the Philippines?

[09~10] 다음 대화를 읽고 물음에 답하시오.

B: Did you watch the news about the flood?
G: Yes, I did. They said a lot of people lost their homes.
B: My club is going to send them some money.
G: How can you do that? Are you going to raise money, Andy?
B: Yes. 우리는 필통을 만들어서 그것들을 팔 거야.

09 다음 영영풀이에 해당하는 단어를 대화에서 찾아 쓰시오.

> to collect money for a particular purpose

➡ _____

10 밑줄 친 우리말을 주어진 단어를 이용하여 영작하시오.

➡ _____

(and, going)

[11~12] 주어진 문장 이후에 이어질 대화의 순서를 바르게 배열하시오.

11

My club is going to hold a green campaign at school next Friday.

(A) It's a campaign to protect the environment. Many students throw trash on the streets. We hope to stop that.
(B) What is a green campaign?
(C) Thanks. I hope so, too.
(D) I hope your campaign goes well.

➡ _____

12

What are you doing, Jason?

(A) That's too bad. I didn't know that.
(B) I'm making a poster about global hunger. Many people are dying of hunger.
(C) I hope more people care about global hunger.

➡ _____

13 우리말에 맞게 주어진 단어를 이용하여 영어로 쓰시오.

> 세상을 위해 뭔가 특별한 일을 하고 싶다면, 우리와 함께 해!
> (if / want / special / something / for)

➡ _____,
   join us!

14 다음 두 문장을 관계대명사를 이용하여 한 문장으로 쓰시오. (that은 쓰지 말 것)

(1) • He is the student.
   • He won the speech contest.
   ➡ _____

(2) • I know the man.
   • He was looking for his dog.
   ➡ _____

(3) • He wrote a novel.
   • It became a best-seller.
   ➡ _____

15 빈칸에 알맞은 것은?

> There is a lady _____ to see you.

① who want   ② who wants
③ which wanted   ④ who wanting
⑤ which to want

16 빈칸에 공통으로 들어갈 말은?

> • Look at the man _____ is wearing blue jeans.
> • There are animals _____ live in the water.

① who   ② that   ③ what
④ which   ⑤ whose

17 밑줄 친 부분의 쓰임이 다른 것은?

① Which one is his laptop computer?
② Can you tell me which book she wants to buy?
③ I don't know which car is Tom's.
④ She asked me which hat was mine.
⑤ Do you know the house which has a beautiful garden?

18 주어진 문장을 어법상 바르게 고친 것이 아닌 것은?

① They are holding bright something.
   ➡ They are holding something bright.
② I invited Tom and his cat who live near my house.
   ➡ I invited Tom and his cat which live near my house.
③ Terry is the girl which went there alone.
   ➡ Terry is the girl that went there alone.
④ If you find sharp something, you should not touch it.
   ➡ If you find something sharp, you should not touch it.
⑤ I like the house whom has big windows.
   ➡ I like the house which has big windows.

19 다음 문장에서 틀린 것을 고치시오.

> Prepare activities that helps people understand the country's culture.

_____ ➡ _____

20 다음 중 어법상 바르지 <u>않은</u> 것은 몇 개인가?

> • She knows a guy who is selling cars.
> • Ben is my neighbor which works in a hospital.
> • I want to buy a bag that has many pockets.
> • I know the man and his dog that are taking a walk in the park.
> • We should take care of the cats which doesn't have a home.

① 1개   ② 2개   ③ 3개
④ 4개   ⑤ 5개

21 다음 빈칸에 들어갈 형태로 알맞은 것은?

> Minsu has a cat _____ cute.

① who is   ② that are
③ who are   ④ which is
⑤ which are

22 다음 문장에서 <u>틀린</u> 곳을 찾아 바르게 고쳐 쓰시오.

(1) Students that is good at painting gathered and painted on some walls of schools and parks.
➡ _____

(2) A musician is a person which play music.
➡ _____

(3) The man is my friend that are working in the garden.
➡ _____

23 다음 중 어법상 바르지 <u>않은</u> 것은?

① He told me that I could be somebody more important.
② She needs somebody strong.
③ I think I ate something bad.
④ My sister likes to eat something sweet.
⑤ There's interesting nothing on TV tonight.

24 다음 중 어법상 올바른 문장을 고르시오.

① There is exciting nothing in that room.
② My grandfather told funny something to us.
③ Mr. Kim sent me an email who was written in French.
④ He is a baker who makes the best apple pie in my town.
⑤ I saw him making beautiful something.

> **Reading**

[25~26] 다음 글을 읽고 물음에 답하시오.

> This is the Global Citizenship Education site. Global Citizenship Education helps us grow as global citizens. Global citizens are people ___ⓐ___ try to understand different cultures. They also care for people in need and work for a better world. Please share your global citizenship education experiences here.

25 위 글의 빈칸 ⓐ에 들어갈 알맞은 말을 <u>모두</u> 고르시오.

① which   ② who
③ whom   ④ what
⑤ that

26 위 글의 내용과 일치하지 <u>않는</u> 것은?

① 세계 시민 교육은 우리가 세계 시민으로 자라도록 도와준다.
② 세계 시민은 다른 문화를 이해하려고 노력하는 사람들이다.
③ 세계 시민은 어려움에 처한 사람들을 보살핀다.
④ 세계 시민은 더 나은 세상을 위해서 일한다.
⑤ 세계 시민은 교육 경험을 공유하는 사람들이다.

28 위 글을 읽고 대답할 수 <u>없는</u> 질문은?

① What is the aim of Minhee's club?
② What did Minhee's club produce?
③ How long did it take to make a video about the lantern festival?
④ How many hits did Minhee's club video get?
⑤ What does Alice think of the lantern festival?

[27~28] 다음 글을 읽고 물음에 답하시오.

Hello. I am Minhee from Korea. I am a member of the Global Community Club. My club aims to communicate with people from around the world. A week ago we produced a video about the lantern festival in our village. We uploaded it to the Internet and amazingly, we got nearly 5,000 hits. Click here for our video.

└ **Alice:** Wow, your lantern festival looks fantastic!
└ **Sunan:** We have a water festival in our village. I'd like to make a video like yours.

[29~30] 다음 글을 읽고 물음에 답하시오.

Hi, my name is Jo. I am from Australia. A few weeks ago, my teacher showed us pictures of students in Kenya. Sadly, they were all using plastic bags to carry their books. ⓐ우리 반은 그들에게 새로운 책가방을 보내기 위해서 기금을 모금하기로 결정했어. We sold cookies and drinks and raised 600 dollars. We hope the Kenyan students are happy with the new bags.

29 위 글의 밑줄 친 ⓐ의 우리말에 맞게 한 단어를 보충하여, 주어진 어휘를 알맞게 배열하시오.

new school bags / money / decided / my class / to send / to / them

➡ _____

_____

27 본문의 내용과 일치하도록 다음 빈칸 (A)와 (B)에 알맞은 단어를 쓰시오.

Minhee's club made a video about (A)_____ _____ _____ in their village, and Sunan wants to produce a video about (B)_____ _____ _____ in their village.

30 위 글의 제목으로 알맞은 것을 고르시오.

① Fund Raising for Sending School Bags
② Pictures of the Kenyan Students
③ The Weak Point of Using Plastic Bags
④ How to Raise Money Effectively
⑤ The Strong Point of New School Bags

출제율 100%

01 다음 〈보기〉와 같은 관계가 되도록 빈칸에 알맞은 말을 쓰시오.

┌─── 보기 ───┐
China – Chinese
└──────────┘

(1) America – _____
(2) Kenya – _____

출제율 90%

02 다음 밑줄 친 부분과 의미와 가장 가까운 것을 주어진 철자로 시작하여 쓰시오.

┌──────────────────────┐
We should not harm any animals.
└──────────────────────┘

➡ h_____

출제율 95%

03 다음 우리말 해석에 맞게 빈칸을 완성하시오.

(1) My house is _____ from yours.
(우리 집은 너희 집에서 멀다.)
(2) The _____ can change a culture. (환경은 문화를 바꿀 수 있다.)
(3) I want to become an _____ lawyer. (나는 국제 변호사가 되고 싶다.)

출제율 90%

04 다음 중 단어의 영영풀이가 바르지 않은 것은?

① celebrate: to do something enjoyable on a special occasion
② environment: the nature where there are land, sea, air, plants, and animals
③ community: a group of people who live in the same area or who are similar in some way
④ fight: to contend in a battle or physical combat
⑤ gather: to share or exchange information or emotion with someone

[05~08] 다음 대화를 읽고 물음에 답하시오.

Karl: Jiho, isn't that too much? (A)너 그걸 다 먹을 거니?
Jiho: I'm not sure, but Bulgogi is my favorite. (①)
Karl: Hey! Look at the campaign poster. "Think, Eat, Save!" (②)
Jiho: What does that mean?
Karl: It means "Think first before you eat and save the Earth."
Jiho: I think I took too much Bulgogi. (③) Let's share it. (④)
Karl: Okay. That's a good idea.
Jiho: (⑤) My clean plate makes me feel good.
Karl: Let's not waste food from now on. I hope we can ___(B)___ the Earth.

출제율 100%

05 위 대화의 ①~⑤ 중 주어진 문장이 들어갈 알맞은 곳은?

┌──────────────────────┐
We ate it all.
└──────────────────────┘

①   ②   ③   ④   ⑤

출제율 90%

06 밑줄 친 (A)와 의미가 같도록 주어진 단어를 이용해 문장을 완성하시오.

➡ _____

(of, going, that)

출제율 90%

07 빈칸 (B)에 들어갈 알맞은 말을 위 대화에서 찾아 쓰시오.

➡ _____

출제율 90%

08 다음 영영풀이에 해당하는 단어를 대화에서 찾아 쓰시오.

┌──────────────────────┐
the nature where there are land, sea, air, plants, and animals
└──────────────────────┘

➡ _____

[09~11] 다음 대화를 읽고 물음에 답하시오.

> G: ⓐMy club is going to hold a green campaign at school next Friday. (①)
>
> B: What is a green campaign? (②)
>
> G: (③) It's a campaign to ___(A)___ the environment. Many students ___(B)___ trash on the streets. (④)
>
> B: I hope your campaign ___(C)___ well. (⑤)
>
> G: Thanks. I hope so, too.

09 위 대화의 ①~⑤ 중 주어진 문장이 들어갈 알맞은 곳은?

> We hope to stop that.

①   ②   ③   ④   ⑤

10 밑줄 친 ⓐ와 같은 의미를 가진 문장으로 쓰고자 한다. 괄호 안에 주어진 단어를 알맞게 배열하시오

(1) (a, club, to, hold, campaign, at, planning, my, Friday, is, green, next, school)

➡ _____

_____

(2) (next, hold, green, at, my, school, will, Friday, a, campaign, club)

➡ _____

_____

11 빈칸(A)~(C)를 〈보기〉에 주어진 단어를 이용해서 채우시오. (형태 변화 가능)

> ┌ 보기 ┐
> come   go   protect   raise
> send   throw   visit

➡ (A) _____ (B) _____ (C) _____

12 다음 대화의 (A)~(D)에 어울리는 말을 골라 쓰시오.

> B: Did you watch the news about the flood?
>
> G: Yes, I did. They said a lot of people (A)[lose / lost / are going to lose] their homes.
>
> B: My club is going to (B)[spend / sell / send] them some money.
>
> G: How can you do that? Are you going to (C)[raise / rise / arise] money, Andy?
>
> B: Yes. We're going to make pencil cases and (D)[sell / to sell / selling] them.

➡ (A) _____ (B) _____ (C) _____

(C) _____

13 다음 대화의 흐름상 어색한 것을 고르시오.

> Karl: Jiho, isn't that too much? Are you going to eat all of that?
>
> Jiho: ①I'm not sure, but Bulgogi is my favorite.
>
> Karl: Hey! Look at the campaign poster. "Think, Eat, Save!"
>
> Jiho: ②What does that mean?
>
> Karl: ③It means "Think first before you eat and save the Earth."
>
> Jiho: ④I think I took too much Bulgogi. Let's share it.
>
> Karl: Okay. That's a good idea.
>
> Jiho: We ate it all. My clean plate makes me feel good.
>
> Karl: ⑤Let's waste food from now on. I hope we can save the Earth.

①   ②   ③   ④   ⑤

14 다음 문장의 빈칸에 알맞은 것은?

> Do you know the girl _____ is sitting on the bench?

① when ② who ③ what
④ which ⑤ whose

15 다음 빈칸에 공통으로 들어갈 말로 알맞은 것은?

> • I want to buy a backpack _____ has many big pockets.
> • The girl _____ is standing under the tree looks like my sister.

① that ② who ③ which
④ she ⑤ it

16 다음 두 문장을 관계대명사를 이용하여 한 문장으로 바꾸시오.

> • The man is my friend.
> • He is working in the garden.

➡ _____

17 다음 중 어법상 어색한 것은?

① I want to buy something special for my mom.
② Did I do anything wrong?
③ Mr. Jackson is planning to eat something nice in the evening.
④ They have nothing special to do this weekend.
⑤ If you want to experience special something, come and enjoy the Songkran festival.

18 다음 글에서 어법상 어색한 것을 찾아 바르게 고치시오.

> My advice is to always think before you speak, especially when you want to say bad something about someone else.

_____ ➡ _____

19 다음 문장에서 생략된 관계대명사를 보충하여 다시 쓰시오.

> I will buy the novels written by Ernest Hemingway.

➡ _____

20 다음 글의 빈칸에 들어갈 말이 알맞게 짝지어진 것은?

> • Thery are many pets ___(A)___ require a lot of care and attention.
> • My role model is a woman ___(B)___ won a gold medal in the Olympics.

① that – which ② who – who
③ which – who ④ who – which
⑤ which – which

[21~23] 다음 글을 읽고 물음에 답하시오.

> This is the Global Citizenship Education site. ⓐ세계 시민 교육은 우리가 세계 시민으로 자라도록 도와줍니다. Global citizens are people who try to understand different cultures. They also care for people in need and work for a better world. Please ___ⓑ___ your global citizenship education experiences here.

21 위 글의 밑줄 친 ⓐ의 우리말에 맞게 주어진 어휘를 이용하여 9 단어로 영작하시오.

> as

➡ _____
_____

22 다음 영영풀이를 참고하여 위 대화의 빈칸 ⓑ에 철자 s로 시작하는 단어를 쓰시오. 〈출제율 90%〉

> have in common or use in common

➡ _____

23 위 글을 읽고 대답할 수 <u>없는</u> 질문은? 〈출제율 95%〉

① What site is this?
② How does Global Citizenship Education help us grow as global citizens?
③ What do global citizens try to understand?
④ Whom do global citizens care for?
⑤ What do global citizens work for?

[24~26] 다음 글을 읽고 물음에 답하시오.

Hello. I am Minhee from Korea. I am a member of the Global Community Club. ⓐ우리 동아리는 전 세계의 사람들과 소통하는 것을 목표로 해. A week ago we produced a video about the lantern festival in our village. We uploaded ⓑit to the Internet and amazingly, we got nearly 5,000 hits. Click here for our video.
└ **Alice:** Wow, your lantern festival looks fantastic!
└ **Sunan:** We have a water festival in our village. I'd like ⓒto make a video like yours.

24 위 글의 밑줄 친 ⓐ의 우리말에 맞게 한 단어를 보충하여, 주어진 어휘를 알맞게 배열하시오. 〈출제율 95%〉

> to / world / club / around / aims / people / the / communicate / from / my

➡ _____
_____

25 위 글의 밑줄 친 ⓑit이 가리키는 것을 본문에서 찾아 영어로 쓰시오. 〈출제율 90%〉

➡ _____

26 아래 보기에서 위 글의 밑줄 친 ⓒto make와 to부정사의 용법이 <u>다른</u> 것의 개수를 고르시오. 〈출제율 100%〉

> ┤ 보기 ├
> ① She went there to meet him.
> ② Did he promise to study hard?
> ③ It's time to start from the station.
> ④ Is there something wrong to correct?
> ⑤ What do you need to make the food?

① 1개 ② 2개 ③ 3개 ④ 4개 ⑤ 5개

[27~28] 다음 글을 읽고 물음에 답하시오.

I am Afig from Malaysia. My school started a wall painting campaign to make our village look better. Students who are good at ⓐ gathered and painted on some walls of schools and parks. Thanks to this campaign, our village looks ⓑ nicer. Now everyone can enjoy walking alongside the ⓒ walls.

27 위 글의 빈칸 ⓐ와 ⓒ에 paint를 각각 알맞은 형태로 쓰시오. 〈출제율 95%〉

➡ ⓐ _____ ⓒ _____

28 빈칸 ⓑ에 들어갈 수 <u>없는</u> 것은? 〈출제율 95%〉

① far   ② very
③ even   ④ still
⑤ a lot

[01~02] 주어진 영영풀이에 해당하는 단어를 이용하여 다음 대화의 빈칸을 채우시오. (내용상이나 어법상 단어 추가 가능)

01

A: Are you going _____ bottles?
B: Yes, I am.

to process used or waste materials so as to make suitable for reuse

➡ _____

02 중요

A: I hope people _____ animals.
B: I hope so, too. Let's hold a Love Animals campaign.
A: That's a good idea.

to injure or cause pain to a part of someone's body

➡ _____

03 괄호 안의 단어를 이용하여 밑줄 친 우리말을 바르게 영작하시오. (if로 시작할 것)

W: Every day, many students leave some food on their plates. So, our club is going to hold a campaign about it. 만약 여러분이 접시에 담은 음식을 다 먹는다면, 작은 선물을 받을 것이다. I hope many students join our campaign.

➡_____
_____

(finish, small, if, get, gift, all)

04 다음 우리말에 맞게 주어진 단어를 이용하여 빈칸에 들어갈 알맞은 말을 쓰시오.

(1) 우리 계획에는 잘못된 것이 있어.
➡ There is _____ _____ with our plan. (wrong, something)

(2) 거기에 재미있는 게 있니?
➡ Is there _____ _____ there? (anything, interesting)

(3) 우리는 중요한 모든 것을 복사해야 한다.
➡ We must take a copy of _____ _____. (important, everything)

05 중요 다음 문장에서 어법상 틀린 부분을 찾아 바르게 고쳐 쓰시오.

(1) This is the girl who like to play the violin.
_____ ➡ _____

(2) The man which teach English is my father.
_____ ➡ _____

06 다음 두 문장을 관계대명사를 이용하여 한 문장으로 바꾸시오.

(1) • I like my house.
• It is by the lake.
➡ _____

(2) • Look at my dog.
• It is playing with a ball.
➡ _____

07 다음 문장은 생략 가능한 부분이 있다. 생략하여 문장을 다시 쓰시오.

> Look at the bird that is flying in the sky.

➡ _____

[08~10] 다음 글을 읽고 물음에 답하시오.

Hello. I am Minhee from Korea. I am a member of the Global Community Club. My club aims to communicate with people from around the world. A week ago we produced a video about the lantern festival in our village. We (A)[uploaded / downloaded] it to the Internet and amazingly, we got (B)[near / nearly] 5,000 hits. Click here for our video.

└ Alice: Wow, your lantern festival looks fantastic!

└ Sunan: We have a water festival in our village. I'd like (C)[to make / making] a video like yours.

08 위 글의 괄호 (A)~(C)에서 문맥이나 어법상 알맞은 낱말을 골라 쓰시오.

➡ (A) _____ (B) _____ (C) _____

09 다음 빈칸 (A)와 (B)에 알맞은 단어를 넣어 Global Community Club에 대한 소개를 완성하시오. (본문의 단어를 이용할 것.)

> It is a club whose ____(A)____ is to communicate with people from around the world. The club members made a video introducing a local festival and ____(B)____ it to the Internet.

➡ (A) _____ (B) _____

10 다음 문장에서 위 글의 내용과 <u>다른 부분</u>을 찾아서 고치시오.

> A week ago Minhee's club made a video about the lantern festival in the world.

_____ ➡ _____

[11~13] 다음 글을 읽고 물음에 답하시오.

I am Afig from Malaysia. My school started a wall painting campaign ⓐ<u>우리 마을을 더 좋아 보이게 하기 위해서.</u> Students who are good at painting gathered and painted on some walls of schools and parks. Thanks to ⓑ<u>this campaign,</u> ⓒ<u>our village looks very nicer.</u> Now everyone can enjoy walking alongside the painted walls.

11 위 글의 밑줄 친 ⓐ의 우리말에 맞게 주어진 어휘를 이용하여 6 단어로 영작하시오.

> to, better

➡ _____

12 다음 빈칸 (A)와 (B)에 알맞은 단어를 넣어 ⓑthis campaign 에 대한 설명을 완성하시오.

> It is a (A)_____ _____ campaign which Afig's school started, and students who (B)_____ well gathered and painted on some walls of schools and parks.

➡ (A) _____ _____ (B) _____

13 위 글의 밑줄 친 ⓒ에서 어법상 틀린 부분을 찾아 고치시오.

_____ ➡ _____

01 다음 그림을 보고 여름 방학에 하려고 계획하는 일에 대한 대화의 빈칸을 완성하시오. (주어진 단어를 활용할 것)

Karen – vegetable garden

Yuri – do volunteer work, library

> **Yuri:** Do you have any plans for _____, Karen?
>
> **Karen:** Yes. _____. (going) How about you?
>
> **Yuri:** _____. (planning)
>
> **Karen:** That's a good idea.

02 〈보기〉를 참고하여 주어진 단어와 관계대명사를 이용하여 사람을 묘사하는 문장 3개를 만드시오.

> ─── 보기 ───
> A thief is a person who steals things.

> a thief / a musician / a dentist / a genius / a patient
> steals things / sees a doctor / plays music / takes care of your teeth / is very intelligent

03 다음 세계 시민 교육을 실천하기 위해 어떤 활동을 할지에 관한 내용을 바탕으로 세계 시민 교육 활동의 참가자를 모집하는 공고문을 만드시오.

> **A:** What kind of activity do you like?
>
> **B:** What do you think about sending shoes to poor children?
>
> **C:** Good. I hope they are happy with them.
>
> **D:** Let's make a poster about the activity to find people who want to help.

> Why   To help poor children who don't have ___(A)___
>
> How   1. Bring shoes from home.
>
>   2. ___(B)___ pictures or ___(C)___ caring words on them.
>
>   3. Send them to children in ___(D)___.
>
> When   July 3rd
>
> If you want to do something ___(E)___ for the world, join us!

단원별 모의고사

01 주어진 문장의 밑줄 친 hold의 뜻과 같은 의미로 쓰이지 <u>않</u>은 것을 고르시오.

> A: I hope the air gets cleaner.
> B: I hope so, too. Let's <u>hold</u> a Plant More Trees campaign.
> A: That's a good idea.

① I <u>held</u> a party this morning.
② The kite festival is <u>held</u> every year.
③ He <u>held</u> her by the arm.
④ The fans <u>held</u> an online contest last year.
⑤ We <u>held</u> a celebration for his promotion.

02 다음 우리말 해석에 맞게 빈칸을 완성하시오. (철자가 주어진 경우 그 철자로 시작할 것)

(1) Tickets are $2 for a_____ and $1 for children. (티켓은 어른은 2달러이고 아이들은 1달러이다.)
(2) Tom a_____ to be back to work in time, but was _____. (Tom은 제시간에 직장에 돌아가려고 목표했지만 늦었다.)
(3) We should know the value of _____. (우리는 교육의 가치를 알아야 한다.)
(4) Members of the charity r_____ money for people _____ _____. (그 자선 단체 회원들은 어려움에 처한 사람들을 위해 모금한다.)

[03~04] 다음 글을 읽고 물음에 답하시오.

> W: Every day, many students ___(A)___ some food on their plates. So, our club is going to ___(B)___ a campaign about it. If you ___(C)___ all the food on your plate, you will get a small gift. 나는 많은 학생들이 우리 캠페인에 참여하기를 바란다.

03 다음 〈보기〉에서 빈칸 (A)~(C)에 들어갈 단어를 골라 쓰시오.

> ┤ 보기 ├
> hold hope mean save volunteer
> leave finish hurt get

➡ (A) _____ (B) _____ (C) _____

04 괄호 안의 단어를 이용하여 밑줄 친 우리말을 바르게 영작하시오.

➡ _____

(join, hope, many)

[05~06] 다음 대화를 읽고 물음에 답하시오.

> B: Did you watch the news about the flood?
> G: Yes, I did. They said a lot of people lost their homes.
> B: My club is going to send them some money.
> G: How can you do that? Are you going to raise money, Andy?
> B: Yes. We're going to make pencil cases and sell them.

05 다음 영영풀이에 해당하는 단어를 대화에서 찾아 쓰시오.

> to give goods in exchange for money

➡ _____

06 위 대화를 읽고 답할 수 <u>없는</u> 질문을 고르시오.

① Did the boy watch the news about the flood?
② Why did many people lose their homes?
③ Is the boy a member of the club?
④ How will the boy raise the money?
⑤ Does the girl know how to make pencil cases?

[07~09] 다음 대화를 읽고 물음에 답하시오.

> B: What's your plan ⓐfor the weekend, Sumin? Are you going to do ⓑspecial anything? (①)
> G: Yes. (②) ⓒOn Saturday, ⓓI was going to visit my grandmother.
> B: ⓔHow about on Sunday? (③)
> G: (④) I have no plans for Sunday. Why?
> B: I'm going to ___(A)___ volunteer work at the library on Sunday. (⑤)
> G: Sure.

07 위 대화의 ①~⑤ 중 주어진 말이 들어갈 알맞은 곳은?

> Would you like to come with me?

①   ②   ③   ④   ⑤

08 ⓐ~ⓔ 중 어법상 어색한 부분을 모두 골라 고치시오.

➡ _____

_____

09 위 대화의 빈칸 (A)에 알맞은 말을 대화에서 찾아 쓰시오.

➡ _____

[10~11] 다음 대화를 읽고 물음에 답하시오.

> G: What are you doing, Jason?
> B: I'm making a poster about global hunger. Many people are (A)die of hunger.
> G: That's too bad. I didn't know that.
> B: (B)더 많은 사람들이 세계의 기아 문제에 관심을 갖기를 바라.

10 밑줄 친 (A)를 알맞은 형으로 고치시오.

➡ _____

11 괄호 안의 단어를 이용하여 밑줄 친 우리말을 바르게 영작하시오.

➡ _____

(care, global, hope, more)

12 ⓐ~ⓔ 중 어법상 어색한 부분을 모두 골라 고치시오.

> G: Dad, my class decided ⓐmaking a vegetable garden.
> M: A vegetable garden? ⓑWhat will you grow there, Sena?
> G: Carrots. We'll grow them and share ⓒit ⓓby others.
> M: That's a good idea.
> G: I hope the carrots grow ⓔgood.

➡ _____

_____

13 다음 괄호 안의 단어를 알맞은 곳에 넣어 문장을 다시 쓰시오.

(1) She wanted to do something. (different)
   ➡ _____
(2) I did nothing last year. (special)
   ➡ _____
(3) Your daughter will never do anything again. (stupid)
   ➡ _____

14 두 문장을 한 문장으로 바꾸어 쓸 때 빈칸에 알맞은 말은?

> • She bought an expensive watch.
> • It was made in Switzerland.
> ➡ She bought an expensive watch
> _____ made in Switzerland.

① which
② which were
③ who was
④ which was
⑤ who

15 다음 중 어법상 틀린 문장을 바르게 고친 것이 아닌 것은?

① The film who was based on a true story impressed many people.
  ➡ The film which was based on a true story impressed many people.
② We need delicious something.
  ➡ We need something delicious.
③ Look at the girl who are playing the violin on the stage.
  ➡ Look at the girl who is playing the violin on the stage.
④ The car who is parked here is mine.
  ➡ The car which is parked here is mine.
⑤ Is there strong somebody to carry this box?
  ➡ Is there strong anybody to carry this box?

16 다음 문장의 빈칸에 알맞은 말을 쓰시오.

> Abraham Lincoln was the sixteenth President _____ succeeded in freeing black slaves.

➡ _____

17 다음 글을 읽고 밑줄 친 부분을 바르게 고치시오.

> Sori has bought the latest cell phone. The cell phone whose has a camera is really small. My cousin who live in California has the same cell phone.

➡ _____ ➡ _____
_____ ➡ _____

18 다음 두 문장을 한 문장으로 알맞게 바꾼 것은?

> • I bought a car.
> • It was made in Germany.

① I bought a car which made in Germany.
② I bought a car who was made in Germany.
③ I bought a car who made in Germany.
④ I bought a car which was made in Germany.
⑤ I bought a car that made in Germany.

19 다음 중 어법상 어색한 것은?

① There are people who make noises in public places.
② She lives in the house which has seven bedrooms.
③ He has the dog that has brown eyes.
④ Summer is the season that comes after spring.
⑤ I read the letter who was written in French.

[20~21] 다음 글을 읽고 물음에 답하시오.

> This is the Global Citizenship Education site. Global Citizenship Education helps us grow as global citizens. Global citizens are people who try ⓐto understand different cultures. ⓑ 그들은 또한 어려움에 처한 사람들을 보살핀다 and work for a better world. Please share your global citizenship education experiences here.

20 위 글의 밑줄 친 ⓐto understand와 to부정사의 용법이 같은 것을 모두 고르시오.

① She worked hard to pass the test.
② What's the fast way to buy the ticket?
③ It is important to finish your work.
④ She decided to meet her sister.
⑤ He was happy to meet her.

21 위 글의 밑줄 친 ⓑ의 우리말에 맞게 한 단어를 보충하여, 주어진 어휘를 알맞게 배열하시오.

> for / they / care / need / people / also

➡ _____

[22~23] 다음 글을 읽고 물음에 답하시오.

> Hello. I am Minhee from Korea. (①) I am a member of the Global Community Club. (②) My club aims to communicate with people from around the world. (③) We uploaded it to the Internet and amazingly, we got nearly 5,000 hits. (④) Click here for our video. (⑤)
> └ **Alice:** Wow, your lantern festival looks fantastic!
> └ **Sunan:** We have a water festival in our village. I'd like to make a video like ⓐyours.

22 위 글의 흐름으로 보아, 주어진 문장이 들어가기에 가장 적절한 곳은?

> A week ago we produced a video about the lantern festival in our village.

①   ②   ③   ④   ⑤

23 위 글의 밑줄 친 ⓐyours가 가리키는 것을 영어로 쓰시오.

➡ _____

[24~25] 다음 글을 읽고 물음에 답하시오.

> I am Afig from Malaysia. My school started a wall painting campaign to make our village (A)[look / to look] better. Students who are good at painting gathered and painted on some walls of schools and parks. Thanks to this campaign, our village looks much nicer. Now everyone can enjoy (B)[to walk / walking] alongside the painted walls.
> └ **Junho:** (C)[How / What] a nice idea!

24 위 글의 괄호 (A)~(C)에서 어법상 알맞은 낱말을 골라 쓰시오.

➡ (A) _____ (B) _____ (C) _____

25 위 글을 읽고 대답할 수 없는 질문은?

① Where is Afig from?
② What did Afig's school start?
③ Who gathered and painted?
④ How many students joined it?
⑤ Where did the students paint?

Interesting Facts Are Around Us

Words & Expressions

Key Words

- **adult**[ədʌ́lt] 명 성인, 어른
- **again**[əgén] 부 다시
- **average**[ǽvəridʒ] 명 보통, 평균
- **bite**[bait] 동 물다
- **blood**[blʌd] 명 피
- **bone**[boun] 명 뼈
- **completely**[kəmplíːtli] 부 완전히
- **during**[djúəriŋ] 전 ~ 동안, ~ 중에
- **enough**[inʌ́f] 형 충분한
- **expand**[ikspǽnd] 동 팽창하다
- **false**[fɔːls] 형 거짓의
- **female**[fíːmeil] 명 여성, 암컷
- **fewer**[fjúːər] 형 (**few**의 비교급) 보다 적은
- **gravity**[grǽvəti] 명 중력
- **grow**[grou] 동 (사람·동식물 등이) 자라다, 성장하다
- **guess**[ges] 동 추측하다
- **heat**[hiːt] 명 열, 열기
- **inventor**[invéntər] 명 발명가
- **item**[áitəm] 명 항목, 물품

- **lay**[lei] 동 (새·곤충 등이) [알을] 낳다
- **lightning**[láitniŋ] 명 번개, 벼락
- **male**[meil] 명 남성, 수컷
- **Mars**[maːrz] 명 화성
- **metal**[métl] 명 금속
- **mosquito**[məskíːtou] 명 모기
- **next**[nekst] 형 다음의 부 그 다음에
- **produce**[prədjúːs] 동 (자식·새끼를) 낳다
- **rest**[rest] 동 쉬다, 휴식하다
- **same**[seim] 형 같은, 똑같은
- **strike**[straik] 동 부딪치다, 충돌하다
- **tongue**[tʌŋ] 명 혀
- **topic**[tápik] 명 화제, 주제
- **toward**[tɔːrd] 전 (위치·방향) ~쪽으로
- **twice**[twais] 부 두 번, 두 배
- **Venus**[víːnəs] 명 금성
- **weaken**[wíːkən] 동 약화시키다, 약화되다
- **weigh**[wei] 동 무게가 ~ 나가다, 무게를 달다
- **whale**[hweil] 명 고래

Key Expressions

- **a few** 약간의, 조금
- **be full of** ~로 가득 차다
- **due to** ~ 때문에
- **find out** 알아보다, 찾아보다
- **go away** 사라지다
- **in fact** 사실상, 실제로

- **join together** ~와 이어지다
- **on average** 평균적으로
- **over and over** 여러 번, 몇 번이고
- **such as** ~와 같은
- **up to** (특정한 수 또는 정도) ~까지
- **with time** 시간이 지남에 따라

Word Power

※ 뒤에 접미사 'en'을 붙여 형용사가 동사로 바뀌는 단어

☐ **bright**(밝은) → **brighten**(밝히다)

☐ **dark**(어두운) → **darken**(어둡게 하다)

☐ **straight**(똑바른) → **straighten**(똑바르게 하다)

☐ **weak**(약한) → **weaken**(약화시키다)

☐ **broad**(넓은) → **broaden**(넓어지다)

☐ **deep**(깊은) → **deepen**(깊게 하다)

☐ **short**(짧은) → **shorten**(줄이다, 짧아지다)

☐ **tight**(꽉 조인) → **tighten**(꽉 조이다)

※ 서로 반대되는 뜻을 가진 단어

☐ **false**(거짓의) ↔ **true**(사실인)

☐ **same**(같은, 똑같은) ↔ **different**(다른)

☐ **female**(여성, 암컷) ↔ **male**(남성, 수컷)

☐ **weaken**(약화시키다, 약화되다) ↔ **strengthen**(강화하다)

※ 서로 비슷한 뜻을 가진 단어

☐ **enough**(충분한) : **sufficient**(충분한)

☐ **next**(다음의) : **following**(다음의, 다음에 계속되는)

☐ **guess**(추측하다) : **estimate**(평가하다, 추정하다)

☐ **topic**(화제, 주제) : **subject**(주제, 당면 과제)

English Dictionary

☐ **average** 보통, 평균
→ the usual amount, extent, quality, number, etc.
보통[평균]의 양, 정도, 질, 수 등

☐ **bite** 물다
→ to seize or grasp something with teeth
이를 이용해 무언가를 붙잡거나 움켜잡다

☐ **blood** 피
→ a red fluid in living things
살아있는 것 안에 있는 빨간 액체

☐ **bone** 뼈
→ a white piece of tissue providing structural support for the body
몸에 구조적 지지를 제공하는 하얀 조직

☐ **completely** 완전히
→ to a complete degree or to the full or entire extent
완전한 정도로 또는 완전히 또는 전적으로

☐ **expand** 팽창하다
→ to increase in size, number, or importance
크기, 수 또는 중요성에서 증가하다

☐ **false** 거짓의
→ not real, because it is not true
진실이 아니기 때문에 사실이 아닌

☐ **female** 여성, 암컷
→ the gender which has the ability to give birth to children
아이를 낳을 수 있는 성

☐ **gravity** 중력
→ the force that a planet pulls things towards the center of it
행성이 그것의 중심 쪽으로 당기는 힘

☐ **inventor** 발명가
→ a person who creates something that does not exist
존재하지 않는 어떤 것을 창조하는 사람

☐ **male** 남성, 수컷
→ the gender which does not give birth
출산할 수 없는 성

☐ **metal** 금속
→ a hard substance such as lead, iron, gold, etc.
납, 철, 금 등과 같은 단단한 물질

☐ **mosquito** 모기
→ a small flying insect which bites and sucks blood
물고, 피를 빠는 날아다니는 작은 곤충

☐ **rest** 쉬다, 휴식하다
→ to spend a period of time relaxing or sleeping after doing something tiring
무엇인가 피곤한 일을 한 후에 쉬거나 자면서 일정한 시간을 보내다

☐ **strike** 부딪치다, 충돌하다
→ to come or bring into heavy contact with someone or something
어떤 사람이나 물체와 강하게 접촉하다

☐ **weigh** 무게가 ~ 나가다, 무게를 달다
→ to find how heavy a person or thing is
사람이나 물건이 얼마나 무거운지 알아보다

Interesting Facts Are Around Us

Welcome to "Ask Dr. Lawrence"! The world is full of interesting
~로 가득 차다 = is filled with
things. Take this quiz and find out how much you know about them.
의문문이 다른 문장의 일부가 되어 목적어로 쓰이는 것을 간접의문문
이라고 한다. 간접의문문은 '의문사+주어+동사'의 어순으로 쓴다.
Are you ready?

Quiz

1. The Eiffel Tower gets taller during the summer.
'get+비교급'은 '더 ~하게 되다, 더 ~해진다'는 의미로 상태의 변화를 포함하는 표현이다.
2. Babies have fewer bones than adults. 여기서는 '더 커진다'는 의미로 쓰였다.
형용사 'few'의 비교급인 'fewer'와 'than'을 사용하여 어린아이와 어른의 뼈의 수를 비교하였다.
3. Only female mosquitoes bite people.
여성의, 암컷의   모기
4. Lightning never strikes the same place twice.
'never'는 'not'처럼 문장 전체를 부정문으로 만드는 부정어이다. 의미상 'not' 보다 강한 부정을 나타내어 '결코 두 번
5. The elephant is the biggest animal on the Earth. 내리치지 않는다'는 의미로 쓰였다.
셋 이상의 사물과 사람 중 '가장 ~하다'는 최상의 의미: the+최상급
6. There is no gravity in space.
'no'는 뒤에 오는 명사를 부정으로 수식해 주므로 '중력이 없다'는 의미가 된다.

1. Metal expands in heat. Due to summer heat, the metal of the Eiffel
'expand'는 '팽창하다'라는 의미의 자동사와 '~을 확장시키다'라는 의미의 타동사로 모두 쓰인다. 여기서는 '금속이 팽창한다'라는 의미의 자동사로 쓰였다.
Tower expands. In summer, the Eiffel tower gets 15cm taller than in

winter.

2. Adults have 206 bones, but babies have about 300 bones. With time,
약   '시간이 지남에 따라'
some of the babies' bones join together, so adults have fewer bones
'so'는 인과 관계를 나타내는 접속사로 앞뒤 내용이 원인과 결과로 이어질 때 쓴다.
than babies.

female 여성의, 암컷의; 여성, 암컷

mosquito 모기

strike 치다, 때리다

gravity 중력

be full of ~로 가득 차다
(= be filled with)

false 거짓의

metal 금속

expand 팽창하다, 확장하다

due to ~ 때문에

with time 시간이 지남에 따라

확인문제

- 다음 문장이 본문의 내용과 일치하면 T, 일치하지 않으면 F를 쓰시오.

1   The world is full of interesting things. ☐

2   Due to winter cold, the metal of the Eiffel Tower expands. ☐

3   In winter, the Eiffel tower gets 15cm taller than in summer. ☐

4   Adults have 206 bones, but babies have about 300 bones. ☐

5   With time, some of the babies' bones join together. ☐

6   Adults have more bones than babies. ☐

'알을 낳기 위하여'라는 의미로 to부정사의 부사적 용법

3. Only female mosquitoes will bite you. They need blood to produce

They = female mosquitoes

eggs. After a female mosquito gets enough blood, she'll rest for a

부사절 / after는 부사적 접속사 　　　　　　　　　　　　　쉬다, 휴식하다

few days and lay her eggs.

lay–laid–laid. 놓다, (새·곤충·어류가) (알을) 낳다

4. Lightning can strike the same place over and over again. The Empire

반복해서

State Building gets hit by lightning 23 times a year on average.

보통, 평균

5. The biggest animal on the Earth is the blue whale. It can weigh

최상급: the+형용사-est 　　　　　　　　　　　　　　'weigh'는 '~만큼 무게가 나가다'라는 동사

up to 180 tons and grow up to 30 meters long. Its tongue alone can

up to'는 '~까지'라는 의미로, 'weigh up to'가　　'grow up to'는 '~까지 자라다'라는 의미이다.　　~만으로도
게 쓰여 '~까지 무게가 나가다'라는 의미로 쓰였다.

weigh as much as an average African elephant.

as+부사+as: 원급비교

6. In fact, there is gravity everywhere in space. As you get farther from

사실　　　　　　　　　　　　　　　　　'as'는 '~함에 따라'라는 의미의 접속사로 쓰였다.

the Earth, the gravity of the Earth weakens, but it never goes away

weaken: 약해지다　　'but'은 등위접속사로, 앞문장과
반대되는 내용을 연결해 준다.

completely. When you get closer to another planet, such as Mars or

완전히　　　　　　　　　　　　　'such as'는 '~와 같은'이라는 의미로, 'like'와 바꿔 쓸 수 있다.　　화성

Venus, its gravity becomes stronger than that of the Earth.

금성　　'another planet'을 가리키는 소유격

Which of these quiz items is the most interesting to you? There will

항목　　　3음절 이상의 형용사는 앞에 the most를 붙여 최상급을 만듦

be another quiz soon. Guess what the next topic will be. See you next

'의문사(what)+주어(the next topic)+동사(will be)'의
간접의문문으로 'guess'의 목적어

month.

rest 쉬다, 휴식을 취하다

lightning 번개

average 평균의

whale 고래

weigh 무게가 나가다, ~의 무게를 달다

tongue 혀

up to ~까지

weaken 약화시키다

completely 완전히

Mars 화성

Venus 금성

item 항목, 물품

📎 **확인문제**

● 다음 문장이 본문의 내용과 일치하면 T, 일치하지 않으면 F를 쓰시오.

1 Female mosquitoes need blood to produce eggs. ☐

2 Lightning never strikes the same place twice. ☐

3 The elephant is the largest animal on the Earth. ☐

4 The blue whale can weigh up to 180 tons. ☐

5 The blue whale's tongue alone can weigh as much as an average African elephant. ☐

6 As you get farther from the Earth, the gravity of the Earth weakens, and it goes away completely. ☐

● 우리말을 참고하여 빈칸에 알맞은 말을 쓰시오.

1 _____ _____ Are _____ Us

2 _____ _____ "Ask Dr. Lawrence"!

3 The world _____ _____ _____ interesting things.

4 Take this quiz and find out _____ _____ _____ _____ about them.

5 Are you _____?

6 _____

7 The Eiffel Tower _____ _____ during the summer.

8 Babies have _____ bones _____ adults.

9 _____ female mosquitoes _____ people.

10 Lightning _____ _____ the same place twice.

11 The elephant is _____ _____ _____ on the Earth.

12 There is _____ _____ in space.

13 Metal expands _____ _____.

14 _____ _____ summer heat, the metal of the Eiffel Tower _____.

15 In summer, the Eiffel tower _____ 15cm _____ _____ in winter.

16 _____ have 206 bones, but babies have _____ 300 bones.

17 _____ _____, some of the babies' bones _____ _____, so adults have fewer bones than babies.

1	흥미로운 사실들은 우리 주위에 있다
2	"Lawrence 박사에게 물어 보세요"에 오신 것을 환영합니다!
3	세상은 흥미로운 것들로 가득 차 있습니다.
4	퀴즈를 풀어보고 그것들에 대해 얼마나 아는지 알아보세요.
5	준비 됐나요?
6	퀴즈
7	에펠 타워는 여름에 키가 더 커진다.
8	아기들은 어른보다 더 적은 수의 뼈를 가지고 있다.
9	암컷 모기만이 사람을 문다.
10	번개는 결코 같은 곳을 내리치지 않는다.
11	코끼리는 지구에서 가장 큰 동물이다.
12	우주에는 중력이 없다.
13	금속은 열에 팽창한다.
14	여름의 열기 때문에, 에펠 타워의 금속은 팽창한다.
15	여름에 에펠 타워는 겨울보다 15센티미터 정도 더 커진다.
16	어른은 206개의 뼈를 가지고 있고, 아기는 대략 300개의 뼈를 가지고 있다.
17	시간이 흐르면서, 아기의 몇몇 뼈들은 붙는다. 그래서 어른들은 아기보다 더 적은 수의 뼈를 가지고 있다.

18 _____ _____ _____ will bite you.

19 They need blood _____ _____ _____.

20 After a female mosquito gets _____ _____, she'll _____ for a few days and _____ her eggs.

21 Lightning can strike the same place _____ _____ _____ _____.

22 The Empire State Building _____ _____ _____ lightning 23 times a year _____ _____.

23 _____ _____ _____ on the Earth is the blue whale.

24 It can weigh _____ _____ 180 tons and grow _____ _____ 30 meters _____.

25 Its tongue _____ can weigh _____ _____ _____ an average African elephant.

26 _____ _____, there is gravity everywhere in space.

27 As you _____ _____ from the Earth, the gravity of the Earth _____, but it never goes away _____.

28 When you _____ _____ to another planet, _____ _____ Mars or Venus, its gravity becomes stronger than _____ _____ the Earth.

29 _____ of these quiz items is _____ _____ _____ to you?

30 There will be _____ _____ soon.

31 Guess _____ _____ _____ _____ _____ _____.

32 _____ _____ next month.

18 오직 암컷 모기만이 당신을 물 것이다.

19 그들은 알을 생산하기 위해서 피가 필요하다.

20 암컷 모기는 충분히 흡혈을 한 뒤, 며칠 동안 쉬고 알을 낳는 다.

21 번개는 같은 곳을 반복해서 칠 수 있다.

22 엠파이어스테이트 빌딩은 한 해 평균 스물세 번 번개를 맞는다.

23 지구상에서 가장 큰 동물은 흰 긴수염고래이다.

24 그것은 무게가 180톤까지 나갈 수 있으며 길이는 30미터까지 자랄 수 있다.

25 이 고래의 혀의 무게만 해도 아 프리카 코끼리의 평균 무게만큼 무겁다.

26 사실, 중력은 우주의 어디에나 있다.

27 지구에서 멀어 질수록 지구의 중력은 약해지지만, 결코 그것 이 완전히 사라지는 것은 아니 다.

28 당신이 화성이나 금성 같은 다 른 행성에 더 가까워진다면, 그 들의 중력은 지구의 그것보다 더 강해진다.

29 이 퀴즈들 중 어떤 퀴즈가 가장 흥미로웠나요?

30 곧 또 다른 퀴즈가 있을 것입니 다.

31 다음 주제는 무엇일지 맞춰보세 요.

32 다음 달에 만나요.

● 우리말을 참고하여 본문을 영작하시오.

1 흥미로운 사실들은 우리 주위에 있다

➡ _____

2 "Lawrence 박사에게 물어 보세요"에 오신 것을 환영합니다!

➡ _____

3 세상은 흥미로운 것들로 가득 차 있습니다.

➡ _____

4 퀴즈를 풀어보고 그것들에 대해 얼마나 아는지 알아보세요.

➡ _____

5 준비 됐나요?

➡ _____

6 퀴즈

➡ _____

7 에펠 타워는 여름에 키가 더 커진다.

➡ _____

8 아기들은 어른보다 더 적은 수의 뼈를 가지고 있다.

➡ _____

9 암컷 모기만이 사람을 문다.

➡ _____

10 번개는 결코 같은 곳을 내리치지 않는다.

➡ _____

11 코끼리는 지구에서 가장 큰 동물이다.

➡ _____

12 우주에는 중력이 없다.

➡ _____

13 금속은 열에 팽창한다.

➡ _____

14 여름의 열기 때문에, 에펠 타워의 금속은 팽창한다.

➡ _____

15 여름에 에펠 타워는 겨울보다 15센티미터 정도 더 커진다.

➡ _____

16 어른은 206개의 뼈를 가지고 있고, 아기는 대략 300개의 뼈를 가지고 있다.

➡ _____

17 시간이 흐르면서, 아기의 몇몇 뼈들은 붙는다. 그래서 어른들은 아기보다 더 적은 수의 뼈를 가지고 있다.

➡ _____

18 오직 암컷 모기만이 당신을 물 것이다.

➡ _____

19 그들은 알을 생산하기 위해서 피가 필요하다.

➡ _____

20 암컷 모기는 충분히 흡혈을 한 뒤, 며칠 동안 쉬고 알을 낳는다.

➡ _____

21 번개는 같은 곳을 반복해서 칠 수 있다.

➡ _____

22 엠파이어스테이트 빌딩은 한 해 평균 스물세 번 번개를 맞는다.

➡ _____

23 지구상에서 가장 큰 동물은 흰긴수염고래이다.

➡ _____

24 그것은 무게가 180톤까지 나갈 수 있으며 길이는 30미터 까지 자랄 수 있다.

➡ _____

25 이 고래의 혀의 무게만 해도 아프리카 코끼리의 평균 무게만큼 무겁다.

➡ _____

26 사실, 중력은 우주의 어디에나 있다.

➡ _____

27 지구에서 멀어 질수록 지구의 중력은 약해지지만, 결코 그것이 완전히 사라지는 것은 아니다.

➡ _____

28 당신이 화성이나 금성 같은 다른 행성에 더 가까워진다면, 그들의 중력은 지구의 그것보다 더 강해진다.

➡ _____

29 이 퀴즈들 중 어떤 퀴즈가 가장 흥미로웠나요?

➡ _____

30 곧 또 다른 퀴즈가 있을 것입니다.

➡ _____

31 다음 주제는 무엇일지 맞춰보세요.

➡ _____

32 다음 달에 만나요.

➡ _____

01 다음 〈보기〉와 같은 관계가 되도록 빈칸에 주어진 철자로 시작하여 알맞은 말을 쓰시오.

┌─── 보기 ───┐
weaken – strengthen
└──────────┘

(1) true – f_____
(2) male – f_____
(3) different – s_____

02 다음 괄호 안의 단어를 문맥에 맞게 알맞은 형태로 고쳐 쓰시오.

(1) English has _____ words than any other language. (few)
(2) Alcohol can _____ heart muscle. (weak)

03 다음 주어진 우리말에 맞게 빈칸을 채우시오.

(1) 작은 개가 큰 뼈다귀를 갖고 있다.
➡ The small dog has a big _____.
(2) 그것은 완전히 다르다.
➡ It is completely _____.
(3) 모기들은 사람과 동물의 피를 빨아먹는다.
➡ _____ suck the _____ of people and animals.
(4) 시간이 지남에 따라, 그는 그것을 깨달을 것이다.
➡ _____ _____, he will realize it.
(5) 사실, 많은 사람들이 집에서 애완 토끼를 키웁니다.
➡ _____ _____, many people keep pet rabbits at home.

04 다음 빈칸에 알맞은 단어를 〈보기〉에서 골라 쓰시오.

┌─── 보기 ───┐
strike   guess   expand   go
└──────────┘

(1) The problem will not _____ away.
(2) The ship might _____ a rock in this storm.
(3) Can you _____ what they are talking about?
(4) Metals _____ when they are heated.

05 다음 밑줄 친 부분과 바꿔 쓸 수 있는 말을 쓰시오.

┌────────────────────────┐
The event was delayed for a week
because of bad weather.
└────────────────────────┘

➡ _____

06 주어진 어구를 이용하여 우리말을 영어로 옮기시오.

(1) 여름에 에펠 탑은 겨울보다 15 cm까지 더 커진다. (in summer, the Eiffel Tower, get, tall, than, winter)
➡ _____
_____

(2) 코끼리는 지구에서 가장 큰 동물이다.
(the elephant, big, on the Earth)
➡ _____
_____

07 다음 문장에서 어법상 <u>틀린</u> 부분을 찾아 바르게 고쳐 쓰시오.

(1) Guess what will the next topic be.

➡ _____

(2) Please tell me who that is girl.

➡ _____

(3) My brother can run the faster in our family.

➡ _____

08 다음 빈칸에 알맞은 말을 〈보기〉에서 찾아 쓰시오.

┌─ 보기 ─┐
who   when   what   whether
└────────┘

(1) Please tell me _____ you can come to the party.

(2) Do you know _____ the concert starts?

(3) Guess _____ I met yesterday.

[09~10] 다음 글을 읽고 물음에 답하시오.

Some people say that brown eggs are good than white eggs. However, there are no differences in the taste or nutritional value between them. 무엇이 달걀 색깔을 결정하는지 아니? It's the breed of chicken which lay the egg.

09 위 글에서 어법상 <u>틀린</u> 부분을 찾아 바르게 고치시오. (두 개)

_____ ➡ _____ , _____ ➡ _____

10 위 글의 밑줄 친 우리말에 맞게 주어진 단어를 알맞은 순서로 배열하시오.

┌────────────────────────────┐
│ what, do, the, you, determines, of, know, │
│ an egg, color   │
└────────────────────────────┘

➡ _____

_____

[11~13] 다음 글을 읽고 물음에 답하시오.

Welcome to "Ask Dr. Lawrence"! The world is full of interesting things. Take this quiz and find out ⓐ그것들에 대해 얼마나 아는지. Are you ready?

Quiz

1. The Eiffel Tower gets taller (A)[during / for] the summer. Ⓣ Ⓕ

2. ⓑBabies have fewer bones than adults. Ⓣ Ⓕ

3. Only female mosquitoes bite people. Ⓣ Ⓕ

4. (B)[Lightning / Lightening] never strikes the same place twice. Ⓣ Ⓕ

5. The elephant is the (C)[bigest / biggest] animal on the Earth. Ⓣ Ⓕ

6. There is no gravity in space. Ⓣ Ⓕ

11 위 글의 밑줄 친 ⓐ의 우리말에 맞게 한 단어를 보충하여, 주어진 어휘를 알맞게 배열하시오.

┌────────────────────────────┐
│ them / know / about / much / you │
└────────────────────────────┘

➡ _____

12 위 글의 괄호 (A)~(C)에서 문맥이나 어법상 알맞은 낱말을 골라 쓰시오.

➡ (A) _____ (B) _____ (C) _____

13 위 글의 밑줄 친 ⓑ를 Adults로 시작하여 바꿔 쓰시오.

➡ _____

출제율 85%

01 다음 짝지어진 낱말의 관계가 나머지 넷과 <u>다른</u> 것은?

① deep – deepen
② loose – loosen
③ weak – weaken
④ strength – strengthen
⑤ straight – straighten

출제율 95%

02 다음 주어진 우리말에 맞게 빈칸을 채우시오.

(1) 엄마는 내가 손톱을 물어뜯곤 했다고 말씀하셨다.

➡ My mom said that I used _____ _____ my nails.

(2) 지구상의 모든 것은 중력의 영향을 받는다.

➡ Everything on Earth is affected by its _____.

(3) Thomas Edison은 위대한 발명가였다.

➡ Thomas Edison _____ a great _____.

(4) 경기장은 사람들로 가득 찼었다.

➡ The stadium _____ full _____ people.

출제율 95%

03 다음 빈칸에 알맞은 말이 순서대로 바르게 나열된 것은?

- Let's read and find _____ the topic and situation.
- He plays the same songs over and _____.

① at – over
② out – under
③ as – under
④ out – over
⑤ at – under

출제율 90%

04 다음 우리말에 맞게 주어진 단어를 바르게 배열하시오.

(1) 암컷 모기들만 피를 빨아먹는다.

(suck, blood, female, only, mosquitoes)

➡ _____

(2) 피는 물보다 진하다.

(thicker, blood, water, than, is)

➡ _____

(3) 너는 몸무게가 얼마 나가니?

(much, weigh, how, you, do)

➡ _____

(4) 십대의 문화는 성인의 문화와 다르다.

(culture, culture, adult, from, teenage, is, different)

➡ _____

출제율 95%

05 다음 〈보기〉의 단어를 사용하여 자연스러운 문장을 만들 수 <u>없는</u> 것은?

┤ 보기 ├
to   with   of

① _____ average, he goes to bed around 12 o'clock.
② I hope this year will be full _____ happiness.
③ Read up _____ page 100.
④ The painting will lose its color _____ time.
⑤ The flight is delayed due _____ bad weather.

06 다음 중 어법상 옳은 것은?

① Take this quiz and find out how much do you know about them.
② The bigger animal on the Earth is the blue whale.
③ Its tongue alone can weigh as more as an average African elephant.
④ Tell me when the dance contest will start.
⑤ This is the difficultest problem in this book.

07 다음 빈칸에 알맞은 것은?

> • Sumi's bag is _____ in our class.
> • Minho gets up _____ in the morning in our class.

① the most heavy – earlier
② the heaviest – earliest
③ heavier – earlier
④ more heavy – the earliest
⑤ the most heaviest – more earlier

08 다음 주어진 두 문장을 〈보기〉처럼 하나의 문장으로 바꾸어 쓰시오.

> ┤ 보기 ├
> • Please tell me.   • Who is that girl?
> ➡ Please tell me who that girl is.

(1) • Can you tell me.
   • How old is your brother?
   ➡ _____

(2) • I know.
   • Where does she live?
   ➡ _____

(3) • Please tell me.
   • Does he like baseball?
   ➡ _____

09 다음 문장의 밑줄 친 부분과 문장의 쓰임이 <u>다른</u> 하나는?

> Welcome to "Ask Dr. Lawrence"! The world is full of interesting things. Take this quiz and find out <u>how much you know about them</u>. Are you ready?

① Tell me <u>when the concert starts</u>.
② Can you tell me <u>who that boy is</u>?
③ <u>How long does it take</u> to go to the bank?
④ I wonder <u>when they will arrive</u>.
⑤ I don't know <u>what I should do</u>.

10 다음 우리말에 맞게 영작한 문장 중 <u>잘못된</u> 것은?

① 이 퀴즈 항목 중에서 어느 것이 가장 흥미로웠나요?
   ➡ Which of these quiz items was the most interesting to you?
② 다음 주제가 무엇일지 추측해 보세요.
   ➡ Guess what the next topic will be.
③ 이 퀴즈를 풀고 그것들에 관해 얼마나 많이 알고 있는지 알아보세요.
   ➡ Take this quiz and find out how much you know about them.
④ 시간이 지남에 따라 아기의 뼈 중 몇몇은 서로 합쳐진다. 그래서 어른들은 아기들보다 더 적은 개수의 뼈를 가지고 있다.
   ➡ With time, some of the babies' bones join together, so adults have few bones than babies.
⑤ 그것의 혀의 무게만 해도 아프리카 코끼리의 평균 무게만큼 무겁다.
   ➡ Its tongue alone can weigh as much as an average African elephant.

11 다음 문장의 밑줄 친 부분 중 어법상 <u>어색한</u> 것은? (출제율 90%)

In fact, ①there is gravity everywhere in space. As you ②get farther from the Earth, the gravity of the Earth weakens, but it never goes away ③completely. When you get closer to another planet, such as Mars or Venus, its gravity becomes ④stronger than ⑤those of the Earth.

①   ②   ③   ④   ⑤

12 다음 문장의 빈칸에 들어갈 말을 글의 흐름에 맞게 쓰시오. (출제율 95%)

Metal expands in heat. Due to summer heat, the metal of the Eiffel Tower expands. In summer, the Eiffel Tower gets 15cm _____ than in winter.

➡ _____

13 다음 문장의 괄호 안에 주어진 단어를 알맞은 형태로 고치시오. (출제율 95%)

The (A)(big) animal on the Earth is the blue whale. It can weigh up to 180 tons and grow up to 30 meters long. Its tongue alone can weigh as (B)(many) as an average African elephant.

➡ (A) _____ (B) _____

14 다음 문장 중 어법상 <u>잘못된</u> 것은? (출제율 100%)

① He is the strongest man of the three.
② This book is thickest among the books I have ever read.
③ Do you know if she can speak French?
④ She works hardest in my company.
⑤ I like this color most.

15 다음 중 형용사의 최상급이 바르게 된 것은? (출제율 85%)

① fast – most fast   ② large – largeest
③ big – biggest   ④ famous – famousest
⑤ popular – popularest

16 다음 빈칸에 알맞은 말을 올바른 형태로 쓰시오. (출제율 95%)

My sisters are all pretty. But, among my sisters, Jenny is the _____ girl.

➡ _____

[17~19] 다음 글을 읽고 물음에 답하시오.

Welcome to "Ask Dr. Lawrence"! ⓐThe world is full of interesting things. Take this quiz and find out how much you know about them. Are you ready?
Quiz
1. The Eiffel Tower ⓑgets taller during the summer. Ⓣ Ⓕ
2. Babies have fewer bones than adults. Ⓣ Ⓕ
3. Only female mosquitoes bite people. Ⓣ Ⓕ
4. Lightning never strikes the same place twice. Ⓣ Ⓕ
5. ⓒThe elephant is the biggest animal on the Earth. Ⓣ Ⓕ
6. There is no gravity in space. Ⓣ Ⓕ

17 위 글의 밑줄 친 ⓐ를 다음과 같이 바꿔 쓸 때 빈칸에 들어갈 알맞은 말을 쓰시오. *출제율 90%*

➡ The world is _____ with interesting things.

18 위 글의 밑줄 친 ⓑgets와 바꿔 쓸 수 있는 말을 고르시오. *출제율 85%*

① brings ② becomes ③ makes
④ takes ⑤ happens

19 밑줄 친 ⓒ를 다음과 같이 바꿔 쓸 때 빈칸에 들어갈 알맞은 말을 고르시오. *출제율 95%*

> The elephant is _____ any other animal on the Earth.

① so big as ② the same as
③ bigger than ④ as big as
⑤ less big than

[20~23] 다음 글을 읽고 물음에 답하시오.

> 1. Metal expands in ___ⓐ___. Due to summer heat, the metal of the Eiffel Tower expands. ⓑIn summer, the Eiffel tower gets 15cm shorter than in winter.
> 2. Adults have 206 bones, but babies have about 300 bones. ___ⓒ___ time, some of the babies' bones join together, so adults have fewer bones than babies.

20 위 글의 빈칸 ⓐ에 들어갈 알맞은 말을 본문에서 찾아 쓰시오. *출제율 85%*

➡ _____

21 위 글의 밑줄 친 ⓑ에서 흐름상 어색한 부분을 찾아 고치시오. *출제율 95%*

_____ ➡ _____

22 위 글의 빈칸 ⓒ에 들어갈 알맞은 전치사를 고르시오. *출제율 95%*

① With ② On ③ At
④ To ⑤ By

23 다음 질문에 대한 알맞은 대답을 빈칸에 쓰시오. *출제율 90%*

> Q: Why do adults have fewer bones than babies?
> A: Because as time goes by, some of the babies' bones _____ _____.

[24~26] 다음 글을 읽고 물음에 답하시오.

> 3. Only female mosquitoes will bite you. They need blood to produce eggs. After a female mosquito gets enough blood, she'll ⓐrest for a few days and lay her eggs.
> 4. Lightning can strike the same place ⓑover and over again. The Empire State Building gets hit ___ⓒ___ lightning 23 times a year ___ⓓ___ average.

24 위 글의 밑줄 친 ⓐrest와 같은 의미로 쓰인 것을 고르시오. *출제율 90%*

① He had a good night's rest.
② Did he rest his chin in his hands?
③ The final decisions rest with you.
④ I want to rest from my work.
⑤ I spent the rest of the day sleeping.

25 위 글의 밑줄 친 ⓑover and over again와 바꿔 쓸 수 없는 말을 고르시오. *출제율 95%*

① again and again ② time after time
③ step by step ④ repeatedly
⑤ time and time again

출제율 95%

26 위 글의 빈칸 ⓒ와 ⓓ에 들어갈 전치사가 바르게 짝지어진 것은?

① in – for ② by – on

③ in – on ④ for – to

⑤ by – for

[27~29] 다음 글을 읽고 물음에 답하시오.

Quiz: There is no gravity in space. Ⓣ Ⓕ

Answer: False

_____ ⓐ _____, there is gravity everywhere in space. As you get farther from the Earth, the gravity of the Earth ___ⓑ___, but it never goes away completely. When you get closer to another planet, such as Mars or Venus, ⓒ its gravity becomes stronger than that of the Earth.

출제율 100%

27 위 글의 빈칸 ⓐ에 들어갈 알맞은 말을 고르시오.

① For example ② Therefore

③ In addition ④ In fact

⑤ In other words

출제율 85%

28 위 글의 빈칸 ⓑ에 weak을 알맞은 형태로 쓰시오.

➡ _____

출제율 90%

29 위 글의 밑줄 친 ⓒ가 가리키는 것을 본문에서 찾아 쓰시오.

➡ _____

[30~32] 다음 글을 읽고 물음에 답하시오.

3. Only female mosquitoes will bite you. They need blood ⓐto produce eggs. After a female mosquito (A)[will get / gets] enough blood, she'll rest for a few days and (B)[lay / lie] her eggs.

4. Lightning can strike the same place over and over again. The Empire State Building gets hit by lightning 23 times a year on average.

5. The biggest animal on the Earth is the blue whale. It can weigh ___ⓑ___ 180 tons and grow ___ⓒ___ 30 meters long. Its tongue (C)[alone / only] can weigh as much as an average African elephant.

출제율 100%

30 위 글의 괄호 (A)~(C)에서 문맥이나 어법상 알맞은 낱말을 골라 쓰시오.

➡ (A) _____ (B) _____ (C) _____

출제율 95%

31 위 글의 밑줄 친 ⓐto produce와 to부정사의 용법이 다른 것을 모두 고르시오.

① I want a chair to sit on.

② He hoped to succeed in life.

③ She was pleased to read the letter.

④ You must be a fool to say so.

⑤ He has too much work to do.

출제율 85%

32 위 글의 빈칸 ⓑ와 ⓒ에 공통으로 들어갈 알맞은 말을 쓰시오.

➡ _____

INSIGHT
on the textbook

교과서 파헤치기

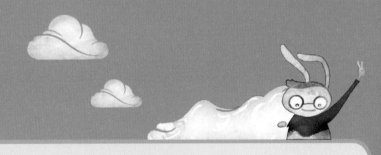

※ 다음 영어를 우리말로 쓰시오.

01 always	_____	22 again	_____
02 warm	_____	23 try	_____
03 due	_____	24 finish	_____
04 easily	_____	25 attention	_____
05 appointment	_____	26 focus	_____
06 worried	_____	27 regularly	_____
07 help	_____	28 wisely	_____
08 prepare	_____	29 nervous	_____
09 helpful	_____	30 recipe	_____
10 lesson	_____	31 achieve	_____
11 history	_____	32 posting	_____
12 remember	_____	33 practice	_____
13 check	_____	34 save	_____
14 while	_____	35 all day long	_____
15 instead	_____	36 stop -ing	_____
16 join	_____	37 take[have] a lesson	_____
17 schedule	_____	38 get along with	_____
18 quiz	_____	39 make a plan	_____
19 monthly	_____	40 set the alarm	_____
20 free time	_____	41 at a time	_____
21 planner	_____	42 put aside	_____
		43 put off	_____

※ 다음 우리말을 영어로 쓰시오.

01 연습하다 _____

02 ~하기 전에 _____

03 규칙적으로 _____

04 끝내다 _____

05 긴장되는, 불안한 _____

06 교과서 _____

07 주의, 집중 _____

08 현명하게 _____

09 성취하다, 달성하다 _____

10 (SNS에 올리는) 글 _____

11 집중하다 _____

12 중요한 _____

13 잊다 _____

14 요리사 _____

15 매주의; 매주 _____

16 ~을 완전히 익히다 _____

17 걸음, 단계 _____

18 조리[요리]법 _____

19 절약하다, 구하다 _____

20 피곤한 _____

21 (시간을) 소비하다 _____

22 (목적·준비) ~을 위해 _____

23 아마 _____

24 기억하다 _____

25 도움이 되는 _____

26 대신에 _____

27 약속 _____

28 따뜻한 _____

29 준비하다 _____

30 쉽게 _____

31 일정 _____

32 매월의; 매월 _____

33 자유 시간 _____

34 확인하다 _____

35 ~ 때문에 _____

36 ~ 앞에 _____

37 온종일 _____

38 알람을 맞춰 놓다 _____

39 요즘 _____

40 목표를 세우다 _____

41 ~하는 것을 멈추다 _____

42 ~에 대해 걱정하다 _____

43 ~을 한쪽에 두다 _____

※ 다음 영영풀이에 알맞은 단어를 <보기>에서 골라 쓴 후, 우리말 뜻을 쓰시오.

1 _____ : a set of instructions for making food: _____

2 _____ : to use money to pay for something: _____

3 _____ : to get or reach something by working hard: _____

4 _____ : to learn something completely: _____

5 _____ : to make yourself ready for something that you will be doing: _____

6 _____ : an arrangement to meet with someone at a particular time _____

7 _____ : to become a member of a group or organization: _____

8 _____ : to keep something from being lost or wasted: _____

9 _____ : an activity that you do in order to learn something: _____

10 _____ : expected to happen or arrive at a particular time: _____

11 _____ : to direct your attention or effort at something specific: _____

12 _____ : a plan of things that will be done and the times when they will be done: _____

13 _____ : the period of time that will come after the present time: _____

14 _____ : making it easier to do a job, deal with a problem, etc.: _____

15 _____ : the act of listening to, looking at, or thinking about something or someone carefully: _____

16 _____ : something that you give to someone especially as a way of showing affection or thanks: _____

보기			
prepare	schedule	spend	future
present	achieve	due	helpful
appointment	master	focus	attention
join	recipe	lesson	save

※ 다음 우리말과 일치하도록 빈칸에 알맞은 말을 쓰시오.

Listen & Speak 1 - A

1. **G:** You _____ _____, Sam. What's the _____?

   B: I _____ _____ my alarm in the morning _____ _____.

   G: _____ _____ you _____ _____ _____ on your clock and on your smartphone?

   B: That's a _____ _____.

2. **G:** Phew, _____ _____ I _____?

   B: _____ the matter, Julie?

   G: I _____ money too _____.

   B: Well, I _____ _____ a plan _____ I _____ things.

   G: Maybe I _____ do the _____.

Listen & Speak 2 - A

1. **G:** Jason, are you _____? You _____ _____ _____ today.

   B: I _____ _____ _____.

   G: That's _____ _____. I _____ you _____ _____ a doctor.

   B: _____ _____. Thank you.

2. **G:** You _____ _____. What's _____ _____?

   B: I'm _____ _____ tomorrow's history quiz. _____ _____ _____ _____?

   G: I _____ you _____ _____ your textbook again.

   B: That's _____ _____ _____.

3. **B:** I'm _____ _____.

   G: Why?

   B: I _____ _____ well _____ _____.

   G: _____ _____ you _____ _____ _____ _____ _____ warm milk _____ you sleep. It _____ _____.

   B: Okay, I _____ _____.

1. G: 걱정이 있어 보여, Sam. 무슨 일 있니?
   B: 요즘 아침에 알람을 못 들어.
   G: 네 시계와 스마트폰에 알람을 맞춰 놓는 게 어때?
   B: 좋은 생각이야.

2. G: 휴, 어떻게 해야 하지?
   B: 무슨 일인데, Julie?
   G: 나는 돈을 너무 빨리 써.
   B: 음, 난 항상 물건을 사기 전에 계획을 세워.
   G: 나도 똑같이 해야 할 것 같아.

1. G: Jason, 괜찮니? 오늘 안 좋아 보여.
   B: 감기에 걸렸어.
   G: 그거 참 안됐구나. 내 생각에 너는 병원에 가 봐야 할 것 같아.
   B: 네 말이 맞아. 고마워.

2. G: 걱정 있어 보여. 무슨 일이야?
   B: 내일 역사 시험이 걱정돼. 어떻게 해야 하지?
   G: 내 생각에 너는 교과서를 다시 읽어야 할 것 같아.
   B: 좋은 생각이야.

3. B: 나 너무 피곤해.
   G: 왜?
   B: 요즘 잠을 잘 못 자.
   G: 내 생각에는 너는 잠을 자기 전에 따뜻한 우유 한 잔을 마셔야 할 것 같아. 그것은 도움이 될 거야.
   B: 알았어, 한번 해 볼게.

Conversation A

B: This is a _____ of book. I write my _____, weekly, and _____ plans here. I also write important dates _____ my friends' birthdays and homework _____ _____ here. Every night, I _____ this for the next day. Do you want _____ _____ things _____? Then I think you _____ _____ this.

Conversation B

Hana: _____ _____ _____, Jiho?

Jiho: I _____ _____ my uniform. I _____ I _____ _____ _____ today.

Hana: Again?

Jiho: My _____ _____ in middle school is _____ _____ my _____ _____, and I _____ _____ things.

Hana: I think _____ _____ _____ a planner. Here's _____.

Jiho: Oh, _____ _____ _____ it?

Hana: Sure. I write my class _____ and _____ in my planner.

Jiho: That's great. _____ I _____ _____ one.

Wrap Up - ❶

W: _____ the matter, Sam? _____ you _____?

B: Ms. Green, _____ _____ I _____ _____ _____ _____.

W: Did you _____ _____ _____ _____ _____ _____ _____?

B: Yes. She _____ I _____ _____ _____ go to the hospital. _____ I _____ school now?

W: Okay, Sam. I'll _____ your mom and _____ _____ about it.

Wrap Up - ❷

B: I'm so _____.

G: Why? Is it _____ _____ the dance contest?

B: Yes. I practiced _____ many days, but I'm _____ nervous. What _____ I _____?

G: I _____ you _____ practice _____ _____ _____ your family. It will be very _____.

B: That's _____ _____ _____. Thank you.

B: 이것은 일종의 책이야. 나는 여기에 매일, 매주, 그리고 월간 계획을 써. 나는 또한 여기에 내 친구들의 생일이나 숙제 예정일과 같은 중요한 날짜를 적어. 매일 밤, 나는 다음 날을 위해 이것을 확인해. 무언가를 쉽게 기억하고 싶니? 그러면 내 생각에 너는 이것을 사용해야 할 것 같아.

하나: 무슨 일 있니, 지호야?
지호: 나는 내 유니폼을 가져오지 않았어. 오늘 축구 연습이 있다는 걸 잊고 있었어.
하나: 또?
지호: 중학교 2학년은 1학년보다 더 바쁘고, 나는 종종 어떤 것들을 잊어버려.
하나: 내 생각에는 너는 일정 계획표를 사용해야 할 것 같아. 여기 내 것이 있어.
지호: 오, 내가 봐도 될까?
하나: 물론. 나는 일정 계획표에 나의 수업 일정과 약속을 적어.
지호: 정말 좋구나. 나도 하나 사야 할까 봐.

W: 무슨 일이야, Sam? 어디 아파?
B: Green 선생님, 제가 감기에 걸린 것 같아요.
W: 보건 선생님한테 갔었니?
B: 네. 보건 선생님이 병원에 갈 필요가 있다고 하셨어요. 지금 하교를 해도 될까요?
W: 그럼, Sam. 내가 어머니한테 전화해서 그것에 대해 말할게.

B: 나 너무 긴장돼.
G: 왜? 댄스 경연 대회 때문이니?
B: 응. 며칠 동안 연습을 했지만 여전히 긴장돼. 어떻게 해야 하지?
G: 내 생각에 너는 가족 앞에서 연습을 해야 할 것 같아. 그것은 아주 도움이 될 거야.
B: 좋은 생각이야. 고마워.

※ 다음 우리말에 맞도록 대화를 영어로 쓰시오.

 해석

Listen & Speak 1 - A

1. G: _____

   B: _____

   G: _____

   B: _____

2. G: _____

   B: _____

   G: _____

   B: _____

   G: _____

1. G: 걱정이 있어 보여, Sam. 무슨 일 있니?
   B: 요즘 아침에 알람을 못 들어.
   G: 네 시계와 스마트폰에 알람을 맞춰 놓는 게 어때?
   B: 좋은 생각이야.

2. G: 휴, 어떻게 해야 하지?
   B: 무슨 일인데, Julie?
   G: 나는 돈을 너무 빨리 써.
   B: 음, 난 항상 물건을 사기 전에 계획을 세워.
   G: 나도 똑같이 해야 할 것 같아.

Listen & Speak 2 - A

1. G: _____

   B: _____

   G: _____

   B: _____

2. G: _____

   B: _____

   G: _____

   B: _____

3. B: _____

   G: _____

   B: _____

   G: _____

   B: _____

1. G: Jason, 괜찮니? 오늘 안 좋아 보여.
   B: 감기에 걸렸어.
   G: 그거 참 안됐구나. 내 생각에 너는 병원에 가 봐야 할 것 같아.
   B: 네 말이 맞아. 고마워.

2. G: 걱정 있어 보여. 무슨 일이야?
   B: 내일 역사 시험이 걱정돼. 어떻게 해야 하지?
   G: 내 생각에 너는 교과서를 다시 읽어야 할 것 같아.
   B: 좋은 생각이야.

3. B: 나 너무 피곤해.
   G: 왜?
   B: 요즘 잠을 잘 못 자.
   G: 내 생각에는 너는 잠을 자기 전에 따뜻한 우유 한 잔을 마셔야 할 것 같아. 그것은 도움이 될 거야.
   B: 알았어, 한번 해 볼게.

Conversation A

B: _____
_____
_____
_____

Conversation B

Hana: _____
Jiho: _____
Hana: _____
Jiho: _____
_____
Hana: _____
Jiho: _____
Hana: _____
Jiho: _____

Wrap Up - ❶

W: _____
B: _____
W: _____
B: _____
W: _____

Wrap Up - ❷

B: _____
G: _____
B: _____
G: _____
B: _____

B: 이것은 일종의 책이야. 나는 여기에 매일, 매주, 그리고 월간 계획을 써. 나는 또한 여기에 내 친구들의 생일이나 숙제 예정일과 같은 중요한 날짜를 적어. 매일 밤, 나는 다음 날을 위해 이것을 확인해. 무언가를 쉽게 기억하고 싶니? 그러면 내 생각에 너는 이것을 사용해야 할 것 같아.

하나: 무슨 일 있니, 지호야?
지호: 나는 내 유니폼을 가져오지 않았어. 오늘 축구 연습이 있다는 걸 잊고 있었어.
하나: 또?
지호: 중학교 2학년은 1학년보다 더 바쁘고, 나는 종종 어떤 것들을 잊어버려.
하나: 내 생각에는 너는 일정 계획표를 사용해야 할 것 같아. 여기 내 것이 있어.
지호: 오, 내가 봐도 될까?
하나: 물론. 나는 일정 계획표에 나의 수업 일정과 약속을 적어.
지호: 정말 좋구나. 나도 하나 사야 할까 봐.

W: 무슨 일이야, Sam? 어디 아파?
B: Green 선생님, 제가 감기에 걸린 것 같아요.
W: 보건 선생님한테 갔었니?
B: 네. 보건 선생님이 병원에 갈 필요가 있다고 하셨어요. 지금 하교를 해도 될까요?
W: 그럼, Sam. 내가 어머니한테 전화해서 그것에 대해 말할게.

B: 나 너무 긴장돼.
G: 왜? 댄스 경연 대회 때문이니?
B: 응. 며칠 동안 연습을 했지만 여전히 긴장돼. 어떻게 해야 하지?
G: 내 생각에 너는 가족 앞에서 연습을 해야 할 것 같아. 그것은 아주 도움이 될 거야.
B: 좋은 생각이야. 고마워.

※ 다음 우리말과 일치하도록 빈칸에 알맞은 것을 골라 쓰시오.

1 _____ _____ the new _____ _____ .

A. year   B. to   C. school   D. welcome

2 _____ the _____ grade, you will have more work _____ _____ .

A. do   B. to   C. second   D. in

3 You_____ _____ _____ your time _____ .

A. well   B. to   C. need   D. manage

4 _____ do you _____ _____ ?

A. that   B. do   C. how

5 Subin: I _____ small _____ and _____ them _____ day.

A. every   B. set   C. achieve   D. goals

6 I do _____ say, "I _____ _____ English."

A. master   B. will   C. not

7 With _____ a big goal, I will probably _____ _____ working on it _____ tomorrow, next week, on next month.

A. until   B. off   C. put   D. such

8 _____ , I say, "I will learn _____ _____ English words _____ day.

A. every   B. new   C. three   D. instead

9 I will _____ my big _____ , one _____ at a time.

A. goal   B. achieve   C. step

10 Minsu: _____ I do something, I give it my _____ _____ .

A. attention   B. full   C. when

11 I _____ _____ read SNS postings _____ I was _____ my homework.

A. doing   B. to   C. while   D. used

1 새 학년이 된 걸 환영해.

2 2학년에서, 여러분은 할 일이 더 많을 거야.

3 여러분은 시간을 잘 관리할 필요가 있어.

4 여러분은 시간 관리를 어떻게 하는가?

5 수빈: 나는 작은 목표들을 세우고 매일 그것들을 성취해.

6 나는 "나는 영어를 마스터할 거야."라고 말하지 않아.

7 그렇게 큰 목표를 가지면, 나는 아마 그것을 위해 노력하는 걸 내일, 다음 주, 혹은 다음 달까지 미룰 거야.

8 대신에 나는 "나는 매일 세 개의 새로운 영어 단어를 배울 거야."라고 말해.

9 나는 한 번에 한 단계씩 나의 큰 목표를 달성할 거야.

10 민수: 나는 무언가를 할 때 그것에 모든 주의를 기울여.

11 나는 숙제를 하는 동안 SNS 게시 글을 읽곤 했어.

12 It _____ me _____ because I couldn't _____.

A. focus   B. down   C. slowed

13 Now, I _____ _____ my smartphone _____ I do my homework.

A. when   B. aside   C. put

14 It _____ me a _____ of _____.

A. time   B. lot   C. saves

15 These _____, I _____ my homework quickly and _____ my _____ time.

A. free   B. finish   C. enjoy   D. days

16 John: I _____ _____ time _____ toward my dream.

A. working   B. spend   C. regularly

17 I _____ to _____ a _____.

A. chef   B. become   C. want

18 _____ Saturday morning, I go to cooking _____ or _____ _____ recipes.

A. for   B. classes   C. search   D. every

19 I think that _____ my time _____ _____ for my future _____ important.

A. is   B. to   C. using   D. prepare

20 _____ is a _____.

A. present   B. time

21 Everyone _____ the same _____ _____ _____ every day.

A. spend   B. to   C. present   D. has

22 _____ your time well, _____ you will _____ _____ in the new school year!

A. happier   B. and   C. manage   D. be

---

12 집중할 수 없었기 때문에 그것은 나의 속도를 늦추었어.

13 지금 나는 숙제를 할 때 스마트폰을 한쪽에 치워 놔.

14 그렇게 하면 시간이 많이 절약돼.

15 요즈음, 나는 숙제를 빨리 끝내고 자유 시간을 즐겨.

16 John: 나는 내 꿈을 위해 노력하며 규칙적으로 시간을 사용해.

17 나는 요리사가 되고 싶어.

18 토요일 아침마다 나는 요리 강습에 가거나 요리법을 찾아봐.

19 나는 나의 미래를 준비하기 위해 시간을 쓰는 것이 중요하다고 생각해.

20 시간은 선물이다.

21 모든 사람은 매일 소비할 똑같은 선물을 가지고 있다.

22 시간을 잘 관리하면 여러분은 새 학년에 더 행복해질 것이다!

※ 다음 우리말과 일치하도록 빈칸에 알맞은 말을 쓰시오.

1 ＿＿＿＿＿ ＿＿＿＿＿ the new ＿＿＿＿＿ ＿＿＿＿＿.

2 ＿＿＿＿ the ＿＿＿＿ ＿＿＿＿, you will have ＿＿＿＿ ＿＿＿＿ ＿＿＿＿ ＿＿＿＿.

3 You＿＿＿＿ ＿＿＿＿ ＿＿＿＿ your time ＿＿＿＿.

4 ＿＿＿＿ do you ＿＿＿＿ that?

5 Subin: I ＿＿＿＿ ＿＿＿＿ ＿＿＿＿ and ＿＿＿＿ them every day.

6 I ＿＿＿＿ ＿＿＿＿ ＿＿＿＿, "I ＿＿＿＿ ＿＿＿＿ English."

7 ＿＿＿＿ such a big goal, I will probably ＿＿＿＿ ＿＿＿＿ ＿＿＿＿ ＿＿＿＿ it ＿＿＿＿ tomorrow, next week, ＿＿＿＿ next month.

8 ＿＿＿＿, I s a y, "I ＿＿＿＿ ＿＿＿＿ ＿＿＿＿ ＿＿＿＿ ＿＿＿＿ words ＿＿＿＿ ＿＿＿＿.

9 I ＿＿＿＿ ＿＿＿＿ my big goal, ＿＿＿＿ ＿＿＿＿ ＿＿＿＿ ＿＿＿＿ ＿＿＿＿.

10 Minsu: ＿＿＿＿ I do something, I ＿＿＿＿ it ＿＿＿＿ ＿＿＿＿ ＿＿＿＿.

11 I ＿＿＿＿ ＿＿＿＿ ＿＿＿＿ SNS postings ＿＿＿＿ I ＿＿＿＿ ＿＿＿＿ my homework.

1 새 학년이 된 걸 환영해.

2 2학년에서, 여러분은 할 일이 더 많을 거야.

3 여러분은 시간을 잘 관리할 필요가 있어.

4 여러분은 시간 관리를 어떻게 하는가?

5 수빈: 나는 작은 목표들을 세우고 매일 그것들을 성취해.

6 나는 "나는 영어를 마스터할 거야."라고 말하지 않아.

7 그렇게 큰 목표를 가지면, 나는 아마 그것을 위해 노력하는 걸 내일, 다음 주, 혹은 다음 달까지 미룰 거야.

8 대신에 나는 "나는 매일 세 개의 새로운 영어 단어를 배울 거야."라고 말해.

9 나는 한 번에 한 단계씩 나의 큰 목표를 달성할 거야.

10 민수: 나는 무언가를 할 때 그것에 모든 주의를 기울여.

11 나는 숙제를 하는 동안 SNS 게시 글을 읽곤 했어.

12 It _____ me down _____ I _____ _____ .

13 Now, I _____ _____ my smartphone _____ I do my homework.

14 It _____ me _____ _____ _____ time.

15 _____ _____ , I finish my homework _____ and _____ _____ _____ _____ .

16 John: I _____ _____ time _____ toward my dream.

17 I _____ _____ _____ a chef.

18 _____ Saturday morning, I go to _____ _____ or _____ _____ _____ .

19 I think that _____ my time _____ _____ _____ my future is important.

20 _____ is a _____ .

21 Everyone _____ the _____ present _____ _____ every day.

22 _____ your time well, _____ you will _____ _____ in the _____ _____ _____ !

12 집중할 수 없었기 때문에 그것은 나의 속도를 늦추었어.

13 지금 나는 숙제를 할 때 스마트폰을 한쪽에 치워 놔.

14 그렇게 하면 시간이 많이 절약돼.

15 요즘, 나는 숙제를 빨리 끝내고 자유 시간을 즐겨.

16 John: 나는 내 꿈을 위해 노력하며 규칙적으로 시간을 사용해.

17 나는 요리사가 되고 싶어.

18 토요일 아침마다 나는 요리 강습에 가거나 요리법을 찾아봐.

19 나는 나의 미래를 준비하기 위해 시간을 쓰는 것이 중요하다고 생각해.

20 시간은 선물이다.

21 모든 사람은 매일 소비할 똑같은 선물을 가지고 있다.

22 시간을 잘 관리하면 여러분은 새 학년에 더 행복해질 것이다!

※ 다음 문장을 우리말로 쓰시오.

1   Welcome to the new school year.

  ➡ _____

2   In the second grade, you will have more work to do.

  ➡ _____

3   You need to manage your time well.

  ➡ _____

4   How do you do that?

  ➡ _____

5   Subin: I set small goals and achieve them every day.

  ➡ _____

6   I do not say, "I will master English."

  ➡ _____

7   With such a big goal, I will probably put off working on it until tomorrow, next week, or next month.

  ➡ _____

8   Instead, I say, "I will learn three new English words every day."

  ➡ _____

9   I will achieve my big goal, one step at a time.

  ➡ _____

10   Minsu: When I do something, I give it my full attention.

  ➡ _____

11   I used to read SNS postings while I was doing my homework.

  ➡ _____

12 It slowed me down because I couldn't focus.

➡ _____

13 Now, I put aside my smartphone when I do my homework.

➡ _____

14 It saves me a lot of time.

➡ _____

15 These days, I finish my homework quickly and enjoy my free time.

➡ _____

16 John: I regularly spend time working toward my dream.

➡ _____

17 I want to become a chef.

➡ _____

18 Every Saturday morning, I go to cooking classes or search for recipes.

➡ _____

19 I think that using my time to prepare for my future is important.

➡ _____

20 Time is a present.

➡ _____

21 Everyone has the same present to spend every day.

➡ _____

22 Manage your time well, and you will be happier in the new school year!

➡ _____

※ 다음 괄호 안의 단어들을 우리말에 맞도록 바르게 배열하시오.

1 (to / welcome / new / the / year. / school)

➡ _____

2 (the / grade, / in / second / will / you / have / work / do. / to / more)

➡ _____

3 (need / you / to / your / manage / well. / time)

➡ _____

4 (you / do / how / that? / do)

➡ _____

5 (Subin: / set / I / goals / small / and / them / achieve / day. / every)

➡ _____

6 (do / I / say, / not / "I / master / English." / will)

➡ _____

7 (such / with / goal, / big / a / I / probably / will / off / put / working / on / until / it / tomorrow, / next / month. / or / week / next)

➡ _____

8 (say, / I / instead, / "I / learn / will / new / three / words / English / day." / every)

➡ _____

9 (I / achieve / will / my / goal, / big / step / one / time. / a / at)

➡ _____

10 (Minsu: / I / do / when / something, / I / it / give / attention. / full / my)

➡ _____

11 (I / read / to / used / postings / SNS / while / was / I / doing / homework. / my)

➡ _____

1 새 학년이 된 걸 환영해.

2 2학년에서, 여러분은 할 일이 더 많을 거야.

3 여러분은 시간을 잘 관리할 필요가 있어.

4 여러분은 시간 관리를 어떻게 하는가?

5 수빈: 나는 작은 목표들을 세우고 매일 그것들을 성취해.

6 나는 "나는 영어를 마스터할 거야."라고 말하지 않아.

7 그렇게 큰 목표를 가지면, 나는 아마 그것을 위해 노력하는 걸 내일, 다음 주, 혹은 다음 달까지 미룰 거야.

8 대신에 나는 "나는 매일 세 개의 새로운 영어 단어를 배울 거야."라고 말해.

9 나는 한 번에 한 단계씩 나의 큰 목표를 달성할 거야.

10 민수: 나는 무언가를 할 때 그것에 모든 주의를 기울여.

11 나는 숙제를 하는 동안 SNS 게시 글을 읽곤 했어.

12 (slowed / it / down / me / because / I / focus. / couldn't)

➡ _____

13 (now, / I / aside / my / put / smartphone / when / do / I / homework. / my)

➡ _____

14 (it / me / saves / lot / time. / of / a)

➡ _____

15 (days, / these / finish / I / homework / my / quickly / and / my / time. / enjoy / free)

➡ _____

16 (John: / I / spend / regularly / working / time / toward / dream. / my)

➡ _____

17 (I / become / to / want / chef. / a)

➡ _____

18 (Saturday / every / morning, / I / cooking / to / go / classes / or / recipes. / for / search)

➡ _____

19 (think / I / using / that / time / my / prepare / to / for / future / my / important. / is)

➡ _____

20 (present. / a / is / time)

➡ _____

21 (has / everyone / the / present / same / spend / to / day. / every)

➡ _____

22 (your / manage / well, / time / and / will / you / be / in / the / happier / year! / school / new)

➡ _____

12 집중할 수 없었기 때문에 그것
은 나의 속도를 늦추었어.

13 지금 나는 숙제를 할 때 스마트
폰을 한쪽에 치워 놔.

14 그렇게 하면 시간이 많이 절약돼

15 요즈음, 나는 숙제를 빨리 끝내
고 자유 시간을 즐겨.

16 John: 나는 내 꿈을 위해 노력하
며 규칙적으로 시간을 사용해.

17 나는 요리사가 되고 싶어.

18 토요일 아침마다 나는 요리 강
습에 가거나 요리법을 찾아봐.

19 나는 나의 미래를 준비하기 위
해 시간을 쓰는 것이 중요하다
고 생각해.

20 시간은 선물이다.

21 모든 사람은 매일 소비할 똑같
은 선물을 가지고 있다.

22 시간을 잘 관리하면 여러분은
새 학년에 더 행복해질 것이다!

※ 다음 우리말을 영어로 쓰시오.

1 새 학년이 된 걸 환영해.

➡ _____

2 2학년에서, 여러분은 할 일이 더 많을 거야.

➡ _____

3 여러분은 시간을 잘 관리할 필요가 있어.

➡ _____

4 여러분은 시간 관리를 어떻게 하는가?

➡ _____

5 수빈: 나는 작은 목표를 세우고 매일 그것들을 성취해.

➡ _____

6 나는 "나는 영어를 마스터할 거야."라고 말하지 않아.

➡ _____

7 그렇게 큰 목표를 가지면, 나는 아마 그것을 위해 노력하는 걸 내일, 다음 주, 혹은 다음 달까지 미룰 거야.

➡ _____

8 대신에 나는 "나는 매일 세 개의 새로운 영어 단어를 배울 거야."라고 말해.

➡ _____

9 나는 한 번에 한 단계씩 나의 큰 목표를 달성할 거야.

➡ _____

10 민수: 나는 무언가를 할 때 그것에 모든 주의를 기울여.

➡ _____

11 나는 숙제를 하는 동안 SNS 게시 글을 읽곤 했어.

➡ _____

12 집중할 수 없었기 때문에 그것은 나의 속도를 늦추었어.

➡ _____

13 지금 나는 숙제를 할 때 스마트폰을 한쪽에 치워 놔.

➡ _____

14 그렇게 하면 시간이 많이 절약돼.

➡ _____

15 요즈음, 나는 숙제를 빨리 끝내고 자유 시간을 즐겨.

➡ _____

16 John: 나는 내 꿈을 위해 노력하며 규칙적으로 시간을 사용해.

➡ _____

17 나는 요리사가 되고 싶어.

➡ _____

18 토요일 아침마다 나는 요리 강습에 가거나 요리법을 찾아봐.

➡ _____

19 나는 나의 미래를 준비하기 위해 시간을 쓰는 것이 중요하다고 생각해.

➡ _____

20 시간은 선물이다.

➡ _____

21 모든 사람은 매일 소비할 똑같은 선물을 가지고 있다.

➡ _____

22 시간을 잘 관리하면 여러분은 새 학년에 더 행복해질 것이다!

➡ _____

Step1

※ 다음 우리말과 일치하도록 빈칸에 알맞은 말을 쓰시오.

Enjoy Writing B

1. My Goals for _____ _____

2. I have three _____ _____ _____ this year.

3. The _____ goal is _____ _____ _____ _____ my new _____.

4. The _____ goal is _____ _____ an A _____ the English speaking test.

5. The _____ goal is to _____ _____ smartphone games.

6. I hope _____ this year is _____ _____ last year.

1. 올해의 나의 목표
2. 나는 올해 달성해야 할 목표가 세 가지 있다.
3. 첫 번째 목표는 새로운 반 친구들과 잘 지내는 것이다.
4. 두 번째 목표는 영어 말하기 시험에서 A를 받는 것이다.
5. 마지막 목표는 스마트폰 게임을 중단하는 것이다.
6. 나는 올해가 작년보다 더 낫기를 희망한다.

Project - Step 1

1. A: I _____ we _____ make our group's motto _____ _____ and _____.

2. B: That's a good idea. I _____ that _____ _____ _____ are different.

3. C: Yes. I think that doing _____ _____ _____ _____ dreaming.

4. D: That's _____.

1. A: 나는 우리가 꿈을 꾸고 행동하는 것에 대한 우리 모둠의 좌우명을 만들어야 한다고 생각해.
2. B: 좋은 생각이야. 나는 꿈과 행동이 다르다고 믿어.
3. C: 맞아. 나는 꿈을 꾸는 것보다 하는 것이 더 중요하다고 생각해요.
4. D: 맞아.

Wrap Up - Writing

1. Jenny is _____ to go to the _____ _____ today.

2. She is _____ to buy three apples _____ _____.

3. She is going to buy _____ _____ _____ water _____ _____.

4. She is going to buy _____ _____ _____ _____ _____.

1. Jenny는 오늘 식료품점에 갈 거야.
2. 그녀는 먹을 사과 세 개를 살 거야.
3. 그녀는 마실 물 두 병을 살 거야.
4. 그녀는 읽을 패션 잡지를 하나 살 거야.

※ 다음 우리말을 영어로 쓰시오.

Enjoy Writing B

1. 올해의 나의 목표

➡ _____

2. 나는 올해 달성해야 할 목표가 세 가지 있다.

➡ _____

3. 첫 번째 목표는 새로운 반 친구들과 잘 지내는 것이다.

➡ _____

4. 두 번째 목표는 영어 말하기 시험에서 A를 받는 것이다.

➡ _____

5. 마지막 목표는 스마트폰 게임을 중단하는 것이다.

➡ _____

6. 나는 올해가 작년보다 더 낫기를 희망한다.

➡ _____

Project - Step 1

1. A: 나는 우리가 꿈을 꾸고 행동하는 것에 대한 우리 모둠의 좌우명을 만들어야 한다고 생각해.

➡ _____

2. B: 좋은 생각이야. 나는 꿈과 행동이 다르다고 믿어.

➡ _____

3. C: 맞아. 나는 꿈을 꾸는 것보다 하는 것이 더 중요하다고 생각해요.

➡ _____

4. D: 맞아.

➡ _____

Wrap Up - Writing

1. Jenny는 오늘 식료품점에 갈 거야.

➡ _____

2. 그녀는 먹을 사과 세 개를 살 거야.

➡ _____

3. 그녀는 마실 물 두 병을 살 거야.

➡ _____

4. 그녀는 읽을 패션 잡지를 하나 살 거야.

➡ _____

※ 다음 영어를 우리말로 쓰시오.

01 shoulder	_____
02 luckily	_____
03 brave	_____
04 lower	_____
05 chest	_____
06 dangerous	_____
07 skill	_____
08 degree	_____
09 chance	_____
10 floor	_____
11 training	_____
12 announcer	_____
13 shake	_____
14 practice	_____
15 protect	_____
16 greatly	_____
17 heart	_____
18 audience	_____
19 around	_____
20 save	_____
21 late	_____

22 zoo keeper	_____
23 remember	_____
24 excited	_____
25 suddenly	_____
26 scared	_____
27 experience	_____
28 CPR	_____
29 carefully	_____
30 angle	_____
31 earthquake	_____
32 wet	_____
33 forget	_____
34 perform	_____
35 push down	_____
36 bump into	_____
37 as ~ as possible	_____
38 fall down	_____
39 all the time	_____
40 get under	_____
41 in case of	_____
42 hit ~ on the shoulder	_____
43 hold on to	_____

※ 다음 우리말을 영어로 쓰시오.

01 낮게; 낮은	
02 각도	
03 주의 깊게	
04 외치다	
05 심폐소생술	
06 경험	
07 숨을 쉬다, 호흡하다	
08 십대	
09 지진	
10 무서워하는, 겁먹은	
11 젖은	
12 무서운, 겁나는	
13 장비, 복장	
14 잇다	
15 학년	
16 세게, 힘껏; 어려운	
17 중요한	
18 인상적인	
19 ~ 이내에, ~ 안에	
20 함께하다	
21 막혀 있지 않은, 개방된	

22 행하다, 실시하다	
23 안전	
24 유지하다	
25 (가볍게) 톡톡 두드리다[치다]	
26 가슴	
27 낮추다, 낮아지다	
28 위험한	
29 용감한	
30 교육, 훈련	
31 청중, 시청자	
32 흔들리다	
33 기억하다	
34 보호하다	
35 ~을 꽉[꼭] 누르다	
36 넘어지다	
37 가능한 한 ~한[하게]	
38 ~에 부딪히다	
39 항상	
40 ~을 입다	
41 ~의 경우에	
42 위아래로	
43 ~에서 내리다	

※ 다음 영영풀이에 알맞은 단어를 <보기>에서 골라 쓴 후, 우리말 뜻을 쓰시오.

1 _____ : not yet dry: _____

2 _____ : feeling or showing no fear: _____

3 _____ : the front part of the body between the neck and the stomach: _____

4 _____ : to keep someone or something safe from death, harm, loss, etc.: _____

5 _____ : a sudden, violent shaking of the earth's surface: _____

6 _____ : the people who watch, read, or listen to something: _____

7 _____ : a unit for measuring the size of an angle: _____

8 _____ : to keep someone or something from being harmed, lost, etc.: _____

9 _____ : to move air into and out of your lungs: _____

10 _____ : the ability to do something that comes from training, experience, or practice: _____

11 _____ : to hit someone or something quickly and lightly: _____

12 _____ : to do an action or activity that usually requires training or skill: _____

13 _____ : a person who takes care of the animals in a zoo: _____

14 _____ : the process of doing and seeing things and of having things happen to you: _____

15 _____ : to reduce something in amount, degree, strength etc, or to become less: _____

16 _____ : to move sometimes violently back and forth or up and down with short, quick movements: _____

보기			
save	audience	earthquake	lower
protect	degree	skill	chest
tap	perform	brave	breathe
wet	zoo keeper	experience	shake

※ 다음 우리말과 일치하도록 빈칸에 알맞은 말을 쓰시오.

해석

Listen & Speak 1 A-1

B: Mom, _____ I _____ some apple juice?

W: Sure, Chris. _____ _____ _____ check the food label.

B: The _____ _____ ?

W: Yes. Too much sugar is _____ _____ _____ you.

B: Okay, I _____ _____ it.

Listen & Speak 1 A-2

G: Dad, I'm _____ .

M: You _____ _____ _____ this, Julie. There is _____ _____ _____ _____ in the air today.

G: Oh, I _____ _____ that.

M: It will _____ _____ _____ your health. So _____ _____ _____ this mask.

G: _____ _____ . Thank you.

Listen & Speak 2 A-1

B: Hi, Amy. _____ _____ ?

G: I'm here _____ _____ a shirt. _____ _____ you?

B: I _____ a lunch meeting _____ this shopping center. Oh, I _____ _____ now. I'm _____ .

G: Okay, but _____ _____ _____ _____ . The sign _____ the floor is _____ .

B: I _____ _____ it. Thanks.

Listen & Speak 2 A-2

G: What _____ the sign _____ ?

B: It means that _____ _____ _____ look at your smartphone _____ you _____ _____ .

G: That's _____ , _____ why?

B: You can _____ _____ people and _____ _____ many cars _____ here. It's so _____ .

G: Now I _____ .

Conversation A

B: I was _____ a good time _____ my family last night. Suddenly everything started _____ _____. I _____ stand still and almost _____ _____. Dad shouted, "_____ under the table. _____ _____ to protect your head." _____, the shaking soon _____. It was a _____ _____.

Conversation B

Teacher: I _____ you _____ _____ safety rules for earthquakes today. Now, _____ _____. Are you _____?

Amy & Jiho: Yes.

Teacher: Everything _____ _____. Don't _____ _____ _____ _____ the desk and _____ your body first.

Jiho: It's so _____.

Amy: You're doing fine, Jiho. _____ _____ _____ the leg of the desk.

Jiho: Oh, the shaking stopped _____ _____. Let's get _____!

Teacher: Remember! You'd _____ _____ _____ the elevator. _____ _____ _____.

Amy: _____ _____ we _____ now?

Teacher: You _____ _____ find an open area _____ _____ _____.

Jiho: Then, _____ _____ _____ the park.

Wrap Up - Listening 1

G: Many people use this _____ every day. People _____ _____ _____ to enter this. They _____ _____ others to _____ _____ before they enter. They use this to _____ _____ and _____ floors in a building. _____ _____ _____ _____ this _____ _____ _____ a fire.

Wrap Up - Listening 2

B: I'm _____ _____ _____ _____ _____ Jiri Mountain _____ my dad tomorrow.

G: It _____ great.

B: I'm _____ _____ we are going to stay there _____ two days and _____ _____.

G: That'll be great, but _____ _____ to check the weather.

B: Okay.

B: 나는 어젯밤에 가족과 즐거운 시간을 보내고 있었다. 갑자기 모든 것이 흔들리기 시작했다. 나는 가만히 있을 수가 없어서 하마터면 넘어질 뻔했다. 아빠는 "테이블 밑으로 들어가. 머리를 보호하는 걸 잊지 마."라고 소리쳤다. 다행히도, 흔들림은 곧 멈추었다. 그것은 무서운 경험이었다.

선생님: 오늘 지진에 대한 몇 가지 안전 수칙들을 말했죠. 자, 실습해 봅시다. 준비됐나요?

Amy와 지호: 네.

선생님: 모든 것이 흔들리고 있어요. 책상 밑에 들어가서 먼저 여러분의 몸을 보호하는 것을 잊지 마세요.

지호: 너무 무서워요.

Amy: 너는 잘하고 있어, 지호야. 책상 다리를 꽉 잡아.

지호: 오, 떨림이 잠시 멈췄어. 나가자!

선생님: 기억하세요! 엘리베이터를 이용하면 안 돼요. 계단을 이용하세요.

Amy: 이제 우린 어디로 가야 하죠?

선생님: 건물이 없는 확 트인 곳을 찾아야 해요.

지호: 그럼, 공원에 가자.

G: 많은 사람들이 거의 매일 이것을 사용한다. 사람들이 이것에 들어가기 위해 줄을 선다. 그들은 다른 사람들이 들어오기 전에 내리기를 기다린다. 그들은 건물의 층을 위아래로 움직이기 위해 이것을 사용한다. 화재가 났을 때는 이것을 사용하면 안 된다.

B: 나는 내일 아빠와 지리산에 갈 거야.

G: 멋진데.

B: 우리는 1박 2일 동안 묵을 예정이어서 신나.

G: 그거 좋겠네. 하지만, 날씨를 확인하는 걸 잊지 마.

B: 알았어.

※ 다음 우리말에 맞도록 대화를 영어로 쓰시오.

Listen & Speak 1 A-1

B: _____

W: _____

B: _____

W: _____

B: _____

B: 엄마, 사과 주스 좀 사도 돼요?
W: 물론, Chris. 식품 라벨을 확인하는 것을 잊지 마라.
B: 식품 라벨이요?
W: 그래. 너무 많은 설탕은 너에게 좋지 않아.
B: 네, 확인해 볼게요.

Listen & Speak 1 A-2

G: _____

M: _____

G: _____

M: _____

G: _____

G: 아빠, 저 나가요.
M: Julie, 이걸 쓸 필요가 있어. 오늘은 공기 중에 미세먼지가 많아.
G: 오, 전 몰랐어요.
M: 그것은 건강에 나쁠 거야. 그러니 이 마스크 쓰는 걸 잊지 마.
G: 알겠습니다. 감사합니다.

Listen & Speak 2 A-1

B: _____

G: _____

B: _____

G: _____

B: _____

B: 안녕, Amy. 왠일이야?
G: 셔츠를 사러 왔어. 너는?
B: 이 쇼핑센터에서 점심 모임이 있어. 오, 이만 가 봐야겠어. 늦었어.
G: 그래, 하지만 뛰지 않는 게 좋겠어. 표지판에 바닥이 젖었다고 적혀 있어.
B: 난 못 봤어. 고마워.

Listen & Speak 2 A-2

G: _____

B: _____

G: _____

B: _____

G: _____

G: 그 표지판은 무슨 뜻이니?
B: 걷는 동안 스마트폰을 보지 않는 게 낫다는 뜻이야.
G: 재미있네, 그런데 왜지?
B: 사람들과 부딪힐 수 있고 이 근처에는 차도 많아. 너무 위험해.
G: 이제 알겠어.

Conversation A

B: _____

_____

_____

_____

Conversation B

Teacher: _____

_____

Amy & Jiho: _____

Teacher: _____

_____

Jiho: _____

Amy: _____

Jiho: _____

Teacher: _____

Amy: _____

Teacher: _____

Jiho: _____

Wrap Up - Listening 1

G: _____

_____

_____

Wrap Up - Listening 2

B: _____

G: _____

B: _____

G: _____

B: _____

B: 나는 어젯밤에 가족과 즐거운 시간을 보내고 있었다. 갑자기 모든 것이 흔들리기 시작했다. 나는 가만히 있을 수가 없어서 하마터면 넘어질 뻔했다. 아빠는 "테이블 밑으로 들어가. 머리를 보호하는 걸 잊지 마."라고 소리쳤다. 다행히도, 흔들림은 곧 멈추었다. 그것은 무서운 경험이었다.

선생님: 오늘 지진에 대한 몇 가지 안전 수칙들을 말했죠. 자, 실습해 봅시다. 준비됐나요?
Amy와 지호: 네.
선생님: 모든 것이 흔들리고 있어요. 책상 밑에 들어가서 먼저 여러분의 몸을 보호하는 것을 잊지 마세요.
지호: 너무 무서워요.
Amy: 너는 잘하고 있어, 지호야. 책상 다리를 꽉 잡아.
지호: 오, 떨림이 잠시 멈췄어. 나가자!
선생님: 기억하세요! 엘리베이터를 이용하면 안 돼요. 계단을 이용하세요.
Amy: 이제 우린 어디로 가야 하죠?
선생님: 건물이 없는 확 트인 곳을 찾아야 해요.
지호: 그럼, 공원에 가자.

G: 많은 사람들이 거의 매일 이것을 사용한다. 사람들이 이것에 들어가기 위해 줄을 선다. 그들은 다른 사람들이 들어오기 전에 내리기를 기다린다. 그들은 건물의 층을 위아래로 움직이기 위해 이것을 사용한다. 화재가 났을 때는 이것을 사용하면 안 된다.

B: 나는 내일 아빠와 지리산에 갈 거야.
G: 멋진데.
B: 우리는 1박 2일 동안 묵을 예정이어서 신나.
G: 그거 좋겠네. 하지만, 날씨를 확인하는 걸 잊지 마.
B: 알았어.

※ 다음 우리말과 일치하도록 빈칸에 알맞은 것을 골라 쓰시오.

1 Announcer: Yesterday, a teenager _____ the _____ of an _____ man.

    A. old   B. life   C. saved

2 The _____ student is _____ the studio _____ us today.

    A. with   B. in   C. brave

3 Please _____ _____.

    A. yourself   B. introduce

4 Sejin: _____ name _____ Kim Sejin.

    A. is   B. my

5 I'm _____ the _____ grade _____ Hanguk Middle School.

    A. at   B. second   C. in

6 Announcer: Could you _____ _____ your _____?

    A. experience   B. us   C. tell

7 Sejin: Sure. I was _____ _____ the bus _____ my friend, Jinho.

    A. for   B. waiting   C. with

8 A man _____ _____ in _____ of us.

    A. front   B. fell   C. suddenly

9 _____ knew _____ to _____.

    A. do   B. what   C. nobody

10 I was _____ _____ as the _____ at first.

    A. others   B. scared   C. as

11 Then, I _____ to him and _____ him _____ the shoulder.

    A. on   B. tapped   C. ran

12 He _____ _____ or _____.

    A. breathing   B. moving   C. wasn't

13 I _____ to Jinho, "_____ 119," and started _____.

    A. CPR   B. call   C. said

14 _____: That's _____.

    A. impressive   B. announcer

1 아나운서: 어제, 한 십대가 ○ 노인의 생명을 구했습니다.

2 그 용감한 학생이 오늘 우○ 함께 스튜디오에 있습니다.

3 자기소개를 해 보세요.

4 세진: 제 이름은 김세진입니○

5 저는 한국중학교 2학년입니○

6 아나운서: 당신의 경험을 우○ 게 말해 줄 수 있나요?

7 세진: 물론이죠. 저는 친구 ○ 와 버스를 기다리고 있었어○

8 갑자기 한 남자가 우리 앞에 러졌어요.

9 아무도 무엇을 해야 할지 몰랐○

10 저는 처음엔 다른 사람들처 겁이 났어요.

11 그리고 나서, 저는 그에게 ○ 가서 그의 어깨를 두드렸어○

12 그는 움직이지도 숨을 쉬게 않았어요.

13 저는 진호에게 "119에 전화 라고 말하고 심폐소생술을 ○ 했습니다.

14 아나운서: 인상적이네요.

15 _____ did you learn _____ _____ important _____?

    A. skill   B. an   C. such   D. when

16 Sejin: We had _____ _____ Day at school _____ week.

    A. last   B. Training   C. Safety

17 I _____ _____ to do CPR and had a _____ to _____.

    A. practice   B. how   C. chance   D. learned

18 Announcer: Can you _____ the audience _____ to _____ CPR?

    A. perform   B. how   C. show

19 Sejin: Yes. _____ your arms _____.

    A. straight   B. keep

20 Your arms and the _____ person's _____ must be _____ a 90 degree _____.

    A. angle   B. chest   C. at   D. other

21 _____ _____ in the center of the chest _____ and fast _____ an ambulance comes.

    A. down   B. until   C. hard   D. push

22 Announcer: Are _____ any _____ things _____ _____?

    A. remember   B. to   C. other   D. there

23 Sejin: Yes. You _____ to _____ the four _____ of "Golden Time."

    A. minutes   B. remember   C. need

24 It means that you _____ start CPR _____ four minutes _____ someone's heart _____.

    A. stops   B. within   C. should   D. after

25 To begin CPR _____ _____ that will greatly _____ the chances of _____ someone's life.

    A. saving   B. than   C. lower   D. later

26 Announcer: _____ is as _____ as _____ CPR.

    A. doing   B. important   C. timing

27 Thank you _____ _____ _____.

    A. us   B. joining   C. for

28 Sejin: _____ _____.

    A. pleasure   B. my

---

15 언제 그런 중요한 기술을 배웠나요?

16 세진: 지난주에 학교에서 '안전 교육의 날'이 있었어요.

17 저는 심폐소생술을 하는 방법을 배웠고 연습할 기회도 가졌어요.

18 아나운서: 청중들에게 심폐소생술을 어떻게 하는지 보여줄 수 있나요?

19 세진: 네. 팔을 쭉 펴세요.

20 당신의 팔과 다른 사람의 가슴은 90도 각도여야 합니다.

21 구급차가 올 때까지 가슴 중앙을 세게 그리고 빨리 누르세요.

22 아나운서: 기억해야 할 다른 것이 있나요?

23 세진: 네. "골든타임" 4분을 기억해야 합니다.

24 그것은 여러분이 누군가의 심장이 멈춘 후 4분 안에 심폐소생술을 시작해야 한다는 것을 의미합니다.

25 그보다 늦게 심폐소생술을 시작하는 것은 누군가의 생명을 구할 가능성을 크게 낮출 것입니다.

26 아나운서: 타이밍은 심폐소생술을 하는 것만큼이나 중요하군요.

27 저희와 함께 해 주셔서 감사합니다.

28 세진: 제가 더 고맙습니다.

※ 다음 우리말과 일치하도록 빈칸에 알맞은 말을 쓰시오.

1 Announcer: Yesterday, a teenager _____ the _____ of an
_____ _____ .

2 The _____ student is in the studio _____ _____ today.

3 Please _____ _____ .

4 Sejin: _____ name _____ Kim Sejin.

5 I'm _____ the _____ grade _____ Hanguk Middle School.

6 Announcer: Could you _____ _____ _____ _____ ?

7 Sejin: Sure. I _____ _____ the bus _____ my
friend, Jinho.

8 A man _____ _____ _____ _____ _____ us.

9 _____ knew _____ _____ _____ .

10 I was _____ _____ the others _____ first.

11 Then, I _____ to him and _____ him _____ the shoulder.

12 He _____ _____ or _____ .

13 I _____ _____ Jinho, "Call 119," and _____ _____ .

14 Announcer: That's _____ .

1 아나운서: 어제, 한 십대가 어
노인의 생명을 구했습니다.

2 그 용감한 학생이 오늘 우리
함께 스튜디오에 있습니다.

3 자기소개를 해 보세요.

4 세진: 제 이름은 김세진입니다

5 저는 한국중학교 2학년입니다

6 아나운서: 당신의 경험을 우리
게 말해 줄 수 있나요?

7 세진: 물론이죠. 저는 친구 진
와 버스를 기다리고 있었어요

8 갑자기 한 남자가 우리 앞에
러졌어요.

9 아무도 무엇을 해야 할지 몰랐어

10 저는 처음엔 다른 사람들처
겁이 났어요.

11 그러고 나서, 저는 그에게 달
가서 그의 어깨를 두드렸어요

12 그는 움직이지도 숨을 쉬지
않았어요.

13 저는 진호에게 "119에 전화하
라고 말하고 심폐소생술을 시
했습니다.

14 아나운서: 인상적이네요.

15 When did you learn _____ _____ important _____?

16 Sejin: We had _____ _____ Day _____ school last week.

17 I _____ _____ _____ _____ CPR and had a _____ _____ _____.

18 Announcer: Can you _____ the audience _____ _____ _____ _____?

19 Sejin: Yes. _____ your _____ _____.

20 Your arms and the _____ person's chest _____ be _____ _____ _____ _____ _____.

21 _____ _____ in the center of the chest _____ and fast _____ _____ _____ _____.

22 Announcer: _____ _____ any other things _____ _____?

23 Sejin: Yes. You _____ _____ _____ the _____ _____ of "Golden Time."

24 It means _____ you _____ start CPR _____ four minutes _____ _____ _____ _____.

25 _____ _____ CPR _____ _____ that will greatly lower the _____ _____ _____ someone's life.

26 Announcer: Timing is _____ _____ _____ doing CPR.

27 _____ _____ _____ _____ us.

28 Sejin: My _____.

15 언제 그런 중요한 기술을 배웠나요?

16 세진: 지난주에 학교에서 '안전 교육의 날'이 있었어요.

17 저는 심폐소생술을 하는 방법을 배웠고 연습할 기회도 가졌어요.

18 아나운서: 청중들에게 심폐소생술을 어떻게 하는지 보여줄 수 있나요?

19 세진: 네. 팔을 쭉 펴세요.

20 당신의 팔과 다른 사람의 가슴은 90도 각도여야 합니다.

21 구급차가 올 때까지 가슴 중앙을 세게 그리고 빨리 누르세요.

22 아나운서: 기억해야 할 다른 것이 있나요?

23 세진: 네. "골든타임" 4분을 기억해야 합니다.

24 그것은 여러분이 누군가의 심장이 멈춘 후 4분 안에 심폐소생술을 시작해야 한다는 것을 의미합니다.

25 그보다 늦게 심폐소생술을 시작하는 것은 누군가의 생명을 구할 가능성을 크게 낮출 것입니다.

26 아나운서: 타이밍은 심폐소생술을 하는 것만큼이나 중요하군요.

27 저희와 함께 해 주셔서 감사합니다.

28 세진: 제가 더 고맙습니다.

※ 다음 문장을 우리말로 쓰시오.

1 Announcer: Yesterday, a teenager saved the life of an old man.

➡ _____

2 The brave student is in the studio with us today.

➡ _____

3 Please introduce yourself.

➡ _____

4 Sejin: My name is Kim Sejin.

➡ _____

5 I'm in the second grade at Hanguk Middle School.

➡ _____

6 Announcer: Could you tell us your experience?

➡ _____

7 Sejin: Sure. I was waiting for the bus with my friend, Jinho.

➡ _____

8 A man suddenly fell in front of us.

➡ _____

9 Nobody knew what to do.

➡ _____

10 I was as scared as the others at first.

➡ _____

11 Then, I ran to him and tapped him on the shoulder.

➡ _____

12 He wasn't moving or breathing.

➡ _____

13 I said to Jinho, "Call 119," and started CPR.

➡ _____

14 Announcer: That's impressive.

➡ _____

15 When did you learn such an important skill?

➡ _____

16 Sejin: We had Safety Training Day at school last week.

➡ _____

17 I learned how to do CPR and had a chance to practice.

➡ _____

18 Announcer: Can you show the audience how to perform CPR?

➡ _____

19 Sejin: Yes. Keep your arms straight.

➡ _____

20 Your arms and the other person's chest must be at a 90 degree angle.

➡ _____

21 Push down in the center of the chest hard and fast until an ambulance comes.

➡ _____

22 Announcer: Are there any other things to remember?

➡ _____

23 Sejin: Yes. You need to remember the four minutes of "Golden Time."

➡ _____

24 It means that you should start CPR within four minutes after someone's heart stops.

➡ _____

25 To begin CPR later than that will greatly lower the chances of saving someone's life.

➡ _____

26 Announcer: Timing is as important as doing CPR.

➡ _____

27 Thank you for joining us.

➡ _____

28 Sejin: My pleasure.

➡ _____

※ 다음 괄호 안의 단어들을 우리말에 맞도록 바르게 배열하시오.

1 (Announcer: / a / yesterday, / teenager / the / saved / life / of / man. / old / an)

➡ _____

2 (brave / the / student / is / the / in / with / studio / today. / us)

➡ _____

3 (yourself. / introduce / please)

➡ _____

4 (Sejin: / name / my / Sejin. / is / Kim)

➡ _____

5 (in / I'm / second / the / grade / School. / at / Middle / Hanguk)

➡ _____

6 (Announcer: / you / could / us / tell / experience? / your)

➡ _____

7 (Sejin: sure. // I / waiting / was / the / for / with / bus / Jinho. / friend, / my)

➡ _____

8 (man / a / fell / suddenly / front / us. / in / of)

➡ _____

9 (knew / nobody / do. / to / what)

➡ _____

10 (was / as / I / scared / as / others / the / first. / at)

➡ _____

11 (then, / ran / I / him / to / and / him / tapped / shoulder. / the / on)

➡ _____

12 (wasn't / he / breathing. / or / moving)

➡ _____

13 (said / I / Jinho, / to / "call / and / 119," / CPR. / started)

➡ _____

14 (Announcer: / impressive. / that's)

➡ _____

1 아나운서: 어제, 한 십대가 노인의 생명을 구했습니다.

2 그 용감한 학생이 오늘 우 함께 스튜디오에 있습니다.

3 자기소개를 해 보세요.

4 세진: 제 이름은 김세진입니

5 저는 한국중학교 2학년입니

6 아나운서: 당신의 경험을 우 게 말해 줄 수 있나요?

7 세진: 물론이죠. 저는 친구 와 버스를 기다리고 있었어

8 갑자기 한 남자가 우리 앞이 러졌어요.

9 아무도 무엇을 해야 할지 몰랐

10 저는 처음엔 다른 사람들 겁이 났어요.

11 그러고 나서, 저는 그에게 가서 그의 어깨를 두드렸어

12 그는 움직이지도 숨을 쉬 않았어요.

13 저는 진호에게 " 119에 전화 라고 말하고 심폐소생술을 했습니다.

14 아나운서: 인상적이네요.

15 (you / when / did / learn / an / such / skill? / important)

➡ _____

16 (Sejin: / had / we / Training / Safety / Day / school / week. / at / last)

➡ _____

17 (learned / I / to / how / do / CPR / and / a / had / practice. / to / chance)

➡ _____

18 (Announcer: / you / can / show / audience / the / to / how / CPR? / perform)

➡ _____

19 (Sejin: / yes. // your / straight. / keep / arms)

➡ _____

20 (arms / your / the / and / other / chest / person's / must / at / be / 90 / a / angle. / degree)

➡ _____

21 (down / push / the / in / center / of / chest / the / hard / and / until / fast / comes. / ambulance / an)

➡ _____

22 (Announcer: / there / are / other / any / to / remember? / things)

➡ _____

23 (Sejin: / yes. // need / you / remember / to / four / the / minutes / Time." / of / "Golden)

➡ _____

24 (that / means / it / should / you / start / within / CPR / minutes / four / after / stops. / heart / someone's)

➡ _____

25 (begin / to / CPR / than / later / will / that / lower / greatly / the / saving / of / chances / life. / someone's)

➡ _____

➡ _____

26 (Announcer: / is / important / as / timing / CPR. / doing / as)

➡ _____

27 (you / thank / for / us. / joining)

➡ _____

28 (Sejin: / pleasure. / my)

➡ _____

15 언제 그런 중요한 기술을 배웠나요?

16 세진: 지난주에 학교에서 '안전 교육의 날'이 있었어요.

17 저는 심폐소생술을 하는 방법을 배웠고 연습할 기회도 가졌어요.

18 아나운서: 청중들에게 심폐소생술을 어떻게 하는지 보여줄 수 있나요?

19 세진: 네. 팔을 쭉 펴세요.

20 당신의 팔과 다른 사람의 가슴은 90도 각도여야 합니다.

21 구급차가 올 때까지 가슴 중앙을 세게 그리고 빨리 누르세요.

22 아나운서: 기억해야 할 다른 것이 있나요?

23 세진: 네. "골든타임" 4분을 기억해야 합니다.

24 그것은 여러분이 누군가의 심장이 멈춘 후 4분 안에 심폐소생술을 시작해야 한다는 것을 의미합니다.

25 그보다 늦게 심폐소생술을 시작하는 것은 누군가의 생명을 구할 가능성을 크게 낮출 것입니다.

26 아나운서: 타이밍은 심폐소생술을 하는 것만큼이나 중요하군요.

27 저희와 함께 해 주셔서 감사합니다.

28 세진: 제가 더 고맙습니다.

※ 다음 우리말을 영어로 쓰시오.

1 아나운서: 어제, 한 십대가 어떤 노인의 생명을 구했습니다.

➡ _____

2 그 용감한 학생이 오늘 우리와 함께 스튜디오에 있습니다.

➡ _____

3 자기소개를 해 보세요.

➡ _____

4 세진: 제 이름은 김세진입니다.

➡ _____

5 저는 한국중학교 2학년입니다.

➡ _____

6 아나운서: 당신의 경험을 우리에게 말해 줄 수 있나요?

➡ _____

7 세진: 물론이죠. 저는 친구 진호와 버스를 기다리고 있었어요.

➡ _____

8 갑자기 한 남자가 우리 앞에 쓰러졌어요.

➡ _____

9 아무도 무엇을 해야 할지 몰랐어요.

➡ _____

10 저는 처음엔 다른 사람들처럼 겁이 났어요.

➡ _____

11 그러고 나서, 저는 그에게 달려가서 그의 어깨를 두드렸어요.

➡ _____

12 그는 움직이지도 숨을 쉬지도 않았어요.

➡ _____

13 저는 진호에게 "119에 전화해."라고 말하고 심폐소생술을 시작했습니다.

➡ _____

14 아나운서: 인상적이네요.

➡ _____

15 언제 그런 중요한 기술을 배웠나요?

➡ _____

16 세진: 지난주에 학교에서 '안전 교육의 날'이 있었어요.

➡ _____

17 저는 심폐소생술을 하는 방법을 배웠고 연습할 기회를 가졌어요.

➡ _____

18 아나운서: 청중들에게 심폐소생술을 어떻게 하는지 보여줄 수 있나요?

➡ _____

19 세진: 네. 팔을 쭉 펴세요.

➡ _____

20 당신의 팔과 다른 사람의 가슴은 90도 각도여야 합니다.

➡ _____

21 구급차가 올 때까지 가슴 중앙을 세게 그리고 빨리 누르세요.

➡ _____

22 아나운서: 기억해야 할 다른 것이 있나요?

➡ _____

23 세진: 네. "골든타임" 4분을 기억해야 합니다.

➡ _____

24 그것은 여러분이 누군가의 심장이 멈춘 후 4분 안에 심폐소생술을 시작해야 한다는 것을 의미합니다.

➡ _____

25 그보다 늦게 심폐소생술을 시작하는 것은 누군가의 생명을 구할 가능성을 크게 낮출 것입니다.

➡ _____

26 아나운서: 타이밍은 심폐소생술을 하는 것만큼이나 중요하군요.

➡ _____

27 저희와 함께 해 주셔서 감사합니다.

➡ _____

28 세진: 제가 더 고맙습니다.

➡ _____

※ 다음 우리말과 일치하도록 빈칸에 알맞은 말을 쓰시오.

My Writing B

1. _____ Your Life from a _____

2. Do you know _____ _____ _____ when _____ _____ a fire?

3. You _____ _____, "Fire!"

4. You _____ _____ _____ your face and body _____ _____ _____ _____.

5. You _____ _____ _____ as low _____ possible and _____ _____.

6. Also, you need to call 119 _____ _____ _____ _____ _____.

7. _____ _____ _____ _____ the stairs, _____ the elevator.

1. 화재로부터 여러분의 생명을 구하라
2. 불이 나면 너는 무엇을 해야 하는지 아니?
3. 여러분은 "불이야!"라고 외쳐야 한다.
4. 여러분은 젖은 수건으로 얼굴과 몸을 가려야 한다.
5. 가능한 한 낮게 유지하고 밖으로 나가야 한다.
6. 또한, 가능한 한 빨리 119에 전화해야 한다.
7. 엘리베이터가 아니라 계단을 이용하는 것을 잊지 마라.

Wrap Up

1. Safety _____ Day

2. Today we had _____ Training Day _____ _____.

3. Teachers _____ _____ _____ _____ _____ when an earthquake hits.

4. We learned _____ _____ _____ our heads and bodies.

5. We also learned _____ _____ _____ when the _____ _____.

1. 안전 교육의 날
2. 오늘은 학교에서 안전 교육의 날이었다.
3. 선생님들은 우리에게 지진이 일어났을 때 무엇을 해야 하는지 가르쳐 주셨다.
4. 우리는 머리와 몸을 보호하는 법을 배웠다.
5. 우리는 또한 흔들림이 멈추었을 때 어디로 가야 하는지 배웠습니다.

Project - Step 3

1. We'll _____ _____ _____ _____ _____ for safety in the science room.

2. First, _____ _____ _____ use _____ _____.

3. Second, you'd _____ _____ run _____.

1. 과학실에서 안전을 위해 무엇을 해야 하는지 알려드리겠습니다.
2. 첫째, 보안경을 쓰는 것을 잊지 마세요.
3. 둘째, 뛰어다니면 안 됩니다.

※ 다음 우리말을 영어로 쓰시오.

My Writing B

1. 화재로부터 여러분의 생명을 구하라

   ➡ _____

2. 불이 나면 너는 무엇을 해야 하는지 아니?

   ➡ _____

3. 여러분은 "불이야!"라고 외쳐야 한다.

   ➡ _____

4. 여러분은 젖은 수건으로 얼굴과 몸을 가려야 한다.

   ➡ _____

5. 가능한 한 낮게 유지하고 밖으로 나가야 한다.

   ➡ _____

6. 또한, 가능한 한 빨리 119에 전화해야 한다.

   ➡ _____

7. 엘리베이터가 아니라 계단을 이용하는 것을 잊지 마라.

   ➡ _____

Wrap Up

1. 안전 교육의 날

   ➡ _____

2. 오늘은 학교에서 안전 교육의 날이었다.

   ➡ _____

3. 선생님들은 우리에게 지진이 일어났을 때 무엇을 해야 하는지 가르쳐 주셨다.

   ➡ _____

4. 우리는 머리와 몸을 보호하는 법을 배웠다.

   ➡ _____

5. 우리는 또한 흔들림이 멈추었을 때 어디로 가야 하는지 배웠습니다.

   ➡ _____

Project - Step 3

1. 과학실에서 안전을 위해 무엇을 해야 하는지 알려드리겠습니다.

   ➡ _____

2. 첫째, 보안경을 쓰는 것을 잊지 마세요.

   ➡ _____

3. 둘째, 뛰어다니면 안 됩니다.

   ➡ _____

※ 다음 영어를 우리말로 쓰시오.

01 position _____

02 pull _____

03 stretch _____

04 difficult _____

05 nature _____

06 advice _____

07 push _____

08 exercise _____

09 understand _____

10 place _____

11 count _____

12 second _____

13 shoulder _____

14 activity _____

15 however _____

16 life _____

17 pour _____

18 switch _____

19 back _____

20 massage _____

21 neck _____

22 download _____

23 backward _____

24 put _____

25 show _____

26 waist _____

27 comfortable _____

28 bend _____

29 lower _____

30 habit _____

31 fresh _____

32 usually _____

33 simple _____

34 warm _____

35 each other _____

36 team up with _____

37 block out _____

38 get over _____

39 from top to bottom _____

40 focus on _____

41 loosen up _____

42 straighten up _____

43 be good for _____

※ 다음 우리말을 영어로 쓰시오.

01	벌써, 이미		22	~을 낮추다	
02	~ 뒤에		23	간단한, 단순한	
03	편안한		24	신선한	
04	부드럽게		25	스트레스를 받다[주다]	
05	걸음		26	빛	
06	길		27	~와 같은, ~처럼	
07	움직이다		28	줄이다	
08	넘어지다		29	보통, 대개	
09	~을 향하다; 얼굴		30	그릇	
10	낚시		31	스트레칭하다	
11	습관		32	뒤로	
12	따뜻한		33	목	
13	둘 다		34	자세	
14	유지하다		35	준비 운동을 하다	
15	구부리다		36	위에서 아래까지	
16	운동하다		37	~에 집중하다	
17	자연		38	몇 초 동안	
18	어려운		39	~에 대해 걱정하다	
19	활동		40	~을 준비하다	
20	(근육 등의) 긴장이 풀리다		41	(빛을) 가리다[차단하다]	
21	건강한, 건강에 좋은		42	똑바로 하다	
			43	회복[극복]하다	

Step3

※ 다음 영영풀이에 알맞은 단어를 <보기>에서 골라 쓴 후, 우리말 뜻을 쓰시오.

1 _____ : to say numbers in order: _____

2 _____ : not hard to understand or do: _____

3 _____ : making you feel physically relaxed: _____

4 _____ : to make something smaller in size, amount, number, etc.: _____

5 _____ : an opinion or suggestion about what someone should do: _____

6 _____ : either of the two parts of the body between the top of each arm and the neck : _____

7 _____ : to change or replace something with another thing: _____

8 _____ : the part of the body between the head and the shoulders: _____

9 _____ : to move your body so that it is not straight: _____

10 _____ : the way someone stands, sits, or lies down: _____

11 _____ : to become or to cause something to become less tense, tight, or stiff: _____

12 _____ : something that a person does often in a regular and repeated way: _____

13 _____ : to put your arms, legs, etc., in positions that make the muscles long and tight: _____

14 _____ : to do gentle physical exercises to prepare your body for a sport or other activity: _____

15 _____ : to hold something firmly and use force in order to move it or try to move it toward yourself: _____

16 _____ : the action of rubbing and pressing a person's body with the hands to reduce pain in the muscles and joints: _____

보기

stretch	bend	count	habit
advice	position	switch	massage
relax	reduce	neck	comfortable
warm up	shoulder	pull	simple

※ 다음 우리말과 일치하도록 빈칸에 알맞은 말을 쓰시오.

Listen & Speak 1-A-1

B: I want to eat _____ _____. Do you _____ any _____?

G: I _____ _____ fresh salad. It _____ me _____ _____.

B: Really? Do you know _____ _____ _____ it?

G: Yes, it's quite _____. First, _____ many vegetables _____ small pieces. Next, _____ them _____ a bowl. Then, _____ some lemon juice on them. Finally, _____ everything together.

B: That's it? I _____ _____ it.

Listen & Speak 1-A-2

B: People say that we should walk _____ _____ 10,000 _____ every day _____ _____ _____. I can't _____ the number of my _____ _____.

G: You _____ _____ this smartphone app. Do you know _____ _____ _____ it?

B: No. _____ you _____ _____ _____?

G: Sure. First, _____ the app. Then, walk _____ your smartphone. Later, you can _____ the number of _____ _____ _____.

B: Thank you. I _____ _____ _____ it today.

Listen & Speak 2-A-1

G: _____ do you _____ _____ after school?

B: I _____ _____ _____ _____ _____.

G: _____ cool. What _____ you _____?

B: I _____ _____ salad, Bibimbap, and vegetable juice.

Listen & Speak 2-A-2

B: What do you do _____ _____?

G: I _____ _____.

B: _____ _____ of pictures do you _____ _____?

G: I _____ _____ pictures _____ nature, _____ trees and flowers. The beautiful pictures _____ _____ _____.

Listen & Speak 2-A-3

G: Do you _____ _____ _____?

B: Yes. _____ name is Coco. I _____ _____ her.

G: _____ do you do _____ _____?

B: I _____ _____ a walk with her. It _____ me _____.

Conversation A

B: Tomorrow, I _____ an English _____ contest. I started _____ _____ the contest two weeks _____. I enjoy _____ _____ English, but I _____ _____ _____ the contest. I _____ _____ well.

Conversation B

Karl: Hana, _____ the _____?

Hana: Well, I'm _____ _____ the test _____ _____.

Karl: I understand. I _____ my longboard _____ I'm stressed. Do you _____ _____ _____ _____ a longboard?

Hana: _____, I _____.

Karl: Let's _____ _____! I _____ teach you. _____ one foot _____ the board and _____ hard _____ the other.

Hana: _____ this? Wow! This is fun. I _____ _____ already.

Karl: See? I _____ _____ my longboard _____ it _____ my stress.

Hana: That's _____!

Wrap Up 1

B: You _____ _____. _____ the matter?

G: Well, I _____ _____ _____.

B: Did you _____ _____ _____?

G: Not _____. Do you know how to _____ _____ a cold?

B: Well, I usually drink _____ water _____ I have a cold. It _____ _____ _____ _____.

G: _____ good. I _____ _____ _____ it.

Wrap Up 2

B: My family _____ many activities. My dad enjoys _____. _____ in the morning, he goes to the lake and _____ _____ with some fish. My mom _____ _____ pictures. She likes _____ _____ beautiful mountains and lakes. My brother and I _____ _____ soccer.

G: 너는 강아지를 기르고 있니?

B: 응. 그녀의 이름은 코코야. 난 코코를 아주 좋아해.

G: 너는 코코와 함께 무엇을 하니?

B: 난 코코와 산책하는 걸 즐겨. 그것은 나를 건강하게 만들어.

B: 내일 영어 말하기 대회가 있어. 나는 2주 전에 대회를 준비하기 시작했어. 나는 영어로 말하는 것을 즐기지만, 난 그 대회가 걱정돼. 나는 잠을 잘 못 자.

Karl: 하나야, 무슨 일 있니?

하나: 음. 다음 주에 있을 시험 때문에 스트레스를 받아.

Karl: 난 이해돼. 나는 스트레스를 받을 때 롱보드를 타. 넌 롱보드를 어떻게 타는지 아니?

하나: 아니, 몰라.

Karl: 나가자! 내가 가르쳐 줄 수 있어. 한 발을 보드 위에 올려놓고 다른 한 발로 세게 밀어.

하나: 이렇게? 와! 이거 재밌다. 벌써 기분이 좋아졌어.

Karl: 봤지? 나는 롱보드를 타는 것이 나의 스트레스를 줄여주기 때문에 즐겨.

하나: 정말 멋진데!

B: 너 아파 보여. 무슨 일 있니?

G: 음, 감기에 걸렸어.

B: 병원에 가봤니?

G: 아직. 넌 감기가 나아지는 방법을 아니?

B: 음, 나는 감기에 걸렸을 때 보통 따뜻한 물을 마셔. 그것은 내 기분을 좋아지게 해.

G: 좋아. 한번 해 볼게.

B: 우리 가족은 많은 활동을 즐겨. 우리 아빠는 낚시를 즐기셔. 이른 아침, 그는 호수에 가셔서 약간의 물고기를 가지고 돌아오셔. 우리 엄마는 그림 그리기를 즐기셔. 그녀는 아름다운 산과 호수를 그리는 것을 좋아하셔. 나의 형과 나는 축구를 즐겨.

※ 다음 우리말에 맞도록 대화를 영어로 쓰시오.

Listen & Speak 1-A-1

B: _____

G: _____

B: _____

G: _____

_____

_____

B: _____

Listen & Speak 1-A-2

B: _____

_____

G: _____

B: _____

G: _____

_____

B: _____

Listen & Speak 2-A-1

G: _____

B: _____

G: _____

B: _____

Listen & Speak 2-A-2

B: _____

G: _____

B: _____

G: _____

_____

해석

B: 나는 건강에 좋은 것을 먹고 싶어. 말해 줄 조언이 있니?

G: 나는 신선한 샐러드를 자주 먹어. 그것은 나를 기분 좋게 만들어.

B: 정말? 그것을 어떻게 만드는지 아니?

G: 응, 아주 간단해. 먼저, 많은 채소들을 작은 조각으로 잘라. 다음으로 그것들을 그릇에 담아. 그런 다음, 레몬 주스를 조금 부어. 마지막으로 모든 것을 함께 섞어.

B: 그게 다야? 한번 해 봐야겠다.

B: 사람들은 우리가 건강해지기 위해서 매일 10,000 걸음 이상을 걸어야 한다고 말해. 나는 내 걸음 수를 쉽게 셀 수 없어.

G: 너는 이 스마트폰 앱을 사용할 수 있어. 어떻게 사용하는지 아니?

B: 아니. 내게 보여줄 수 있니?

G: 물론. 먼저 앱을 다운로드해. 그런 다음 스마트폰을 가지고 걸어. 나중에 네가 걸은 걸음 수를 확인할 수 있어.

B: 고마워. 오늘부터 그것을 쓰기 시작해야겠어.

G: 너는 방과 후에 뭐 하는 걸 즐기니?

B: 나는 건강에 좋은 음식을 요리하는 것을 즐겨.

G: 멋지구나. 너는 무엇을 만들 수 있니?

B: 나는 샐러드, 비빔밥 그리고 야채 주스를 만들 수 있어.

B: 너는 주말에 무엇을 하니?

G: 나는 사진을 찍어.

B: 너는 보통 어떤 종류의 사진을 찍니?

G: 나는 나무와 꽃 같은 자연의 사진을 찍는 것을 좋아해. 그 아름다운 사진들은 내 스트레스를 줄여주거든.

Listen & Speak 2-A-3

G: _____

B: _____

G: _____

B: _____

Conversation A

B: _____

_____

Conversation B

Karl: _____

Hana: _____

Karl: _____

_____

Hana: _____

Karl: _____

_____

Hana: _____

Karl: _____

Hana: _____

Wrap Up 1

B: _____

G: _____

B: _____

G: _____

B: _____

G: _____

Wrap Up 2

B: _____

_____

_____

G: 너는 강아지를 기르고 있니?
B: 응. 그녀의 이름은 코코야. 난 코코를 아주 좋아해.
G: 너는 코코와 함께 무엇을 하니?
B: 난 코코와 산책하는 걸 즐겨. 그것은 나를 건강하게 만들어.

B: 내일 영어 말하기 대회가 있어. 나는 2주 전에 대회를 준비하기 시작했어. 나는 영어로 말하는 것을 즐기지만, 난 그 대회가 걱정돼. 나는 잠을 잘 못 자.

Karl: 하나야, 무슨 일 있니?
하나: 음, 다음 주에 있을 시험 때문에 스트레스를 받아.
Karl: 난 이해돼. 나는 스트레스를 받을 때 롱보드를 타. 넌 롱보드를 어떻게 타는지 아니?
하나: 아니, 몰라.
Karl: 나가자! 내가 가르쳐 줄 수 있어. 한 발을 보드 위에 올려놓고 다른 한 발로 세게 밀어.
하나: 이렇게? 와! 이거 재밌다. 벌써 기분이 좋아졌어.
Karl: 봤지? 나는 롱보드를 타는 것이 나의 스트레스를 줄여주기 때문에 즐겨.
하나: 정말 멋진데!

B: 너 아파 보여. 무슨 일 있니?
G: 음, 감기에 걸렸어.
B: 병원에 가봤니?
G: 아직. 넌 감기가 나아지는 방법을 아니?
B: 음, 나는 감기에 걸렸을 때 보통 따뜻한 물을 마셔. 그것은 내 기분을 좋아지게 해.
G: 좋아. 한번 해 볼게.

B: 우리 가족은 많은 활동을 즐겨. 우리 아빠는 낚시를 즐기셔. 이른 아침, 그는 호수에 가셔서 약간의 물고기를 가지고 돌아오셔. 우리 엄마는 그림 그리기를 즐기셔. 그녀는 아름다운 산과 호수를 그리는 것을 좋아하셔. 나의 형과 나는 축구를 즐겨.

※ 다음 우리말과 일치하도록 빈칸에 알맞은 것을 골라 쓰시오.

1 _____ school you sit _____ many _____.
A. hours   B. for   C. at

2 _____ you _____ _____?
A. tired   B. get   C. do

3 Why _____ you massage _____ and _____?
A. stretch   B. yourself   C. don't

4 _____ begin _____ the eyes.
A. with   B. let's

5 _____ your eyes and _____ them _____ with your fingers.
A. softly   B. massage   C. close

6 It _____ _____ your eyes.
A. relax   B. will

7 _____ you finish, _____ your eyes with your hands to _____ _____ the light.
A. out   B. cover   C. block   D. when

8 It will _____ your eyes _____ more _____.
A. comfortable   B. feel   C. make

9 Next, _____ your _____.
A. neck   B. massage

10 _____ your fingers _____ the _____ of your neck.
A. back   B. on   C. put

11 Draw small _____ with your _____ to _____ your neck.
A. massage   B. fingers   C. circles

12 Massage from _____ to _____.
A. bottom   B. top

13 The massage will _____ you _____ _____.
A. better   B. feel   C. help

14 _____ work _____ your _____.
A. waist   B. on   C. let's

15 _____ _____ with a friend.
A. up   B. team

1 학교에서 너는 오랜 시간에 걸쳐 앉아 있다.

2 여러분은 피곤한가?

3 마사지와 스트레칭을 하는 게 어떤가?

4 눈부터 시작하자.

5 눈을 감고 손가락으로 눈을 부드럽게 마사지해라.

6 그것은 여러분의 눈을 편안하게 해줄 것이다.

7 끝나면, 빛을 차단하기 위해 손으로 눈을 가려라.

8 그것은 여러분의 눈을 더 편안하게 해줄 것이다.

9 다음으로, 여러분의 목을 마사지해라.

10 여러분의 목 뒤에 손가락을 대라.

11 여러분의 목을 마사지하기 위해 손가락으로 작은 원을 그려라.

12 위에서 아래로 마사지해라.

13 마사지는 여러분의 기분이 좋아지도록 도울 것이다.

14 허리 운동을 하자.

15 친구와 짝을 이루어라.

16 Stand _____ to each _____ and _____ your partner.
A. face　　　　　B. other　　　　　C. close

17 _____ each _____ wrists.
A. other's　　　　B. hold

18 Slowly _____ your head and _____ _____.
A. backward　　　B. body　　　　　C. stretch

19 _____ that position _____ three _____.
A. seconds　　　　B. for　　　　　C. hold

20 Then, slowly _____ each other _____ a standing position.
A. to　　　　　　B. pull

21 You and your partner _____ _____ at the same _____.
A. speed　　　　　B. move　　　　　C. should

22 _____ you don't, _____ of you will _____ !
A. fall　　　　　　B. both　　　　　C. if

23 _____ the _____ of your right foot _____ the desk _____ you.
A. behind　　　　B. top　　　　　C. on　　　　　D. place

24 Then, slowly _____ your left leg and _____ _____.
A. yourself　　　　B. lower　　　　　C. bend

25 _____ it for a _____ seconds and slowly _____ _____.
A. up　　　　　　B. few　　　　　C. straighten　　　D. hold

26 This _____ will _____ _____ your right leg.
A. up　　　　　　B. loosen　　　　　C. position

27 _____ your legs and _____ the _____.
A. exercise　　　　B. repeat　　　　　C. switch

28 _____ do you _____ now?
A. feel　　　　　　B. how

29 If you _____ yourself and _____ every day, you will _____ _____.
A. healthier　　　B. stretch　　　　C. massage　　　D. feel

30 Also, you can _____ _____ your _____ better.
A. studies　　　　B. on　　　　　C. focus

16 서로 가까이 서서 여러분의 파트너를 마주 보아라.

17 서로의 손목을 잡아라.

18 천천히 여러분의 머리와 몸을 뒤로 뻗어라.

19 3초 동안 그 자세를 유지해라.

20 그러고 나서, 천천히 서로 선 자세로 끌어 당겨라.

21 너와 너의 파트너는 같은 속도로 움직여야 한다.

22 그렇지 않으면, 너희 둘 다 넘어질 것이다!

23 여러분의 뒤에 있는 책상 위에 오른쪽 발등을 올려놓아라.

24 그러고 나서, 천천히 왼쪽 다리를 구부리고 몸을 낮추어라.

25 몇 초 동안 그 자세를 유지하다가 천천히 몸을 펴라.

26 이 자세는 여러분의 오른쪽 다리를 풀어 줄 것이다.

27 다리를 바꿔서 운동을 반복해라.

28 지금 기분이 어떤가?

29 매일 마사지와 스트레칭을 하면, 여러분은 더 건강해지는 것을 느낄 것이다.

30 또한, 여러분은 공부에 더 집중할 수 있을 것이다.

※ 다음 우리말과 일치하도록 빈칸에 알맞은 말을 쓰시오.

1 _____ _____ you sit _____ many hours.

2 Do you _____ _____?

3 _____ _____ you massage _____ and _____?

4 _____ _____ _____ the eyes.

5 _____ your eyes and _____ them softly _____ your
_____.

6 It _____ _____ your eyes.

7 _____ you finish, _____ your eyes _____ your hands to
_____ _____ the light.

8 It will _____ your eyes _____ _____ _____.

9 Next, _____ _____ _____.

10 _____ your fingers _____ the _____ of your neck.

11 _____ small circles _____ your fingers _____ _____
your neck.

12 Massage _____ _____ _____ _____.

13 The massage will _____ _____ _____ _____.

14 _____ _____ _____ your _____.

15 _____ _____ _____ a friend.

---

1 학교에서 너는 오랜 시간에 걸쳐 앉아 있다.

2 여러분은 피곤한가?

3 마사지와 스트레칭을 하는 게 어떤가?

4 눈부터 시작하자.

5 눈을 감고 손가락으로 눈을 부드럽게 마사지해라.

6 그것은 여러분의 눈을 편안하게 해줄 것이다.

7 끝나면, 빛을 차단하기 위해 손으로 눈을 가려라.

8 그것은 여러분의 눈을 더 편안하게 해줄 것이다.

9 다음으로, 여러분의 목을 마사지해라.

10 여러분의 목 뒤에 손가락을 대라.

11 여러분의 목을 마사지하기 위해 손가락으로 작은 원을 그려라.

12 위에서 아래로 마사지해라.

13 마사지는 여러분의 기분이 좋아지도록 도울 것이다.

14 허리 운동을 하자.

15 친구와 짝을 이루어라.

16 Stand close to _____ _____ and _____ your partner.

17 _____ each other's _____.

18 _____ _____ your head and body _____.

19 _____ that position _____ _____ _____.

20 Then, slowly _____ each other _____ a standing position.

21 You and _____ partner should move _____ the same speed.

22 _____ you don't, _____ _____ you _____ _____!

23 _____ the _____ of your right foot _____ the desk _____ you.

24 Then, _____ _____ your left leg and _____ yourself.

25 _____ it for _____ _____ _____ and slowly _____ _____.

26 _____ _____ will _____ _____ your right leg.

27 _____ your legs and _____ _____ _____.

28 _____ do you _____ now?

29 If you _____ yourself and _____ _____ _____, you will _____ _____.

30 Also, you _____ _____ _____ your studies _____.

16 서로 가까이 서서 여러분의 파트너를 마주 보아라.

17 서로의 손목을 잡아라.

18 천천히 여러분의 머리와 몸을 뒤로 뻗어라.

19 3초 동안 그 자세를 유지해라.

20 그리고 나서, 천천히 서로 선 자세로 끌어 당겨라.

21 너와 너의 파트너는 같은 속도로 움직여야 한다.

22 그렇지 않으면, 너희 둘 다 넘어질 것이다!

23 여러분의 뒤에 있는 책상 위에 오른쪽 발등을 올려놓아라.

24 그리고 나서, 천천히 왼쪽 다리를 구부리고 몸을 낮추어라.

25 몇 초 동안 그 자세를 유지하다가 천천히 몸을 펴라.

26 이 자세는 여러분의 오른쪽 다리를 풀어 줄 것이다.

27 다리를 바꿔서 운동을 반복해라.

28 지금 기분이 어떤가?

29 매일 마사지와 스트레칭을 하면, 여러분은 더 건강해지는 것을 느낄 것이다.

30 또한, 여러분은 공부에 더 집중할 수 있을 것이다.

※ 다음 문장을 우리말로 쓰시오.

1 At school you sit for many hours.

➡ _____

2 Do you get tired?

➡ _____

3 Why don't you massage yourself and stretch?

➡ _____

4 Let's begin with the eyes.

➡ _____

5 Close your eyes and massage them softly with your fingers.

➡ _____

6 It will relax your eyes.

➡ _____

7 When you finish, cover your eyes with your hands to block out the light.

➡ _____

8 It will make your eyes feel more comfortable.

➡ _____

9 Next, massage your neck.

➡ _____

10 Put your fingers on the back of your neck.

➡ _____

11 Draw small circles with your fingers to massage your neck.

➡ _____

12 Massage from top to bottom.

➡ _____

13 The massage will help you feel better.

➡ _____

14 Let's work on your waist.

➡ _____

15 Team up with a friend.

➡ _____

16 ▶ Stand close to each other and face your partner.

➡ _____

17 ▶ Hold each other's wrists.

➡ _____

18 ▶ Slowly stretch your head and body backward.

➡ _____

19 ▶ Hold that position for three seconds.

➡ _____

20 ▶ Then, slowly pull each other to a standing position.

➡ _____

21 ▶ You and your partner should move at the same speed.

➡ _____

22 ▶ If you don't, both of you will fall!

➡ _____

23 ▶ Place the top of your right foot on the desk behind you.

➡ _____

24 ▶ Then, slowly bend your left leg and lower yourself.

➡ _____

25 ▶ Hold it for a few seconds and slowly straighten up.

➡ _____

26 ▶ This position will loosen up your right leg.

➡ _____

27 ▶ Switch your legs and repeat the exercise.

➡ _____

28 ▶ How do you feel now?

➡ _____

29 ▶ If you massage yourself and stretch every day, you will feel healthier.

➡ _____

30 ▶ Also, you can focus on your studies better.

➡ _____

※ 다음 괄호 안의 단어들을 우리말에 맞도록 바르게 배열하시오.

1 (school / you / at / sit / hours. / many / for)
➡ _____

2 (get / do / tired? / you)
➡ _____

3 (you / don't / why / massage / stretch? / and / yourself)
➡ _____

4 (begin / with / let's / eyes. / the)
➡ _____

5 (eyes / close / your / and / them / massage / fingers. / with / softly / your)
➡ _____

6 (will / it / relax / eyes. / your)
➡ _____

7 (you / finish, / when / your / cover / with / eyes / hands / your / block / to / light. / the / out)
➡ _____

8 (will / it / make / eyes / your / feel / comfortable. / more)
➡ _____

9 (next, / neck. / your / massage)
➡ _____

10 (fingers / put / your / the / on / back / neck. / your / of)
➡ _____

11 (small / draw / circles / your / with / fingers / massage / neck. / to / your)
➡ _____

12 (from / bottom. / to / massage / top)
➡ _____

13 (massage / the / help / will / better. / feel / you)
➡ _____

14 (work / on / waist. / let's / your)
➡ _____

15 (up / team / friend. / a / with)
➡ _____

1 학교에서 너는 오랜 시간에 걸쳐 앉아 있다.

2 여러분은 피곤한가?

3 마사지와 스트레칭을 하는 게 어떤가?

4 눈부터 시작하자.

5 눈을 감고 손가락으로 눈을 부드럽게 마사지해라.

6 그것은 여러분의 눈을 편안하게 해줄 것이다.

7 끝나면, 빛을 차단하기 위해 손으로 눈을 가려라.

8 그것은 여러분의 눈을 더 편안하게 해줄 것이다.

9 다음으로, 여러분의 목을 마사지해라.

10 여러분의 목 뒤에 손가락을 대라.

11 여러분의 목을 마사지하기 위해 손가락으로 작은 원을 그려라.

12 위에서 아래로 마사지해라.

13 마사지는 여러분의 기분이 좋아지도록 도울 것이다.

14 허리 운동을 하자.

15 친구와 짝을 이루어라.

16 (close / to / stand / other / each / and / partner. / your / face)

➡ _____

17 (each / wrists. / hold / other's)

➡ _____

18 (stretch / slowly / head / your / and / backward. / body)

➡ _____

19 (that / hold / for / position / seconds. / three)

➡ _____

20 (slowly / then, / each / pull / other / to / position. / standing / a)

➡ _____

21 (your / and / you / partner / move / should / the / at / speed. / same)

➡ _____

22 (don't, / you / if / of / you / both / fall! / will)

➡ _____

23 (the / place / of / top / right / your / foot / on / the / desk / you. / behind)

➡ _____

24 (slowly / then, / your / bend / leg / left / yourself. / lower / and)

➡ _____

25 (it / hold / a / for / seconds / few / and / slowly / up. / straighten)

➡ _____

26 (position / this / loosen / will / up / leg. / right / your)

➡ _____

27 (your / switch / legs / and / exercise. / the / repeat)

➡ _____

28 (you / do / how / now? / feel)

➡ _____

29 (you / massage / if / yourself / and / stretch / day, / every / will / you / healthier. / feel)

➡ _____

30 (can / you / also, / on / focus / better. / studies / your)

➡ _____

16 서로 가까이 서서 여러분의 트너를 마주 보아라.

17 서로의 손목을 잡아라.

18 천천히 여러분의 머리와 몸 뒤로 뻗어라.

19 3초 동안 그 자세를 유지해라.

20 그리고 나서, 천천히 서로 선 세로 끌어 당겨라.

21 너와 너의 파트너는 같은 속도 움직여야 한다.

22 그렇지 않으면, 너희 둘 다 넘 질 것이다!

23 여러분의 뒤에 있는 책상 위 오른쪽 발등을 올려놓아라.

24 그리고 나서, 천천히 왼쪽 다 를 구부리고 몸을 낮추어라.

25 몇 초 동안 그 자세를 유지하 가 천천히 몸을 펴라.

26 이 자세는 여러분의 오른쪽 다 리를 풀어 줄 것이다.

27 다리를 바꿔서 운동을 반복해라

28 지금 기분이 어떤가?

29 매일 마사지와 스트레칭을 하 면, 여러분은 더 건강해지는 것 을 느낄 것이다.

30 또한, 여러분은 공부에 더 집중 할 수 있을 것이다.

※ 다음 우리말을 영어로 쓰시오.

1 학교에서 여러분은 오랜 시간에 걸쳐 앉아 있다.

➡ _____

2 여러분은 피곤한가?

➡ _____

3 마사지와 스트레칭을 하는 게 어떤가?

➡ _____

4 눈부터 시작하자.

➡ _____

5 눈을 감고 손가락으로 눈을 부드럽게 마사지해라.

➡ _____

6 그것은 여러분의 눈을 편안하게 해줄 것이다.

➡ _____

7 끝나면, 빛을 차단하기 위해 손으로 눈을 가려라.

➡ _____

8 그것은 여러분의 눈을 더 편안하게 해줄 것이다.

➡ _____

9 다음으로, 여러분의 목을 마사지해라.

➡ _____

10 여러분의 목 뒤에 손가락을 대라.

➡ _____

11 여러분의 목을 마사지하기 위해 손가락으로 작은 원을 그려라.

➡ _____

12 위에서 아래로 마사지해라.

➡ _____

13 마사지는 여러분의 기분이 좋아지도록 도울 것이다.

➡ _____

14 허리 운동을 하자.

➡ _____

15 친구와 짝을 이루어라.

➡ _____

16 서로 가까이 서서 여러분의 파트너를 마주 보아라.

➡ _____

17 서로의 손목을 잡아라.

➡ _____

18 천천히 여러분의 머리와 몸을 뒤로 뻗어라.

➡ _____

19 3초 동안 그 자세를 유지해라.

➡ _____

20 그리고 나서, 천천히 서로 선 자세로 끌어 당겨라.

➡ _____

21 너와 너의 파트너는 같은 속도로 움직여야 한다.

➡ _____

22 그렇지 않으면, 너희 둘 다 넘어질 것이다!

➡ _____

23 여러분의 뒤에 있는 책상 위에 오른쪽 발등을 올려놓아라.

➡ _____

24 그리고 나서, 천천히 왼쪽 다리를 구부리고 몸을 낮추어라.

➡ _____

25 몇 초 동안 그 자세를 유지하다가 천천히 몸을 펴라.

➡ _____

26 이 자세는 여러분의 오른쪽 다리를 풀어 줄 것이다.

➡ _____

27 다리를 바꿔서 운동을 반복해라.

➡ _____

28 지금 기분이 어떤가?

➡ _____

29 매일 마사지와 스트레칭을 하면, 여러분은 더 건강해지는 것을 느낄 것이다.

➡ _____

30 또한, 여러분은 공부에 더 집중할 수 있을 것이다.

➡ _____

※ 다음 우리말과 일치하도록 빈칸에 알맞은 말을 쓰시오.

Enjoy Writing C

1. My Plan _____ _____ _____

2. _____ _____ my plan to be healthier.

3. I will exercise _____ _____ _____ _____ a week.

4. I will eat breakfast _____ _____.

5. If I exercise more than _____ _____ _____ _____, I will _____ _____.

6. Also, _____ I eat breakfast every day, I _____ _____ _____ in the morning.

7. I will change my _____, and it will _____ _____ _____ a healthy life.

1. 더 건강해지기 위한 나의 계획
2. 여기 더 건강해지기 위한 나의 계획이 있다.
3. 나는 일주일에 세 번 이상 운동을 할 것이다.
4. 나는 매일 아침을 먹을 것이다.
5. 일주일에 세 번 이상 운동을 하면 더 강해질 것이다.
6. 또한, 매일 아침을 먹으면 아침에 기분이 나아질 것이다.
7. 나는 습관을 바꿀 것이고, 그것은 나를 건강한 삶을 살게 할 것이다.

Project - Step 2

1. Do you know _____ _____ _____ your shoulders?

2. Our _____ _____ _____ _____ "Number Stretching."

3. First, make a number "I" _____ your arm _____ _____ _____.

4. _____, make a number "2" _____ your arms.

5. It _____ _____ your _____.

6. Now, _____ a number "3".

7. If you move your arms _____ _____ _____, it will _____ _____.

8. _____, make a number "4".

9. It is _____ _____ _____ difficult, but it will _____ _____ _____ your shoulders.

1. 여러분은 여러분의 어깨를 어떻게 스트레칭하는지 아니?
2. 우리의 스트레칭 운동은 "숫자 스트레칭"이라고 부른다.
3. "첫 번째, 준비 운동을 하기 위해 팔로 숫자 "1"를 만들어라.
4. 그런 다음, 팔로 숫자 2를 만들어라.
5. 그것은 여러분의 어깨를 쫙 펴줄 것이다.
6. 이제 숫자 3을 만들어라.
7. 팔을 동그랗게 움직이면 기분이 좋아질 것이다.
8. 마지막으로, 숫자 4를 만들어라.
9. 그것은 조금 어렵긴 하지만, 여러분의 어깨에 좋을 것이다.

Wrap Up - Writing

1. Sumi: I feel stressed _____ _____. What _____ I _____?

2. Jiae: When I _____ _____, I listen to music. It _____ _____ _____ better.

3. If you don't know _____ _____ _____ music, I will show you.

1. 수미: 나는 요즘 스트레스를 받고 있어. 어떻게 해야 하지?
2. 지애: 스트레스를 받을 때, 나는 음악을 들어. 그건 내 기분을 좋아지게 해.
3. 음악을 다운로드하는 방법을 모르면, 내가 가르쳐 줄게.

※ 다음 우리말을 영어로 쓰시오.

Enjoy Writing C

1. 더 건강해지기 위한 나의 계획
   ➡ _____

2. 여기 더 건강해지기 위한 나의 계획이 있다.
   ➡ _____

3. 나는 일주일에 세 번 이상 운동을 할 것이다.
   ➡ _____

4. 나는 매일 아침을 먹을 것이다.
   ➡ _____

5. 일주일에 세 번 이상 운동을 하면 더 강해질 것이다.
   ➡ _____

6. 또한, 매일 아침을 먹으면 아침에 기분이 나아질 것이다.
   ➡ _____

7. 나는 습관을 바꿀 것이고, 그것은 나를 건강한 삶을 살게 할 것이다.
   ➡ _____

Project - Step 2

1. 여러분은 여러분의 어깨를 어떻게 스트레칭하는지 아니?
   ➡ _____

2. 우리의 스트레칭 운동은 "숫자 스트레칭"이라고 부른다.
   ➡ _____

3. "첫 번째, 준비 운동을 하기 위해 팔로 숫자 "1"를 만들어라.
   ➡ _____

4. 그런 다음, 팔로 숫자 2를 만들어라.
   ➡ _____

5. 그것은 여러분의 어깨를 쫙 펴줄 것이다.
   ➡ _____

6. 이제 숫자 3을 만들어라.
   ➡ _____

7. 팔을 동그랗게 움직이면 기분이 좋아질 것이다.
   ➡ _____

8. 마지막으로, 숫자 4를 만들어라.
   ➡ _____

9. 그것은 조금 어렵긴 하지만, 여러분의 어깨에 좋을 것이다.
   ➡ _____

Wrap Up - Writing

1. 수미: 나는 요즘 스트레스를 받고 있어. 어떻게 해야 하지?
   ➡ _____

2. 지애: 스트레스를 받을 때, 나는 음악을 들어. 그건 내 기분을 좋아지게 해.
   ➡ _____

3. 음악을 다운로드하는 방법을 모르면, 내가 가르쳐 줄게.
   ➡ _____

※ 다음 영어를 우리말로 쓰시오.

01	hunger	
02	recycle	
03	environment	
04	celebrate	
05	save	
06	aim	
07	education	
08	far	
09	flood	
10	hurt	
11	gather	
12	produce	
13	send	
14	adult	
15	share	
16	join	
17	trash	
18	messy	
19	nothing	
20	raise	
21	waste	

22	lantern	
23	awesome	
24	global	
25	community	
26	communicate	
27	garden	
28	poor	
29	alongside	
30	plate	
31	citizen	
32	protect	
33	hold	
34	international	
35	care for	
36	thanks to	
37	watch out (for)	
38	die of	
39	go well	
40	be good at	
41	throw away	
42	in need	
43	share A with B	

※ 다음 우리말을 영어로 쓰시오.

01 시민

02 미국의, 미국인

03 가난한

04 싸움; 싸우다

05 ~ 옆에, 나란히

06 공동체, 사회

07 굉장한, 감탄할 만한

08 캠페인, 조직적 활동

09 정원

10 접시

11 팔다

12 업로드하다, 올리다

13 전 세계적인, 지구상의

14 (회의, 시합 등을) 열다

15 국제적인

16 당황한

17 남기다

18 의사소통하다

19 보호하다

20 (컴퓨터의) 사이트

21 가져가다

22 자연환경, 환경

23 모으다

24 쓰레기

25 교육

26 다치게 하다

27 어른

28 살리다, 구하다

29 (폐기물을) 재활용하다

30 생산하다

31 홍수

32 축하하다, 기념하다

33 기아, 배고픔

34 (자금 등을) 모금하다

35 ~에 관심을 가지다

36 샤워를 하다

37 어려움에 처한

38 (~에 대해서) 조심하다

39 ~을 버리다

40 ~을 잘하다

41 ~ 덕분에

42 ~을 돌보다, 신경 쓰다

43 ~으로 죽다

※ 다음 영영풀이에 알맞은 단어를 <보기>에서 골라 쓴 후, 우리말 뜻을 쓰시오.

1 _____ : a grown-up person: _____

2 _____ : an overflow of water: _____

3 _____ : a place where you can grow plants: _____

4 _____ : untidy or dirty: _____

5 _____ : having very little money: _____

6 _____ : to give goods in exchange for money: _____

7 _____ : to plan or hope to achieve something: _____

8 _____ : including the whole world: _____

9 _____ : to process used or waste materials so as to make suitable for reuse:

_____

10 _____ : emotionally disturbed or agitated: _____

11 _____ : to fail to use time, money, energy, etc. fully or in the sensible or useful

way: _____

12 _____ : to collect money for a particular purpose: _____

13 _____ : to do something enjoyable on a special occasion: _____

14 _____ : to bring people together or collect things together: _____

15 _____ : a person who lives in a country or town legally: _____

16 _____ : to share or exchange information or emotion with someone: _____

보기			
citizen	recycle	poor	celebrate
raise	upset	flood	sell
aim	communicate	adult	garden
gather	waste	global	messy

대화문 Test

※ 다음 우리말과 일치하도록 빈칸에 알맞은 말을 쓰시오.

 해석

Listen & Speak 1 A

1. **B:** Did you _____ the news _____ _____ _____?
   G: Yes, _____ _____. They said _____ _____ _____ people _____ their homes.
   B: My club is _____ _____ _____ them some money.
   G: _____ can you do that? _____ _____ going _____ _____ money, Andy?
   B: Yes. We're _____ _____ _____ pencil cases and _____ them.

2. **B:** Do you have any _____ for the summer _____, Suji?
   G: Yes. I'm _____ _____ the Philippines to _____ _____ _____ _____ _____ my family.
   B: Oh, I _____ there and _____ some children study last year. _____ _____ _____ _____ _____ that, too?
   G: Yes. And I'll _____ _____ walls _____ the children.
   B: That _____ _____.

Listen & Speak 1 B

1. **G:** _____ you _____ _____ _____ a short shower?
   B: Yes, I _____, / No, _____ _____.

2. **G:** Are you _____ _____ _____ _____?
   B: Yes, _____ _____. / No, _____ _____.

Listen & Speak 2 A

1. **G:** _____ are you doing, Jason?
   B: I'm _____ a poster _____ global _____. Many people are _____ _____ _____.
   G: That's _____ _____. I didn't know that.
   B: I _____ more people _____ _____ _____ hunger.

1. **B:** 홍수에 대한 뉴스를 보았니?
   G: 응, 보았어. 많은 사람들이 집을 잃었다고 하더라.
   B: 우리 동아리는 그들에게 약간의 돈을 보낼 거야.
   G: 그것을 어떻게 할 수 있니? 돈을 모금할 거니, Andy?
   B: 응. 우리는 필통을 만들어서 그것들을 팔 거야.

2. **B:** 여름 방학에 어떤 계획이 있니, 수지야?
   G: 응. 나는 나의 가족들과 봉사활동을 하러 필리핀에 갈 거야.
   B: 오, 나는 작년에 그 곳에 가서 몇몇 아이들이 공부하는 것을 도와줬어. 너도 그렇게 할 거니?
   G: 응, 그리고 나는 또한 아이들과 벽화를 그릴 거야.
   B: 정말 좋겠다.

1. **A:** 너는 샤워를 짧게 할 거니?
   B: 응, 그럴 거야. / 아니, 그러지 않을 거야.

2. **A:** 너는 병을 재활용할 거니?
   B: 응, 그럴 거야. / 아니, 그러지 않을 거야.

1. **G:** 무엇을 하고 있니, Jason?
   B: 세계의 기아 문제에 대한 포스터를 만드는 중이야. 많은 사람들이 기아로 죽어가고 있어.
   G: 정말 안됐다. 난 몰랐어.
   B: 더 많은 사람들이 세계의 기아 문제에 관심을 갖기를 바라.

2. **G:** Dad, my class _____ _____ _____ a vegetable _____.

   M: A _____ _____? What _____ you grow there, Sena?

   G: Carrots. We'll _____ them and _____ them _____ others.

   M: That's a _____ _____.

   G: I _____ the carrots _____ _____.

Listen & Speak 2 B

1. **A:** I _____ people _____ _____ _____ _____ _____.

   B: I _____ _____, too. _____ _____ a Keep the World Clean _____.

   A: That's a good idea.

2. **A:** _____ _____ _____ _____ _____ _____ animals.

   B: I _____ _____, too. _____ _____ a Love Animals campaign.

   A: That's a _____ _____.

Wrap Up

1. **B:** _____ _____ _____ for the weekend, Sumin? _____ you _____ _____ _____ _____ _____?

   G: Yes. _____ Saturday, I'm _____ _____ _____ my grandmother.

   B: _____ _____ Sunday?

   G: I _____ _____ for Sunday. Why?

   B: I'm _____ _____ _____ _____ _____ at the library on Sunday. Would you _____ _____ _____ with me?

   G: Sure.

2. **G:** My club is _____ _____ _____ a green campaign _____ _____ _____ _____.

   B: _____ _____ a green campaign?

   G: It's a _____ _____ _____ the environment. Many students _____ _____ _____ the streets. We hope _____ _____ that.

   B: I _____ your campaign _____ well.

   G: Thanks. I _____ _____, _____.

---

2. **G:** 아빠, 우리 반은 채소밭을 가꾸기로 했어요.

   M: 채소밭? 거기서 무엇을 기를 거니, 세나야?

   G: 당근이요. 우리는 그것을 길러서 사람들과 나눌 거예요.

   M: 좋은 생각이구나.

   G: 당근이 잘 자랐으면 좋겠어요.

1. **A:** 나는 사람들이 쓰레기를 버리지 않기를 바라.

   B: 나도 그렇게 생각해. '세상을 깨끗하게 하라'라는 캠페인을 열자.

   A: 좋은 생각이야.

2. **A:** 나는 사람들이 동물을 해치지 않기를 바라.

   B: 나도 그렇게 생각해. '동물을 사랑하라'라는 캠페인을 열자.

   A: 좋은 생각이야.

1. **B:** 너의 주말 계획은 뭐니, 수민아? 특별한 걸 할 거니?

   G: 응. 토요일에 할머니를 방문할 거야.

   B: 일요일은 어때?

   G: 일요일은 아무 계획 없어. 왜?

   B: 나는 일요일에 도서관에서 봉사활동을 할 거야. 나와 함께 갈래?

   G: 물론이지.

2. **G:** 우리 동아리는 다음 주 금요일에 학교에서 그린 캠페인을 열 거야.

   B: 그린 캠페인이 뭐야?

   G: 환경을 보호하기 위한 캠페인이야. 많은 학생들이 길에 쓰레기를 버려. 우리는 그걸 멈추길 바라.

   B: 네 캠페인이 잘 되길 바라.

   G: 고마워. 나도 그러길 바라

※ 다음 우리말에 맞도록 대화를 영어로 쓰시오.

Listen & Speak 1 A

1. B: _____
   G: _____
   B: _____
   G: _____
   B: _____

2. B: _____
   G: _____
   B: _____

   G: _____
   B: _____

1. B: 홍수에 대한 뉴스를 보았나니?
   G: 응, 보았어. 많은 사람들이 집을 잃었다고 하더라.
   B: 우리 동아리는 그들에게 약간의 돈을 보낼 거야.
   G: 그것을 어떻게 할 수 있니? 돈을 모금할 거니, Andy?
   B: 응. 우리는 필통을 만들어서 그것들을 팔 거야.

2. B: 여름 방학에 어떤 계획이 있니, 수지야?
   G: 응. 나는 나의 가족들과 봉사활동을 하러 필리핀에 갈 거야.
   B: 오, 나는 작년에 그 곳에 가서 몇몇 아이들이 공부하는 것을 도와줬어. 너도 그렇게 할 거니?
   G: 응, 그리고 나는 또한 아이들과 벽화를 그릴 거야.
   B: 정말 좋겠다.

Listen & Speak 1 B

1. G: _____
   B: _____

2. G: _____
   B: _____

1. A: 너는 샤워를 짧게 할 거니?
   B: 응, 그럴 거야. / 아니, 그러지 않을 거야.

2. A: 너는 병을 재활용할 거니?
   B: 응, 그럴 거야. / 아니, 그러지 않을 거야.

Listen & Speak 2 A

1. G: _____
   B: _____
   G: _____
   B: _____

1. G: 무엇을 하고 있니, Jason?
   B: 세계의 기아 문제에 대한 포스터를 만드는 중이야. 많은 사람들이 기아로 죽어가고 있어.
   G: 정말 안됐다. 난 몰랐어.
   B: 더 많은 사람들이 세계의 기아 문제에 관심을 갖기를 바라.

2. G: _____

   M: _____

   G: _____

   M: _____

   G: _____

2. G: 아빠, 우리 반은 채소밭을 가꾸기
      로 했어요.
   M: 채소밭? 거기서 무엇을 기를 거
      니, 세나야?
   G: 당근이요. 우리는 그것을 길러서
      사람들과 나눌 거예요.
   M: 좋은 생각이구나.
   G: 당근이 잘 자랐으면 좋겠어요.

Listen & Speak 2 B

1. A: _____

   B: _____

   A: _____

2. A: _____

   B: _____

   A: _____

1. A: 나는 사람들이 쓰레기를 버리지
      않기를 바라.
   B: 나도 그렇게 생각해. '세상을 깨끗
      하게 하라'라는 캠페인을 열자.
   A: 좋은 생각이야.

2. A: 나는 사람들이 동물을 해치지 않
      기를 바라.
   B: 나도 그렇게 생각해. '동물을 사랑
      하라'라는 캠페인을 열자.
   A: 좋은 생각이야.

Wrap Up

1. B: _____

   _____

   G: _____

   B: _____

   G: _____

   B: _____

   G: _____

2. G: _____

   B: _____

   G: _____

   B: _____

   G: _____

1. B: 너의 주말 계획은 뭐니, 수민아?
      특별한 걸 할 거니?
   G: 응. 토요일에 할머니를 방문할 거
      야.
   B: 일요일은 어때?
   G: 일요일은 아무 계획 없어. 왜?
   B: 나는 일요일에 도서관에서 봉사
      활동을 할 거야. 나와 함께 갈래?
   G: 물론이지.

2. G: 우리 동아리는 다음 주 금요일에
      학교에서 그린 캠페인을 열 거야.
   B: 그린 캠페인이 뭐야?
   G: 환경을 보호하기 위한 캠페인이
      야. 많은 학생들이 길에 쓰레기를
      버려. 우리는 그걸 멈추길 바라.
   B: 네 캠페인이 잘 되길 바라.
   G: 고마워. 나도 그러길 바라

※ 다음 우리말과 일치하도록 빈칸에 알맞은 것을 골라 쓰시오.

1 _____ Citizenship _____
   A. Education   B. Global

2 _____ is the Global _____ Education _____ .
   A. Citizenship   B. site   C. this

3 Global Citizenship Education _____ us _____ _____ global citizens.
   A. grow   B. helps   C. as

4 Global citizens are people who _____ to _____ different _____ .
   A. understand   B. cultures   C. try

5 They also _____ _____ people _____ _____ and work for a better world.
   A. need   B. for   C. in   D. care

6 Please _____ your _____ citizenship education _____ here.
   A. experiences   B. share   C. global

7 Hello. I _____ Minhee _____ _____ .
   A. Korea   B. from   C. am

8 I am _____ _____ _____ the Global Community Club.
   A. a   B. of   C. member

9 My club _____ to _____ _____ people from around the world.
   A. with   B. communicate   C. aims

10 A week _____ we _____ a video about the _____ festival in our village.
   A. ago   B. produced   C. lantern

11 We _____ it to the Internet and _____ , we got _____ 5,000 _____ .
   A. amazingly   B. uploaded   C. hits   D. nearly

12 _____ here _____ our _____ .
   A. video   B. for   C. click

13 Alice: Wow, _____ lantern festival _____ _____ !
   A. fantastic   B. your   C. looks

14 Sunan: We _____ a water festival _____ our _____ .
   A. village   B. have   C. in

15 I'd like to _____ a video _____ _____ .
   A. yours   B. like   C. make

---

1 세계 시민 교육

2 이곳은 세계 시민 교육 사이 입니다.

3 세계 시민 교육은 우리가 세 시민으로 자라도록 도와줍니

4 세계 시민은 다른 문화를 이 하려고 노력하는 사람들입니

5 그들은 또한 어려움에 처한 람들을 보살피고 더 나은 세 을 위해서 일합니다.

6 당신의 세계 시민 교육 경험 이곳에 공유해 주세요.

7 안녕. 나는 한국의 민희야.

8 나는 세계 공동체 동아리의 원이야.

9 우리 동아리는 전 세계의 사 들과 소통하는 것을 목표로 하

10 일주일 전에 우리는 우리 마 의 등 축제에 관한 비디오를 작했어.

11 우리는 그것을 인터넷에 올렸 데, 놀랍게도 거의 5,000개의 회 수를 획득했어.

12 우리 비디오를 보려면 이곳 클릭해.

13 Alice: 와, 너희 등 축제는 환 적으로 보인다!

14 Sunan: 우리 마을에는 물 축 가 있어.

15 나도 너희 것과 같은 비디오 만들고 싶어.

16 Hi, _____ _____ is Jo.

A. name   B. my

17 I _____ _____ Australia.

A. from   B. am

18 A _____ weeks _____, my teacher _____ us pictures _____ students in Kenya.

A. few   B. showed   C. ago   D. of

19 Sadly, they were _____ _____ plastic bags _____ _____ their books.

A. using   B. all   C. carry   D. to

20 My class _____ to _____ money to _____ them new school bags.

A. raise   B. decided   C. send

21 We _____ cookies and _____ and _____ 600 dollars.

A. drinks   B. sold   C. raised

22 We _____ the Kenyan students are _____ _____ the new bags.

A. with   B. hope   C. happy

23 Wang: _____! I'm _____ they _____ like the bags.

A. sure   B. awesome   C. will

24 Kozo: You did _____ _____!

A. wonderful   B. something

25 I _____ Afig _____ Malaysia.

A. from   B. am

26 My school started a wall _____ campaign to _____ our village _____ _____.

A. make   B. better   C. look   D. painting

27 Students who are _____ at painting _____ and _____ on some walls of schools and parks.

A. good   B. painted   C. gathered

28 _____ to this campaign, our village looks _____ _____.

A. nicer   B. thanks   C. much

29 Now everyone can enjoy _____ _____ the _____ walls.

A. walking   B. painted   C. alongside

30 Junho: _____ _____ _____ idea!

A. nice   B. what   C. a

16 안녕. 내 이름은 Jo야.

17 나는 호주 출신이야.

18 몇 주 전에, 선생님이 우리에게 케냐에 있는 학생들의 사진을 보여주셨어.

19 슬프게도, 그들은 모두 책을 들고 다니기 위해서 비닐 봉지를 사용하고 있었어.

20 우리 반은 그들에게 새로운 책가방을 보내기 위해서 기금을 모금하기로 결정했어.

21 우리는 쿠키와 음료를 팔아서 600달러를 모았어.

22 우리는 케냐의 학생들이 그들의 새 가방을 좋아하기를 바라.

23 Wang: 멋지다! 분명 그들이 가방을 좋아할 거야.

24 Kozo: 훌륭한 일을 했구나!

25 난 말레이시아의 Afig야.

26 우리 학교는 우리 마을을 좀 더 좋아 보이게 하기 위해서 벽화 캠페인을 시작했어.

27 그림을 잘 그리는 학생들이 모여서 학교와 공원 벽에 그림을 그렸어.

28 이 캠페인 덕분에, 우리 마을은 훨씬 멋져 보여.

29 이제 모든 사람들이 그림이 그려진 벽을 따라서 산책하는 것을 즐길 수 있어.

30 Junho: 정말 멋진 생각이다!

※ 다음 우리말과 일치하도록 빈칸에 알맞은 말을 쓰시오.

1 _____ Citizenship _____

2 _____ is the Global _____ _____ _____ .

3 Global Citizenship Education _____ us _____ _____
_____ _____ .

4 Global citizens are people who _____ _____ _____
different _____ .

5 They also _____ _____ people _____ _____ and
work for _____ _____ _____ .

6 Please _____ your _____ citizenship education _____
here.

7 Hello. I _____ Minhee _____ _____ .

8 I am _____ _____ _____ the Global Community Club.

9 My club _____ _____ _____ _____ people from
_____ the world.

10 _____ _____ _____ we produced a video _____ _____
_____ _____ in our village.

11 We _____ it to the Internet and _____ , we _____
_____ 5,000 _____ .

12 _____ here _____ our _____ .

13 Alice: Wow, _____ lantern festival _____ _____ !

14 Sunan: We _____ a water festival _____ our _____ .

15 I'd _____ _____ _____ a video _____ _____ .

---

1 세계 시민 교육

2 이곳은 세계 시민 교육 사◯
입니다.

3 세계 시민 교육은 우리가 ◯
시민으로 자라도록 도와줍니◯

4 세계 시민은 다른 문화를 ◯
하려고 노력하는 사람들입니◯

5 그들은 또한 어려움에 처한◯
람들을 보살피고 더 나은 ◯
을 위해서 일합니다.

6 당신의 세계 시민 교육 경◯
이곳에 공유해 주세요.

7 안녕. 나는 한국의 민희야.

8 나는 세계 공동체 동아리의◯
원이야.

9 우리 동아리는 전 세계의 ◯
들과 소통하는 것을 목표로 ◯

10 일주일 전에 우리는 우리 ◯
의 등 축제에 관한 비디오를◯
작했어.

11 우리는 그것을 인터넷에 올◯
데, 놀랍게도 거의 5,000개의◯
회 수를 획득했어.

12 우리 비디오를 보려면 이◯
클릭해.

13 Alice: 와, 너희 등 축제는 ◯
적으로 보인다!

14 Sunan: 우리 마을에는 물 ◯
가 있어.

15 나도 너희 것과 같은 비디◯
만들고 싶어.

---

16 Hi, _____ _____ is Jo.

17 I _____ _____ Australia.

18 A _____ weeks _____, my teacher _____ _____ _____ _____ students in Kenya.

19 _____, they were _____ _____ plastic bags _____ _____ their books.

20 My class _____ to _____ _____ _____ _____ them new school bags.

21 We _____ cookies and _____ and _____ 600 dollars.

22 We _____ the Kenyan students _____ _____ _____ the new bags.

23 Wang: _____! I'm _____ they _____ _____ the bags.

24 Kozo: You _____ _____ _____!

25 I _____ Afig _____ _____.

26 My school started a _____ _____ campaign _____ _____ our village _____ _____.

27 Students who _____ _____ _____ painting _____ and _____ on some walls of schools and parks.

28 _____ _____ this campaign, our village _____ _____ _____.

29 Now everyone can _____ _____ the _____ walls.

30 Junho: _____ _____ _____ _____!

---

16 안녕, 내 이름은 Jo야.

17 나는 호주 출신이야.

18 몇 주 전에, 선생님이 우리에게 케냐에 있는 학생들의 사진을 보여주셨어.

19 슬프게도, 그들은 모두 책을 들고 다니기 위해서 비닐 봉지를 사용하고 있었어.

20 우리 반은 그들에게 새로운 책 가방을 보내기 위해서 기금을 모금하기로 결정했어.

21 우리는 쿠키와 음료를 팔아서 600달러를 모았어.

22 우리는 케냐의 학생들이 그들의 새 가방을 좋아하기를 바라.

23 Wang: 멋지다! 분명 그들이 가방을 좋아할 거야.

24 Kozo: 훌륭한 일을 했구나!

25 난 말레이시아의 Afig야.

26 우리 학교는 우리 마을을 좀 더 좋아 보이게 하기 위해서 벽화 캠페인을 시작했어.

27 그림을 잘 그리는 학생들이 모여서 학교와 공원 벽에 그림을 그렸어.

28 이 캠페인 덕분에, 우리 마을은 훨씬 멋져 보여.

29 이제 모든 사람들이 그려진 벽을 따라서 산책하는 것을 즐길 수 있어.

30 Junho: 정말 멋진 생각이다!

※ 다음 문장을 우리말로 쓰시오.

1 Global Citizenship Education

➡ _____

2 This is the Global Citizenship Education site.

➡ _____

3 Global Citizenship Education helps us grow as global citizens.

➡ _____

4 Global citizens are people who try to understand different cultures.

➡ _____

5 They also care for people in need and work for a better world.

➡ _____

6 Please share your global citizenship education experiences here.

➡ _____

7 Hello. I am Minhee from Korea.

➡ _____

8 I am a member of the Global Community Club.

➡ _____

9 My club aims to communicate with people from around the world.

➡ _____

10 A week ago we produced a video about the lantern festival in our village.

➡ _____

11 We uploaded it to the Internet and amazingly, we got nearly 5,000 hits.

➡ _____

12 Click here for our video.

➡ _____

13 Alice: Wow, your lantern festival looks fantastic!

➡ _____

14 Sunan: We have a water festival in our village.

➡ _____

15 I'd like to make a video like yours.

➡ _____

16 Hi, my name is Jo.

➡ _____

17 I am from Australia.

➡ _____

18 A few weeks ago, my teacher showed us pictures of students in Kenya.

➡ _____

19 Sadly, they were all using plastic bags to carry their books.

➡ _____

20 My class decided to raise money to send them new school bags.

➡ _____

21 We sold cookies and drinks and raised 600 dollars.

➡ _____

22 We hope the Kenyan students are happy with the new bags.

➡ _____

23 Wang: Awesome! I'm sure they will like the bags.

➡ _____

24 Kozo: You did something wonderful!

➡ _____

25 I am Afig from Malaysia.

➡ _____

26 My school started a wall painting campaign to make our village look better.

➡ _____

27 Students who are good at painting gathered and painted on some walls of schools and parks.

➡ _____

28 Thanks to this campaign, our village looks much nicer.

➡ _____

29 Now everyone can enjoy walking alongside the painted walls.

➡ _____

30 Junho: What a nice idea!

➡ _____

※ 다음 괄호 안의 단어들을 우리말에 맞도록 바르게 배열하시오.

1 (Education / Citizenship / Global)
➡ _____

2 (is / this / Global / the / site. / Education / Citizenship)
➡ _____

3 (Citizenship / Global / Education / us / helps / grow / citizens. / global / as)
➡ _____

4 (citizens / global / people / are / try / who / understand / to / cultures. / different)
➡ _____

5 (also / they / for / care / people / need / in / and / for / work / world. / better / a)
➡ _____

6 (share / please / global / your / citizenship / here. / experiences / education)
➡ _____

7 (hello. // Minhee / am / I / Korea. / from)
➡ _____

8 (am / I / member / a / the / of / Club. / Community / Global)
➡ _____

9 (club / my / aims / communicate / to / people / with / around / from / world. / the)
➡ _____

10 (week / a / ago / produced / we / video / a / about / lantern / the / in / festival / village. / our)
➡ _____

11 (uploaded / we / to / it / Internet / the / and / we / amazingly, / nearly / got / hits. / 5,000)
➡ _____

12 (here / click / our / video. / for)
➡ _____

13 (Alice: / your / wow, / lantern / fantastic! / looks / festival)
➡ _____

14 (Sunan: / have / we / water / a / in / festival / village. / our)
➡ _____

15 (like / I'd / make / to / a / yours. / like / video)
본문 ➡ _____

1 세계 시민 교육

2 이곳은 세계 시민 교육 사이트 입니다.

3 세계 시민 교육은 우리가 세 시민으로 자라도록 도와줍니

4 세계 시민은 다른 문화를 이 하려고 노력하는 사람들입니

5 그들은 또한 어려움에 처한 람들을 보살피고 더 나은 세 을 위해서 일합니다.

6 당신의 세계 시민 교육 경험 이곳에 공유해 주세요.

7 안녕. 나는 한국의 민희야.

8 나는 세계 공동체 동아리의 원이야.

9 우리 동아리는 전 세계의 사 들과 소통하는 것을 목표로 해

10 일주일 전에 우리는 우리 마 의 등 축제에 관한 비디오를 작했어.

11 우리는 그것을 인터넷에 올렸 데, 놀랍게도 거의 5,000개의 회 수를 획득했어.

12 우리 비디오를 보려면 이곳 클릭해.

13 Alice: 와, 너희 등 축제는 환 적으로 보인다!

14 Sunan: 우리 마을에는 물 축 가 있어.

15 나도 너희 것과 같은 비디오 만들고 싶어.

16 (my / hi, / is / Jo. / name)

➡ _____

17 (am / I / Australia. / from)

➡ _____

18 (few / a / ago, / weeks / teacher / my / us / showed / pictures / students / of / Kenya. / in)

➡ _____

19 (they / sadly, / were / using / all / bags / plastic / carry / to / books. / their)

➡ _____

20 (class / my / to / decided / money / raise / send / to / new / them / bags. / school)

➡ _____

21 (sold / we / drinks / and / cookies / and / dollars. / 600 / raised)

➡ _____

22 (hope / we / Kenyan / the / are / students / with / happy / the / bags. / new)

➡ _____

23 (Wang: / awesome! / sure / I'm / will / they / bags. / the / like)

➡ _____

24 (Kozo: / did / you / wonderful! / something)

➡ _____

25 (am / I / Malaysia. / from / Afig)

➡ _____

26 (school / my / started / wall / a / campaign / painting / make / to / village / our / better. / look)

➡ _____

27 (who / students / good / are / painting / at / and / gathered / on / painted / walls / some / parks. / and / schools / of)

➡ _____

28 (to / thanks / campaign, / this / village / our / nicer. / much / looks)

➡ _____

29 (everyone / now / enjoy / can / walking / the / alongside / walls. / painted)

➡ _____

30 (Junho: / a / idea! / what / nice)

➡ _____

16 안녕, 내 이름은 Jo야.

17 나는 호주 출신이야.

18 몇 주 전에, 선생님이 우리에게 케냐에 있는 학생들의 사진을 보여주셨어.

19 슬프게도, 그들은 모두 책을 들고 다니기 위해서 비닐 봉지를 사용하고 있었어.

20 우리 반은 그들에게 새로운 책 가방을 보내기 위해서 기금을 모금하기로 결정했어.

21 우리는 쿠키와 음료를 팔아서 600달러를 모았어.

22 우리는 케냐의 학생들이 그들의 새 가방을 좋아하기를 바라.

23 Wang: 멋지다! 분명 그들이 가방을 좋아할 거야.

24 Kozo: 훌륭한 일을 했구나!

25 난 말레이시아의 Afig야.

26 우리 학교는 우리 마을을 좀 더 좋아 보이게 하기 위해서 벽화 캠페인을 시작했어.

27 그림을 잘 그리는 학생들이 모여서 학교와 공원 벽에 그림을 그렸어.

28 이 캠페인 덕분에, 우리 마을은 훨씬 멋져 보여.

29 이제 모든 사람들이 그림이 그려진 벽을 따라서 산책하는 것을 즐길 수 있어.

30 Junho: 정말 멋진 생각이다!

※ **다음 우리말을 영어로 쓰시오.**

1 세계 시민 교육

➡ _____

2 이곳은 세계 시민 교육 사이트입니다.

➡ _____

3 세계 시민 교육은 우리가 세계 시민으로 자라도록 도와줍니다.

➡ _____

4 세계 시민은 다른 문화를 이해하려고 노력하는 사람들입니다.

➡ _____

5 그들은 또한 어려움에 처한 사람들을 보살피고 더 나은 세상을 위해서 일합니다.

➡ _____

6 당신의 세계 시민 교육 경험을 이곳에 공유해 주세요.

➡ _____

7 안녕. 나는 한국의 민희야.

➡ _____

8 나는 세계 공동체 동아리의 회원이야.

➡ _____

9 우리 동아리는 전 세계의 사람들과 소통하는 것을 목표로 해.

➡ _____

10 일주일 전에 우리는 우리 마을의 등 축제에 관한 비디오를 제작했어.

➡ _____

11 우리는 그것을 인터넷에 올렸는데, 놀랍게도 거의 5,000개의 수를 획득했어.

➡ _____

12 우리 비디오를 보려면 이곳을 클릭해.

➡ _____

13 Alice: 와, 너희 등 축제는 환상적으로 보인다!

➡ _____

14 Sunan: 우리 마을에는 물 축제가 있어.

➡ _____

15 나도 너희 것과 같은 비디오를 만들고 싶어.

➡ _____

16 안녕, 내 이름은 Jo야.

➡ _____

17 나는 호주 출신이야.

➡ _____

18 몇 주 전에, 선생님이 우리에게 케냐에 있는 학생들의 사진을 보여주셨어.

➡ _____

19 슬프게도, 그들은 모두 책을 들고 다니기 위해서 비닐 봉지를 사용하고 있었어.

➡ _____

20 우리 반은 그들에게 새로운 책가방을 보내기 위해서 기금을 모금하기로 결정했어.

➡ _____

21 우리는 쿠키와 음료를 팔아서 600달러를 모았어.

➡ _____

22 우리는 케냐의 학생들이 그들의 새 가방을 좋아하기를 바라.

➡ _____

23 Wang: 멋지다! 분명 그들이 가방을 좋아할 거야.

➡ _____

24 Kozo: 훌륭한 일을 했구나!

➡ _____

25 난 말레이시아의 Afig야.

➡ _____

26 우리 학교는 우리 마을을 좀 더 좋아 보이게 하기 위해서 벽화 캠페인을 시작했어.

➡ _____

27 그림을 잘 그리는 학생들이 모여서 학교와 공원 벽에 그림을 그렸어.

➡ _____

28 이 캠페인 덕분에, 우리 마을은 훨씬 멋져 보여.

➡ _____

29 이제 모든 사람들이 그림이 그려진 벽을 따라서 산책하는 것을 즐길 수 있어.

➡ _____

30 Junho: 정말 멋진 생각이다!

➡ _____

※ 다음 우리말과 일치하도록 빈칸에 알맞은 말을 쓰시오.

Conversation B

1. Karl: Jiho, _____ that _____ _____? Are you _____ _____ eat _____ _____ that?

2. Jiho: I'm _____ _____, but Bulgogi is my _____.

3. Karl: Hey! _____ _____ the campaign poster. "_____, Eat, _____!"

4. Jiho: _____ _____ _____ _____?

5. Karl: _____ _____ "Think first before you eat and save the Earth."

6. Jiho: I _____ I _____ too much Bulgogi. _____ _____ it.

7. Karl: Okay. _____ _____ _____ _____.

8. Jiho: We _____ it _____. My clean plate _____ _____ _____ _____.

9. Karl: _____ _____ _____ food _____ _____ _____. I hope we _____ _____ the Earth.

Project

1. A: _____ _____ _____ _____ do you like?

2. B: _____ _____ _____ _____ _____ _____ _____ _____ shoes to poor children?

3. C: Good. I hope they _____ _____ _____ them.

4. D: _____ _____ a poster about the activity _____ _____ _____ _____ _____ _____ _____.

5. Sending _____ _____ _____

6. Why: To help poor _____ _____ _____ _____ _____ _____

7. How: 1. _____ shoes _____ _____.

8. 2. _____ pictures or _____ _____ _____ _____ on them.

9. 3. Send them to children _____ _____.

10. When: _____ _____

11. _____ you want _____ _____ _____ _____ _____ for the world, _____ us!

1. Karl: 지호야, 너무 많지 않니? 너 그걸 다 먹을 거니?
2. 지호: 잘 모르겠어, 그렇지만 불고기는 내가 가장 좋아하는 음식이야.
3. Karl: 저기! 캠페인 포스터를 봐. "생각하라, 먹어라, 구하라!"
4. 지호: 저게 무슨 뜻이야?
5. Karl: 그것은 먹기 전에 먼저 생각하고 지구를 살리자는 뜻이야.
6. 지호: 나 불고기를 너무 많이 담아온 것 같아. 나눠 먹자.
7. Karl: 그래. 좋은 생각이야.
8. 지호: 우리 다 먹었네. 내 깨끗한 그릇을 보니 기분이 좋아.
9. Karl: 이제부터 음식을 낭비하지 말자. 나는 우리가 지구를 살리기를 바라.

1. A: 어떤 활동을 하고 싶니?
2. B: 가난한 아이들에게 신발을 보내는 게 어때?
3. C: 좋아. 그들이 그것들을 좋아하길 바라.
4. D: 도움을 주고 싶어 하는 사람들을 찾기 위해서 이 활동에 대한 포스터를 만들자.
5. 희망의 신발 보내기
6. 왜: 신발이 없는 가난한 아이들을 돕기 위해
7. 어떻게: 1. 집에서 신발을 가져오세요.
8. 2. 신발에 그림을 그리거나 배려의 말을 쓰세요.
9. 3. 그것들을 어려움에 처한 아이들에게 보내세요.
10. 언제: 7월 3일
11. 세상을 위해 뭔가 특별한 일을 하고 싶다면, 우리와 함께 해요!

구석구석 지문 Test

※ 다음 우리말을 영어로 쓰시오.

Conversation B

1. Karl: 지호야, 너무 많지 않니? 너 그걸 다 먹을 거니?
➡ _____

2. 지호: 잘 모르겠어, 그렇지만 불고기는 내가 가장 좋아하는 음식이야.
➡ _____

3. Karl: 저기! 캠페인 포스터를 봐. "생각하라, 먹어라, 구하라!"
➡ _____

4. 지호: 저게 무슨 뜻이야?
➡ _____

5. Karl: 그것은 먹기 전에 먼저 생각하고 지구를 살리자는 뜻이야.
➡ _____

6. 지호: 나 불고기를 너무 많이 담아온 것 같아. 나눠 먹자.
➡ _____

7. Karl: 그래. 좋은 생각이야.
➡ _____

8. 지호: 우리 다 먹었네. 내 깨끗한 그릇을 보니 기분이 좋아.
➡ _____

9. Karl: 이제부터 음식을 낭비하지 말자. 나는 우리가 지구를 살리기를 바라.
➡ _____

Project

1. A: 어떤 활동을 하고 싶니?
➡ _____

2. B: 가난한 아이들에게 신발을 보내는 게 어때?
➡ _____

3. C: 좋아. 그들이 그것들을 좋아하길 바라.
➡ _____

4. D: 도움을 주고 싶어 하는 사람들을 찾기 위해서 이 활동에 대한 포스터를 만들자.
➡ _____

5. 희망의 신발 보내기
➡ _____

6. 왜: 신발이 없는 가난한 아이들을 돕기 위해
➡ _____

7. 어떻게: 1. 집에서 신발을 가져오세요.
➡ _____

8. 2. 신발에 그림을 그리거나 배려의 말을 쓰세요.
➡ _____

9. 3. 그것들을 어려움에 처한 아이들에게 보내세요.
➡ _____

10. 언제: 7월 3일
➡ _____

11. 세상을 위해 뭔가 특별한 일을 하고 싶다면, 우리와 함께 해요!
➡ _____

※ 다음 영어를 우리말로 쓰시오.

01 topic _____

02 during _____

03 male _____

04 toward _____

05 again _____

06 gravity _____

07 twice _____

08 grow _____

09 bone _____

10 weigh _____

11 Mars _____

12 item _____

13 lightning _____

14 metal _____

15 fewer _____

16 produce _____

17 rest _____

18 mosquito _____

19 tongue _____

20 weaken _____

21 expand _____

22 female _____

23 inventor _____

24 enough _____

25 average _____

26 guess _____

27 false _____

28 completely _____

29 blood _____

30 adult _____

31 bite _____

32 whale _____

33 Venus _____

34 same _____

35 be full of _____

36 in fact _____

37 due to _____

38 over and over _____

39 such as _____

40 up to _____

41 find out _____

42 go away _____

43 a few _____

※ 다음 우리말을 영어로 쓰시오.

01	완전히	
02	고래	
03	피	
04	거짓의	
05	여성, 암컷	
06	팽창하다	
07	금성	
08	같은, 똑같은	
09	부딪치다, 충돌하다	
10	추측하다	
11	열, 열기	
12	(새·곤충 등이) 알을 낳다	
13	보통, 평균	
14	발명가	
15	다음의; 그 다음에	
16	충분한	
17	성인, 어른	
18	물다	
19	약화시키다, 약화되다	
20	중력	
21	번개, 벼락	

22	두 번, 두 배	
23	모기	
24	항목, 물품	
25	화제, 주제	
26	화성	
27	쉬다, 휴식하다	
28	(자식·새끼를) 낳다	
29	혀	
30	남성, 수컷	
31	뼈	
32	금속	
33	(위치·방향) ~쪽으로	
34	~ 동안, ~ 중에	
35	사실상, 실제로	
36	평균적으로	
37	알아보다, 찾아보다	
38	~로 가득 차다	
39	~와 같은	
40	~ 때문에	
41	사라지다	
42	여러 번, 몇 번이고	
43	~와 이어지다	

※ 다음 영영풀이에 알맞은 단어를 <보기>에서 골라 쓴 후, 우리말 뜻을 쓰시오.

1 _____ : a red fluid in living things: _____

2 _____ : not real, because it is not true: _____

3 _____ : the gender which does not give birth: _____

4 _____ : to seize or grasp something with teeth: _____

5 _____ : a hard substance such as lead, iron, gold, etc.: _____

6 _____ : to find how heavy a person or thing is: _____

7 _____ : to increase in size, number, or importance: _____

8 _____ : a small flying insect which bites and sucks blood: _____

9 _____ : the usual amount, extent, quality, number, etc.: _____

10 _____ : a white piece of tissue providing structural support for the body:

_____

11 _____ : a person who creates something that does not exist: _____

12 _____ : to a complete degree or to the full or entire extent: _____

13 _____ : the force that a planet pulls things towards the center of it: _____

14 _____ : the gender which has the ability to give birth to children: _____

15 _____ : to come or bring into heavy contact with someone or something:

_____

16 _____ : the soft organ in the mouth used in tasting, swallowing, etc. and by

people in speaking: _____

보기			
strike	metal	false	inventor
expand	female	mosquito	tongue
bone	completely	gravity	male
blood	weigh	bite	average

※ 다음 우리말과 일치하도록 빈칸에 알맞은 것을 골라 쓰시오.

1 _____ _____ Are _____ Us
A. Around　　　　B. Facts　　　　C. Interesting

2 _____ _____ "_____ Dr. Lawrence"!
A. to　　　　B. ask　　　　C. welcome

3 The world is _____ _____ interesting _____ .
A. things　　　　B. full　　　　C. of

4 _____ this quiz and find _____ how _____ you know about them.
A. much　　　　B. out　　　　C. take

5 _____ you _____ ?
A. ready　　　　B. are

6 Quiz: The Eiffel Tower _____ _____ _____ the summer.
A. get　　　　B. during　　　　C. taller

7 Babies have _____ bones _____ adults.
A. than　　　　B. fewer

8 _____ female mosquitoes _____ people.
A. bite　　　　B. only

9 Lightning _____ _____ the same place _____ .
A. never　　　　B. twice　　　　C. strikes

10 The elephant is _____ _____ animal _____ the Earth.
A. on　　　　B. biggest　　　　C. the

11 _____ is _____ gravity _____ space.
A. no　　　　B. in　　　　C. there

12 Metal _____ _____ heat.
A. in　　　　B. expands

13 _____ _____ summer heat, the metal of the Eiffel Tower _____ .
A. expands　　　　B. to　　　　C. due

14 In summer, the Eiffel tower _____ 15cm _____ _____ in winter.
A. taller　　　　B. gets　　　　C. than

15 _____ have 206 bones, _____ babies have _____ 300 bones.
A. about　　　　B. but　　　　C. adults

16 _____ time, some of the babies' bones _____ _____ , so adults have _____ bones than babies.
A. fewer　　　　B. with　　　　C. together　　　　D. join

1　흥미로운 사실들은 우리 주위에 있다

2　"Lawrence 박사에게 물어 보세요"에 오신 것을 환영합니다!

3　세상은 흥미로운 것들로 가득 차 있습니다.

4　퀴즈를 풀어보고 그것들에 대해 얼마나 아는지 알아보세요.

5　준비 됐나요?

6　퀴즈: 에펠 타워는 여름에 키가 더 커진다.

7　아기들은 어른보다 더 적은 수의 뼈를 가지고 있다.

8　암컷 모기만이 사람을 문다.

9　번개는 결코 같은 곳을 내리치지 않는다.

10　코끼리는 지구에서 가장 큰 동물이다.

11　우주에는 중력이 없다.

12　금속은 열에 팽창한다.

13　여름의 열기 때문에, 에펠 타워의 금속은 팽창한다.

14　여름에 에펠 타워는 겨울보다 15센티미터 정도 더 커진다.

15　어른은 206개의 뼈를 가지고 있고, 아기는 대략 300개의 뼈를 가지고 있다.

16　시간이 흐르면서, 아기의 몇몇 뼈들은 붙는다. 그래서 어른들은 아기보다 더 적은 수의 뼈를 가지고 있다.

17 _____ _____ mosquitoes will _____ you.
  A. bite   B. female   C. only

18 They _____ blood _____ _____ eggs.
  A. produce   B. to   C. need

19 After a female mosquito gets _____ _____, she'll _____ for a few days and _____ her eggs.
  A. blood   B. lay   C. enough   D. rest

20 Lightning _____ _____ the _____ place over and _____ again.
  A. same   B. over   C. strike   D. can

21 The Empire State Building _____ hit _____ lightning 23 times a year _____ _____.
  A. by   B. gets   C. average   D. on

22 _____ _____ animal _____ the Earth is the blue _____.
  A. whale   B. biggest   C. the   D. on

23 It can _____ _____ to 180 tons and _____ up to 30 meters _____.
  A. long   B. grow   C. weigh   D. up

24 Its tongue _____ can weigh as _____ _____ an average African elephant.
  A. alone   B. as   C. much

25 _____ fact, there is _____ everywhere in _____.
  A. in   B. space   C. gravity

26 As you get _____ from the Earth, the gravity of the Earth _____, but it never _____ _____ completely.
  A. away   B. weakens   C. farther   D. goes

27 When you _____ closer to another planet, _____ _____ Mars or Venus, its gravity becomes stronger than _____ of the Earth.
  A. as   B. that   C. such   D. get

28 _____ of _____ quiz items is the _____ interesting to you?
  A. most   B. these   C. which

29 _____ will be _____ quiz _____.
  A. another   B. there   C. soon

30 _____ _____ the next topic will _____.
  A. be   B. guess   C. what

31 _____ you _____ month.
  A. next   B. see

---

17 오직 암컷 모기만이 당신을 물 것이다.

18 그들은 알을 생산하기 위해서 피가 필요하다.

19 암컷 모기는 충분히 흡혈을 한 뒤, 며칠 동안 쉬고 알을 낳는다.

20 번개는 같은 곳을 반복해서 칠 수 있다.

21 엠파이어스테이트 빌딩은 한 해 평균 스물세 번 번개를 맞는다.

22 지구상에서 가장 큰 동물은 흰 긴수염고래이다.

23 그것은 무게가 180톤까지 나갈 수 있으며 길이는 30미터까지 자랄 수 있다.

24 이 고래의 혀의 무게만 해도 아프리카 코끼리의 평균 무게만큼 무겁다.

25 사실, 중력은 우주의 어디에나 있다.

26 지구에서 멀어 질수록 지구의 중력은 약해지지만, 결코 그것이 완전히 사라지는 것은 아니다.

27 당신이 화성이나 금성 같은 다른 행성에 더 가까워진다면, 그들의 중력은 지구의 그것보다 더 강해진다.

28 이 퀴즈들 중 어떤 퀴즈가 가장 흥미로웠나요?

29 곧 또 다른 퀴즈가 있을 것입니다.

30 다음 주제는 무엇일지 맞춰보세요.

31 다음 달에 만나요.

※ 다음 우리말과 일치하도록 빈칸에 알맞은 말을 쓰시오.

1 _____ _____ Are _____ Us

2 _____ _____ "_____ Dr. Lawrence"!

3 The world _____ _____ _____ interesting _____.

4 _____ this quiz and _____ _____ _____ _____ you
   know about them.

5 _____ you _____?

6 _____

7 The Eiffel Tower _____ _____ _____ the summer.

8 Babies have _____ _____ _____ _____.

9 _____ _____ mosquitoes _____ people.

10 Lightning _____ _____ the _____ _____ _____.

11 The elephant is _____ _____ animal _____ the Earth.

12 _____ is _____ _____ _____ space.

13 Metal _____ _____ _____.

14 _____ _____ _____ _____, the metal of the Eiffel
   Tower _____.

15 In summer, the Eiffel tower _____ 15cm _____ _____
   _____ _____.

16 _____ have 206 _____, _____ _____ have _____
   300 bones.

17 _____ _____, some of the babies' bones _____ _____,
   so adults have _____ _____ _____ _____.

1 흥미로운 사실들은 우리 주위에
   있다

2 "Lawrence 박사에게 물어 보세
   요"에 오신 것을 환영합니다!

3 세상은 흥미로운 것들로 가득
   차 있습니다.

4 퀴즈를 풀어보고 그것들에 대해
   얼마나 아는지 알아보세요.

5 준비 됐나요?

6 퀴즈

7 에펠 타워는 여름에 키가 더 커
   진다.

8 아기들은 어른보다 더 적은 수
   의 뼈를 가지고 있다.

9 암컷 모기만이 사람을 문다.

10 번개는 결코 같은 곳을 내리치
   지 않는다.

11 코끼리는 지구에서 가장 큰 동
   물이다.

12 우주에는 중력이 없다.

13 금속은 열에 팽창한다.

14 여름의 열기 때문에, 에펠 타워
   의 금속은 팽창한다.

15 여름에 에펠 타워는 겨울보다
   15센티미터 정도 더 커진다.

16 어른은 206개의 뼈를 가지고 있
   고, 아기는 대략 300개의 뼈를
   가지고 있다.

17 시간이 흐르면서, 아기의 몇몇
   뼈들은 붙는다. 그래서 어른들
   은 아기보다 더 적은 수의 뼈를
   가지고 있다.

18 _____ _____ mosquitoes _____ _____ you.

19 They _____ blood _____ _____ _____ .

20 After a female mosquito gets _____ _____ , she'll _____ _____ _____ _____ and _____ her eggs.

21 Lightning _____ _____ the _____ place _____ _____ _____ _____ .

22 The Empire State Building _____ hit _____ lightning 23 _____ _____ _____ _____ _____ .

23 _____ _____ animal _____ the Earth is the blue _____ .

24 It _____ _____ _____ _____ 180 tons and _____ _____ 30 meters _____ .

25 Its tongue _____ can _____ _____ _____ _____ an average African elephant.

26 _____ _____ , there is _____ everywhere in _____ .

27 As you get _____ from the Earth, the gravity of the Earth _____ , but it _____ _____ _____ _____ .

28 When you _____ closer to another planet, _____ _____ Mars or Venus, its gravity _____ _____ _____ of the Earth.

29 _____ of _____ quiz items is _____ _____ _____ to you?

30 _____ will _____ _____ quiz _____ .

31 _____ _____ the next topic _____ _____ .

32 _____ you _____ _____ .

18 오직 암컷 모기만이 당신을 물 것이다.

19 그들은 알을 생산하기 위해서 피가 필요하다.

20 암컷 모기는 충분히 흡혈을 한 뒤, 며칠 동안 쉬고 알을 낳는다.

21 번개는 같은 곳을 반복해서 칠 수 있나.

22 엠파이어스테이트 빌딩은 한 해 평균 스물세 번 번개를 맞는다.

23 지구상에서 가장 큰 동물은 흰 긴수염고래이다.

24 그것은 무게가 180톤까지 나갈 수 있으며 길이는 30미터까지 자랄 수 있다.

25 이 고래의 혀의 무게만 해도 아 프리카 코끼리의 평균 무게만큼 무겁다.

26 사실, 중력은 우주의 어디에나 있다.

27 지구에서 멀어 질수록 지구의 중력은 약해지지만, 결코 그것이 완전히 사라지는 것은 아니다.

28 당신이 화성이나 금성 같은 다 른 행성에 더 가까워진다면, 그 들의 중력은 지구의 그것보다 더 강해진다.

29 이 퀴즈들 중 어떤 퀴즈가 가장 흥미로웠나요?

30 곧 또 다른 퀴즈가 있을 것입니다.

31 다음 주제는 무엇일지 맞춰보세요.

32 다음 달에 만나요.

※ 다음 문장을 우리말로 쓰시오.

1 Interesting Facts Are Around Us

➡ _____

2 Welcome to "Ask Dr. Lawrence"!

➡ _____

3 The world is full of interesting things.

➡ _____

4 Take this quiz and find out how much you know about them.

➡ _____

5 Are you ready?

➡ _____

6 Quiz

➡ _____

7 The Eiffel Tower gets taller during the summer.

➡ _____

8 Babies have fewer bones than adults.

➡ _____

9 Only female mosquitoes bite people.

➡ _____

10 Lightning never strikes the same place twice.

➡ _____

11 The elephant is the biggest animal on the Earth.

➡ _____

12 There is no gravity in space.

➡ _____

13 Metal expands in heat.

➡ _____

14 Due to summer heat, the metal of the Eiffel Tower expands.

➡ _____

15 In summer, the Eiffel tower gets 15cm taller than in winter.

➡ _____

16 Adults have 206 bones, but babies have about 300 bones.

➡ _____

17 With time, some of the babies' bones join together, so adults have fewer bones than babies.

➡ _____

18 Only female mosquitoes will bite you.

➡ _____

19 They need blood to produce eggs.

➡ _____

20 After a female mosquito gets enough blood, she'll rest for a few days and lay her eggs.

➡ _____

21 Lightning can strike the same place over and over again.

➡ _____

22 The Empire State Building gets hit by lightning 23 times a year on average.

➡ _____

23 The biggest animal on the Earth is the blue whale.

➡ _____

24 It can weigh up to 180 tons and grow up to 30 meters long.!

➡ _____

25 Its tongue alone can weigh as much as an average African elephant.

➡ _____

26 In fact, there is gravity everywhere in space.

➡ _____

27 As you get farther from the Earth, the gravity of the Earth weakens, but it never goes away completely.

➡ _____

28 When you get closer to another planet, such as Mars or Venus, its gravity becomes stronger than that of the Earth.

➡ _____

29 Which of these quiz items is the most interesting to you?

➡ _____

30 There will be another quiz soon.

➡ _____

31 Guess what the next topic will be.

➡ _____

32 See you next month.

➡ _____

Step4

※ 다음 괄호 안의 단어들을 우리말에 맞도록 바르게 배열하시오.

1 (Facts / Interesting / Us / Around / Are)
➡ _____

2 (to / welcome / Lawrence"! / Dr. / "Ask)
➡ _____

3 (world / the / full / is / of / things. / interesting)
➡ _____

4 (this / take / quiz / and / out / find / much / how / know / you / them. / about)
➡ _____

5 (ready? / you / are)
➡ _____

6 (quiz: / Eiffel / The / Tower / taller / gets / the / during / summer.)
➡ _____

7 (have / babies / bones / fewer / adults. / than)
➡ _____

8 (female / only / mosquitoes / people. / bite)
➡ _____

9 (never / lightening / the / strikes / twice. / place / same)
➡ _____

10 (elephant / the / is / the / animal / biggest / Earth. / the / on)
➡ _____

11 (no / is / there / gravity / space. / in)
➡ _____

12 (expands / heat. / in / metal)
➡ _____

13 (to / due / summer / heat, / metal / the / of / Eiffel / expands. / Tower)
➡ _____

14 (summer, / in / Eiffel / the / gets / tower / 15cm / in / winter. / than / taller)
➡ _____

15 (have / adults / bones, / 206 / babies / but / about / have / bones. / 300)
➡ _____

16 (time, / with / of / some / babies' / the / join / bones / together, / adults / so / fewer / have / bones / babies. / than)
➡ _____

1 흥미로운 사실들은 우리 주위에 있다

2 "Lawrence 박사에게 물어 보세요"에 오신 것을 환영합니다!

3 세상은 흥미로운 것들로 가득 차 있습니다.

4 퀴즈를 풀어보고 그것들에 대해 얼마나 아는지 알아보세요.

5 준비 됐나요?

6 퀴즈: 에펠 타워는 여름에 키가 더 커진다.

7 아기들은 어른보다 더 적은 수의 뼈를 가지고 있다.

8 암컷 모기만이 사람을 문다.

9 번개는 결코 같은 곳을 내리치지 않는다.

10 코끼리는 지구에서 가장 큰 동물이다.

11 우주에는 중력이 없다.

12 금속은 열에 팽창한다.

13 여름의 열기 때문에, 에펠 타워의 금속은 팽창한다.

14 여름에 에펠 타워는 겨울보다 15센티미터 정도 더 커진다.

15 어른은 206개의 뼈를 가지고 있고, 아기는 대략 300개의 뼈를 가지고 있다.

16 시간이 흐르면서, 아기의 몇몇 뼈들은 붙는다. 그래서 어른들은 아기보다 더 적은 수의 뼈를 가지고 있다.

17 (female / only / mosquitoes / you. / bite / will)
➡ _____

18 (need / they / to / blood / eggs. / produce)
➡ _____

19 (a / after / mosquito / female / enough / gets / blood, / rest / she'll / for / a / days / few / and / eggs. / her / lay)
➡ _____
_____

20 (can / lightning / strike / same / the / over / place / and / again. / over)
➡ _____

21 (Empire / the / Building / State / hit / gets / lightning / by / times / 23 / average. / on / year / a)
➡ _____

22 (biggest / the / animal / the / Earth / on / the / is / whale. / blue)
➡ _____

23 (can / it / up / weigh / 180 / to / tons / grow / and / to / up / long. / meters / 30)
➡ _____

24 (tongue / its / can / alone / as / weigh / much / as / an / African / average / elephant.)
➡ _____

25 (fact, / in / is / there / everywhere / gravity / space. / in)
➡ _____

26 (you / as / farther / get / the / from / Earth, / gravity / the / of / Earth / the / weakens, / it / but / goes / never / completely. / away)
➡ _____
_____

27 (you / when / closer / get / another / to / planet, / as / such / Venus, / or / Mars / gravity / its / stronger / becomes / than / of / that / Earth. / the)
➡ _____
_____

28 (of / these / which / items / quiz / is / most / the / interesting / you? / to)
➡ _____

29 (will / there / another / be / soon. / quiz / is / most / the / interesting / you? / to)
➡ _____

30 (what / guess / next / the / be. / will / topic)
➡ _____

31 (you / see / month. / next)
➡ _____

17 오직 암컷 모기만이 당신을 것이다.

18 그들은 알을 생산하기 위해 피가 필요하다.

19 암컷 모기는 충분히 흡혈을 뒤, 며칠 동안 쉬고 알을 낳는

20 번개는 같은 곳을 반복해서 수 있다.

21 엠파이어스테이트 빌딩은 한 평균 스물세 번 번개를 맞는다

22 지구상에서 가장 큰 동물은 긴수염고래이다.

23 그것은 무게가 180톤까지 나 수 있으며 길이는 30미터까지 랄 수 있다.

24 이 고래의 혀의 무게만 해도 프리카 코끼리의 평균 무게만 무겁다.

25 사실, 중력은 우주의 어디에 있다.

26 지구에서 멀어 질수록 지구 중력은 약해지지만, 결코 그것 완전히 사라지는 것은 아니다.

27 당신이 화성이나 금성 같은 른 행성에 더 가까워진다면, 들의 중력은 지구의 그것보 더 강해진다.

28 이 퀴즈들 중 어떤 퀴즈가 가 흥미로웠나요?

29 곧 또 다른 퀴즈가 있을 것입니다

30 다음 주제는 무엇일지 맞춰보세요

31 다음 달에 만나요.

※ 다음 우리말을 영어로 쓰시오.

1 흥미로운 사실들은 우리 주위에 있다

➡ _____

2 "Lawrence 박사에게 물어 보세요"에 오신 것을 환영합니다!

➡ _____

3 세상은 흥미로운 것들로 가득 차 있습니다.

➡ _____

4 퀴즈를 풀어보고 그것들에 대해 얼마나 아는지 알아보세요.

➡ _____

5 준비 됐나요?

➡ _____

6 퀴즈

➡ _____

7 에펠 타워는 여름에 키가 더 커진다.

➡ _____

8 아기들은 어른보다 더 적은 수의 뼈를 가지고 있다.

➡ _____

9 암컷 모기만이 사람을 문다.

➡ _____

10 번개는 결코 같은 곳을 내리치지 않는다.

➡ _____

11 코끼리는 지구에서 가장 큰 동물이다.

➡ _____

12 우주에는 중력이 없다.

➡ _____

13 금속은 열에 팽창한다.

➡ _____

14 여름의 열기 때문에, 에펠 타워의 금속은 팽창한다.

➡ _____

15 여름에 에펠 타워는 겨울보다 15센티미터 정도 더 커진다.

➡ _____

16 어른은 206개의 뼈를 가지고 있고, 아기는 대략 300개의 뼈를 가지고 있다.

➡ _____

17 시간이 흐르면서, 아기의 몇몇 뼈들은 붙는다. 그래서 어른들은 아기보다 더 적은 수의 뼈를 가지고 있다.

➡ _____

18 오직 암컷 모기만이 당신을 물 것이다.

➡ _____

19 그들은 알을 생산하기 위해서 피가 필요하다.

➡ _____

20 암컷 모기는 충분히 흡혈을 한 뒤, 며칠 동안 쉬고 알을 낳는다.

➡ _____

21 번개는 같은 곳을 반복해서 칠 수 있다.

➡ _____

22 엠파이어스테이트 빌딩은 한 해 평균 스물세 번 번개를 맞는다.

➡ _____

23 지구상에서 가장 큰 동물은 흰긴수염고래이다.

➡ _____

24 이것은 무게가 180톤까지 나갈 수 있으며 길이는 30미터 까지 자랄 수 있다.

➡ _____

25 이 고래의 혀의 무게만 해도 아프리카 코끼리의 평균 무게만큼 무겁다.

➡ _____

26 사실, 중력은 우주의 어디에나 있다.

➡ _____

27 지구에서 멀어 질수록 지구의 중력은 약해지지만, 결코 그것이 완전히 사라지는 것은 아니다.

➡ _____

_____

28 당신이 화성이나 금성 같은 다른 행성에 더 가까워진다면, 그들의 중력은 지구의 그것보다 더 강해진다.

➡ _____

_____

29 이 퀴즈들 중 어떤 퀴즈가 가장 흥미로웠나요?

➡ _____

30 곧 또 다른 퀴즈가 있을 것입니다.

➡ _____

31 다음 주제는 무엇일지 맞춰보세요.

➡ _____

32 다음 달에 만나요.

➡ _____

MEMO

영어 기출 문제집

적중 100 plus

1학기

정답 및 해설

시사 | 박준언

중 2

적중 100

Lesson 1

Manage Yourself!

01 ③은 -ous를 붙여 형용사형을 만들고, 나머지는 -ful을 붙여 형용사형을 만든다.

02 in front of: ~ 앞에 / because of: ~ 때문에

03 열심히 일해 뭔가를 얻거나 이루다: 성취하다(achieve)

04 반의어 관계이다. 쉬운 : 어려운 = 기억하다 : 잊다

05 set the alarm: 알람을 맞춰 놓다 / make a plan: 계획을 세우다

06 음식을 만들기 위한 일련의 지시 사항: recipe(조리법)

07 all day long: 하루 종일, 온종일

08 prepare for: ~을 준비하다 / put off: ~을 미루다

서술형 시험대비
p.09

01 (1) warm   (2) present   (3) helpful
02 (1) be good at   (2) get along with   (3) stop playing
03 (1) appointment   (2) future   (3) manage   (4) achieve
04 (1) wisely   (2) carefully   (3) regularly
05 (1) because of   (2) put off   (3) at a time   (4) put aside
06 (1) (l)esson   (2) (s)ave   (3) (f)ocus   (4) (d)ue

01 (1) 반의어 관계이다. ~ 전에 : ~ 후에 = 따뜻한 : 서늘한 (2) 유의어 관계이다. 맛있는 = 선물 (3) '명사 - 형용사' 관계이다. 구름 : 흐린 = 도움 : 도움이 되는

02 (1) be good at: ~에 능숙하다 (2) get along with: ~와 잘 지내다 (3) stop -ing: ~하는 것을 멈추다

03 (1) appointment: 약속 (2) future: 미래 (3) manage: 관리하다 (4) achieve: 달성하다, 성취하다

04 (1) wisely: 현명하게 (2) carefully: 주의 깊게 (3) regularly: 규칙적으로

05 (1) because of: ~ 때문에 (2) put off: ~을 미루다 (3) at a time: 한 번에 (4) put aside: ~을 치우다, ~을 한쪽에 두다

06 (1) lesson: 수업, 강습 (2) save: 절약하다 (3) focus: 집중하다 (4) due: ~하기로 되어 있는[예정된]

[교과서]
Conversation

핵심 Check
p.10~11

1 (1) matter / lost / too bad
 (2) with / hurt, finger / I'm sorry
2 (1) toothache / think, should go
 (2) Let's / better
 (3) Why don't / should drink
 (4) play / ought to

교과서 대화문 익히기

Check(√) True or False
p.12

1 F   2 T   3 F   4 T

교과서 확인학습
p.14~15

Listen & Speak 1 - A
1 worried, matter / hear, these days / Why don't, set / idea
2 should / What's / spend, fast / make, before / should, same

Listen & Speak 2 - A
1 okay, don't look / cold / think, should see / right
2 worried, going on / worried about, What, do / should read / idea
3 tired / these days / I think, a glass of, before, help / will try

Conversation A
type, daily, monthly, like, due dates, check, to remember, easily, should use

Conversation B
matter / didn't bring, forgot / second, busier than, first / you should use, mine / can / schedule, appointment / Maybe, should

Wrap Up - ❶
What's, Are, sick / have a cold / school nurse / need to, Can, leave / call, tell her

Wrap Up - ❷
nervous / because of / for, still, should, do / think, should, in front of, helpful / a good idea

---

01 ①　　　02 ④　　　03 ②　　　04 ⓓ - ⓑ
- ⓒ - ⓐ

01 What's the matter?는 어떤 문제점이 있는지 물어보는 표현으로 What's wrong? / What's the problem? 등으로 바꿔 쓸 수 있다.

02 감기에 걸린 친구에게 알맞은 충고는 ④ '병원에 가보는 게 좋겠다.'가 알맞다.

03 나머지는 모두 '진수에게 무슨 일 있니?'라는 뜻으로 문제점을 파악하는 표현인데, ②는 '진수에 대해서 어떻게 생각하니?'라는 뜻으로 의견을 묻고 있다.

04 ⓓ 너 아파 보여. 괜찮니? - ⓑ 아니. 난 심한 감기에 걸렸어. - ⓒ 너는 병원에 가봐야 해. ⓐ 오, 네 말이 맞아.

01 problem　02 busier　03 ③　　04 a
planner　05 ③　　06 on　　07 ④
08 better read　09 She thinks the boy should read his
textbook again.　　10 ③　　11 of
12 소년이 자기 가족 앞에서 연습하는 것　　13 ⑤
14 ⑤　　　15 ②

01 What's the matter?는 What's the problem?으로 바꿔 쓸 수 있다.

02 비교급+than: ~보다 더 …한

03 제안이나 권유하는 표현인 「I think you should +동사원형 ~」은 Why don't you ~?로 바꿔 쓸 수 있다.

04 인칭대명사 it은 앞 문장에 나온 단수명사를 가리킨다.

05 ③ 지호가 축구 연습을 하는 장소는 알 수 없다.

06 What's going on?: 무슨 일 있니?

07 What should I do?는 상대방에게 제안이나 충고를 구할 때 사용하는 표현이다.

08 I think you should + 동사원형 ~은 You'd better + 동사원형 ~으로 바꿔 쓸 수 있다.

09 소녀는 소년이 그의 교과서를 다시 읽어야 한다고 생각한다.

10 주어진 문장은 제안이나 충고를 구하는 표현으로 '가족 앞에서 연습해야 한다고 생각해.'라는 문장 앞에 와야 한다.

11 ⓐ because of: ~ 때문에 ⓑ in front of: ~ 앞에서

13 Sam이 요즘 아침에 알람을 듣지 못한다고 말한 것으로 보아 상대방의 상태가 안 좋아 보일 때 무슨 일인지 묻는 표현이 들어가야 한다.

14 Why don't you ~?는 '~하는 게 어때?'라는 말이다.

15 That's a good idea.는 제안이나 권유에 동의하는 표현이다.

01 |모범답안| What's wrong? / What's the matter [problem]? / Is (there) something wrong? 등

02 Why don't

03 그는 내일 역사 시험을 걱정한다.

04 |모범답안| I'm sorry to hear that. / That sounds bad. / What a pity! 등

05 She thinks Jason should see a doctor.

06 I think I have a cold.

07 (A) matter (B) Can

08 She said Sam needs to go to the hospital.

09 감기에 걸린 것 같아 일찍 하교해서 병원에 가는 것

01 슬픔, 불만족, 실망의 원인을 묻는 표현에는 What's wrong? / What's the problem? / What's the matter? / Is (there) something wrong? 등이 있다.

02 I think you should + 동사원형 ~.은 제안이나 충고하기 표현으로 Why don't you + 동사원형 ~?로 바꿔 쓸 수 있다.

03 소년이 'I'm worried about tomorrow's history quiz.'라고 했다.

04 That's too bad.는 유감을 나타낼 때 사용하는 표현으로 I'm sorry to hear that. / That sounds bad. / What a pity! / That's a pity! 등으로 바꿔 쓸 수 있다.

05 소녀는 Jason이 병원에 가야 한다고 충고한다.

06 I think ~: 내 생각에는 ~하다 / have a cold: 감기에 걸리다

07 What's the matter? = What's wrong? / Can I + 동사원형 ~?: 제가 ~해도 될까요?

08 양호 선생님은 Sam에게 병원에 가야 할 필요가 있다고 말했다.

1 (1) to go　(2) to help　(3) to write with　(4) cold to drink
2 (1) to visit　(2) to tell　(3) to listen
3 (1) that　(2) that
4 (1) heard ˅she　(2) thought ˅we　(3) says ˅the

01 ③　　　　02 (1) many things to do　(2) to help
us　　　03 (1) that Jenny is at home　(2) believed
that he would come back.　(3) didn't think that Alice

would like Mason   04 (1) to change   (2) to visit   (3) to solve.

01 접속사 that절 이하의 내용과 자연스럽게 어울리지 않는 단어는 mind이다.
02 (1) '해야 할 많은 일'이라는 뜻으로 to do가 명사 many things를 뒤에서 수식해 준다. (2) to부정사구(to help us)는 앞에 나온 명사 the only person을 꾸며주는 형용사 역할을 한다.
03 that이 접속사로 동사의 목적어가 되는 명사절을 이끄는 경우이다.
04 to부정사구가 앞에 나온 명사(구)를 꾸며주는 형용사 역할을 한다.

01 ⑤   02 ⑤   03 that   04 ①
05 ⑤   06 believe that   07 ③
08 to eat   09 ②   10 ⑤   11 didn't know that   12 ③   13 I think that Jinwoo will be a great leader.   14 ③   15 Do you have something interesting to read?   16 ③
17 ④   18 something cold to drink 19 a chair to sit on[in]   20 ⑤   21 ③   22 I think (that) James went on a trip. 23 ③   24 The girl has some food to feed the dog.

01 to부정사인 to save가 앞의 명사 a way를 꾸며주는 형용사 역할을 한다.
02 ⑤에서 made 다음에 that이 이끄는 명사절이 나오는 것은 어색하다.
03 절과 절을 연결해 주는 것은 접속사 that이다.
04 빈칸에는 some books를 수식하는 표현이나 책을 산 목적을 나타내는 표현이 올 수 있다.
05 ⑤는 목적어 역할을 하는 to부정사의 명사적 용법으로 쓰였고, 나머지는 to부정사의 형용사적 용법으로 쓰였다.
06 '~라고 믿는다.'라는 의미를 가진 I believe that이 오는 것이 적합하다.
07 ①, ②, ④, ⑤는 명사절을 이끄는 접속사 that이고, ③은 지시형용사이다.
08 명사 snacks을 수식하는 형용사 역할의 to부정사로 써야 한다.
09 good news를 수식하는 to부정사가 와야 한다. (to부정사의 형용사적 용법)
10 ①, ②, ③, ④의 that은 접속사의 목적어 역할로 쓰여서 생략이 가능하고, ⑤는 지시형용사로 쓰였으므로 생략할 수 없다.
11 목적어절을 이끄는 접속사 that이 필요하다.
12 ③은 '~하기 위하여'라는 목적을 나타내는 to부정사의 부사적 용법이고, 나머지는 '~할'의 뜻으로 앞의 명사를 수식하는 to부정사의 형용사적 용법이다.

13 '나는 ~라고 생각한다'는 I think that을 이용해서 나타낸다.
14 ③ something reading → something to read / 그녀는 읽을 것을 찾고 있는 중이다.
15 대명사 something을 수식하기 위해 동사 read를 형용사 역할로 바꿔 준다. (to read)
16 ③은 지시형용사이고, 나머지는 모두 명사절을 이끄는 접속사로 쓰였다.
17 부정사인 to write가 앞의 명사 paper를 수식한다. 이때 paper는 write on의 목적어이므로 write 다음에 전치사 on을 반드시 붙여야 한다.
18 「-thing+형용사+to부정사」의 어순으로 쓴다.
19 to부정사의 수식을 받는 명사가 전치사의 목적어일 경우 to부정사 뒤에 반드시 전치사를 써야 한다.
20 주어신 문장과 ⑤의 that은 접속사로 목적어절을 이끄는 억할을 한다.
21 think 뒤에 절이 올 경우 「that+주어+동사」의 어순으로 쓰고, 이때 접속사 that은 생략 가능하다. ③은 의문문의 어순으로 되어 있으므로 that절 뒤에 이어질 수 없다.
22 여행을 갔다는 것이 목적어이므로 that을 사용한 명사절을 써야 한다.
23 to부정사의 수식을 받는 명사가 전치사의 목적어일 경우 to부정사 뒤에 전치사를 쓴다. ③은 to talk with[to]라고 해야 옳다.
24 주어는 the girl이고 동사는 has, to부정사의 형용사적 용법을 이용하여 some food to feed the dog를 목적어로 쓴다.

01 to   02 that
03 (1) I bought some cookies to eat in the afternoon.
   (2) They need four chairs to sit on.
04 (1) My brother says that he didn't eat the bananas.
   (2) They think that they are proud of themselves.
05 (1) to eat   (2) to drink
   (3) sit on[in]   (4) talk with[to]
06 (1) that you can do everything
   (2) you think that she is pretty
07 (1) a pen to write → a pen to write with
   (2) visiting → to visit
08 (1) I know, she is a wise wife
   (2) I think, he is Chinese
   (3) We believe, we can change the world
09 She needs something to put on.
10 (1) She thinks that her daughter is sick.
   (2) I don't believe that Nick will come to the party.
11 a hotel to stay at[in]
12 (1) She has a strong desire to be a singer.

(2) We had something to talk about.

(3) I want a sheet[piece] of paper to write on.

(4) Please give me something hot to drink.

13 (1) I think (that) my English teacher is pretty.

(2) Many people believe (that) the earth is round.

14 (1) I have a lot of homework to do.

(2) It is your turn to introduce your family.

01 앞의 명사를 수식하는 형용사적 용법의 to부정사가 필요하다.

02 첫 번째 문장의 that은 접속사, 두 번째 문장은 관계대명사, 세 번째 문장은 지시형용사이다.

03 (2) 의미상 to부정사구 뒤에 전치사 on이 와야 한다.

04 주절의 동사 뒤에 접속사 that이 이끄는 목적어절을 쓴다.

05 앞의 명사를 꾸며주는 to부정사의 형용사적 용법을 이용한다.

06 that이 목적어가 되는 명사절을 이끄는 문장이다.

07 (1) to부정사의 수식을 받는 명사가 전치사의 목적어일 경우 to부정사 뒤에 반드시 전치사를 써야 한다. (2) '~할'이라는 의미로 명사를 수식하는 to부정사가 와야 한다. (형용사적 용법)

08 접속사 that은 동사의 목적어절을 이끄는 역할을 한다.

09 명사[대명사]를 수식하는 형용사 역할의 to부정사는 명사[대명사]의 뒤에 위치한다.

10 접속사 that 이하의 내용이 부정일 때, that 앞에 있는 주절의 동사를 부정으로 만든다.

11 stay at[in] a hotel의 구조이다.

12 (1), (2) to부정사의 형용사적 용법을 이용해 「명사[대명사]+to부정사」의 형태로 쓴다. (3) to부정사의 목적어가 있고 to부정사의 동사가 자동사일 때는 전치사가 필요하다. (4) -thing으로 끝나는 부정대명사는 「-thing+형용사+to부정사」의 어순을 따른다.

13 (2) 주어 + believe (that): ~라고 믿다

14 (1) 나는 해야 할 숙제가 많다. (2) 네 가족을 소개할 차례야.

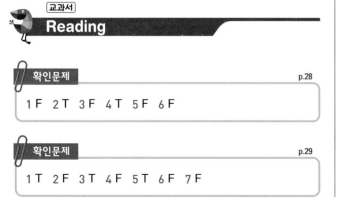

교과서

Reading

확인문제 　　　　　　　　　　　　　　　　　p.28

1 F　2 T　3 F　4 T　5 F　6 F

확인문제 　　　　　　　　　　　　　　　　　p.29

1 T　2 F　3 T　4 F　5 T　6 F　7 F

교과서 확인학습 A 　　　　　　　　　　　　p.30~31

01 Welcome to　02 In, second, to do

03 need to, well　04 How, do　　05 set, achieve

06 will master　　07 With, put off, until, or

08 Instead, will learn, every day

09 will achieve, at a time

10 When, full attention

11 used to read, while

12 slowed, because

13 put aside, when　　　　　14 a lot of

15 These days, free time

16 spend, working　　　　　17 to become

18 Every, classes, search for

19 that, to prepare　　　　　20 present

21 has, to spend　22 Manage, and, be happier

교과서 확인학습 B 　　　　　　　　　　　　p.32~33

1 Welcome to the new school year.

2 In the second grade, you will have more work to do.

3 You need to manage your time well.

4 How do you do that?

5 Subin: I set small goals and achieve them every day.

6 I do not say, "I will master English."

7 With such a big goal, I will probably put off working on it until tomorrow, next week, or next month.

8 Instead, I say, "I will learn three new English words every day."

9 I will achieve my big goal, one step at a time.

10 Minsu: When I do something, I give it my full attention.

11 I used to read SNS postings while I was doing my homework.

12 It slowed me down because I couldn't focus.

13 Now, I put aside my smartphone when I do my homework.

14 It saves me a lot of time.

15 These days, I finish my homework quickly and enjoy my free time.

16 John: I regularly spend time working toward my dream.

17 I want to become a chef.

18 Every Saturday morning, I go to cooking classes or search for recipes.

19 I think that using my time to prepare for my future is important.

20 Time is a present.

21 Everyone has the same present to spend every day.

22 Manage your time well, and you will be happier in the new school year!

시험대비 실력평가　　　　　　p.34~37

01 ②	02 small goals		03 ④
04 ③	05 ⑤	06 to	07 ①
08 working	09 ③	10 ④	11 ④
12 to	13 ⑤	14 숙제를 하는 동안 SNS 게시 글을 읽은 것	
	15 ⑤	16 ③	
17 ③	18 to become	19 ①	20 ②
21 are → is	22 ②	23 ④	24 ⑤
25 ③	26 set, achieve, big goal, achieve		
27 ②	28 (a)ttention	29 ④	30 ⑤
31 ④	32 He enjoys his free time.		

01 set a goal: 목표를 세우다

02 인칭대명사 them은 앞에 나온 복수명사를 가리킨다.

03 put off: 미루다(=postpone)

04 instead: 대신에

05 수빈이는 한 번에 한 걸음씩 그녀의 큰 목표를 달성할 것이라고 했다.

06 welcome to: ~이 된 것을 환영하다

07 밑줄 친 ⓑ는 to부정사의 형용사적 용법이다. ① 형용사적 용법 ② 명사적 용법 ③ 부사적 용법 ④ 명사적 용법 ⑤ 부사적 용법

08 spend time -ing: ~하는 데 시간을 소비하다

09 think 다음에 나오는 내용이 목적어의 역할을 하고 있으므로 명사절을 이끄는 접속사 that이 와야 한다.

10 토요일 아침에 요리법을 찾아본다고 했다.

11 주어진 문장의 It은 '숙제를 할 때 스마트폰을 한 쪽에 치워 놓는 것'을 가리키므로 ④에 와야 한다.

12 수여동사 give는 3형식에서 전치사 to를 쓴다.

13 「used to+동사원형」은 과거에 반복적으로 일어난 행위를 나타낸다.

14 인칭대명사 It은 앞에 나온 문장을 받는다.

15 because: ~ 때문에

16 ③ 스마트폰을 이용해서 숙제를 했는지는 알 수 없다.

17 toward: ~을 위해

18 want는 to부정사를 목적어로 취한다.

19 ⓒ, ①: 수업, 강습 ②, ③, ④: 학급 ⑤: 반 학생들

20 search for: ~을 찾다

21 동명사 주어는 단수 취급하므로 are를 is로 고쳐야 한다.

22 ⓐ, ②: 학년, ①, ③: 성적, ④: 등급, ⑤: 학점

23 2학년에서는 해야 할 일이 많아서 시간을 잘 관리해야 한다는 의미가 자연스러우므로 manage(관리하다)가 알맞다.

24 put off: 미루다

25 문맥상 until(~까지)이 알맞다.

27 주어진 문장의 It은 '숙제를 할 때 SNS 게시 글을 읽었던 것'을 가리키므로 ②에 오는 것이 알맞다.

28 어떤 것 또는 어떤 사람에 대해 주의 깊게 듣고, 보고, 생각하는 행위: attention(주의)

29 used to와 would는 과거에 반복적으로 일어났던 행위를 나타낼 때 쓸 수 있는 표현이다.

30 시간의 접속사 while이 알맞다.

31 ④④: 절약하다, ①③: 구조하다, ②⑤: 저장하다

32 민수는 숙제를 빨리 끝내고 그의 여가 시간을 즐긴다고 했다.

서술형 시험대비　　　　　　p.38~39

01 you will have more work to do

02 너의 시간을 관리하다

03 She sets small goals and achieves them every day.

04 working

05 She will learn three new English words.

06 나는 한 번에 한 단계씩 나의 큰 목표를 달성할 거야.

07 something

08 (A) used to (B) because

09 숙제할 때 스마트폰을 한 쪽에 치워 두는 것

10 He used to read SNS postings (while he was doing his homework.)

11 (A) to do (B) working

12 We need to manage our time well.

13 He wants to become a chef.

14 that, is

15 He goes to cooking classes or search for recipes.

16 선물　　　17 the same present to spend

01 work를 to do로 수식하여 표현한다.

02 do that = manage your time

03 수빈이는 작은 목표를 세우고 매일 그것들을 성취한다고 했다.

04 put off는 동명사를 목적어로 취한다.

05 수빈이는 매일 세 개의 새로운 단어를 배울 것이라고 했다.

06 achieve: 달성하다, 성취하다 / goal: 목표 / one step at a

time: 한 번에 한 단계씩

07 인칭대명사 it은 something을 가리킨다.

08 (A) used to+동사원형: ~하곤 했다 (B) because: ~ 때문에

09 인칭대명사 It은 앞 문장을 받는다.

10 민수는 그의 숙제를 하는 동안 SNS 게시 글들을 읽곤 했다.

11 (A) work을 꾸며주는 형용사 역할을 하는 to부정사의 형태가 되어야 한다. (B) spend time -ing: ~하는 데 시간을 보내다

12 2학년에서는 시간 관리를 잘해야 한다고 언급되었다.

13 John은 요리사가 되고 싶어 한다고 했다.

14 명사절을 이끄는 접속사 that과 「동명사 주어+동사」 어순이므로 be동사가 들어가는데, 동명사 주어는 단수 취급하므로 is가 알맞다.

15 John은 토요일 아침마다 요리 강습에 가거나 요리법을 찾아본 다고 했다.

16 present: 선물

17 to spend가 앞에 있는 명사구 the same present를 꾸며주는 형용사적 용법이다.

영역별 핵심문제　　　　　　　p.41~45

01 ④	02 ②	03 present	04 ③
05 ③	06 ②	07 ⑤	08 ④
09 (D) – (A) – (C) – (B)		10 ②, ⑤	11 I'm worried about the math test.		12 ④
13 ④	14 ③	15 in	16 He is nervous because of the dance contest.		17 ①
18 ⑤	19 that	20 ③	21 ⑤
22 ②	23 Jane didn't believe that Kevin would come to the party.		24 to write → to write with		25 that → if	26 ③	27 ④
28 ④	29 ③	30 would	31 (f)ocus
32 지금 나는 숙제를 할 때 스마트폰을 한쪽에 치워 놔.			
33 ④	34 ②	35 ③	36 ③
37 with	38 playing	39 ②	40 ④

01 ④는 형용사이고 나머지는 부사이다.

02 관심이나 노력을 특정한 대상에 기울이다: focus(집중하다)

03 동의어 관계이다. 아마 : 아마 = 선물 : 선물

04 be good at: ~을 잘하다, ~에 능숙하다 / at a time: 한 번에

05 • 나는 나의 큰 목표를 달성할 것이다. • 나는 오늘 축구 연습이 있다. • 그는 6학년이다. • 너는 시간을 잘 관리해야 해.

06 put off: 연기하다, 미루다(=postpone)

07 상대방에게 무언가 제안하거나 권유하는 표현을 고른다. ⑤는 '왜 너는 조리법을 찾지 않았니?'라는 의미이다.

08 What's wrong with ~?는 어떤 문제점이 있는지 물을 때 사용하는 표현이므로 ④는 어울리지 않는다.

09 (D) Jason, 너 괜찮니? 오늘 안 좋아 보여. - (A) 감기에 걸렸

어. (C) 그거 참 안됐구나. 내 생각에 너는 병원에 가 봐야 할 것 같아.- (B) 네 말이 맞아. 고마워.

10 B가 좋지 않은 소식을 전하는 것으로 보아 A에는 Kevin에게 무슨 문제가 있느냐고 물어보는 표현이 오는 게 맞다.

11 be worried about: ~에 대해 걱정하다

12 주어진 문장의 It은 '가족 앞에서 연습하는 것'을 가리키므로 ④에 와야 한다.

13 ⓐ because of: ~ 때문에 ⓑ for many days: 여러 날 동안

14 앞뒤 내용이 상반되므로 역접의 접속사 but이 알맞다.

15 in front of: ~ 앞에서

16 소년은 춤 경연대회 때문에 긴장된다고 했다.

17 think 다음에 나오는 내용이 목적어의 역할을 하고 있으므로 명사절을 이끄는 접속사 that이 와야 한다.

18 to부정사인 to live가 앞의 명사 a good house를 수식한다. 수식을 받는 명사가 전치사의 목적어인 경우 to부정사 뒤에 전치사가 와야 한다.

19 명사절을 이끄는 접속사 that이 필요하다.

20 ③은 '~하기 위하여'라는 의미로 목적을 나타내는 to부정사의 부사적 용법이고, 나머지는 앞의 명사를 꾸며주는 to부정사의 형용사적 용법이다.

21 목적어가 되는 명사절을 이끄는 접속사 that은 생략할 수 있다

22 <보기>와 ②는 to부정사의 형용사적 용법 ①, ⑤ 부사적 용법 (목적) ③, ④ 명사적 용법

24 to write가 앞의 명사 a pen을 수식한다. 이때는 write with a pen이라는 전치사의 목적어 관계이므로 write 다음의 전치사 with를 빠뜨리지 않도록 주의한다.

25 don't know의 목적어가 되는 명사절은 접속사 if를 쓴다.

26 ③의 to부정사는 '~하기 위하여'라는 의미로 목적을 나타내는 부사적 용법으로 쓰였고, 나머지는 모두 '~할, ~하는'이라는 뜻으로 앞에 오는 명사나 대명사를 꾸며주는 형용사적 용법으로 쓰였다.

27 ①, ②, ③, ⑤: that / ④: 접속사 when

28 ⓐ, ⓒ to부정사의 형용사적 용법 ⓑ to부정사의 명사적 용법 ⓓ to부정사의 부사적 용법

29 때를 나타내는 접속사 when이 알맞다

30 used to는 '~하곤 했다'는 의미로 would와 바꿔 쓸 수 있다.

31 관심이나 노력을 특정한 대상에 기울이다: 집중하다(focus)

32 put aside: 한쪽에 치워 놓다

33 these days: 요즈음(=nowadays)

34 ⓕ, ②: 자유로운 ①: 사용 중이 아닌, ③: ~이 없는, ④, ⑤: 무료로

35 ③ 민수가 하루에 얼마나 오랫동안 스마트폰을 사용하는지는 알 수 없다.

36 ⓐ와 ③은 형용사적 용법의 to부정사이고, ①, ②, ④는 명사적 용법, ⑤는 부사적 용법의 to부정사이다.

37 get along with: ~와 잘 지내다

38 stop -ing: ~하는 것을 멈추다

39 hope 다음에 나오는 내용이 목적어의 역할을 하고 있으므로 명사절을 이끄는 접속사 that이 와야 한다.

34 ④ 글쓴이가 작년에 성취한 목표가 무엇인지는 알 수 없다.

단원별 예상문제   p.46~49

01 ③	02 ⑤	03 (1) in front of (2) all
day long (3) used to (4) because of		04 ④
05 ③	06 ①	07 ④ 08 worried
09 ⑤	10 ⑤	11 ④ 12 ③
13 hang my coat → hang my coat on		14 ③
15 if → that	16 something hot to drink	17 ⑤
18 ①	19 작은 목표들	20 such a big goal
21 put off	22 영어를 마스터하는 것	23 ①
24 ①	25 and	26 She says, "I will learn
three new English words every day."		27 recipes
28 ②	29 ③	

01 ③은 유의어 관계이고 나머지는 반의어 관계이다.

02 get along with: ~와 잘 지내다 / put aside: ~을 한쪽으로 치우다

03 (1) in front of: ~ 앞에서 (2) all day long: 하루 종일 (3) used to: ~하곤 했다 (4) because of: ~ 때문에

04 ④는 spend(소비하다)의 영영풀이이다.

05 What should I do?는 상대방에게 충고를 구할 때 사용하는 표현이다.

06 감기에 걸렸을 때 병원에 가보라고 하는 충고가 어울린다.

07 ④ 필기를 하는 게 어떠냐며 조언을 하는데 아직 아니라며 무엇을 해야 하는지 묻는 건 어색하다.

08 ⓐ look+형용사: ~하게 보이다 ⓑ I'm worried about~: 나는 ~이 걱정이다

09 What's going on?은 '무슨 일 있니?'라는 의미로 문제점을 파악할 때 사용하는 표현이다.

10 '내일 역사 시험이 걱정돼. 어떻게 해야 할까?' 다음에 충고의 의미를 담은 ③ 'Why don't you ~?'가 가장 알맞다.

11 ①, ②, ③ 명사적 용법 ④ 형용사적 용법 ⑤ 부사적 용법

12 첫 번째 빈칸에는 hope의 목적어로 쓰이면서 주절과 종속절을 이어주는 명사절 접속사 that이 적절하다. 두 번째 빈칸에는 '그것(그 말)'이라는 뜻의 지시대명사 that이 적절하다.

13 to부정사의 수식을 받는 명사가 전치사의 목적어일 경우 뒤에 전치사가 온다.

14 ①, ②, ④, ⑤: 지시형용사 / ③: 접속사 that

15 hope 다음에는 접속사 that이 이끄는 명사절이 와야 한다.

16 -thing으로 끝나는 대명사는 형용사가 뒤에서 수식하며, 이를 다시 to부정사가 뒤에서 수식한다.

17 목적어 역할을 하는 명사절을 이끄는 that은 생략 가능하다.

18 ①에서 sit은 자동사이므로 chair를 목적어로 취하기 위해서는 전치사 in이나 on이 필요하다.

19 them은 small goals를 가리킨다.

20 「such + a + 형용사 + 명사」 어순이다.

21 특정 시간에 하기로 계획된 일을 나중에 하기로 결정하다: put off(연기하다, 미루다)

23 at a time: 한 번에

24 본문의 to spend는 형용사적 용법의 to부정사이다. ①은 형용사적 용법, ③은 명사적 용법, ②④⑤는 모두 부사적 용법의 to부정사이다.

25 명령문 ~, and ...: ~해라, 그러면 ...

26 수빈이는 영어를 마스터하는 대신에 매일 세 개의 새로운 영어 단어를 배울 것이라고 말한다고 했다.

27 음식을 만들기 위한 일련의 지시 사항 : 요리법, 조리법(recipe)

28 ②는 형용사적 용법이고 ⓑ와 나머지는 부사적 용법이다.

29 John이 요리 강습을 어디에서 듣는지는 알 수 없다.

서술형 실전문제   p.50~51

01 ⓐ What's the matter   ⓑ What should I do

02 (B) – (C) – (D) – (A)

03 |모범답안| What's wrong with you? / What's the problem with you? / Is (there) something wrong with you? 등

04 |모범답안| You'd better drink some water. / Why don't you drink some water?/ I advise you to drink some water. / How[What] about drinking some water?

05 (1) He believes that it will be a lot of fun.
(2) I think that he is honest.
(3) I know that she was a teacher.

06 to play with

07 I think that he enjoys playing soccer.

08 (1) to tell (2) to live in

09 (1) to answers → to answer
(2) to talk → to talk with[to]
(3) anything drink → anything to drink

10 three goals to achieve

11 to play → playing

12 It is to learn taegwondo.

13 regularly   **14** chef

15 for   **16** using[to use]

17 He goes to cooking classes every Saturday morning.

01 ⓐ '무슨 일이 있니?'라는 뜻의 What's the matter (with

you)?가 알맞다. ⓑ '내가 어떻게 해야 할까?'라는 뜻의 What should I do?가 알맞다.

02 (B) 무슨 문제 있니? - (C) 음, 이가 아파. - (D) 그것 참 안됐구나. 치과에 가 보는 게 어때? - (A) 알았어. 그럴게.

03 어떤 문제점이 있는지 물을 때 사용하는 표현에는 What's wrong with ~? / What's the matter[problem] with ~? / Is (there) something wrong with ~? 등이 있다.

04 I think you should+동사원형 ~.은 제안이나 충고하기 표현으로 You'd better+동사원형 ~. / Why don't you+동사원형 ~? / How[What] about -ing ~? 등으로 바꿔 쓸 수 있다.

05 that: 명사절(목적어)을 이끄는 접속사

06 앞의 명사를 수식하는 to부정사를 이용하여 한 문장으로 만들도록 한다. 수식을 받는 명사가 전치사의 목적어인 경우 to부정사 뒤에 전치사가 와야 한다.

07 enjoy는 동명사를 목적어로 취하는 동사이다. I think that ~: 나는 ~라고 생각한다

08 (1) to tell이 앞에 있는 명사 good news를 꾸며주는 형용사적 용법이다. (2) to live 앞에 있는 명사 house는 전치사 in의 목적어이므로 in을 써야 한다.

09 (1) 앞에 있는 명사 the questions를 꾸며주는 to부정사(to+동사원형) 형태가 되어야 한다. (2) to부정사의 형용사적 용법으로 앞의 명사 some friends와 연결되려면 전치사 with[to]가 필요하다. (3) '마실 것'의 의미가 되어야 하므로 앞에 나온 대명사 뒤에서 꾸며주는 '대명사+to부정사' 형태가 되어야 한다.

10 to achieve가 앞에 있는 명사구 three goals를 꾸며주는 형용사적 용법이다.

11 stop -ing: ~하는 것을 멈추다 cf. stop + to부정사: ~하기 위해 멈추다

12 글쓴이의 마지막 목표는 태권도를 배우는 것이다.

13 동사 spend를 수식하므로 부사가 되어야 한다.

14 전문 요리사, 특히 식당, 호텔 등에서 가장 상급의 요리사

15 search for: ~을 찾다 / prepare for: ~을 준비하다

16 주어 역할을 하는 동명사나 to부정사 형태가 되어야 한다.

창의사고력 서술형 문제 p.52

|모범답안|

01 (1) I need something to drink.
  (2) I need a chair to sit on[in].
  (3) He needs friends to talk with[to].

02 (1) He thinks that Jenny is kind.
  (2) She heard that they needed help.
  (3) Mike says that it's delicious.
  (4) They know that many children are hungry.

03 (1) I need a chair to sit on.

  (2) I need friends to talk with.
  (3) I need ski gloves to wear.

01 앞의 명사를 꾸며주는 to부정사의 형용사적 용법을 이용한다.

02 동사의 목적어가 되는 명사절을 이끄는 접속사 that을 사용하여 내용상 어울리는 것끼리 연결한다.

03 앞의 명사를 꾸며주는 to부정사의 형용사적 용법을 이용한다.

단원별 모의고사 p.53~56

01 ④	02 ②	03 ④	
04 remember	05 master	06 ⑤	07 Why
don't you	08 wrong	09 ①	
10 (a) ppointment		11 She thinks he should	
use a planner.	12 ③	13 ②	14 ⑤
15 I think that my English teacher is pretty.			16 ⑤
17 to stay in[at]		18 ④	19 ②
20 ④	21 slowed down me → slowed me		
down	22 ③	23 much	24 No, he
finishes his homework quickly.			25 ②
26 working	27 manage	28 ③	29 different
30 If	31 ④		

01 앞으로 하려는 일을 위해 스스로를 준비시키다: prepare(준비하다)

02 put off: 미루다

03 save: 절약하다; 구하다

04 반의어 관계이다. 미래 : 과거 = 잊다 : 기억하다

05 어떤 것을 완전히 익히다

06 ⑤ A가 B에게 슬퍼 보인다며 무슨 일 있느냐고 물었는데, B가 도와주겠다고 대답하는 것은 어색하다.

07 You'd better+동사원형 ~.과 유사한 표현에는 I think you should+동사원형 ~. / I advise you to+동사원형 ~. / I suggest you+동사원형 ~. / Why don't you+동사원형 ~? / How[What] about ~? 등이 있다.

08 What's the matter? = What's wrong?

09 I think you should ~는 상대방에게 제안이나 충고를 하는 표현으로 You had better ~와 바꿔 쓸 수 있다.

10 특정한 때에 어떤 사람을 만나기로 하는 약속: appointment (약속)

11 하나는 지호가 일정 계획표를 사용해야 한다고 생각한다.

12 문맥상 '함께 여행할 친구를 찾고 있다'는 흐름이 자연스러우므로, 빈칸에는 '~와 함께'에 해당하는 with가 알맞다.

13 ①, ③, ④, ⑤의 that은 know, hope, believe 등의 타동사 다음에 목적어가 되는 명사절을 이끄는 접속사 that으로 쓰였으나 ②의 that은 관계대명사이다.

14 to부정사의 형용사적 용법이다.

15 I think that: ~라고 생각한다

16 ⑤ -thing이나 -body로 끝나는 부정대명사의 경우 형용사와 to부정사의 수식을 동시에 받으면 「대명사+형용사+to부정사」의 순서로 써야 한다. something important to tell

17 앞의 명사를 수식해야 하므로 to부정사 형태가 되어야 하고, 호텔 안에 머무는 것이므로 전치사 in[at]을 함께 써야 한다.

18 ①, ②, ③, ⑤: 명사절을 이끄는 접속사 ④: 지시형용사

19 ⓐ, ⓒ: to부정사의 형용사적 용법 ⓑ, ⓓ: to부정사의 명사적 용법 ⓔ to부정사의 부사적 용법

20 「used to+동사원형」은 과거에 반복적으로 일어난 행위를 나타낸다.

21 「타동사 + 부사」의 이어동사의 목적어가 인칭대명사인 경우 「동사 + 인칭대명사 + 부사」의 어순이 된다.

22 밑줄 친 It은 앞에 나온 문장을 받는다.

23 time은 셀 수 없는 명사이므로 much와 바꿔 쓸 수 있다.

24 요즈음 민수는 숙제를 빨리 끝낸다고 했다

25 ⓐ와 ②는 '~할, ~하는'의 의미로 앞의 명사를 수식해 주는 to부정사의 형용사적 용법이고, 나머지는 to부정사의 명사적 용법이다.

26 spend time -ing: ~하는 데 시간을 쓰다

27 시간, 돈 등을 낭비하지 않고 현명하게 사용하다: manage (관리하다)

28 '~하기 위하여'라는 목적을 나타내는 to부정사가 와야 한다.

29 same(같은)의 반의어는 different(다른)이다.

30 「명령문, and ~」구문은 if 조건문으로 바꿔 쓸 수 있다.

31 ④ John이 왜 요리사가 되고 싶어 하는지는 알 수 없다.

All about Safety

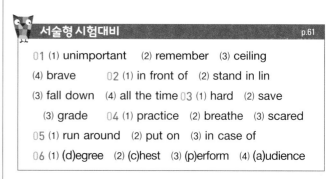

01 ⑤　　02 possible　03 ④　　04 wet
05 ④　　06 earthquake　07 ②
08 save

01 <보기>와 ⑤는 동사에 -ive를 붙여 형용사가 되는 단어이다.

02 as soon as you can(가능한 한 빨리 = as soon as possible)

03 공기를 폐 안으로 들이마셨다가 내쉬다: 숨을 쉬다(breathe)

04 반의어 관계이다. 잘못된 : 옳은 = 마른 : 젖은

05 bump into: ~에 부딪히다 / wait for: ~을 기다리다

06 지구 표면의 갑작스럽고 격렬한 진동: 지진(earthquake)

06 get off: 내리다 / get under: ~ 밑에 들어가다

08 save: 구하다; 절약하다

01 (1) unimportant　(2) remember　(3) ceiling
(4) brave　02 (1) in front of　(2) stand in lin
(3) fall down　(4) all the time 03 (1) hard　(2) save
(3) grade　04 (1) practice　(2) breathe　(3) scared
05 (1) run around　(2) put on　(3) in case of
06 (1) (d)egree　(2) (c)hest　(3) (p)erform　(4) (a)udience

01 (1), (2), (3) 반의어 관계이다. (1) 늦게 : 일찍 = 중요한 : 중요하지 않은 (2) 쉬운 : 어려운 = 잊다 : 기억하다 (3) 강한 : 약한 = 바닥 : 천장 (4) 쓰레기 : 쓰레기 = 용감한 : 겁이 없는

02 (1) in front of: ~ 앞에 (2) stand in line: 한 줄로 서다 (3) fall down: 넘어지다 (4) all the time: 항상

03 (1) hard: 어려운; 세게 (2) save: 구하다; 저축하다 (3) grade: 학년; 성적

04 (1) 그들은 보통 방과 후에 축구를 연습한다. practice: 연습하다 (2) 사람은 숨쉬기 위해 산소가 필요하다. breathe: 숨을 쉬다 (3) 그 토끼는 사자를 만났을 때 겁을 먹었다. scared: 겁먹은, 무서워하는

05 (1) run around: 뛰어다니다 (2) put on: ~을 입다 (3) in case of: ~의 경우에

06 (1) degree: (각도의 단위인) 도 (2) chest: 가슴 (3) perform: 수행하다 (4) audience: 청중, 시청자

Conversation

핵심 Check

p.62~63

1 (1) don't forget to   (2) borrow / remember to / will

(3) Make[Be] sure / won't

2 (1) think, cold / better not drink   (2) Don't eat

(3) shouldn't use / sorry

교과서 대화문 익히기

Check(√) True or False

p.64

1 T   2 F   3 F   4 T

교과서 확인학습

p.66~67

Listen & Speak 1 A-1

can, buy / forget to / food label / for / will check

Listen & Speak 1 A-2

leaving / wear, find dust / didn't know / bad for, don't forget / All right

Listen & Speak 2 A-1

up / to buy, about / have, in, should go, late / better not, says, wet / didn't

Listen & Speak 2 A-2

does, mean / you'd better not, while / but / bump into, there are, around, dangerous / see

Conversation A

having, with, to shake, couldn't, fell down, Get, Don't forget, Luckily, scary experience

Conversation B

told, a few / let's, ready / is shaking, forget to get, protect / scary, Hold on to / for now, out / better not use, Use / should, go / need to, with / let's, to

Wrap Up - Listening 1

almost, stand in line, wait for, get off, move up, down, You'd better, in case of

Wrap Up - Listening 2

going to, with / sounds / because, for, one night / don't forget to check

---

시험대비 기본평가

p.68

01 ⑤   02 ⑤   03 ④   04 ②

01 상대에게 상기시키는 표현을 할 때, 「don't forget to+동사원형」의 표현을 써서 잊지 말 것을 당부한다.

02 You'd better not+동사원형 ~은 '~하지 않는 게 좋겠다'라는 뜻의 금지하는 표현으로 You shouldn't + 동사원형 ~.으로 바꿔 쓸 수 있다.

03 Don't forget to + 동사원형: '~하는 것을 잊지 마'라는 의미의 상기시킬 때 사용하는 표현이다.

04 B의 답변으로 보아, 빈칸에는 금지를 나타내는 should not을 사용한 문장이 들어가야 한다.

시험대비 실력평가

p.69~70

01 is   02 ③   03 ④   04 ⑤

05 ④   06 ①   07 ②   08 They

are practicing a few safety rules for earthquakes.

09 ①   10 Remember 11 ③   12 ①, ③

13 ③   14 ③   15 걷는 동안 스마트폰을

보지 않는 게 낫다는 뜻이다.

01 주어 a lot of fine dust가 셀 수 없는 명사이므로 동사는 is가 되어야 한다.

02 so: 그래서

03 잊지 말라고 상기시키는 말이다.

04 ⑤ 소녀는 아빠가 당부하는 말에 알겠다고 했으므로 마스크를 쓸 것이다

05 a few+셀 수 있는 명사의 복수형

06 hold on to: ~을 꼭 잡다

07 계단을 이용하라고 했으므로 빈칸에는 '엘리베이터를 타면 안 된다.'는 금지의 표현이 알맞다.

08 Amy와 지호는 지진에 대한 안전 수칙들을 실습하고 있다.

09 주어진 문장은 '갑자기 모든 것이 흔들리기 시작했다.'라는 뜻으로 나는 가만히 서 있을 수 없었고 거의 넘어질 뻔 했다.는 문장 앞에 오는 것이 자연스럽다.

10 Don't forget to + 동사원형 ~: ~하는 것을 잊지 마라 (=Remember+동사원형 ~)

11 ③ 필자와 그의 가족이 어디에 있었는지는 알 수 없다

12 you'd better not ~은 금지를 나타내는 표현으로 ①, ③과 바꿔 쓸 수 있다. you don't have to ~는 '너는 ~할 필요가 없다'는 의미이다.

13 but: 그러나

14 bump into: ~에 부딪히다

11

01 Don't forget to wear your gloves.

02 Make sure to bring your trash back.

03 you'd better not play　　04 (B) – (D) – (C) – (A)

05 you shouldn't use / you must not use / don't [do not] use / you can't use

06 to buy　　07 She came to buy a shirt.

08 Because the floor is wet.

01 Don't forget to+동사원형 ～: ～하는 것을 잊지 마라.

02 Make sure to + 동사원형 ～: ～하는 것을 명심해라.

03 You'd better not ～.: 너는 ～하지 않는 게 좋겠다.

04 A: 나는 내일 아빠와 지리산에 갈 거야. (B) 멋진데. (D) 우리는 1박 2일 동안 묵을 예정이어서 신나. (C) 그거 좋겠네. 하지만, 날씨를 확인하는 걸 잊지 마. (A) 알았어.

05 You'd better not + 동사원형 ～은 금지하는 표현으로 You shouldn't + 동사원형 ～ / You must not + 동사원형 ～ / Don't[Do not] + 동사원형 ～ / You can't + 동사원형 ～ 등으로 바꿔 쓸 수 있다.

06 목적을 나타내는 to부정사의 부사적 용법이다.

07 소녀는 셔츠를 사러 이 쇼핑센터에 왔다.

08 바닥이 젖었기 때문이다.

교과서
Grammar

핵심 Check　　　　　　p.72~73

1 (1) how　(2) which　(3) where　(4) when　(5) where

2 (1) as fast as Bora　(2) as new as mine
　　(3) not as long as the yellow one

시험대비 기본평가　　　　　　p.74

01 (1) where to go　(2) how to make
　　(3) what to eat　(4) when to open

02 (1) as heavy as mine
　　(2) run as fast as
　　(3) as Seoul's (population)
　　(4) not as[so] delicious as
　　(5) as difficult

03 (1) where I should park
　　(2) how they should use the computer

---

01 (1) where+to부정사: 어디로 ～할지 (2) how+to부정사: ～하는 방법 (3) what+to부정사: 무엇을 ～할지 (4) when+to부정사: 언제 ～할지

02 (1) your bag과 my bag을 비교하는 것이므로 me를 mine으로 고친다. (2) fast의 정도를 비교하는 것이므로 run as fast as ～가 맞다. (3) 도쿄의 인구와 서울의 인구를 비교하는 것이므로 Seoul은 적절하지 않다. (4) as ～ as의 부정문은 not as/so ～ as로 쓴다. (5) 뒤의 비교 대상 앞에 as가 있으므로 동등비교로 만들어야 한다.

03 「의문사+to부정사」는 「의문사+주어+should+동사원형」으로 바꾸어 쓸 수 있다.

시험대비 실력평가　　　　　　p.75~77

01 ①　02 ②　03 ②　04 ③

05 ②　06 as tall as Ted　07 ①

08 where to go　09 as, as　10 ②

11 ②　12 ②　13 they shoul 14 not

as[so] cheap as　15 ④　16 (1) cold

(2) hotter, than　17 ⑤　18 ②

19 She is not as[so] popular as you.　20 ②

21 ④　22 Can you show me how to use a camera?　23 ④　24 ③

01 '～만큼 …한'의 뜻을 나타내는 동등비교이다.

02 how+to부정사: ～하는 방법, what+to부정사: 무엇을 ～ 할지

03 as ～ as … 동등비교를 쓴다.

04 「의문사+to부정사」 구문으로 첫 번째 문장은 문맥상 '무엇을 입어야 할지'가 되어야 하므로 what이 알맞고, 두 번째 문장은 '～하는 방법'이라는 의미가 되어야 하므로 how가 알맞다.

05 「의문사+to부정사」는 should를 써서 명사절로 바꿔 쓸 수 있다.

06 Eric과 Ted는 키가 같으므로 동등비교 「as + 형용사 + as」를 이용하여 문장을 완성한다.

07 「의문사+to부정사」 구문을 이용한다.

08 '어디로 가야 할지'는 「의문사 where+to부정사」로 나타낼 수 있다.

09 less ～ than …은 not as ～ as 구문으로 바꿔 쓸 수 있다.

10 ② 동사 eat의 목적어로 what이 왔으므로, 뒤에 lunch가 또 올 수 없다. (what → where[when] 또는 lunch → for lunch

11 빨리 달리는 순서는 Mike>Mina>Eric>Junho이다.

12 ②의 what to read는 동사 is의 보어로 쓰였고, 나머지 「의문사+to부정사」는 모두 목적어로 쓰였다.

13 의문사+to부정사 = 「의문사+주어+should+동사원형」

14 A is ～ than B: …보다 더 ～하다 = B is not as[so] ～ as A: …만큼 ～하지 않다

15 ④ how to make의 목적어가 될 수 있는 말이 와야 한다.

16 (1) 비교급의 문장을 not as ~ as ...의 문장으로 바꾼다. (2) not as ~ as ...의 문장을 비교급의 문장으로 바꾼다.

17 ⑤ as ~ as 사이에 동사 speak를 수식하는 부사인 well을 써야 한다.

18 ②에서 '카메라를 사용하는 방법'은 「의문사+to부정사」 구문으로 나타내야 한다.

19 「be동사+not as[so]+형용사 원급+as」: …만큼 ~하지 않다

20 첫 번째 문장은 '~만큼 많이'의 동등비교 표현이고, 두 번째는 'more+원급+than ...'의 비교 표현이다.

21 '서울은 인천보다 크다.'라는 표현은 '인천은 서울만큼 크지 않다.'는 의미이다. not as[so]+형용사의 원급+as: ~만큼 …하지 않은

22 가르쳐 주실래요?: Can you show me ~? / 카메라 사용법: how to use a camera

23 ④ who가 주어로 사용될 때 「who+to부정사」 구문은 사용하지 않는다. Will you tell me who will invite Jack?으로 나타낸다.

24 ③은 문맥으로 보아 who가 동사 take의 주어 역할을 하므로 조동사 should가 들어가야 한다. 나머지는 모두 to가 적절하다.

🦉 서술형 시험대비
p.78~79

01 (1) how   (2) what   (3) which   (4) where

02 (1) as tall as   (2) taller than   (3) as old as
(4) not as old as

03 (1) I can't decide what to buy[what I should buy] for my mother's birthday.
(2) Bill didn't tell us where to stay.

04 (1) Jimin is not as[so] tall as Taemin.
(2) Jane isn't as[so] heavy as Kirk.

05 (1) as much as I do
(2) as fast as I could
(3) not as comfortable as that bed

06 (1) My brother doesn't know where he should go.
(2) Alice doesn't know what she should cook.
(3) Please tell me when I should help you.
(4) The problem is how I should escape from here.

07 (1) where to practice   (2) when to visit
(3) who(m) to go   (4) what to buy
(5) which, to buy

08 (1) Ella has as many hats as I have.
(2) This new tool is as useful as that old one.
(3) Tom drank as much wine as water.

09 she to take ➡ she should take 또는 to take

10 better, as[so] well as

11 (1) I didn't know when to leave.

(2) Do you know how to play the guitar?
(3) I don't know where to meet her.

12 (1) just   (2) wise   (3) twice   (4) early

01 (1) 방법을 나타낼 때는 「how+to부정사」를 쓴다. (2) '몇 시'는 what time ~을 쓴다. (3) '어느 책'은 which book ~으로 나타낸다. (4) '이름을 적을 곳'은 장소를 나타내므로 where가 알맞다.

02 (1) Brian은 Kevin만큼 키가 크다. (2) 준호는 Kevin보다 키가 크다. (3) Brian은 준호만큼 나이가 많다. (4) Kevin은 준호와 Brian만큼 나이가 많지 않다.

03 (1) '무엇을 사야 할지'의 의미이므로 「의문사+to부정사」 또는 「의문사+주어+should+동사원형」의 형태로 고쳐야 한다. (2) 「의문사+to부정사」 구문이므로, to 다음에 동사원형 stay가 와야 한다.

04 (2) 'A는 B보다 덜 ~하다'는 A not as[so] ~ as B로 바꾸어 쓸 수 있다.

05 as ~ as ... 구문을 쓴다.

06 「의문사+to부정사」 구문을 「의문사+주어+should+동사」 구문으로 바꿔 쓸 수 있다.

07 (3) 목적격 whom 대신 주격 who를 써도 좋다. (5) 'which+명사+to부정사'의 형태이다.

08 (1) Ella has ~와 I have를 동등 비교한다. (2) This new tool과 That old one을 동등 비교한다. one은 tool의 반복을 피하기 위해 쓴 대명사이다. (3) wine과 water를 비교한다.

09 어느 길을 택해야 하는지는 「의문사+to부정사」 구문이나 「의문사+주어+should+동사」 구문을 써서 나타낸다.

10 A 비교급 than B=B not as[so] 원급 as A

11 (1) 의문사(when)+to leave (2) 의문사(how) + to play the guitar (3) 의문사(where)+to meet her

12 (1) 비교 대상의 정도가 완전히 같을 때는 as 앞에 just를 붙인다. (2) '예전만큼 현명하지 않다'의 뜻이므로 wise가 적절하다. (3) '몇 배의 ~'는 배수사를 as 앞에 둔다. (4) 'Ann 만큼 일찍'이므로 early를 쓴다.

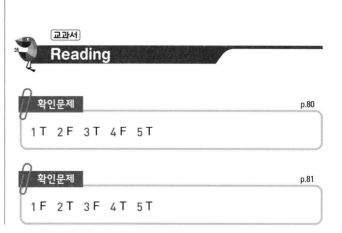

교과서
🐦 Reading

📎 **확인문제**
p.80

1 T   2 F   3 T   4 F   5 T

📎 **확인문제**
p.81

1 F   2 T   3 F   4 T   5 T

01 saved, life   02 brave, with us

03 yourself   04 My, is   05 in, second, at

06 tell us, experience

07 waiting for, with   08 in front of

09 what to do   10 as, as, at

11 ran, tapped, on

12 wasn't, breathing   13 said to, CPR

14 impressive   15 did, such an

16 Safety Training, at

17 how to do, to practice   18 show, how to

19 Keep, straight   20 other, must, at, angle

21 Push down, hard, until

22 Are there, to remember

23 need to, minutes

24 that, should, within, after, stops

25 To begin, later than, saving

26 as important as   27 for joining

28 pleasure

1 Announcer: Yesterday, a teenager saved the life of an old man.

2 The brave student is in the studio with us today.

3 Please introduce yourself.

4 Sejin: My name is Kim Sejin.

5 I'm in the second grade at Hanguk Middle School.

6 Announcer: Could you tell us your experience?

7 Sejin: Sure. I was waiting for the bus with my friend, Jinho.

8 A man suddenly fell in front of us.

9 Nobody knew what to do.

10 I was as scared as the others at first.

11 Then, I ran to him and tapped him on the shoulder.

12 He wasn't moving or breathing.

13 I said to Jinho, "Call 119," and started CPR.

14 Announcer: That's impressive.

15 When did you learn such an important skill?

16 Sejin: We had Safety Training Day at school last week.

17 I learned how to do CPR and had a chance to practice.

18 Announcer: Can you show the audience how to perform CPR?

19 Sejin: Yes. Keep your arms straights,

20 Your arms and the other person's chest must be at a 90 degree angle.

21 Push down in the center of the chest hard and fast until an ambulance comes.

22 Announcer: Are there any other things to remember?

23 Sejin: Yes. You need to remember the four minutes of "Golden Time."

24 It means that you should start CPR within four minutes after someone's heart stops.

25 To begin CPR later than that will greatly lower the chances of saving someone's life.

26 Announcer: Timing is as important as doing CPR.

27 Thank you for joining us.

28 Sejin: My pleasure.

01 ④   02 in   03 ⑤   04 Nobody knew what to do.   05 ④   06 ⑤

07 the four minutes of "Golden Time"   08 ⑤

09 (l)ower   10 such an important skill   11 to

12 ③   13 perform   14 Our arms and the other person's chest must be at a 90 degree angle.

15 ②   16 a man   17 ③   18 breathing

19 CPR   20 She was waiting for the bus with her friend, Jinho.   21 Is → Are   22 ③

23 4분   24 of   25 ⑤   26 joining

27 ②   28 chest   29 at   30 ③

01 명령문의 주어가 You이므로, 주어 You의 재귀대명사는 yourself 이다.

02 be in the second grade: 2학년이다

03 suddenly: 갑자기(=unexpectedly)

04 nobody: 아무도 ~ 않다 / what+to부정사: 무엇을 ~해야 할지

05 ④ 그 남자의 직업은 알 수 없다.

06 ⓐ 명사구 any other things를 꾸며주는 to부정사의 형용사적 용법이므로 to remember가 알맞다. ⓓ 문장의 주어의 역할을 하는 to부정사나 동명사가 와야 한다.

07 인칭대명사 It은 앞 문장의 the four minutes of "Golden Time"을 가리킨다.

08 문맥상 심장이 멈춘 후가 알맞다.

09 어떤 것을 양, 정도, 강도 등을 줄이거나 적게 되다: lower

10 such + a/an + 형용사 + 명사

11 how+to부정사: ~하는 방법, 어떻게 ~해야 할지

12 ⓒ와 ③은 to부정사의 형용사적 용법으로 쓰인 문장이다.

13 대개 훈련이나 기술이 필요한 행동이나 활동을 하다: 행하다, 실시하다(perform)

14 90도 각도가 되어야 한다고 언급되었다.

15 아무도 무엇을 해야 할지 몰랐다고 했으므로 세진이도 처음에는 다른 사람들처럼 겁이 났을 것이다.

16 him은 a man을 가리킨다.

17 tap ~ on the shoulder: ~의 어깨를 가볍게 두드리다

18 or는 앞에 있는 moving과 같은 구조의 단어로 이루어져야 하므로 breathe의 현재분사형 breathing이 되어야 한다.

19 호흡이 멈추고 심장 박동이 정지된 사람의 생명을 구하려고 시행하는 방법: 심폐소생술(CPR)

20 세진이는 그녀의 친구 진호와 함께 버스를 기다리고 있었다.

21 Are there + 복수명사 ~?: ~이 있나요?

22 within: ~ 이내에[안에]

23 the four minutes를 가리킨다.

24 「명사+of+동명사구」 구문으로 이때의 of는 동격을 나타낸다.

25 타이밍은 심폐소생술을 하는 것만큼 중요하다가 문맥상 알맞다.

26 전치사의 목적어로 동명사가 쓰인다.

27 세진이는 심폐소생술 과정을 보여 주고 있다.

28 목과 위 사이의 몸의 앞부분: 가슴(chest)

29 at a 90 degree angle: 90도 각도로

30 문맥상 push down(~을 누르다)이 알맞다.

서술형 시험대비 p.90~91

01 She is in the second grade.

02 Could you tell your experience to us?

03 in front of

04 I was as scared as the others at first.

05 on   06 She said to him, "Call 119."

07 to remember   08 that

09 누군가의 심장이 멈춘 후 4분 안에 심폐소생술을 시작해야 한다는 것을 의미한다.

10 (c)hances 11 as important as doing CPR

12 so

13 She had Safety Training Day at school last week.

14 I learned how to do CPR.

15 audience 16 will come → comes

17 팔을 쭉 펴고, 팔과 다른 사람의 가슴은 90도 각도로 하고, 구급차가 올 때까지 가슴 중앙을 세게 그리고 빨리 누른다.

01 세진이는 2학년이다.

02 tell+간접목적어+직접목적어 = tell+직접목적어+to+간접목적어

03 in front of: ~ 앞에

04 as + 형용사의 원급 +as: ~만큼 …한

05 tap ~ on the shoulder: ~의 어깨를 톡톡 치다

06 세진이는 진호에게 119에 전화하라고 말한 후, 심폐소생술을 시작했다.

07 any other things를 꾸며주는 to부정사의 형용사적 용법이다.

08 명사절을 이끄는 접속사 that이 알맞다.

09 It means that you should start CPR within four minutes after someone's heart stops.를 통해서 알 수 있다.

10 어떤 일이 일어날 가능성: 가능성(chance)

11 as + 형용사의 원급 +as: ~만큼 …한

12 such+a/an+형용사+명사 = so+형용사+a/an+명사

13 지난주 학교에서 안전 교육의 날이 있었다고 언급되었다.

14 how+to부정사: ~하는 방법

15 무언가를 보거나 듣기 위해 모인 사람들(연극, 콘서트, 말하는 사람 등): 청중(audience)

16 때를 나타내는 부사절은 미래의 일이라도 현재시제를 쓴다.

영역별 핵심문제 p.93~97

01 ⑤	02 ④	03 fall down
04 impressive	05 ③	06 ②
07 ②	08 ①, ②, ④	09 ⑤ 10 ②
11 ①	12 Don't forget to check the food label.	
13 ④	14 the food label	15 as[so], as
16 to	17 ③	18 ⑤
19 He plays tennis as well as Tom.		20 should begin
21 ②	22 ③	23 ⑤
24 not as[so] diligent as	25 ④	26 ①
27 yourself	28 Could you tell your experience to us?	
29 ③	30 Nobody knew what to do.	
31 ①	32 ③	33 are → is
34 ⑤	35 as low as you can	
36 Remember	37 ⑤	

01 ⑤는 유의어 관계이고, 나머지는 반의어 관계이다.

02 in front of: ~ 앞에 / in case of: ~의 경우에

03 fall down: 넘어지다

04 impressive: 인상적인

05 • 너는 "불이야!"라고 소리쳐야 한다. • 그 표지판은 무엇을 의미하니? • 날씨를 확인하는 것을 잊지 마라. • 너는 젖은 수건으로 너의 얼굴과 몸을 가려야 한다.

06 대개 훈련이나 기술이 필요한 행동이나 활동을 하다: 수행하다 (perform)

07 A가 태권도 수업에 간다고 하는 것에 대해 B는 '도복을 입고 가는 것을 잊지 마.'라고 하는 것이 자연스럽다.

08 빈칸에는 대화의 흐름상 상대방에게 상기시키거나 당부를 하는 말이 들어가는 것이 알맞다. 상기를 시키거나 당부를 하는 말에는 「Don't forget to+동사원형 ~.」, 「Make sure to+동사원

형 ~.」, 「Remember to+동사원형 ~.」이 있다.

09 금지의 표현은 명령문 「Don't+동사원형 ~.」을 사용하거나 「You shouldn't + 동사원형 ~. / You'd better not + 동사원형 ~.」으로 바꿔 쓸 수 있다.

10 상대에게 무엇인가 상기시키거나 당부하는 표현인 「Don't forget to+동사원형 ~.」에 대한 답은 Okay, thanks., Okay, I see., No, I won't. 등으로 한다.

11 사과 주스를 좀 사도 되겠냐는 요청의 말에 "Sure."는 '물론이지.'라는 뜻으로, 승낙하는 말이다. ①은 승낙의 표현이다.

12 부정명령문은 「Don't + 동사원형 ~.」으로 시작한다. '~하는 것을 잊다'는 「forget + to부정사」로 쓴다.

13 be good for: ~에 좋다

14 인칭대명사 it은 the food label을 가리킨다.

15 not as[so] ~ as: …만큼 ~하지 않다

16 to부정사는 의문사와 함께 쓰여 '~해야 하는지'의 뜻을 나타낸다.

17 「as+형용사+a(n)+명사 as ~」의 어순이므로 as great a statesman as ~가 되어야 한다.

18 ⑤ 「의문사+to부정사」 또는 「의문사+주어+should+동사원형」 (where should go → where to go 또는 where they should go)

19 '~만큼 잘'은 as well as로 나타낸다.

20 「의문사+to부정사」 구문은 「의문사+주어+should+동사원형」으로 바꿔 쓸 수 있다.

21 ②에서 두 번째 as 뒤에 오는 절의 주어가 George로 3인칭 단수이므로 do를 does로 바꾸어야 한다.

22 ⓓ 「who+to부정사」는 어색한 표현이므로, Do you know who will tell me about it?으로 바꿔 쓴다. ⓔ when to move는 언제 움직일지 시간에 관한 물음인데, yesterday와 쓰이면, 시간을 나타내는 부사가 중복되어 어색한 문장이 된다.

23 ⑤는 '~할 때'라는 뜻의 접속사이고 나머지는 as ~ as ... 구문의 부사로 쓰였다.

24 A is more+형용사의 원급+than B. = B is not as[so]+ 형용사의 원급+as A.

25 「what+to부정사 ~」는 「what+주어+should+동사원형 ~」으로 바꿔 쓸 수 있다.

26 just the same as는 as ~ as로 바꿔 쓸 수 있다.

27 명령문의 주어는 You이므로, You의 재귀대명사 yourself가 알맞다.

28 수여동사가 있는 3형식 문장은 「tell+직접목적어+to+간접목적어」 어순이다.

29 ⓒ wait for: ~을 기다리다 ⓓ in front of: ~ 앞에서

30 nobody: 아무도 ~ 않다 / what+to부정사: 무엇을 ~해야 할지

31 '~만큼 …한'의 뜻을 나타내는 동등비교이다.

32 그 노인이 어디를 가는 중이었는지는 알 수 없다.

33 there is + 단수명사: ~이 있다

34 with: ~으로

35 as ~ as possible: 가능한 한 ~하게(=as ~ as you can)

36 Don't forget to+동사원형 ~은 상대방에게 상기시키거나 당부하는 표현으로 Remember to+동사원형 ~.으로 바꿔 쓸 수 있다.

37 엘리베이터보다 계단을 이용해야 한다고 상기시키고 있다.

단원별 예상문제　　　　　　　　p.98~101

01 ②	02 putting on	03 ④	04 (b)reathe
05 ④	06 dangerous	07 ③	08 ⑤
09 you'd better not run		10 the sign	11 ⑤
12 buys → buy			13 ④
14 I am not as[so] pretty as you.			15 how to cook
16 ①	17 ③	18 as much as he used to	
19 ②	20 had a chance to practice		
21 ⑤	22 ④		
23 She learned how to do CPR.			24 ④
25 "골든타임" 4분	26 ③	27 (1) Begin → To begin[Beginning]　(2) save → saving	28 Timing

01 <보기>와 ②는 동사에 -ive를 붙여 형용사가 되는 단어들이다.

02 take off: ~을 벗다(↔ put on: ~을 입다)

03 ④는 degree의 영영풀이이다.

04 breathe: 호흡하다, 숨을 쉬다

05 at first: 처음에 / in case of: ~의 경우에

06 반의어 관계이다. 바닥 : 천장 = 위험한 : 안전한

07 You'd better not + 동사원형 ~은 '~하지 않는 게 좋겠다.'라는 의미로 금지하는 표현이다.

08 어떤 일을 상기시켜 주는 표현인 Don't forget to ~는 Remember to ~로 바꿔 쓸 수 있다.

09 You'd better not + 동사원형 ~: 너는 ~하지 않는 게 좋을 거야.

10 인칭대명사 it은 앞에 나온 단수명사를 받는다.

11 must be chosen을 수식해야 하므로 부사 형태가 알맞다.

12 「what to+동사원형」 형태이다.

13 모두 「의문사+to부정사」 구문으로 to가 빈칸에 들어가고, ④는 too ~ to부정사 구문으로 빈칸에 too가 들어간다.

14 A is not as[so] ~ as B: A는 B만큼 ~하지 않다

15 '요리하는 방법'을 배우고 싶다는 뜻이므로 「how+to부정사」로 나타낼 수 있다.

16 ① 두 번째의 as 뒤에 오는 절의 주어가 Mike로 3인칭 단수이므로 do를 does로 바꾸어야 한다.

17 '언제 꺼야 할지'라는 뜻으로 목적어 역할을 하는 「의문사 +to부정사」 형태가 되어야 한다.

18 '예전만큼 많이'는 as much as he used to로 나타낸다.

19 how to+동사원형: ~하는 방법

20 to부정사 to practice가 명사 a chance를 꾸며주는 역할을 한다.

21 「keep+목적어+목적격보어」 순으로 와야 한다.

22 until: ~할 때까지

23 세진이는 안전 교육의 날에 심폐소생술을 배웠다고 했다.

24 ④는 to부정사의 부사적 용법으로 목적을 나타내지만, ⓐ와 나머지는 앞에 나온 명사를 수식하는 형용사적 용법으로 사용되었다.

25 인칭대명사 It은 the four minutes of "Golden Time"을 가리킨다.

26 누군가의 심장이 멈춘 후가 되어야 하므로 after가 알맞다.

27 (1) 동사 will의 주어 역할을 해야 하므로 To begin[Beginning]이 되어야 한다. (2) 전치사의 목적어로 동명사 형태가 되어야 한다.

28 특히 결과에 좋거나 나쁜 영향을 미칠 것으로 여겨지는 어떤 것이 일어나거나 행해지는 시간: 타이밍(timing)

너무 많은 설탕은 너에게 좋지 않아. - (B) 네, 확인해 볼게요.

05 as ~ as ...는 동등비교를 나타낸다.

06 (1) '어느 것을 ~할 것인지'는 which to ~로 쓴다. make up one's mind 결정하다 (2) '언제 공부해야/놀아야 하는지'는 when to study/play로 나타낸다.

07 when: ~할 때 / there is + 단수명사: ~이 있다

08 with: ~으로

09 마르지 않은: 젖은(wet)

10 우리는 엘리베이터 대신에 계단을 사용해야 한다.

11 ⓐ how to+동사원형: ~하는 방법 ⓑ a chance를 꾸며 주는 형용사적 용법의 to부정사가 되어야 한다.

12 keep+목적어+목적격보어: ~을 …하게 유지하다

13 우리는 심폐소생술을 할 때 가슴 중앙을 눌러야 한다고 언급되었다.

서술형 실전문제 p.102~103

01 Remember / Don't forget

02 you shouldn't eat / you must not eat / don't eat

03 Don't forget to wear safety gear.

04 (C) – (E) – (A) – (D) – (B)

05 (1) Meg sings as well as you (do).

(2) This street is just as wide as that one.

(3) Seoul Tower is about three times as high as this tower.

(4) I can't[cannot] cook as well as my sister.

06 (1) I couldn't make up my mind which to choose.

(2) He doesn't know when to study/play and when to play/study.

07 when there is a fire

08 with   09 wet

10 No, we should use the stairs.

11 to   12 Keep your arms straight.

13 We push down in the center of the chest when we perform CPR.

01 '~하는 것을 잊지 마.'라는 표현은 「Make sure to+동사원형 ~.」, 「Remember to+동사원형 ~.」, 「Don't forget to+동사원형 ~.」 등이다.

02 You'd better not + 동사원형 ~.은 금지를 나타내는 표현으로 You shouldn't + 동사원형 ~. / You must not + 동사원형 ~. / Don't+동사원형 ~. 등으로 나타낼 수 있다.

03 Don't forget to + 동사원형 ~: ~하는 것을 잊지 마라.

04 (C) 엄마, 사과 주스 좀 사도 돼요? - (E) 물론, Chris. 식품 라벨을 확인하는 것을 잊지 마라. - (A) 식품 라벨요? - (D) 그래.

창의사고력 서술형 문제 p.104

|모범답안|

01 A: Excuse me. May I use this computer?

B: Yes, you may. But don't forget to turn it off.

A: All right.

A: Excuse me. May I borrow this book?

B: Yes, you may. But don't forget to return it.

A: All right.

A: Excuse me. May I ride my bike?

B: Yes, you may. But don't forget to ride slowly.

A: All right.

A: Excuse me. May I use my cell phone here?

B: Yes, you may. But don't forget to talk quietly.

A: All right.

A: Excuse me. May I eat here?

B: Yes, you may. But don't forget to pick up any trash.

A: All right.

02 (1) I am as popular as you.

(2) I run as fast as my brother does.

(3) I study as hard as you do.

(4) I am not as beautiful as Kate.

03 (1) I want to know how to make *gimbap*.

(2) I didn't know what to choose.

(3) I didn't decide where to stay during my trip.

(4) I told him when to leave.

02 「as+형용사/부사의 원급+as」와 「not as+형용사/부사의 원급+as」의 구문을 활용하여 자신의 입장에서 자유롭게 써 보도록 한다.

01 ④	02 ④	03 zoo keeper	04 ⑤
05 wait for	06 as, as possible		07 ②
08 ④	09 ③	10 ②, ④	11 ①, ③
12 ④	13 ①	14 ④	15 what to

15 what to say 16 ⑤ 17 should go there 18 harder → hard 19 ④ 20 as fast as 21 ⑤ 22 what to do 23 (s)cared 24 ⑤ 25 ③ 26 the four minutes of "Golden Time" 27 ⑤ 28 where 29 They taught us what to do when an earthquake hits

01 ④는 유의어 관계이고 나머지는 반의어 관계이다.

02 hold on to: ~을 꽉 잡다 / bump into: ~에 부딪히다

03 특히 동물원에서 동물을 돌보는 일을 하는 사람 : 동물원 사육사 [관리인](zoo keeper)

04 wear: 입다, 쓰다 / touch: 만지다 / pick: 고르다 / cross: 건너다

05 wait for: ~을 기다리다

06 as ~ as possible: 가능한 한 ~하게

07 상기시키거나 당부하는 말에 대한 대답은 OK, I won't (forget). / Don't worry. I won't forget. 등으로 표현한다.

08 You'd better not to ~는 금지하는 표현으로 You're not permitted to로 바꿔 쓸 수 있다.

09 Don't forget to ~. (~하는 것을 잊지 마.)는 꼭 해야 할 중요한 것을 상기시킬 때 쓰는 표현이다.

10 '~하는 것을 잊지 마라'라는 표현은 「Don't forget to+동사원형」, 「Remember to+동사원형」, 「Make sure to+ 동사원형」으로 한다.

11 '~하는 것을 잊지 마라'라는 「Don't forget to+동사원형」에 대한 응답은 Okay, I see., Thank you for reminding me., No, I won't. 등으로 한다.

12 B가 자기의 행동을 사과하고 있으므로 잘못된 행동을 금지하는 말이 와야 알맞다. ④ leave computers on: 컴퓨터를 켠 채로 두다

13 '어디서 경기 하는지', '어떻게 가는지'라는 의미로 where와 how가 알맞다.

14 ④ 원급 비교 「as+원급+as」: as와 as 사이에는 형용사나 부사의 원급이 와야 한다. heavier를 heavy로 고쳐야 한다.

15 「의문사+주어+should+동사원형」은 「의문사+to부정사」와 같은 의미이다.

16 ⑤ 동등 비교이므로 as ~ as ... 구문이 되어야 한다.

17 의문사 why는 to부정사와 함께 쓰이지 않는다. 대신 why로 「의문사+to부정사」의 의미를 나타내고자 할 때는 「why+주어 +should+동사」로 나타낸다.

18 동등 비교 as와 as 사이에는 형용사/부사의 원급 형태가 와야 한다.

19 ④ 「what+to부정사」의 구문으로 what이 to read의 목적어가 되므로 a book은 삭제해야 한다

20 '~만큼 …할 수 있다'는 as ~ as를 이용한 원급 비교로 나타낼 수 있다.

21 ⓐ be in the second grade: 2학년이다 ⓓ tap ~ on the shoulder: ~의 어깨를 가볍게 두드리다

22 what to+동사원형: 무엇을 ~해야 할지

23 뭔가를 두려워하거나 뭔가 나쁜 일이 일어날까봐 두려워하는: scared(무서워하는, 두려워하는)

24 세진이는 그 남자의 어깨를 가볍게 두드렸고 그가 움직이거나 숨을 쉬고 있지 않다는 것을 알게 되었다.

25 (A) such an + 형용사 + 명사 (B) keep + 목적어 + 목적격 보어(형용사) (C) any other things를 꾸며주는 to부정사의 형용사적 용법이다.

26 인칭대명사 It은 the four minutes of "Golden Time"을 가리킨다.

28 뒤에 go가 나왔으므로, 장소에 관한 내용이 와야 한다. 따라서 where to go가 어울린다.

29 선생님들은 우리에게 지진이 일어났을 때 무엇을 해야 하는지 가르쳐 주셨다고 언급되었다.

Lesson 3
Living a Healthy Life

시험대비 실력평가
p.112

01 ④ 02 ② 03 warm 04 ②
05 Both of 06 warm up 07 ② 08 second

01 ④는 -ive를 붙여 형용사형을 만들고 나머지는 -able을 붙여 형용사형을 만든다.

02 be good for: ~에 좋다 / focus on: ~에 집중하다

03 반의어 관계이다. 강한 : 약한 = 서늘한 : 따뜻한

04 신체적으로 편안함을 느끼게 하는: 편안한(comfortable)

05 both of: ~ 둘 다

06 운동이나 다른 활동을 위해 당신의 몸을 준비하기 위해 가벼운 운동을 하다: 준비 운동을 하다(warm up)

07 get over: 회복하다

08 second: (시간 단위인) 초; 두 번째의

서술형 시험대비
p.113

01 (1) forward (2) increase (3) advice (4) uncomfortable
02 (1) each other (2) more than (3) a little bit
03 (1) ride (2) reduce (3) count (4) download
04 (1) healthy (2) movable (3) comfortable
05 (1) get over (2) prepare for (3) am worried about
06 (1) (s)tretch (2) (h)abit (3) (s)witch (4) (r)elax

01 (1) 반의어 관계이다. ~ 전에 : ~ 후에 = 뒤로 : 앞으로 (2) 반의어 관계이다. 잘못된 : 틀린 = 줄다 : 증가하다 (3) 유의어 관계이다. 맛있는 : 맛있는 = 조언 : 조언 (4) 나타나다 : 사라지다 = 편안한 : 불편한

02 (1) each other: 서로 (2) more than: ~ 이상 (3) a little bit: 조금

03 (1) ride: 타다 (2) reduce: 줄이다 (3) count: 세다 (4) download: 다운로드하다

04 (1) healthy: 건강에 좋은 (2) movable: 움직이는 (3) comfortable: 편안한

05 (1) get over: 회복하다 (2) prepare for: ~을 준비하다 (3) be worried about: ~에 대해 걱정하다

06 (1) stretch: 스트레칭하다 (2) habit: 습관 (3) switch: 바꾸다 (4) relax: (근육 등의) 긴장을 풀다

교과서 Conversation

핵심 Check
p.114~115

1 (1) how to / not good at (2) how to make
2 (1) What / like to / riding
  (2) what, enjoy doing / fishing
  (3) do you do / enjoy drawing / How

교과서 대화문 익히기

Check(√) True or False
p.116

1 T 2 F 3 T 4 F

교과서 확인학습
p.118~119

Listen & Speak 1 A-1
something healthy, have, adivce / often eat, makes, good / how to / cut, into, put, into, pour, mix / should try

Listen & Speak 1 A-2
more than / to be, count, steps / can use, how to use / Can, show / download, with, check / will, using

Listen & Speak 2 A-1
What, doing / enjoy cooking / Sounds, can / can make

Listen & Speak 2 A-2
on weekends / take / What kind, take / taking, of, like / reduce

Listen & Speak 2 A-3
puppy / Her, really / with / enjoy taking, makes, healthy

Conversation A
have, speaking, preparing, for, ago, speaking in, about, cannot sleep

Conversation B
matter / stressed about / ride, when / how to ride / go out, can, Put, on, push, with / Like, feel better / riding, because

시험대비 기본평가   p.120

01 ②   02 ⑤   03 ②   04 ⓒ - ⓑ - ⓐ - ⓓ

01 건강에 좋은 주스를 만드는 방법을 아는지 묻고 있으므로 how to make가 들어가야 한다.

02 건강해지기 위해 하는 것으로 적절하지 않은 것을 고른다

03 Do you know how to + 동사원형 ~?은 능력 여부를 묻는 표현으로 Can you + 동사원형 ~?으로 바꿔 쓸 수 있다.

04 ⓒ 너는 강아지가 있니? - ⓑ 응. 그 강아지의 이름은 코코야. 난 강아지를 정말 좋아해. - ⓐ 너는 강아지와 함께 무엇을 하니? - ⓓ 난 강아지와 산책하는 걸 즐겨. 그것은 나를 건강하게 만들어.

시험대비 실력평가   p.121~122

01 ⑤   02 ⑤   03 ⓑ to ride ⓓ riding

04 riding[to ride] my longboard   05 ②

06 ③   07 ③   08 (감기에 걸렸을 때) 따뜻한 물을 마시는 것   09 I want to eat something healthy.

10 Eating[To eat] fresh salad   11 ①, ③

12 ②   13 ②   14 ③

01 주어진 문장은 '난 벌써 기분이 더 좋아졌어.'라는 의미로 롱보드를 타는 것이 재미있다는 문장 다음에 와야 한다.

02 ⓐ be stressed about: ~에 대해 스트레스를 받다 ⓒ with: ~로

03 ⓑ how+to부정사: ~하는 방법 ⓓ enjoy -ing: ~하는 것을 즐기다

04 인칭대명사 it은 riding[to ride] my longboard를 가리킨다.

05 ② 하나가 스트레스를 받을 때 무엇을 하는지는 알 수 없다.

06 How have you been?은 안부를 묻는 표현이고, 나머지는 슬픔, 불만족, 실망의 원인을 묻는 표현이다.

07 Do you know how to ~?: 상대방에게 어떤 일을 할 수 있는지 묻는 표현이다.

08 인칭대명사 It은 drinking warm water를 의미한다.

09 -thing으로 끝나는 부정대명사는 형용사가 뒤에서 수식한다.

10 인칭대명사 It은 Eating[To eat] fresh salad를 가리킨다.

11 능력 여부를 묻는 문장에는 Do you know how to ~?, Can you ~?, Are you good at ~? 등이 있다.

12 ⓐ prepare for: ~을 준비하다 ⓒ be worried about: ~에 대해 걱정하다

13 앞뒤 내용이 상반되므로 but이 알맞다.

14 글쓴이는 내일 있을 영어 시험이 걱정된다고 했으므로 스트레스를 받고 있을 것이다.

서술형 시험대비   p.123

01 People say that we should walk more than 10,000 steps.

02 너는 그것(스마트폰 앱)을 어떻게 사용하는지 아니? / 모범답안 Can you use it? / Are you good at using it?

03 app   04 It is to download the app.

05 taking

06 She enjoys taking pictures of nature, like trees and flowers.

07 such as   08 (r)educe

01 매일 10,000 걸음 이상을 걸어야 한다고 말한다.

02 Do you know how to + 동사원형 ~?은 능력 여부를 묻는 표현으로 Can you + 동사원형 ~? / Are you good at + (동)명사 ~? 등으로 바꿔 쓸 수 있다.

03 특정한 일을 하도록 고안된 컴퓨터 프로그램, 특히 스마트폰에서 사용할 수 있는 프로그램: app(앱)

04 스마트폰 앱을 사용하는 첫 번째 단계는 앱을 다운로드하는 것이라고 언급되었다.

05 enjoy는 동명사를 목적어로 취한다.

06 소녀는 나무와 꽃 같은 자연의 사진을 찍는 것을 즐긴다고 했다.

07 like: ~ 같은(=such as)

08 어떤 것의 크기, 양, 수 등이 작아지게 하다: reduce(줄이다)

교과서
Grammar

핵심 Check   p.124~125

1 (1) melt   (2) do   (3) ring   (4) to come

2 (1) will give   (2) If   (3) takes   (4) drink

01 (1) If I go to France　(2) If it rains tomorrow

02 (1) to look → look　(2) to write → write

　(3) to go → go

03 (1) Unless you leave　(2) If it doesn't rain

04 (1) me go out after dinner

　(2) the children play outside

　(3) the bear stand on the ball

01 조건의 부사절은 「If+주어+동사 ~」의 어순으로 쓴다.

02 사역동사 have, make, let은 목적격 보어로 동사원형을 취한다.

03 「if+주어+don't[doesn't]+동사원형 ~」은 「unless+주어+동사의 현재형 ~」으로 바꿔 쓸 수 있 다.

04 「사역동사(let, have, make)+목적어+동사원형」의 형태에 유의하여 주어진 문장을 「목적어+동사원형」 형태로 완성한다.

01 ③　　02 ①　　03 ⑤　　04 ⑤

05 to do → do　　06 ③　　07 I helped

my mom (to) do the dishes. 08 ③　　09 ③

10 ④　　11 ④　　12 will rain → rains

13 ③　　14 His smile always makes me smile.

15 ③　　16 ①　　17 ②　　18 you

stop　　19 ②　　20 Judy makes her

brother study math.　21 ③　　22 Unless

you like the food　　23 My father helped me

carry the heavy bag.　24 ⑤

01 「주어+동사+목적어+목적격보어」로 구성된 5형식 문장이므로 사역동사 have의 목적격보어로 쓰일 수 있는 동사원형의 형태가 알맞다.

02 '만약 ~하면'의 조건절을 이끄는 접속사와 '~인지 아닌지'의 명사절을 이끄는 접속사 역할을 하는 if가 적절하다.

03 make가 5형식 문장에 쓰이면 목적격 보어로 형용사 또는 동사원형이 올 수 있다.

04 가까운 미래의 상황을 가정하거나 조건을 나타낼 때 if절은 현재시제로, 종속절은 미래시제로 써야 한다.

05 사역동사 make는 목적격 보어로 동사원형을 취한다.

06 if 조건절은 의미가 미래이더라도 현재시제를 쓴다.

07 help는 준사역동사로 목적격 보어로 동사원형이나 to부정사 둘 다 취할 수 있다.

08 조건을 나타내는 if절에서는 현재시제가 미래의 일을 나타내므로 ③이 알맞다.

09 let, have, make, help는 모두 목적격보어로 동사원형을 취한다. want는 to부정사를 목적격보어로 취한다.

10 If ~ not은 Unless와 의미가 같다.

11 ④는 4형식 문장에 쓰인 수여동사이며, 나머지는 5형식 문장에 쓰인 불완전 타동사이다.

12 조건을 나타내는 if는 미래시제 will과 쓰지 못한다.

13 조건을 나타내는 if 부사절에서는 미래의 일이라도 현재시제를 사용한다.

14 make+목적어+동사원형

15 두 빈칸 모두 동사의 자리이고, 다음에 him이라는 목적어가 나온다. 목적격보어로 'to+동사원형'이 나왔으므로 get이 들어가야 맞다. 동사원형이 목적격보어로 오는 경우 사역동사는 해당되지 않는다. help는 의미상 어울리지 않는다.

16 if ~ not = unless: 만약 ~하지 않으면

17 첫 번째 빈칸에는 사역동사가 들어가야 하고, 두 번째 빈칸에는 사역동사의 목적격보어인 동사원형이 들어가야 한다. 사역동사 let, have, make는 모두 뒤에 동사원형을 동반한다. take care of: ~를 돌보다

18 if ~ not = unless

19 사역동사 make, let과 help는 모두 목적격보어로 동사원형을 쓴다. (② to go → go) ③ 「ask+목적어+to부정사」 형태이다.

21 ③ 조건을 나타내는 if절에서는 현재시제가 미래시제를 대신한다. will leave → leave

22 '만약 ~하지 않는다면'이라는 의미의 「If+주어+don't [doesn't]+동사원형 ~」은 「Unless+주어+동사의 현재형 ~」으로 바꿔 쓸 수 있다.

23 사역동사 help 다음에는 동사원형이나 to부정사가 쓰인다.

24 대화 속의 밑줄 친 make와 ⑤는 사역동사이다.

01 (1) (to) carry　(2) get　(3) help　(4) to show

02 (1) If　(2) when　(3) Unless

03 (1) to explain → explain　(2) fell → fall

　(3) played → play

04 (1) If I am late for class, my teacher gets very angry.

　(2) If the weather is nice, I always walk to school.

　(3) If it rains on weekends, we watch TV.

05 Mom doesn't let me go out at night.

06 I made my younger[little] brother turn off the TV.

07 (1) If you study hard　(2) If it rains

08 (1) Finally, the police let the thief go.

　(2) Love makes people do unusual things.

　(3) I got my dog to wear strange glasses.

　(4) My English teacher helps us (to) write a diary every day.

09 (1) you'll pass → you pass

　(2) I won't be → I'm not / I am not

21

10 (1) My parents let me play computer games every Friday.

(2) My teacher made me wash my hands.

(3) My mom didn't let me go out.

11 (1) If it rains tomorrow, we won't go hiking.

(2) Unless you hurry, you will miss the train.

12 (1) Eddie lets his brother play with his toys.

(2) She makes her children study English.

(3) Dad has us cook breakfast on Sundays.

13 If she doesn't study hard, she will fail the exam.

01 (1) help+목적어+(to)동사원형 (2) get+목적어+to부정사 (3) let+목적어+동사원형 (4) 보여줄 그림들이라는 의미의 to부정사의 형용사적 용법이 적절하다.

02 when은 때, if는 조건을 나타낸다. unless는 if ~ not의 뜻이다.

03 5형식 문장에서 사역동사 let, make, have의 목적격보어는 동사원형을 써야 한다.

04 if는 종속절을 이끄는 접속사이다.

06 「사역동사+목적어+목적격보어(동사원형)」 어순으로 써야 한다.

07 '만약 ~한다면'이라는 의미로 조건을 나타내는 표현은 「if+ 주어+동사의 현재형」으로 나타낸다.

08 (1), (2) let, make는 사역동사로 목적격보어 자리에는 동사원형이 와야 한다. (3) get은 목적격보어 자리에 'to+동사원형'이 온다. (4) help는 목적격보어로 동사원형 또는 to부정사를 쓴다.

09 조건의 if절에서는 미래의 일을 현재시제로 나타낸다.

10 (1) 「let+목적어+동사원형(…이 ~하도록 허락하다)」 (2) 「make+목적어+동사원형(…이 ~하게 하다)」 (3) 「don't let+목적어+동사원형(…이 ~하도록 허락하지 않다)」

11 (1) if 이하가 조건절이므로, 현재시제가 미래시제를 대신한다. (2) unless는 '만약 ~하지 않으면'의 뜻이므로 not을 붙일 필요가 없다

12 사역동사 have, make, let은 목적격 보어로 동사원형을 사용한다.

13 콤마가 있으므로 if절을 주절 앞에 둔다.

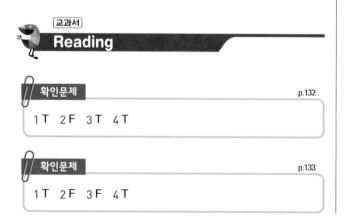

교과서 Reading

확인문제   p.132

1 T 2 F 3 T 4 T

확인문제   p.133

1 T 2 F 3 F 4 T

01 At, for   02 get tired

03 Why don't, yourself   04 Let's, with

05 Close, massage, with   06 will relax

07 When, cover, with, block out

08 make, feel, comfortable   09 massage

10 Put, on   11 Draw, with, to 12 from, to

13 help, feel   14 Let's, waist   15 Team up

16 each other, faces   17 Hold

18 stretch, backward   19 Hold, for

20 pull, to   21 your, at   22 If, both of

23 Place, on, behind   24 bend, lower

25 Hold, a few, up   26 loosen up

27 Switch, repeat 28 How, feel

29 massage, stretch, feel healthier 30 focus on, better

교과서 확인학습 B   p.136~137

1 At school you sit for many hours.

2 Do you get tired?

3 Why don't you massage yourself and stretch?

4 Let's begin with the eyes.

5 Close your eyes and massage them softly with your fingers.

6 It will relax your eyes.

7 When you finish, cover your eyes with your hands to block out the light.

8 It will make your eyes feel more comfortable.

9 Next, massage your neck.

10 Put your fingers on the back of your neck.

11 Draw small circles with your fingers to massage your neck.

12 Massage from top to bottom.

13 The massage will help you feel better.

14 Let's work on your waist.

15 Team up with a friend.

16 Stand close to each other and face your partner.

17 Hold each other's wrists.

18 Slowly stretch your head and body backward.

19 Hold that position for three seconds.

20 Then, slowly pull each other to a standing position.

21 You and your partner should move at the same speed.

22 If you don't, both of you will fall!

23 Place the top of your right foot on the desk behind you.

24 Then, slowly bend your left leg and lower yourself.

25 Hold it for a few seconds and slowly straighten up.

26 This position will loosen up your right leg.

27 Switch your legs and repeat the exercise.

28 How do you feel now?

29 If you massage yourself and stretch every day, you will feel healthier.

30 Also, you can focus on your studies better.

시험대비 실력평가　　　　　p.138~141

01 ③	02 ②	03 your eyes	04 stretch
05 ⑤	06 ③	07 ⓑ for　ⓔ of	
08 position	09 ②	10 ⑤	11 ③
12 ③	13 slowly	14 ④	15 ⓑ → ⓒ → ⓐ
16 softly	17 눈을 감고 손으로 눈을 부드럽게 마사지하는 것	18 ③	19 ④
20 make your eyes feel more comfortable		21 ②	
22 ③	23 feeling → feel[to feel]		24 waist
25 ③	26 ②	27 ⑤	28 ③
29 yourself	30 switch	31 ⑤	

01 for many hours: 오랜 시간 동안 / block out: (빛을) 차단하다

02 get tired: 피곤하다

03 인칭대명사 them은 your eyes를 가리킨다.

04 팔, 다리 등을 근육이 길고 단단해지도록 하는 자세에 놓다: stretch(스트레칭하다)

05 인칭대명사 It은 앞에 나온 문장 cover your eyes with your hands to block out the light를 가리킨다.

06 ⓐ, ③: 마주보다, ①, ④: 얼굴, ②: 직면하다, ⑤: 표면

07 for three seconds: 3초 동안 / both of: ~ 둘 다

08 어떤 사람이 서거나 앉거나 눕는 방식 : position(자세)

09 '만약 ~하면'의 뜻으로 조건절을 이끄는 접속사 if가 알맞다.

10 두 사람이 같은 속도로 움직이지 않으면, 두 사람은 넘어질 것이라고 언급되어 있다.

11 명령문은 상대방, 즉 2인칭에게 하는 말이므로 재귀대명사는 yourself가 되어야 한다.

12 ③ bend(구부리다): 몸을 움직여 구부리다 ① mix ② switch ④ place ⑤ stretch

13 동사를 수식하는 부사 형태가 되어야 한다

14 straighten up: 똑바로 하다 / loosen up: (몸·근육을) 풀어 주다

15 뒤에 있는 책상 위에 오른쪽 발등을 올려놓고 천천히 왼쪽 다리를 구부리고 몸을 낮추고 그 상태로 몸을 낮춘 상태로 몇 초 동안 유지한다.

16 동사를 수식하는 부사 형태가 되어야 한다.

17 인칭대명사 It은 앞 문장 Close your eyes and massage them softly with your fingers.를 가리킨다.

18 빛을 차단하기 위해 눈을 가려라가 문맥상 적절하므로 cover가 알맞다.

19 목적을 나타내는 부사적 용법의 to부정사 형태가 되어야 한다.

20 make + 목적어 + 목적격 보어(동사원형): ~을 …하게 하다 / feel+형용사: ~하게 느끼다

21 목을 마사지하는 방법은 '목 뒤에 손가락을 대고(Put), 목을 마사지하기 위해 손가락으로 작은 원을 그리고(Draw), 위에서 아래로 마사지해라(Massage)'는 순서가 알맞다.

22 <보기>와 ③은 목적을 나타내는 부사적 용법의 to부정사이다. 나머지는 명사적 용법이다

23 동사 help는 목적격 보어로 동사원형이나 to부정사를 쓸 수 있다.

24 갈비뼈와 엉덩이 사이의 신체 중앙 부분: 허리

25 머리와 몸을 뒤로 뻗어라가 알맞다. forward → backward

26 ⓑ, ②: (시간 단위인) 초 ①: 두 번째로 ③,⑤: 두 번째의 ④: 둘째의[제2의]

27 ⓒ should: ~해야 한다 ⓓ 조건을 나타내는 접속사 if 문장에서 주절에는 미래형을 쓴다.

28 주어진 문장의 it은 왼쪽 다리를 구부리고 몸을 낮춘 자세를 가리키므로 ③이 알맞다.

29 재귀대명사 yourself가 되어야 한다.

30 어떤 것에서 다른 것으로 바꾸다[전환하다]: 바꾸다 (switch)

31 문맥상 몸을 풀어 주다라는 의미를 가진 loosen up이 알맞다.

서술형 시험대비　　　　　p.142~143

01 Why don't you massage

02 massage　03 comfortably → comfortable

04 We can cover our eyes with our hands.

05 to massage　　　　　06 from

07 The massage will help you feel better.

08 ⓒ → ⓐ → ⓑ　　　　09 (l)ower

10 왼쪽 다리를 구부리고 몸을 낮춘 자세　　11 up

12 이 자세는 여러분의 오른쪽 다리를 풀어 줄 것이다.

13 (f)ace　　14 여러분의 머리와 몸을 뒤로 뻗은 자세

15 push → pull　　　　16 They will fall.

01 Why don't you + 동사원형 ~?: ~하는 게 어때?

02 근육의 긴장을 풀어 주거나 근육과 관절의 통증을 완화 시키기

위해 몸을 문지르거나 눌러 주다: 마사지하다 (massage)

03 feel+형용사: ~하게 느끼다

04 빛을 막기 위해 우리는 우리의 눈을 가릴 수 있다고 언급되었다.

05 목적을 나타내는 to부정사의 부사적 용법이다.

06 from A to B: A부터 B까지

07 help+목적어+목적격보어(동사원형/to+동사원형); ~가 …하는 것을 돕다 / feel better: 기분이 나아지다

08 목 뒷부분에 손가락을 대고, 목을 마사지하기 위해 손가락으로 작은 원을 그린 후, 위에서 아래로 마사지한다.

09 뭔가를 위쪽에서 아래로 이동시키다: 낮추다(lower)

11 straighten up: 똑바로 하다

12 loosen up: 몸을 풀어 주다

13 얼굴과 몸을 어떤 것 또는 어떤 사람을 향해 서거나 앉다: 마주 보다

14 밑줄 친 부분은 stretching your head and body backward 를 가리킨다.

15 천천히 서로 서 있는 위치로 끌어당겨라가 문맥상 알맞다. push → pull

16 같은 속도로 움직이지 않으면, 두 사람은 넘어질 것이라고 언급 되어 있다.

영역별 핵심문제

p.145~149

01 ④	02 ②	03 team up	
04 massage	05 ③	06 ⑤	07 ④
08 ②	09 ③	10 ③	11 (C) –

(A) – (D) – (B)　　12 ⓐ feel ⓑ to make

13 ④　　14 ③　　15 It is to put small pieces of vegetables into a bowl.　　16 ③

17 ⑤　　18 ③　　19 What will you do if he visits your home tomorrow? 20 ②　　21 ②

22 She has the children play soccer.　　23 ④

24 ③　　25 changing → change　　26 If Jenny does not get up now, she will miss the train. 또는 Jenny will miss the train if she does not get up now.　　27 ⑤　　28 ②　　29 with

30 ④　　31 make your eyes feel　　32 ④

33 wrists　　34 ④　　35 ⑤　　36 how to stretch　　37 (A) First (B) Then (C) Finally

38 너의 팔로 숫자 2를 만드는 것　　39 ④

01 ④는 유의어 관계이고 나머지는 반의어 관계이다.

02 몸을 움직여 구부리다: 구부리다(bend)

03 team up with: ~와 협력하다

04 근육과 관절의 통증을 줄이기 위해 손으로 사람의 몸을 문지르고 누르는 행동: 마사지(massage)

05 • 시청에 가려면 어떤 방법이 가장 좋을까요?. • 나는 경기장으

로 가는 길을 모른다.

06 loosen up: (몸을) 풀어 주다 / block out: (햇빛을) 차단하다

07 방과 후에 무엇을 하는 것을 즐기냐고 물었으므로, 대답으로는 방과 후에 할 수 있는 활동에 대해 말하는 것이 적절하다.

08 '~하는 방법'은 「how to+동사원형」으로 나타낸다.

09 음악의 종류로 답했으므로 '너는 어떤 종류의 음악을 좋아하니?'라고 묻는 것이 알맞다.

10 A: 수학 문제 푸는 것 잘하니? B: 아니, 나 수학 잘 못해.

11 (C) 방과 후에 뭐 하는 걸 즐기니? (A) 나는 건강에 좋은 음식을 요리하 는 것을 즐겨. (D) 멋지구나. 너는 무엇을 만들 수 있니? (B) 나는 샐러드, 비빔 밥 그리고 야채 주스를 만들 수 있어.

12 ⓐ 사역동사 make의 목적격보어로 동사원형을 쓴다. ⓑ how+to부정사: ~하는 방법

13 cut A into B: A를 B로 자르다

14 순서를 열거하는 문장이므로 First, Then, Finally 순으로 오는 것이 알맞다.

15 신선한 샐러드를 만드는 두 번째 단계는 채소의 작은 조각들을 그릇에 담는 것이다.

16 문장의 구조로 보아 목적어와 목적격보어(원형부정사)를 갖는 5형식 문장이므로 사역동사 made가 빈칸에 들어가야 한다.

17 접속사 if가 '~한다면'으로 해석되면 부사절을 이끌고, '~인지 아닌지'로 해석되면 명사절을 이끈다. 주어진 문장과 ⑤의 if는 명사절을 이끄는 접속사이다.

18 ①, ②, ④, ⑤의 밑줄 친 동사는 모두 사역동사로 쓰였으나, ③의 have는 '가지고 있다'의 일반동사로 쓰였다.

19 미래의 일이므로 주절에서는 미래시제를 나타낸다.

20 ①, ③, ④, ⑤는 사역동사 구문인데, ②의 told는 목적격보어로 to부정사를 사용하는 동사이다.

21 '만약 ~하면'의 뜻으로 조건절을 이끄는 접속사와 '~인지 아닌지'의 뜻으로 명사절을 이끄는 접속사 역할을 하는 if가 알맞다.

22 사역동사 have는 목적격보어로 동사원형을 쓴다.

23 <보기>와 ④는 사역동사로 '(목적어)를 ~하게 만들다'라는의미로 쓰였다. ① make it: 해내다 ② make money: 돈을 벌다 ③ make: 만 들어 주다(수여동사) ⑤ make an effort: 노력하다

24 ③ 조건을 나타내는 if절에서는 현재시제가 미래시제를 대신한다.

25 어떤 것도 나의 마음을 바꾸게 하지 않을 것이다.

26 첫 문장이 두 번째 문장의 조건이 되므로 접속사 if를 이용하여 연결한다.

27 ①~④는 내용상 조건을 나타내는 접속사 if가 와야 하고, ⑤는 동사 think의 목적어 역할을 하는 접속사 that이 적절하다.

28 (A) for + 숫자를 나타내는 기간 (B) 목적어가 주어 자신이 므로 재귀대명사 yourself가 알맞다. (C) 목적을 나타내는 to부정사 형태가 되어야 한다.

29 ⓐ begin with: ~부터 시작하다 ⓑ with: ~으로

---

30 빛을 차단하기 위해서 눈을 가리라는 의미가 되는 것이 흐름상 알맞다. open → close

31 make+목적어+목적격 보어(동사원형)

32 team up with: ~와 협력하다

33 손과 팔이 잇닿은 부분: 손목(wrist)

34 that position은 여러분의 머리와 몸을 뒤로 뻗는 것을 가리키므로 ④번이 알맞다.

35 미래를 표현할 때 주절에서는 미래시제를 쓴다.

36 '~하는 방법'이라는 뜻으로 「how to+동사원형」을 쓴다.

37 순서를 열거할 때 First(우선, 먼저), Then(그런 다음), Finally(마지막으로) 순으로 표현한다.

38 인칭대명사 It은 앞 문장의 내용을 받는다.

39 앞뒤 내용이 상반되는 내용이므로 but이 알맞다.

단원별 예상문제
p.150~153

01 ③	02 bottom	03 ⑤	04 ④

05 (1) a few seconds (2) take a walk (3) What kind of   06 ③   07 ②   08 to be

09 Do you know how to use it?   10 Later

11 the smartphone app   12 ⑤   13 ④

14 ②   15 ④   16 ⑤   17 ⑤

18 If it is, will go   19 had Martin read

20 top   21 ④   22 ⑤   23 ④

24 to   25 warm up   26 for   27 ⓐ Place

ⓑ bend ⓒ Hold   28 ①   29 ⑤

30 ④

---

01 <보기>와 ③은 -able를 붙여 형용사형이 되는 단어이고, 나머지는 -ive를 붙여 형용사가 되는 단어들이다.

02 반의어 관계이다. 단순한 : 복잡한 = 꼭대기 : 맨 아래

03 focus on: ~에 집중하다 / straighten up: 똑바로 하다

04 어떤 것이 긴장, 팽팽함, 경직성이 줄어들게 하다: relax(근육 등의) 긴장을 풀다

05 (1) for a few seconds: 몇 초 동안 (2) take a walk: 산책하다 (3) what kind of: 어떤 종류의

06 Do you know how to + 동사원형 ~?은 능력 여부를 묻는 표현이다.

07 여가 시간에 무엇을 하느냐는 질문에 나는 영어와 수학 공부하는 것을 싫어한다는 대답은 어색하다.

08 목적을 나타내는 to부정사의 부사적 용법이다.

09 Do you know how to + 동사원형 ~?: ~하는 방법을 아니?(능력 여부를 묻는 표현)

10 later: 나중에

11 인칭대명사 it은 the smartphone app을 가리킨다.

12 사역동사 let은 목적격보어로 동사원형을 취한다.

13 ④ make는 5형식을 이끄는 사역동사이므로 practicing을

---

14 if로 시작하는 조건절에서는 현재시제가 미래시제를 대신한다.

15 ④ 사역동사 make는 목적어 다음에 목적격보어로 동사원형이 온다.

16 '주말마다'는 반복적인 습관을 나타내므로 현재시제를 사용한다.

17 첫 번째 문장은 이유, 두 번째 문장은 조건을 나타낸다.

18 조건의 부사절에서는 현재시제가 미래시제를 대신한다. 날씨를 말할 때는 비인칭 주어 it을 사용한다.

19 「have+목적어+동사원형」의 사역동사 구문이다.

20 어떤 것의 윗면

21 place A on B: A를 B 위에 놓다

22 a few+복수 명사

23 주어진 문장의 This position은 몇 초 동안 왼쪽 다리를 구부리고 몸을 낮추는 자세를 가리키므로 ④번이 알맞다.

24 ⓐ how to부정사: ~하는 방법 ⓑ 목적을 나타내는 to부정사의 부사적 용법

25 스포츠나 그 밖의 활동을 준비하려고 하는 운동이나 일련의 운동을 하다: 준비 운동을 하다(warm up)

26 be good for: ~에 좋다

27 ⓐ place: 놓다, 두다 ⓑ bend: 구부리다 ⓒ hold: 유지하다

28 straighten up: 똑바로 하다 / focus on: ~에 집중하다

29 문맥상 여러분의 오른쪽 다리를 풀어줄 것이라는 내용이 알맞다.

30 also: 또한

서술형 실전문제
p.154~155

01 Do you know how to massage

02 I enjoy playing catch.

03 I am not good at math.

04 (D)−(C)−(A)−(B)

05 (1) I will have my brother clean my room.

(2) Inhui made her daughter do the dishes.

(3) My mother let me watch the TV drama.

06 (1) If you have a fever, you should see a doctor.

(2) If it rains tomorrow, I will go to a movie.

(3) If you add yellow to blue, it becomes green.

07 (1) My mother makes me clean my room.

(2) The librarian helped me find a book.

(3) They let her go safely.

08 We massage our eyes softly.

09 그것은 여러분의 눈을 더 편안하게 해 줄 것이다.

10 We can draw small circles with our fingers.

11 The massage will help you feel better.

12 are → is

13 He[She] plans to exercise more than three times a week.

14 나의 습관을 바꾸는 것

15 make me live a healthy life

01 Do you know how to + 동사원형 ～?: 너는 ～하는 방법을 아니?

02 I enjoy -ing ～.: 나는 ～하는 것을 즐긴다.

03 능력을 부인하는 표현으로 I'm not good at을 사용할 수 있다.

04 (D) 너는 방과 후에 뭐 하는 걸 즐기니? (C) 나는 건강에 좋은 음식을 요리하는 것을 즐겨. (A) 멋지구나. 너는 무엇을 만들 수 있니? (B) 나는 샐러드, 비빔밥 그리고 야채 주스를 만들 수 있어.

05 have, make, let 등 사역동사는 목적어 다음에 목적격보어로 동사원형을 쓴다.

06 (1) see a doctor: 진찰을 받다 (2) go to a movie: 영화 보러 가다 (3) add A to B: B에 A를 섞다

07 (1) makes가 사역동사이므로 목적격보어로 clean이 들어 가야 한다. (2) help는 목적격보어로 동사원형을 쓴다. (3) let은 사역동사로 목적격보어는 동사원형이 온다.

08 눈을 손가락으로 부드럽게 마사지한다.

09 사역동사 make+목적어+목적격보어(동사원형): ～을 …하게 만들다 / feel+형용사: ～하게 느끼다

10 목을 마사지하기 위해 손가락으로 작은 원을 그릴 수 있다.

11 help+목적어+목적격보어(동사원형/to부정사): ～가 …하는 것을 돕다 / feel better: 기분이 좋아지다

12 Here is + 단수 명사 ～: 여기 ～이 있다

13 글쓴이는 일주일에 세 번 이상 운동할 것이라고 했다.

14 인칭대명사 it은 changing[to change] my habits를 가리킨다.

15 사역동사 make+목적어+목적격보어(동사원형) / live a healthy life: 건강한 삶을 살다

창의사고력 서술형 문제
p.156

|모범답안|

01 (1) Do you know how to shop on the Internet? / No, I don't know how to shop on the Internet.

(2) Do you know how to cook instant noodles? / Yes, I know how to cook instant noodles.

02 (1) If I go to Paris, I can see the Eiffel Tower.

(2) If it is sunny tomorrow, I will go hiking with my friends.

(3) If I find an abandoned dog on the street, I will take it to the animal center.

03 (1) My mother let me go to the amusement park.

(2) Jenny made my brother run fast.

(3) My friend helped me (to) do my homework.

(4) My grandparents had me wait so long.

단원별 모의고사
p.157~160

01 ⑤	02 ③	03 ④	04 simple
05 (a)dvice	06 ⑤	07 ②, ⑤	08 ②
09 ②, ④	10 ③	11 한쪽 발을 보드 위에 올려 놓고 다른 한 발로 세게 민다.	12 ③
13 feels → feel		14 ①	15 ④
16 My brother had me clean[sweep] the room.			
17 Unless	18 ②	19 ①	20 ①
21 ④	22 ①	23 Massage from top to bottom.	24 ④
25 ③	26 position		
27 won't → don't		28 ⑤	29 ②
30 to feel → feel			

01 각각의 팔 끝과 목 사이에 있는 신체의 두 부분 중 하나: 어깨 (shoulder)

02 ③ for a few seconds: 수 초 동안

03 face: 얼굴; ～와 마주 보다

04 반의어 관계이다. 배고픈 : 배부른 = 복잡한 : 단순한

05 누군가에게 어떻게 하라고 알려 주는 말이나 제안: 조언, 충고 (advice)

06 능력 여부를 묻는 말에는 Do you know how to ～?, Can you ～?, Are you good at ～? 등이 있다.

07 I enjoy -ing ～는 좋아하는 것을 말하는 표현으로 I like to + 동사원형 ～. / I feel great when I + 동사원형 ～ 으로 바꿔 쓸 수 있다.

08 when: ～할 때 / because: ～이기 때문에

09 Do you know how to + 동사원형 ～?은 능력 여부를 묻는 표현으로 ①, ③, ⑤와 바꿔 쓸 수 있다.

10 the other: (둘 중에서) 다른 하나

11 Put one foot on the board and push hard with the other.에서 알 수 있다.

12 '～하면'이라는 조건의 접속사가 필요하다.

13 make는 사역동사로 목적격보어로 동사원형을 쓴다. 따라서 동사 feels는 원형인 feel로 써야 한다.

14 사역동사 let은 목적격보어로 동사원형(cross)을 쓴다.

15 ④ 조건을 나타내는 if절은 미래의 의미이더라도 현재시제로 써야 한다.

16 사역동사 have+목적어+동사원형: ～하도록 시키다

17 If ～ not은 '～하지 않는다면'이라는 의미로 Unless와 같다.

18 ②는 직접목적어와 간접목적어가 있는 4형식 문장이고 나머지는 모두 5형식 문장이다.

19 ② 미래의 일이므로 조건을 나타내는 문장의 주절은 미래시제를 사용한다.

20 문맥상 오른쪽 발등이 되어야 한다. ⓐ bottom → top

21 loosen up: (근육을) 풀어 주다

22 put A on B: A를 B 위에 놓다[대다]

23 from top to bottom: 위에서 아래로

24 파트너를 마주 보고(face), 머리와 몸을 뒤로 뻗고 (stretch), 서로 서 있는 자세로 끌어당긴다(pull)가 옳다.

25 for three seconds: 3초 동안 / at the same speed: 같은 속도로

26 어떤 사람이 서거나 앉거나 눕는 방식: 자세(position)

27 조건의 부사절에서는 미래시제 대신 현재시제를 사용한다.

28 주어진 문장의 It은 massaging[to massage] your eyes softly with your fingers를 가리키므로 ⑤번이 알맞다.

29 block out: (빛을) 차단하다

30 make+목적어+목적격보어(동사원형)

To Be a Global Citizen

시험대비 실력평가   p.164

01 far	02 ①	03 ④	04 ④
05 ②	06 ③	07 (E)ducation	
08 (g)lobal	09 (1) kind, bag	(2) sell	

01 둘은 반의어 관계이다. more: 더 많이 less: 더 적게 far: 멀리; 먼 near: 가까운

02 flood: 홍수 / 그 폭우로 홍수가 났다.

03 community: 공동체, 지역[공동] 사회 / 매우 큰 지역 사회는 도시라고 불린다.

04 upload: 업로드하다 / 인터넷을 사용해서 문서나 프로그램을 컴퓨터에서 더 큰 시스템으로 보내다

05 citizen: 시민 / 합법적으로 어떤 나라나 마을에 살고 있는 사람

06 ① garden: 정원 / 너는 올해 정원에 장미를 심을 거니? ② Kenyan: 케냐의 / Charlie는 케냐의 중학교에 입학했다. ③ hold: (회의나 시합 등을) 열다 / 올해 그 마을은 축제를 열 것이다. ④ lantern: 랜턴, 제등 / 그녀는 멀리서 랜턴 불빛을 보았다. ⑤ poor: 가난한 / 많은 근로자들은 빈곤 지역 출신이다.

07 education: 교육

08 global: 전 세계적인, 지구상의

09 (1) kind: 종류 bag: 가방 (2) sell: 팔다

서술형 시험대비   p.165

01 (1) The cars are moving alongside us.
  (2) Citizens of the same country have the same nationality.
  (3) The heavy rain resulted in the flood.
  (4) We decided to raise money for the needy people.

02 (1) rcommunicate   (2) gathered   (3) celebrated
(4) left   03 (1) hunger   (2) national   04 care
05 (1) is good at solving   (2) Thanks to   (3) going, turn down   (4) (c)elebrate

01 (1) alongside: ~ 옆에, ~와 나란히 (2) citizen: 시민 (3) flood: 홍수 (4) raise: (자금 등을) 모으다, 모금하다

02 (1) communicate: 의사소통하다 / 우리는 서로 영어로 의사

소통한다. (2) gather: 모으다 / 그는 인터넷에서 정보를 모았다. (3) celebrate: (특별한 날·경사 등을) 축하하다, 기념하다 / 그녀는 작년에 내 생일을 축하해줬다. (4) leave: 남기다 / 그는 어제 접시에 음식을 남겼다.

03 (1) hunger: 기아, 배고픔 / 그들은 굶주림과 공기 오염으로 고통받을 것이다. (2) national: 국가적인 / 이것은 국가적인 문제가 아니라 국제적인 문제이다

04 care for: ~을 돌보다, 신경 쓰다 care about: ~에 관심을 가지다

05 (1) be good at: ~을 잘하다 (2) thanks to: ~ 덕분에 (3) be going to 동사원형: ~할 것이다 turn down the heat: (실내) 온도를 낮추다 (4) celebrate: 기념하다, 축하하다

교과서

Conversation

핵심 Check   p.166~167

1 (1) you (p)lanning to / am   (2) What are you, to do / I'm, to   2 (B) → (A) → (C)
3 (1) Are you (p)lanning / to swim   (2) I hope she
4 ①, ③

교과서 대화문 익히기

Check(√) True or False   p.168

1 F   2 F   3 T   4 T

교과서 확인학습

p.170~171

Listen & Speak 1 A

1 about the flood / I did, lot, lost / to send / How, Are you, to raise / going to, sell

2 plans, vacation / going to, do, with / went, helped, Are you going to do / paint walls

Listen & Speak 1 B

1 to take / am, I'm not

2 going to recycle / I am

Listen & Speak 2 A

1 What / making, about, hunger, dying / too bad / hope, care about global

2 to make, garden / vegetable garden, will / grow, share, with / hope, grow

Listen & Speak 2 B

1 hope, don't throw away / hope so, Let's hold / campaign

2 I hope people don't / so, Let's hold

Wrap Up

1 What's your plan, Are, to do anything special / On, going to / about on / have / going to do volunteer work, like to come

2 going to hold, at / What is / protect, throw trash on, to stop / hope, goes

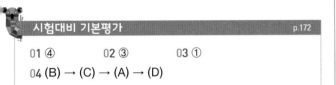

시험대비 기본평가   p.172

01 ④   02 ③   03 ①

04 (B) → (C) → (A) → (D)

01 의도나 앞으로의 할 일 물을 때는 Are you going to ~?로 물을 수 있다. 대답을 할 때 긍정이면 Yes, I am., 부정이면 No, I'm not.으로 대답한다.

02 I hope (that) 주어 can 동사 ~.: 나는 ~하기를 바라 hurt: 다치게 하다

03 be going to 동사원형 = be planning to 동사원형: ~할 것이다

04 (B) 반에서 채소밭을 만들기로 했다고 말하자 (C) 채소밭에서 무엇을 기르는지 질문한다. (A) 채소밭에 당근을 길러서 사람들과 나눌 거라고 대답한다. (D) 좋은 생각이라고 상대방의 의견에 동의한다. decide: 결정하다 garden: 정원 will: ~할 것이다 grow: 기르다, 재배하다 share A(사물) with B(사람): A를 B와 나누다[나눠 가지다]

시험대비 실력평가   p.173~174

01 ④   02 ②, ⑤   03 ④   04 ④

05 garden   06 ④   07 ②, ④   08 ①

09 ④   10 waste   11 ②   12 ②, ④

01 남자아이가 현재진행형(be동사의 현재형+동사ing)을 사용하여 대답하고 있으므로, 빈칸에는 현재진행형을 사용해 지금 하고 있는 일이 무엇인지 질문한다.

02 많은 사람들이 기아로 죽어가고 있다는 사실에 안타까움을 표현하고 있다.

03 about: ~에 관하여 die of: ~으로 죽다 care about: ~에 관심을 가지다

04 공기가 깨끗해지기를 바라며, '더 많은 나무를 심어라'라는 캠페인을 열자는 말에, '정말 안됐다.'라는 것은 어색하다. That's

too bad. → That's a good idea.

05 식물을 기를 수 있는 장소 / garden: 정원

06 ⓐ, ⓑ, ⓒ, ⓔ: 당근 ⓓ others: 다른 사람들

07 의도나 계획을 묻는 표현으로 'Are you planning to 동사원형 ~?', 'Are you going to 동사원형 ~?', 'Are you trying to 동사원형 ~?' 등이 있으며, '너는 ~할 계획이니?' 또는 '너는 ~할 거니?'의 의미로 쓰인다.

08 공기가 깨끗해지기를 바란다는 말에 어울리는 캠페인은 '더 많은 나무를 심어라'라는 캠페인이다.

09 주어진 문장에서 it은 지호가 가져온 불고기를 의미한다. 불고기를 많이 담아온 것 같아 나눠 먹자는 말의 대답으로, That's a good idea.(좋은 생각이야.)가 어울리므로 ④가 적절하다.

10 시간, 돈, 에너지를 완전히 또는 합리적이거나 유용한 방법으로 사용하지 못하다 / waste: 낭비하다, 허비하다

11 from now on: 앞으로는, 지금부터는

12 ① "생각하라, 먹어라, 구하라!"는 포스터에 쓰여져 있다. ② '불고기를 다 먹을 거니?'라는 질문에 지호는 '잘 모르겠어.'라고 대답했으므로, 다 먹을 거라는 확신이 없었다. ③ 불고기는 지호가 좋아하는 음식이다. ④ 지호와 Karl은 음식을 다 먹었다. ⑤ Karl은 지구를 살리기를 바란다.

서술형 시험대비   p.175

01 (1) (g)oing   (2) (p)lanning   02 plans

03 she will visit her grandmother, she will do volunteer work at the library

04 Are you going to use your own cup?   05 flood

06 My club is going to send them some money.

07 How   08 I hope people don't throw away trash.

01 의도나 계획을 표현할 때 'I'm planning to 동사원형 ~.(나는 ~할 것이다)' 또는 'I'm going to 동사원형 ~.'을 사용한다.

02 plan: 계획

03 수민이는 토요일에 할머니를 방문하고, 일요일에는 남자아이와 같이 도서관에서 봉사 활동을 할 것이다. do volunteer work: 자원 봉사를 하다

04 의도나 계획을 묻는 표현으로 'Are you going to 동사원형 ~?'을 사용할 수 있으며, '너는 ~할 계획이니?' 또는 너는 ~할 거니?'의 의미로 쓰인다.

05 물의 넘쳐흐름 / flood: 홍수

06 be going to 동사원형: ~할 것이다 send+간접목적어(사람)+직접목적어(사물): ~에게 ~을 보내다

07 홍수로 집을 잃은 사람들에게 돈을 줄 방법을 물어보고 있다. How: 어떻게

08 throw away: ~을 버리다 trash: 쓰레기 I hope (that) 주어 동사 ~: 나는 ~하기를 바라

핵심 Check   p.176~177

1 (1) who   (2) has   (3) that   **2** (1) nothing strange
(2) anything delicious   (3) something bright
3 (1) something cool   (2) nothing exciting   (3) anything
sweet

시험대비 기본평가   p.178

01 (1) which → who[that]
(2) wonderful something → something wonderful
(3) which → who[that]
(4) delicious anything → anything delicious
02 ④   03 ②, ④   04 ③

01 (1) 선행사가 사람인 people이므로 관계대명사는 who가 적절
하다. (2) 대명사 something은 형용사가 뒤에서 수식한다. (3)
선행사가 사람인 girl이므로 관계대명사는 who가 적절하다.
(4) 대명사 anything은 형용사가 뒤에서 수식한다.
02 선행사가 a huge clock인 사물이고 단수 명사이므로 which
is가 적절하다.
03 선행사가 사람인 a woman이고 주격인 she를 대신하므로 주격
인 who가 적절하고, that은 who 대신 사용 가능하다.
04 -thing으로 끝나는 대명사는 뒤에서 형용사의 수식을 받는다.
그리고 긍정문에서는 something을 사용하고, 부정문과 의문문
에서는 anything을 사용한다.

시험대비 실력평가   p.179~181

01 ①
02 (1) Do you know anybody famous?
(2) I want to do something different.
(3) Do you have anything new?
(4) He met someone beautiful yesterday.
03 which / who   04 (1) who   (2) who are
(3) who   05 ⑤   06 ②   07 ④
08 ④   09 (1) special nothing → nothing
special   (2) something → anything   (3) who are →
which[that] is   10 ①   11 ③
12 ⑤   13 (1) which   (2) who   (3) which
(4) who   14 ②   15 I want to eat
something sweet.   16 someone tall
17 who   18 ①   19 ③   20 ⑤
21 (1) who   (2) that

01 -thing으로 끝나는 대명사는 형용사가 뒤에서 수식을 한다.
02 -thing, -one, -body로 끝나는 대명사는 형용사가 뒤에서 수식
을 한다.
03 선행사가 the lion과 doctor이므로 which와 who가 적절하다.
04 (1) 선행사가 사람이므로 who가 적절하다. (2) 선행사가 복수
명사 students이므로 주격 관계대명사 뒤의 동사는 복수동사
are가 적절하다. (3) 동사 was가 관계대명사 뒤에 있기 때문에
주격 who가 적절하다.
05 선행사가 단수명사인 The girl(사람)이므로 관계대명사는 who,
동사는 단수 lives가 적절하다.
06 주격 관계대명사는 뒤에 동사가 온다. 즉, 'who[which/that]+동
사 ~'의 형태를 취한다.
07 보기의 who와 같은 쓰임은 ④번의 관계대명사다. 나머지는 모
두 의문대명사 who나.
08 선행사가 복수 명사인 two daughters이기 때문에 주격 관계대
명사 뒤의 동사는 복수 동사인 are가 되어야 한다.
09 (1) -thing으로 끝나는 대명사는 형용사가 뒤에서 수식한다.
(2) 의문문에서는 something이 아니라 anything을 사용한다.
(3) 100년 된 집에 산다는 의미로 선행사가 사물이므로 who를
which로 바꾸고, 동사도 단수 동사 is로 바꾼다.
10 many people을 수식하고, 동사 want의 주어 역할을 하는 관계
대명사절을 이끄는 who가 적절하다.
11 선행사가 사람이면 who, 사물이면 which를 사용하고, 주격 관
계대명사 뒤의 동사는 선행사의 수에 일치시킨다.
12 ①은 선행사가 the girl이므로 who가 적절하다. ②는 선행사
가 a book이므로 which를 쓴다. ③은 선행사가 Ms. Ha이고
동사 is의 주어 역할을 하는 who를 쓴다. ④는 선행사가 the
phone이고 동사 is의 주어 역할을 하는 which를 쓴다.
13 선행사가 사람이면 who를, 사물이면 which를 사용한다.
14 사물 선행사인 the movie를 수식하는 관계대명사절을 이끄는
주격 관계대명사 which가 적절하다.
15 something은 형용사가 뒤에서 수식한다.
16 someone은 형용사가 뒤에서 수식을 한다.
17 선행사가 사람 people이기 때문에 관계대명사 that을 who로 바
꾸어 쓸 수 있다.
18 something은 형용사가 뒤에서 수식한다.
19 관계대명사를 이용하여 두 문장을 한 문장으로 바꿀 때, 두 번째
문장의 중복되는 명사를 관계대명사로 바꾸어 준다. 중복되는 명
사(선행사)가 사물인 stamps이므로 관계대명사 which로 바꾸
어 준다.
20 명사는 형용사가 명사 앞에서 수식을 하지만, -thing으로 끝나는
대명사는 형용사가 뒤에서 수식한다.
21 (1), (2)는 모두 선행사가 사람이므로 관계대명사는 who 또는
that을 사용할 수 있다.

01 valuable anything → anything valuable

02 (1) Both paintings show a couple who[that] are dancing

   (2) In 1883, Renoir completed two paintings which[that] look very similar.

   (3) Jake is wearing a hat which[that] looks very old.

03 (1) who → which[that]   (2) who are → which[that] is   (3) whom → who[that]

04 (1) which has   (2) who is

   (3) which has

05 (1) Yesterday I met a girl who is from Mexico.

   (2) I want to buy a smartphone which has a large screen.

   (3) John read an article which was written by his friend.

06 (1) nothing special   (2) something nice

07 (1) The teacher talked about something different.

   (2) Sam is wearing shoes that are too big for him.

   (3) Are you going to do anything special during the summer vacation?

08 which aim → which aims

   special something → something special

09 We need someone smarter than us.

10 (1) There is something strange on the roof of the house.

   (2) He liked to draw ballet dancers who[that] were moving.

   (3) He fell in love with a lady who[that] taught music at the nursing home.

01 anything은 형용사가 뒤에서 수식을 한다.

02 (1) 선행사가 a couple이므로 which를 who로 바꾼다. (2) 선행사가 two paintings이므로 whose를 which로 바꾼다. (3) 선행사가 a hat이므로 who를 which로 바꾸고, 동사도 선행사의 수에 맞추어 단수 동사 looks로 고친다.

03 (1) 선행사가 사물인 the tea이므로 who를 which[that]로 고친다. (2) 선행사가 사물인 a house이므로 who를 which[that]으로 고치고, 동사를 단수형인 is로 고친다. (3) 선행사가 사람인 painter이고, 동사 is의 주어 역할을 하는 주격 관계대명사가 필요하므로 whom을 who로 고친다.

04 선행사의 종류에 따라 관계대명사를 선택하고, 주격 관계대명사절의 동사는 선행사의 수에 일치시킨다.

05 두 문장에서 중복되는 명사를 찾고, 사람이 중복되면 who를, 사물이 중복되면 which를 사용한다.

06 대화의 흐름상 B는 주말에 특별한 일이 없다는 것을 알 수 있

다. 그래서 빈칸 (1)은 nothing special이 자연스럽고, (2)는 이번 주말에 Jenny와 근사한 것을 먹을 계획이라고 했으므로 something nice가 적절하다.

07 (1) '~에 관해 말하다'는 talk about이고, 다른 무언가는 something 뒤에 형용사 different를 사용한다. (2) shoes를 수식하는 관계대명사절을 만들 때 선행사가 사물이므로 관계대명사는 that을 쓰고 동사 are를 사용한다. (3) '~할 것이니?'라는 표현으로 'are you going to+동사원형'을 이용한다. do의 목적어로 anything을 쓰고 형용사 special이 뒤에서 수식한다. 마지막으로 전치사 during과 명사 the summer vacation을 쓴다.

08 a poster가 선행사이므로 which 뒤에 동사는 단수 동사 aims가 되어야 한다. 그리고 something은 형용사 special이 뒤에서 수식해야 한다.

09 '주어(We)+동사(need)+목적어(someone)+형용사 비교급(smarter) than ~' 어순으로 쓴다.

10 (1) something은 형용사 strange가 뒤에서 수식해야 한다. (2) 선행사가 사람이고 복수 명사인 dancers이므로 who[that] were로 바꾸어야 한다. (3) 선행사가 a lady이기 때문에 관계대명사 which를 who 또는 that으로 고쳐야 한다.

Reading

확인문제   p.184

1 T   2 F   3 F   4 T   5 T   6 F   7 T

확인문제   p.185

1 F   2 T   3 F   4 T   5 T   6 F   7 F   8 T

교과서 확인학습 A   p.186~187

01 Global Citizenship   02 This is

03 helps us grow   04 who try to understand

05 care for, in need   06 share, experiences

07 from Korea   08 a member of

09 to communicate with

10 about the lantern festival

11 uploaded it, 5,000 hits   12 for our video

13 looks fantastic   14 a water festival

15 like yours   16 my name

17 am from   18 showed us pictures

19 they were all, to carry their books

20 to raise money 21 raised 600 dollars
22 are happy with 23 Awesome, I'm sure
24 something wonderful 25 from
26 a wall painting, look better
27 are good at, gathered, painted
28 Thanks to, much nicer
29 walking alongside, painted
30 What a nice idea

25 I am Afig from Malaysia.
26 My school started a wall painting campaign to make our village look better.
27 Students who are good at painting gathered and painted on some walls of schools and parks.
28 Thanks to this campaign, our village looks much nicer.
29 Now everyone can enjoy walking alongside the painted walls.
30 Junho: What a nice idea!

교과서 확인학습 B
p.188~189

1 Global Citizenship Education
2 This is the Global Citizenship Education site.
3 Global Citizenship Education helps us grow as global citizens.
4 Global citizens are people who try to understand different cultures.
5 They also care for people in need and work for a better world.
6 Please share your global citizenship education experiences here.
7 Hello. I am Minhee from Korea.
8 I am a member of the Global Community Club.
9 My club aims to communicate with people from around the world.
10 A week ago we produced a video about the lantern festival in our village.
11 We uploaded it to the Internet and amazingly, we got nearly 5,000 hits.
12 Click here for our video.
13 Alice: Wow, your lantern festival looks fantastic!
14 Sunan: We have a water festival in our village.
15 I'd like to make a video like yours.
16 Hi, my name is Jo.
17 I am from Australia.
18 A few weeks ago, my teacher showed us pictures of students in Kenya.
19 Sadly, they were all using plastic bags to carry their books.
20 My class decided to raise money to send them new school bags.
21 We sold cookies and drinks and raised 600 dollars.
22 We hope the Kenyan students are happy with the new bags.
23 Wang: Awesome! I'm sure they will like the bags.
24 Kozo: You did something wonderful!

시험대비 실력평가
p.190~193

01 ④	02 ③	03 Global citizens	
04 ③	05 ①	06 ⑤	07 ④
08 ①	09 (1) How nice the idea is!		
(2) It is a very nice idea.	10 hit(s)	11 ②	
12 ⑤	13 ①, ④	14 which 또는 that	
15 ③	16 ③	17 ①, ⑤	18 Kenyan
19 ④	20 ③	21 ③ raising → to raise	
22 students in Kenya	23 ②		
24 ① knowing → know	25 ⑤		
26 ①, ③, ⑤			

01 ④ 위 글은 '웹 사이트에 게시된 글'이다. ② review (책·연극·영화 등에 대한) 논평[비평], 감상문, ③ article (신문·잡지의) 글, 기사, ⑤ summary 요약, 개요

02 ⓐ와 ③번은 ~로서, ~으로, ① 이유, ② ~만큼, ④ ~하다시피[~이듯이], ⑤ ~함에 따라, ~할수록

03 '세계 시민'을 가리킨다.

04 ⓐ와 ②, ④, ⑤는 명사적 용법, ① 부사적 용법, ③ 형용사적 용법

05 ⓑ upload A to ~: A를 ~에 업로드하다, ⓒ for our video: 우리 비디오를 보려면

06 ⑤ 위 글은 민희가 동아리의 목표를 말하면서 마을의 등 축제에 관한 비디오를 제작한 것을 소개하는 내용의 글이므로, 제목으로는 '우리 동아리의 활동을 소개할게'가 적절하다.

07 이 글은 'Afig의 학교가 벽화 캠페인을 시작해서 마을을 더 보기 좋게 만들었다'는 내용의 글이다.

08 very는 비교급을 강조할 수 없다.

09 How+형용사[부사]+주어+동사! (2) What을 very로 고치고 '주어+동사'의 순서로 쓰면 된다.

10 hit: 조회 수, 웹 사이트를 한 번 방문하는 것

11 ② '좋아하다', ⓑ와 나머지는 다 '~와 비슷한', '~와 같이, ~처럼'이라는 뜻이다. ① 그녀는 내 것과 비슷한 드레스를 입고 있다. ③ 그는 술을 많이 마신다. ④ 나는 너처럼 요리를 잘하지

못한다. ⑤ 그녀는 배우처럼 보인다.

12 Sunan은 자기 마을의 물 축제에 관한 비디오를 만든 것이 아니라 만들고 싶다고 했을 뿐이다.

13 ⓐ와 ①, ④번: 즐겁게 보내다, 즐거운 시간을 갖다, ② 놀리다, ③ (음식 등을) 마음대로 드시오. ⑤ 코믹한 표정을 짓다

14 선행사가 사물이고 주어 자리이므로, 주격 관계대명사 which나 that이 적절하다.

15 물싸움을 즐길 수 있다.

16 주어진 문장의 new school bags에 주목한다. ③번 앞 문장의 plastic bags 대신에 쓸 수 있도록 책가방을 보내려는 것이므로 ③번이 적절하다.

17 ⓐ와 ②, ③, ④는 부사적 용법, ① 형용사적 용법, ⑤ 명사적 용법

18 Kenya의 형용사형을 쓰는 것이 적절하다. Kenyan: [형용사, 명사] 케냐의, 케냐인

19 ④ Jo의 반이 어디에서 쿠키와 음료를 팔았는지는 대답할 수 없다. ① From Australia. ② Pictures of students in Kenya. ③ No. ⑤ 600 dollars.

20 위 글은 케냐에 있는 학생들에게 새로운 책가방을 보내기 위해서 기금을 모금하는 것에 관한 글이므로, 주제로는 '새 책가방을 보내기 위해서 기금을 모금하기'가 적절하다.

21 decide는 목적어 자리에 동명사가 아니라 to부정사를 써야 한다

22 '케냐의 학생들'을 가리킨다.

23 ② 'Jo의 선생님이 보여주신 사진의 숫자'는 알 수 없다. ① 호주, ③ 비닐 봉지, ④ 쿠키와 음료를 팔았다. ⑤ 600달러.

24 사역동사 let은 목적격보어 자리에 원형부정사를 쓰는 것이 적절하다.

25 이 글은 Sunan이 친구 민희에게 보내는 송크란 축제의 '초대장'이다. ③ order: 명령하다, ④ force: 강요하다

26 송크란 축제에서는 물싸움, 퍼레이드 구경, 그리고 태국 전통 음식을 맛볼 수 있다.

---

11 make their village look better

12 Students who are good at painting gathered and painted on some walls of schools and parks.

13 (A) New Year   (B) water fight   14 Thai

---

01 (A) 세계 시민 교육 '(웹)사이트'라고 해야 하므로 site가 적절하다. cite: 인용하다, site: (웹)사이트, 장소, (B) 'help+목적어+원형부정사 또는 to부정사'이므로 grow가 적절하다. (C) care for와 병렬구문을 이루도록 work가 적절하다.

02 '세계 시민'은 다른 문화를 이해하려고 노력하고 또한 어려움에 처한 사람들을 보살피고 더 나은 세상을 위해서 일한다.

03 care for = take care of = look after: 돌보다

04 hits: 조회 수

05 감각동사 look+형용사, look like+명사: ~하게 보이다

06 Sunan은 '민희의 동아리'가 그들 마을의 등 축제에 관한 비디오를 제작한 것처럼 그들 마을의 물 축제에 관한 '비디오를 만들고' 싶어 한다.

07 그들은 비닐 봉지를 사용하고 있었다.

08 Jo의 반은 비닐 봉지 대신 사용할 새로운 '책가방'을 보내기 위해서 기금을 모금했다.

09 'hope+목적어+to부정사'는 쓸 수 없다. 'hope+(that)+주어+동사'로 쓰는 것이 적절하다.

10 send는 'to'를 사용하여 3형식으로 고친다.

11 Afig의 학교는 '그들의 마을을 좀 더 좋아 보이게 하기 위해서' 벽화 캠페인을 시작했다.

12 'at'을 보충하면 된다. be good at: ~에 능숙하다

13 송크란은 태국의 큰 축제이고 전통적인 태국의 '설날'을 축하하기 위해 개최된다. 축제에서 여러분은 큰 '물싸움'을 즐길 수 있고 송크란 퍼레이드를 볼 수 있다.

14 Thai: (형용사) 태국(인, 어)의, (명사) 태국인, 타이어

서술형 시험대비
p.194~195

01 (A) site   (B) grow   (C) work

02 (1) 다른 문화를 이해하려고 노력하는 사람들이다.

(2) 어려움에 처한 사람들을 보살피고 더 나은 세상을 위해서 일하는 사람들이다.

03 take care of 또는 look after

04 we got nearly(또는 almost) 5,000 hits

05 looks like fantastic → looks fantastic

06 (A) make a video   (B) Minhee's club

07 were using plastic bags   08 plastic → school

09 ⑤ to be → are(또는 will be)

10 to send new school bags to them

영역별 핵심문제
p.197~201

01 ⑤   02 ①   03 ⑤   04 ③

05 ②   06 (A) going   (B) to do   (C) helped

07 Are you going to do that, too?   08 ④

09 raise

10 We're going to make pencil cases and sell them.

11 (B) → (A) → (D) → (C)   12 (B) → (A) → (C)

13 If you want to do something special for the world

14 (1) He is the student who won the speech contest.

(2) I know the man who was looking for his dog.

(3) He wrote a novel which became a best-seller.

15 ②   16 ②   17 ⑤   18 ②

01 ⓔ를 제외한 <보기>의 단어들은 모두 동의어 관계이다. ⓐ gather: 모으다 collect: 모으다 ⓑ global: 전 세계적인, 지구상의 worldwide: 세계적인 ⓒ save: 살리다, 구하다 rescue: 구출하다, 구조하다 ⓓ upset: 당황한 worried: 걱정스러운, 당황하는 ⓔ far: 멀리, 먼 near: 가까운

02 awesome: 굉장한, 감탄할 만한, 엄청난 impressive: 인상적인, 감동적인

03 finish: (남아 있는 것을) 마저 먹다

04 ① bags, bag: 가방 / 음식 담을 비닐봉지가 필요하세요? ② trash, trash: 쓰레기 / 공원은 10분 후에 폐장합니다. 쓰레기를 남기고 가면 안 됩니다. ③ fight, fight: 싸움, 싸우다 / 너는 너의 친구들과 자주 싸우니? ④ campaign, campaign: 캠페인, 조직적 활동 / 나는 네가 우리의 새로운 캠페인에 참여하기를 원한다. ⑤ garden, garden: 정원 / 너는 정원에 장미를 심을 거니?

05 save: 아끼다, 구하다

06 (A) 현재진행형으로 가까운 미래의 일을 표현하고 있다. (B) to부정사의 부사적 용법 중 목적(~하기 위해서)을 사용한다. to do some volunteer work: 봉사활동을 하기 위해서 (C) 접속사 and로 went와 helped는 병렬구조를 이루고 있다.

07 Are you going 동사원형 ~?: 너는 ~할 거니?

08 ① 남자아이는 필리핀에 작년에 갔었다. ② 여자아이는 이번 여름 방학에 필리핀에 갈 것이다. ③ 남자아이는 필리핀에 가서 아이들이 공부하는 것을 도와줬다. ④ 남자아이의 여름 방학 계획에 대해서는 대화에서 언급되지 않았다. ⑤ 여자아이는 여름 방학에 필리핀에 갈 것이다.

09 특정한 목적을 위한 돈을 모으다 / raise: (자금 등을) 모으다, 모금하다

10 be going to 동사원형: ~할 것이다 sell: 팔다

11 동아리가 다음 주 금요일에 그린 캠페인을 연다는 말에, (B) 그린 캠페인이 무엇인지 질문한다. (A) 환경을 보호하기 위한 캠페인이라고 얘기하며, 많은 학생들이 길에 쓰레기를 버리는 것을 멈추기를 바란다는 희망을 표현하자. (D) 캠페인이 잘되길 빌어주고, (C) 감사를 표하며 캠페인이 잘되기를 바란다고 대답한다.

12 무엇을 하고 있는지 질문하자 (B) 세계 기아 문제에 대한 포스터를 만들고 있다고 말하며, 많은 사람들이 기아로 죽어가고 있다고 말한다. (A) 기아로 많은 사람들이 죽어가는 것에 대해 안타까움을 표현하면서, 그러한 사실을 몰랐다고 얘기한다. (C) 더 많은 사람들이 세계의 기아 문제에 관심을 갖기를 바라는 희망을 표현한다.

13 대명사 something은 형용사의 수식을 뒤에서 받는다.

14 선행사가 사람이면 who를, 사물이면 which를 사용한다.

15 선행사가 a lady이므로 who wants가 적절하다.

16 사람과 사물, 동물을 선행사로 가질 수 있는 관계대명사는 that이다.

17 ①~④는 의문형용사이고 ⑤는 관계대명사이다.

18 ② 선행사가 '사람+동물'일 때는 관계대명사 that을 사용한다. which를 that으로 고쳐야 한다.

19 선행사가 복수 명사 activities이므로 주격 관계대명사절의 동사는 선행사에 일치하여 복수 동사가 되어야 한다.

20 두 번째 문장에서 선행사가 neighbor로 사람이므로 which를 who로 바꾸어야 하며, 마지막 문장에서 선행사가 the cats로 복수 명사이므로 주격 관계대명사절의 동사는 복수형인 don't가 되어야 한다.

21 선행사가 a cat이므로 관계대명사는 which 또는 that이 적절하고 동사는 단수 동사 is가 와야 한다.

22 관계대명사는 선행사의 종류에 따라 결정되므로 (1) 선행사가 students이므로 who나 that을 쓰고 복수 동사 are로 고친다. (2) 선행사가 a person이므로 which를 who로 고치고 단수 동사 plays로 고친다. (3) 선행사가 my friend이므로 that이나 who를 쓰고 단수 동사 is로 고친다.

23 ⑤ nothing은 형용사 interesting이 뒤에서 수식해야 한다.

24 ①, ②, ⑤번은 '–thing+형용사' 형태의 문장이 되어야 한다. ③은 선행사가 an email이므로 who를 which나 that으로 고쳐야 한다.

25 선행사가 사람이고 주어 자리이므로 주격 관계대명사 who나 that이 적절하다.

26 '세계 시민은 교육 경험을 공유하는 사람들이다.'가 아니라, '당신의 세계 시민 교육 경험을 이곳에 공유해 주세요.'라고 했다.

27 민희의 동아리는 그들 마을의 '등 축제'에 관한 비디오를 제작했고, Sunan은 자기 마을의 '물 축제'에 관한 비디오를 만들고 싶어 한다.

28 ③ '등 축제에 관한 비디오를 만드는 데 얼마나 오래 걸렸는지'는 대답할 수 없다. ① To communicate with people from around the world. ② A video about the lantern festival in their village. ④ Nearly 5,000 hits. ⑤ She thinks it looks fantastic.

29 'raise'를 보충하면 된다.

30 이 글은 케냐에 있는 학생들에게 새로운 책가방을 보내기 위해서 기금을 모금하는 것에 관한 글이므로, 제목으로는 '책가방을 보내기 위한 모금'이 적절하다.

01 (1) American   (2) Kenyan   02 (h)urt

03 (1) far   (2) environment   (3) international

04 ⑤   05 ⑤   06 Are you going to eat
all of that?   07 save   08 environment   09 ④

10 (1) My club is planning to hold a green campaign
     at school next Friday.

    (2) My club will hold a green campaign at school
     next Friday.

11 (A) protect   (B) throw   (C) goes

12 (A) lost   (B) send   (C) raise   (C) sell   13 ⑤

14 ②   15 ①   16 The man who[that] is
working in the garden is my friend.   17 ⑤

18 bad something → something bad

19 I will buy the novels which[that] were written by
    Ernest Hemingway.

20 ③   21 Global Citizenship Education helps
us grow as global citizens.   22 share   23 ②

24 My club aims to communicate with people from
    around the world.

25 a video about the lantern festival in our village

26 ④   27 ⓐ painting   ⓒ painted   28 ②

---

01 China: 중국 Chinese: 중국의 (1) American: 미국의; 미국
인 (2) Kenyan: 케냐의

02 hurt: 다치게 하다

03 (1) far: 멀리; 먼 (2) environment: 자연환경, 환경 (3)
international: 국제적인

04 ⑤의 영영풀이는 'communicate'이다. gather의 영영풀이는
'to bring people together or collect things together'이다.

05 주어진 문장은 음식을 다 먹고 나서 얘기할 수 있는 말로 ⑤번
다음의 clean plate로 보아 ⑤번이 적절하다.

06 be going to 동사원형: ~할 것이다

07 save: 살리다, 구하다

08 육지, 바다, 공기, 식물 및 동물이 있는 자연 / environment:
자연환경, 환경

09 주어진 문장의 that이 ④번 앞 문장의 내용을 가리키므로 ④번이
적절하다. I hope to 동사원형 ~: 나는 ~하고 싶어

10 'I'm planning to 동사원형 ~.'은 '나는 ~할 계획이다.'라는 의
미로 미래의 계획이나 의도에 대해 사용하는 표현으로 to 다음
에 동사원형이 온다. 비슷한 표현으로 'I'm going to 동사원형
~.', 'I'll 동사원형 ~.' 등이 있다.

11 (A) protect: 보호하다 (B) throw: 버리다 (C) go well: 잘
되다

12 (A) lost는 lose의 과거형이다. 과거의 사실을 말하고 있으므
로 과거형을 사용해야 한다. (B) send: 보내다 spend는 4형식

을 사용할 수 없고, 내용상 집을 잃은 사람들에게 돈을 보낸다는
것이 적절하다. (C) raise: (자금 등을) 모으다, 모금하다 (D)
make와 sell은 등위접속사 and에 의해 연결되어 있다.

13 Let's waste food from now on. → Let's not waste food
from now on.

14 선행사가 사람이고 주격이므로 관계대명사 who가 적절하다.

15 사물과 사람을 선행사로 가질 수 있는 관계대명사는 that이다.

16 두 문장에서 동일한 대상을 가리키는 단어를 찾는다. 그 다음 뒤
문장의 대명사를 관계대명사(who, which, that)로 바꾼다. 마
지막으로 관계대명사가 이끄는 문장을 선행사 바로 뒤에 붙여
쓴다.

17 ⑤ 'something, anything, nothing, everything'은 형용사
가 뒤에서 꾸며 준다.

18 'something'은 형용사가 뒤에서 꾸며 준다.

19 주격 관계대명사와 be동사는 동시에 생략할 수 있다.

20 (A)는 선행사가 many pets이므로 which가 적절하고, (B)는 선
행사가 a woman이므로 who가 적절하다.

21 help+목적어+원형부정사

22 share: 공유하다, 공통으로 가지다, 공동으로 가지거나 또는 공
통으로 사용하다

23 ② 세계 시민 교육이 어떻게 우리가 세계 시민으로 자라도록 도
와주는지는 대답할 수 없다. ① It is the Global Citizenship
Education site. ③ Different cultures. ④ People in
need. ⑤ A better world.

24 'with'를 보충하면 된다.

25 '우리 마을의 등 축제에 관한 비디오'를 가리킨다.

26 ⓒ와 ② 명사적 용법(목적어), ①과 ⑤ 부사적 용법(목적), ③
형용사적 용법 (It은 비인칭 주어), ④ 형용사적 용법

27 ⓐ 전치사의 목적어이므로 동명사로 쓰는 것이 적절하다. ⓑ
'그림이 그려진' 벽이라고 해야 하므로 'painted'가 적절하다.

28 very는 비교급을 수식할 수 없다.

---

01 to recycle   02 don't hurt

03 If you finish all the food on your plate, you will
    get a small gift.

04 (1) something wrong   (2) anything interesting
(3) everything important   05 (1) like → likes
(2) which teach → who[that] teaches

06 (1) I like my house which[that] is by the lake.

    (2) Look at my dog which[that] is playing with a
     ball.

07 Look at the bird flying in the sky.

08 (A) uploaded   (B) nearly   (C) to make

09 (A) aim   (B) uploaded

10 in the world → in their village

11 to make our village look better

12 (A) wall painting   (B) paint

13 very → much[far, even]

01 사용된 재료나 폐기물을 재사용에 알맞게 되도록 처리하다 / recycle: (폐기물을) 재활용하다 be going to 동사원형: ~할 것이다

02 어떤 사람의 신체 일부에 부상을 입히거나 고통을 유발하다 / hurt: 다치게 하다 / 내용상 동물을 해치지 않기를 바란다는 것이 들어가야 하므로, 'don't'를 추가해야 한다.

03 finish: (남아 있는 것을) 마저 먹다

04 'something, anything, nothing, everything'은 형용사가 뒤에서 꾸며 준다.

05 (1) 주격 관계대명사 who의 선행사가 단수 명사 the girl이므로 like를 likes로 고친다. (2) 선행사가 사람인 the man이므로 which를 who로, 그리고 선행사가 단수 명사이므로 동사 teach를 단수 동사 teaches로 고친다.

06 두 문장에서 동일한 대상을 가리키는 단어를 찾는다. 그 다음 뒤 문장의 대명사를 관계대명사(who, which, that)로 바꾼다. 마지막으로 관계대명사가 이끄는 문장을 선행사 바로 뒤에 붙여 쓴다.

07 주격 관계대명사와 be동사는 동시에 생략할 수 있다.

08 (A) 인터넷에 '올렸다'고 해야 하므로 uploaded가 적절하다. download: (데이터를) 다운로드하다[내려받다], (B) '거의' 5,000 조회 수라고 해야 하므로 nearly가 적절하다. near: 가까운, (거리상으로) 가까이, (C) would like는 목적어로 동명사가 아닌 to부정사를 써야 하므로 to make가 적절하다.

09 그것은 전 세계의 사람들과 소통하는 것이 '목표'인 동아리이다. 동아리 회원들이 지역 축제를 소개하는 비디오를 만들어서 그것을 인터넷에 '올렸다.'

10 일주일 전에 민희의 동아리는 '그들 마을의' 등 축제에 관한 비디오를 만들었다.

11 사역동사(make)+목적어+원형부정사(look)

12 그것은 Afig의 학교가 시작한 '벽화' 캠페인이고, '그림을 잘 그리는' 학생들이 모여서 학교와 공원 벽에 그림을 그렸다. who are good at painting = who paint well

13 very는 원급을 강조하고, much, far, even, still 등은 비교급을 강조한다. nicer를 nice로 고치는 것도 가능하지만, 본문의 앞부분에 나오는 look better에 일치시켜 비교급으로 쓰는 것이 더 적절하다.

창의사고력 서술형 문제 p.208

|모범답안|

01 the summer vacation / I'm going to make a vegetable garden / I'm planning to do volunteer work at the library

---

02 (1) A musician is a person who plays music.

(2) A patient is a person who sees a doctor.

(3) A dentist is a person who takes care of your teeth.

(4) A genius is a person who is very intelligent.

03 (A) shoes   (B) Draw   (C) write   (D) need

(E) special

01 summer vacation: 여름 방학 be going to 동사원형 = be planning to 동사원형: ~할 것이다 do volunteer work: 자원 봉사를 하다

단원별 모의고사 p.209~212

01 ③   02 (1) (a)dults   (2) (a)imed, late

(3) education   (4) (r)aise, in need

03 (A) leave   (B) hold   (C) finish

04 I hope (that) many students join our campaign.

05 sell   06 ⑤   07 ⑤

08 ⓑ special anything → anything special

ⓓ I was going to → I'm going to

09 do   10 dying   11 I hope (that) more people care about global hunger.

12 ⓐ making → to make   ⓒ it → them   ⓓ by → with   ⓔ good → well

13 (1) She wanted to do something different.

(2) I did nothing special last year.

(3) Your daughter will never do anything stupid again.

14 ④   15 ⑤   16 who[that]

17 whose → which[that] / who live → who lives

18 ④   19 ⑤   20 ③, ④

21 They also care for people in need   22 ③

23 your video   24 (A) look   (B) walking   (C) What

25 ④

01 ③ 잡다, 쥐다 / 이외의 보기는 '(회의, 시합 등을) 열다'의 의미로 사용되었다.

02 (1) adult: 어른 (2) aim: ~을 목표로 삼다, 지향하다 late: 늦은 (3) education: 교육 (4) raise: (자금 등을) 모으다, 모금하다 in need: 어려움에 처한

03 leave: 남기다 hold: (회의, 시합 등을) 열다 finish: (남아 있는 것을) 마저 먹다

04 I hope (that) 주어 동사 ~: 나는 ~하기를 바란다 campaign: 캠페인, 조직적 활동

05 돈과 교환하여 물건을 주다 / sell: 팔다

06 ⑤ 남자아이가 필통을 만들어서 판다는 말은 나왔지만, 여자아

이가 필통을 만들 수 있는지 없는지에 대해서는 언급되어 있지 않다.

07 주어진 문장은 함께 가자고 제안하는 질문이다. 이에 'Sure.(물론이지)'란 긍정의 대답이 어울린다.

08 ⓑ '-thing', '-body', '-one'으로 끝나는 대명사는 형용사가 뒤에서 수식한다. ⓓ 'Are you going to 동사원형 ~? (너는 ~할 거니?)'으로 질문하였으므로, 과거형 동사로 대답하는 것은 어색하다.

09 do volunteer work: 자원 봉사를 하다

10 die의 현재분사형은 dying이다.

11 I hope (that) 주어 동사 ~: 나는 ~하기를 바란다 care about: ~에 관심을 가지다 global: 전 세계적인, 지구상의

12 ⓐ decide는 to부정사를 목적어로 취하는 동사이다. ⓒ carrots를 받기 때문에 복수형 대명사 them이 적절하다. ⓓ share A(사물) with B(사람): A를 B와 나누다[나눠 가지다] ⓔ grow: 자라다, 크다

13 'something, anything, nothing, everything'은 형용사가 뒤에서 꾸며 준다.

14 두 문장을 관계대명사를 이용하여 한 문장으로 만들 때, 두 번째 문장의 중복되는 단어를 관계대명사로 바꾸어 준다. 사물이 중복되므로 which를 사용하고 뒤의 문장은 그대로 쓰면 된다.

15 ⑤ anybody는 형용사가 뒤에서 꾸며준다. anybody strong이 되어야 한다.

16 '아브라함 링컨은 흑인 노예를 해방하는 데 성공한 16대 대통령이었다.' 선행사가 사람이므로 관계대명사는 who 또는 that을 사용할 수 있다.

17 선행사가 the cell phone이고 관계대명사절에 주어가 없이 동사 has가 있기 때문에 주격 관계대명사 which가 적절하다. 두 번째는 My cousin이 선행사이므로 단수 동사 lives가 적절하다.

18 선행사가 a car이므로 관계대명사 which나 that을 이용하여 한 문장으로 만든다.

19 ⑤번의 선행사는 the letter이므로 관계대명사는 which[that]가 적절하다.

20 ⓐ와 ③, ④는 명사적 용법, ①과 ⑤ 부사적 용법, ② 형용사적 용법

21 'in'을 보충하면 된다. in need: 어려움에 처한

22 ③번 다음 문장의 it에 주목한다. 주어진 문장의 'a video about the lantern festival in our village'를 받고 있으므로 ③번이 적절하다.

23 '너희 비디오'를 가리킨다.

24 (A) 사역동사(make)+목적어+원형부정사(look), (B) enjoy는 목적어로 동명사를 취한다. (C) What+a+형용사+명사(+주어+동사)! How+형용사[부사] (+주어+동사)!

25 ④ 몇 명의 학생들이 참가했는지는 대답할 수 없다. ① Malaysia. ② A wall painting campaign. ③ Students who are good at painting. ⑤ On some walls of schools and parks.

Interesting Facts Are Around Us

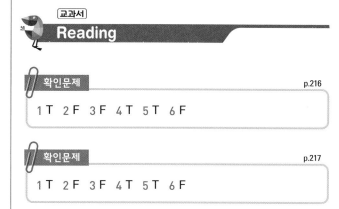

교과서
Reading

확인문제   p.216

1 T   2 F   3 F   4 T   5 T   6 F

확인문제   p.217

1 T   2 F   3 F   4 T   5 T   6 F

교과서 확인학습 A   p.218~219

01 Interesting Facts, Around   02 Welcome to
03 is full of   04 how much you know
05 ready   06 Quiz   07 gets taller
08 fewer, than   09 Only, bite   10 never strikes
11 the biggest animal   12 no gravity
13 in heat   14 Due to, expands
15 gets, taller than   16 Adults, about
17 With time, join together
18 Only female mosquitoes   19 to produce eggs
20 enough blood, rest, lay   21 over and over again
22 gets hit by, on average   23 The biggest animal
24 up to, up to, long   25 alone, as much as
26 In fact   27 get farther, weakens, completely
28 get closer, such as, that of
29 Which, the most interesting
30 another quiz   31 what the next topic will be
32 See you

교과서 확인학습 B   p.220~221

1 Interesting Facts Are Around Us
2 Welcome to "Ask Dr. Lawrence"!
3 The world is full of interesting things.
4 Take this quiz and find out how much you know about them.
5 Are you ready?
6 Quiz
7 The Eiffel Tower gets taller during the summer.

8 Babies have fewer bones than adults.

9 Only female mosquitoes bite people.

10 Lightning never strikes the same place twice.

11 The elephant is the biggest animal on the Earth.

12 There is no gravity in space.

13 Metal expands in heat.

14 Due to summer heat, the metal of the Eiffel Tower expands.

15 In summer, the Eiffel tower gets 15cm taller than in winter.

16 Adults have 206 bones, but babies have about 300 bones.

17 With time, some of the babies' bones join together, so adults have fewer bones than babies.

18 Only female mosquitoes will bite you.

19 They need blood to produce eggs.

20 After a female mosquito gets enough blood, she'll rest for a few days and lay her eggs.

21 Lightning can strike the same place over and over again.

22 The Empire State Building gets hit by lightning 23 times a year on average.

23 The biggest animal on the Earth is the blue whale.

24 It can weigh up to 180 tons and grow up to 30 meters long.

25 Its tongue alone can weigh as much as an average African elephant.

26 In fact, there is gravity everywhere in space.

27 As you get farther from the Earth, the gravity of the Earth weakens, but it never goes away completely.

28 When you get closer to another planet, such as Mars or Venus, its gravity becomes stronger than that of the Earth.

29 Which of these quiz items is the most interesting to you?

30 There will be another quiz soon.

31 Guess what the next topic will be.

32 See you next month.

🦉 서술형 실전문제
p.222~223

01 (1) (f)alse (2) (f)emale (3) (s)ame

02 (1) fewer (2) weaken   03 (1) bone (2) different
(3) Mosquitoes, blood (4) With time (5) In fact

04 (1) go (2) strike (3) guess (4) expand 05 due to

06 (1) In summer, the Eiffel Tower gets 15cm taller
than in winter.
(2) The elephant is the biggest animal on the Earth.

07 (1) Guess what the next topic will be.
(2) Please tell me who that girl is.
(3) My brother can run the fastest in our family.

08 (1) whether (2) when (3) who

09 good → better, lay → lays

10 Do you know what determines the color of an

egg?

11 how much you know about them

12 (A) during (B) Lightning (C) biggest

13 Adults have more bones than babies.

01 주어진 보기는 반의어 관계이다. weaken: 약화시키다, 약화되다 strengthen: 강화하다 (1) true: 사실인 false: 거짓의 (2) male: 남성 female: 여성 (3) different: 다른 same: 같은

02 (1) fewer: (few의 비교급) 보다 적은 / 영어는 다른 언어보다 어휘 수가 적다. (2) weaken: 약화시키다, 약화되다 / 알코올은 심장 근육을 약화시킬 수 있다.

03 (1) bone: 뼈 (2) different: 다른 (3) mosquito: 모기 blood: 피 (4) with time: 시간이 지남에 따라 (5) in fact: 사실상, 실제로

04 (1) go away: 사라지다 / 그 문제는 사라지지 않을 것이다. (2) strike: 부딪치다, 충돌하다 / 배는 이 폭풍으로 바위에 부딪칠지도 모른다. (3) guess: 추측하다 / 그들이 무엇에 관해 이야기하고 있는지 추측할 수 있나요? (4) expand: 팽창하다 / 금속은 열을 받으면 팽창한다.

05 because of: ~ 때문에 due to: ~ 때문에 / 그 행사는 나쁜 날씨 때문에 일주일 동안 지연되었다.

06 (1) get+형용사: '~해지다'는 의미이고, '비교급+than' 구문을 이용한다. (2) '가장 ~한'의 의미는 최상급으로, 형태는 'the 최상급+단수명사'이다. big처럼 '단모음+단자음'으로 끝나는 단어는 자음을 한 번 더 쓰고 –est를 붙인다.

07 (1) 'what the next topic will be'는 '의문사(what)+주어(the next topic)+동사(will be)'의 간접의문문으로 'guess'의 목적어 역할을 한다. (2) 의문사 who가 이끄는 문장이 tell의 직접목적어 자리에 사용되기 때문에 '의문사+주어+동사'의 어순이 되어야 한다. (3) 셋 이상의 사물과 사람 중에서 '가장 ~한'은 the fastest를 사용한다.

08 (1) 의문사가 없는 의문문은 '~인지 아닌지'를 의미하는 'if'나 'whether'가 명사절을 이끌어 'if[whether]+주어+동사'의 어순으로 쓴다. (2) know의 목적어 자리에 사용된 간접의문문으로 의미상 의문사 when이 적절하다. (3) Guess의 목적어 자리에 사용된 간접의문문으로 의문사 who가 적절하다.

09 than은 비교급과 호응하여 사용하기 때문에 good을 비교급인 better로 고친다. 주격 관계대명사 which 앞의 선행사가 chicken(단수명사)이기 때문에 주격 관계대명사절의 동사 lay는 단수 동사 lays로 고친다.

10 'Do you know'의 목적어 자리에 '의문사+주어+동사' 어순의 간접의문문을 사용한다. 여기서 의문사 what은 의문사이면서 동시에 주어 역할을 한다.

11 'how'를 보충하면 된다.

12 (A) during+특정 기간을 나타내는 명사, for+숫자가 붙은 기간, (B) '번개'라고 해야 하므로 Lightning이 적절하다. lightening: lighten(가볍게 해주다, 밝아지다)의 동명사/현재분사 형태임. (C) '단모음+단자음'으로 이루어진 1음절 단어는 최상급을 만들 때 마지막 자음을 한 번 더 쓰고 '-est'를 붙여야 하므로 biggest가 적절하다.

13 어른들은 아기들보다 '더 많은' 수의 뼈를 가지고 있다.

01 ④   02 (1) to bite   (2) gravity   (3) was, inventor   (4) was, of   03 ④

04 (1) Only female mosquitoes suck blood.
   (2) Blood is thicker than water.
   (3) How much do you weigh?
   (4) Teenage culture is different from adult culture.

05 ①   06 ④   07 ②

08 (1) Can you tell me how old your brother is?
   (2) I know where she lives.
   (3) Please tell me if[whether] he likes baseball.

09 ③   10 ④   11 ⑤   12 taller
13 (A) biggest   (B) much   14 ②   15 ③
16 prettiest   17 filled   18 ②   19 ③
20 heat   21 shorter → taller   22 ①
23 join together   24 ④   25 ③
26 ②   27 ④   28 weakens
29 another planet   30 (A) gets   (B) lay
(C) alone   31 ①, ②, ⑤   32 up to

01 ④번은 명사와 동사의 관계이고 나머지는 형용사와 동사의 관계이다. ① deep: 깊은 deepen: 깊게 하다 ② loose: 느슨한 loosen: 느슨해지다 ③ weak: 약한 weaken: 약화시키다 ④ strength: 힘 strengthen: 강화하다 ⑤ straight: 똑바른 straighten: 똑바르게 하다

02 (1) used to 동사원형: ~하곤 했다 bite: 물다 (2) gravity: 중력 (3) inventor: 발명가 (4) be full of: ~로 가득 차다

03 find out: 알아보다, 찾아보다 over and over: 여러 번, 몇 번이고

04 (1) female: 여성의, 암컷의 (2) blood: 피 (3) weigh: 무게가 ~ 나가다, 무게를 달다 (4) adult: 성인, 어른

05 ① On, on average: 평균적으로 / 보통 그는 12시쯤에 잔다. ② of, be full of: ~로 가득 차다 / 나는 올해가 행복으로 가득하기를 바란다. ③ to, up to: (특정한 수 또는 정도) ~까지 / 100쪽까지 읽어라. ④ with, with time: 시간이 지남에 따라 / 그 그림은 시간이 흐름에 따라 색이 바랠 것이다. ⑤ to, due to: ~ 때문에 / 악천후로 항공기가 지연되고 있습니다.

06 ①은 find out의 목적어 자리에 사용된 간접 의문문으로 Take this quiz and find out how much you know about them.이 되어야 한다. ②는 셋 이상의 사물을 나타낼 때 최상급 형태가 되어야 하므로 the biggest가 적절하다. ③은 'as 원급 as' 형태로 more를 much로 고쳐야 한다. ⑤는 difficult의 최상급 형태는 the most difficult를 쓴다.

07 셋 이상의 사물과 사람 중에서 '가장 ~하다'는 최상급의 의미로 heavy는 heaviest, early는 earliest가 적절하다.

08 간접의문문은 '의문사+주어+동사'의 어순으로 사용되고, 의문사가 없는 의문문은 접속사 if나 whether를 사용한다.

09 주어진 문장의 밑줄은 동사의 목적어 자리에 사용된 간접의문문이다. ③번은 직접의문문으로 '의문사+동사+주어 ~?'의 형태로 사용된 문장이다.

10 ④ than이 있으면 앞에는 비교급이 와야 한다. few를 비교급 fewer로 고친다.

11 ① 'there is+단수명사'로 맞다. ② get+비교급: 점점 ~해지다, ③ 부사로 동사 goes away를 수식한다. ④ '비교급(stronger) than' 구문이다. ⑤ 지구의 그것(gravity)을 가리키는 단수 명사로 those를 that으로 바꾸어야 한다.

12 첫 번째 문장에서 '금속은 열에 팽창한다.'라고 했으므로 여름에 에펠 탑은 겨울보다 15cm까지 더 커진다는 의미가 적절하다.

13 (A)는 지구상에서 가장 큰 동물이란 의미로 최상급 biggest가 적절하고, (B)는 'as+원급+as' 형태로 동사 weigh를 수식하는 부사 much가 적절하다.

14 ② 최상급 앞에 정관사 the를 사용해서 the thickest로 써야 한다. ④, ⑤번의 hardest와 most는 부사의 최상급으로 부사가 최상급이 될 때는 보통 정관사 the를 안 붙인다.

15 ① fastest ② largest ④, ⑤ 3음절어 이상의 형용사나 2음절어 중에서 -ful, -ous, -ive, -less, ing 등으로 끝나는 단어는 최상급을 만들 때 'most+원급' 형태를 사용한다.

16 내 여동생들은 모두 예쁘다. 하지만 내 여동생들 중에서, Jenny가 가장 예쁜 소녀다.

17 be full of = be filled with: ~로 가득 차다

18 'get[become]+비교급'은 '더 ~하게 되다, 더 ~해진다'는 의미로 상태의 변화를 포함하는 표현이다. 여기서는 '더 커진다'는 의미로 쓰였다.

19 '비교급+than any other+단수명사'는 최상급의 뜻을 나타낸다.

20 뒤에 이어지는 문장의 내용과 일치하도록, 금속은 '열'에 팽창한다고 하는 것이 적절하다.

21 여름의 열기 때문에, 에펠 타워의 금속은 팽창한다고 했으므로, 여름에 에펠 타워는 겨울보다 15센티미터 정도 더 '커진다'로 고쳐야 한다.

22 With time: 시간이 흐르면서

23 시간이 흐르면서, 아기의 몇몇 뼈들은 '붙기' 때문에, 어른들은 아기보다 더 적은 수의 뼈를 갖게 된다.

24 ⓐ와 ④번은 쉬다, ① 휴식, 수면, ② (어떤 것에) 받치다[기대다], ③ (결정 등이) ~에 달려 있다, ⑤ (어떤 것의) 나머지

25 ③ 한 걸음 한 걸음, 점차로, ⓑ와 나머지: 반복해서

26 ⓒ gets hit 'by' lightning: 번개를 맞는다, ⓓ 'on' average: 평균적으로

27 앞의 내용을 추가해서 설명하고 있으므로 In fact가 가장 적절하다. ① 예를 들어, ② 그러므로, ③ 게다가, ⑤ 다시 말해

28 weak의 동사 형태를 쓰는 것이 적절하다. 주어가 3인칭 단수(the gravity)이므로 끝에 s를 붙여야 한다.

29 화성이나 금성 같은 '다른 행성'을 가리킨다.

30 (A) 때를 나타내는 부사절에서는 현재시제가 미래시제를 대신하므로 gets가 적절하다. (B) 알을 '낳는다'고 해야 하므로 lay가 적절하다. lay: 놓다, (새, 곤충, 어류가) (알을) 낳다, lie: 눕다, 거짓말하다, (C) 혀의 무게'만' 해도라고 해야 하므로 alone이 적절하다. alone: ~만으로도(명사·대명사 뒤에 쓰여 특정한 그것 하나만을 가리킴을 강조함), only: (명사 앞에 써서) 유일한, 오직[겨우]

31 ⓐ와 ③, ④는 부사적 용법, ①, ⑤ 형용사적 용법, ② 명사적 용법

32 180톤'까지', 30미터'까지'라고 해야 하므로 up to가 적절하다. up to: ~까지

교과서 파헤치기

Lesson
1

01 항상	02 따뜻한	
03 ~하기로 되어 있는[예정된]		04 쉽게
05 약속	06 걱정하는	07 도움이 되다; 도움
08 준비하다	09 도움이 되는	10 수업, 강습
11 역사	12 기억하다	13 확인하다
14 ~하는 동안	15 대신에	16 가입하다
17 일정	18 퀴즈, 시험	19 매월의; 매월
20 자유 시간	21 일정 계획표, 플래너	
22 다시	23 해 보다, 노력하다	24 끝내다
25 주의, 집중	26 집중하다	27 규칙적으로
28 현명하게	29 긴장되는, 불안한	30 조리[요리]법
31 성취하다, 달성하다		
32 (인터넷이나 SNS에 올리는) 글, 포스팅		33 연습하다
34 절약하다, 구하다	35 온종일	
36 ~하는 것을 멈추다		37 수업[강습]을 받다
38 ~와 잘 지내다	39 계획을 세우다	40 알람을 맞춰 놓다
41 한 번에	42 ~을 한쪽에 두다	43 미루다, 연기하다

01 practice	02 before	03 regularly
04 finish	05 nervous	06 textbook
07 attention	08 wisely	09 achieve
10 posting	11 focus	12 important
13 forget	14 chef	15 weekly
16 master	17 step	18 recipe
19 save	20 tired	21 spend
22 toward	23 probably	24 remember
25 helpful	26 instead	27 appointment
28 warm	29 prepare	30 easily
31 schedule	32 monthly	33 free time
34 check	35 because of	36 in front of
37 all day long	38 set the alarm	39 these days
40 set a goal	41 stop -ing	41 be worried about
43 put aside		

1 recipe, 요리[조리]법   2 spend, (돈을) 쓰다
3 achieve, 성취하다, 달성하다   4 master, ~을 완전히 익히다
5 prepare, 준비하다   6 appointment, 약속
7 join, 가입하다   8 save, 절약하다   9 lesson, 수업, 강습
10 due, ~하기로 되어 있는[예정된]   11 focus, 집중하다
12 schedule, 일정   13 future, 미래
14 helpful, 도움이 되는   15 attention, 주의
16 present, 선물

Listen & Speak 1 - A
1 look worried, matter / don't hear, these days / Why don't, set the alarm / good idea
2 what should, do / What's / spend, fast / always make, before, buy / should, same

Listen & Speak 2 - A
1 okay, don't look good / have a cold / too bad, think, should see / You're right
2 look worried, going on / worried about, What should I do / think, should read / a good idea
3 so tired / don't sleep, these days / I think, should drink a glass of, before, will help / will try

Conversation A
type, daily, monthly, like, due dates, check, to remember, easily, should use

Conversation B
What's the matter / didn't bring, forgot, have soccer practice / second year, busier than, first year, often forget / you should use, mine / can I see / schedule, appointment / Maybe, should buy

Wrap Up - ❶
What's, Are, sick / I think, have a cold / go to the school nurse / said, need to, Can, leave / call, tell her

Wrap Up - ❷
nervous / because of / for, still, should, do / think, should, in front of, helpful / a good idea

Listen & Speak 1 - A
1 G: You look worried, Sam. What's the matter?
   B: I don't hear my alarm in the morning these days.
   G: Why don't you set the alarm on your clock and on your smartphone?

B: That's a good idea.

2 G: Phew, what should I do?

B: What's the matter, Julie?

G: I spend money too fast.

B: Well, I always make a plan before I buy things.

G: Maybe I should do the same.

Listen & Speak 2 - A

1 G: Jason, are you okay? You don't look good today.

B: I have a cold.

G: That's too bad. I think you should see a doctor.

B: You're right. Thank you.

2 G: You look worried. What's going on?

B: I'm worried about tomorrow's history quiz. What should I do?

G: I think you should read your textbook again.

B: That's a good idea.

3 B: I'm so tired.

G: Why?

B: I don't sleep well these days.

G: I think you should drink a glass of warm milk before you sleep. It will help.

B: Okay, I will try.

Conversation A

B: This is a type of book. I write my daily , weekly, and monthly plans here. I also write important dates like my friends' birthdays and homework due dates here. Every night, I check this for the next day. Do you want to remember things easily? Then I think you should use this.

Conversation B

Hana: What's the matter, Jiho?

Jiho: I didn't bring my uniform. I forgot I have soccer practice today.

Hana: Again?

Jiho: My second year in middle school is busier than my first year, and I often forget things.

Hana: I think you should use a planner. Here's mine.

Jiho: Oh, can I see it?

Hana: Sure. I write my class schedule and appointment in my planner.

Jiho: That's great. Maybe I should buy one.

Wrap Up - ❶

W: What's the matter, Sam? Are you sick?

B: Ms. Green, I think I have a cold.

W: Did you go to the school nurse?

B: Yes. She said I need to go to the hospital. Can I leave school now?

W: Okay, Sam. I'll call your mom and tell her about it.

Wrap Up - ❷

B: I'm so nervous.

G: Why? Is it because of the dance contest?

B: Yes. I practiced for many days, but I'm still nervous. What should I do?

G: I think you should practice in front of your family. It will be very helpful.

B: That's a good idea. Thank you.

본문 TEST Step 1   p.09~10

01 Welcome to, school year   02 In, second, to do

03 need to manage, well   04 How, do that

05 set, goals, achieve, every

06 not, will master

07 such, put off, until

08 Instead,three new, every

09 achieve, goal, step

10 When, full attention

11 used to, while, doing

12 slowed, down, focus

13 put aside, when

14 saves, lot, time

15 days, finish, enjoy, free

16 regularly spend, working

17 want, become, chef

18 Every, classes, search for

19 using, to prepare, is   20 Time, present

21 has, present to spend

22 Manage, and, be happier

본문 TEST Step 2   p.11~12

01 Welcome to, school year

02 In, second grade, more work to do

03 need to manage, well   04 How, do

05 set small goals, achieve

06 do not say, will master

07 With put off working on, until, or

08 Instead, will learn three new English, every day

09 will achieve, one step at a time

10 When, give, my full attention

11 used to read, while, was doing

12 slowed, because, couldn't focus

13 put aside, when   14 saves, a lot of

15 These days, quickly, enjoy my free time

16 regularly spend, working
17 want to become
18 Every, cooking classes, search for recipes
19 using, to prepare for   20 Time, present
21 has, same, to spend
22 Manage, and, be happier, new school year

1 새 학년이 된 걸 환영해.
2 2학년에서, 여러분은 할 일이 더 많을 거야.
3 여러분은 시간을 잘 관리할 필요가 있어.
4 여러분은 시간 관리를 어떻게 하는가?
5 수빈: 나는 작은 목표를 세우고 매일 그것들을 성취해.
6 나는 "나는 영어를 마스터할 거야."라고 말하지 않아.
7 그렇게 큰 목표를 가지면, 나는 아마 그것을 위해 노력하는 걸 내일, 다음 주, 혹은 다음 달까지 미룰 거야.
8 대신에 나는 "나는 매일 세 개의 새로운 영어 단어를 배울 거야."라고 말해.
9 나는 한 번에 한 단계씩 나의 큰 목표를 달성할 거야.
10 민수: 나는 무언가를 할 때 그것에 모든 주의를 기울여.
11 나는 숙제를 하는 동안 SNS 게시 글을 읽곤 했어.
12 집중할 수 없었기 때문에 그것은 나의 속도를 늦추었어.
13 지금 나는 숙제를 할 때 스마트폰을 한쪽에 치워 놔.
14 그렇게 하면 시간이 많이 절약돼.
15 요즈음, 나는 숙제를 빨리 끝내고 자유 시간을 즐겨.
16 John: 나는 내 꿈을 위해 노력하며 규칙적으로 시간을 사용해.
17 나는 요리사가 되고 싶어.
18 토요일 아침마다 나는 요리 강습에 가거나 요리법을 찾아봐.
19 나는 나의 미래를 준비하기 위해 시간을 쓰는 것이 중요하다고 생각해.
20 시간은 선물이다.
21 모든 사람은 매일 소비할 똑같은 선물을 가지고 있다.
22 시간을 잘 관리하면 여러분은 새 학년에 더 행복해질 것이다!

1 Welcome to the new school year.
2 In the second grade, you will have more work to do.
3 You need to manage your time well.
4 How do you do that?
5 Subin: I set small goals and achieve them every day.
6 I do not say, "I will master English."
7 With such a big goal, I will probably put off

working on it until tomorrow, next week, or next month.
8 Instead, I say, "I will learn three new English words every day."
9 I will achieve my big goal, one step at a time.
10 Minsu: When I do something, I give it my full attention.
11 I used to read SNS postings while I was doing my homework.
12 It slowed me down because I couldn't focus.
13 Now, I put aside my smartphone when I do my homework.
14 It saves me a lot of time.
15 These days, I finish my homework quickly and enjoy my free time.
16 John: I regularly spend time working toward my dream.
17 I want to become a chef.
18 Every Saturday morning, I go to cooking classes or search for recipes.
19 I think that using my time to prepare for my future is important.
20 Time is a present.
21 Everyone has the same present to spend every day.
22 Manage your time well, and you will be happier in the new school year!

Enjoy Writing B
1. This Year
2. goals to achieve
3. first, to get along with, classmates
4. second, to get, on
5. last, stop playing
6. that, better than

Project - Step 1
1. think, should, about dreaming, doing
2. believe, dreaming and doing
3. is more important than
4. right

Wrap Up - Writing
1. going, grocery store
2. going, to eat
3. two bottles of, to drink
4. one fashion magazine to read

Enjoy Writing B

1. My Goals for This Year

2. I have three goals to achieve this year.

3. The first goal is to get along with my new classmates.

4. The second goal is to get an A on the English speaking test.

5. The last goal is to stop playing smartphone games.

6. I hope that this year is better than last year.

Project - Step 1

1. A: I think we should make our group's motto about dreaming and doing.

2. B: That's a good idea. I believe that dreaming and doing are different.

3. C: Yes. I think that doing is more important than dreaming.

4. D: That's right.

Wrap Up - Writing

1. Jenny is going to go to the grocery store today.

2. She is going to buy three apples to eat.

3. She is going to buy two bottles of water to drink.

4. She is going to buy one fashion magazine to read.

Lesson **2**

01 어깨	02 다행히도	03 용감한
04 낮추다, 낮아지다	05 가슴	06 위험한
07 기술	08 (각도의 단위인) 도	09 기회, 가능성
10 바닥	11 교육, 훈련	12 아나운서
13 흔들리다	14 연습하다	15 보호하다
16 대단히, 크게	17 심장	18 청중, 시청자
19 ~ 주위에	20 구하다	21 늦게
22 동물원 사육사	23 기억하다	24 신이 난
25 갑자기	26 무서워하는, 겁먹은	
27 경험	28 심폐소생술	29 주의 깊게
30 각도	31 지진	32 젖은
33 잊다	34 행하다, 실시하다	35 ~을 꽉[꼭] 누르다
36 ~에 부딪히다	37 가능한 한 ~한[하게]	
38 넘어지다	39 항상	
40 밑에 들어가다, 밑에 숨다		41 ~의 경우에
42 ~의 어깨를 치다	43 ~을 꼭 잡다, ~을 붙잡다	

01 low	02 angle	03 carefully
04 shout	05 CPR	06 experience
07 breathe	08 teenager	09 earthquake
10 scared	11 wet	12 scary
13 gear	14 forget	15 grade
16 hard	17 important	18 impressive
19 within	20 join	21 open
22 perform	23 safety	24 stay
25 tap	26 chest	27 lower
28 dangerous	29 brave	30 training
31 audience	32 shake	33 remember
34 protect	35 push down	36 fall down
37 as ~ as possible		38 bump into
39 all the time	40 put on	41 in case of
42 up and down	43 get off	

1 wet, 젖은   2 brave, 용감한   3 chest, 가슴

4 save, 구하다   5 earthquake, 지진

6 audience, 청중, 시청자   7 degree, (각도의 단위인) 도

8 protect, 보호하다   9 breathe, 숨을 쉬다, 호흡하다

10 skill, 기술　11 tap, (가볍게) 톡톡 두드리다[치다]
12 perform, 행하다, 실시하다　13 zoo keeper, 동물원 사육사
14 experience, 경험　15 lower, 낮추다, 낮아지다
16 shake, 흔들리다

대화문 TEST Step 1　　　　p.24~25

Listen & Speak 1 A-1

can, buy / Don't forget to / food label / not good for / will check

Listen & Speak 1 A-2

leaving / need to wear, a lot of find dust / didn't know / be bad for, don't forget to wear / All right

Listen & Speak 2 A-1

What's up / to buy, What about / have, in, should go, late / you'd better not run, says, wet / didn't see

Listen & Speak 2 A-2

does, mean / you'd better not, while, are walking / interesting, but / bump into, there are, around, dangerous / see

Conversation A

having, with, to shake, couldn't, fell down, Get, Don't forget, Luckily, scary experience

Conversation B

told, a few / let's practice, ready / is shaking, forget to get under, protect / scary / Hold on to / for now, out / better not use, Use the stairs / Where should, go / need to, with no buildings / let's go to

Wrap Up - Listening 1

almost, stand in line, wait for, get off, move up, down, You'd better not use, in case of

Wrap Up - Listening 2

going to go to, with / sounds / excited because, for, on night / don't forget

대화문 TEST Step 2　　　　p.26~27

Listen & Speak 1 A-1

B: Mom, can I buy some apple juice?
W: Sure, Chris. Don't forget to check the food label.
B: The food label ?
W: Yes. Too much sugar is not good for you.
B: Okay, I will check it.

Listen & Speak 1 A-2

G: Dad, I'm leaving.
M: You need to wear this, Julie. There is a lot of fine dust in the air today.

G: Oh, I didn't know that.
M: It will be bad for your health. So don't forget to wear this mask.
G: All right . Thank you.

Listen & Speak 2 A-1

B: Hi, Amy. What's up?
G: I'm here to buy a shirt. What about you?
B: I have a lunch meeting in this shopping center. Oh, I should go now. I'm late .
G: Okay, but you'd better not run . The sign says the floor is wet.
B: I didn't see it. Thanks.

Listen & Speak 2 A-2

G: What does the sign mean?
B: It means that you'd better not look at your smartphone while you are walking.
G: That's interesting, but why?
B: You can bump into people and there are many cars around here. It's so dangerous.
G: Now I see .

Conversation A

B: I was having a good time with my family last night. Suddenly everything started to shake. I couldn't stand still and almost fell down. Dad shouted, "Get under the table. Don't forget to protect your head." Luckily, the shaking soon stopped. It was a scary experience.

Conversation B

Teacher: I told you a few safety rules for earthquakes today. Now, let's practice. Are you ready?
Amy & Jiho: Yes.
Teacher: Everything is shaking. Don't forget to get under the desk and protect your body first.
Jiho: It's so scary.
Amy: You're doing fine, Jiho. Hold on to the leg of the desk.
Jiho: Oh, the shaking stopped for now. Let's get out!
Teacher: Remember! You'd better not use the elevator. Use the stairs .
Amy: Where should we go now?
Teacher: You need to find an open area with no buildings.
Jiho: Then, let's go to the park.

Wrap Up - Listening 1

G: Many people use this almost every day. People stand in line to enter this. They wait for others to get off before they enter. They use this to move up and down floors in a building. You'd better not use this in case of a fire.

Wrap Up - Listening 2

B: I'm going to go to Jiri Mountain with my dad tomorrow.

G: It sounds great.

B: I'm excited because we are going to stay there for two days and one night.

G: That'll be great, but don't forget to check the weather.

B: Okay.

본문 TEST Step 1　　　　　　　　　　　　p.28~29

01 saved, life, old 02 brave, in, with

03 introduce yourself　　　　04 My, is

05 in, second, at 06 tell us, experience

07 waiting for, with

08 suddenly, fell, front

09 Nobody, what, do

10 as, scared, others

11 ran, tapped, on

12 wasn't moving, breathing

13 said, Call, CPR

14 Announcer, impressive

15 When, such as, skill

16 Safety Training, last

17 learned how, chance, practice

18 show, how, perform　　　19 Keep, straight

20 other, chest, at, angle

21 Push down, hard, until

22 there, other, to remember

23 need, remember, minutes

24 should, within, after, stops

25 later than, lower, saving

26 Timing, important, doing　　27 for joining us

28 My pleasure

본문 TEST Step 2　　　　　　　　　　　　p.30~31

01 saved, life, old man　　　　02 brave, with us

03 introduce yourself　　　　04 My, is

05 in, second, at 06 tell us your experience

07 was waiting for, with

08 suddenly fell in front of

09 Nobody, what to do

10 as scared as, at

11 ran, tapped, on

12 wasn't moving, breathing

13 said to, started CPR　　　14 impressive

15 such as, skill

16 Safety Training, at

17 learned how to do, chance to practice

18 show, how to perform CPR

19 Keep, arms straight

20 other, must, at a 90 degree angle

21 Push down, hard, until an ambulance comes

22 Are there, to remember

23 need to remember, four minutes

24 that, should, within, after someone's heart stops

25 To begin, later than, chances of saving

26 as important as

27 Thank you for joining　　　21 pleasure

본문 TEST Step 3　　　　　　　　　　　　p.32~33

1 아나운서: 어제, 한 십대가 어떤 노인의 생명을 구했습니다.

2 그 용감한 학생이 오늘 우리와 함께 스튜디오에 있습니다.

3 자기소개를 해 보세요.

4 세진: 제 이름은 김세진입니다.

5 저는 한국중학교 2학년입니다.

6 아나운서: 당신의 경험을 우리에게 말해 줄 수 있나요?

7 세진: 물론이죠. 저는 친구 진호와 버스를 기다리고 있었어요.

8 갑자기 한 남자가 우리 앞에 쓰러졌어요.

9 아무도 무엇을 해야 할지 몰랐어요.

10 저는 처음엔 다른 사람들처럼 겁이 났어요.

11 그리고 나서, 저는 그에게 달려가서 그의 어깨를 두드렸어요.

12 그는 움직이지도 숨을 쉬지도 않았어요.

13 저는 진호에게 "119에 전화해."라고 말하고 심폐소생술을 시작했습니다.

14 아나운서: 인상적이네요.

15 언제 그런 중요한 기술을 배웠나요?

16 세진: 지난주에 학교에서 '안전 교육의 날'이 있었어요.

17 저는 심폐소생술을 하는 방법을 배웠고 연습할 기회를 가졌어요.

18 아나운서: 청중들에게 심폐소생술을 어떻게 하는지 보여줄 수 있나요?

19 세진: 네. 팔을 쭉 펴세요.

20 당신의 팔과 다른 사람의 가슴은 90도 각도여야 합니다.

21 구급차가 올 때까지 가슴 중앙을 세게 그리고 빨리 누르세요.

22 아나운서: 기억해야 할 다른 것이 있나요?

23 세진: 네. "골든타임" 4분을 기억해야 합니다.

24 그것은 여러분이 누군가의 심장이 멈춘 후 4분 안에 심폐소생술을

시작해야 한다는 것을 의미합니다.

25 그보다 늦게 심폐소생술을 시작하는 것은 누군가의 생명을 구할 가능성을 크게 낮출 것입니다.

26 아나운서: 타이밍은 심폐소생술을 하는 것만큼이나 중요하군요.

27 저희와 함께 해 주셔서 감사합니다.

28 세진: 제가 더 고맙습니다.

본문 TEST Step 4 - Step 5 　　　　　　p.34~37

1 Announcer: Yesterday, a teenager saved the life of an old man.

2 The brave student is in the studio with us today.

3 Please introduce yourself.

4 Sejin: My name is Kim Sejin.

5 I'm in the second grade at Hanguk Middle School.

6 Announcer: Could you tell us your experience?

7 Sejin: Sure. I was waiting for the bus with my friend, Jinho.

8 A man suddenly fell in front of us.

9 Nobody knew what to do.

10 I was as scared as the others at first.

11 Then, I ran to him and tapped him on the shoulder.

12 He wasn't moving or breathing.

13 I said to Jinho, "Call 119," and started CPR.

14 Announcer: That's impressive.

15 When did you learn such an important skill?

16 Sejin: We had Safety Training Day at school last week.

17 I learned how to do CPR and had a chance to practice.

18 Announcer: Can you show the audience how to perform CPR?

19 Sejin: Yes. Keep your arms straights.

20 Your arms and the other person's chest must be at a 90 degree angle.

21 Push down in the center of the chest hard and fast until an ambulance comes.

22 Announcer: Are there any other things to remember?

23 Sejin: Yes. You need to remember the four minutes of "Golden Time."

24 It means that you should start CPR within four minutes after someone's heart stops.

25 To begin CPR later than that will greatly lower the chances of saving someone's life.

26 Announcer: Timing is as important as doing CPR.

27 Thank you for joining us.

28 Sejin: My pleasure.

구석구석지문 TEST Step 1 　　　　　　p.38

My Writing B

1. Save, Fire

2. what to do, there is

3. should shout

4. need to cover, with a wet towel

5. have to stay, as, get out

6. as soon as you can

7. Don't forget to use, not

Wrap Up

1. Training

2. Safety, at school

3. taught us what to do

4. how to protect

5. where to go, shaking stops

Project - Step 3

1. tell you what to do

2. don't forget to, safety glasses

3. better not, around

구석구석지문 TEST Step 2 　　　　　　p.39

My Writing B

1. Save Your Life from a Fire

2. Do you know what to do when there is a fire?

3. You should shout, "Fire!"

4. You need to cover your face and body with a wet towel.

5. You have to stay as low as possible and get out.

6. Also, you need to call 119 as soon as you can.

7. Don't forget to use the stairs, not the elevator.

Wrap Up

1. Safety Training Day

2. Today we had Safety Training Day at school.

3. Teachers taught us what to do when an earthquake hits.

4. We learned how to protect our heads and bodies.

5. We also learned where to go when the shaking stops.

Project - Step 3

1. We'll tell you what to do for safety in the science room.

2. First, don't forget to use safety glasses.

3. Second, you'd better not run around.

Lesson **3**

단어 TEST Step 1   p.40

01 자세	02 끌다, 당기다	03 스트레칭하다
04 어려운	05 자연	06 조언, 충고
07 밀다	08 운동하다	09 이해하다, 알다
10 놓다, 두다	11 세다	12 (시간 단위인) 초
13 어깨	14 활동	15 그러나
16 삶	17 붓다	18 바꾸다
19 뒤쪽, 뒷부분	20 마사지; 마사지를 하다	
21 목	22 다운로드하다	23 뒤로
24 놓다, 두다	25 보여[가르쳐] 주다	
26 허리	27 편안한	28 구부리다
29 ~을 낮추다, ~을 낮게 하다		30 습관
31 신선한	32 보통, 대개	33 간단한, 단순한
34 따뜻한	35 서로	36 ~와 협력하다
37 (빛을) 가리다[차단하다]		38 회복[극복]하다
39 위에서 아래까지	40 ~에 집중하다	41 몸을 풀어 주다
42 똑바로 하다	43 ~에 좋다	

단어 TEST Step 2   p.41

01 already	02 behind	03 comfortable
04 softly	05 step	06 way
07 move	08 fall	09 face
10 fishing	11 habit	12 warm
13 both	14 hold	15 bend
16 exercise	17 nature	18 difficult
19 activity	20 relax	21 healthy
22 lower	23 simple	24 fresh
25 stress	26 light	27 like
28 reduce	29 usually	30 bowl
31 stretch	32 backward	33 neck
34 position	35 warm up	
36 from top to bottom		37 focus on
38 for a few seconds		39 be worried about
40 prepare for	41 block out	42 straighten up
43 get over		

단어 TEST Step 3   p.42

1 count, 세다   2 simple, 간단한   3 comfortable, 편안한
4 reduce, 줄이다   5 advice, 조언   6 shoulder, 어깨
7 switch, 바꾸다   8 neck, 목   9 bend, 구부리다
10 position, 자세   11 relax, (근육 등의) 긴장을 풀다
12 habit, 습관   13 stretch, 스트레칭하다
14 warm up, 준비 운동을 하다   15 pull, 당기다
16 massage, 마사지

대화문 TEST Step 1   p.43~44

Listen & Speak 1 A-1

something healthy, have, adivce / often eat, makes, feel / how to make / simple, cut, into, put, into, pour, mix / should try

Listen & Speak 1 A-2

more than / steps, to be healthy, count, steps easily / can use, how to use / Can, show me / download, with, check, steps you took / will start using

Listen & Speak 2 A-1

What, enjoy doing / enjoy cooking healthy food / Sounds, can, make / can make

Listen & Speak 2 A-2

on weekends / take pictures / What kind, usually take / enjoy taking, of, like / reduce my stress

Listen & Speak 2 A-3

have a puppy / Her, really like / What, with her / enjoy taking, makes, healthy

Conversation A

have, speaking, preparing, for, ago, speaking in, am worried about, cannot sleep

Conversation B

what's matter / stressed about, next week / ride, when / know how to ride / No, don't / go out, can, Put, on, push, with / Like, feel better / enjoy, riding, because, reduces / great

Wrap Up 1

look sick, What's / have a cold / see a doctor / yet, get over / warm, when, makes me feel better / Sounds, will try

Wrap Up 2

enjoys, fishing, Early, comes back, enjoys drawing, to draw, enjoy playing

대화문 TEST Step 2   p.45~46

Listen & Speak 1 A-1

B: I want to eat something healthy. Do you have any adivce?
G: I often eat fresh salad. It makes me feel good.

B: Really? Do you know how to make it?

G: Yes, it's quite simple. First, cut many vegetables into small pieces. Next, put them into a bowl. Then, pour some lemon juice on them. Finally, mix everything together.

B: That's it? I should try it.

Listen & Speak 1 A-2

B: People say that we should walk more than 10,000 steps every day to be healthy. I can't count the number of my steps easily.

G: You can use this smartphone app. Do you know how to use it?

B: No. Can you show me?

G: Sure. First, download the app. Then, walk with your smartphone. Later, you can check the number of steps you took.

B: Thank you. I will start using it today.

Listen & Speak 2 A-1

G: What do you enjoy doing after school?

B: I enjoy cooking healthy food.

G: Sounds cool. What can you make?

B: I can make salad, Bibimbap, and vegetable juice.

Listen & Speak 2 A-2

B: What do you do on weekends?

G: I take pictures.

B: What kind of pictures do you usually take?

G: I enjoy taking pictures of nature, like trees and flowers. The beautiful pictures reduce my stress.

Listen & Speak 2 A-3

G: Do you have a puppy?

B: Yes. Her name is Coco. I really like her.

G: What do you do with her?

B: I enjoy taking a walk with her. It makes me healthy.

Conversation A

B: Tomorrow, I have an English speaking contest. I started preparing for the contest two weeks ago. I enjoy speaking in English, but I am worried about the contest. I cannot sleep well.

Conversation B

Karl: Hana, what's the matter?

Hana: Well, I'm stressed about the test next week.

Karl: I understand. I ride my longboard when I'm stressed. Do you know how to ride a longboard?

Hana: No, I don't.

Karl: Let's go out! I can teach you. Put one foot on the board and push hard with the other.

Hana: Like this? Wow! This is fun. I feel better already.

Karl: See? I enjoy riding my longboard because it reduces my stress.

Hana: That's great!

Wrap Up 1

B: You look sick. What's the matter?

G: Well, I have a cold.

B: Did you see a doctor?

G: Not yet. Do you know how to get over a cold?

B: Well, I usually drink warm water when I have a cold. It makes me feel better.

G: Sounds good. I will try it.

Wrap Up 2

B: My family enjoys many activities. My dad enjoys fishing . Early in the morning, he goes to the lake and comes back with some fish. My mom enjoys drawing pictures. She likes to draw beautiful mountains and lakes. My brother and I enjoy playing soccer.

본문 TEST Step 1   p.47~48

01 At, for, hours   02 Do, get tired

03 don't, yourself, stretch   04 Let's, with

05 Close, massage, softly   06 will relax

07 When, cover, block out

08 make, feel, comfortable

09 massage, neck   10 Put, on, back

11 circles, fingers, massage   12 top, bottom

13 help, feel better

14 Let's, on, waist   15 Team up

16 close, other, faces   17 Hold, other's

18 stretch, body backward

19 Hold, for, seconds   20 pull, to

21 should move, speed   22 If, both, fall

23 Place, top, on, behind

24 bend, lower yourself

25 Hold, few, straighten up

26 position, loosen up

27 Switch, repeat, exercise   28 How, feel

29 massage, stretch, feel healthier

30 focus on, studies

본문 TEST Step 2   p.49~50

01 At school, for 02 get tired

03 Why don't, yourself, stretch

04 Let's begin with

05 Close, massage, with, fingers   06 will relax

07 When, cover, with, block out

08 make, feel more comfortable

09 massage your neck   10 Put, on, back

11 Draw, with to massage

12 from top to bottom

13 help you feel better

14 Let's work on, waist   15 Team up, with

16 each other, faces   17 Hold, wrists

18 Slowly stretch, backward

19 Hold, for three seconds   20 pull, to

21 your, at   22 If, both of, will fall

23 Place, top, on, behind

24 slowly bend, lower

25 Hold, a few seconds, straighten up

26 The position, loosen up

27 Switch, repeat the exercise   28 How, feel

29 massage, stretch every day, feel healthier

30 can focus on, better

---

1 학교에서 여러분은 오랜 시간에 걸쳐 앉아 있다.

2 여러분은 피곤한가?

3 마사지와 스트레칭을 하는 게 어떤가?

4 눈부터 시작하자

5 눈을 감고 손가락으로 눈을 부드럽게 마사지해라.

6 그것은 여러분의 눈을 편안하게 해줄 것이다.

7 끝나면, 빛을 차단하기 위해 손으로 눈을 가려라.

8 그것은 여러분의 눈을 더 편안하게 해줄 것이다.

9 다음으로, 여러분의 목을 마사지해라.

10 여러분의 목 뒤에 손가락을 대라.

11 여러분의 목을 마사지하기 위해 손가락으로 작은 원을
   그려라.

12 위에서 아래로 마사지해라.

13 마사지는 여러분의 기분이 좋아지도록 도울 것이다.

14 허리 운동을 하자.

15 친구와 짝을 이루어라.

16 서로 가까이 서서 여러분의 파트너를 마주 보아라.

17 서로의 손목을 잡아라.

18 천천히 여러분의 머리와 몸을 뒤로 뻗어라.

19 3초 동안 그 자세를 유지해라.

20 그리고 나서, 천천히 서로 선 자세로 끌어 당겨라.

21 너와 너의 파트너는 같은 속도로 움직여야 한다.

22 그렇지 않으면, 너희 둘 다 넘어질 것이다!

---

23 여러분의 뒤에 있는 책상 위에 오른쪽 발등을 올려놓아라.

24 그리고 나서, 천천히 왼쪽 다리를 구부리고 몸을 낮추어라.

25 몇 초 동안 그 자세를 유지하다가 천천히 몸을 펴라.

26 이 자세는 여러분의 오른쪽 다리를 풀어 줄 것이다.

27 다리를 바꿔서 운동을 반복해라.

28 지금 기분이 어떤가?

29 매일 마사지와 스트레칭을 하면, 여러분은 더 건강해지는
   것을 느낄 것이다.

30 또한, 여러분은 공부에 더 집중할 수 있을 것이다.

---

1 At school you sit for many hours.

2 Do you get tired?

3 Why don't you massage yourself and stretch?

4 Let's begin with the eyes.

5 Close your eyes and massage them softly with
  your fingers.

6 It will relax your eyes.

7 When you finish, cover your eyes with your hands
  to block out the light.

8 It will make your eyes feel more comfortable.

9 Next, massage your neck.

10 Put your fingers on the back of your neck.

11 Draw small circles with your fingers to massage
   your neck.

12 Massage from top to bottom.

13 The massage will help you feel better.

14 Let's work on your waist.

15 Team up with a friend.

16 Stand close to each other and face your partner.

17 Hold each other's wrists.

18 Slowly stretch your head and body backward.

19 Hold that position for three seconds.

20 Then, slowly pull each other to a standing position.

21 You and your partner should move at the same
   speed.

22 If you don't, both of you will fall!

23 Place the top of your right foot on the desk
   behind you.

24 Then, slowly bend your left leg and lower
   yourself.

25 Hold it for a few seconds and slowly straighten
   up.

26 This position will loosen up your right leg.

27 Switch your legs and repeat the exercise.

28 How do you feel now?

29 If you massage yourself and stretch every day, you will feel healthier.

30 Also, you can focus on your studies better.'

Enjoy Writing C

1. to Be Healthier

2. Here is

3. more than three times

4. every day

5. three times a week, become stronger

6. if, will feel better,

7. habits, make me live

Project - Step 2

1. how to stretch

2. stretching exercise is called

3. with, to warm up

4. Then, with

5. will stretch, shoulders

6. make

7. in a circle, feel nice

8. Finally

9. a little bit, be good for

Wrap Up - Writing

1. these days, should, go

2. get stressed, makes me feel

3. how to download

Enjoy Writing C

1. My Plan to Be Healthier

2. Here is my plan to be healthier

3. I will exercise more than three times a week.

4. I will eat breakfast every day.

5. If I exercise more than three times a week, I will become stronger.

6. Also, if I eat breakfast every day, I will feel better in the morning.

7. I will change my habits, and it will make me live a healthy life.

Project - Step 2

1. Do you know how to stretch your shoulders?

2. Our stretching exercise is called "Number Stretching."

3. First, make a number "I" with your arm to warm up.

4. Then, make a number "2" with your arms. 5

5. It will stretch your shoulders.

6. Now, make a number "3".

7. If you move your arms in a circle, it will feel nice.

8. Finally, make a number "4".

9. It is a little bit difficult, but it will be good for your shoulders.

Wrap Up - Writing

1. Sumi: I feel stressed these days. What should I do?

2. Jiae: When I get stressed, I listen to music. It makes me feel better.

3. If you don't know how to download music, I will show you.

Lesson 4

단어 TEST Step 1 　　　　　　　　　　p.59

01 기아, 배고픔　　02 (폐기물을) 재활용하다
03 자연환경, 환경　　04 (특별한 날·경사 등을) 축하하다, 기념하다
05 살리다, 구하다　　06 ~을 목표로 삼다, 지향하다
07 교육　　08 멀리; 먼　　09 홍수
10 다치게 하다　　11 모으다　　12 생산하다
13 보내다, 전하다　　14 어른　　15 같이 쓰다, 공유하다
16 참여하다　　17 쓰레기　　18 엉망진창의
19 아무것도 ~ 아니다　　20 (자금 등을) 모금하다
21 낭비하다, 허비하다　　22 랜턴, 등불, 등
23 굉장한, 감탄할 만한, 엄청난　　24 전 세계적인 지구상의
25 공동체, 사회　　26 의사소통하다　　27 정원
28 가난한　　29 ~ 옆에, 나란히　　30 접시
31 시민　　32 보호하다　　33 (회의·시합 등을) 열다
34 국제적인　　35 ~을 돌보다, 신경 쓰다
36 ~ 덕분에　　37 (~에 대해서) 조심하다
38 ~으로 죽다　　39 잘 되다　　40 ~을 잘하다
41 ~을 버리다　　42 어려움에 처한
43 A를 B와 나누다[나눠 가지다]

단어 TEST Step 2 　　　　　　　　　　p.60

01 citizen　　02 American　　03 poor
04 fight　　05 alongside　　06 community
07 awesome　　08 campaign　　09 garden
10 plate　　11 sell　　12 upload
13 global　　14 hold　　15 international
16 upset　　17 leave　　18 communicate
19 protect　　20 site　　21 take
22 environment　　23 gather　　24 trash
25 education　　26 hurt　　27 adult
28 save　　29 recycle　　30 produce
31 flood　　32 celebrate　　33 hunger
34 raise　　35 care about　　36 take a shower
37 in need　　38 watch out (for)
39 throw away　　40 be good at　　41 thanks to
42 care for　　43 die of

단어 TEST Step 3 　　　　　　　　　　p.61

1 adult, 어른　　2 flood, 홍수　　3 garden, 정원
4 messy, 엉망진창의　　5 poor, 가난한　　6 sell, 팔다

---

7 aim, ~을 목표로 삼다, 지향하다
8 global, 전 세계적인, 지구상의
9 recycle, 폐기물을 재활용하다　　10 upset, 당황한
11 waste, 낭비하다, 허비하다
12 raise, (자금 등을) 모금하다
13 celebrate, (특별한 날·경사 등을) 축하하다, 기념하다
14 gather, 모으다　　15 citizen, 시민
16 communicate, 의사소통하다

대화문 TEST Step 1 　　　　　　　　　　p.62~63

Listen & Speak 1 A

1 watch, about the flood / I did, a lot of, lost / going to send / How, Are you, to raise / going to make, sell
2 plans, vacation / going to, do some volunteer work with / went, helped, Are you going to do / also paint, with / sounds nice

Listen & Speak 1 B

1 Are, going to take / am, I'm not
2 going to recycle bottles / I am, I'm not

Listen & Speak 2 A

1 What / making, about, hunger, dying of hunger / too bad / hope, care about global
2 decided to make, garden / vegetable garden, will / grow, share, with / good idea / hope, grow well

Listen & Speak 2 B

1 hope, don't throw away trash / hope so, Let's hold / campaign
2 I hope people don't hurt / hope so, Let's hold / good idea

Wrap Up

1 What's your plan, Are, going to do anything special / On, going to visit / How about on / have no plans / going to do volunteer work, like to come
2 going to hold, at school next Friday / What is / campaign to protect, throw trash on, to stop / hope, goes / hope so, too

대화문 TEST Step 2 　　　　　　　　　　p.64~65

Listen & Speak 1 A

1 B: Did you watch the news about the flood?
　 G: Yes, I did. They said a lot of people lost their homes.

51

B: My club is going to send them some money.

G: How can you do that? Are you going to raise money, Andy?

B: Yes. We're going to make pencil cases and sell them.

2 B: Do you have any plans for the summer vacation, Suji?

G: Yes. I'm going to the Philippines to do some volunteer work with my family.

B: Oh, I went there and helped some children study last year. Are you going to do that, too?

G: Yes. And I'll also paint walls with the children.

B: That sounds nice.

Listen & Speak 1 B

1 G: Are you going to take a short shower?

B: Yes, I am. / No, I'm not.

2 G: Are you going to recycle bottles?

B: Yes, I am. / No, I'm not.

Listen & Speak 2 A

1 G: What are you doing, Jason?

B: I'm making a poster about global hunger. Many people are dying of hunger.

G: That's too bad. I didn't know that.

B: I hope more people care about global hunger.

2 G: Dad, my class decided to make a vegetable garden.

M: A vegetable garden? What will you grow there, Sena?

G: Carrots. We'll grow them and share them with others.

M: That's a good idea.

G: I hope the carrots grow well.

Listen & Speak 2 B

1 A: I hope people don't throw away trash.

B: I hope so, too. Let's hold a Keep the World Clean campaign.

A: That's a good idea.

2 A: I hope people don't hurt animals.

B: I hope so, too. Let's hold a Love Animals campaign.

A: That's a good idea.

Wrap Up

1 B: What's your plan for the weekend, Sumin? Are you going to do anything special?

G: Yes. On Saturday, I'm going to visit my grandmother.

B: How about on Sunday?

G: I have no plans for Sunday. Why?

B: I'm going to do volunteer work at the library on Sunday. Would you like to come with me?

G: Sure.

2 G: My club is going to hold a green campaign at school next Friday.

B: What is a green campaign?

G: It's a campaign to protect the environment. Many students throw trash on the streets. We hope to stop that.

B: I hope your campaign goes well.

G: Thanks. I hope so, too.

본문 **TEST** Step 1   p.66~67

01 Global Citizenship   02 This, Citizenship, site
03 helps, grow as   04 try, understand, cultures
05 care for, in need
06 share, global, experiences
07 am, from Korea   08 a member of
09 aims, communicate with
10 ago, produced, lantern
11 uploaded, amazingly, nearly, hits
12 Click, for, video   13 yours, looks fantastic
14 have, in, village   15 make, like yours
16 my name   17 am from
18 few, ago, showed, of   19 all using, to carry
20 decided, raise, send   21 sold, drinks, raised
22 hope, happy with   23 Awesome, sure, will
24 something wonderful   25 am, from
26 painting, make, look better
27 good, gathered, painted
28 Thanks, much nicer
29 walking alongside, painted 30 What a nice

본문 **TEST** Step 2   p.68~69

01 Global, Education
02 This, Citizenship Education site
03 helps, grow as global citizens
04 try to understand, cultures
05 care for, in need, a better world
06 share, global, experiences
07 am, from Korea   08 a member of
09 aims to communicate with, around
10 A week ago, about the lantern festival
11 uploaded, amazingly, got nearly, hits

12 Click, for, video   13 your, looks fantastic

14 have, in, village   15 like to make, like yours

16 my name   17 am from

18 few, ago, showed us pictures of

19 Sadly, all using, to carry

20 decided, raise money to send

21 sold, drinks, raised

22 hope, are happy with

23 Awesome, sure, will like

24 did something wonderful

25 am, from Malaysia

26 wall painting, to make, look better

27 are good at, gathered, painted

28 Thanks to, looks much nicer

29 enjoy walking alongside, painted

30 What a nice idea

본문 TEST Step 3   p.70~71

1 세계 시민 교육

2 이곳은 세계 시민 교육 사이트입니다.

3 세계 시민 교육은 우리가 세계 시민으로 자라도록 도와줍니다.

4 세계 시민은 다른 문화를 이해하려고 노력하는 사람들입니다.

5 그들은 또한 어려움에 처한 사람들을 보살피고 더 나은 세상을 위해서 일합니다.

6 당신의 세계 시민 교육 경험을 이곳에 공유해 주세요.

7 안녕. 나는 한국의 민희야.

8 나는 세계 공동체 동아리의 회원이야.

9 우리 동아리는 전 세계의 사람들과 소통하는 것을 목표로 해.

10 일주일 전에 우리는 우리 마을의 등 축제에 관한 비디오를 제작했어.

11 우리는 그것을 인터넷에 올렸는데, 놀랍게도 거의 5,000개의 조회 수를 획득했어.

12 우리 비디오를 보려면 이곳을 클릭해.

13 Alice: 와, 너희 등 축제는 환상적으로 보인다!

14 Sunan: 우리 마을에는 물 축제가 있어.

15 나도 너희 것과 같은 비디오를 만들고 싶어.

16 안녕, 내 이름은 Jo야.

17 나는 호주 출신이야.

18 몇 주 전에, 선생님이 우리에게 케냐에 있는 학생들의 사진을 보여주셨어.

19 슬프게도, 그들은 모두 책을 들고 다니기 위해서 비닐 봉지를 사용하고 있었어.

20 우리 반은 그들에게 새로운 책가방을 보내기 위해서 기금을 모금하기로 결정했어.

21 우리는 쿠키와 음료를 팔아서 600달러를 모았어.

22 우리는 케냐의 학생들이 그들의 새 가방을 좋아하기를 바라.

---

23 Wang: 멋지다! 분명 그들이 가방을 좋아할 거야.

24 Kozo: 훌륭한 일을 했구나!

25 난 말레이시아의 Afig야.

26 우리 학교는 우리 마을을 좀 더 좋아 보이게 하기 위해서 벽화 캠페인을 시작했어.

27 그림을 잘 그리는 학생들이 모여서 학교와 공원 벽에 그림을 그렸어.

28 이 캠페인 덕분에, 우리 마을은 훨씬 멋져 보여.

29 이제 모든 사람들이 그림이 그려진 벽을 따라서 산책하는 것을 즐길 수 있어.

30 Junho: 정말 멋진 생각이다!

본문 TEST Step 4-Step 5   p.72~75

1 Global Citizenship Education

2 This is the Global Citizenship Education site.

3 Global Citizenship Education helps us grow as global citizens.

4 Global citizens are people who try to understand different cultures.

5 They also care for people in need and work for a better world.

6 Please share your global citizenship education experiences here.

7 Hello. I am Minhee from Korea.

8 I am a member of the Global Community Club.

9 My club aims to communicate with people from around the world.

10 A week ago we produced a video about the lantern festival in our village.

11 We uploaded it to the Internet and amazingly, we got nearly 5,000 hits.

12 Click here for our video.

13 Alice: Wow, your lantern festival looks fantastic!

14 Sunan: We have a water festival in our village.

15 I'd like to make a video like yours.

16 Hi, my name is Jo.

17 I am from Australia.

18 A few weeks ago, my teacher showed us pictures of students in Kenya.

19 Sadly, they were all using plastic bags to carry their books.

20 My class decided to raise money to send them new school bags.

21 We sold cookies and drinks and raised 600 dollars.

22 We hope the Kenyan students are happy with the

new bags.

23 Wang: Awesome! I'm sure they will like the bags.

24 Kozo: You did something wonderful!

25 I am Afig from Malaysia.

26 My school started a wall painting campaign to make our village look better.

27 Students who are good at painting gathered and painted on some walls of schools and parks.

28 Thanks to this campaign, our village looks much nicer.

29 Now everyone can enjoy walking alongside the painted walls.

30 Junho: What a nice idea!

구석구석지문 TEST Step 1

p.76

Conversation B

1. isn't, too much, going to, all of
2. not sure, favorite
3. Look at, Think, Save
4. What does that mean
5. It means
6. think, took, Let's share
7. That's a good idea
8. ate, all, makes me feel good
9. Let's not waste, from now on, can save

Project

1. What kind activity
2. What do you think about sending
3. are happy with
4. Let's make, to find people who want to help
5. Shoes of Hope
6. children who don't have shoes
7. Bring, from home
8. Draw, write caring words
9. in need
10. July 3rd
11. If, to do something special, join

구석구석지문 TEST Step 2

p.77

Conversation B

1. Karl: Jiho, isn't that too much? Are you going to eat all of that?
2. Jiho: I'm not sure, but Bulgogi is my favorite.
3. Karl: Hey! Look at the campaign poster. "Think,

Eat, Save!"

4. Jiho: What does that mean?
5. Karl: It means "Think first before you eat and save the Earth."
6. Jiho: I think I took too much Bulgogi. Let's share it.
7. Karl: Okay. That's a good idea.
8. Jiho: We ate it all. My clean plate makes me feel good.
9. Karl: Let's not waste food from now on. I hope we can save the Earth.

Project

1. A: What kind activity do you like?
2. B: What do you think about sending shoes to poor children?
3. C: Good. I hope they are happy with them.
4. D: Let's make a poster about the activity to find people who want to help.
5. Sending Shoes of Hope
6. Why: To help poor children who don't have shoes
7. How: 1. Bring shoes from home.
8. 2. Draw pictures or write caring words on them.
9. 3. Send them to children in need.
10. When: July 3rd
11. If you want to do something special for the world, join us!

11 inventor, 발명가　12 completely, 완전히

13 gravity, 중력　14 female, 여성, 암컷

15 strike, 부딪치다, 충돌하다　16 tongue, 혀

단어 TEST Step 1　　　　　p.78

01 화제, 주제　02 ~ 동안, ~ 중에　03 남성, 수컷

04 (위치 · 방향) ~쪽으로　05 다시

06 중력　07 두 번, 두 배

08 (사람 · 동식물 등이) 자라다, 성장하다　09 뼈

10 무게가 ~ 나가다, 무게를 달다　11 화성

12 항목, 물품　13 번개, 벼락　14 금속

15 (few의 비교급) 보다 적은　16 (자식 · 새끼를) 낳다

17 쉬다, 휴식하다　18 모기　19 혀

20 약화시키다, 약화되다 21 팽창하다　22 여성, 암컷

23 발명가　24 충분한　25 보통, 평균

26 추측하다　27 거짓의　28 완전히

29 피　30 성인, 어른　31 물다

32 고래　33 금성　34 같은, 똑같은

35 ~로 가득 차다　36 사실상, 실제로　37 ~ 때문에

38 여러 번, 몇 번이고 39 ~와 같은　40 (특정한 수 또는 정도) ~까지

41 알아보다, 찾아보다 42 사라지다

43 약간의, 조금

단어 TEST Step 2　　　　　p.79

01 completely　02 whale　03 blood

04 false　05 female　06 expand

07 Venus　08 same　09 strike

10 guess　11 heat　12 lay

13 average　14 inventor　15 next

16 enough　17 adult　18 bite

19 weaken　20 gravity　21 lightning

22 twice　23 mosquito　24 item

25 topic　26 Mars　27 rest

28 produce　29 tongue　30 male

31 bone　32 metal　33 toward

34 during　35 in fact　36 on average

37 find out　38 be full of　39 such as

40 due to　41 go away　42 over and over

43 join together

단어 TEST Step 3　　　　　p.80

1 blood, 피　2 false, 거짓의　3 male, 남성, 수컷

4 bite, 물다　5 metal, 금속

6 weigh, 무게가 ~나가다, 무게를 달다　7 expand, 팽창하다

8 mosquito, 모기　9 average, 보통, 평균　10 bone, 뼈

본문 TEST Step 1　　　　　p.81~82

01 Interesting Facts, Around

02 Welcome to, Ask　03 full of, things

04 Take, out, much　05 Are ready

06 gets taller during　07 fewer, than

08 Only, bite　09 never strikes, twice

10 the biggest, on　11 There, no, in

12 expands in　13 Due to, expands

14 gets, taller than

15 Adults, but, about

16 With, join together, fewer

17 Only female, bite　18 need, to produce

19 enough blood, rest, lay

20 can strike, same, over

21 gets, by, on average

22 The biggest, on, whale

23 weigh up, grow, long　24 alone, much as

25 In, gravity, space

26 farther, weakens, goes away

27 get, such as, that　28 Which, these, most

29 There, another, soon　30 Guess what, be

31 See, next

본문 TEST Step 2　　　　　p.83~84

01 Interesting Facts, Around

02 Welcome to, Ask　03 is full of, things

04 Take, find out how much　05 Are, ready

06 Quiz　07 gets taller during

08 fewer bones than adults

09 Only female, bite

10 never strikes, same place twice

11 the biggest, on

12 There, no gravity in　13 expands in heat

14 Due to summer heat, expands

15 gets, taller than in winter

16 Adults, bones, but babies, about

17 With time, join together, fewer bones than babies

18 Only female, will bite

19 need, to produce eggs

55

20 enough blood, rest for a few days, lay

21 can strike, same, over and over again

22 gets, by, times a year on average

23 The biggest, on, whale

24 can weigh up to, grow up to, long

25 alone, weigh as much as　26 In fact, gravity, space

27 farther, weakens, never goes away completely

28 get, such as, becomes stronger than that

29 Which, these, the most interesting

30 There, be another, soon　31 Guess what, will be

32 See, next month

본문 TEST Step 3　p.85~86

1 흥미로운 사실들은 우리 주위에 있다

2 "Lawrence 박사에게 물어 보세요"에 오신 것을 환영합니다!

3 세상은 흥미로운 것들로 가득 차 있습니다.

4 퀴즈를 풀어보고 그것들에 대해 얼마나 아는지 알아보세요.

5 준비 됐나요?

6 퀴즈

7 에펠 타워는 여름에 키가 더 커진다.

8 아기들은 어른보다 더 적은 수의 뼈를 가지고 있다.

9 암컷 모기만이 사람을 문다.

10 번개는 결코 같은 곳을 내리치지 않는다.

11 코끼리는 지구에서 가장 큰 동물이다.

12 우주에는 중력이 없다.

13 금속은 열에 팽창한다.

14 여름의 열기 때문에, 에펠 타워의 금속은 팽창한다.

15 여름에 에펠 타워는 겨울보다 15센티미터 정도 더 커진다.

16 어른은 206개의 뼈를 가지고 있고, 아기는 대략 300개의 뼈를 가지고 있다.

17 시간이 흐르면서, 아기의 몇몇 뼈들은 붙는다. 그래서 어른들은 아기보다 더 적은 수의 뼈를 가지고 있다.

18 오직 암컷 모기만이 당신을 물 것이다.

19 그들은 알을 생산하기 위해서 피가 필요하다.

20 암컷 모기는 충분히 흡혈을 한 뒤, 며칠 동안 쉬고 알을 낳는다.

21 번개는 같은 곳을 반복해서 칠 수 있다.

22 엠파이어스테이트 빌딩은 한 해 평균 스물세 번 번개를 맞는다.

23 지구상에서 가장 큰 동물은 흰긴수염고래이다.

24 그것은 무게가 180톤까지 나갈 수 있으며 길이는 30미터 까지 자랄 수 있다.

25 이 고래의 허의 무게만 해도 아프리카 코끼리의 평균 무게만큼 무겁다.

26 사실, 중력은 우주의 어디에나 있다.

27 지구에서 멀어 질수록 지구의 중력은 약해지지만, 결코 그것이 완전히 사라지는 것은 아니다.

28 당신이 화성이나 금성 같은 다른 행성에 더 가까워진다면, 그들의 중력은 지구의 그것보다 더 강해진다.

29 이 퀴즈들 중 어떤 퀴즈가 가장 흥미로웠나요?

30 곧 또 다른 퀴즈가 있을 것입니다.

31 다음 주제는 무엇일지 맞춰보세요.

32 다음 달에 만나요.

본문 TEST Step 4　p.87~88

1 Interesting Facts Are Around Us

2 Welcome to "Ask Dr. Lawrence"!

3 The world is full of interesting things.

4 Take this quiz and find out how much you know about them.

5 Are you ready?

6 Quiz: The Eiffel Tower gets taller during the summer.

7 Babies have fewer bones than adults.

8 Only female mosquitoes bite people.

9 Lightning never strikes the same place twice.

10 The elephant is the biggest animal on the Earth.

11 There is no gravity in space.

12 Metal expands in heat.

13 Due to summer heat, the metal of the Eiffel Tower expands.

14 In summer, the Eiffel tower gets 15cm taller than in winter.

15 Adults have 206 bones, but babies have about 300 bones.

16 With time, some of the babies' bones join together, so adults have fewer bones than babies.

17 Only female mosquitoes will bite you.

18 They need blood to produce eggs.

19 After a female mosquito gets enough blood, she'll rest for a few days and lay her eggs.

20 Lightning can strike the same place over and over again.

21 The Empire State Building gets hit by lightning 23 times a year on average.

22 The biggest animal on the Earth is the blue whale.

23 It can weigh up to 180 tons and grow up to 30 meters long.

24 Its tongue alone can weigh as much as an average African elephant.

25 In fact, there is gravity everywhere in space.

26 As you get farther from the Earth, the gravity of the Earth weakens, but it never goes away completely.

27 When you get closer to another planet, such as Mars or Venus, its gravity becomes stronger than that of the Earth.

28 Which of these quiz items is the most interesting to you?

29 There will be another quiz soon.

30 Guess what the next topic will be.

31 See you next month.

본문 TEST Step 5　p.89~90

정답은 p.220~221 Reading 교과서 확인학습 B와 동일

1학기 전과정

적중100 plus

영어 기출 문제집

정답 및 해설

시사 | 박준언

적중 **100** + 특별부록

Plan B

우리학교 최신기출

시사 · 박준언 교과서를 배우는

학교 시험문제 분석 · 모음 · 해설집

전국단위 학교 시험문제 수집 및 분석
출제 빈도가 높은 문제 위주로 선별
문제 풀이에 필요한 상세한 해설

중2-1
영어

시사 · 박준언

◎ 선택형 문항의 답안은 컴퓨터용 수정 싸인펜을 사용하여 OMR 답안지에 바르게 표기하시오.
◎ 서술형 문제는 답을 답안지에 반드시 검정 볼펜으로 쓰시오.
◎ 총 30문항 100점 만점입니다. 문항별 배점은 각 문항에 표시되어 있습니다.

[경기 ○○중]

1. 다음 영영 풀이에 해당하는 단어는?   (3점)

knowledge or skill in a particular job or activity, which you have gained because you have done that job or activity for a long time

① experience
② attention
③ experiment
④ impression
⑤ emergency

[서울 강남구○○중]

3. ⓐ와 ⓑ에 들어갈 표현으로 알맞은 것은?   (3점)

• Tom goes to his uncle's house every Sunday. He visits him _____ ⓐ _____.
• The quiz is not difficult. Anyone can solve it _____ ⓑ _____.

	ⓐ		ⓑ
①	really	–	easily
②	easily	–	finally
③	easily	–	regularly
④	finally	–	really
⑤	regularly	–	easily

[서울 광진구 ○○중]

2. 빈칸에 가장 알맞은 단어를 찾아 문장을 완성하시오. (단어는 한 번씩만 사용할 것)   (3점)

stretch	volunteer	advice
attention	appointment	achieve
remember		

(1) How often do you do _____ work?
(2) Can you give me some _____?
(3) You must pay _____ to the teacher.

[충북 ○○중]

4. 다음 상황에 맞추어 볼 때 빈칸 (A)에 들어갈 가장 적절한 말은?   (4점)

• I make a plan to save time.
• I always listen to on-line classes right away.
• I never (A)_____ my daily schedule.

① finish   ② remind
③ put off   ④ check over
⑤ hand in

5. 다음 밑줄 친 that 중 생략할 수 없는 것은? (4점)

① I hope <u>that</u> my sister is safe.

② Imagine <u>that</u> you won the lottery.

③ It is true <u>that</u> they like the same guy.

④ I think <u>that</u> this shirt looks better than that one.

⑤ Emma believes <u>that</u> she can do better next year.

6. 다음 중 짝지어진 대화가 <u>어색한</u> 것은? (3점)

① A: I often forget things.

 B: I think you should use a textbook.

② A: I want to be good at speaking English.

 B: You'd better join an English club.

③ A: I have a cold.

 B: That's too bad.

④ A: I'm worried about the history quiz. What should I do?

 B: I think you should read your textbook again.

⑤ A: Why are you so sad?

 B: I lost my cat.

[7-9] 다음 대화를 읽고 물음에 답하시오.

Hana: (A)What's the matter, Jiho?

Jiho: I didn't bring my uniform. I forgot I have soccer practice today.

Hana: Again?

Jiho: My second year in middle school is busier than my first year, and I often forget things.

Hana: I think you should use a planner. Here's mine.

Jiho: Oh, can I see it?

Hana: Sure. I write my class schedule and appointments in my planner.

Jiho: That's great. Maybe I should buy one.

7. 위 대화에서 알 수 있는 것은? (3점)

① Jiho will probably buy a planner.

② Jiho is giving Hana some advice.

③ Jiho has soccer practice tomorrow.

④ Jiho never forgets that he has soccer practice.

⑤ Jiho's second year in middle school is as busy as his first year.

8. 밑줄 친 (A)와 바꿔 쓸 수 있는 표현은? (4점)

① What's wrong, Jiho?

② How have you been, Jiho?

③ What does it mean, Jiho?

④ How do you like it, Jiho?

⑤ What are you doing, Jiho?

9. 위 대화를 읽고 답할 수 <u>없는</u> 질문은? (4점)

① What didn't Jiho bring today?

② What does Hana think Jiho should use?

③ What does Hana do with her planner?

④ What is Jiho probably going to do after the conversation?

⑤ What does Hana do with her uniform?

10. 자연스러운 대화가 되도록 (A)~(C)를 바르게 배열한 것은? (3점)

Somi: I'm so nervous.

(A) I think you should practice in front of your family. It will be very helpful.   (B) Why? Is it because of the dance contest?   (C) Yes. I practiced for many days, but I'm still nervous. What should I do?   Somi: That's a good idea. Thank you.

① (A) – (C) – (B)

② (B) – (A) – (C)

③ (B) – (C) – (A)

④ (C) – (A) – (B)

⑤ (C) – (B) – (A)

11. 빈칸에 들어갈 표현으로 알맞지 <u>않은</u> 것은? (2점)

A: _____ Are you sick?   B: Ms. Green, I think I have a cold.   A: Did you go to the school nurse?   B: Yes. She said I need to go to the hospital. Can I leave school now?   A: Okay, Sam. I'll call your mom and tell her about it.

① What's the matter?

② What's the problem?

③ You don't look good.

④ You look good today.

⑤ What's wrong with you?

12. 다음 빈칸에 어울리는 질문은? (2점)

G: You look worried, Sam.   _____   B: I don't hear my alarm in the morning these days.   G: Why don't you set the alarm on your clock and on your smartphone?   B: That's a good idea.

① What are you doing?

② Why don't you hear?

③ What's the matter?

④ Why should I do?

⑤ What do you do?

13. 다음 중 어법상 옳은 것은?　　　　　(3점)

① Jaemin is good to speaking English.

② I don't forget important things easy.

③ Focus on your work, and you will succeed.

④ That was the last class from the teacher.

⑤ Everyone has different thoughts to this book.

> Nick: I'm so nervous.
> Nancy: Why? Is it because (A)_____ the dance contest?
> Nick: Yes. I practiced for many days, but I'm still nervous. What should I do?
> Nancy: I think you should practice in front __(B)__ your family. It will be very helpful.
> Nick: That's a good idea. Thank you.

15. 위 대화의 빈칸 (A), (B)에 공통으로 알맞은 것은?　　　　　(3점)

① in　　　　② for

③ from　　　④ of

⑤ with

14. 밑줄 친 that의 쓰임이 다른 것은?　　　(3점)

① I have a pet dog that is 15 years old.

② I believe that you will keep the secret.

③ He knows that I can speak Chinese well.

④ I hope that I will visit the city next year.

⑤ Imagine that you can fly like a bird in the sky.

16. 위 대화를 읽고 질문에 답할 수 없는 것은?　　(4점)

① Why is Nick nervous?

② Will Nick join the dance contest?

③ How many days did Nick practice?

④ What is Nancy's idea?

⑤ Do you think Nick will follow Nancy's advice?

17. 다음 영어 문장을 우리말로 해석하시오. (4점)

Mary used to wear glasses when she was a child.

→ _____

[18-23] 다음 글을 읽고 물음에 답하시오.

> Minsu: When I do something, I give it my full attention. I used to read SNS postings while I was doing my homework. It slowed me down because I couldn't focus. Now, I put aside my smartphone when I do my homework. (A)It saves me a lot of time. These days, I finish my homework quickly and enjoy my free time.
>
> John: I regularly spend time working toward my dream. I want to become a chef. Every Saturday morning, I go to cooking classes or search for recipes. I think @that using my time to prepare for my future is important.
>
> Time is a present. Everyone has the same present (B)to spend every day. Manage your time well, and you will be happier in the new school year!

18. 위 글을 읽고 아래 제시된 질문에 영어로 답하시오. (5점)

What does John do every Saturday morning?

→ He _____.

19. 위 글의 주제로 가장 적절한 것은? (4점)

① Time is gold.

② You'd better not use smartphones when you study.

③ It is important to manage your time well.

④ Start small steps at a time to achieve big goals.

⑤ Working hard regularly for your future job is important.

20. 위 글의 내용과 일치하는 것은? (3점)

① Minsu still reads SNS postings while he does homework.

② Reading SNS postings helps Minsu concentrate on his homework.

③ Minsu puts away his smartphone when he does his homework.

④ John rarely spends time working on his dream.

⑤ John thinks using the time to prepare for his future is not a good thing.

21. 위 글의 밑줄 친 @와 쓰임이 다른 것은? (3점)

① I know the man that is smart.

② He accepted that he made a mistake.

③ I think that she is an honest person.

④ Everyone knows that he loves music.

⑤ She believes that he doesn't get what she said.

22. 밑줄 친 (A)It(그것)이 가리키는 의미를 우리말로 서술하시오. (4점)

(한글로): _____

23. 위 글의 밑줄 친 (B)의 쓰임과 같은 것은? (3점)

① It is hard to master English in a short time.

② David wants to play soccer after school.

③ Samuel came to see me yesterday.

④ You are very kind to take me to the station.

⑤ He gave his brother some toys to play with.

24. 다음 빈칸에 들어갈 표현으로 적절한 것은? (2점)

A: I spend money too fast.
_____
B: Usually I make a shopping list before I buy things.

① Can I see it?

② What's wrong?

③ What's going on?

④ What should I do?

⑤ Could you say that again?

25. 다음 중 문장의 의미가 옳지 않은 것은? (3점)

① I walked all day long.

　: 나는 하루 종일 걸었다.

② The movie is a true story.

　: 그 영화는 실화이다.

③ Anyone can solve it easily.

　: 누구나 그것을 쉽게 풀 수 있다.

④ I looked for my smartphone for an hour.

　: 나는 한 시간 동안 스마트폰을 찾았다.

⑤ Why don't you set the alarm on your clock?

　: 왜 시계에 알람을 설정했니?

[26-30] 다음 글을 읽고 물음에 답하시오.

Welcome to the new school year. (A)[In / On] the second grade, you will have more work (가)to do. You need to manage your time well. How do you do that?

Subin: I set small goals and achieve them every day, I do not say, "I will master English." With (B)[such big a goal / such a big goal], I will probably put off working on it until tomorrow, next week, or next month. Instead, I say, "I will learn three new English words every day." I will achieve my big goal, (C)[one step at a time / one step at the time].

Minsu: When I do something, I give it my full attention. ⓐ I used to read SNS postings while I was doing my homework. ⓑ It slowed me down because I couldn't focus. ⓒ It saves me a lot of time. ⓓ These days, I finish my homework quickly and enjoy my free time. ⓔ

26. 위 글의 (가)의 to부정사의 용법과 쓰임이 _다른_ 것은?
(3점)

① Jinho told her <u>to finish</u> the project.

② Jake wants a key <u>to open</u> the door.

③ Would you like something <u>to drink</u>?

④ I have some magazines <u>to read</u> today.

⑤ Julie bought a skateboard <u>to ride</u> in the park.

27. 위 글의 괄호 (A), (B), (C)에 알맞은 말이 바르게 연결된 것은?
(4점)

	(A)	(B)	(C)
①	In	such a big goal	one step at a time
②	On	such a big goal	one step at the time
③	In	such big a goal	one step at a time
④	On	such big a goal	one step at a time
⑤	In	such a big goal	one step at the time

28. 다음 ⓐ~ⓔ 중 주어진 문장이 들어가기에 가장 적절한 곳은?
(4점)

> Now, I put aside my smartphone when I do my homework.

① ⓐ   ② ⓑ   ③ ⓒ

④ ⓓ   ⑤ ⓔ

29. 위 글에 대한 설명으로 가장 옳은 것은?
(3점)

① Minsu was tired of SNS and quit it now.

② Subin writes down her plans in her planner.

③ Luckily, Subin is good at memorizing words.

④ Subin's big goal is to become an English teacher.

⑤ Minsu knows how to concentrate on his homework.

30. Why does Minsu put aside his smartphone when he does his homework?
(4점)

① He wants to read SNS postings.

② He wants to slow it down.

③ He wants to focus on his homework

④ He wants to finish his homework later.

⑤ He wants to enjoy his free time.

반		점수	
이			
름			

문항수 : 선택형(27문항) 서술형(2문항)   20   .   .   .

◎ 선택형 문항의 답안은 컴퓨터용 수정 싸인펜을 사용하여 OMR 답안지에 바르게 표기하시오.
◎ 서술형 문제는 답을 답안지에 반드시 검정 볼펜으로 쓰시오.
◎ 총 29문항 100점 만점입니다. 문항별 배점은 각 문항에 표시되어 있습니다.

[서울 광진구 ○○중]

1. 다음 밑줄 친 단어 중 문맥에 맞지 않은 것은? (3점)

① We need to <u>manage</u> our time well.

② Carrie never <u>puts off</u> doing her homework.

③ The first goal is <u>to along with</u> Jiho and Sujin.

④ Nancy does many things at the same time, but Paul does only one thing <u>at a time</u>.

⑤ The movie is a true story. It <u>really</u> happened last year.

[서울 광진구 ○○중]

2. 다음 빈칸 (A), (B), (C)에 들어갈 적절한 것은? (3점)

(1) I need a pencil to write ____(A)____.
(2) They were looking for a house to live ____(B)____.
(3) She wants a chair to sit ____(C)____.

	(A)	(B)	(C)
①	with	in	on
②	with	to	on
③	at	to	in
④	at	in	for
⑤	for	to	in

[서울 강남구 ○○중]

3. ⓐ~ⓒ에 들어갈 표현으로 알맞은 것은? (4점)

• Carrie never ____ⓐ____ doing her homework.
• Suji ____ⓑ____ wear glasses when she was a child.
• Tod ____ⓒ____ the books and papers on the desk.

① puts off – used to – put aside
② puts off – put aside – used to
③ used to – puts off – put aside
④ put aside – puts off – used to
⑤ put aside – used to – puts off

[서울 영등포구 ○○중]

4. 두 단어의 관계가 보기와 같은 것을 <u>두 개</u> 고르면? (4점)

real – really

① love – lovely
② final – finally
③ time – timely
④ friend – friendly
⑤ different – differently

- 8 -

5. 대화의 흐름상 빈칸에 사용될 수 <u>없는</u> 단어는? (3점)

Girl: Phew, what should I _____?
Boy: What's _____ on, Julie?
Girl: I _____ money too fast.
Boy: I always _____ a plan before I _____ things.
Girl: Maybe I should do the same.

① go
② do
③ buy
④ make
⑤ spend

7. 다음 밑줄 친 'that' 중 생략할 수 있는 것은? (4점)

① Where did you buy <u>that</u>?

② I think <u>that</u> is a best time.

③ Believe <u>that</u> you can be a pilot.

④ <u>That</u> he was in error was beyond doubt.

⑤ A long time passed in a silence like <u>that</u> of the grave.

8. 다음 대화의 마지막에 이어질 말로 적절한 것은? (3점)

A: Are you sick?
B: Ms. Green, I think I have a cold.
A: Did you go to the school nurse?
B: Yes. She said I need to go the hospital. Can I leave school now?
A: Okay, Sam. _____

① We can't live at school.

② You can do your homework well.

③ I am going to give you some bread.

④ He will come and help you to go home.

⑤ I will call your mother and tell her about it.

6. 다음 짝지어진 대화 중 가장 <u>어색한</u> 것은? (3점)

① A: Emily, you look sad. What's the matter?
  B: I lost my cat.

② A: I think you should see a doctor.
  B: You're right. Thank you.

③ A: I want to be good at swimming.
  B: I think you should take swimming lessons.

④ A: Why don't you take soccer lessons?
  B: I watched the game last night.

⑤ A: I think you should use a planner. Here's mine.
  B: I'll take a look at it.

9. 밑줄 친 부분의 쓰임이 <u>어색한</u> 것은? (3점)

① Do you want to a chair <u>to sit</u>?

② Does Kelly need a bike <u>to ride</u>?

③ My homework is <u>to make</u> a toy car.

④ He has many books <u>to read</u> at night.

⑤ I needed some paper <u>to write</u> on yesterday.

10. 빈칸에 들어갈 말로 적절한 것은? (3점)

A: You look worried. _____
B: My best friend is going to move to America soon.
A: Oh, I'm sorry to hear that.
B: I'm going to miss him a lot.

① How much is it?
② What's the matter?
③ How's the weather?
④ What makes you happy?
⑤ What are you going to eat?

11. (a)와 (b)에 들어갈 말로 가장 적절한 것은? (3점)

• I want to be (____a____) speaking English.
 (나는 영어 말하기를 잘하고 싶어요.)
• I spend 30 minutes practicing (____b____).
 (나는 방과 후에 30분 동안 연습한다.)

	(a)	(b)
①	well	school
②	good at	after school
③	good at	after practice
④	poor at	before practice
⑤	poor at	before practicing

[12-13] 다음 글을 읽고 물음에 답하시오.

I set small goals and ⓐachieve them every day. I do not say, "I will master English." With ⓑsuch a big goal, I will probably ⓒput off working on it until tomorrow, next week, or next month. Instead, I say, "I will learn ⓓthree new English word every day." I will achieve my big goal, ⓔone step at a time.

12. 밑줄 친 ⓐ~ⓔ 중 어법상 옳지 않은 것은? (3점)

① ⓐ 　　② ⓑ 　　③ ⓒ
④ ⓓ 　　⑤ ⓔ

13. 위 글의 제목으로 알맞은 것은? (4점)

① Making Big Goals
② The Importance of English
③ Achieving Our Future Dreams
④ To Become An English Teacher
⑤ The Importance of Setting Small Goals

14. 밑줄 친 to부정사의 쓰임이 다른 하나는? (3점)

① Kelly needs some water to drink now.

② I don't have time to practice this question.

③ Anna came here to meet her uncle yesterday.

④ My father bought many books to read for me.

⑤ I will have more homework to do for my math class.

15. 위 대화의 빈칸 (A)에 들어갈 말로 적절하지 않은 것은? (4점)

① What's wrong, Jiho?

② What should I do, Jiho?

③ What's the matter, Jiho?

④ What's the problem, Jiho?

⑤ You look worried. What happened?

16. 위 대화를 읽고 답할 수 없는 것은? (3점)

① What did Jiho forget to bring?

② Why does Jiho forget things?

③ How does Hana use her planner?

④ Where will Jiho buy his planner?

⑤ Who recommends a planner to Jiho?

[15-17] 다음 대화를 읽고 물음에 답하시오.

Hana: (A)_____
Jiho: I didn't bring my uniform. I forgot I have soccer practice today.
Hana: Again?
Jiho: My second year in middle school is busier than my first year, and I often forget things.
Hana: I think you should use a planner. Here's mine.
Jiho: Oh, can I see it?
Hana: Sure. I write my class schedule and appointments in my planner.
Jiho: That's great. Maybe I should buy one.

17. Jiho에 대한 설명으로 알맞은 것은? (4점)

① Jiho는 중학교 2학년이다.

② Jiho는 유니폼을 잃어버렸다.

③ Jiho는 오늘 축구 시합이 있다.

④ Jiho는 Hana와 같은 동아리이다.

⑤ Jiho는 Hana에게 플래너를 선물할 것이다.

[18-19] 다음 글을 읽고 물음에 답하시오.

ⓐ When I do something, I give it my full attention. ⓑ I used to read SNS postings while I was doing my homework. ⓒ (A)It slowed me down because I couldn't focus. ⓓ Now, I put aside my smartphone when I do my homework. ⓔ These days, I finish my homework quickly and enjoy my free time.

[경기 ○○중]

18. ⓐ~ⓔ 중 다음 문장이 들어갈 가장 적절한 곳은? (4점)

It saves me a lot of time.

① ⓐ   ② ⓑ   ③ ⓒ
④ ⓓ   ⑤ ⓔ

[20-21] 다음 글을 읽고 물음에 답하시오.

I regularly spend time working toward my dream. I want to become a chef. Every Saturday morning, I go to cooking classes or search for recipes. I think (A)that using my time to prepare for my future is important.

[경기 ○○중]

20. 밑줄 친 (A)와 쓰임이 같은 것은? (3점)
① We cannot walk that far.
② That is my English teacher.
③ Do you believe that he is lying?
④ What is that interesting thing?
⑤ This is my bag, and that is yours.

[경기 ○○중]

21. 위 글의 내용을 다음과 같이 요약할 때 빈칸 ⓐ~ⓒ에 알맞은 영어를 위 글을 참고하여 쓰시오. (5점)

My Dream Job : ⓐ_____

- On Saturdays :
1. ⓑ_____ _____ _____ _____
2. Searching for recipes

- Important Thing :
Spending time ⓒ_____ _____ my future

ⓐ _____

ⓑ _____ _____ _____ _____

ⓒ _____ _____

[경기 ○○중]

19. (A)가 지칭하는 내용으로 가장 적절한 것은? (3점)
① 숙제하면서 휴대 전화를 사용하는 것
② 숙제를 밀리지 않고 제때 하는 것
③ 학원에 가서 숙제를 다 끝마치는 것
④ 열심히 방과 후에 축구 연습을 하는 것
⑤ 숙제를 다 끝마치고 자유 시간을 갖는 것

22. 다음 중 글의 흐름상 적절하지 않은 문장은? (4점)

A planner is a type of book. ①I write my daily, weekly, and monthly plans here. ②I also write important dates like my friend's birthdays and homework due dates here. ③There is too much homework these days. ④Every night, I check this for the next day. ⑤Do you want to remember things easily? Then I think you should use this.

23. 다음 빈칸에 들어갈 내용으로 가장 알맞은 것은? (3점)

B: I'm so nervous.
G: Why? Is it because of the dance contest?
B: Yes. I practiced for many days, but I'm still nervous. What should I do?
G: I think you should _____.
   It will be very helpful.
B: That's a good idea. Thank you.

① do your homework
② take singing lessons
③ practice more at home
④ join a conversation club
⑤ read your textbook again

24. 다음의 밑줄 친 that과 다른 용법으로 쓰인 것은? (3점)

We believed that the man was honest.

① I think that it will rain.
② I didn't know that you won the match.
③ He said that he wanted to be a police officer.
④ He didn't believe the thing that he was told.
⑤ Imagine that you can communicate with animals.

[25-29] 다음 글을 읽고 물음에 답하시오.

Welcome to the new school year. In the second grade, you will have more work to do. You need to manage your time well. How do you do that?

Subin : I set small goals and achieve them every day. I do not say, "I will master English." With such a big goal, I will probably (A)_____ working on it until tomorrow, next week, or next month. Instead, I say, "I will learn three new English words every day." I will achieve my big goal, one step (B)_____.

Minsu : When I do something, I give it my full attention. I used to read SNS postings while I was doing my homework. It slowed me down because I couldn't focus. Now, I (C)_____ my smartphone when I do my homework. ⓐIt saves me a lot of time. These days, I finish my homework quickly and enjoy my free time.

John : I regularly spend time working toward my dream. I want to become a chef. Every Saturday morning, I go to cooking classes or search for recipes. I think that using my time to prepare for my future is important.

(D)_____ Everyone has the same present to spend every day. Manage your time well, and you will happier in the new school year!

25. 위 글의 빈칸 (A)～(C)에 들어갈 말로 올바르게 짝지어진 것은? (4점)

	(A)	(B)	(C)
①	put off	at a time	put aside
②	at a time	put off	put aside
③	put off	put aside	at a time
④	put aside	put off	at a time
⑤	put aside	at a time	put off

26. 위 글 내용의 흐름상 빈칸 (D)에 들어갈 말로 적절한 것은? (3점)

① Time is a present.

② Managing time is impressive.

③ You should achieve your goal.

④ You'd better finish your homework quickly.

⑤ You have more work to do in the second grade.

27. 위 글의 주제로 올바른 것은? (3점)

① what to do for cooking

② what to do in English classes

③ how to manage your time well

④ how to become a chef

⑤ how to do your homework quickly

28. 위 글의 내용과 일치하지 <u>않는</u> 것은? (4점)

① John wants to become a chef.

② Subin does not say, "I will master English."

③ These days, Minsu finishes his homework quickly.

④ Subin sets big goals and achieve them every day.

⑤ Minsu used to read SNS postings while he was doing his homework.

29. 위 글의 밑줄 친 ⓐIt이 가리키는 의미를 우리말로 쓰시오. (4점)

[정답]: _____

2학년 영어 1학기 중간고사(2과) 1회

반		점수	
이			
름			

문항수 : 선택형(27문항) 서술형(3문항)   20 . . .

◎ 선택형 문항의 답안은 컴퓨터용 수정 싸인펜을 사용하여 OMR 답안지에 바르게 표기하시오.
◎ 서술형 문제는 답을 답안지에 반드시 검정 볼펜으로 쓰시오.
◎ 총 30문항 100점 만점입니다. 문항별 배점은 각 문항에 표시되어 있습니다.

[경남 ○○중]

1. 짝지어진 두 단어의 관계가 〈보기〉와 다른 것은? (3점)

> 보기
>
> impress : impressive

① act : active
② invent : inventive
③ pass : passive
④ create : creative
⑤ attract : attractive

[서울 강남구 ○○중]

2. 다음 빈칸에 공통으로 들어갈 말로 알맞은 것은?
(3점)

> • Learn CPR. You will _____ people's lives.
> • I will _____ money to buy a new bike.

① tap
② call
③ save
④ stop
⑤ experience

[경기 ○○중]

3. 빈칸에 들어갈 말로 가장 적절한 것은?   **(2점)**

> A: I'm going to make fried eggs.
> B: Don't forget to turn _____ the fan.
>   (환풍기를 켜는 것을 잊지 마세요.)

① on   ② to   ③ in
④ for   ⑤ off

[서울 영등포구 ○○중]

4. 밑줄 친 단어의 의미가 다른 것은?   **(2점)**

① If you are in the third grade of middle school, you need to think more about your dreams.
② I want to get a high grade on the English test.
③ Students learn how to read from the first grade of school.
④ Q: What grade are you in?
A: I'm in the second grade at Youngwon middle school.
⑤ Mr. Kim is the head teacher of the third grade classes.

[경기 ○○중]

5. 다음 빈칸에 들어갈 말로 가장 적절한 것은?   **(3점)**

> A: Dad, I am leaving.
> B: _____ wear this mask.
> There is a lot of fine dust in the air today.

① You must not
② Don't forget to
③ You should not
④ You'd better not
⑤ You don't need to

― 15 ―

I was having dinner with my ⓐfamily last night. ⓑSuddenly everything started to shake. I couldn't stand ⓒstill and almost fell down. Dad shouted, "Get under the table. ⓓProtect your head. We all got under the table." Then, my little sister began to cry. Luckily, the shaking soon stopped. It was a scary ⓔexperience.

[서울 광진구 ○○중]

6. 위 글에 드러난 I의 심정으로 가장 적절한 것은?
(4점)

① happy

② lonely

③ bored

④ angry

⑤ scared

[경기 ○○중]

7. 위 글의 밑줄 친 ⓐ~ⓔ의 의미가 옳은 것은? (3점)

① ⓐ - 학생

② ⓑ - 안전하게

③ ⓒ - 흔들리는

④ ⓓ - 파괴하다

⑤ ⓔ - 경험

Teacher: I told you a few safety rules for earthquakes today. Now, let's practice. Are you ready?
Amy & Jiho: Yes.
Teacher: Everything is shaking. Get under the desk and protect your body first.
Jiho: It's so scary.
Amy: You're doing fine, Jiho. Hold on to the leg of the desk.
Jiho: Oh, the first shaking stopped. Let's get out!
Teacher: _____ (A) _____
Amy: Where should we go now?
Teacher: _____ (B) _____
Amy: Then, let's go to the park.

[경기 ○○중]

8. (A)와 (B)에 들어갈 말을 <보기>에서 바르게 짝지은 것은? (4점)

보기

ⓐ You need to find an open area with no buildings.

ⓑ You need to go into the library and keep yourself safe.

ⓒ Wait! You should use the elevator. It'll keep you out safely.

ⓓ Remember! You should not use the elevator. Use the stairs.

① ⓐ, ⓓ
② ⓑ, ⓒ
③ ⓓ, ⓐ
④ ⓓ, ⓑ
⑤ ⓒ, ⓑ

9. 위 대화의 내용과 일치하는 것은? (4점)

① The teacher tells students some dangerous situations to happen if the earthquake hits.

② The earthquake actually happens.

③ To hold on to the leg of the desk is the first thing to do.

④ Students need to use the stairs for safety instead of the elevators.

⑤ Students will go to the library to find an open area without buildings.

10. 다음 ①~⑤ 중 글의 흐름과 관련 없는 것은? (3점)

> Save Your Life from a Fire!
> Do you know what you should do when there is a fire? ①If you find out there is a fire, you should not cross the street on a red light. ②You should shout. "Fire!" ③You need to cover your face and body with a wet towel. ④You have to stay low and get out. ⑤Also, you need to call 119 and tell them the address. Don't forget to use the stairs, not the elevator.

11. 우리말과 뜻이 같도록 빈칸을 완성하시오. (5점)

(1) 시간 관리를 하는 것은 목표를 이루는 것만큼 쉽지 않다.

→ Managing _____.

(2) 그가 거짓말을 하고 있다는 것은 놀라워.

→ It _____.

12. 다음 중 우리말과 연결된 영어 표현이 잘못된 것은? (3점)

① 난 너와 이야기하는 것을 즐겼어.

= I have enjoyed to talk with you.

② 난 계란 프라이를 만들 거야.

= I'm going to make fried eggs.

③ 자전거를 타고 있는 동안에는 스마트폰을 쓰지 마라.

= Don't use your smartphone while you're riding a bike.

④ 이제 우린 어디로 가야 하는 거야?

= Where should we go now?

⑤ 난 다음 주 시험 때문에 스트레스를 받고 있어.

= I'm stressed about the test next week.

13. 다음 문장을 영어로 가장 적절하게 옮긴 것은? (4점)

> 모든 사람은 매일 쓸 똑같은 시간을 갖고 있다.

① No one has same time to spend.

② Anyone has same time spend every day.

③ Anyone has the same time spend every day.

④ Everyone has the same time to spend every day.

⑤ Everyone have the same time to spend every day.

14. 다음 괄호 안의 단어들을 바르게 배열하여 문장을 완성하시오. (3점)

가슴 중앙을 세게 누르세요.
(in / the / of / push / down / center / the / chest / hard)

→ _____

15. 다음 밑줄 친 ⓐ~ⓔ 중 글의 흐름상 어색한 문장은? (3점)

Announcer: Are there any other things to remember?

Sejin: Yes. ⓐYou need to remember the four minutes of "Golden Time." ⓑIt means that you should start CPR within four minutes after someone's heart stops. ⓒThis is the golden time of the day, and those who succeeded make the most of it. ⓓTo begin CPR later than that will greatly lower the chances of saving someone's life.

Announcer: ⓔTiming is as important as doing CPR. Thank you for joining us.

Sejin: My pleasure.

① ⓐ   ② ⓑ   ③ ⓒ
④ ⓓ   ⑤ ⓔ

16. 다음 중 어법상 옳지 <u>않은</u> 것은? (2점)

① Everything are shaking.

② Her speech was impressive.

③ They met in front of the cinema.

④ He was a very creative artist.

⑤ He was waiting for the bus there.

A: Dad, I'm leaving. (A)
B: (B) You need to wear this _____, Julie. There is a lot of fine dust in the air today.
A: Oh, I didn't know that. (C)
B: It will be bad for your health. (D)
A: (E) All right. Thank you.

17. 위 대화의 흐름으로 보아 주어진 문장이 들어가기에 가장 적절한 곳은? (4점)

Be sure to wear it.

① (A)   ② (B)   ③ (C)
④ (D)   ⑤ (E)

18. 위 대화의 빈칸에 들어갈 말은? (3점)

① helmet

② mask

③ gloves

④ glasses

⑤ swimming cap

19. 안전 수칙을 바르게 이야기한 사람을 묶은 것은?
(4점)

> • James - "Don't cross the street on a red light."
> • Mike - "You should wear a swimming cap in the swimming pool."
> • Jane - "Don't forget to pick plants and eat them on the mountains."
> • Amy - "You need to find an open area with no buildings in case of an earthquake."
> • John - "When there is an earthquake, you shouldn't get under the table and protect your head."

① James, John

② Mike, Jane

③ Jane, Amy

④ Mike, Jane, John

⑤ James, Mike, Amy

20. 문장의 의미가 옳게 연결된 것은? (4점)

① It's so dangerous.

: 그것은 정말 안전하다.

② He should wear a safety vest.

: 그는 안전 조끼를 착용해야 한다.

③ It will be bad for your health.

: 그것은 네 건강에 도움이 된다.

④ Hold on to the leg of the desk.

: 책상 다리를 꼭 잡으면 안 된다.

⑤ There is a lot of fine dust in the air.

: 공기 중에 습기가 많이 있다.

[21-25] 다음 대화를 읽고 물음에 답하시오.

> **Announcer:** That's impressive. When did you learn such an important skill?
> **Sejin:** We had Safety Training Day at school last week. I learned how to do CPR and had a chance to practice.
> **Announcer:** Can you show the audience ⓐ_____ to perform CPR?
> **Sejin:** Yes. Keep your arms straight. Your arms and the other person's chest must be at a 90 degree angle. Push down in the center of the chest hard and fast ⓑ_____ an ambulance comes.
>
> **Announcer:** Are there any other things to remember?
> **Sejin:** Yes. You need to remember the four minutes of "Golden Time." It means that you should start CPR within four minutes after someone's heart stops. (A)_____
> _____.
> **Announcer:** (B)타이밍이 CPR을 하는 것만큼 중요하군요. Thank you for joining us.
> **Sejin:** My pleasure.

21. 위 대화의 빈칸 ⓐ에 들어갈 말로 적절한 것은? (3점)

① who

② how

③ when

④ what

⑤ where

22. 위 대화의 흐름상, 빈칸 ⓑ에 들어갈 말로 가장 적절한 것은? (3점)

① when

② if

③ that

④ because

⑤ until

- 19 -

23. 위 대화의 빈칸 (A)에 들어갈 말로 적절한 것은?

(4점)

① If you begin CPR in a right way, someone will lose his or her life.

② If you remember where to do CPR, someone's heart will never stop.

③ If you don't forget "Golden Time", you will surely find gold under the ground.

④ If you start CPR later than four minutes, the chances of saving someone's life will lower.

⑤ If you want to save someone's life, you can perform CPR before someone's heart stops.

24. 밑줄 친 (B)를 영어로 바르게 영작한 것은?　(3점)

① Timing is as important as doing CPR.

② Timing is not as important as doing CPR.

③ Timing is more important than doing CPR.

④ Doing CPR is more important than timing.

⑤ Doing CPR is not as important as timing.

25. 위 대화에서 언급되지 않은 것은?　　　　(4점)

① 세진이가 심폐소생술을 배운 장소

② 심폐소생술시 팔과 다른 사람 가슴과의 각도

③ 심폐소생술시 분당 압박 횟수

④ 심폐소생술을 실시할 때 압박 부위

⑤ 심폐소생술에 있어서 골든타임의 중요성

26. 다음 중 상황과 조언이 가장 어울리지 않는 것은?

(4점)

① A: I'm leaving now. Bye.

　B: There is a lot of fine dust in the air today. So don't forget to wear this mask.

② A: I'm going to go to Jiri Mountain with my dad tomorrow.

　B: It sounds great. Don't forget to check the weather.

③ A: I want to buy some apple juice.

　B: Don't forget to check the food label. Too much sugar is not good for you.

④ A: There was an earthquake last night. The shaking soon stopped but it was scary.

　B: You'd better not run. The sign says the floor is wet.

⑤ A: I want to check my smartphone while I am walking down the street.

　B: You'd better not look at your smartphone while you are walking. You can bump into people and there are many cars around here. It's dangerous.

[27-30] 다음 글을 읽고 물음에 답하시오.

Announcer: Yesterday, a teenager ⓐsaved the life of an old man. The brave student ⓑis in the studio with us today. Can you introduce yourself?

Sejin: My name is Kim Sejin. I'm in the second grade at Hanguk Middle School.

Announcer: Could you tell us your experience?

Sejin: Sure. I ⓒwas waiting for the bus with my friend, Jinho. A man suddenly ⓓfalled in front of us. Nobody ⓔknew (A)_____ to do. I was (B)as scared as the others at first. Then, I ran to him and tapped him on the shoulder. He wasn't moving or breathing. I said to Jinho. "Call 119," and started CPR.

28. 위 글의 내용과 일치하는 것은?　　　　(2점)

① 어제, 20대 청년이 한 노인의 목숨을 구했다.
② 세진이는 한국 중학교 2학년 학생이다.
③ 진호는 세진이의 오빠이다.
④ 세진이가 택시를 기다리고 있을 때, 한 남자가 갑자기 쓰러졌다.
⑤ 119에 전화한 사람은 바로 세진이였다.

29. 위 글의 밑줄 친 ⓐ~ⓔ 중, 쓰임이 <u>어색한</u> 것은?
　　　　(3점)

① ⓐ　　　　② ⓑ　　　　③ ⓒ
④ ⓓ　　　　⑤ ⓔ

27. (A)에 들어갈 말로 가장 적절한 것은?　　　(3점)

① how
② who
③ what
④ when
⑤ where

30. 위 글의 (B)as scared as를 참고하여 다음 문장을 영어로 쓰시오.　　　　(5점)

| 그녀는 그녀의 남동생만큼 열심히 공부한다. |

정답: _____

◎ 선택형 문항의 답안은 컴퓨터용 수정 싸인펜을 사용하여 OMR 답안지에 바르게 표기하시오.
◎ 서술형 문제는 답을 답안지에 반드시 검정 볼펜으로 쓰시오.
◎ 총 30문항 100점 만점입니다. 문항별 배점은 각 문항에 표시되어 있습니다.

[서울 강남구 ○○중]

1. 다음 글이 설명하는 것은?　　(3점)

Many people use this almost every day. People stand in line to enter this. They wait for others to get off before they enter. They use this to move up and down floors in a building. You'd better not use it in case of a fire.

① car
② stair
③ elevator
④ ambulance
⑤ smartphone

[서울 강남구 ○○중]

2. 다음 중 두 문장이 의미상 일치하는 것은?　　(3점)

① Tony is as tall as Julie.
　 Tony is shorter than Sam.
② Tom can run as fast as Mike.
　 Tom can run faster than Mike.
③ Yesterday was as cold as today.
　 Yesterday was colder than today.
④ Skiing is as difficult as skating.
　 Skiing is more difficult than skating.
⑤ Come to my house as fast as possible.
　 Come to my house as fast as you can.

[경남 ○○중]

3. 영영풀이가 올바르게 연결된 단어의 개수는?　　(3점)

- few: a large number of
- breathe: to take the air in and out of lungs
- protect: to do and finish an action or activity
- emergency: a dangerous situation which is needed to be dealt with quickly

① 0개　　② 1개　　③ 2개
④ 3개　　⑤ 4개

[서울 강남구 ○○중]

4. ⓐ~ⓒ에 들어갈 표현으로 알맞은 것은?　　(3점)

- Sohee's speech was _____ⓐ_____ . I was moved.
- Picasso was a very _____ⓑ_____ artist. He painted in a new style.
- Tony is a very _____ⓒ_____ boy. He is full of energy all the time.

① impress　　－　creative　　－　active
② impress　　－　create　　－　active
③ impressive　　－　creative　　－　active
④ impressive　　－　creative　　－　act
⑤ impressive　　－　create　　－　act

[경남 ○○중]

5. 우리말 의미에 맞도록 빈칸에 알맞은 말을 넣으시오.　　(5점)

(1) Don't _____ get under the desk.
　 (책상 아래로 들어갈 것을 잊지 마라.)
(2) You'd _____ use the elevator.
　 (엘리베이터를 이용하지 않는 것이 좋겠다.)

- 22 -

6. 짝지어진 대화가 자연스럽지 <u>않은</u> 것은? (3점)

① A: I'm worried about tomorrow's history quiz.

B: I think you should read your textbook again.

② A: Did you go to the school nurse?

B: Yes. She said I need to go to the hospital. Can I leave school now?

③ A: What does the sign mean?

B: It means that you should not look at your smartphone while you are walking.

④ A: I don't hear my alarm in the morning these days.

B: Why don't you set the alarm on your clock and on your smartphone?

⑤ A: I practiced dancing for many days because of the dance contest, but I'm still nervous.

B: You need to write your class schedule and appointments in this planner.

7. 위 글과 관계 있는 것은? (3점)

① Plants
② View points
③ Hiking
④ Oxygen
⑤ Earthquake

8. 위 글에서 다음 문장이 들어갈 적합한 위치는? (3점)

Luckily, the shaking soon stopped.

① (가) ② (나)
③ (다) ④ (라)
⑤ (마)

[7–8] 다음 글을 읽고 물음에 답하시오.

(가) I was having a good time with my family last night. (나) Suddenly everything started to shake. I couldn't stand still and almost fell down. (다) Dad shouted, "Get under the table. Don't forget to protect your head." (라) It was a scary experience. (마)

9. 대화의 흐름으로 보아 밑줄 친 부분에 들어가기에 적절하도록 단어를 배열하시오. (4점)

A: What does the sign mean?
B: It means that (<u>you / not / at / your / you'd / look / walking / smartphone / while / better / are</u>).
A: That's interesting, but why?
B: You can bump into people and there are many cars around here. It's so dangerous.
A: Now I see.

[정답] : _____

10. 주어진 말에 이어질 대화의 순서로 알맞은 것은?

(3점)

> A: Dad, I'm leaving.

> ⓐ Oh, I didn't know that.
> ⓑ Wait. You need to wear a mask. There is a lot of fine dust in the air today.
> ⓒ It will be bad for your health. So wear this.
> ⓓ All right. Thank you.

① ⓑ, ⓐ, ⓒ, ⓓ

② ⓑ, ⓐ, ⓓ, ⓒ

③ ⓒ, ⓐ, ⓓ, ⓑ

④ ⓒ, ⓓ, ⓐ, ⓑ

⑤ ⓓ, ⓑ, ⓒ, ⓐ

11. 다음 글의 제목으로 가장 적절한 것은? (4점)

> 1. If you're in a car, slow down and drive to a safe place. Stay in the car until the shaking stops.
> 2. Stay away from windows.
> 3. You'd better not use the elevator.
> 4. You need to find an open area with no buildings.

① How to Use an Elevator

② Safety Rules for Buildings

③ Rules of the Road for Safe Driving

④ Four Tips that Could Save Your Life

⑤ How to Stay Safe During an Earthquake

12. 〈보기〉의 단어를 사용하여 다음 우리말과 뜻이 같도록 영어 문장을 쓰시오. (필요한 단어는 추가할 것) (3점)

> **보기**
>
> know / where
> 그녀는 어디로 가야 할지 몰랐다.
> = She didn't _____ _____ _____ _____.

[13-17] 다음 글을 읽고 물음에 답하시오.

> **Sejin**: We had Safety Training Day at school last week. ⓐ<u>I learned how to do CPR and had a chance practice.</u>
> **Announcer**: Can you show the audience how to perform CPR?
> **Sejin**: Yes. Keep your arms straight. ⓑ<u>Your arms and the other person's chest must be at a 90 degree angle.</u> Push down in the center of the chest hard and fast until an ambulance comes.
> **Announcer**: ⓒ<u>Is there any other things to remember?</u>
> **Sejin**: Yes. You need to remember the four minutes of "Golden Time." (A)<u>It means that you should start CPR within four minutes after someone's heart stops.</u> ⓓ<u>To begin CPR later than that will greatly low the chances of saving someone's life.</u>
> **Announcer**: Timing is as important as doing CPR. ⓔ<u>Thank you for join us.</u>
> **Sejin**: My pleasure.

13. 다음 심폐소생술의 내용이 글에서 언급되지 않은 것은? (3점)

① 팔을 곧게 유지하라.

② 당신의 팔과 환자의 가슴은 90도 각도가 되어야 한다.

③ 사람의 심장이 멈춘 뒤 4분 안에 심폐소생술을 시작해야 한다.

④ 구급차가 오기 전까지 환자의 가슴 중앙을 강하고 빠르게 눌러라.

⑤ 사람의 심장이 멈춘 뒤 구급차가 오기 전까지 환자에게 인공호흡을 해야 한다.

14. ⓐ～ⓔ 중 어법상 맞는 문장은? (3점)

① ⓐ   ② ⓑ   ③ ⓒ

④ ⓓ   ⑤ ⓔ

15. CPR을 하는 방법을 정리한 포스터이다. (A)～(E)에 알맞은 말을 위 글에 맞게 서술하시오. (5점)

> *How to do CPR*
>
>   CPR is very important because it can save people's lives. Please keep these in mind for emergency.
>
>   First, you should keep your arms (A)_____. Second, your arms and the other person's (B)_____ a 90 degree angle. Third, (C)_____ in the center of the chest hard and fast until an (D)_____ comes.
>
>   CPR should be done (E)_____ minutes of "Golden Time."

(A) _____

(B) _____

(C) _____

(D) _____

(E) _____

16. 위 글의 (A)를 우리말로 해석하시오. (4점)

→ _____

17. 위 글의 내용에 관한 질문과 답이 바르게 연결되지 않은 것은? (3점)

① Q: What did Sejin learn on Safety Training Day?

   A: She learned how to call an ambulance.

② Q: At what degree should your arms and the other person's chest be?

   A: They must be at a 90 degree angle.

③ Q: Where on the body do we push down when we perform CPR?

   A: We push down in the center of the chest when we perform CPR.

④ Q: What does the four minutes of "Golden Time" mean?

   A: It means that you should begin CPR in four minutes after someone's heart stops.

⑤ Q: What is as important as doing CPR?

   A: Timing is as important as doing CPR.

18. 주어진 문장 다음에 이어질 대화의 순서로 가장 적절한 것은? (4점)

> Hi, Chris. What's up?

> (A) Watch out! Didn't you see that sign?
> (B) It says the floor is wet.
> (C) I have a lunch meeting in this shopping center. Oh, I think I'd better leave now. I'm late.
> (D) I didn't see it. What does the sign mean?
> (E) I'm here to buy a shirt. What about you?

① (E)–(C)–(A)–(D)–(B)
② (C)–(E)–(A)–(D)–(B)
③ (E)–(C)–(D)–(B)–(A)
④ (C)–(A)–(D)–(E)–(B)
⑤ (C)–(E)–(D)–(B)–(A)

19. 그림을 참고하여 빈칸 ⓐ～ⓑ에 알맞은 말을 영어로 쓰시오. (4점)

Seho   Kate   Jack   Minji

> Q) What do they need?
> A) Seho needs water to drink.
>   Kate needs bread ⓐ_____ _____.
>   Jack needs a cap to wear.
>   Minji needs ⓑ_____ _____ _____ _____.

20. 다음 글의 빈칸 (A), (B), (C)에 들어갈 단어로 올바르게 짝지어진 것은? (4점)

> **Announcer:** Are there any other things to remember?
> **Sejin:** Yes. You need to remember the four minutes of Golden Time. It means that you should start CPR (A)_____ four minutes after someone's heart stops. To begin CPR (B)_____ than that will greatly (C)_____ the chances of saving someone's life.
> **Announcer:** Timing is as important as doing CPR. Thank you for joining us.
> **Sejin:** My pleasure.

	(A)	(B)	(C)
①	with	later	lower
②	with	late	low
③	within	late	lower
④	within	later	lower
⑤	within	later	low

[21-22] 다음 대화를 읽고 물음에 답하시오.

> M: Hi, Amy. What's up?
> A: Hi, Max. I'm here to buy a shirt. What about you?
> M: I have a lunch meeting in this shopping center. Oh, I should go now. I'm late.
> A: Okay, but (A)_____. The sign says the floor is wet.
> M: I didn't see it. Thanks.

21. 빈칸 (A)에 들어갈 말로 알맞은 것은? (3점)

① you'd better not run
② you need to buy a shirt
③ let's have lunch together
④ you can find an open area
⑤ hold on to the leg of the desk

22. 위 대화의 내용과 일치하는 것은? (3점)

① Amy has a lunch meeting today.

② Max already had lunch when he met Amy.

③ Amy and Max are talking about their school.

④ Max told Amy to see a sign in a shopping center.

⑤ Amy has a reason to come to a shopping center.

23. 다음 문장을 영어로 가장 적절하게 옮긴 것은? (3점)

> 제가 그에게 달려가서, 그의 어깨를 두드렸어요.

① I ran and tap her shoulder.

② I run him and tap him shoulder.

③ I run to him and tapped his on shoulder.

④ I ran to his and tapped her on the shoulder.

⑤ I ran to him and tapped him on the shoulder.

24. 다음 중 장소에 어울리는 안전 수칙은? (3점)

① Zoo – You should touch the animals.

② Mountain – Pick plants and eat them.

③ Car – Put your hand out of the car window.

④ Swimming pool – Stay in the water for a long time.

⑤ Street – You'd better not use your smartphone while you are riding a bike.

[25-30] 다음 글을 읽고 물음에 답하시오.

Announcer: Yesterday, a teenager saved the life of an old man. The brave student is in the studio with us today. Can you (a)introduce yourself?

Sejin: My name is Kim Sejin. I'm in the second grade at Hanguk Middle School.

Announcer: Could you tell us your experience?

Sejin: Sure. I (b)was waiting for the bus with my friend, Jinho. A man suddenly fell in front of us. Nobody knew what to do. I was (c)as scaring as the others at first. Then, I ran to him and asked if he was okay. And I also tapped him on the shoulder. He was not (d)moving or breathe. I said to Jinho, Call 119, and started CPR.

Announcer: That's impressive. When did you learn (e)such an important skill?

Sejin: We had Safety Training Day at school last week. I learned how to do CPR and had (f)a chance to practice.

Announcer: Can you show the audience how to perform CPR?

Announcer: Are there any other (g)things to remember?

Sejin: Yes. You need to remember the four minutes of Golden Time. It means that you should start CPR within four minutes after someone's heart stops. To begin CPR later than (A)that will greatly lower the chances of saving someone's life.

Announcer: (B) (as, do, important, time, is, CPR, as). Thank you for joining us.

Sejin: My pleasure.

25. (a)~(g) 중에서 어법상 옳지 <u>않은</u> 것의 개수는?
(3점)

① 1개   ② 2개   ③ 3개

④ 4개   ⑤ 5개

26. 위 글을 읽고 답할 수 있는 질문으로 적절하지 <u>않은</u> 것은? (2점)

① Whose life did Sejin save yesterday?

② What is as important as doing CPR?

③ What did Sejin learn on Safety Training Day?

④ When did Sejin have a chance to practice CPR?

⑤ Why did an old man suddenly fall in front of people?

27. 위 글에 나타난 세진이의 모습을 말하고자 한다. 빈칸에 가장 적절한 것은? (3점)

> Sejin showed the audience how to do CPR very impressively and asked them to remember _____.

① her role

② the safety rule

③ the role of '119'

④ the importance of life

⑤ the kinds of school training

28. 위 글을 읽고 보일 수 있는 반응으로 적절한 것은? (3점)

① Kane: You shouldn't help someone if he falls.

② Vardy: Middle school students cannot save people.

③ Sancho: When you check whether someone is awake, you should tap on his stomach.

④ Raul: If someone falls and doesn't move, you have to do CPR before you call 119.

⑤ Henry: Something that you learn at school can help you in real life.

29. 위 글의 (A)가 지칭하는 것은? (3점)

① CPR   ② four minutes

③ call 119   ④ how to do CPR

⑤ someone's heart stops

30. (B)를 조건에 맞추어 문맥에 맞게 배열하여 문장을 완성하시오. (4점)

> **조건**
> 다른 단어를 추가할 수 없고, 단어를 한 번씩만 이용하되, 문장의 구성에 필요한 형태의 변화를 시킬 것.

→ _____

◎ 선택형 문항의 답안은 컴퓨터용 수정 싸인펜을 사용하여 OMR 답안지에 바르게 표기하시오.
◎ 서술형 문제는 답을 답안지에 반드시 검정 볼펜으로 쓰시오.
◎ 총 29문항 100점 만점입니다. 문항별 배점음 각 문항에 표시되어 있습니다.

[울산 ○○중]

1. 빈칸 ⓐ～ⓒ에 들어갈 단어들이 알맞게 짝지어진 것은? (3점)

• Stand next to your partner and ⓐ_____ each other.
• He smiles when he looks at his baby's ⓐ_____.
• Can you press the ⓑ_____ to turn on the light?
• I will ⓑ_____ my dress with my sister's.
• Please ⓒ_____ your hands on your shoulders.
• Where is a good ⓒ_____ to go on a trip?

     ⓐ   –   ⓑ   –   ⓒ

① face – switch – place
② face – key – world
③ hold – button – put
④ hold – switch – put
⑤ hand – key – place

[경기 ○○중]

2. 다음 중 밑줄 친 단어의 의미가 나머지 넷과 <u>다른</u> 것은? (2점)

① Please <u>close</u> your eyes.
② Please come <u>close</u> to each other.
③ He <u>closed</u> the window when it rained.
④ You have to <u>close</u> your book during the test.
⑤ We came back home when we saw the sign "<u>Closed</u>".

[서울 양천구 ○○중]

3. 다음 〈보기〉의 단어들을 활용하여 쓴 문장 중 옳지 <u>않</u>은 것은? (3점)

> **보기**
> • comfort – comfortable
> • use – usable
> • change – changeable
> • move – movable

① I can still use my old bike.
② My old longboard is still usable.
③ The robot has movable arms and legs.
④ The weather in the mountain changes a lot.
⑤ We should wear comfort shoes for walking for a long time.

[서울 도봉구 ○○중]

4. 다음 중 어법상 또는 문맥상 옳은 문장은? (4점)

① I'll go jog if I get up early tomorrow.
② She let the painter draw her portrait.
③ My rival makes me practice play the piano.
④ I want to buy a bag which have many pockets.
⑤ My teacher helped me to find some informations on the topic.

5. 자연스러운 대화가 되도록 ⓐ~ⓔ를 바르게 배열한 것은? (4점)

> ⓐ That's it? I should try it.
> ⓑ I want to eat something healthy. Do you have any advice?
> ⓒ Really? Can you make it?
> ⓓ I often eat fresh salad. When I eat it, I feel good.
> ⓔ Yes, it's quite simple. First, cut many vegetables into small pieces. Next, put them into a bowl. Then, pour some lemon juice on them. Finally, mix everything together.

① ⓑ – ⓓ – ⓔ – ⓒ – ⓐ
② ⓑ – ⓓ – ⓒ – ⓔ – ⓐ
③ ⓒ – ⓔ – ⓓ – ⓑ – ⓐ
④ ⓓ – ⓔ – ⓒ – ⓑ – ⓐ
⑤ ⓓ – ⓒ – ⓔ – ⓑ – ⓐ

6. 위 대화의 빈칸 ⓐ에 공통으로 알맞은 것은? (3점)

① bored   ② excited
③ scary   ④ stressed
⑤ interesting

7. 위 대화의 ⓑ가 가리키는 것으로 가장 적절한 것은? (2점)

① the other test
② the other board
③ the other foot
④ the other hand
⑤ the other finger

[6-8] 다음 대화를 읽고 물음에 답하시오.

> Karl: Hana, what's the matter?
> Hana: Well, I'm ⓐ_____ about the test next week.
> Karl: I understand. I ride my longboard when I'm ⓐ_____. Can you ride a longboard?
> Hana: No, I can't.
> Karl: Let's go out! I can teach you. Put one foot on the board and push hard with ⓑthe other.
> Hana: Like this? Wow! This is fun. I feel better already.
> Karl: See? I enjoy riding my longboard because (A)_____.
> Hana: That's great!

8. 위 대화의 흐름상 (A)에 알맞은 말은? (3점)

① it reduces my stress
② it makes my left leg healthier
③ it makes me sad when I'm down
④ there is a longboard festival soon
⑤ I'm really good at riding my longboard

9. 괄호 안의 단어를 모두 이용하여 제시된 우리말에 맞게 if 조건문을 쓰시오. (5점)

> 만약 내일 화창하다면, 우리는 자전거를 타러 갈 수 있어. (bike ride, for, a, go, sunny)
> (1)_____
>
> 만약 그가 패스트푸드 먹는 것을 멈추지 않는다면, 그는 아플 것이다. (sick, fast food, get, stop)
> (2)_____

11. 위 대화의 밑줄 친 (A)의 우리말을 주어진 단어를 활용하여 어법상 완전한 문장으로 쓰시오. (4점)

┌─ 조건 ─────────────────────
• 주어진 단어를 모두 사용할 것.
• 필요한 경우 단어를 추가할 것.
└────────────────────────────

┌─ 보기 ─────────────────────
know / how / it / use / to
└────────────────────────────

정답: _____

[10-11] 다음 대화를 읽고 물음에 답하시오.

> B: People say that we should walk more than 10,000 steps every day to be healthy. I can't count the number of my steps easily.
> G: You can use this smartphone app. (A)너는 그것을 어떻게 사용하는지 아니?
> B: No. Can you show me?
> G: Sure. First download the app. Then, walk with your smartphone. Later you can check the number of steps you took.
> B: Thank you. I will start using ⓐit today.

10. 위 대화의 밑줄 친 ⓐit이 가리키는 것은? (4점)

① walking
② to be healthy
③ to count
④ smartphone app
⑤ the number of my steps

12. 다음 그림의 동작에 대한 설명이 바르지 <u>못한</u> 것은? (3점)

①

②

③

④

⑤

① Straighten your arms.
② Bend your back and hold your feet with your hands.
③ Stand close to each other and face your partner.
④ Slowly bend your left leg and lower yourself.
⑤ Cover your eyes with your hands.

- 31 -

Next, massage your neck. Put your fingers on the back of your neck. Draw small circles (a)[with / of] your fingers to massage your neck. Massage from top to bottom.

Let's work on your waist. (A) Team up with a friend, (B) Stand (b)[close / closely] to each other and face your partner. (C) Hold each other's wrists. Slowly stretch your head and body (c)[forward / backward]. (가)Hold that position for three seconds. Then, slowly pull each other to a standing position. (D) If you don't, both of you will fall! (E)

[충북 ○○중]

13. 위 글의 흐름으로 보아 주어진 문장이 들어가기에 가장 적절한 곳은? (3점)

You and your partner should move at the same speed.

① (A) 　　② (B) 　　③ (C)

④ (D) 　　⑤ (E)

[서울 영등포구 ○○중]

14. (a)~(c)에 들어갈 말로 가장 적절한 것은? (4점)

	(a)	(b)	(c)
①	with	close	backward
②	with	closely	backward
③	with	close	forward
④	of	closely	forward
⑤	of	close	forward

[서울 도봉구 ○○중]

15. 위 글에서 밑줄 친 (가)의 풀이로 알맞은 것은? (3점)

① 유지해라　　　② 잡아라

③ 멈추어라　　　④ 쥐어라

⑤ 안아라

[충북 ○○중]

16. 위 글의 허리 운동에 대한 설명에 맞게 순서를 바르게 연결한 것은? (3점)

ⓐ 선 자세로 서로를 천천히 잡아당긴다.
ⓑ 친구와 팀을 이룬다.
ⓒ 자세를 3초간 유지한다.
ⓓ 짝과 가까이 서서 서로 마주본다.
ⓔ 서로 손목을 잡고 머리와 몸을 뒤로 천천히 늘린다.

① ⓐ-ⓑ-ⓒ-ⓓ-ⓔ
② ⓑ-ⓐ-ⓓ-ⓒ-ⓔ
③ ⓑ-ⓓ-ⓔ-ⓒ-ⓐ
④ ⓓ-ⓔ-ⓐ-ⓒ-ⓑ
⑤ ⓔ-ⓐ-ⓑ-ⓓ-ⓒ

17. 위 글을 읽고, 다음 질문에 대한 답을 영어로 쓰시오. (3점)

> Q: If two people move at different speeds, what will happen?
>
> A: _____ _____ _____

19. 밑줄 친 (a)의 의미에 맞게 주어진 단어를 이용하여 완전한 문장으로 쓰시오. (4점)

> yourself, stretch, every, healthier

→ If _____.

[18-20] 다음 글을 읽고 물음에 답하시오.

> ⓐPlace the top of your right foot on the desk behind you. Then, slowly ⓑbend your left leg and ⓒlower yourself. Hold it for a few seconds and slowly straighten up. This position will loosen up your right leg. ⓓSwitch your legs and repeat the exercise.
>
> How do you feel now? If (a)네가 매일 네 자신을 마사지하고 스트레칭을 하면, 너는 더 건강해지는 것을 느낄 것이다. Also, you can ⓔfocus on your studies better.

18. 위 글의 흐름상 ⓐ~ⓔ의 밑줄 친 부분의 의미가 어색한 것은? (4점)

① ⓐ Place : 두다
② ⓑ bend : 구부리다
③ ⓒ lower : 더 낮은
④ ⓓ Switch : 바꾸다
⑤ ⓔ focus on : ~에 집중하다

20. 위 글의 내용으로 보아 〈보기〉의 빈칸 (A)와 (B)에 들어갈 말로 알맞은 것은? (3점)

> 보기
>
> After we place the top of our right foot on the desk behind us, we slowly bend our (A)_____ leg and (B)_____ ourselves.

	(A)	(B)
①	right	pull
②	left	lower
③	right	lower
④	left	stand
⑤	right	massage

21. 다음 대화의 흐름에 맞게 괄호 안의 단어를 이용하여 빈칸에 알맞은 말을 쓰시오. (9단어로 쓸 것) (4점)

> B: You look sick. What's the matter?
> G: Well, I have a cold.
> B: Did you see a doctor?
> G: Not yet. _____?
>   (get, how, know, do)
> B: Well, I usually drink warm water when I have a cold.
> G: Sounds good.

[22–25] 다음 글을 읽고 물음에 답하시오.

> Let's begin with the eyes. Close your eyes and massage (a)them softly with your fingers. (b)It will relax your eyes. When you finish, cover your eyes with your hands to (A)_____ the light. (c)그것은 당신의 눈을 더 편안하게 할 것이다.

22. 다음 중 빈칸 (A)에 들어갈 자연스러운 말은? (3점)

① take off

② begin with

③ loosen up

④ put on

⑤ block out

23. 눈의 피로를 풀어주는 방법이 순서대로 알맞게 된 것은? (3점)

> (a) 손가락으로 눈을 부드럽게 마사지한다.
> (b) 손으로 눈을 가린다.
> (c) 눈을 감는다.

① (a) – (c) – (b)

② (c) – (b) – (a)

③ (b) – (a) – (c)

④ (c) – (a) – (b)

⑤ (b) – (c) – (a)

24. 밑줄 친 (a)와 (b)가 각각 가리키는 것은? (4점)

	(a)	(b)
①	your eyes	– to massage your eyes
②	your eyes	– to relax your eyes
③	your hands	– to block out the light
④	your hands	– to massage your eyes
⑤	your fingers	– to block out the light

25. 밑줄 친 (c)의 의미가 되도록 주어진 단어들을 배열하여 문장을 완성하시오. (4점)

> → It _____.
> (feel / make / more comfortable / will / your eyes)

At school you sit for many hours. ⓐDo you get tired? Why don't you massage yourself and stretch?

Let's begin with the eyes. Close your eyes and massage them softly with your fingers. ⓑIt will relax your eyes. When you finish, cover your eyes with your hands to block out the light. ⓒIt will make your eyes to feel more comfortable.

Next, massage your neck. Put your fingers on the back of your neck. ⓓDraw small circles with your fingers to massage your neck. Massage from top to bottom. ⓔThe massage will help you feel better.

Let's work on your waist. Team up with a friend. Stand close to each other and face your partner. Hold each other's wrists. Slowly stretch your head and body backward. Hold that position for three seconds. Then, slowly pull each other to a standing position. You and your partner should move at the same speed. (a)_____ you don't, both of you will fall!

(A) Place the top of your right foot on the desk behind you. (B) Hold it for a few seconds and slowly straighten up. (C) This position will loosen up your (b)_____ leg. (D) Switch your legs and repeat the exercise. (E)

How do you feel now? (a)_____ you massage yourself and stretch every day, you will feel healthier. Also, you can focus on your studies better.

---

26. 위 글의 빈칸 (a)에 공통으로 들어갈 말로 가장 적절한 것은? (3점)

① Because   ② When

③ If   ④ Until

⑤ Before

27. 위 글의 빈칸 (b)에 문맥상 들어갈 말을 찾아 쓰시오. (3점)

답: _____

28. 위 글의 (A)~(E) 중 다음 문장이 들어갈 위치로 알맞은 것은? (4점)

> Then, slowly bend your left leg and lower yourself.

① (A)   ② (B)   ③ (C)

④ (D)   ⑤ (E)

29. 위 글의 밑줄 친 ⓐ~ⓔ 중 어법상 어색한 것을 골라 어색한 부분을 바르게 고치시오. (5점)

(1) 어색한 문장 기호: _____

(2) 어색한 부분: _____

(3) 바르게 고친 것: _____

◎ 선택형 문항의 답안은 컴퓨터용 수정 싸인펜을 사용하여 OMR 답안지에 바르게 표기하시오.

◎ 서술형 문제는 답을 답안지에 반드시 검정 볼펜으로 쓰시오.

◎ 총 29문항 100점 만점입니다. 문항별 배점은 각 문항에 표시되어 있습니다.

[울산 ○○중]

1. 〈보기〉의 단어 생성 규칙이 잘못 적용된 단어는?   (2점)

> **보기**
> 동사 + able = 형용사

① usable

② lovable

③ enable

④ movable

⑤ changeable

[서울 양천구 ○○중]

2. 다음 밑줄 친 단어의 의미가 같은 것끼리 짝지어진 것은?   (3점)

① - We're going to <u>raise</u> money to help poor children in India.

  - <u>Raise</u> your hands if you have a question.

② - <u>Close</u> your eyes and massage them softly with your fingers.

  - Stand <u>close</u> to each other.

③ - <u>Face</u> your partner and hold each other's hands.

  - She smiles when she looks at the baby's <u>face</u>.

④ - You should not <u>waste</u> water.

  - We cannot finish the work if we <u>waste</u> time.

⑤ - Where is a good <u>place</u> to visit?

  - Please <u>place</u> your books on the desk.

[경기 ○○중]

3. 빈칸에 들어갈 말로 바르게 짝지어진 것은?   (3점)

> • I finished my project thanks _____ Jason.
> • His brother is good _____ speaking English.

① to - at   ② to - to

③ in - at   ④ in - in

⑤ to - with

[경기 ○○중]

4. 다음 짝지어진 대화 중 <u>어색한</u> 것은?   (3점)

① A: I enjoy cooking healthy food.

  B: Sounds cool. What can you make?

② A: What kind of pictures do you usually take?

  B: The beautiful pictures reduce my stress.

③ A: What do you do with her?

  B: I enjoy taking a walk with her. It makes me healthy.

④ A: Put one foot on the board and push hard with the other.

  B: Like this? Wow! This is fun.

⑤ A: Do you know how to get over a cold?

  B: Well, I usually drink warm water when I have a cold.

5. 다음 글의 "I"의 기분으로 가장 알맞은 것은? (3점)

> Tomorrow, I have an English speaking contest. I started preparing for the contest two weeks ago. I love speaking in English, but I am nervous because of the contest. I cannot sleep well.

① bored

② excited

③ stressed

④ surprised

⑤ disappointed

[6-8] 다음 대화를 읽고 물음에 답하시오.

> Karl: Hana, what's the matter?
> Hana: Well, I'm ⓐ_____ about the test next week. I started preparing for the test three weeks ago. I like to speak in English, but I'm nervous about the test. I cannot sleep well.
> Karl: I understand. I ride my longboard when I feel nervous. Do you know how to ride it?
> Hana: No, I don't.
> Karl: Let's go out! I will teach you. First, put one foot on the board and push hard with ⓑ_____.
> Hana: Like this? Wow! This is fun. I feel better already.
> Karl: See? I enjoy riding my longboard because it can ⓒ_____ my stress.
> Hana: That's great!

6. 위 대화의 ⓐ, ⓑ, ⓒ에 들어갈 적절한 말은? (4점)

	ⓐ	ⓑ	ⓒ
①	stressed	others	increase
②	stressed	the other	decrease
③	stressing	the other	decrease
④	stressing	others	increase
⑤	stressing	others	decrease

7. 위 대화의 내용과 일치하는 것은? (3점)

① Karl is not interested in Hana's feeling.

② Hana feels better when she makes a board.

③ Hana teaches Karl how to ride a longboard.

④ Riding a longboard helps Karl reduce his stress.

⑤ Only one foot is needed when Karl rides a board.

8. 위 대화를 읽고 대답할 수 없는 질문은? (4점)

① Why is Hana stressed?

② What does Karl enjoy doing?

③ How does Karl reduce his stress?

④ Where did Karl learn to ride a longboard?

⑤ Why does Karl like to ride his longboard?

B: I want to eat healthy food. Do you have any advice?

G: I often eat fresh salad. It makes me feel good.

B: Really? Can you tell me how to make it?

G: Yes, it is quite simple. First, cut many vegetables ⓐ small pieces. Next, put them ⓑ a bowl. Then, pour some lemon juice on them. Finally, mix everything together.

B: That's it? I should try it.

[부산 ○○중]

9. 빈칸 ⓐ, ⓑ에 공통으로 들어갈 전치사는? (2점)

① in   ② for   ③ with
④ into   ⑤ from

[인천 ○○중]

10. 위 대화를 읽고, 샐러드 만드는 방법을 바르게 배열한 것은? (3점)

(가) 모두 함께 섞는다.
(나) 썬 야채 재료를 모두 그릇에 담는다.
(다) 썬 야채 재료에 레몬주스를 붓는다.
(라) 야채를 작은 조각으로 썬다.

① (가) – (나) – (다) – (라)
② (가) – (다) – (나) – (라)
③ (나) – (가) – (다) – (라)
④ (다) – (나) – (가) – (라)
⑤ (라) – (나) – (다) – (가)

At school you sit for many hours. Do you get tired? Why don't you massage yourself and stretch?

Let's begin with the eyes. Close your eyes and massage them softly with your fingers. It will relax your eyes. When you finish, cover your eyes with your hands to block out the light. (a)그것은 당신의 눈이 더욱 편안하게 느끼게 해줄 것이다.

Next, massage your neck. Put your fingers on the back of your neck. Draw small circles with your fingers (b)to massage your neck. Massage from top to bottom. The massage will help you (가)_____ better.

[인천 ○○중]

11. Which can be the title of this text? (4점)

① Block Out Light to Relax
② How to Stretch Your Legs
③ The Reason Why Students Are Tired
④ The Reason Why Eyes Are Important
⑤ How to Massage Your Eyes and Neck

[울산 ○○중]

12. 빈칸 (가)에 들어갈 feel의 알맞은 형태는? (정답 2개) (3점)

① feel   ② felt
③ feels   ④ feeling
⑤ to feel

13. 밑줄 친 (a)의 뜻이 되도록 〈보기〉의 단어를 배열하여 쓰시오. (5점)

> **보기**
>
> it / eyes / comfortable / feel / make / will / your / more

> **조건**
>
> 1. 완벽한 문장이 되도록 쓸 것.
> 2. 대·소문자에 유의할 것.

답: _____

14. 위 글의 내용과 일치하는 문장의 개수는? (3점)

> - You sit for a long time at school.
> - You cover your eyes using your hands to sleep.
> - When you massage your neck, you should start it from the bottom.
> - You use the back of your hands when you massage your eyes.
> - You should draw small circles with your neck before massaging your neck.

① 1개   ② 2개

③ 3개   ④ 4개

⑤ 5개

15. 밑줄 친 (b)의 용법과 같은 것은? (정답 2개) (3점)

① Give me a pencil <u>to write</u> with.

② I need <u>to finish</u> my homework first.

③ Exercise regularly <u>to become</u> stronger.

④ Do you know the way <u>to get</u> to the subway station?

⑤ I use the Internet <u>to communicate</u> with people from other countries.

[16-17] 다음 대화를 읽고 물음에 답하시오.

> B: People say that we should walk more than 10,000 steps every day to be healthy. I can't count ⓐ<u>the number of</u> my steps easily.
>
> G: You can use this smartphone app. Do you know ⓑ<u>what to use</u> it?
>
> B: No. Can you show me?
>
> G: Sure. First, ⓒ<u>download the app</u>. Then, ⓓ <u>walk with</u> your smartphone. Later, you can check the number of steps you took.
>
> B: Thank you. I will ⓔ<u>start using</u> it today.

16. ⓐ~ⓔ 중 어법상 어색한 것은? (4점)

① ⓐ   ② ⓑ   ③ ⓒ

④ ⓓ   ⑤ ⓔ

17. 위 대화를 읽고 답할 수 있는 질문의 개수는? (3점)

- What is the name of the app?
- Does the girl know the way to use the app?
- When is the boy going to start using the app?
- How many steps should we walk to be healthy?
- Can they check how many steps they took with the app?

① 1개　　　　　② 2개

③ 3개　　　　　④ 4개

⑤ 5개

18. 위 글의 내용과 일치하지 <u>않는</u> 것은? (4점)

① When you stretch your waist, you should team up with a friend.

② You should hold each other's waist when you massage your wrist.

③ After you stretch your head and body backward, you should hold it for 3 seconds.

④ If you massage yourself and stretch every day, you can focus on your studies better.

⑤ After you loosen up your right leg, you can switch your legs and repeat the exercise.

[18~21] 다음 글을 읽고 물음에 답하시오.

Let's work on your waist. Team up with a friend. Stand close to each other and ⓐ<u>face</u> your partner. Hold each other's wrists. Slowly stretch your head and body ⓑ<u>backward</u>. Hold that position for three seconds. Then, slowly pull each other to a standing position. You and your partner should move at the same speed. If you don't ＿＿＿ (가) ＿＿＿, both of you will fall!

ⓒ<u>Place</u> the top of your right foot on the desk behind you. Then, slowly bend your left leg and ⓓ<u>lower</u> yourself. ⓔ<u>Hold</u> it for a few seconds and slowly straighten up. This position will loosen up your right leg. Switch your legs and repeat the exercise.

How do you feel now? If you massage yourself and stretch every day, you will feel healthier. Also, you can focus on your studies better.

19. 위 글의 흐름으로 보아 빈칸 (가)에 들어갈 표현으로 가장 알맞은 것은? (3점)

① bend your left leg

② work on your waist

③ move at the same speed

④ hold that position for three seconds

⑤ stretch your head and body backward

20. ⓐ~ⓔ의 우리말 뜻이 글의 흐름과 어울리지 <u>않는</u> 것은? (4점)

① ⓐ face : 마주보다

② ⓑ backward : 뒤쪽으로

③ ⓒ Place : 장소

④ ⓓ lower : 낮추다

⑤ ⓔ Hold : 유지하다

21. 위 글의 내용과 일치하는 것은? (4점)

① They will not fall if they move at different speeds.

② They will fall unless they move at different speeds.

③ Both of them will fall if they move at different speeds.

④ Both of them will fall if they move at the same speed.

⑤ They will not fall unless they move at the same speed.

[22~23] 다음 글을 읽고 물음에 답하시오.

Place the top of your right foot on the desk behind you. Then, slowly bend your left leg and lower yourself. Hold it for a few seconds and slowly (a)_____ up. This position will loosen up your right leg. Switch your legs and repeat the exercise.

How do you feel now? (1) 매일 너 자신을 마사지하고 스트레칭을 하면, 너는 더 건강해지는 것을 느낄 거야. Also, (2) 너는 너 자신을 공부에 더 집중하게 할 수 있어.

22. (a)에 들어갈 말로 옳은 것은? (3점)

① straighten

② straightly

③ straightens

④ straightened

⑤ straightening

---

23. 〈조건〉에 맞게 문장 (1)~(2)를 완성하시오. (5점)

> **조건**
> • 주어진 단어를 활용하여 문장을 쓸 것.
> • (1)은 조건문을, (2)는 사역동사를 꼭 포함할 것.

(1) _____

_____(massage, feel)

(2) _____

_____(more, studying, on)

---

24. 대화의 흐름에 맞게 괄호 안의 단어를 활용하여 빈칸에 알맞은 말을 쓰시오. (4점)

A: I feel stressed these days. What should I do?

B: When I stressed, I listen to music. It (1)_____ better. (make, me) I will show (2)_____ music. (you, how, download)

(1) _____

(2) _____

At school you sit ⓐfor many hours. Do you get tired? Why don't you massage yourself and stretch?

First, let's begin with the eyes. Close your eyes and massage them softly ⓑwith your fingers. It will relax your eyes. When you finish, cover your eyes with your hands to block out the light. It will make your eyes (A)_____ more comfortable.

Next, massage your neck. Put your fingers on the back of your neck. Draw small circles with your fingers to massage your neck. Massage ⓒfrom top to bottom. The massage will help you (B)_____ better.

Let's work on your (C)_____. Team up with a friend. Stand close to each other and face your partner. Hold each other's wrists. Slowly stretch your head and body backward. Hold that position ⓓduring three seconds. Then, slowly pull each other to a standing position. You and your partner should move ⓔat the same speed. (D)_____, both of you will fall!

25. 위 글의 내용과 일치하는 것은? (4점)

① 눈을 마사지할 때 눈을 떠야 한다.

② 목을 마사지할 때는 아래에서부터 위로 한다.

③ 허리 운동을 위해 머리와 몸을 앞쪽으로 구부린다.

④ 허리 운동은 친구와 짝을 지어 등을 맞대고 한다.

⑤ 허리 운동에서 서 있는 위치로 돌아올 때 짝과 같은 속도로 움직여야 한다.

26. 위 글의 빈칸 (A)와 (B)에 들어가기에 공통으로 알맞은 형태는? (3점)

① feel

② to feel

③ feeling

④ felt

⑤ to feeling

27. 위 글의 문맥상 빈칸 (C)에 들어가기에 가장 적절한 것은? (4점)

① wrist

② head

③ body

④ waist

⑤ partner

28. 위 글의 문맥상 빈칸 (D)에 들어갈 말로 가장 적절한 것은? (3점)

① If you don't

② If you move

③ If you do that

④ Unless you don't

⑤ If you hold that position

29. 위 글의 밑줄 친 ⓐ~ⓔ 중, 단어의 사용이 어색한 것은? (4점)

① ⓐ

② ⓑ

③ ⓒ

④ ⓓ

⑤ ⓔ

◎ 선택형 문항의 답안은 컴퓨터용 수정 싸인펜을 사용하여 OMR 답안지에 바르게 표기하시오.
◎ 서술형 문제는 답을 답안지에 반드시 검정 볼펜으로 쓰시오.
◎ 총 30문항 100점 만점입니다. 문항별 배점음 각 문항에 표시되어 있습니다.

[부산 ○○중]

1. 〈보기〉의 빈칸에 들어갈 수 없는 것은?　　(4점)

보기
• We _____ to be there around six.
• Jane _____s a room with her sister.
• Mike was born in Korea, but is an American _____.
• Baby rabbits _____ together with their mother.

① aim
② gather
③ reduce
④ citizen
⑤ share

[경기 ○○중]

2. 다음 글의 내용상 빈칸에 들어갈 적절한 말은? (3점)

Nancy works at a children's hospital. She is always busy because she _____ sick children. She tries to treat them kindly.

① puts on
② cares for
③ blocks out
④ pushes down
⑤ fights against

[부산 ○○중]

3. 다음 두 문장을 관계대명사를 이용하여 한 문장으로 만드시오.　　(6점)

조건
완벽한 문장으로 쓸 것.

(1) I know a girl. + She speaks Japanese well.

→ _____

(2) The man is my father. + He is playing soccer there.

→ _____

(3) I played with James and his dog. + They live near my house.

→ _____

[부산 ○○중]

4. 짝지어진 대화가 어색한 것은?　　(2점)

① A: Do you have any plans for the weekend?
　 B: Yes. I'm going to Jeju Island with my family.
② A: Are you going to visit your uncle?
　 B: Yes, I am.
③ A: I hope people save water.
　 B: I hope so, too.
④ A: Let's hold a 'Save the Earth' campaign.
　 B: Oh, that's too bad.
⑤ A: Dad, my class will grow carrots in the garden.
　 B: I hope the carrots grow well.

[5-8] 다음 대화를 읽고 물음에 답하시오.

Karl: Jiho, isn't that too much? Are you (a)_____ eat all of that?

Jiho: I'm not sure, but Bulgogi is my favorite.

Karl: Hey! Look at the campaign poster. "_____(가)_____"

Jiho: What does that (b)_____?

Karl: It means "Think first (c)_____ you eat and save the Earth."

Jiho: I think I took too much Bugogi. Let's (d)_____ it.

Karl: Okay. That's a good idea.

Jiho: We ate it all. My clean plate makes me feel good.

Karl: Let's not (e)_____ food from now on. I hope we can save the Earth.

5. 위 대화의 빈칸 (a)~(e)에 들어갈 말로 어색한 것은? (3점)

① (a) going to
② (b) mean
③ (c) after
④ (d) share
⑤ (e) waste

6. 위 대화의 내용으로 보아 빈칸 (가)에 들어갈 캠페인의 제목으로 가장 알맞은 것은? (4점)

① Plant Trees
② Let's Recycle
③ Think, Eat, Save!
④ Help People in Need
⑤ Send Shoes of Hope

7. 위 대화의 내용과 일치하는 것은? (3점)

① Jiho가 가장 좋아하는 음식은 불고기이다.
② Jiho는 처음에 담은 불고기를 혼자 다 먹었다.
③ Karl은 음식을 남기지 않아서 기분이 좋아졌다.
④ 캠페인 포스터는 '물을 아껴 쓰자'에 관한 것이다.
⑤ Jiho와 Karl은 음식을 재활용해서 지구를 구하고 싶어 한다.

8. 위 대화에서 답을 찾을 수 있는 질문 만을 있는 대로 모두 고른 것은? (3점)

ⓐ What does Karl hope for?
ⓑ What food does Karl like?
ⓒ Why did Karl join the campaign?
ⓓ What did the campaign poster say?
ⓔ What does "Think, Eat, Save" on the poster mean?
ⓕ How did Jiho feel after he finished his Bulgogi all?

① ⓐ, ⓒ, ⓔ
② ⓐ, ⓑ, ⓓ
③ ⓐ, ⓓ, ⓔ, ⓕ
④ ⓑ, ⓒ, ⓓ, ⓔ
⑤ ⓑ, ⓓ, ⓔ, ⓕ

[9-12] 다음 글을 읽고 물음에 답하시오.

Hi, my name is Jo. I ⓐam from Australia. A few weeks ago, (A)나의 선생님은 우리에게 케냐 학생들의 사진들을 보여주었다. Sadly, they were all using plastic bags to carry their books. My class ⓑdecided to raise money to ⓒsend them new school bags. We sold cookies and drinks and (B)raised 600 dollars. We hope the Kenyan students ⓓare happy with the new bags.

    └, Wang: Great! I'm sure they will like the bags.
    └, Kozo: You did ⓔwonderful something!

9. 위 글의 우리말 (A)를 영어로 바르게 바꾼 것은? (3점)

① my teacher showed us pictures of students in Kenya

② my teacher showed pictures of students for us in Kenya

③ my teacher showed to us pictures of students in Kenya

④ my teacher showed pictures of students us in Kenya

⑤ my teacher showed pictures of students of us in Kenya

10. 위 글의 밑줄 친 부분 중, 어법상 어색한 것은? (3점)

① ⓐ   ② ⓑ   ③ ⓒ

④ ⓓ   ⑤ ⓔ

11. 위 글의 밑줄 친 (B)와 의미가 같은 것은? (3점)

① Tom raised his left hand to ask a question.

② It is not easy to raise a child these days.

③ They don't raise chickens on that farm.

④ We raise money for the World Food Program.

⑤ Sumi raises a dog and a cat in her house.

12. 위 글을 다음과 같이 요약할 때 ⓐ~ⓒ에 들어갈 말로 알맞은 것은? (4점)

Jo and his friends in ⓐ_____ sent new bags to ⓑ_____ students because they ⓒ_____ their books in plastic bags.

	ⓐ	ⓑ	ⓒ
①	Australia	Kenya	read
②	Kenya	Kenya	read
③	Australia	Kenyan	read
④	Kenya	Kenyan	carried
⑤	Australia	Kenyan	carried

[13-15] 다음 글을 읽고 물음에 답하시오.

I am Afig from Malaysia. My school started a wall painting campaign (A)[make / to make] our village look better. ⓐ그림을 잘 그리는 학생들 gathered and painted on some walls of schools and parks.

Thanks to this campaign, our village looks (B)[much / very] nicer. Now, everyone can enjoy (C)[to walk / walking] alongside the painted walls.

15. 위 글의 밑줄 친 ⓐ의 우리말을 〈보기〉에 주어진 단어를 사용하여 영어로 옮기시오.   (3점)

보기

good, who, painting

답: Students _____

13. 위 글의 괄호 (A), (B), (C) 안에서 어법상 알맞은 것끼리 짝지어진 것은?   (4점)

	(A)	(B)	(C)
①	make	much	to walk
②	make	very	walking
③	to make	very	walking
④	to make	much	walking
⑤	to make	much	to walk

[16-18] 다음 대화를 읽고 물음에 답하시오.

Karl: Jiho, ⓐ그거 너무 많지 않니?
　　　Are you going to eat all of that?
Jiho: ⓑ잘 모르겠어, but Bulgogi is my favorite.
Karl: Hey! Look at the campaign poster. "Think, Eat, Save!"
Jiho: ⓒ그게 무슨 뜻이지?
Karl: It means "Think first before you eat and save the Earth."
Jiho: I think I took too much Bulgogi. ⓓ나눠 먹자.
Karl: Okay. That's a good idea.
Jiho: We ate it all. My clean plate makes me feel good.
Karl: ⓔ음식을 낭비하지 말자 from now on.
　　　(A)_____

14. According to Afig's education experience, what is the best meaning of the global citizenship? (3점)

*according to: ~에 의하면

① It is saving money for myself.

② It is working for a better world.

③ It is growing citizens who work well.

④ It is caring for our own cultures.

⑤ It is sharing the information of making the village dirty.

16. 위 대화의 ⓐ~ⓔ를 영어로 바르게 표현한 것은?   (3점)

① ⓐ is that too much

② ⓑ I'm not sure

③ ⓒ What does it do

④ ⓓ Let's make it

⑤ ⓔ Let's waste food

17. 위 대화의 내용과 일치하지 <u>않는</u> 것은?　　(3점)

① Jiho likes Bugogi best.

② Jiho didn't leave the food.

③ Jiho took too much Bulgogi.

④ Jiho and Karl shared Bulgogi.

⑤ Jiho understood the campaign poster at first.

19. 위 글의 내용상 빈칸 ⓐ에 들어갈 알맞은 말은? (3점)

① the pictures

② much money

③ the new bags

④ the plastic bags

⑤ cookies and drinks

18. 위 대화의 (A)에 들어갈 표현을 주어진 단어를 <u>모두</u> 활용하여 어법에 맞게 쓰시오.　　(4점)

→ _____.

(can / we / I / save / the Earth / hope)

20. 위 글을 읽고 대답할 수 <u>없는</u> 것은?　　(3점)

① Where is Jo from?

② Why did Jo's class sell cookies and drinks?

③ How did Kenyan students carry their books?

④ What did Jo's teacher show to the students?

⑤ Where did Jo's class sell cookies and drinks?

[19~22] 다음 글을 읽고 물음에 답하시오.

Hi, my name is Jo. I am from Australia. A few weeks ago, my teacher showed us pictures of students in Kenya. Sadly, they were all using plastic bags to carry their books. My class decided to raise money to send them new school bags. We sold cookies and drinks and raised 600 dollars. We hope the Kenyan students are happy with ⓐ_____.

└ Wang: Awesome! I'm sure they will like the bags.

└ Kozo: ⓑ<u>너희 멋진 일을 했구나!</u>

21. 위 글의 우리말 ⓑ를 주어진 단어를 <u>모두</u> 이용하여 영작하시오.　　(3점)

→ _____!

(did / you / wonderful / something)

22. 위 글을 읽고, 다음 질문에 대한 답을 빈칸 수에 맞게 쓰시오. (4점)

> What did Jo's class do to raise money?

→ They _____ _____ _____ _____ _____

_____ _____.

23. 빈칸 (A)에 들어갈 알맞은 단어를 <u>모두</u> 고르면? (3점)

① who   ② this

③ what   ④ which

⑤ that

[23-27] 다음 글을 읽고 물음에 답하시오.

> This is the Global Citizenship Education site. Global citizens are people (A)_____ try to understand different cultures. They also care for people in need and work for a better world. Please share your global citizenship education experiences here.
>
> Hello. I am Minhee from Korea. I am a member of the Global Community Club. My club aims to communicate with people from around the world. (a)일주일 전에 우리는 우리 마을의 유등 축제에 관한 비디오를 제작했다. We uploaded it to the Internet and amazingly, we got nearly 5,000 hits. Click here for our video.
>
> └ Alice: Wow, your lantern festival looks fantastic!
> └ Sunan: We have a water festival in our village. I'd like to make a video like yours.

24. 위 글에서 답을 찾아 쓰시오. (5점)

(1) Who do global citizens care for?

They _____.

(2) What does Minhee's club aim to do?

_____

25. 위 글의 우리말 (a)의 의미에 맞도록 <보기>에 주어진 단어를 바르게 배열하여 문장을 완성하시오. (3점)

> 보기
>
> a / in / our / produced / about the lantern festival / village / video

→ A week ago we _____

_____.

26. 위 글의 내용과 일치하지 <u>않는</u> 것은?   (3점)

① Minhee joined the Global Community Club.

② Global citizens try to understand different cultures.

③ A lot of people watched the video made by Minhee's club.

④ Minhee's club made a video about the festival in her village.

⑤ This site helps people in need to grow as global citizens.

27. 위 글을 읽고 답할 수 <u>없는</u> 질문은?   (3점)

① What can you share on this site?

② How many hits did the video get?

③ What does Minhee's club aim to do?

④ What does Global Citizenship Education do?

⑤ Why did Minhee join the Global Community Club?

28. 위 글의 ⓐ~ⓔ 중 어법이 바르지 <u>않은</u> 것은? (3점)

① ⓐ   ② ⓑ   ③ ⓒ

④ ⓓ   ⑤ ⓔ

29. 위 글의 (A)who와 용법이 <u>다른</u> 것은?   (3점)

① I don't know <u>who</u> is telling the truth.

② The girl <u>who</u> is cleaning the floor is Susan.

③ He is the man <u>who</u> made this table.

④ He is the boy <u>who</u> broke the window.

⑤ You need a friend <u>who</u> can understand you.

[28-30] 다음 글을 읽고 물음에 답하시오.

I am Afig from Malaysia. My school started a wall painting campaign to make our village ⓐ<u>looks</u> better. Students (A)<u>who</u> are good at ⓑ<u>painting</u> gathered and painted on some walls of schools and parks. ⓒ<u>Thanks to</u> this campaign, our village looks much nicer. Now everyone can enjoy ⓓ<u>walking</u> alongside the painted walls.

└ Junho : ⓔ<u>What a nice idea!</u>

30. 위 글의 내용과 일치하지 <u>않는</u> 것은?   (3점)

① Afig은 말레이시아 출신이다.

② 학교에서 벽화 캠페인을 시작했다.

③ 벽화 덕분에 마을은 훨씬 멋지게 보인다.

④ 그림을 좋아하는 학생들이 벽화를 그렸다.

⑤ 사람들이 벽화 길 걷는 것을 즐길 수 있다.

◎ 선택형 문항의 답안은 컴퓨터용 수정 싸인펜을 사용하여 OMR 답안지에 바르게 표기하시오.
◎ 서술형 문제는 답을 답안지에 반드시 검정 볼펜으로 쓰시오.
◎ 총 30문항 100점 만점입니다. 문항별 배점은 각 문항에 표시되어 있습니다.

[서울 도봉구 ○○중]

1. 다음 밑줄 친 단어와 바꾸어 쓸 수 있는 것은?
(2점)

He wants to be the CEO of a <u>worldwide</u> company.

① global　　　　② whole
③ particular　　　④ same
⑤ able

[충북 ○○중]

2. 다음 보기의 빈칸에 필요 <u>없는</u> 표현은?　　(4점)

• I finished my project _____ Susan.
• Sam tries to _____ before taking the test.
• He could play basketball _____.
• It can weigh _____ 180 tons.

① with time　　　　② loosen up
③ thanks to　　　　④ in need
⑤ up to

[울산 ○○중]

3. 다음 중 어법상 옳은 것은?　　(3점)

① He owns a dog has a long tail.
② Mike is wearing a hat that look old.
③ The man teaching history is my uncle.
④ Suho is reading a book who has a red cover.
⑤ My sister and her cat that was in her bed fell asleep together.

[울산 ○○중]

4. 문맥상 빈칸에 들어갈 말로 가장 <u>어색한</u> 것은? (3점)

A: I hope _____.
B: I hope so, too. Let's hold a Save the Earth campaign.
A: That's a good idea.

① the air gets cleaner
② people don't waste water
③ people turn down the heat
④ people often take a shower
⑤ people don't throw away trash

[부산 ○○중]

5. 환경을 위해 우리가 할 수 있는 일을 잘못 말하고 있는 사람들만 짝지은 것은?　　(4점)

- John : I always finish all my food.
- Andy : I use a paper cup when I drink coffee.
- Sophia : I walk to school instead of taking a bus.
- Jinhee : I buy a plastic bag when I go shopping.
- Minsu : I usually take a short shower to save water.

① John, Andy　　　② John, Jinhee
③ Andy, Jinhee　　④ Andy, Minsu
⑤ Sophia, Minsu

6. 다음 우리말에 맞게 영어로 쓰시오. (5점)

Jake는 오래되어 보이는 모자(hat)를 쓰고 있습니다.
→ Jake is _____ _____ _____

_____ _____ _____.

7. 괄호 안의 우리말과 일치하도록 빈칸에 알맞은 말을 쓰시오. (4점)

B: What's your plan for this weekend?

_____

<특별한 무언가를 할 예정이니?>
G: Yes. On Sunday, I'm going to go for a picnic with my family.
B: How about on Saturday?
G: I have no plans for Saturday. Why?
B: I'm going to do volunteer work at the library on Saturday. Would you like to come with me?
G: Sure.

・Are you going to ~를 활용할 것.
・완벽한 문장으로 서술할 것.

→ _____

8. 다음은 세계시민교육 활동 자원봉사자를 모집하는 포스터이다. 포스터의 내용을 바르게 해석한 사람은? (3점)

> **Sending Shoes of Hope**
> Why: To help poor children who don't have shoes
> How: 1. Bring shoes from home.
> 2. Draw pictures or write caring words on them.
> 3. Send them to children in need
> When: July 3rd
> **If you want to do something special for the world, join us!**

① Sean: The poor children can get the shoes before July 3rd.

② Josh: This poster aims to help poor children who lost their homes.

③ Ian: Volunteers will also send the poor children some cards with caring words.

④ Amy: If volunteers want to do something for the poor children, they can bring some pictures.

⑤ Mark: Volunteers are going to draw pictures or write caring words on the shoes.

9. What is the campaign about? (3점)

> Every day, many students leave some food on their plates. So, our club is going to hold a campaign about it. If you finish all the food on your plate, you will get a small gift. I hope many students join our campaign.

① To get a gift

② Not to leave food

③ To grow vegetables

④ To make healthy food

⑤ To join the cooking club

I am Afig from Malaysia. My school started a wall painting campaign to make our village look better. Students ⓐwhich ⓑis good at painting gathered and painted on some walls of schools and parks. Thanks to this campaign, our village looks ⓒmuch nicer. Now everyone can enjoy ⓓto walk alongside the painted walls.

└, Junho: ⓔHow a nice idea!

10. 위 글의 밑줄 친 부분 중, 어법상 옳은 것은? (2점)

① ⓐ   ② ⓑ   ③ ⓒ

④ ⓓ   ⑤ ⓔ

11. 위 글을 읽고 답할 수 없는 것은? (4점)

① Where does Afig come from?

② When did students paint the wall paintings?

③ Thanks to the campaign, what can everyone enjoy?

④ Why did Afig's school start the wall painting?

⑤ What did Afig's school do to make his village look better?

12. Which is NOT something you can do for the Earth? (3점)

① I'm going to walk to school.

② I'm going to recycle bottles.

③ I'm going to leave some food.

④ I'm going to taking a short shower.

⑤ I'm going to take a cotton shopping bag.

13. ⓐ~ⓔ가 가리키는 것이 잘못된 것은? (3점)

B: Did you watch the news about the flood?

G: Yes, I did. ⓐThey said a lot of people lost their homes.

B: My club is going to send ⓑthem some money.

G: How can you do ⓒthat? Are you going to raise money, Andy?

B: Yes. ⓓWe're going to make pencil cases and sell ⓔthem.

① ⓐ They: the news

② ⓑ them: people who lost their homes

③ ⓒ that: to send Andy's club some money

④ ⓓ We: Andy and his club members

⑤ ⓔ them: pencil cases

Karl: Jiho, isn't that too much? ⓐ<u>Are you going to eat all of that</u>?

Jiho: I'm not sure, but Bulgogi is my favorite.

Karl: Look at the campaign poster. "Think, Eat, Save!"

Jiho: ⓑ<u>What does that mean</u>?

Karl: It means "Think first before you eat and save the Earth."

Jiho: I think I took too much Bulgogi. ⓒ <u>Let's share it.</u>

Karl: Okay. That's a good idea.

Jiho: We ate it all. ⓓ<u>My clean plate makes me feel good.</u>

Karl: ⓔ<u>Let's waste food from now on.</u> I hope we can save the Earth.

[서울 ○○중]

14. 위 대화의 흐름상 ⓐ~ⓔ 중 어색한 것은? (4점)

① ⓐ 　　② ⓑ 　　③ ⓒ

④ ⓓ 　　⑤ ⓔ

[서울 양천구 ○○중]

15. 위 대화의 내용과 일치하는 것은? (3점)

① Bulgogi is Karl's favorite food.

② Jiho knows the meaning of the campaign poster.

③ Karl is holding a campaign about saving the Earth.

④ Jiho doesn't think he took too much food.

⑤ Jiho and Karl finished all the food on the plate.

[서울 영등포구 ○○중]

16. 위 대화를 읽고 질문에 답할 수 <u>없는</u> 것은? (3점)

① What does Karl hope for?

② Why does Jiho feel good?

③ Did Jiho finish his food all alone?

④ What food does Karl like most?

⑤ Who knows the meaning of "Think, Eat, Save!"?

[17-19] 다음 글을 읽고 물음에 답하시오.

Hi, my name is Jo. I am from Australia. (A) A few weeks ago, my teacher showed us pictures of ⓐ<u>students</u> in Kenya. (B) My class decided to raise money to send ⓑ<u>them</u> new school bags. (C) We sold cookies and drinks. And we raised 600 dollars. (D) We hope ⓒ<u>they</u> are happy with the new bags. (E)

└, Wang: Awesome! I'm sure ⓓ<u>they</u> will like the bags.

└, Kozo: ⓔ<u>You</u> did something wonderful!

[서울 양천구 ○○중]

17. 위 글의 흐름상 (A)~(E) 중 주어진 문장이 들어갈 위치는? (3점)

Sadly, they were all using plastic bags to carry their books.

① (A) 　　② (B) 　　③ (C)

④ (D) 　　⑤ (E)

18. 위 글의 밑줄 친 ⓐ~ⓔ 중 가리키는 것이 다른 하나는? (2점)

① ⓐ   ② ⓑ   ③ ⓒ

④ ⓓ   ⑤ ⓔ

21. 위 글 ⓐ~ⓔ 중 우리말 뜻이 옳지 않은 것은? (3점)

① ⓐ 세계 시민 교육

② ⓑ 다른 문화들

③ ⓒ 좋아하다

④ ⓓ 어려움에 처한

⑤ ⓔ 경험들

19. 위 글을 읽고 다음 질문의 답을 본문에서 찾아 영어로 쓰시오. (4점)

Q: What did Jo's class do to raise money?

답: They _____ .

22. 위 글의 소재는? (3점)

① global citizenship

② global cities

③ a better world

④ people in need

⑤ caring for people

[20-24] 다음 글을 읽고 물음에 답하시오.

This is the Global Citizenship Education site. ⓐGlobal Citizenship Education helps us grow (A)_____ global citizens. Global citizens are people (a)that try to understand ⓑdifferent cultures. They also ⓒcare for people ⓓin need and work (B)_____ a better world. Please share your global citizenship education ⓔexperiences here.

20. 빈칸 (A)와 (B)에 들어갈 전치사가 바르게 짝지어진 것은? (3점)

① by – for   ② as – for

③ to – at   ④ as – off

⑤ in – without

23. 다음 질문에 알맞은 답을 본문에서 찾아 쓰시오. (5점)

Q: What does Global citizens do in the passage?

A: They try to (A)_____ .

    They also (B)_____ and

    (C)_____ .

(A)_____

(B)_____

(C)_____

24. 위 글의 (a)와 쓰임이 같은 것은? (정답 2개) (3점)

① That is my favorite color.

② Do you remember that boy?

③ I know that he is very honest.

④ I like the girl that is wearing a red dress.

⑤ The man that is wearing blue pants is my brother.

25. 다음 대화의 내용과 일치하지 않는 것은? (3점)

Bob: Do you have any plans for the summer vacation, Suji?

Suji: Yes, I'm going to the Philippines to do some volunteer work with my family.

Bob: Oh, I went there and helped some children study last year. Are you going to do that, too?

Suji: Yes. And I'll also paint walls with the children.

Bob: That sounds nice.

① Suji는 여름방학 중에 특별한 계획이 있다.

② Suji는 필리핀에서 자원봉사를 할 예정이다.

③ Suji는 가족들과 함께 필리핀으로 갈 것이다.

④ Suji는 아이들이 공부하는 것을 도와줄 것이다.

⑤ Suji는 작년에 아이들과 함께 벽에 페인트칠을 하였다.

[26-30] 다음 글을 읽고 물음에 답하시오.

Hello. I am Minhee from Korea. I am a member of the Global Community Club. My club aims to communicate with people from around the world. A week ago we produced a video about the lantern festival in our village. We uploaded it to the Internet and ⓐ amazingly, we got near 5,000 hits. Click here for our video.

Hi, my name is Jo. I am from Australia. A few weeks ago, ⓑmy teacher showed us pictures of students in Kenya. Sadly, they were all using plastic bags to carry their books. ⓒMy class decided raising money to send them new school bags. We hope the Kenyan students are happy with the new bags.

I am Afig from Malaysia. ⓓMy school started a wall painting campaign to make our village to look better. Students ㉠who are good at painting gathered and painted on some walls of schools and parks. Thanks to this campaign, ⓔour village look much nicer. Now everyone can enjoy walking alongside the painted walls.

26. 위 글의 밑줄 친 ⓐ～ⓔ 중, 어법상 옳은 것은? (3점)

① ⓐ   ② ⓑ   ③ ⓒ

④ ⓓ   ⑤ ⓔ

27. 위 글을 읽고 답을 알 수 <u>없는</u> 질문은?　　(4점)

① What does Minhee's club aim to do?

② Why did Jo's class decide to raise money?

③ Thanks to the wall painting campaign, what can everyone enjoy?

④ Where does Jo come from?

⑤ How long did it take to finish the wall painting?

29. 위 글의 내용과 일치하지 <u>않는</u> 것은?　　(3점)

① 케냐의 학생들은 책을 들고 다니기 위해 비닐봉지를 사용한다.

② Jo의 학급은 케냐의 학생들을 돕기 위해 돈을 모았다.

③ 케냐 학생들은 새 가방을 받고 무척 행복해 했다.

④ Afig는 말레이시아 출신이다.

⑤ Afig의 학교는 벽화 캠페인을 통해 멋진 마을을 만들었다.

28. 위 글의 밑줄 친 ㉠who와 그 쓰임이 같은 것은?
　　(3점)

① Anyone <u>who</u> wants to come is welcome.

② I don't care <u>who</u> you are.

③ <u>Who</u> do you think they are?

④ The problem is <u>who</u> will take care of the lion.

⑤ <u>Who</u> else ordered steak?

30. 다음은 세계 시민으로서 민희의 경험을 요약한 글이다. 빈칸에 들어갈 단어를 위 글에서 찾아 글을 완성하시오.　　(5점)

> Minhee's Club (1)_____ a video about the (2)_____ festival in her village. The club members (3)_____ the video to the Internet. They got nearly 5,000 (4)_____.

답: (1) _____

　　(2) _____

　　(3) _____

　　(4) _____

정답 및 해설

Lesson 1 (중간) 1회

01 ① **02** (1) volunteer (2) advice (3) attention
03 ⑤ **04** ③ **05** ③ **06** ① **07** ① **08** ① **09** ⑤
10 ③ **11** ④ **12** ③ **13** ③ **14** ① **15** ④ **16** ③
17 Mary는 그녀가 어렸을 때 안경을 쓰곤 했다.
18 He goes to cooking classes or searches for recipes.
19 ③ **20** ③ **21** ①
22 숙제를 할 때 스마트폰을 한쪽으로 치워 두는 것
23 ⑤ **24** ④ **25** ⑤ **26** ① **27** ① **28** ③ **29** ⑤
30 ③

01 '오랫동안 해 왔던 특정한 일이나 행동에서 얻은 지식이나 능력'이라는 영영 풀이가 가리키는 것은 ① experience (경험)이다.

02 volunteer 자원의; 자원봉사의 / advice 충고, 조언 / attention 주의, 집중

03 regularly 정기적으로 / easily 쉽게

04 시간 관리를 잘한다는 요지의 문장들의 내용으로 미루어 볼 때, 빈칸에 들어갈 말은 (never) put off(절대 미루지 않는다)이다.

05 접속사 that이 문장 안에서 목적어로 쓰인 경우에는 생략할 수 있다. ③that은 진주어로 쓰였다.

06 일들을 잘 잊어버린다는 A의 말에 대해 교과서를 이용해야 한다는 B의 대답은 대화 흐름상 적절하지 않다.

07 Jiho와 Hana가 학교 일정 관리를 위한 일정표 관리에 대해서 이야기하고 있고, Jiho는 Hana처럼 자신도 일정표를 하나 사야겠다고(Maybe I should buy one.) 언급했다.

08 "What's the matter?"는 대화 상대방에게 무슨 일이 있냐고 물어보는 표현으로, "What's wrong?", "What's up?"과 같은 표현으로 대체할 수 있다.

09 Hana가 교복으로 무엇을 하는가(What does Hana do with her uniform?)에 대해서는 위 대화에서 언급되지 않았다.

10 위 대화의 첫 문장에서 Somi가 긴장된다고 말하자 B는 댄스 대회 때문에 긴장되는 것인지 되묻는다. 이에 Somi는 연습을 많이 했지만 떨린다고 말하면서 B에게 조언을 구한다. B는 Somi에게 가족들 앞에서 연습을 해보라고

조언하면서 그것이 매우 도움이 될 것이라고 조언한다. 이에 Somi가 고마워하는 순서로 이어지는 것이 대화 흐름상 가장 적절하다.

11 위 대화의 B의 대답으로 미루어 볼 때, 무슨 일이 있냐고 물어보는 표현이 들어가는 것이 가장 적절하다.

12 위 대화의 B의 대답으로 미루어 볼 때, 무슨 일이 있냐고 물어보는 표현인 "What's the matter?"가 들어가는 것이 가장 적절하다.

13 ① good to → good at ② easy → easily ④ from → of ⑤ to → about

14 ① that은 관계대명사로 쓰였다. 나머지는 모두 that이 접속사로 쓰인 문장들이다.

15 (A) because of: ~ 때문에 (B) in front of: ~ 앞에

16 Nick이 며칠 동안 연습했는지는 알 수 없다.

17 'used to+동사원형'은 과거에는 했지만 현재에는 하지 않는 습관 또는 행동에 대해서 이야기할 때 쓸 수 있는 표현이다.

18 John은 매주 토요일 아침마다 무엇을 하는지에 대해서는 요리 수업에 가거나 요리법을 찾아 본다.(Every Saturday morning, I go to cooking classes or search for recipes.)고 언급되어 있다.

19 위 글의 마지막 문단에 나와 있듯이, 시간은 모두가 매일 쓸 수 있는 선물이므로 시간을 잘 활용하자는 것이 위 글의 주제로 가장 적절하다.

20 Minsu는 숙제를 할 때는 스마트폰을 옆으로 치워 둔다(Now, I put aside my smartphone when I do my homework)고 언급한 바 있다.

21 위 글의 @that은 두 문장을 연결해 주는 접속사로서 쓰였다. ①that은 관계대명사로 사용되었다.

22 첫 문단에서 Minsu는 그것이 많은 시간을 절약해 준다고 이야기하고 있다. 흐름상 그것이 가리키는 것은 앞 문장인 숙제를 할 땐 스마트폰을 한 쪽으로 치워 둔다(I put aside my smartphone when I do my homework)는 내용을 가리킨다.

23 to spend는 the same present를 꾸며주는 to부정사의 형용사적 용법으로 사용 되었다. ①, ②는 to부정사의 명사적 용법, ③, ④는 부사적 용법으로 사용되었다.

24 A의 질문에 대한 B의 대답이 A가 돈을 너무 빨리 쓴다는 말에 대한 조언이다. 따라서 빈칸에 들어갈 말로 가장 적절한 것은 대화 상대방에게 조언을 구하는 표현인 'What should I do?'이다.

25 "Why don't you ~?"는 대화 상대방에게 "~하는 것이 어때?"라고 권유나 조언하는 표현으로 같은 표현으로는

"How about ~?", "What about ~?" 등이 있다.

26 (가)to do는 to부정사의 형용사적 용법으로 사용되었다. ①은 to finish가 to부정사의 명사적 용법으로 사용된 문장이다.

27 (A) in the second grade: 2학년 때에

(B) such a +형+명: 그렇게 ~한 …

(C) one step at a time: 한 번에 한 단계씩

28 위 글의 마지막 문단에서 Minsu는 스마트폰으로 SNS 포스팅을 보곤 했으며 그것 때문에 숙제에 집중하지 못했기 때문에 숙제를 하는 게 느려졌다(I used to read SNS postings while I was doing my homework. It slowed me down because I couldn't focus.)고 말했다. 그리고 나서 바로 그것이 시간을 많이 절약해 준다고 말하였으므로 주어진 문장이 들어가기에 가장 적절한 곳은 ⓒ이다.

29 위 글의 마지막 문단에서 Minsu는 숙제를 할 땐 스마트폰을 옆으로 치워놓고 하며 그것이 시간을 많이 절약해 주었고 따라서 숙제를 빨리 끝내놓고 자유 시간을 즐긴다고(Now I put aside my smartphone when I do my homework. It saves me a lot of time. These days, I finish my homework quickly and enjoy my free time.) 언급하였다.

30 위 글에서 Minsu는 스마트폰으로 SNS 포스팅을 보곤 했으며 그것 때문에 숙제에 집중하지 못했기 때문에 숙제를 하는 게 느려졌다(I used to read SNS postings while I was doing my homework. It slowed me down because I couldn't focus.)고 언급했다.

Lesson 1 (중간)

01 ③	02 ①	03 ①	04 ②, ⑤		05 ①	06 ④
07 ③	08 ⑤	09 ①	10 ②	11 ②	12 ④	13 ⑤
14 ③	15 ②	16 ④	17 ①	18 ⑤	19 ①	20 ③

21 ⓐ chef ⓑ Going to cooking classes
　　ⓒ preparing for

22 ③	23 ③	24 ④	25 ①	26 ①	27 ③	28 ④

29 SNS를 안 보며 숙제하는 것

01 along with는 전치사 to 뒤에 올 수 없다. 문맥상 to 뒤에는 동사원형이 오는 것이 적절하다 / get along with ~와 잘 지내다

02 to부정사는 문장 안에서 명사, 형용사, 부사의 역할을 한다. 형용사적 용법의 경우 명사 또는 명사구를 뒤에서 꾸며

준다. 이때 to부정사 뒤에 전치사가 쓰이기도 한다.

03 put off ~을 미루다, 연기하다 / used to ~ (과거에) ~하곤 했다 / put aside ~을 옆으로 치워 두다

04 주어진 real과 really는 형용사-부사 관계이다. 나머지 ①, ③, ④는 모두 명사-형용사 관계이다.

05 위에서부터 순서대로, do - going - spend - make - buy가 들어가야 흐름상 적절하다.

06 축구 수업을 듣는 것이 어떠냐고 조언하는 A의 말에 '난 어젯밤에 그 경기를 봤어.'라고 대답하는 B의 말은 흐름상 자연스럽지 않다.

07 접속사 that이 문장 안에서 목적어로 쓰인 경우에는 생략할 수 있다.

08 위 대화에서 A는 몸이 좋지 않아 조퇴를 해야겠다고 선생님인 B에게 이야기한다. 따라서 빈칸에 들어갈 말로 가장 적절한 것은 '내가 너희 어머니께 조퇴한다고 말씀 드릴게'(I will call your mother and tell her about it.)이다.

09 ①에서 to부정사 to sit은 a chair를 꾸며주는 형용사적 역할을 한다. 따라서 to sit on이 되어야 어법상 적절하다.

10 위 대화에서 B의 대답인 '내 친구가 곧 미국으로 이사가.'로 미루어 볼 때, A가 할 말로 가장 적절한 것은 "무슨 일 있니?"(What's the matter?)이다.

11 be good at ~를 잘하다 / after school 방과 후에

12 복수형이므로 word를 words라고 고쳐야 어법상 적절하다.

13 위 글에서는 큰 목표보다는 작은 목표를 세우는 것이 결국에는 큰 목표를 이룰 수 있다고 이야기하고 있다. 따라서 제목으로 가장 적절한 것은 작은 목표를 세우는 것의 중요성(The Importance of Setting Small Goals)이다.

14 ③to meet은 to부정사의 부사적 용법으로 사용되었다. 나머지는 모두 형용사적 용법으로 사용된 문장들이다.

15 위 대화에서 Jiho의 대답으로 미루어 볼 때, Hana가 Jiho에게 한 질문은 무슨 일 있냐고 묻는 것이다. 따라서 내가 어떻게 해야 할까?(What should I do, Jiho?)는 적절하지 않다.

16 Jiho가 어디서 일정표를 사는지(Where will Jiho buy his planner?)에 대해서는 위 대화에서 언급되어 있지 않다.

17 위 대화에서 Jiho는 중학교 2학년 생활이 1학년 때보다 더 바쁘다(My second year in middle school is busier than my first year)고 언급했다.

18 주어진 문장에서 It이 가리키는 내용은 흐름상 숙제할 때는 스마트폰을 옆에 둔다는 것이다. 따라서 ⓔ에 들어가는

19 (A)가 집중하지 못하게 만들고 숙제를 하는 데 있어 속도를 늦춘다는 것이다. 따라서 그것이 가리키는 내용은 흐름상 '숙제를 하면서 휴대 전화를 사용하는 것'이다.

20 (A)that은 두 문장을 연결해 주는 접속사로 사용되었다. ①, ②, ④, ⑤는 모두 한정사 또는 명사 역할을 하는 that으로 '저 ~' 혹은 '저것'이라는 뜻으로 해석된다.

21 위 글에서 화자는 요리사가 되고 싶다고 했으며 매주 토요일에는 요리법을 찾아보거나 요리 수업을 듣는다고 언급한 바 있다.

22 위 글에서는 일정표(A planner)에 대해 설명하고 있다. 따라서 '요즘에는 숙제가 너무 많다'(There is too much homework these days.)는 문장은 글의 흐름상 자연스럽지 않다.

23 대화에서 B는 댄스 대회를 앞두고 긴장하고 있는데 G에게 조언을 구하고 있다. 따라서 G가 B에게 해줄 말로 가장 적절한 것은 집에서 연습을 하는 것이 좋겠다(practice more at home.)이다.

24 주어진 문장에서 that은 두 문장을 연결하는 접속사로 사용되었다. 이때 that이 목적어 역할을 할 경우 생략 가능하다. ④that은 관계대명사로 사용되었다.

25 put off ~을 미루다, 연기하다 / one step at a time 한 번에 한 단계씩 / put aside 옆으로 치워 두다

26 위 글의 내용으로 미루어 볼 때, 시간이 모두에게 주어진 사용할 수 있는 선물이라는 내용이 빈칸에 들어가는 것이 적절하다.

27 위 글에서는 시간을 잘 관리하고 사용하는 법에 대해서 이야기하고 있으므로 제목으로 가장 적절한 것은 ③ 시간을 잘 관리하는 방법(how to manage your time well)이다.

28 Subin이는 '작은 목표를 세우고 그것들을 매일 이룬다'(I set small goals and achieve them every day.)고 언급했다.

29 위 글의 세 번째 문단에서 Minsu는 그것이 많은 시간을 절약해 준다고 이야기했다. 이야기의 흐름상 그것은 스마트폰으로 SNS 게시물을 보지 않고 공부 또는 숙제에 집중하는 것을 가리킨다.

Lesson 2 (중간)

01 ③	**02** ③	**03** ①	**04** ②	**05** ② **06** ⑤ **07** ⑤

08 ③ **09** ④ **10** ①

11 (1) Managing time is not as[so] easy as achieving goals.
(2) It is surprising that he is lying.

12 ① **13** ④

14 Push down in the center of the chest hard.

15 ③ **16** ① **17** ④ **18** ② **19** ⑤ **20** ② **21** ②

22 ⑤ **23** ④ **24** ① **25** ③ **26** ④ **27** ③ **28** ②

29 ④ **30** She studies as hard as her brother.

01 <보기>의 두 단어는 동사와 그 동사의 형용사형의 관계이다. 이와 같이 동사와 형용사의 관계가 아닌 것은 ③ pass : passive로, 이때 pass는 '건네다', '통과하다'라는 뜻이며 passive는 '수동적인'이라는 뜻을 갖는다.

02 첫 번째 문장은 CPR을 배우면 사람의 생명을 살릴 수 있을 것이라는 문장이며, 두 번째 문장은 새 자전거를 사기 위해 돈을 절약할 것이라는 문장이다. 따라서 빈칸에 공통으로 들어갈 수 있는 단어는 ③ save(구하다, 절약하다)이다.

03 'Don't forget to ~'는 상대방에게 무언가를 상기시킬 때 쓸 수 있는 표현으로 to 뒤에는 동사원형을 쓴다 / turn on ~을 켜다

04 ② I want to get a high grade on the English test.에서 grade는 '성적'이라는 뜻인 반면에 나머지 지문에서 grade는 '학년'이라는 뜻을 갖는다.

05 'Don't forget to ~'는 상대방에게 무언가를 상기시킬 때 쓸 수 있는 표현으로 to 뒤에는 동사원형을 쓴다.

06 위 글은 지난밤에 화자가 가족들과 시간을 보내고 있었는데 지진이 발생한 경험에 대해서 이야기하고 있는 내용이다. 따라서 위 글에 드러난 화자 I의 심정으로 가장 적절한 것은 ⑤ scared(무서워하는)이다.

07 ⓐ 가족, ⓑ 갑자기, 갑작스럽게, ⓒ 가만히, ⓓ 보호하다

08 지진이 멈추자 Jiho는 나가자고 했는데, 이에 대해 선생님은 "엘레베이터를 사용하면 안 된다. 계단을 이용해라."(Remember! You should not use the elevator. Use the stairs.)라고 말하는 것이 흐름상 자연스럽다. 또한 "어디로 가야 하지?"(Where should we go now?)라는 Amy의 물음에 대한 선생님의 대답으로 가장 적절한 것은 건물이 없는 개방된 곳을 찾아야 한다(You need to find an open area with no buildings.)는 문장이다.

09 위 대화의 내용으로 미루어 볼 때, 지진이 발생했을 때 엘

레베이터는 위험하므로 대신 계단을 이용해야 한다.

10 당신이 화재를 발견한다면, 빨간 불에 길을 건너서는 안 된다'(If you find out there is a fire, you should not cross the street on a red light.)는 문장은 화재가 발생했을 경우에 대해서 이야기하고 있는 위 글의 흐름과는 어색하다.

11 (1) '~만큼 …한'이라는 동등 비교 표현은 'as (형용사/부사) as ~'의 형태로 쓸 수 있다. (2) 위 문장은 두 문장으로 이루어진 문장으로, 접속사 that을 사용해 두 문장을 연결할 수 있다. 이때 가주어 it을 함께 사용하면 '…하는 것은 ~하다'라는 의미의 'it is ~ that …'의 구문을 만들 수 있다.

12 to talk → talking

13 위 문장에서는 to부정사의 형용사적 용법을 사용해 the same time to spend라는 표현을 만들 수 있다.

14 push down 누르다 / in the centre of ~의 중간, 가운데

15 "이는 하루의 황금 시간대로, 성공한 사람들은 그것을 최대한 이용한다"(This is the golden time of the day, and those who succeeded make the most if it.)는 문장은 응급 상황에서 CPR을 하고 사람의 생명을 살릴 수 있는 골든 타임에 대해서 이야기하고 있는 위 글의 내용과는 관련이 없다.

16 Everything은 단수 명사이기 때문에 동사는 are가 아니라 is가 되어야 어법상 적절하다.

17 "그걸 쓰는 것을 확실히 해라."는 문장은 미세 먼지가 건강에 좋지 않으므로 마스크를 쓰는 것을 확실히 하라는 곳에 위치하는 것이 적절하다.

18 위 대화의 흐름상 미세 먼지가 많기 때문에 마스크를 써야 한다는 내용이 되어야 적절하다. 따라서 빈칸에 들어갈 말로 가장 알맞은 것은 ② mask이다.

19 "Don't cross the street on a red light." (빨간 불에 길을 건너지 마라.), "You should wear a swimming cap in the swimming pool."(수영장에서는 수영 모자를 써야 한다.), "You need to find an open area with no buildings in case of an earthquake."(지진이 발생했을 경우, 건물이 없는 개방된 곳을 찾아야 한다.)는 문장들이 안전에 대한 규칙으로 적절한 문장이다.

20 조동사 should는 '~해야 한다'는 의미로 어떤 일에 대한 의무를 나타낸다. / safety vest 안전 조끼

21 「의문사+to부정사」는 문장에서 주로 목적어로 쓰인다. 이때 의문사가 무엇이냐에 따라 의미가 조금씩 달라진다. 따라서 빈칸에 들어갈 말로 가장 적절한 것은 ② how(어떻게)이다.

22 위 글의 흐름상, CPR을 할 때 구급차가 올 때까지 가슴 중앙을 빠르고 강하게 압박하라는 문장이 되어야 한다. 따라서 빈칸에 들어갈 말로 가장 적절한 것은 ⑤ until(~할 때까지)이다.

23 빈칸 앞 부분에서 "4분간의 골든 타임을 기억해야 한다. 그 말은 누군가의 심장이 멈추고 4분 안에 CPR을 실행해야 한다는 것을 의미한다."(You need to remember the four minutes of "Golden Time." It means that you should start CPR within four minutes after someone's heart stops.)라고 말했다. 따라서 빈칸에 들어갈 문장으로 가장 적절한 것은 ④ If you start CPR later than four minutes, the chances of saving someone's life will lower.(4분보다 늦게 CPR을 하게 되면 누군가의 생명을 살릴 기회는 낮아질 것이다.)라는 문장이다.

24 '~만큼 …한'이라는 동등 비교 표현은 'as (형용사/부사) as ~'의 형태로 쓸 수 있다. 이때 not을 앞에 붙인 'not as[so] (형용사/부사) as ~'는 비교급 문장이 된다. 두 경우 모두 비교하는 두 대상들의 품사가 같아야 한다.

25 위 대화에서 세진이가 심폐소생술(CPR)을 배운 이유와 하는 방법에 대해서 이야기하고 있지만 ③ 심폐소생술시 분당 압박 횟수에 대해서는 언급하지 않았다.

26 어젯밤에 지진이 있었고 흔들림이 곧 멈추었지만 무서웠다는 A의 말에 대해 바닥이 젖었다는 표시가 있어 뛰지 않는 것이 좋다고 말하는 B의 말은 흐름상 적절하지 않다.

27 「의문사+to부정사」는 문장에서 주로 목적어로 쓰인다. 이때 의문사가 무엇이냐에 따라 의미가 달라진다. / what to do: 무엇을 해야 할지

28 세진이는 자신이 한국 중학교 2학년(My name is Kim Sejin. I'm in the second grade at Hanguk Middle School.)이라고 언급했다.

29 ④falled는 fall의 과거형인 fell이 되어야 어법상 자연스럽다.

30 '~만큼 …하게'라는 동등 비교 표현은 'as (형용사/부사) as ~'의 형태로 쓸 수 있다. 이때 not을 앞에 붙인 'not as[so] (형용사/부사) as ~'는 비교급 문장이 된다. 두 경우 모두 비교하는 두 대상들의 품사가 같아야 한다.

Lesson 2 (중간)

01 ③ **02** ⑤ **03** ③ **04** ③

05 (1) forget to (2) better not **06** ⑤ **07** ⑤ **08** ④

09 you'd better not look at your smartphone while you are walking

10 ① **11** ⑤ **12** know where to go **13** ⑤ **14** ②

15 (A) straight (B) chest must be at (C) push down (D) ambulance (E) within four

16 그것은 누군가의 심장이 멈춘 후 당신이 4분 이내에 심폐 소생술을 시작해야 한다는 것을 의미합니다.

17 ① **18** ① **19** ⓐ to eat ⓑ a bike[bicycle] to ride

20 ④ **21** ① **22** ⑤ **23** ⑤ **24** ⑤ **25** ② **26** ⑤

27 ② **28** ⑤ **29** ②

30 Timing is as important as doing CPR.

---

01 위 글에서, 많은 사람들이 거의 매일 이것을 사용하며 건물에서 위아래로 이동하기 위해 사용하는 것이며, 또한 화재가 발생했을 경우엔 사용해서는 안 되는 이것에 대해서 설명하고 있다. 따라서 이것이 가리키는 것으로 가장 적절한 것은 ③ elevator(엘레베이터)이다.

02 '~만큼 …한'이라는 동등 비교 표현은 'as (형용사/부사) as ~'의 형태로 쓸 수 있다. 이때 모두 비교하는 두 대상들의 품사가 같아야 한다. 또한 'as ~ as 주어+can(could)'는 as ~ as possible로 바꿔 쓸 수 있다.

03 few : 거의 없는 / protect : 보호하다

04 impressive 인상적인 / creative 창의적인 / active 활동적인

05 (1) 'Don't forget to~'는 상대방에게 무언가를 상기시킬 때 쓸 수 있는 표현으로 to 뒤에는 동사원형을 쓴다. (2) 'You'd better not ~'은 상대방에게 무언가를 금지할 때 쓸 수 있는 표현으로 'You must not ~'으로 바꿔 쓸 수 있다. 이때 not 뒤에는 모두 동사원형을 쓴다.

06 댄스 대회 때문에 며칠 동안 연습했지만 그래도 여전히 떨린다는 A의 말에 대해 이 일정표에 수업 일정과 약속을 쓸 필요가 있다는 B의 대답은 흐름상 적절하지 않다.

07 위 글에서는 모든 것이 흔들려 가만히 서 있을 수 없어 넘어졌고 머리를 보호하면서 테이블 아래로 들어갔던 무서웠던 경험에 대해서 이야기하고 있다. 따라서 위 글에서 이야기하고 있는 것은 ⑤ Earthquake(지진)이다.

08 "운이 좋게도, 흔들림이 곧 멈추었다"는 문장이 들어가기에 가장 적절한 곳은 지진이 일어나서 대피한 상황이 끝난 후인 ④ (라)이다.

09 'You'd better not ~'은 상대방에게 무언가를 금지할 때

쓸 수 있는 표현으로 'You must not ~'으로 바꿔 쓸 수 있다. 이때 not 뒤에는 모두 동사원형을 쓴다. / while ~ 하는 도중에

10 A가 나간다고 말하자 아빠의 대답은 오늘 공기 중에 미세 먼지가 많기 때문에 마스크를 써야 한다고 말한다. 이에 A가 몰랐다고 대답하자 아빠는 미세 먼지가 건강에 나쁘다고 말하면서 마스크를 쓰라고 건네준다. 이에 A는 고맙다고 말하는 순서로 이어지는 것이 대화의 흐름상 가장 자연스럽다.

11 위 글에선 차에 있다면, 속도를 늦추고 안전한 장소로 갈 것과 흔들림이 멈출 때까지 차 안에 있으라고 조언한다. 또한 두 번째로, 창문에서 떨어져 있으라고 말하며 세 번째로는 엘레베이터는 이용하지 않는 것이 좋다고 말한다. 마지막으로 건물이 없는 개방된 공간을 찾아야 한다고 조언한다. 이 내용들로 미루어 볼 때 위 글에서 이야기하고 있는 것은 지진이 발생한 경우의 안전 수칙이다. 따라서 제목으로 가장 적절한 것은 ⑤ How to Stay Safe During an Earthquake(지진 도중에 안전하게 있는 방법)이다.

12 「의문사+to부정사」는 문장에서 주로 목적어로 쓰인다. 이때 의문사가 무엇이냐에 따라 의미가 조금씩 달라진다. / where to 어디로[어디서] ~할지

13 위 글에서 사람의 심장이 멈춘 뒤 구급차가 오기 전까지 환자에게 인공호흡이 아니라 CPR을 시행해야 한다고 했다.

14 ⓐ a chance practice → a chance to practice / ⓒ Is → Are / ⓓ low → lower / ⓔ join → joining

15 위 글의 내용을 미루어 볼 때, CPR을 할 때는 팔을 곧게 펴야 하며, CPR 대상의 가슴과 90도를 이루어야 한다. 또한 가슴 중앙을 압박해야 하고, 구급차가 올 때까지 계속 CPR을 시행해야 한다. 마지막으로 CPR은 골든 타임이라는 4분 내에 시행해야 한다.

16 It means that ~ 그것은 ~를 의미한다 / should ~해야 한다 / within ~이내에

17 세진이는 학교 안전 훈련의 날에 구급차를 부르는 방법(how to call an ambulance)이 아니라 CPR을 하는 법(how to do CPR)을 배웠다고 언급했다.

18 A가 잘 지냈냐("What's up?")고 묻자, Chris는 셔츠를 사기 위해 왔다고 이야기한다. A는 자신은 쇼핑몰에서 점심 모임이 있다고 대답한다. 그리고 나서 늦었다며 빨리 가려고 하자 Chris는 조심하라고 저기 있는 표지판을 보라고 말한다. A는 그 표지판을 못 봤고 무슨 의미냐고 묻자, Chris는 그것이 바닥이 미끄럽다는 뜻이라고 대답하는 순서로 이어지는 것이 대화 흐름상 자연스럽다.

19 위 그림으로 미루어 볼 때, Kate는 빵을 먹고 싶어 하며,

Minji는 자전거를 타고 싶어 한다. 따라서 to부정사의 형용사적 용법을 이용해 bread to eat과 a bike[bicycle] to ride라는 표현을 만들 수 있다.

20 within ~ 안에 / later than ~보다 늦게 / lower 낮추다, 낮게 하다

21 'You'd better not ~'은 상대방에게 무언가를 금지할 때 쓸 수 있는 표현으로 'You must not ~'으로 바꿔 쓸 수 있다. 이때 not 뒤에는 모두 동사원형을 쓴다.

22 위 대화에서 Amy는 셔츠를 사기 위해 여기 쇼핑몰에 왔다("I'm here to buy a shirt.")고 언급했다.

23 run to ~에게로 달려가다 / tap ~ on the shoulder ~의 어깨를 톡톡 두드리다

24 거리에서 자전거를 타고 있을 때 스마트폰을 사용하지 않는 것이 좋다는 안전 수칙이 장소와 연결된 내용으로 가장 적절하다.

25 ⓒas scaring as는 as scared as로, ⓓmoving or breathe는 moving or breathing으로 고쳐야 어법상 적절한 문장이 된다.

26 ⑤ Why did an old man suddenly fall in front of people? (왜 노인이 갑자기 사람들 앞에서 쓰러졌는가?)는 위 글에서 언급되어 있지 않다.

27 위 글에서는 세진이가 관객들에게 CPR하는 방법을 매우 인상적으로 보여 줬고 관객들에게 어떤 것을 기억하라고 요청했다고 한다. 본문의 내용으로 미루어 볼 때 세진이가 관객들에게 기억하라고 한 것은 사람의 생명을 살릴 수 있는 ② the safety rule(안전 수칙)이다.

28 위 글에서 세진이는 학교 안전훈련의 날에 배운 CPR로 인해 사람의 생명을 구하게 되었다. 따라서 ⑤ Something that you learn at school can help you in real life.(학교에서 배운 것이 실생활에서 당신에게 도움을 줄 수도 있다.)라는 Henry의 반응이 적절하다.

29 위 글에서 (A)that(그것)보다 늦게 되면 사람의 생명을 살릴 수 있는 기회가 현저히 낮아질 것이라고 말한다. 따라서 그것이 가리키는 것으로 가장 적절한 것은 앞 문장에서 언급했던 ② four minutes(4분)이다.

30 '~만큼 …한'이라는 동등 비교 표현은 'as (형용사/부사) as ~'의 형태로 쓸 수 있다. 이때 not을 앞에 붙인 'not as (형용사/부사) as ~'는 비교급 문장이 된다. 두 경우 모두 비교하는 두 대상들의 품사가 같아야 한다.

Lesson 3 (기말)

1회

01 ① **02** ② **03** ⑤ **04** ② **05** ② **06** ④ **07** ③
08 ①
09 (1) If it is sunny tomorrow, we can go for a bike ride. (2) If he doesn't stop eating fast food, he will get sick.
10 ④ **11** Do you know how to use it? **12** ④
13 ④ **14** ① **15** ① **16** ③ **17** They will fall.
18 ③
19 you massage yourself and stretch every day, you will feel healthier
20 ② **21** Do you know how to get over a cold?
22 ⑤ **23** ④ **24** ①
25 It will make your eyes feel more comfortable.
26 ③ **27** right **28** ②
29 (1) ⓒ (2) to feel (3) feel

01 ⓐ face 마주보다; 얼굴 ⓑ switch 스위치(버튼); 바꾸다 ⓒ place 두다, 놓다; 장소

02 ② close는 '가깝게'라는 뜻의 부사로 사용되었다. 나머지는 모두 '닫다', '감다'라는 뜻의 동사의 의미로 사용되었다.

03 ⑤ We should wear comfort shoes for walking for a long time.에서 comfort를 명사 shoes를 수식하는 형용사형 comfortable로 고쳐야 어법상 적절한 문장이 된다.

04 ① jog → jogging ③ play → playing
④ have → has ⑤ informations → information

05 위 대화에 A가 B에게 자신은 건강한 음식을 먹고 싶다고 말하면서 조언을 구하자 B는 자신이 때로 신선한 샐러드를 먹으면 기분이 좋다고 대답한다. 이에 A가 만들 수 있냐고 묻자, B는 만드는 법이 간단하다면서 샐러드 만드는 법을 설명해 준다. 이에 A는 자신도 시도해 봐야겠다고 말하는 순서로 이어지는 것이 대화 흐름상 가장 자연스럽다.

06 위 대화에서 하나는 다음주에 있을 시험 때문에 스트레스를 받고 있고, Karl 역시 자신이 스트레스 받을 땐 롱보드를 탄다는 내용이므로 빈칸에 들어갈 말로 알맞은 것은 ④ stressed이다.

07 Karl이 하나에게 롱보드 타는 법을 가르쳐 줄 때, "한 쪽 발은 롱보드에 올려놓고 다른 발은 세게 밀어라"("Put one foot on the board and push hard with the other.")라고 말하고 있다. 따라서 the other가 가리키는 말은 ③ the other foot(다른 쪽 발)이다.

08 위 대화의 내용으로 미루어 볼 때 Karl이 롱보드를 타는 이유는 그것이 스트레스를 줄여주기 때문이라고 말하는 것이 적절하다.

09 조건절은 '~한다면'이라는 의미로, 「If+주어+동사 ~, 주어+조동사(will/can ...)+동사원형 ...」 형태로 쓰인다. 조건절을 문장의 뒤에 위치시켜 「주어+조동사+동사원형 ~ +if+주어+동사 ...」의 형태로 쓸 수도 있다. 이때 조건절은 미래의 일을 말하지만 현재 시제를 사용한다. / stop ~ing: ~하는 것을 멈추다

10 위 대화에선 B가 걸음수를 쉽게 세는 방법에 대해서 조언을 구하자 G가 스마트폰 앱을 추천하고 이용하는 방법에 대해서 설명하고 있다. 따라서 ⓐit이 가리키는 것은 ④ smartphone app이다.

11 위 대화에서 ~하는 방법에 대해서 물어 봤으므로 「의문사+to부정사」를 이용해 문장을 만들 수 있다. 이때 「의문사+to부정사」는 문장에서 주로 목적어로 쓰이며 의문사가 무엇이냐에 따라 의미가 조금씩 달라진다. / how to ~: ~하는 방법, 어떻게 ~할지

12 ④번 그림에서 오른쪽 다리를 구부리고 있으므로 일치하지 않는다.

13 '너와 너의 파트너가 같은 속도로 움직여야 한다'는 문장이 들어가기에 적절한 곳은 짝과 함께 허리 운동을 할 때 같은 속도로 당기지 않으면 쓰러진다는 문장 앞 부분이다.

14 with ~으로, ~을 사용해서 / Stand close 가까이 서다 / backward 뒤 쪽으로

15 hold는 '유지하다', '버티다'라는 뜻으로 사용되었다.

16 위 글에 따르면, 친구와 팀을 이룬 후 가까이 서서 마주보고 손목을 잡고 머리와 몸을 뒤로 천천히 늘리라고 한다. 그 자세를 3초 간 유지한 다음 선 자세로 서로를 천천히 잡아당기라는 순서로 언급되어 있다.

17 두 번째 문단에서 같은 속도로 움직이지 않으면 쓰러진다고(If you don't, both of you will fall!) 언급되어 있다.

18 lower는 동사로 '낮추다', '낮게 하다'라는 뜻으로 사용되었다.

19 '~한다면'이라는 의미의 조건절은 「If+주어+동사 ~, 주어+조동사(will/can ...)+동사원형 ...」 형태로 쓰인다. 이때 조건절은 미래의 일을 말하지만 현재 시제를 사용한다.

20 위 글에 언급되어 있듯이, 오른발을 뒤쪽에 있는 테이블에 올려놓고 천천히 왼쪽 다리를 구부려 몸을 낮추면 스트레칭이 된다. 따라서 빈칸에 들어갈 말로 가장 알맞은 것은 left - lower이다.

21 G가 감기에 걸렸고 B에게 감기를 낮게 하는 방법에 대해서 조언을 구하고 있다. 따라서 의문사+to부정사를 이용해 to get over a cold라는 표현을 쓸 수 있다.

22 위 글에서 눈을 마사지하는 방법을 설명하고 있다. 눈을 손으로 덮고 빛을 가리는 방법이 눈을 편안하게 해 줄 것이라고 언급하고 있다. 따라서 빈칸에 들어갈 말로 가장 적절한 것은 ⑤ block out(가리다, 막다)이다.

23 위 글에 따르면, 우선 눈을 감고(c), 손가락을 이용해 부드럽게 마사지(a)하라고 한다. 마지막으론 손으로 눈을 가려 빛을 막으라고(b) 언급되어 있다.

24 인칭대명사 them과 It이 가리키는 것은 각각 앞서 언급된 복수형 명사, 단수형 명사이다. 따라서 them은 your eyes를, It은 to massage your eyes를 가리킨다.

25 사역 동사 make를 사용할 때 목적보어는 동사원형을 쓴다.

26 '~한다면'이라는 의미의 문장은 조건절로, 「If+주어+동사 ~, 주어+조동사(will/can ...)+동사원형 ...」 형태로 쓰인다. 이때 조건절은 미래의 일을 말하지만 현재 시제를 사용한다.

27 오른쪽 발을 뒤쪽에 있는 테이블에 올리고 왼쪽 다리를 구부려 몸을 낮추는 것은 오른쪽 다리를 스트레칭하는 방법이라고 나와 있다.

28 '그런 다음, 천천히 왼쪽 다리를 구부리고 몸을 낮춰라'라는 문장이 들어가기에 적절한 곳은 오른쪽 다리 스트레칭을 할 때 왼쪽 다리는 어떻게 해야 하는지 설명하는 ② (B)이다.

29 사역동사 make는 목적보어로 동사원형을 취한다. 따라서 to feel을 feel로 고쳐야 어법상 적절한 문장이 된다.

Lesson 3 (기말) 2회

01 ③	**02** ④	**03** ①	**04** ②	**05** ③	**06** ②	**07** ④
08 ④	**09** ④	**10** ⑤	**11** ⑤	**12** ①, ⑤		

13 It will make your eyes feel more comfortable.

14 ①	**15** ③, ⑤		**16** ②	**17** ④	**18** ②	**19** ③
20 ③	**21** ③	**22** ①			

23 (1) If you massage yourself and stretch every day, you will feel healthier.
(2) you can make yourself focus on studying more.

24 (1) makes me feel (2) you how to download

25 ⑤	**26** ①	**27** ④	**28** ①	**29** ④

01 ③ enable은 able에 접두사 en-가 합성되어 만들어진

동사이다. 나머지는 모두 접미사 −able이 합성되어 만들어진 단어들이다.

02 ④번에서 위 문장의 waste와 아래 문장의 waste는 '낭비하다'라는 뜻으로 사용되었다.

03 thanks to ~ ~ 덕분에 / be good at ~ ~을 잘하다

04 보통 무슨 종류의 사진을 찍냐는 A의 질문에 대해 아름다운 사진들이 스트레스를 줄여준다는 B의 대답은 대화 흐름상 자연스럽지 않다.

05 위 글에서 화자 I는 영어 말하기 대회를 앞두고 있고 2주 전부터 준비하기 시작했다고 말한다. 또한 영어로 말하는 것을 좋아하지만, 대회 때문에 긴장되고 잠을 잘 못 잔다고 이야기하고 있다. 따라서 화자의 기분으로 가장 적절한 것은 ③ stressed(스트레스 받은)이다.

06 대화의 흐름상, 하나는 다음주에 있는 대회 때문에 스트레스를 받고 있는 상황에서 Karl은 자신이 스트레스를 해소하는 방법으로 롱보드 타기를 소개하고 하나도 롱보드를 타는 법을 배우면서 스트레스를 해소하는 내용이 그려지고 있다. 따라서 빈칸에 들어갈 말로 가장 적절한 것은 stressed - the other - decrease이다. / stressed 스트레스 받은, decrease 감소시키다

07 Karl은 롱보드가 스트레스를 줄여주기 때문에 롱보드 타는 것을 즐긴다("I enjoy riding my longboard because it can decrease my stress.")고 언급했다.

08 ④ Where did Karl learn to ride a longboard?(Karl은 어디서 롱보드 타는 것을 배웠는가?)라는 질문에 대해서는 위 대화에서 언급되어 있지 않다.

09 ④ into: ~으로, ~에

10 위 대화에서는 B가 신선한 샐러드 만드는 방법에 대해서 묻자 G가 설명해 주고 있다. 우선(First) 채소들을 작은 조각으로 자른다(라). 그 다음(Next) 그것들을 큰 그릇에 넣고(나), 그 후(Then) 그 위에 레몬즙을 뿌린다(다). 마지막으로(Finally) 레몬즙과 샐러드를 모두 섞는다(가)라고 말했다.

11 눈과 목을 마사지 하는 방법에 대해서 이야기하고 있으므로 제목으로 가장 적절한 것은 ⑤ How to Massage Your Eyes and Neck(눈과 목을 마사지 하는 방법)이다.

12 help는 목적보어로 동사원형과 to부정사를 취한다. ① feel과 ⑤ to feel 모두 가능하다.

13 행동의 주체가 자발적으로 어떤 행동을 하는 것이 아니라 '주어가 목적격보어에게 ~하게 하다'라는 뜻으로 쓰이는 동사를 사역동사라고 한다. 이때 「사역동사+목적어+목적격보어(동사원형)」의 순서로 쓴다

14 You sit for a long time at school.(학교에서 당신은 오랜 시간 앉아 있다.)는 문장은 위 글의 첫 문단에서 언급된 문장(At school you sit for many hours.)의 내용과 일치한다.

15 밑줄 친 (b)to massage는 to부정사의 부사적 용법으로 사용되었다. ①, ④는 to부정사의 형용사적 용법으로 사용되었다. ②는 명사적 용법으로 사용되었다.

16 ⓑwhat to use를 ⓑhow to use로 고쳐야 어법상 적절한 문장이 된다.

17 What is the name of the app?(그 앱의 이름은 무엇인가?)에 대한 질문은 대화 중에 언급되지 않았기 때문에 대답할 수 없다.

18 첫 문단에서 '파트너의 손목을 잡아라'(Hold each other's wrists.)라고 언급되어 있다. 따라서 ② You should hold each other's waist when you massage your wrist.(당신은 손목을 마사지할 때 서로의 허리를 잡아야 한다)는 문장은 위 글의 내용과 일치하지 않는다.

19 빈칸에는 앞 문장인 'You and your partner should move at the same speed.'(당신과 파트너는 반드시 같은 속도로 움직여야 한다.)를 줄여 쓴 문장이 들어가야 내용상 적절하다. 따라서 빈칸에 들어갈 말로 가장 적절한 것은 ③ move at the same speed이다.

20 ⓒ Place는 '장소'라는 뜻이 아니라 '두다', '놓다'라는 뜻으로 사용되었다.

21 첫 문단에 나와 있듯이, 두 사람이 같은 속도로 움직이지 않으면, 둘 다 넘어질 것("If you don't, both of you will fall!")이라고 언급되어 있다.

22 글의 내용상 낮추고 있던 자세를 곧게 펴라는 내용이 들어가야 하므로 ① straighten이 빈칸에 가장 알맞다.

23 조건절은 '~한다면'이라는 의미로, 「If+주어+동사 ~, 주어+조동사(will/can ...)+동사원형 ...」 형태로 쓰인다. 조건절을 문장의 뒤에 위치시켜 「주어+조동사+동사원형 ~ +if+주어+동사 ...」의 형태로 쓸 수도 있다. 이때 조건절은 미래의 일을 말하지만 현재 시제를 사용한다.

24 (1) 행동의 주체가 자발적으로 어떤 행동을 하는 것이 아니라 '주어가 목적격보어에게 ~하게 하다'라는 뜻으로 쓰이는 동사를 사역동사라고 한다. 이때 「사역동사+목적어+목적격보어(동사원형)」의 순서로 쓴다. (2) 상대방의 능력 여부를 물을 때 'Do you know how to ~?'라는 표현을 쓸 수 있다. 이때 to 뒤에는 동사원형을 쓴다.

25 마지막 문단에서, '천천히 서로를 잡아 당기면서 서 있는 위치로 돌아오는데, 이때 같은 속도로 돌아와야 한다'(slowly pull each other to a standing position.

You and your partner should move at the same speed.)고 언급되어 있다.

26 빈칸 (A)와 (B)에는 사역동사 make와 help를 수식하는 목적보어가 들어가야 한다. 이때 공통으로 들어갈 수 있는 단어 형태는 동사원형이다. 따라서 빈칸에 들어갈 말로 가장 알맞은 것은 ① feel이다.

27 마지막 문단에서는 친구와 짝을 지어 허리를 스트레칭하는 방법을 설명하고 있다. 따라서 빈칸에 들어갈 말로 가장 적절한 것은 ④ waist(허리)이다.

28 마지막 문단에서, 빈칸 앞 문장에서 서 있는 자세로 돌아올 때 같은 속도로 돌아와야 한다고 조언하고 있다. 그렇지 않으면 넘어지기 때문이다. 따라서 빈칸에 들어갈 말로 알맞은 말은 if 조건절을 사용한 ① If you don't(만약 그렇게 하지 않으면)이다.

29 during은 시간을 의미하는 명사와 쓰여 '~ 동안에'라는 뜻을 갖는다. 그러나 숫자나 시간의 길이를 의미하는 단어와는 함께 쓰이지 않는다. 따라서 숫자나 시간의 길이를 표현할 때 쓰이는 전치사 for(~ 동안에)로 바꾸는 것이 어법상 적절하다.

Lesson 4 (기말)

01 ③ **02** ②

03 (1) I know a girl who[that] speaks Japanese well.
(2) The man who[that] is playing soccer there is my father.
(3) I played with James and his dog that live near my house.

04 ④ **05** ③ **06** ③ **07** ① **08** ③ **09** ① **10** ⑤
11 ④ **12** ⑤ **13** ④ **14** ②
15 who are good at painting **16** ② **17** ⑤
18 I hope we can save the Earth. **19** ③ **20** ⑤
21 You did something wonderful!
22 sold cookies and drinks to raise money
23 ①, ⑤
24 (1) care for people in need
(2) It aims to communicate with people from around the world.
25 produced a video about the lantern festival in our village
26 ⑤ **27** ⑤ **28** ① **29** ① **30** ④

01 위에서부터 순서대로 aim, shares, citizen, gather가 들

어가야 내용상 자연스럽다. 따라서 ③ reduce(감소하다, 감소시키다)는 빈칸에 들어가지 않는다.

02 Nancy는 아동 병원에서 일하고 있고 아픈 아이들을 돌보느라 항상 바쁘다고 말한다. 따라서 빈칸에 들어갈 말로 가장 적절한 것은 ② cares for(~를 보살피다)이다.

03 두 문장을 연결할 때 관계대명사를 이용해 연결할 수 있다. 관계대명사절에서 관계대명사가 주어 역할을 할 때 주격 관계대명사라고 한다. who는 선행사가 사람일 때, which는 선행사가 사물일 때, that은 두 경우 모두 쓸 수 있다.

04 '지구를 아끼자'라는 캠페인을 열자고 제안하는 A의 말에 대해 '안타깝다'라고 대답하는 B의 말은 대화 흐름상 적절하지 않다.

05 위 대화에서 Karl은 '먹기 전에 생각하고 지구를 아끼자'라고 이야기하고 있다. 따라서 (c) after가 아니라 before(~ 전에)가 들어가야 자연스러운 문장이 된다.

06 위 대화에서는 지구를 보호하기 위해 음식물을 먹을 만큼만 가져가서 남기지 말자고 이야기하고 있다. 따라서 캠페인의 제목으로 가장 적절한 것은 ③ Think, Eat, Save! (생각하고 먹고 아끼자!)이다.

07 지호는 불고기가 자신이 가장 좋아하는 음식("Bulgogi is my favorite.")이라고 언급한 바 있다.

08 ⓑ What food does Karl like?(Karl은 어떤 음식을 좋아하는가?)라는 질문과 ⓒ Why did Karl join the campaign?(Karl는 왜 그 캠페인에 참여했는가?)라는 질문에 대한 내용은 위 대화에서 언급되어 있지 않다.

09 show A B A에게 B를 보여주다

10 something, anything, nothing, everything은 형용사가 뒤에서 꾸며 준다. 따라서 ⓔwonderful something이라는 표현은 something wonderful이 되어야 어법상 적절하다.

11 (B)raised는 '(돈을) 모으다'라는 뜻으로 사용되었다. 이와 같은 뜻으로 사용된 문장은 ④ We raise money for the World Food Program.(우리는 세계 식량 프로그램을 위해 모금한다.)라는 문장이다.

12 호주(Australia)에 있는 Jo와 그의 친구들은 케냐 학생들에게 새로운 책가방을 보냈는데, 왜냐하면 케냐 학생들이 책을 비닐 봉지에 넣고 다녔기 때문이다. 따라서 빈칸에 들어갈 말로 적절한 것은 Australia -Kenyan - carried이다.

13 (A) '~하기 위해'라는 의미의 to부정사의 부사적 용법이 들어가는 것이 적절하다. (B) much 훨씬 더 ~, very는 비교급을 수식할 수 없다. (C) 동사 enjoy는 목적어로 명

사나 동명사를 취한다.

14 세계 시민 의식이 무슨 의미냐는 질문에 대한 대답은 Afig
와 친구들이 마을을 위해 했던 벽화 그리기에서 유추할 수
있다. 따라서 ② It is working for a better world.(그
것은 좀 더 나은 세상을 위해 일하는 것이다.)가 세계 시민
의식의 의미로 가장 적절하다.

15 be good at ~를 잘하다

16 ⓐ isn't that too much / ⓒ What does that mean /
ⓓ Let's share it / ⓔ Let's not waste food로 고치는
것이 내용상 적절하다.

17 지호는 캠페인 포스터를 보고 이해하지 못해서 Karl에게
그 의미를 물어 보았다.

18 'I hope ~'는 '~했으면 좋겠다'라는 의미로 희망을 나타
내는 표현이다. / save the Earth 지구를 구하다, 아끼다

19 Jo와 친구들은 쿠키와 음료를 판매해서 모은 돈으로 케냐
친구들에게 새로운 책가방을 선물했다. 따라서 빈칸에 들
어갈 말로 가장 적절한 것은 ③ the new bags(새로운 책
가방)이다.

20 ⑤ Where did Jo's class sell cookies and drinks?
(Jo와 학급 친구들은 어디서 쿠키와 음료를 판매했는가?)
라는 질문에 대한 내용은 위 글에서 언급되어 있지 않다.

21 something, anything, nothing, everything은 형용
사가 뒤에서 꾸며 준다. 또한 something은 긍정문에,
anything은 부정문과 의문문에 주로 쓰인다. 따라서
'You did something wonderful!'의 순서가 되는 것
이 적절하다.

22 Jo와 친구들이 모금을 위해 쿠키와 음료를 팔았고 600달
러를 모았다('We sold cookies and drinks and
raised 600 dollars.')고 언급되어 있다.

23 빈칸 (A)에는 선행사 people을 수식하는 주격 관계대명
사가 들어가는 것이 어법상 적절하다. 따라서 빈칸에 들어
갈 수 있는 관계대명사는 who와 that이다.

24 (1) 첫 문단에 세계 시민은 어려움에 처한 사람들을 보살
핀다(They also care for people in need)고 언급되어
있다. (2) 민희의 동아리는 전 세계 사람들과 소통하는 것
을 목표로 한다(My club aims to communicate with
people from around the world.)고 언급되어 있다.

25 produce 제작하다 / lantern festival 등불 축제

26 위 글에서 세계 시민 교육 웹사이트가 빈곤한 사람들이 세
계 시민으로 성장하도록 돕는다는 언급은 없다.

27 ⑤ Why did Minhee join the Global Community
Club?(왜 민희는 세계 공동체 클럽에 가입했는가?)이라
는 질문에 대한 내용은 위 글에서 언급되어 있지 않다.

28 ⓐlooks는 사역동사 make의 목적보어 역할이므로 동사
원형인 look이 되어야 한다.

29 밑줄 친 (A)who는 주격 관계대명사로 사용되었다. ①
who는 의문사 who로 사용되었다.

30 그림을 잘 그리는 학생들이 모여서 벽화를 그렸다
('Students who are good at painting gathered and
painted on some walls of schools and parks.')고 언
급되어 있다.

Lesson 4 (기말)

> **01** ① **02** ④ **03** ③ **04** ④ **05** ③
> **06** wearing a hat which[that] looks old
> **07** Are you going to do anything special?
> **08** ⑤ **09** ② **10** ③ **11** ② **12** ③ **13** ③ **14** ⑤
> **15** ⑤ **16** ④ **17** ② **18** ⑤
> **19** sold cookies and drinks **20** ② **21** ③ **22** ①
> **23** (A) understand different cultures
> (B) care for people in need
> (C) work for a better world
> **24** ④, ⑤ **25** ⑤ **26** ② **27** ⑤ **28** ① **29** ③
> **30** (1) produced (2) lantern (3) uploaded (4) hits

01 worldwide는 '전세계적인'이라는 뜻으로 ① global(세
계적인)과 바꿔 쓸 수 있다.

02 위에서부터 순서대로, thanks to-loosen up-with
time-up to가 들어가야 내용상 적절하다.

03 ① has → that has / ② look → looks / ④ who →
which / ⑤ that was → that were로 고쳐야 어법상 적
절한 문장이 된다.

04 'I hope ~'는 '~했으면 좋겠다'라는 의미로 희망을 나타
내는 표현이다. B가 '지구를 아끼자'라는 캠페인을 열자
고 제안한 것을 고려해 볼 때, 빈칸에 들어갈 말로 적절하
지 않은 것은 ④ people often take a shower(사람들이
샤워를 자주 했으면 좋겠어.)이다.

05 커피를 마실 때 종이컵을 쓴다("I use a paper cup
when I drink coffee.")는 Andy의 말이나, 쇼핑을 갈
때는 비닐봉지를 사서 쓴다("I buy a plastic bag when
I go shopping.")는 Jinhee의 말은 환경 보호와는 거리
가 멀다.

06 관계대명사가 이끄는 절에서 who는 선행사가 사람일 때,
which는 선행사가 사물일 때, that은 두 경우 모두 쓸 수
있다. 또한 관계대명사 뒤에 나오는 동사는 선행사와 수의

일치가 되어야 한다.

07 'Are you going to ~?'는 '넌 ~할 거니?'라는 의미로 상대방의 의도를 묻는 표현이다. 이때 대답은 'I'm going to ~'로 하며 뜻은 '난 ~할 거야'이다.

08 위 글에서 방법을 설명하는 부분에 신발을 집에서 가져와 그림을 그리거나 문구를 쓰라고 되어 있다.

09 첫 문장과 두 번째 문장에서 매일 학생들이 음식을 많이 남기고 있고 그래서 화자의 동아리가 그것에 대한 캠페인을 열 예정이라고 말하고 있다. 따라서 캠페인은 ② Not to leave food(음식을 남기지 않는 것)에 대한 것이다.

10 ⓐ which → who / ⓑ is → are / ⓓ to walk → walking / ⓔ How → What으로 고쳐야 어법상 적절한 문장이 된다.

11 ② When did students paint the wall paintings?(언제 학생들이 벽에 벽화를 그렸는가?)에 대한 내용은 위 글에서 언급되어 있지 않다.

12 ③ I'm going to leave some food.(음식을 남길 거야.)라는 문장은 지구 보호와는 거리가 먼 문장이다.

13 ⓒ that은 집을 잃은 사람들에게 돈을 보내는 것을 의미한다.

14 ⓔLet's waste food from now on.는 대화의 흐름상 "Let's not waste food from now on."(앞으로 음식을 낭비하지 말자.)가 되어야 한다.

15 지호는 우린 음식을 다 먹었다고("We ate it all.") 언급한 바 있다.

16 ④ What food does Karl like most?(Karl이 제일 좋아하는 음식은 무엇인가?)라는 질문에 대한 내용은 위 대화에서 언급되어 있지 않다.

17 '안타깝게도, 그들은 모두 책을 가져가기 위해 비닐봉지를 이용하고 있었다.'라는 문장이 들어가기에 적절한 곳은 선생님이 케냐 학생들의 사진을 보여주고 그것에 대해 설명하는 부분인 (B)이다.

18 ⓔYou는 화자인 Jo와 친구들을 가리킨다. 나머지는 모두 케냐 학생들을 가리킨다.

19 Jo와 친구들은 모금을 위해 쿠키와 음료를 팔았다고('We sold cookies and drinks.') 언급되어 있다.

20 (A) as(~로서), (B) for(~를 위해)

21 ⓒ'좋아하다'는 뜻이 아니라 '~를 보살피다'라는 뜻을 갖는다.

22 위 글에서는 세계 시민 교육 웹사이트를 소개하면서 세계 시민의 목적과 의미를 설명하고 있고 웹사이트에서는 경험을 공유해 달라고 이야기하고 있다. 따라서 위 글의 소재로 가장 적절한 것은 ① global citizenship(세계 시민

의식)이다.

23 위 글에서 '세계 시민들은 다른 문화를 이해하려고 노력하는 사람들이다. 그들은 또한 어려움에 처한 사람들을 보살피며 좀 더 나은 세상을 위해 일한다'(Global citizens are people that try to understand different cultures. They also care for people in need and work for a better world.)라고 언급되어 있다.

24 (a)that은 주격 관계대명사로 쓰였다. 이와 쓰임이 같은 문장은 ④ I like the girl that is wearing a red dress.(나는 빨간 드레스를 입고 있는 소녀를 좋아한다.)와 ⑤ The man that is wearing blue pants is my brother.(파란 바지를 입고 있는 남자는 내 남동생이다.)이다.

25 Bob이 작년에 아이들의 공부를 도와주었다고 언급되어 있다("I went there and helped some children study last year.").

26 ⓐ near → nearly / ⓒ raising → to raise / ⓓ to look → look / ⓔ look → looks 로 고쳐야 어법상 적절한 문장이 된다.

27 ⑤ How long did it take to finish the wall painting?(벽화를 끝내는 데 시간이 얼마나 걸렸는가?)에 대한 내용은 위 글에서 언급되어 있지 않다.

28 ㉠who는 선행사 students를 수식하는 관계대명사절을 이끄는 주격 관계대명사이다. ②, ③, ④, ⑤는 모두 의문사 역할을 한다.

29 새 가방을 받은 케냐 학생들의 반응은 위 글에 언급되어 있지 않다.

30 produce 제작하다 / lantern 등불 / upload 업로드하다 / hits 조회수

MEMO